Poetry

past and present

Poetry
past and present

Frank Brady
City University of New York

Martin Price
Yale University

 Harcourt Brace Jovanovich, Inc.

New York   Chicago   San Francisco   Atlanta

ISBN: 0-15-570682-9

Library of Congress Catalog Card Number: 73-18759

Printed in the United States of America

Copyrights and Acknowledgments

For permission to use the selections reprinted in this book, the authors are grateful to the following publishers and copyright holders:

GEORGE ALLEN & UNWIN LTD   For "The Peasants" from *Ha Ha Among the Trumpets* by Alun Lewis. Reprinted by permission of George Allen & Unwin Ltd.

ATHENEUM PUBLISHERS   For "The Dover Bitch," "Third Avenue in Sunlight," and "Birdwatchers of America" from *The Hard Hours* by Anthony Hecht. Copyright © 1958, 1959, 1960 by Anthony E. Hecht. "The Dover Bitch" appeared originally in *Transatlantic Review*, and "Third Avenue in Sunlight" appeared originally in *Hudson Review*; for "Movie-Going" from *Movie-Going and Other Poems* by John Hollander. Copyright © 1962 by John Hollander; for "Adam's Task" and "The Bird" from *The Night Mirror* by John Hollander. Copyright © 1970, 1971 by John Hollander. "Adam's Task" appeared originally in *New American Review*, and "The Bird" appeared originally in *Treasury of Modern Yiddish Poetry*; for "Jerome" from *The Woman at the Washington Zoo* by Randall Jarrell. Copyright © 1960 by Randall Jarrell; for "The Broken Home" from *Nights and Days* by James Merrill. Copyright © 1965 by James Merrill. Appeared originally in *The New Yorker*; for "The Owl" and "The Chaff" from *The Carrier of Ladders* by W. S. Merwin. Copyright © 1967, 1970 by W. S. Merwin; for "The Remains" and "From a Litany" from *Darker* by Mark Strand. Copyright © 1968, 1969, 1970 by Mark Strand. "The Remains" appeared originally in *The New Yorker*, and "From a Litany" appeared originally in *Tri-Quarterly*; and for "Keeping Things Whole" and "Eating Poetry" from *Reasons for Moving* by Mark Strand. Copyright © 1963, 1966 by Mark Strand. "Keeping Things Whole" appeared originally in *The New York Review of Books*. All reprinted by permission of Atheneum Publishers.

BIG SKY MUSIC   For "Lay, Lady, Lay" by Bob Dylan. Copyright © 1969 Big Sky Music. Used by permission of Big Sky Music.

ROBERT BLY   For "Laziness and Silence," reprinted from *Silence in the Snowy Fields*, by Robert Bly, Wesleyan University Press, 1962, © copyright 1962 by Robert Bly, by permission of the author.

CHATTO AND WINDUS LTD   For "Dulce et Decorum Est" and "Anthem for Doomed Youth" from *The Collected Poems of Wilfred Owen*, edited by C. Day Lewis. Reprinted by permission of the Executors of the Estate of Harold Owen and Chatto & Windus Ltd.

CITY LIGHTS BOOKS   For "America" from *Howl & Other Poems* by Allen Ginsberg. Copyright © 1956, 1959 by Allen Ginsberg. Reprinted by permission of City Lights Books.

CORINTH BOOKS   For "Preface to a Twenty Volume Suicide Note" from *Preface to a Twenty Volume Suicide Note* by LeRoi Jones. Copyright © 1961 by LeRoi Jones; and for "The Songs of Maximus: #3" from *The Maximus Poems* by Charles Olson. Copyright © 1960 by Charles Olson. Both reprinted by permission of Corinth Books.

CORNELL UNIVERSITY PRESS   For "Corson's Inlet," reprinted from A. R. Ammons: *Corson's Inlet: A Book of Poems*. Copyright © 1965 by Cornell University. Used by permission of Cornell University Press.

J. M. DENT & SONS LTD For "Fern Hill," "Lament," and "The Force That Through the Green Fuse Drives the Flower" from *Collected Poems of Dylan Thomas*. Reprinted by permission of the Trustees for the Copyrights of the late Dylan Thomas.

DOUBLEDAY & COMPANY, INC For "First Confession" and "In A Prominent Bar in Secaucus One Day" from *Nude Descending a Staircase* by X. J. Kennedy, copyright © 1951, 1961 by X. J. Kennedy; and for "Root Cellar," copyright 1943 by Modern Poetry Association, Inc., "My Papa's Waltz," copyright 1942 by Hearst Magazines, Inc., "The Waking," copyright 1953 by Theodore Roethke, and "In a Dark Time," copyright © 1960 by Beatrice Roethke as Administratrix of the Estate of Theodore Roethke, from *The Collected Poems of Theodore Roethke*. All reprinted by permission of Doubleday & Company, Inc.

ALAN DUGAN For "Funeral Oration for a Mouse" and "Actual Vision of Morning's Extrusion" from *Poems* by Alan Dugan, Yale University Press, 1961. Copyright © 1961 by Alan Dugan. Reprinted by permission of the author.

ROBERT DUNCAN For "This Place Rumord to Have Been Sodom" by Robert Duncan. Reprinted by permission of the author.

FABER AND FABER LTD For "Lullaby," "In Memory of W. B. Yeats," "Sonnets from China, XVIII," and "Musée des Beaux Arts" from *Collected Shorter Poems 1927–1957* by W. H. Auden; for "The Love Song of J. Alfred Prufrock," "Preludes," "Sweeney Among the Nightingales," "Gerontion," and "East Coker" from *Collected Poems 1909–1962* by T. S. Eliot; for "On the Move" and "The Corridor" from *The Sense of Movement* by Thom Gunn; for "Modes of Pleasure" from *My Sad Captains* by Thom Gunn; for "Hawk Roosting" and "Pennines in April" from *Lupercal* by Ted Hughes; for "Reveille" from *Wodwo* by Ted Hughes; and for "An Arundel Tomb," "Love Songs in Age," and "A Study of Reading Habits" from *The Whitsun Weddings* by Philip Larkin. All reprinted by permission of Faber and Faber Ltd.

FARRAR, STRAUS & GIROUX, INC For "Dream Song #15" from *77 Dream Songs* by John Berryman, copyright © 1959, 1962, 1963, 1964 by John Berryman; for "A Prayer for the Self" from *Love & Fame* by John Berryman, copyright © 1970 by John Berryman; for "Seascape," "Man-Moth," and "The Prodigal" from *The Complete Poems* by Elizabeth Bishop, copyright © 1933, 1935, 1936, 1937, 1938, 1939, 1940, 1941, 1944, 1945, 1946, 1947, 1948, 1949, 1951, 1952, 1955, 1956, 1957, 1958, 1959, 1960, 1961, 1962, 1963, 1964, 1965, 1966, 1967, 1968, 1969 by Elizabeth Bishop; for "Modes of Pleasure" from *Moly and My Sad Captains* by Thom Gunn, copyright © 1961, 1971, 1973 by Thom Gunn; for "The Death of the Ball Turret Gunner" from *The Complete Poems* by Randall Jarrell, copyright © 1945, 1969 by Mrs. Randall Jarrell; for "Skunk Hour" and "Waking in the Blue" from *Life Studies* by Robert Lowell, copyright © 1958, 1959 by Robert Lowell; and for "For the Union Dead" from *For the Union Dead* by Robert Lowell, copyright © 1960 by Robert Lowell. All reprinted with permission of Farrar, Straus & Giroux, Inc.

GROVE PRESS INC For "Permanently" from *Thank You and Other Poems* by Kenneth Koch. Copyright © 1962 by Kenneth Koch. Reprinted by permission of Grove Press, Inc.

HARCOURT BRACE JOVANOVICH, INC For "pity this busy monster" and "what if a much of a which of a wind," copyright, 1944, by E. E. Cummings, copyright, 1962, by Nancy Andrews; "my sweet old etcetera," copyright, 1926, by Horace Liveright, copyright, 1954, by E. E. Cummings; and "r-p-o-p-h-e-s-s-a-g-r," copyright, 1935, by E. E. Cummings, copyright, 1963, by Marion Morehouse Cummings, from *Complete Poems 1913–1962* by E. E. Cummings; for "The Love Song of J. Alfred Prufrock," "Preludes," "Sweeney Among the Nightingales," "Gerontion," and "East Coker" from *Collected Poems 1909–1962* by T. S. Eliot, copyright, 1936, by Harcourt Brace Jovanovich, Inc.; copyright, © 1943, 1963, 1964, by T. S. Eliot; for "After the Surprising Conversions" and "Mary Winslow" from *Lord Weary's Castle*, copyright, 1946, by Robert Lowell; for "Love Calls Us to the Things of This World," "Beasts," and "Mind" from *Things of This World*, © 1956, by Richard Wilbur; and for "Advice to a Prophet," © 1959 by Richard Wilbur, from his volume *Advice to a Prophet and Other Poems*. First published in *The New Yorker*. All reprinted by permission of Harcourt Brace Jovanovich, Inc.

HARPER & ROW, PUBLISHERS, INC For "Pennines in April" and "Hawk Roosting" from

PREFACE

Poetry Past and Present is a selection of carefully annotated and teachable poems that reflect both our own tastes and the dominant traditions of British and American poetry. It offers an unusually large representation of contemporary poetry as well as a number of other features that should prove helpful to the student and allow the instructor considerable flexibility: an Introduction that provides an extensive, up-to-date discussion of the technical and theoretical aspects of poetry; a thematic and generic table of contents to assist the student in perceiving relationships between poems and the continuity of certain poetic subjects and traditions; and a detailed glossary of critical terms with specific examples.

The Introduction is divided into two parts. Part I, "The Poem Itself," is an essay on practical criticism: it discusses the poem's basic components—sense, imagery, prosody, tone, and so forth, including two topics less often treated, syntax and structure. It also considers certain elements common to a number of poems, such as allegory, symbol, convention, and genre. This essay directs itself to beginning students of poetry and is extensively illustrated with poems. Part II, "The Poem and Poetic Theories," surveys a wide range of critical problems and approaches, such as the questions raised by the conception of poetry as a form of knowledge or as a mode of imitation or expression, the problems of intention and evaluation, and the roles played by biography and psychology in criticism, among others. In addition, it introduces students to new approaches to poetry found in archetypal, phenomenological, and structuralist criticism. This essay will help students clarify and extend their theoretical understanding of poetry after they have grasped the poem's basic elements in Part I.

The anthology selections are divided almost equally between poems of the twentieth century and earlier works. Beginning students usually find contemporary poetry the most accessible in language, attitudes, and sensibility, even though the range of allusion may be as wide in Yeats and Eliot as it is in Milton and Pope. For this reason some instructors may prefer to start with recent selections and work their way back through earlier poems. Others may be more interested in comparing contemporary poems with earlier selections and so may prefer to choose works without regard for their chronological order.

Although flexibility of approach was a highly important consideration in developing this book, we were governed by certain principles in choosing the poems. The anthology illustrates continuity in English poetry from the late medieval period to the present by including poems of the past that can be compared, in various ways, to poems of this century. Such comparisons involve similar or contrasting uses of subject, theme, or technique, and illuminate the development of the genre or form. Marvell's "Pictuie of Little T. C." provides the model for John Ashbery's and Charles Tomlinson's poems of similar titles. E. E. Cummings' "Pity This Busy Monster Manunkind" achieves sharper definition if put in a sonnet tradition running back through Wordsworth and Milton to Renaissance poets. Mark Strand's "From a Litany" imitates Christopher Smart's *Jubilate Agno*; Anthony Hecht's "Dover Bitch" parodies Matthew Arnold's poem. Sometimes contrasts in theme and form are revealing, as in the opposing visions of America present in Walt Whitman's "When Lilacs Last in the Dooryard Bloomed" and Allen Ginsberg's "America" or the widely differing views of marriage expressed in Spenser's *Prothalamion* and Gregory Corso's "Marriage." Many such connections are suggested in the thematic and generic table of contents, and many others will suggest themselves.

Every student of poetry has encountered words and allusions that are unfamiliar and a hindrance to the full enjoyment of poetry. We have tried to eliminate this hindrance as much as possible and to provide annotation wherever we thought the student might need help. Our aim has been to provide enough information to enable both the instructor and the student to concentrate on explication and interpretation without infringing on the reader's prerogative in these areas. To this end, critical or evaluative commentary has been avoided, except that which is occasionally offered by or quoted from the poets themselves.

The student reader was kept in mind on another matter also. We had to choose between concentrating on the work of perhaps a half-dozen contemporary poets and picking a few poems by many writers. We preferred the second alternative on the grounds that students confronting poetry for the first time learn more from examining a wide variety of attitudes toward the world expressed in a range of techniques than from restricting their attention to the work of a few fine poets.

In conclusion we wish to thank Professor Samuel R. Levin for his advice on prosody. Eben Ludlow and his colleagues Sidney Zimmerman and Andrea Haight at Harcourt Brace Jovanovich have been patient and helpful.

F. B.

M. P.

CONTENTS

INTRODUCTION

I: The Poem Itself

When asked to define poetry, the eighteenth-century poet and critic Samuel Johnson remarked, "Why, Sir, it is much easier to say what it is not. We all *know* what light is; but it is not easy to *tell* what it is." The same problem of definition frustrates modern critics, but most would agree that a poem must be written in verse, which, in contrast to prose, is characterized by patterns of varying line length and rhythm. The length of a prose line is a mechanical matter, in which lines are of the same length all down a page; and while good prose shows rhythmic flexibility, if the stress patterns that determine rhythm become too marked they get between the reader and what he is reading. Verse patterning, the stress on certain words or phrases reflected in line length and rhythms, enables poems—good poems, anyway—to express experience more intensely, concisely, and memorably than prose. The following poem, published in 1945, illustrates these qualities:

The Death of the Ball Turret Gunner

From my mother's sleep I fell into the State,
And I hunched in its belly till my wet fur froze.
Six miles from earth, loosed from its dream of life,
I woke to black flak and the nightmare fighters.
When I died they washed me out of the turret with a hose.

RANDALL JARRELL

Briefly summarized in prose, the poem says that from "sleep" in his mother's womb, the speaker became an "embryo" of the state. He hunched in the unheated belly of a World War II bomber, where his sweat-soaked, fur-lined uniform froze in the cold air. Six miles up, under attack by

fighter planes and fired at by antiaircraft guns, he lost the dreams or illusions of everyday life on earth, and woke to the terrible realities of war.
His body was blown into so many pieces that it had to be hosed out of the
gun turret.

This simple summary ignores those aspects of the poem that develop
and reinforce its meaning, and provide its power. The main use of paraphrase is to establish the basic sense of a poem. If we wish to go beyond
the simple sense and find out why the total poem has impact, we have to
look at those elements in it that bring out or intensify the meaning. These
elements, to be explained and illustrated later, include imagery, diction,
metrics, and tone, among others. When we examine these features of a
poem we are actually trying to see how the poem "works" to create its
total effect, just as an auto mechanic takes apart an engine to find out precisely how it functions. But while an engine's parts are neatly separable,
the poem's elements are distinguished, almost arbitrarily, for analytic purposes only. The poem "works" because its elements mesh effectively. Few
readers try for a complete analysis of a complex poem, simply because such
an analysis would quickly run into the law of diminishing returns. Instead,
the experienced reader examines what seems to be the most important
aspect of a particular poem or some problem connected with it.

Some readers object that analysis spoils a poem for them. They are happier, they say, just to know the poem is "beautiful" or that it makes them
"feel good." Analyzing a poem, they argue, is like chopping up a tree. But
poems are not trees. Poems are man-made objects, artifacts; they have
never been known to sprout another line as a tree grows a new branch.
"Pulled apart," a poem nevertheless remains intact. Analysis is valuable
because it tries to show how a poem works, and in the process the reader
often gets a clearer grasp of the poem's meaning and effect. For a good
poem is not a vague attempt to arouse emotions; ordinarily it has as much
precise meaning as a prose work, though the meaning is usually more complex and the language more highly suggestive.

Subject

As "The Death of the Ball Turret Gunner" illustrates, any human experience can be the subject of a poem, as well as non-human objects: both
birds and bulldozers can be the material of poetry. Nor are there any forbidden topics. Jonathan Swift's "Description of a City Shower" (p.
173) vividly depicts an overflowing sewer. The Earl of Rochester's "The
Disabled Debauchee" (p. 171) describes the feelings of an impotent man,
while Shakespeare's plays illustrate the whole range of love from the explicitly sexual to the ideally romantic, as John Donne's "Elegy 19" (p.

107) does in miniature. And, most notoriously, modern poets have often chosen subjects that in Victorian times were considered sordid or obscene. Whatever involves the body, the mind, the spirit, and their relationships, concerns poets. To take a specific example, poets are persistently aware, as W. B. Yeats says in "Crazy Jane Talks with the Bishop" (p. 318), that

> Love has pitched his mansion in
> The place of excrement.
>
> (ll. 15–16)

Naturally the poet is also concerned with the individual's relations to others, to society, to nature, and to God. Perhaps only very scientific and technical subjects are unsuitable to poetry, although some poets have tackled them too, like the eighteenth-century writer, Erasmus Darwin, who used botany as a subject in "The Loves of the Plants."

Sense

The way to approach any poem is first to try to grasp its sense, its basic meaning. But the reader may find that although he understands a poem sentence by sentence, he still does not understand it as a whole. If this happens, it helps to locate the poem's central issue. All works of literature present some kind of conflict, choice, or contrast. Some *narrative poems* (poems that tell a story) may resemble some Western and detective films because the conflict is mainly physical, yet such poems and films usually have some moral dimension, even if at its simplest it is only to contrast the good guys to the bad guys. And in the simplest *lyric* (a short poem, originally meant to be sung), which may seem to offer only a single view of its subject, conflict or choice is always present. When Bob Dylan sings,

> Why wait any longer for the world to begin?
> You can have your cake and eat it too.
> Why wait any longer for the one you love,
> When he's standing in front of you?
>
> ("Lay, Lady, Lay")

the lady has the choice of accepting or not accepting the argument. Andrew Marvell's "To His Coy Mistress" (see pp. 147–48) deals with the same subject in a more complicated way, partly by elaborating the situation and by exaggerating the alternatives:

> Had we but world enough, and time,
> This coyness, lady, were no crime.
> We would sit down, and think which way
> To walk, and pass our long love's day.
> Thou by the Indian Ganges' side

> Shouldst rubies find; I by the tide
> Of Humber would complain. . . .
>
>   (ll. 1–7)

If time didn't matter, the speaker is saying, he and his mistress could take as long as they wanted for an extended courtship. The lady could look for rubies in India, while the speaker "complained" (sang a conventional love song about his mistress's cruelty) beside an English river. "But," the speaker continues,

> at my back I always hear
> Time's wingèd chariot hurrying near;
> And yonder all before us lie
> Deserts of vast eternity.
>
>   (ll. 21–24)

Now the speaker reminds his mistress of the swift passage of time, suggesting that old age and death are menacingly close, while the future turns into a frightening vision of vast emptiness. From here the poem goes on to insist that we must seize pleasure quickly and fiercely.

Theme

Sometimes it is difficult to distinguish between a poem's subject and theme. The subject is what the poem is about, while the theme is the idea or attitude suggested by the subject. This distinction will become clearer by looking at the following poem.

Fire and Ice

> Some say the world will end in fire,
> Some say in ice.
> From what I've tasted of desire
> I hold with those who favor fire.
> But if it had to perish twice,
> I think I know enough of hate
> To say that for destruction ice
> Is also great
> And would suffice.

                                         ROBERT FROST

The apparent subject of the poem can be thought of as an answer to the question, "How will the world end?" But the reader quickly recognizes that Frost's deeper subject is man's nature, driven by desire and hate. The theme of the poem, as is usually the case, is harder to state with assurance than the subject. It may be simply, "Man is possessed by contradictory emotions that equally destroy him." Or, it might be possible to extend the theme to "The world's prospects for survival are dim when people are dominated by destructive emotions." For in Frost's poem, as in many others, the theme may not be clear-cut. Indeed, in long poems there often is more than one theme. Despite the difficulty, however, it is essential to identify a poem's major theme, since it provides the poem's basic organizing principle.

The discussion of sense, subject, and theme may seem to imply that a poem consists of a series of statements, and in a way it does. But these statements are seldom straightforward assertions; rather they are shaped, or at least strongly influenced, by such non-thematic factors as the poem's imagery, diction, syntax, and prosody.

Imagery

Imagery is usually the most important of these factors. An image is any concrete representation of a sense impression or idea. "The brown table" is an image because it directly represents a sense impression. "Justice sat on her throne," where "Justice" expresses an idea concretely, is also an image because it is a *personification,* a word or phrase which represents an idea or abstraction as a person or object, something that can be sensed. But when Alexander Pope writes,

> There are (I scarce can think it, but am told),
> There are, to whom my satire seems too bold:
> ("The First Satire of the Second Book of
> Horace," ll. 1–2, p. 185)

no images occur. Totally imageless lines like these, however, are rare in poetry.

Imagery is the most common way of shaping a poetic statement, of giving it some unusual quality, like freshness, precision, or memorability. The number and kind of images a poet uses vary according to the effect he wants to create. On the simplest level, a poet may seem merely to list impressions that are connected to make a point, but the handling of imagery in a fine poem is seldom as simple as it looks. The poem below can serve as an example.

Cavalry Crossing a Ford

A line in long array where they wind betwixt green islands,
They take a serpentine course, their arms flash in the sun—hark to the
    musical clank,
Behold the silvery river, in it the splashing horses loitering stop to
    drink,
Behold the brown-faced men, each group, each person, a picture, the
    negligent rest on the saddles,
Some emerge on the opposite bank, others are just entering the ford—
    while,

Scarlet and blue and snowy white,
The guidon flags flutter gaily in the wind.

WALT WHITMAN

This poem is like "a picture," as Whitman says. Its effectiveness, however, depends not only on the details he selects but also on their arrangement. Whitman organizes his "picture" almost as a movie director might. The first two lines are a "long shot" of the troops, in which only a general impression emerges of a winding movement of men whose weapons flash and clank. Then Whitman "dollies in" closer, so we can see that the cavalrymen are tanned, that some are entering the water and some coming out on the opposite bank, and that the colors of the flags they carry are clearly distinguishable. The poem does not focus on any individual nor does the poet comment on the scene; instead, he lets the images speak for themselves. The reader draws his own conclusions as to what the scene means.

A twentieth-century group of poets called the Imagists asserted that all poetry should be made up of highly detailed imagery. We might take as the group's motto William Carlos Williams's statement of his own Imagist credo, "No ideas but in things." Poetry often does consist of detailed descriptions of things and actions, as these lines from Williams's "The Yachts" show:

Mothlike in mists, scintillant in the minute

brilliance of cloudless days, with broad bellying sails
they glide to the wind tossing green water
from their sharp prows while over them the crew crawls

ant like, solicitously grooming them, releasing,
making fast as they turn, lean far over and having
caught the wind again, side by side, head for the mark.

(ll. 6–12, pp. 336–37)

At the other extreme, poems may contain very little imagery, or a poet may operate in a gray area between the imagistic and the non-imagistic to advantage, as in the following poem:

Joy

I could look at
an empty hole for hours
thinking it will
get something in it,

will collect
things. There is
an infinite emptiness
placed there.

ROBERT CREELEY

The only concrete elements in the poem—"empty hole," "something," and "things"—are so unspecific as to hardly seem like images. Because they are generalized and can cover so many possibilities, however, they lead directly into the concept of "infinite emptiness" and are thus appropriate to the poet's purpose. If the poet had described a black pothole that collected dead maple leaves, the idea of "infinite emptiness" would seem disproportionate to the specific details.

Metaphor and Simile

The "simple" images discussed so far are distinct from the complex forms of imagery which are based on comparison. The two most important of these complex forms are the figures of speech *metaphor* and *simile*. Metaphor asserts the identity of two objects, as for example in "the man is a lion." Simile compares two objects by using such words as "like" or "as," for example in "the man is like a lion." Some people—critics, teachers, and poets—ignore the difference between the two figures, but it is wise to know the distinction between them: metaphor emphasizes some whole or partial *identity*, and simile some whole or partial *likeness*.

An intense, even shocking kind of metaphor has been highly admired in this century, like this stanza from Donne's "The Canonization" (p. 103):

> Call us what you will, we are made such by love:
>   Call her one, me another fly,
> We are tapers too, and at our own cost die;
> And we in us find the eagle and the dove.
>   The phoenix riddle hath more wit
>   By us; we two being one, are it:
> So to one neutral thing both sexes fit.
>
>   (ll. 19–25)

These violent shifts in metaphor trace the scale of love as the lovers rise from the insect lechery of flies, through the classical contrast and pairing of the masculine eagle and feminine dove, to the mysterious union of the sexes in the riddle of the "neutral" phoenix (the phoenix was supposed to incorporate both sexes, and only one phoenix existed at any one time). But metaphor need not shock; it can make an effective point gently:

> Who would have thought my shriveled heart
> Could have recovered greenness? It was gone
>   Quite under ground; as flowers depart
> To see their mother-root when they have blown.
>
>   (ll. 8–11)

These lines from George Herbert's "The Flower" (p. 124) make two further points: (1) metaphor does not have to be explicitly stated. It can be implicit or "submerged," as in the metaphor of the first two lines identifying the speaker's heart with the life of the flower. (2) The smoothness with which the metaphor of the first two lines shifts into the simile of the third, "as flowers depart," shows how close these two figures of speech can be.

Both metaphor and simile can show a subtlety and ingenuity that extends meaning differently than in the ways just illustrated. Pope writes in *An Essay on Criticism:*

> 'Tis with our judgments, as our watches, none
> Go just alike, yet each believes his own.
>
> (ll. 9–10)

In what ways are judgments like watches? In their accuracy? In their rigidity? In their objectivity? In the fact that no watch keeps perfect time? This last question recalls that all watches keep an approximation of ideal time, Greenwich mean time. By analogy Pope suggests that all judgments try to approximate an ideal judgment, even though each individual must rely on his own subjective judgment.

Diction

Imagery is a distinct and important part of the larger subject called *diction*. Diction refers to the poet's vocabulary, his choice of words. All of us use different vocabularies in different situations; we speak in one way to our classmates and in another to our parents, for example. Although differences in diction are breaking down today, the vocabulary of the prison has not yet become identical with that of the church. Nor is the vocabulary of daily speech the same as that of the essay, even though the two overlap more and more. In earlier periods the literary language tended to be more formal than it is now, and certain levels of diction were considered particularly appropriate to certain kinds of poetry. A "high" or elevated style was used for the epic, a long narrative poem involving a hero in an important action, as in John Milton's *Paradise Lost* (see selection on pp. 143–44). Didactic (instructive) poems, like Pope's *To Richard Boyle . . . Of the Use of Riches* (pp. 179–84), were written in a "middle" or plain style. A "low" style was appropriate to satires, like Thomas Gray's "The Candidate" (p. 195), where everyday or colloquial phrases appear. Of course syntax and prosody also influenced the stylistic level of a poem, but diction was considered its distinguishing factor.

As is true of imagery, the only test for correct diction is appropriateness, or "decorum" as it was once called: the proper matching of manner to matter, of style to content. The following sonnet shows how diction can be used skillfully:

On First Looking into Chapman's Homer

Much have I traveled in the realms of gold
And many goodly states and kingdoms seen;

Round many western islands have I been
Which bards in fealty to Apollo hold.
Oft of one wide expanse had I been told
    That deep-browed Homer ruled as his demesne;
    Yet never did I breathe its pure serene
Till I heard Chapman speak out loud and bold:
Then felt I like some watcher of the skies
    When a new planet swims into his ken;
Or like stout Cortez when with eagle eyes
    He stared at the Pacific—and all his men
Looked at each other with a wild surmise—
    Silent, upon a peak in Darien.

JOHN KEATS

In the *octave* (the first eight lines), Keats uses archaic words like "goodly," "bards," "fealty," and "demesne," and two *periphrastic* (roundabout) expressions, "realms of gold" and "pure serene," to suggest the antiquity, remoteness, and dignity of classical poetry, especially of Homeric epic. The phrase "deep-browed Homer" echoes the *fixed epithets* (constantly paired adjectives and nouns) used by the ancient Greek poet, such as "wine-dark sea" and "rosy-fingered Dawn." In the last line of the octave and the following *sestet* (the last six lines) the diction changes strikingly. The narrator's first reading of Chapman's translation of Homer is compared to an astronomer's discovery of a new planet and to Cortez's (actually Balboa's) discovery of the Pacific, in direct and simple language that suggests vividly the charged excitement of these similar experiences. A good deal of the poem's effectiveness depends on the sharp contrast between these two kinds of language.

    A useful modern method of looking at diction is in terms of its "substantive level."[1] We call a spade a spade, but we can also call it a common garden spade or an agricultural instrument. Arranged in levels these possibilities become:

1. *abstract or general:* agricultural instrument
2. *substantive:* spade
3. *concrete or particular:* common garden spade.

The lines previously quoted from Williams's "The Yachts" (p. 6) operate mainly on the third of these levels. The second stanza from William Wordsworth's "Intimations Ode" (p. 228) offers a contrast:

The rainbow comes and goes,
And lovely is the rose,
The moon doth with delight
Look round her when the heavens are bare,
    Waters on a starry night
    Are beautiful and fair;

---

[1] This discussion is derived from W. K. Wimsatt's essay, "The Substantive Level," in his book *The Verbal Icon* (Lexington: University of Kentucky Press, 1954).

> The sunshine is a glorious birth;
> But yet I know, where'er I go,
> That there hath passed away a glory from the earth.

Wordsworth here sticks close to the middle or substantive level. It is this level of diction which seems to give Wordsworth's best poetry the quality of uniting concreteness with generalization.

As suggested earlier, totally imageless poems, which usually draw on an abstract vocabulary (our first level), are uncommon. There are, however, interesting exceptions, like this short poem.

I Promise Nothing

> I promise nothing: friends will part;
>   All things may end, for all began;
> And truth and singleness of heart
>   Are mortal even as is man.
>
> But this unlucky love should last
>   When answered passions thin to air;
> Eternal fate so deep has cast
>   Its sure foundation of despair.

A. E. HOUSMAN

Just as the shift in levels of diction in the Keats poem is important to its effect, so is the continuity between abstract thought and individual experience here. The series of abstract statements made in Housman's first stanza seem accurate and proper, if for no other reason than that we are used to such generalizations as "all men are mortal." They suggest a universality and inevitability which carries over to the individual experience described in the second stanza, itself so carefully generalized that it could fit almost any reader's case. Yes, we think, although all things are temporary, the pain of unrequited love is lasting and decreed by "eternal fate." We nod our heads and agree that it is a "universal experience."

The danger in poetry characterized by much imagery is that its details will seem to exist for their own sakes rather than for the poem's overall effect. On the other hand, generalized or abstract poetry can seem vague or pompous. The poet must be sensitive to the effect his words will have in the total context of the whole poem. The instances given below are only a few samples of the many ways imagery and diction can go wrong. Sometimes a poet will use a colloquial image for a dignified subject, as when Nathaniel Lee says of thunder:

> The lords above are angry and talk big.
>
> (*Alexander the Great,* quoted in Pope's
Peri Bathous, ch. 10)

At other times the imagery may seem merely ingenious or exaggerated, as in Richard Crashaw's description of Mary Magdalene's eyes:

Two walking baths; two weeping motions;
Portable and compendious oceans.

("Saint Mary Magdalene," ll. 113–14)

But when John Dryden says of the effect of a fatal attack of smallpox,

Each little pimple had a tear in it,
To wail the fault its rising did commit,

("Upon the Death of the Lord Hastings," ll. 59–60)

we are amused, or repelled, not so much by the ingenuity of the image as by its falseness. Poets are traditionally allowed a great deal of license in regard to facts, but no one can persuade us that smallpox pustules feel sorry for their victim.

The choice of exactly the right word or phrase can be striking. Gerard Manley Hopkins's "God's Grandeur" (p. 299) begins:

The world is charged with the grandeur of God.
It will flame out, like shining from shook foil.

In these lines, "shining from shook foil" particularizes Hopkins's idea of God's grandeur, and the special aptness of "shook" becomes obvious when we try to substitute another adjective for it, like "rolled" or "silver."

Certain quasi-imagistic devices, such as juxtaposition, produce special effects. When Pope describes certain dunces,

'Twas chattering, grinning, mouthing, jabbering all,
And noise and Norton, brangling and Breval,

(*Dunciad*, Book II, ll. 238–39)

the immediate juxtaposition of descriptive terms and people suggests that the dunce and his activity not only exist on the same level but are one and the same entity. Norton and noise are identical. Juxtaposition works differently in T. S. Eliot's "Gerontion" (p. 353), where the series "Rocks, moss, stonecrop, iron, merds" suggests the sterile randomness of the world.

Another near-imagistic device is the pun. The whore in Robert Burns's *Love and Liberty* sings:

I once was a maid, though I cannot tell when,
And still my delight is in proper young men.

(ll. 57–58)

"Proper" concentrates three meanings: (1) respectable or chaste; (2) complete; (3) handsome, well built. The song suggests that the "proper" young man for a woman is the "complete," well built one.

The *turn* is a looser play on words, in which one word is repeated in various contexts or two words are sharply contrasted. In *Paradise Lost*, Milton describes the landscape of Hell:

Rocks, caves, lakes, fens, bogs, dens, and shades of death,
A universe of death, which God by curse

Created evil, for evil only good,
Where all life dies, death lives, and Nature breeds,
Perverse, all monstrous, all prodigious things.

                                                (Book II, ll. 621–25)

The basic turn here is on "death," "evil," "good," and "life." Milton is
also playing on the Latin roots of "monstrous" (*monstrum,* an unnatural
growth; an evil omen) and "prodigious" (*prodigium,* monster, also an evil
omen). Further, Milton moves from the concreteness of "rocks, caves
. . ." to the abstractness of "a universe of death" through a phrase, "shades
of death," which can be taken as both concrete and abstract.

An ambiguous statement or image combines various levels or possibilities
of meaning, as in this example of dramatic irony from Shakespeare's
Othello, when Othello resolves to murder Desdemona and says,

It is the cause, it is the cause, my soul.
Let me not name it to you, you chaste stars!
It is the cause.

                                                (Act V, Scene ii, ll. 1–3)

But what is "it"? In Othello's consciousness, "it" is adultery, the act he
cannot name. But to the audience, "it" is both Othello's credulity and the
chaos in his mind as well.

Syntax

Imagery and diction are not isolated parts of a poem; they are given
shape by syntax, the way in which the phrases, sentences and larger units
of a poem are organized grammatically. By defining the relationships of
statement and images, syntax helps to underline the meanings in a poem
and to provide emphasis. The following poem illustrates some of the functions of syntax.

Dream Songs: 15

Let us suppose, valleys & such ago,
one pal unwinding from his labours in
one bar of Chicago,
and this did actual happen. This was so.
And many graces are slipped, & many a sin   5
even that laid man low

but this will be remembered & told over,
that she was heard at last, haughtful & greasy,
to bawl in that low bar:
'You can biff me, you can bang me, get it you'll never.   10
I may only be a Polack   broad but I don't lay easy.
Kiss my ass, that's what you are.'

Women is better, braver. In a foehn of loss
entire, which too they hotter understand,
having had it, 15
we struggle. Some hang heavy on the sauce,
some invest in the past, one hides in the land.
Henry was not his favourite.

JOHN BERRYMAN

"Let us suppose" suggests that what is to follow is an imaginary incident, and like "once upon a time" signals a fictional beginning. But having
aroused one set of expectations, Berryman shifts to "this did actual happen." Grammatically speaking, he has shifted from the subjunctive, "Let
us suppose . . . ," to a form of the indicative, "this did . . . happen,"
which insists that the event he is about to describe actually occurred. And
the following sentence, "This was so," emphasizes by repetition and separation that this event is real and true. At the same time, the easy conversa-
tional phrasing makes the anecdote seem both ordinary and probable.

The next three lines (5–7) stress the difference between this one memorable event and all those incidents involving "graces" and "sin" that have
taken place in every life. The woman's remark is introduced by a colon
(end of line 9), a highly formal mark of punctuation that stands in contrast to the simple and informal punctuation used so far. In terms of syntax, a comma would have introduced her speech just as correctly, but the
colon emphasizes that what is to follow illustrates and, in this case, justifies
the narrator's previous statements. Each of the following three lines (10–12)
is a sentence, a formal division that again suggests the importance of what
is being said while the slang phrases underline its credibility. And the use
of repetition (here in the form of *parallelism,* for a discussion of which see
the Glossary) in "You can biff me, you can bang me" reinforces our sense of
the woman's determination. "Get it you'll never" is clarified in the next
line, where the typographical space between "Polack" and "broad" stresses
the woman's definition of herself. We could elaborate what she says as, "I
may only be a 'Polack broad' in the eyes of the world but I have my self-
respect, a sense of my own value." And her final sentence (line 12) offers
a condensed summary of her opinion of the man.

Unlike the first two stanzas, which merge syntactically, the closing stanza
is a unit in itself, and it brings out the significance of the incident. It starts
with an *antithesis* (a contrast or, often, direct opposition) between women
and men. "Women is," the ungrammatical opening of the first short sentence, keeps the phrasing colloquial or slangy, but the poet's seriousness is
brought out in the second sentence (lines 13–16) where he uses an uncommon word, "foehn" (a treacherous warm wind off a mountain), and
more formal syntax. The inversion of ordinary word order in "loss entire"
draws attention to the inverted phrasing of the sentence as a whole.

(Since the main subject and verb don't appear until the end of the sentence its sense is said to be *suspended,* and it is called a *periodic* sentence.)

The next sentence (lines 16–17) uses a parallel structure, "some . . . some . . . one," to indicate the ways in which men, in contrast to women, avoid facing situations directly. The final "one," as other poems in *Dream Songs* make clear, is the father of Henry (the poem's narrator), who "hides in the land," in other words, committed suicide. The final line expresses Henry's sadness when he thinks about his father.

In their syntax, the first two stanzas of "Dream Songs: 15" more or less imitate the connections and rhythms of ordinary speech. The somewhat more disconnected syntax of the final stanza may seem to imitate the movement of thought as well as speech, as in Robert Browning's "The Bishop Orders his Tomb" (pp. 262–65). The Renaissance Bishop lies on his deathbed wondering if his illegitimate sons, who are gathered there, may cheat him by erecting a cheap monument to him in the church:

> . . . There, leave me, there!
> For ye have stabbed me with ingratitude
> To death—ye wish it—God, ye wish it! Stone—
> Gritstone, a-crumble! Clammy squares which sweat
> As if the corpse they keep were oozing through—
> And no more *lapis* to delight the world!
>
> (ll. 113–18)

All punctuation, except exclamation marks to indicate the Bishop's feelings, and dashes to indicate pauses, have disappeared. Presumably the Bishop is speaking here, but some of these remarks may be thought rather than uttered.

If the poet tries to imitate the flow of mind or idea at a deeper level, the logical connections necessary to make our ideas understandable to someone else tend to drop out, and the resulting pattern is sometimes called "associative":

> Signs are taken for wonders. "We would see a sign!"
> The word within a word, unable to speak a word,
> Swaddled with darkness. In the juvescence of the year
> Came Christ the tiger
>
> In depraved May, dogwood and chestnut, flowering judas,
> To be eaten, to be divided, to be drunk
> Among whispers. . . .
>
> (T. S. Eliot, "Gerontion," ll. 17–23, p. 354)

The lack of logically apparent connections makes associative poetry difficult to follow, and it may take the reader some time to locate the theme, which unifies these statements, in this case that the modern world practices a parody of Christianity.

But syntax may not try to imitate the movements of thought or speech at all. Instead it may take advantage of the complicated possibilities of formal written English. Poets in the seventeenth and eighteenth centuries, for example, developed a verse form called the *heroic couplet* (see Glossary), which exploited precisely and compactly the devices of parallelism and antithesis. Here is Pope's description of a radiantly beautiful young woman named Belinda:

> Bright as the sun, her eyes the gazers strike,
> And, like the sun, they shine on all alike.
> Yet graceful ease, and sweetness void of pride,
> Might hide her faults, if belles had faults to hide.
>
> (*The Rape of the Lock*, Canto II, ll. 13–16)

The syntactic neatness and clarity of these couplets tend to conceal the complexity of Pope's view of Belinda. Certainly he is praising her, but with qualifications that raise questions for the reader: What does the comparison between Belinda's eyes and the sun suggest about her? What are the implications of "yet" and "if"? Do belles have "faults to hide"?

Epic poems ordinarily use the most complex kinds of syntax, as in this passage from Milton's *Paradise Lost*, where Satan first sees Eden:

> Southward through Eden went a river large,
> Nor changed his course, but through the shaggy hill
> Passed underneath engulfed, for God had thrown
> That mountain as his garden mold, high raised
> Upon the rapid current, which through veins
> Of porous earth with kindly thirst up drawn,
> Rose a fresh fountain, and with many a rill
> Watered the garden; thence united fell
> Down the steep glade, and met the nether flood,
> Which from his darksome passage now appears,
> And now divided into four main streams,
> Runs divers, wandering many a famous realm
> And country whereof here needs no account;
> But rather to tell how, if art could tell,
> How from that sapphire fount the crispèd brooks,
> Rolling on orient pearl and sands of gold,
> With mazy error under pendent shades
> Ran nectar, . . .
>
> (Book IV, ll. 223–40, pp. 143–44)

The syntax of this passage is loosely called "Latinate," because it involves very long sentences (this passage occurs in the middle of a sentence forty-six lines long), complicated grammatical constructions, parallel and antithetical phrases, and inverted word order. It is worth noting that the words used in this passage are generally quite simple, which indicates that the effect of resonance and grandeur appropriate to epic here depends chiefly on syntax.

Prosody

So far, this discussion has ignored a central fact about poetry, that it is meant to be heard—either aloud or in the mind—rather than read silently. Actually, experienced students hear everything they read or write, but it is especially important to "hear" poetry. On a basic level, poetry consists of arrangements of sounds, which may be subdivided into meter, verse form, and other sound patterns. These categories are covered by the general term "prosody." Sometimes in the analysis of poetry the importance of prosody is exaggerated, perhaps because metrical effects are the most easily analyzed parts of a poem. Nevertheless, to understand poetry it is essential to have a grasp of the fundamentals of prosody.

Meter

Metrical patterns are established by *scansion* (analysis of the number and kind of units called "feet" in each line of verse). The number of feet will identify the line as trimeter, tetrameter, pentameter, etc. (see *meter* in Glossary). The kind of foot is determined by looking for the relationship of stressed to unstressed syllables in the line. By far the most common pattern in English poetry is *iambic* meter (an unstressed syllable followed by a stressed one). But immediately a basic problem for many students appears: how does one distinguish between unstressed and stressed syllables? One way is to exaggerate the syllables that are ordinarily stressed. As an example, one can read aloud,

> All human things are subject to decay,
> And, when fate summons, monarchs must obey:
> > (John Dryden, "MacFlecknoe," ll. 1–2, p. 159)

(it is best to scan two lines at once, since one line may be irregular) and then mark the stressed syllables with a slant line (◢).

> All húman thíngs are súbject tó decáy,

> And, whén fate súmmons, mónarchs múst obéy.

The remaining syllables, which are the unstressed ones, should then be marked with a cross (x). All syllables must be either stressed or unstressed.

> All húman thíngs are súbject tó decáy,

> And, whén fate súmmons, mónarchs múst obéy.

The metrical pattern, which consists of recurrences, is then considered separately from the words. All feet must contain at least one stressed syllable.

x⋆ x⋆ x⋆ x⋆ x⋆

The pattern in the above example is iambic, unsurprisingly, and since there are five feet in each line, the meter is iambic pentameter.

Three major variations of this pattern occur. One, the *trochee*, simply reverses the iambic pattern:

> Lay your sleeping head, my love, ⌃
>
> Human on my faithless arm. ⌃
>
> (W. H. Auden, "Lullaby," ll. 1–2, p. 383)

Since each line has four feet, the meter is identified as trochaic tetrameter. But as in many trochaic lines, the last syllable in each line is missing and is indicated by a caret (⌃). The last foot, in this case, is called defective. An alert student may notice that these lines can be scanned equally well with the defective foot at the beginning, which creates what is called a "headless" line:

> ⌃ Lay your sleeping head, my love.

But conventionally such lines are scanned as trochaic.

The other two major patterns are *anapest* (xx⋆) and *dactyl* (⋆xx).

> When sly/Jemmy Twit/cher had smugged/up his face
>
> With a lick/of Court white/wash, and pi/ous grimace
>
> (Thomas Gray, "The Candidate," ll. 1–2, p. 195)

Here the first foot of the first line is an iamb; but since the other three feet are anapests, the line is identified as anapestic tetrameter. Finally,

> This is the/forest prim/eval. The/murmuring pines and the/hemlocks,
>
> Bearded with/moss, and in/garments/green, indis/tinct in the/twilight, ⌃
>
> (Henry Wadsworth Longfellow, *Evangeline*, ll. 1–2)

is an example of dactylic hexameter.

Most of the lines cited so far scan regularly, but many lines in English poetry do not:

> Brandy/and ripe/in my bright,/bass prime,
>
> No spring/tailed tom/in the red/hot town
>
> (Dylan Thomas, "Lament," ll. 28–29, p. 399)

Here a number of irregularities occur. Both lines contain a mixture of feet, but since iambs are the most common the lines are described as iambic tetrameter. The first foot of the first line is a trochee, a very common occurrence in largely iambic verse, and is known as a trochaic "substitution." Also, the last foot in each line contains two more or less equally stressed syllables. For the moment each has been scanned as a *spondee* (′′), an unusual foot, but conventionally the spondee is reserved for syllables that are felt to be quite distinct:

$$\text{Ó dárk,} \,/ \text{dárk, dárk,} \,/ \overset{x}{\text{amíd}} \,/ \overset{x}{\text{the bláze}} \,/ \overset{x}{\text{of noón.}}$$

(Milton, *Samson Agonistes*, l. 80)

Most traditional metrists would scan "bass prime" in Thomas's poem as having either a secondary accent (‵) on "bass" or a hovering accent (⌢) on "bass prime." Scanned either way, the emphasis on these syllables calls attention to them.

A poem's metrical pattern and its deviations help to make clear how rhythm, or beat, reinforces meaning. Meaning, however, determines meter in a fundamental way, for as we read the poem aloud, we naturally stress important words and pass more lightly and quickly over unimportant ones. What meter, considered separately from meaning, does establish is a pattern of expectation. If the first three lines of a poem are written in iambic tetrameter, for example, the reader will expect, consciously or unconsciously, the same pattern in the fourth line. But a beat that is too regular is like a monotonous voice; it both irritates and dulls the ear, as the opening lines of John Greenleaf Whittier's *Snow-Bound* illustrate:

> The sun that brief December day
> Rose cheerless over hills of gray,
> And, darkly circled, gave at noon
> A sadder light than waning moon.

The sing-song meter here begins to exert a tyranny over meaning.

Skillful poets, however, play on our metrical expectations. They alter the stress so that its variations reflect and underline the meaning of what is said. For example, the poetic passages in *Hamlet* are written in "blank verse" (unrhymed iambic pentameter), but Shakespeare constantly varies this pattern according to speaker and meaning, as in Hamlet's most famous soliloquy:

> To be or not to be, that is the question:
> Whether 'tis nobler in the mind to suffer
> The slings and arrows of outrageous fortune,
> Or to take arms against a sea of troubles
> And, by opposing, end them. To die, to sleep . . .

(Act III, Scene i, ll. 56–60)

One aspect of Shakespeare's genius as a dramatist is his ability to use the blank verse pattern to heighten the movement of ordinary speech. The verse is formal yet natural at the same time, an effect produced by constant shifts in stress. For example, inversion (here, a trochee to replace an iamb) provides emphasis, as in "thát ĭs" (line 1). The stress on "that" throws our attention back to the opening alternative, "To be or not to be." Throughout the play, Hamlet has had trouble in determining his course of action, and indeed in deciding whether to act at all, and here he equates "being" or existence itself with action, as the following lines make plain. But the choice between action and inaction (or passive endurance) is not an easy one for him, and again inversion at the start of the second line ("whéthĕr") underlines Hamlet's questioning of himself. Nor are all stressed syllables equally weighted: the second syllable of "outrageous" gets more emphasis than any of the other stressed syllables in line three, and the word as a whole points up Hamlet's anger at the sequence of events that has led him to this moment of decision. The alternative to passive suffering—positive physical activity—is brought out by the hovering accent in "takĕ arms" (line 4). Finally in line 5, the *caesura* (sharp pause) between "opposing" and "end" has a complex effect: it stresses both words, but where "opposing" troubles should "end" them, Hamlet's next words, "to die, to sleep," show that "end" has suggested his own end to him. Such a brief analysis of these lines can only sketch a few of the metrical effects Shakespeare uses. But it is worth repeating that metrics have very little importance in themselves: they are determined by meaning, and serve mainly to reinforce it.

Verse Form and Sound Patterns

Like meter, verse form establishes a basic pattern, a structure that the poet finds particularly appropriate to what he has to say. Verse forms fall into two major categories, unrhymed and rhymed. Old English verse (up to A.D. 1100) was mainly unrhymed and *alliterative* (repeating the initial sounds of words or syllables within a line); this "native meter," as it is sometimes called, persisted into Middle English (A.D. 1100–1500):

> In a sómer séson, whan sóft was the sónne,
>
> I shópe me into shróudes, as I a shépe were.
> [I clothed myself in garments, as if I were a shepherd]
>> (William Langland, *Piers Plowman*, ll. 1–2)

In Elizabethan times, blank verse became the ordinary unrhymed form, familiar to us from Shakespeare's plays. *Free verse*, in which line length is determined by units of thought or phrasing or rhythmic pattern, first became widely used in the nineteenth century, and poets are still experimenting with it:

> He has only to pass by a tree   moodily walking   head down
> A worried accountant   not with it   and he is swarming
> He is gliding up the underside light of leaves   upfloating
> In a seersucker suit   passing window after window of her building.
> (James Dickey, "The Fiend," ll. 1–4, p. 425)

The origins of rhymed verse in English cannot be determined historically, but most of the common forms of rhymed verse appeared by the late fifteenth century. The shortest unit of rhymed verse is the *couplet* (two consecutive rhyming lines), either *octosyllabic* (iambic tetrameter),

> Offend/ing race/of hum/an kind,
>
> By nat/ure, rea/son, learn/ing, blind;
> (Jonathan Swift, "The Day of Judgment," ll. 11–12, pp. 174–75)

or *heroic* (iambic pentameter):

> She went/from op/era, park,/assem/bly, play,
>
> To morn/ing walks,/and prayers/three hours/a day.
> (Pope, "Epistle to Miss Blount," ll. 13–14, p. 178)

(Note that "opera" is pronounced "op'ra," and "prayers" pronounced "pray'rs." This condensation of two syllables into one is called *elision*.) Rhymed verse is also arranged in larger units than the couplet, such as the four-line *quatrain* and the fourteen-line *sonnet*. In these stanza forms the rhyme scheme becomes increasingly elaborate.

Rhyme is a special form of *assonance*, the repetition of the same vowel sound in one or more lines:

> In Xanadu did Kubla Khan
> (S. T. Coleridge, "Kubla Khan," l. 1)

We can hear the repetition of the vowels in the *a*'s of Xanadu, Kubla, and Khan, the *i*'s of In and did, and the *u*'s of Xanadu and Kubla. *Consonance*, the repetition of the same consonant sound, appears in the *n*'s, *d*'s, and *k*'s of the line just quoted; when consonance occurs at the ends of lines with different vowel sounds, it produces *slant rhyme*, as in

> There's a certain slant of *light*,
> Winter afternoons,

> That oppresses, like the *heft*
> Of cathedral tunes.
>> (Emily Dickinson, "There's a Certain Slant
>> of Light," ll. 1–4, pp. 287–88)

(Note that "—oons" and "tunes" is a perfect rhyme to most American ears, but would be a slant rhyme to many British ones. Shifts in pronunciation make the determination of slant rhyme a subject best left to experts. Pope rhymes "join" with "line," and "seat" with both "feet" and "great." Marvell's contemporaries would have pronounced his famous line "Desárts of vast etárnity.") Put alliteration, assonance, and consonance together, and they can reach the pleasant complications of

> And all the summer through the water saunter.
>> (W. H. Auden, "Look, Stranger," l. 22)

Rhyme itself is either masculine, when the last syllable of a line is stressed (béd-deád), or feminine, when the last syllable is unstressed (bénding-lénding). Usually we think of rhyme as *external*, that is as occurring at the ends of lines, but it can also be *internal*:

> I bring fresh *showers* for the thirsting *flowers*,
> From the seas and the streams;
> I bear light *shade* for the leaves when *laid*
> In their noonday dreams.
>> (P. B. Shelley, "The Cloud," ll. 1–4)

Onomatopoeia refers to a word that imitates the sound it represents, as in hiss, crackle, cuckoo. True onomatopoeia is very unusual; much more common is a quasi-onomatopoeia in which a sound is suggested rather than directly imitated:

> The Trumpet's loud clangor
> Excites us to arms
> With shrill notes of anger
> And mortal alarms.
>> (John Dryden, "A Song for St. Cecilia's
>> Day," ll. 25–28, p. 158)

Even movement can be imitated in verse:

> Little trotty wagtail, he went in the rain,
> And tittering, tottering sideways he ne'er got straight again.
>> (John Clare, "Little Trotty Wagtail," ll. 1–2)

Verse forms and sound patterns, like metrical patterns, have few, if any, intrinsic properties. Octosyllabic couplets, for instance, have often been used in comic or satiric poems, as the example from "The Day of Judgment" (cited on p. 20) shows, but they are also the verse form of such serious poems as Marvell's "The Garden" (pp. 148–50). Occasionally students will assign a fixed meaning to a sound, such as "s," but that meaning will shift helplessly from one poem to another despite the classification. Let us juxtapose two famous passages:

> If th'*assassination*
> Could trammel up the *consequence,* and catch
> With his *surcease success,*
> > (Shakespeare, *Macbeth,* Act I, Scene vii, ll. 2–4)

and

> She *causes* boys to pile new plum*s* and pear*s*
> On disregarded plate. The maiden*s* taste
> And *stray* impa*ssioned* in the littering leave*s.*
> > (Wallace Stevens, "Sunday Morning," ll. 73–75)

The sinister "s" of Macbeth's meditation on murder has no relation to the sensuous "s" of Stevens's description. Form and sound are invariably ways of shaping and reinforcing sense, and cannot be isolated from it.

Tone

So far we have discussed what might be called the "primary" qualities of poetry—sense, theme, imagery, diction, syntax, and prosody—since these aspects of a poem can all be separately identified in it. Taken together, they produce the poem's tone, a "secondary" quality since it depends on their combination. Tone can be defined as the poem's mood, or the attitude that the poem's speaker takes toward his subject or audience, or simply his tone of voice. We might think of it as the poem's emotional coloration, the "feeling" the poem imparts. In many poems, the tone becomes established quickly and remains essentially the same throughout. When Yeats writes,

> I met the Bishop on the road
> And much said he and I.
> "Those breasts are flat and fallen now,
> Those veins must soon be dry;
> Live in a heavenly mansion,
> Not in some foul sty,"
> > ("Crazy Jane Talks with the Bishop," ll. 1–6, p. 318)

it is not difficult to grasp that the Bishop's tone is both admonitory and reproachful. But speakers' attitudes and feelings in poetry, like ours in daily life, are sometimes mixed and hard to sort out. The poem reprinted below illustrates some of the problems involved:

Piano

Softly, in the dusk, a woman is singing to me:
Taking me back down the vista of years, till I see
A child sitting under the piano, in the boom of the tingling strings
And pressing the small, poised feet of a mother who smiles as she sings.

In spite of myself, the insidious mastery of song
Betrays me back, till the heart of me weeps to belong
To the old Sunday evenings at home, with winter outside
And hymns in the cozy parlor, the tinkling piano our guide.

So now it is vain for the singer to burst into clamor
With the great black piano appassionato. The glamour
Of childish days is upon me, my manhood is cast
Down in the flood of remembrance, I weep like a child for the past.

D. H. LAWRENCE

A number of problems that tone can present were interestingly revealed when I. A. Richards, a famous British critic, showed this as an anonymous poem to his students at Cambridge University over forty years ago. Many condemned it out-of-hand as sentimental; as one student said, "The ideas of Motherhood—the past—Sunday evenings etc. all lend themselves to insincere emotion." Others seemed unable to read it accurately, thinking that the speaker was at a concert or that the same piano appears in the first and third stanzas. A third group was literal-minded, objecting, for example, that a child "could sit under the keyboard but not under the piano." And some constructed their own poems, like the reader who said that "its excellence lies in its securing a feeling of ecstasy from a sordid incident, because it happened in the past."

"Piano" gives some readers trouble partly because its subject involves a *stock response* (see Glossary), the irrational power of nostalgia, and partly because it represents a double attitude toward its subject: the speaker yields to the sentimental appeal of the past while acknowledging that he does so at a cost to himself. This double attitude toward a subject appears frequently in the form of verbal *irony*, which occurs when a speaker says one thing and means the opposite. In much irony the double attitudes resolve into a single implied one, as in Lord Byron's description of the "learnèd" Donna Inez:

She knew the Latin—that is, "the Lord's prayer,"
And Greek—the alphabet—I'm nearly sure.

(*Don Juan*, Canto I, Stanza xiii)

Sometimes irony results if the double attitude is sustained, as when

Byron mixes mockery with sympathy in his attitude toward Don Juan as, on shipboard, he mourns his lost mistress:

> He felt that chilling heaviness of heart,
>   Or rather stomach, which, alas! attends,
> Beyond the best apothecary's art,
>   The loss of love, the treachery of friends,
> Or death of those we dote on, when a part
>   Of us dies with them as each fond hope ends:
> No doubt he would have been much more pathetic,
> But the sea acted as a strong emetic.
>
> *   (Don Juan,* Canto II, Stanza xxi)

Here the shifting attitudes make the tones apparent, but where double attitudes combine it is easy for the inexperienced reader mistakenly to overstress one or the other, as in Marvell's portrait of a young child:

> See with what simplicity
> This nymph begins her golden days!
> In the green grass she loves to lie,
> And there with her fair aspect tames
> The wilder flowers, and gives them names;
> But only with the roses plays,
>   And them does tell
> What color best becomes them, and what smell.
>
> ("The Picture of Little T. C.," ll. 1–8, p. 150)

Not all double attitudes are ironic. In this passage, for example, Marvell is not ironic; rather the narrator's attitude toward little T.C. is both playful and serious. Seen in one way, she is a child talking to the flowers which surround her. Seen in another, she is a "nymph" of a Golden Age whose rule over nature is shown by naming the flowers, just as Adam "gave names to all cattle, and to the fowl of the air, and to every beast of the field" in Genesis. One attitude does not cancel the other; little T.C. is at the same time both a young girl and a nature goddess.

Tone, then, can be the hardest aspect of a poem to define accurately, whether mistakes result from stock responses, inexperience, misreadings, or just the blind spots that afflict even the expert critic. Fortunately, mistakes about tone decrease as the reader becomes more familiar with a particular poet, or historical period, or poetry in general.

Levels of Meaning

Symbol and Allegory

In considering "little T.C." both as a young girl and as a nature goddess, we are well on the way to treating her as a symbolic figure. Technically, a symbol is one kind of metaphor—a metaphor with the first term omitted. "The man is a lion" is a metaphor, but just to call the man "a lion" ordinarily turns "lion" into a symbol. While retaining the characteristic concreteness of metaphor, the symbol carries a suggestiveness that cannot be defined completely. The lion usually symbolizes such qualities as courage, power, majesty, and masculinity, but depending on the context it may evoke other qualities.

It is useful to distinguish public from private symbols. Public symbols, like the flag or the cross, are those whose range of significance most readers can grasp, though different poems may alter somewhat the meanings of the symbol. For example, in "Good Friday, 1613," Donne meditates on the full religious meaning of the Crucifixion:

> But that Christ on this cross did rise and fall,
> Sin had eternally benighted all.
> Yet dare I almost be glad I do not see
> That spectacle of too much weight for me.
> Who sees God's face, that is self life, must die;
> What a death where it then to see God die!
>
> (ll. 13–18, pp. 110–11)

In Pope's *The Rape of the Lock*, the cross appears as an ornament for the beautiful, young Belinda:

> On her white breast a sparkling cross she wore,
> Which Jews might kiss, and infidels adore.
>
> (Canto II, ll. 7–8)

Pope's point, of course, is that the cross has no religious significance for Belinda. That is why Jews might kiss and infidels adore it, since what they are worshiping is Belinda's beauty.

Private symbols, like those organized into systems by Blake and Yeats, can be much harder to grasp. The reader often needs to be aware of the poet's general framework of ideas as developed in his other writings to understand the symbols in any one poem. But in many cases, private symbols grow out of public ones, as this poem shows.

A Poison Tree

> I was angry with my friend:
> I told my wrath, my wrath did end.
> I was angry with my foe:
> I told it not, my wrath did grow.
>
> And I watered it in fears,
> Night and morning with my tears;
> And I sunnèd it with smiles,
> And with soft deceitful wiles.
>
> And it grew both day and night,
> Till it bore an apple bright;

And my foe beheld it shine,
And he knew that it was mine,

And into my garden stole
When the night had veiled the pole:
In the morning glad I see
My foe outstretched beneath the tree.

WILLIAM BLAKE

Blake's poem is based in part on the story of Adam's fall, but the apple here symbolizes hidden and deceitful hatred, rather than being the fruit of the tree of knowledge of good and evil. And instead of representing a test of man's obedience to God, the eating (or stealing) of the apple is a trap which not only causes the downfall of the narrator's "foe," but also shows the bad effects of secrecy and hypocrisy on the narrator's own character. Yet it would be hard to give the "apple bright" a precise meaning. It stands for whatever is attractive but poisonous, or whatever underhanded means we use to lure our enemies, and consequently ourselves, to destruction.

Symbolism and allegory are overlapping terms, but though there are isolated allegorical figures (or personifications) like Sin and Death in *Paradise Lost,* an allegory is usually a narrative with significance on two or more levels. The surface or literal level of the story indicates, either explicitly or implicitly, that the poem is to be "read" on other levels as well. The "allegorical" level of the poem can be defined as an extended metaphor which expresses a connected pattern of either specific (historical) or general (philosophical or ethical) meaning. Complex allegories, like Edmund Spenser's *Faerie Queene* (see extract on pp. 84–89), may incorporate both specific and general levels of meaning, but the following poem provides a simpler example:

Up-Hill

Does the road wind up-hill all the way?
   Yes, to the very end.
Will the day's journey take the whole long day?
   From morn to night, my friend.

But is there for the night a resting place?
   A roof for when the slow dark hours begin.
May not the darkness hide it from my face?
   You cannot miss that inn.

Shall I meet other wayfarers at night?
   Those who have gone before.
Then must I knock, or call when just in sight?
   They will not keep you standing at that door.

Shall I find comfort, travel-sore and weak?
   Of labor you shall find the sum.

Will there be beds for me and all who seek?
Yea, beds for all who come.

CHRISTINA ROSSETTI

A curious student might ask, "How do we know this poem is allegorical?" The most immediate answer is that the two questions of the first stanza don't mean very much if only interpreted literally. Of course, roads do wind up-hill all the way if they go up a mountain, but to ask about such a road and to get the answer, "Yes, to the very end," seems hardly worth the trouble. Then too, the word "end" seems slightly exaggerated in the context. The second question, whether a day's journey takes a whole day is, in literal terms, almost redundant. Unless we abandon the poem as a piece of nonsense, these questions force us to seek another level of meaning: to infer that the up-hill road stands for something like our struggle through existence and a day's journey represents our life span.

Our curious student might now ask a harder question: "Is the difference between symbol and allegory one of precision?" Is the difference merely that it is harder to say what Blake's "apple" represents than Rossetti's "road" and "journey"? Some modern critics do distinguish between symbol and allegory in just this way, and are inclined to assert that symbol is more valuable than allegory because it is more suggestive and less clearcut. But it is more helpful to realize that, in general, symbol and allegory differ in the kinds of consideration they ask for. A symbol demands careful examination as an image in itself before we can approximate its meaning, and complex symbols, like Yeats's city of Byzantium (see pp. 313 and 314), may need to be studied in a series of poems before we can come close to defining them. The symbol insists, so to speak, on its own concreteness.

Allegory, on the other hand, is a short cut to meaning, like the personifications it often uses. It dispenses with much of the "irrelevant concreteness" of a realistic poem to get more directly at the generalizations or events with which it is concerned. The literal narrative in allegory may be complex and exciting—a good prose example is J. R. R. Tolkien's *Lord of the Rings*—but the emphasis in allegory is placed ultimately on its nonliteral levels.

Allusion

The symbol's great merit is its power and range of suggestiveness; its typical limitation is that it tends to be vague or obscure. These attributes it shares with allusion: the use of explicit or implicit references to persons, places, history, works of art, etc., that lie outside the immediate experience presented in the poem. Allusion can operate like a massive image or symbol, sometimes providing the framework for a poem as in Blake's "A Poison Tree" or Yeats's "Byzantium" (pp. 314–15), or it can offer a crucial illustration for its theme like the mention of Brueghel's painting of Icarus in Auden's "Musée des Beaux Arts" (pp. 382–83). Also, we can consider allusion, like allegory, as both a short cut to meaning and a way of giving depth and resonance to a poem. For example, when Robert Lowell writes in "For the Union Dead":

> . . . a commercial photograph
> shows Hiroshima boiling
>
> over a Mosler Safe, the "Rock of Ages"
> that survived the blast,
>   (ll. 55–58, p. 410)

he is evoking the horror of Hiroshima, and the way in which an advertisement asks us to replace faith in God, the "Rock of Ages" of the hymn, with faith in a mechanical marvel, a safe that survived the first atomic bomb. These allusions reinforce the question posed by the poem, whether the sacrifices made by both whites and blacks in the Civil War have been made in vain.

Conventions and Genres

Though every poem is an individual and whole object in itself, it is invariably affected by conventions and genres. Conventions are ways of formalizing reality. It is a convention, for example, for a bride to wear white and a mourner to wear black. Poetry includes many kinds of conventions: patterns or procedures agreed upon by poet and audience. They are, so to speak, the rules of the game. In Elizabethan drama it is understood that a soliloquy represents the inner thoughts of the speaker and expresses his view of his situation as he grasps it: it would violate convention for Iago to tell a lie in one of his soliloquies, though he may not understand his own motivations. Poetic forms involve conventions, such as that the octave of an Italian sonnet states a problem and that the sestet resolves it. Themes and situations may be conventionalized, as in the Petrarchan lament where the idealized mistress disdains her humble lover. And stock characters in comedies, like the interfering old man and the resourceful servant, are conventional.

A genre is a literary kind or species. The study of genres is based on a knowledge of conventions, because genres are distinguished by the conventions they build on. But the term, genre, is confusing at first because genres sometimes are classified by content or attitude, sometimes by form, and sometimes by a mixture of both. In this essay, type designates classifications determined primarily by content or attitude, as when we call *Moby Dick* an "epic," and genre refers to classifications determined primarily by form. Comedy, as a term applied equally to poem, play, or novel, is a type; comedy, when it refers to a group of plays sharing certain structural principles, is a genre.

Genres are distinguished by different kinds of conventions. For example, the ancient distinction among lyric, dramatic, and epic poetry was based on, among other factors, the role of the speaker in each genre: the lyric uses a first-person speaker, the drama third-person speakers, and the epic a mixture of the two. Certain genres, like the ballad, sonnet, or ode, are classified primarily according to stanzaic form; others, like elegy, according to subject and attitude as well as form, which means they hover between type and genre.

Despite its complexity, the study of genres is very useful. First, it provides categories with which to order the thousands of existing poems. In turn, the categories, as they are viewed historically, present traditions in which poets work and which help us to better understand particular poems. For example, contemporary ignorance of the conventions of pastoral poetry leads to a rejection of what is seen as impossibly idealized shepherds and shepherdesses, who roam unnaturally beautiful landscapes and spend their time whining about love. The usually unstated assumption behind such criticism is that all literature should be "realistic." This sort of demand is irrelevant to the pastoral. One can like a horse better than a cow, but one cannot blame the cow for not being a horse nor examine the cow as though it were a poorly put-together horse.

On the other hand, a certain amount of knowledge about a genre like the pastoral enables us to see how various poets use its conventions for different purposes. Essentially a pastoral is a poem about a simple, pure existence, a Garden of Eden or a Golden Age in the remote past, or some later equivalent. It praises the life of nature as contrasted to the life of society or civilization. The basic appeal of the pastoral shows itself in the opening stanzas of Christopher Marlowe's "The Passionate Shepherd to His Love":

> Come live with me and be my love,
> And we will all the pleasures prove
> That valleys, groves, hills, and fields,
> Woods, or steepy mountain yields.
>
> And we will sit upon the rocks,
> Seeing the shepherds feed their flocks,
> By shallow rivers, to whose falls
> Melodious birds sing madrigals.
>
> (ll. 1–8, p. 94)

Everyone would like, or thinks he would like, the simple life Marlowe suggests here so attractively. At the same time, the vision of the pastoral clashes with our sense of what the daily, complicated routine of ordinary existence involves, and the contrast is apt to provoke the kind of response to Marlowe that appears in Sir Walter Ralegh's "The Nymph's Reply to the Shepherd":

> If all the world and love were young,
> And truth in every shepherd's tongue,
> These pretty pleasures might me move
> To live with thee and be thy love.
>
> . . .
>
> The flowers do fade, and wanton fields
> To wayward winter reckoning yields;
> A honey tongue, a heart of gall,
> Is fancy's spring, but sorrow's fall.
>
> (ll. 1–4, 9–12, p. 91)

If the pastoral is as easily discredited as Ralegh's poem implies, we might ask why poets have been writing pastorals since the time of ancient Greece. Part of the answer is that the ideal is as "true" as the actual; part that the belief in the happy country life is still very strong; and part that the pastoral is a flexible genre, allowing the poet considerable range of expression. It can reflect a sense of the complex relationship of nature to man, as in Marvell's "Picture of Little T. C." (p. 150), and it has often been used as a vehicle for elegy, as in Milton's *Lycidas* (p. 136). The dead Lycidas and the speaker who mourns for him are conventionalized as shepherds:

> Under the opening eyelids of the morn,
> We drove afield, and both together heard
> What time the gray-fly winds her sultry horn.
>
> (ll. 26–28)

But Milton extends the pastoral to include satire. Invoking the old metaphor of the religious leader as "the pastor of his flock," he unexpectedly introduces a digression in which St. Peter attacks self-seeking clergymen:

> Blind mouths! that scarce themselves know how to hold
> A sheep-hook, or have learned aught else the least
> That to the faithful herdman's art belongs!
>
> (ll. 119–21)

Even here Milton is careful not to violate the pastoral conventions he has established for the poem.

In more recent times, pastoral has dropped the trappings of shepherds and flocks, while retaining its old mixture of realistic and symbolic elements. Whitman's elegy for Abraham Lincoln, *When Lilacs Last in the*

Dooryard Bloomed (p. 275), describes the countryside through which the funeral train passes in realistic terms:

> Amid lanes and through old woods, where lately the violets peeped
>   from the ground, spotting the gray debris,
>
> Passing the yellow-speared wheat, every grain from its shroud in the
>   dark-brown fields uprisen.
>
> (ll. 27, 29)

But in the same poem, the great star drooping in the west and the hermit thrush singing of death from the swamp are also symbolic elements which represent nature mourning.

A recent commentator has defined the poems of Robert Frost, the most famous pastoral poet of this century, as a "mode of viewing common experience through the medium of the rural world." In Frost's poems the old pastoral ideas of the beauty and simplicity of country life recur regularly, though often streaked with a consciousness of its harsher aspects. Frost also exploits the allegorical possibilities that pastoral has always offered, as in "Mowing":

> There was never a sound beside the wood but one,
> And that was my long scythe whispering to the ground.
> What was it it whispered? I know not well myself;
> Perhaps it was something about the heat of the sun,
> Something, perhaps, about the lack of sound.
>
> (ll. 1–5, pp. 323–24)

A more complicated modern use of pastoral occurs in Auden's "In Memory of W. B. Yeats" (p. 384), an elegy, like *Lycidas* and *When Lilacs Last in the Dooryard Bloomed*. In Auden's poem, the pastoral setting itself has disappeared, but Auden echoes it in his metaphors of valley, river, and country:

> For poetry makes nothing happen: it survives
> In the valley of its saying where executives
> Would never want to tamper; it flows south
> From ranches of isolation and the busy griefs.
>
> (ll. 36–39)

One result of studying poetry is a sense of genre and its conventions that most modern readers have only in the detective story and science-fiction novel. Ignorance of genre not only limits a reader's access to past literature, it also handicaps his understanding of modern poetry. If he fails, for instance, to recognize that E. E. Cummings's "Pity This Busy Monster, Manunkind" (p. 368) is a slant-rhymed Italian sonnet, he may not recognize that the poem pivots, as such sonnets traditionally do, on its eighth and ninth lines:

A world of made
is not a world of born.

A particular victim of this reduced sense of genre is parody. Without
knowledge of the epic, half the fun and point of a mock-epic like *The
Rape of the Lock* disappear.

Structure

Another way of characterizing conventions is to say that they are the
structural properties of a genre: their presence helps determine what
genre a poem belongs to. But each poem taken by itself also has a structure. We can define structure as the relation of part to part or parts to a
whole. The structure of a poem, then, is made up of a number of subordinate patterns. In some ways it resembles the structure of the human
body, which includes the skeleton, cardiovascular system, central nervous
system, and autonomic nervous system. Similarly poems contain patterns
of narrative, idea, imagery, sound, etc. The analogy is inexact, of course,
since humans, as organic beings, grow and decay, and poems do not. Also,
all human physical systems, apart from differences based on gender, function in much the same way, while the patterns of poetry vary a great deal
from poem to poem.

It is vital to grasp the structure of a poem because then we can understand how its parts—sense, imagery, diction, prosody, and so forth—make
up a whole. In theory it would be possible to examine all the patterns involved in the structure of a poem, but in practice any such examination
would be clumsy, repetitive, and very boring. Hence most discussions of
structure concentrate on the part or parts of a poem that most clearly
shape it and provide its particular effect. The genre here is helpful in
locating the poem's most important structural features. In an epic, like
Paradise Lost, the narrative structure is highly significant and the patterns
of imagery somewhat less so. But in a lyric like Donne's "A Valediction
Forbidding Mourning" (pp. 104–05), the reverse is true, since the narrative
structure is simple and the complex imagery patterns carry most of the
poem's meaning. Shifts in diction are significant to Keats's "On First
Looking into Chapman's Homer" (see discussion, pp. 8–9) and shifts
in tone to Marvell's "To His Coy Mistress" (pp. 147–48). There are even
poems dominated by sound patterns, sometimes to the detriment of sense,
like these lines from A. C. Swinburne's *Atalanta in Calydon*:

> Before the beginning of years
>   There came to the making of man
> Time, with a gift of tears;
>   Grief, with a glass that ran;

Pleasure, with pain for leaven;
Summer, with flowers that fell.
("Chorus," ll. 1–6)

There is space here to mention only a few elements of poetic structure, but their interrelationships can be illustrated by examining the poem reprinted below.

Mind

Mind in its purest play is like some bat
That beats about in caverns all alone,
Contriving by a kind of senseless wit
Not to conclude against a wall of stone.

It has no need to falter or explore;
Darkly it knows what obstacles are there,
And so may weave and flitter, dip and soar,
In perfect courses through the blackest air.

And has this simile a like perfection?
The mind is like a bat. Precisely. Save
That in the very happiest intellection
A graceful error may correct the cave.

RICHARD WILBUR

Perhaps the first structural feature of "Mind" to strike the reader is the poem's stanzaic division into three quatrains, in each of which a single idea is presented. The first quatrain states that the mind is like a bat, the second explores the ways in which mind and bat are alike, and the third turns to examine the truth of the simile and to stress one significant way in which mind and bat differ.

Syntactically, each of the first two stanzas of the poem is made up of a single sentence. The third stanza, however, is divided into four sentences: the first asks a question, the second restates the original simile, and the third consists of a single adverb, "Precisely." On this word the poem pivots, since the fourth sentence modifies what has been said up to this point. The bat is enclosed in its physical surroundings, while the mind is occasionally able to alter its world ("caverns," "cave") by some "graceful error." The unexpectedness of this last phrase calls attention to it: how can an error correct a cave? The double meaning of "error" helps to solve this problem. "To err" originally meant "to wander," as both bat and mind do within their limitations. But a "graceful error," which means something like a "fortunate mistake," shows the mind that its boundaries are not fixed, though it takes "the very happiest intellection" to reach this result. In terms of diction, "intellection" is a highly abstract word which contrasts to the concrete terms, "weave and flitter, dip and soar," that develop the parallel between "bat" and "mind." The bat, we know, operates almost uncannily through its sensory apparatus to avoid flying against a "wall of stone" which a man moving in "the blackest air" would almost surely blunder into. But through "intellection," a capacity that distinguishes man from bat, the human mind can accomplish a change far beyond the bat's ability. Wilbur characterizes the mind as having a "senseless wit," a pun which defines the mind's movement in two different ways: man's "wit" or intellect can seem senseless or foolish, but also to some extent it operates independently of the senses and thus can alter its limitations. Finally, the allusion to the "cave" will recall to the knowledgeable reader Plato's comparison of the world to a cave in which man sits and mistakes the passing shadows on the cave's walls for the "real" world outside. Plato's point is that the mind can penetrate through the material world perceived by the senses to the "reality" which the senses only shadow forth.

A more complete structural analysis of "Mind" would surely explore the mind-bat comparison and the allusions to Plato's cave at greater length. Sound patterns here are much less important, though the reader might remark that "bat" and "wit" (lines 1 and 3) make up the one slant rhyme in the poem—perhaps an ingenious hint that the analogy between "bat" and man's "wit" is only accurate in part. Since the elegant, playfully serious tone of the poem does not vary, it asks for comparatively little analysis and requires but that we note it. The poem's structure depends basically on its stanzaic organization and on its central mind-bat simile to bring out its subject: the operation of the mind at its most abstract.

With this brief illustration of structural analysis, we have finished considering the major parts of the poem, taking the poem as an object in itself. But a poem is never quite an isolated object; it has connections that the sketch below illustrates:

It is the concern of Part II of the Introduction to consider some of the relationships this sketch indicates.

II: The Poem and Poetic Theories

One way to explore the form and function of poetry is to consider the differences between poetry and discursive prose, such as the report or the editorial. Let us start with the definition of poetry framed by Samuel Taylor Coleridge.

> A poem is that species of composition which is opposed to works of science by proposing for its *immediate* object pleasure, not truth; and from all other species having *this* object in common with it it is discriminated by proposing to itself such delight from the *whole* as is compatible with a distinct gratification from each component *part*.
>
> (*Biographia Literaria*, Ch. XIV)

Coleridge speaks of the *immediate* object of the poem as pleasure rather than truth. By pleasure he means more than "entertainment." He is not making a case for poetry as the graceful accomplishment of light minds. Rather, what he means is that we read poetry for its own sake and not as a means to some other end, as we would a piece of expository prose. We may, of course, read poems in order to gain information about what people of a given time felt or thought, and we may read them in order to learn about the mind of the poet who wrote them. But these are possible uses to which we may put the poems rather than their proper object. We can gain such information from other sources, and these need not be poetic in form.

If we feel that "pleasure" is too trivial a word, we may choose to speak of poems as existing for the sake of contemplation. The word "contemplation" denotes a disinterested activity, from which we seek no ulterior benefit and to which we come with an open mind. A poem, like a painting, may require some puzzling out, but it is not a puzzle that loses interest as soon as we have solved it. It may resemble a game in its lack of practical purpose, but it is a game that involves our feelings and our thought to a greater degree than most games can. It presents us with a complex structure, composed in varying degrees of statement and image, which suggests meanings and teases us into exploring them further.

This brings us to the second main point of Coleridge's statement: that a poem, compared with other kinds of writing, has great formal complexity. The words have intricate relationships with each other—patterns of sound, of syntax, and of imagery among others—and require a great deal of attention in themselves. They are not "transparent" in the sense that we look through them to the ideas or things they denote, as we usually do in reading a report. We cannot substitute one word for another in a poem without disrupting the intricate structure the words create with each other. In fact, each word tends to be part of more than one pattern. It is the sense of multiple function that each part of a poem carries, as well as the unity that holds all these functions together in one structure, that has led many critics to speak of the poem as an organism. This can be a misleading analogy if we take it in too strict a sense. We might better compare the structure of a poem with that which we find in a system of ecological balance; all the elements of the system are so subtly interdependent that each change may introduce incalculable dislocations.

The two aspects of a poem that Coleridge singles out—its being an end in itself and its having a complex internal structure—both serve to "frame" the poem somewhat as a painting is framed. This frame does not cut off the poem from human feeling. The framing effect of the poem simply allows us to free our feelings and ideas of their urgency and their immediate reference to specific events in the world outside. Those feelings and ideas become, for the moment, tentative, experimental, provisional. We explore what it is like to hold a given idea; we try out the feelings the poem awakens and see where they may lead. In a similar way, when we watch a film, we may have deep feelings about the characters in it; but we do not expect to affect their lives or stop the action, nor do we want to. We are, instead, exploring the possibilities that the film releases.

The framing effect of a poem is produced both by the close attention required to respond to its complex structure and by the expectations we bring to it. One may use another analogy. Museums often frame, by placing in glass cases and mounting for display, useful everyday objects—spoons, typewriters, pencil-sharpeners—so as to allow us to look at their form, to consider the economy of the structure or the shapeliness of the design. We must be wrenched away from our customary, utilitarian view of such objects in order to see those qualities of design we often take for granted and respond to, if at all, only unconsciously. This "arrest" of mind is created in part by what we expect an art museum to display. We bring to the museum a kind of attention that concentrates on the form and design of objects. So it is with a poem. We might read the same words, if they were written as prose, without the attention to "each component part" (in Coleridge's terms) that produces a full response.

The arrest of mind enables us to see things freshly. Our habitual responses are inhibited and we can look more fully at those elements that we might otherwise consider solely for their utilitarian function. In a display of typography, we cease for a moment to read words and are enabled to see the design of letters. We do not altogether forget the words, for the value of the type design will depend upon the ease and grace with which letters relate to each other and form an appropriate medium for a given kind of subject matter. We may admire a certain typeface as a medium for advertising, another for the printing of the Bible. But we are concentrating for the moment, as we rarely do when we read, upon the shape of the type itself.

What a poem can do is to free us of habitual responses, both to words and to experience, and to restore the sense of freshness with which we encounter a moving experience for the first time. A poem may deal with a familiar experience, but it forces us to respond more fully to what we ordinarily hurry past or take for granted. The poem, in fact, may enable us to see in the familiar what we have never before been able to recognize, just as a portrait of someone we think we know very well may reveal aspects we have never before been able to see clearly. It has been said that the language of poetry seeks to "defamiliarize" experience. One could also say it tries to awaken us to a full response that most of us seldom attain, and it does this by making words act differently than they ordinarily do. What has been an ordinary event becomes a "happening," something that commands attention and rewards it by making us use our powers of perception in a new way.

Poetry and Knowledge

Even if the "immediate object" of poetry is pleasure, we must recognize that poetry seems to provide a kind of knowledge—not merely knowledge of the poet's feelings or of his imagined world but of the larger world we share with him. Some critics have claimed that poetry gives us "the world's body," that is, the immediacy and complexity of experience as opposed to the schematic categories and necessary abstractions that more scientific knowledge requires. Others have spoken of the power of poetry to refine and mature our awareness, to give us a language in which to frame experience we might otherwise be unable to articulate and therefore to reflect upon.

What these critics are expressing is the sense that poetry is "true to" our experience, not that it gives us "truth about" that experience. Poetry can extend or sharpen our awareness of objects that have grown familiar and are taken for granted. These it presents with new intensity, and the intensity is not simply an emotional one. We are made to feel more intensely because we are made to see more intensely. What we see is a new shape in our experience, a shape into which objects fit in a new way. The shape may, for example, be a sense of unity in all things that is the outward counterpart of an inward sense of joy; or it may be the fragmentation that a dejected or alienated mind finds in the world about it. In each case, there is a "vision," a shaping of experience according to a pattern. The emotions we bring to the "vision" vary from reader to reader, and they may vary from time to time within the same reader. What remains constant is the power of the poem to summon up a pattern of awareness. It is "true to" experience seen in a certain aspect or a certain way.

Such a vision may have an influence on all our later responses. Our reading of Wordsworth may alter our response to all landscape and, as a result, we may say that the poem shapes the reality we perceive or gives us a kind of truth nowhere else available. But this "truth to" experience does not offer itself as a factual assertion. As the Elizabethan poet and critic Sir Philip Sidney said, "The poet, he nothing affirmeth, and therefore never lieth." Poetry does not offer us verifiable knowledge of the sort that may be tested empirically and cited as evidence. It offers us "knowledge by acquaintance," that sense of what it is like to see things in a certain way or to envisage experience from a certain point of view. We "entertain" the vision that poetry offers; that is, we try the vision on and explore its possibilities. This gives us a broader or deeper awareness without necessarily informing us of new objective facts. To claim value for such insight does not require us to claim all value for it or to deny the distinction between this kind of insight and what we usually mean by empirical knowledge.

Let us consider the example of the following poem:

A Study of Reading Habits

When getting my nose in a book
Cured most things short of school,
It was worth ruining my eyes
To know I could still keep cool,
And deal out the old right hook
To dirty dogs twice my size.

Later, with inch-thick specs,
Evil was just my lark:
Me and my cloak and fangs
Had ripping times in the dark.
The women I clubbed with sex!
I broke them up like meringues.

Don't read much now: the dude
Who lets the girl down before
The hero arrives, the chap
Who's yellow and keeps the store,
Seem far too familiar. Get stewed:
Books are a load of crap.

PHILIP LARKIN

The poem provides us with three stages of the speaker's reading habits. First we have the small boy finding escape from his feelings of powerlessness in fantasies of physical strength. His escape is not quite complete, for it cannot "cure" the frustrations he finds in school. In the second stanza we move on to adolescence, where aggressive sexual fantasies—the cloak and the fangs suggest Dracula, and there are overtones of the Victorian murderer of prostitutes, Jack the Ripper—seem to compensate for the retiring life behind "inch-thick specs." Finally, these uses of reading lose their power. The typical themes of adult romantic fiction are too close to the disenchanting life of actuality. Life cannot live up to fantasies, and fantasies no longer have a commanding power. Drink must take their place.

It is a poem about the misuse of literature as a substitute for life, and it is also a poem about growing up. Or about not growing up. For the bitterness of the last line is not simply a mature man's rejection of fantasy. It is rather the disappointment of someone who can neither endure actuality nor sustain his daydreams. He has dwindled into the "chap/Who's yellow and keeps the store," a weak man locked in a routine. One may find in the poem implicit "truths about" the uses of literature: for example, escapist fantasies only leave one dissatisfied with actual life and unprepared to meet it. The poem suggests this without needing to assert it. What it does is to give us a compressed little drama in three acts, with the last bursting out in a memorable final line that is at once bitter and fatuous. Does such a poem give us knowledge? Does it teach a lesson? Not in any direct way. Yet it is so constructed that we are teased by questions and moved to reflection; we may be led to seek knowledge about ourselves and others.

Another brief poem raises similar questions.

Nothing Gold Can Stay

Nature's first green is gold,
Her hardest hue to hold.
Her early leaf's a flower;
But only so an hour.
Then leaf subsides to leaf.
So Eden sank to grief,
So dawn goes down to day.
Nothing gold can stay.

ROBERT FROST

Gold has traditionally been a symbol of the precious and the pure. Frost gives to it new qualities of freshness and fragility, attributes that are hardly associated with gold as a metal. There is another way in which Frost upsets traditional ideas. The "first green" of the tree is not properly a leaf but a blossom, and, while it is green, it is a tender golden green that lasts a short time. "Then leaf subsides to leaf." The blossom is replaced by the true leaf, at once sturdier and darker, the true green that endures for the summer. Why does Frost put it so? Is he suggesting that we deceive ourselves by thinking of the blossom as a leaf, that the leaf it "subsides to" is what, after all, we must expect? Is Eden only a myth that we cannot expect actuality to match? Dawn is a moving sight but a momentary one; we must live most of our lives in day. We are left with a double sense: we recognize with regret that the precious may be fragile and unstable, but we recognize also that we may invest its evanescent beauty with so much value that we underrate most of our other experience.

Here the fantasies, if that is the word for them, are not an escape from a sense of personal incompetence or insufficiency, as in Larkin's poem. They are far more universal and are built into man's temperament. In a later poem, "There Are Roughly Zones" (p. 326), Frost deals with the foolishness that tries to cultivate a peach tree too far north. It is a somewhat destructive foolishness but also a rather heroic one, a "limitless trait in the hearts of men." In the earlier poem the regret of the last line, "Nothing gold can stay," is a recognition of this limitlessness, the yearning for that which cannot be kept. In short, this poem awakens us, here by puzzles of language rather than by dramatic reversal, to a pattern of opposition: a momentary glimpse of unlimited good or beauty vs. the substantial, enduring second-best. In what sense does the poem give us knowledge? It shapes an experience so as to leave us with two opposed or contrary views of it, one stressing a restless idealism, the other stressing reconciliation to what in fact we are given. The difficulty of choosing between them is what remains before us.

Poetry as Imitation

When we speak of poetry as a form of knowledge, we imply a theory of poetry as an imitation of nature. A theory of poetry as *mimesis*, that is, as representation or copying, can be used either to exalt or condemn poetry. The crucial question is how we define "nature." For Plato, true reality lay in those Forms or Ideas which were, at best, imperfectly realized in the world of natural objects. No actual man is a perfect embodiment of the Idea of man, for each man is in some way warped, stunted, or distorted (whether physically or morally) by the material circumstances of his existence. To represent an actual man in a work of art, then, means, according to Plato, to create an imitation, an image twice removed from the Idea. Art becomes the imitation of appearances rather than of reality, and it may serve to produce a dangerous appetite for the vivid and immediate at the expense of that which is real and permanent. A simpler illustration of the process would be the power of a popular art form to generate a strong taste for uncritical fantasies (such as Philip Larkin presents in "A Study of Reading Habits") that makes impossible the acceptance of reality.

Whereas Plato condemned the imitative poet and banned him from his ideal republic, Aristotle reclaimed both the status of poetry and the theory of imitation. For Aristotle there was no supersensible world of Forms to which the mind had direct access, and imitation was not twice-removed from reality. On the contrary, poetry might give a meaningful order to events that actuality could not provide. Aristotle's view freed the idea of imitation from that of mere deception. Poetry inevitably alters actuality in order to represent it, but it may surpass—at least in formal coherence, probability, and universality—the stuff of actual experience. Aristotle's theory can even give rise, with extension, to the view that poetry recovers those Forms of things that are not accessible in everyday experience. Such a view, which is to be found in its fullest form in Neoplatonism, turns from the idea of imitation to one of discovery or revelation, for what poetry reveals has never in fact been available to us in the literal world. The poet becomes a discoverer, a creator, a maker.

Sir Philip Sidney, in *An Apology for Poetry*, stressed the idea of the poet as "maker" and set him apart from those who are limited to mere literal imitation of nature:

> Only the poet, disdaining to be tied to any such subjection, lifted up with the vigor of his own invention, doth grow in effect into another nature, in making things either better than nature bringeth forth, or quite anew . . . so as he goeth hand in hand with nature, not enclosed within the narrow warrant of her gifts, but freely ranging only within the zodiac of his own wit. . . . Her world is brazen, the poets only deliver a golden.

In this conception the poet no longer imitates created nature but the creative power itself; he is a second maker, whose golden world redeems the actual one by realizing man's values more completely. The world the poet creates may be called a heterocosm, "not a part, nor yet a copy, of the real world . . . [but] a world by itself, independent, complete, autonomous." To "possess it fully you must enter that world, conform to its laws, and ignore for a time the beliefs, aims, and particular conditions which belong to you in the other world of reality," as the nineteenth-century scholar A. C. Bradley said in "Poetry for Poetry's Sake."

In this view poetry ceases to be imitation and becomes analogy. It neither offers us a copy of the actual world, nor does it claim to reveal a world more "real" than the actual one. What it creates could be called a "model" of our world constructed so as to allow us to test certain beliefs. Or it could be called an extended metaphor, an imagined world with which to compare our own in order to see ours in a certain light. Our world may never be the same again once we have lived imaginatively in Dostoevsky's or Kafka's fictional world, and the same may be said of the worlds created by the poets.

Whether we call the world of the poem a golden world, a model, or an extended metaphor, we do not mistake it for a literal imitation. It makes reference to our world through analogy, and to do that it must reproduce certain structures and features of this world; but, like all analogies, it contains elements of difference as well as of sameness, of strangeness as well as of familiarity. And, like all analogies, it invites being explored "as if" it were real. This may permit an escape from our confusions and difficulties into a world that seems to foster our hearts' desires. Or it may provide a critique of the imperfections and errors of our actual world.

Poetry as Expression

To speak of the poet as a second maker is to shift attention from the creation to the creator, and to shift our metaphor for poetry from a mirror that reflects nature to a lamp that shines from within, its glow a product of deep feeling and imaginative power. This shift becomes most dramatic with the emergence of Romantic poetry at the end of the eighteenth century. Wordsworth, when he speaks of poetry as "the spontaneous overflow of powerful feelings," implies that the poet has greater intensity of feeling than most men and that the feelings are strong enough to force themselves out, literally to "ex-press" themselves. Byron describes this pressure even more sharply when he says that poetry "is the lava of the imagination whose eruption prevents an earthquake." Earlier, eighteenth-century critics had been less respectful of this process. They could speak satirically of "poetical evacuation," a "vent of unruly passions," a "natural or morbid secretion from the brain." In fact, both Pope and Swift play ironically with the question of whether a given poem is "issue" or "excrement," a new and independent life or a mere discharge of excesses. The problem, as they see it, is to make the act of expression an act of creation as well. This is achieved by giving form to what otherwise might be mere "overflow."

Cries of pain and squeals of joy express powerful feelings and communicate them to others, but they are seldom works of art. To create a poem, the expression of feeling must involve as well the shaping power of imagination. In a weak but passionate poem Keats records his feeling for Fanny

Brawne. He expresses intense feeling, but he hardly gives it form or creates a memorable structure:

I Cry Your Mercy

I cry your mercy—pity—love—aye, love!
  Merciful love that tantalizes not,
One-thoughted, never-wandering, guileless love,
  Unmasked, and being seen—without a blot!
O! let me have thee whole,—all—all—be mine!
  That shape, that fairness, that sweet minor zest
Of love, your kiss,—those hands, those eyes divine,
  That warm, white, lucent, million-pleasured breast,—
Yourself—your soul—in pity give me all,
  Withhold no atom's atom or I die,
Or living on perhaps, your wretched thrall,
  Forget, in the mist of idle misery,
Life's purposes,—the palate of my mind
Losing its gust, and my ambition blind!

                                         JOHN KEATS

This power of creation, of shaping experience in memorable form, has been given various names. "Wit" was the most common term for this creative power among Renaissance critics like Sidney, and it persisted until it was displaced by the Romantic idea of "imagination." Wit, in its broadest sense, meant the discovery of insightful analogies, the power to discover hidden but significant resemblances in things that are apparently dissimilar. It was, therefore, a unifying power. But it could impose deceptive unity through strained or false analogies. There was a need to distinguish "true wit" from "false wit," and the latter term came to be applied to a shallow cleverness that produced ingenious half-truths. Alexander Pope defined true wit in a famous pair of couplets:

> True wit is nature to advantage dressed,
> What oft was thought, but ne'er so well expressed;
> Something whose truth convinced at sight we find,
> That gives us back the image of our mind.
>
> (*An Essay on Criticism*, ll. 297–300)

What Pope stresses is "truth to" experience. The poet uncovers what we have, at some deep level of consciousness, always known, although we have not until now been able quite to say it and therefore to see it. The poet's wit shapes our experience of nature in a way that makes its meaning clear; what he reveals strikes us as true, as something we have always, as it were, been about to realize. In that sense, poetic wit tells us about ourselves as well as about the world—it reveals to us what has been latent in our thought, "the image of our mind."

Imagination, in its earliest sense, meant the image-making power of the mind. Like false wit, it could be misleading or deceptive, framing wishful fantasies or delusions rather than images of reality. But, as the Romantics conceived imagination, it became the highest forming power of the mind. Like true wit, imagination can both reveal us to ourselves and reveal new dimensions in nature. Imagination tended to act under the pressure of strong feeling, and, under that pressure, it created new wholes of elements formerly seen as distinct and separate. The nineteenth-century critic William Hazlitt shows imagination at work in *King Lear*. When Lear exclaims in his madness, "The little dogs and all, Tray, Blanche, and Sweetheart, see, they bark at me," Hazlitt points out that we see Lear's "passion lending occasion to imagination to make every creature in league against him." Imagination, in this instance, creates a world shaped by one prevailing passion, and it approaches mania, which gives a single design to all experience.

Lear's passion is an extreme case. Equally important in the Romantic view is the stress upon imagination as a full and active power of man's mind (rather than as a passive instrument of forces beyond its control). Wordsworth saw this power at the heart of man's myth-making. He described the way in which the goddess of the moon—Artemis, the chaste huntress—might have been born of man's imagination:

> The nightly hunter, lifting a bright eye
> Up towards the crescent moon, with grateful heart
> Called on the lovely wanderer who bestowed
> That timely light, to share his joyous sport;
> And hence, a beaming goddess with her nymphs,
> Across the lawn and through the darksome grove,
> Not unaccompanied with tuneful notes
> By echo multiplied from rock or cave,
> Swept in the storm of chase. . . .
>
> (*The Excursion*, Book IV, ll. 861–69)

The mind, stirred by feeling but not overcome by it, invests nature with mysterious presences that transform and humanize man's outer world.

As we have seen, the mimetic and expressive theories of poetry approach the poetic process from different directions. It is their meeting point that concerns us. The expressive theory accounts for the origin of the poem in the poet's feelings, but those feelings are attached to the world outside the poet and require some vision of that world in which to find their full expression. The mimetic theory can account for the materials which the poet shapes and it can tell us about the relation of the poem—imitative or metaphoric—to the world, but it does not account for the inner motive and intention in shaping a poem, which arise from the feelings of the poet. The expressive and mimetic functions of the poem meet in the poet's vision, rendered in narrative or metaphor. This makes the poem at once more than an expression of private feeling and more than impersonal description. The poem includes elements of both. It challenges us to explore the vision it presents, accepting it to the extent that we can, modifying or rejecting it to the extent that we must, but in either case reexamining experience in its light.

The Poet and the Poem

When discussing expressive theories of poetry we encounter the difficult problem of the poet's relation to his poem. First of all, we must distinguish between what a poem means and what the poet intended it to mean. Not every poet accomplishes what he intends and the creation of his poem is often more a mixture of accident and intuition than a process of rational control. "The poet is entitled to whatever you can find in him," Robert Frost has said, and this implies the poet may not be aware of all he has achieved. On the other hand, he *may* be an excellent interpreter of his own meaning. But as interpreter of what the poem achieves (in contrast with what he intended) he does not have unique authority. He often learns from his critics both what he has done and what he has failed to do.

Second, we must recognize that, just as the poet shapes the poem, so the poem in some sense shapes the poet. Once the author is embarked on a poem his writing may be determined by the logic of the work itself. This is most striking when the form of the poem is a strict one. Poets have often valued rhyme precisely because it does not permit them a free choice of words. In the search for a word that must meet arbitrary conditions of sound as well as of meaning, the poet may be forced into greater depths and rewarded with a happier discovery than before. And when he has found the rhyming word, he must often recast the preceding lines to make that word seem the necessary or inevitable one.

How much of the process of composition is conscious, how much it draws upon unconscious or pre-conscious impulses and associations, will vary from poet to poet, and we cannot always trust the poet's own account of how he writes. In Edgar Allan Poe's "The Philosophy of Composition," for example, we are offered a coldly deductive procedure that would, if it were truly Poe's practice, lead him to write the same poem ("The Raven") whenever he took up his pen. Some poets have tended to exaggerate the conscious control they exercise over their work; others have tended to minimize it and to suggest complete spontaneity and lack of forethought. We often have extensively revised manuscripts to undermine the claim to casual improvisation, such as Byron liked to make, but we should also keep in mind that a skill earned through long practice may seem to the poet to come as second nature with little sense of effort.

Psychoanalysis has deepened our conception of the poetic process. Sigmund Freud showed the mind, as one critic put it, to be "a poetry-making organ." In his analysis of dreams and jokes, Freud studied processes that are very similar to those of poetry. In the expression of impulses which must be disguised in order to be expressed at all, the mind finds techniques by which to conceal and reveal at the same time, techniques of ambiguity which can accommodate both a latent (or hidden) and a manifest (or surface) meaning. Freud sees the poet drawing upon regressive, sometimes even infantile, wishes and fantasies but giving them a formal structure or an acceptable surface that will allow them to escape that censorship exercised by the superego in behalf of traditional or social values. The psychoanalytic interpreter of dreams often seeks to uncover those impulses that present themselves in a disguised form, and this can lead to a dismissal of that form as merely the means of evading suppression. The literary interpreter of a poem, on the other hand, is equally interested in all of its elements, for the total structure of the poem is what produces its complexity of meaning and its richness of implication. The poem's interest lies not merely in a hidden meaning or an emotional drive but in the full balance of impulse and order. There is a potential conflict, therefore, between the effort to read the poem as symptomatic of the poet's internal conflicts and the effort to read it as a literary work. The theorist and historian of art Arnold Hauser presented the problem well in his *Philosophy of Art History*.

> Briefly, the closer we go to the origin of a work of art, the farther we may get from its artistic meaning. A too close relating of the work to the biography of the artist may lead to an abuse of psychology—to psychologism. The life-history of an artist is, at any rate, as definitely determined by his work as his work is determined by his life-history. They are interrelated and condition one another in many ways. The life of the artist is an expression of his talent, as his talent is a product of his life. He experiences, by a kind of anticipation, the material adequate for his works, that is to say, he makes of his life what he is able to represent and interpret as an artist.

The nineteenth-century essayist Charles Lamb, in "Sanity of True Genius," wrote: "The true poet dreams being awake. He is not possessed by his subject but has dominion over it. . . ." All men have their fantasies, but most "do not create, which implies shaping and consistency. Their imaginations are not active—for to be active is to call something into act and form—but passive, as men in sick dreams." What distinguishes the successful poet is the shaping power by which he gives his experience form and objectifies it, making it meaningful to other men and relevant to other experiences.

One way to trace this shaping power is to recover the raw materials with which the poet works. The American scholar and critic John Livingston Lowes, in a famous study called *The Road to Xanadu*, retraced the reading of Coleridge in order to study the process by which his vicarious experience of foreign places (often drawn from travel books) was transformed in *The Ancient Mariner* and "Kubla Khan." In a different way Professor David Erdman has studied, in *Prophet Against Empire*, the social milieu of William Blake in order to see how contemporary political events obliquely contributed to his visionary poems. In both cases one needs a theory of transformation: an explanation of the imaginative process that used the materials of the poet's world and gave them the different shapes they took in the poems. Such a theory will be necessarily complex. We can see just how complex when we consider the processes by which Freud interprets the simpler materials of dreams and jokes; for the materials may arise from associations built at a much earlier time in the poet's mind, from immediate events in his life, from all the devices of concealment and disguises that Freud explores. If we try to recover the intentions that govern the transformation of the raw material, we are confronted with the contexts of the poem—personal, social, and artistic.

Context and Interpretation

We can try to study the poet's intentions in terms of his working out his deepest conflicts, or we may stop short of this attempt to reach an inaccessible level of his mind and instead trace meaningful patterns of images throughout his works. Such a study cannot remain too external; it cannot concern itself with the surface content of the images—stars, apples, doors— but must consider recurrent metaphorical patterns, that is, what stars, for example, mean in various contexts and what common tendencies their use reveals. These image-patterns, particularly strong in lyric poets, have their counterparts in the recurrent and typical characters or episodes of the dramatist and the novelist. Such patterns reveal the poet's mind working at a level that is scarcely conscious. Working at the level of conscious activity, we can study the poet's relationship to his literary traditions, his use of received forms (epic, tragedy, or the sonnet), where he may depart from tradition in ways that are a significant part of his meaning (as in Milton and the classical epic, for example). There is also the problem of a single poem's relationship to the poet's whole body of work. Poets often create a "canon," an authorized sequence in which their works are to be read or divisions into which their works are meant to fall. Wordsworth divided his poems into such groups as Poems Founded on the Affections, Poems of the Fancy, and Poems of the Imagination.

Whether or not we find these categories useful, they become in some

degree part of the meaning of the work. They induce an appropriate response. It is this function that the titles of poems, generally, may be said
to serve. They may state the occasion ("Lines Composed a Few Miles above
Tintern Abbey, on Visiting the Banks of the Wye during a Tour, July 13,
1798," "A Refusal to Mourn the Death, by Fire, of a Child in London"),
indicate a form ("The Indian Serenade," "Satires of Circumstance,"
"Eclogue on a Five-Barred Gate"), or tease us with a suggestive description or metaphor ("Neutral Tones," "The Equilibrists," "Angel Surrounded by Paysans").

There are ways, moreover, of studying poems as if they were the product
of an idea or of an age. If we isolate a traditional idea which has wide and
continual currency, we can study poems of different authors and ages as if
they were generated by the idea itself. This is only to say that the idea remains a relatively stable constant as it is transmitted, and we may be as
much interested in the creative power of this idea as in that of any given
poet's personality. The idea may, in fact, be a commanding image (the
earthly paradise) or a mythical motif (the fall of Icarus) or a theme (the
pleasures of country life). One of the most extensive of such studies is
the intellectual historian A. O. Lovejoy's *The Great Chain of Being*, which
traces a major metaphysical idea (or related set of ideas) through its appearance in philosophers and poets as it undergoes alteration in different
ages but remains identifiable as a pattern of Western thought. Another such
study, C. S. Lewis's *The Discarded Image*, traces the rise and decline of
the medieval model of the universe.

Lewis's book suggests another kind of "authorship" we may seek in
poems, that is, the impress of an age. We may be interested in seeing
poems as the product of a Renaissance or a Romantic mind. Any such
large abstractions tend to be vague, and the problem grows all the more
complex if one extends such a term, like the Age of the Baroque, to encompass all the arts or, indeed, all the institutions man creates. There have
been discussions of the baroque state by historians of political thought as
well as of baroque painting and of baroque poetry by critics of the arts.
A term which applies with reasonable precision to one kind of achievement
is extended as a metaphor to refer to others. Behind this metaphorical extension is the faith that a whole culture, like a single personality, has unity
and coherence at some level in its imaginative activities.

The Question of Intention

Behind these various frames of reference for studying a poem is the issue
of intention. When we interpret a law, for example, we try to determine
the precise meaning of its terms. If these seem unclear or double-edged,

we may go on to raise the question of what the law-makers intended the law to accomplish when they passed it. One may look at a poem in the same way, but, as we have seen, a poem is often a work in which the poet's intention is not altogether conscious and not always perfectly realized. We usually cannot fall back on questioning the author, but we may feel more secure in "questioning" his other works or his age. Could he have meant this, we ask ourselves? Can we give to this poem an interpretation that nothing in his other work supports? Can we properly assume this poem to be making a statement that no one in the eighteenth century would have made? We soon find ourselves in a circular pattern. We derive our knowledge of what an author could mean from our interpretation of all his works, and yet our interpretation of any one of those works must be guided by what all of them as a whole can mean.

How real is the difficulty? There is always some danger of importing into a poem a meaning that the author could not have conceived. This may arise through the changes in the meanings of words, as in this example from Dryden's translation of Virgil:

> I yield to fate, unwillingly retire;
> And, loaded, up the hill convey my sire.
> (Aeneid, Book II, ll. 1095–96)

Such cases are clear enough, but they shade into others that are more delicate. To what extent can we fully recover the meanings that certain terms ("imagination," "wit," "nature") had for a given poet or a given age? How much do we lose of a poem's meaning if we have lost the full sense of its occasion—that is, of which other poems were current and very possibly in the poet's and the readers' minds at the time a given poem was written and first read? Or which public events may lie behind the peculiar tone of a given poetic phrase? Or, indeed, what private associations of the poet? Clearly we must draw the line somewhere and accept limits to what we can know of the poet's intention.

One way of meeting the problem is to ask what we do with an anonymous poem. By studying the idiom we can place it with fair accuracy at a certain date. Through a historical dictionary, such as the *Oxford English Dictionary*, we can get rough guidelines to when certain meanings were current for a given word or phrase. By studying the form or conventions of the poem we can make surmises as to the kind of poem it seeks to be—lyric, satire, pastoral, etc.—and adopt expectations that are appropriate to its genre. Having placed it in the coordinates of period and genre, we can proceed to interpret it tentatively, perhaps correcting our placement of it as we go along. If there are telltale signs of a particular author—those distinctive "signatures" we recognize in a poet's or a painter's style—we may be able to assign it to a given writer and to relate it to his other works.

To approach the poem in this way is to leave open the question of whether it will necessarily conform with other works by the same author. He may introduce some novelty or discordancy that will complicate our conception of that poet or even of his age. Once we have placed the poem with accuracy and find sufficient confirming evidence from other sources that it is the work of a given poet, we may be able to see implications in the words that have previously escaped us, reference to particular events or people or instances of a recurring image in that poet's work. But we must always ask ourselves whether these further implications are a valuable enrichment of the meaning or an unnecessary restriction of it.

The task of choosing a text for a poem reveals these issues more sharply. The poet's revisions—not the mere corrections of printer's errors but substantial changes of meaning—may be genuine improvements, or they may seem excessively guarded afterthoughts (especially when poets undergo a change of social or religious attitude), or they may become mere impositions of a later mind upon an earlier one at the expense of the full expression of either. Several poets have presented this question, notably Wordsworth by his revisions of *The Prelude* and Yeats and Auden by their revision of earlier published poems. An editor, at any rate, must decide whether to present the poet's final decisions or whether to preserve what seems to him the best version of the poem, and he may sometimes be led to present a poem that combines eclectically the best versions of each textual variant. This may yield a poem that was never the poet's own choice at any one stage of composition, but rather a selection from various possibilities the poet has entertained at different stages. Since revisions may mark a fundamental change in conception, they may impose a new coherence upon the text at each stage; it becomes dangerous, therefore, to ignore the stages of composition in making selections from the variants. We can see this in the editing of a Shakespeare play, where the quarto texts of the individual plays may be more or less trustworthy than the folio collection edited after Shakespeare's death. In some cases, such as *Hamlet*, there are vast differences that may have resulted from a fundamentally new conception of the play.

Revisions may sometimes reveal not a change of conception but a groping toward more precise meaning. The discarded versions mark the failure to attain that full complexity or simplicity, that interplay of elements that gives us the sense of sureness and inevitability in the final version. One may compare two versions of the opening of W. B. Yeats's "Leda and The Swan" (see p. 319 for the complete poem).

> A rush, a sudden wheel, and hovering still
> The bird descends, and her frail thighs are pressed
> By the webbed toes, and that all-powerful bill
> Has laid her helpless face upon his breast . . .

> A sudden blow: the great wings beating still
> Above the staggering girl, her thighs caressed
> By the dark webs, her nape caught in his bill,
> He holds her helpless breast upon his breast.

Or one may see in a line of Pope the movement toward metaphor and energy:

> Tis all my joy in rhyme to speak as plain

> I love in verse to speak my mind as plain

> I love to pour out all myself, as plain.

And in the following line, there is a corresponding growth in force, as Pope revises

> As Master Shippen, or as old Montaigne

to

> As downright Shippen, or as old Montaigne.
> (*The First Satire of the Second Book of
> Horace*, ll. 51–52, p. 186)

Poetry and Society

If the revisions of poems are stages of a private process, the published poem is a social act. The poet has at one time or another in history been a public servant, celebrating great occasions in courtly tributes, pleading an official cause, deriding and thus disarming public enemies, or more simply providing entertainment of various kinds. Chaucer read his poems at court. In some ways they may seem to support the attitudes of the court but in others the poems seem to question and challenge courtly attitudes as well. The poet may help to forge a sense of national greatness, but he may also seek to redirect national purpose or to question its assumptions. He may be a licensed critic at court, like the jester, or he may be an intransigent critic outside society and even opposed to the very idea of participation in social concerns. It has been said that in ages when poets have high and respectable status, the theory of poetry tends to be moral, but that when they have low status or feel their own alienation from society, the theory of poetry tends to be aesthetic. In our own age, however, we can see poets finding their isolation from political power perhaps all the more a goad to moral intensity.

A poet like Pope may see himself as a man of independence intransigently opposed to the corruptions of the court, trying through his satire to restore a sense of conscience and freedom to people who have been bribed into silence or depressed into indifference. While a poet like Pope states his opposition in universal moral terms, he may find himself in alliance with a given social class, for example, the landed aristocracy that resisted the growth to power of a middle class whose wealth came from capital investment. In any age historical forces and class interests tend to be imagined in mythical terms: in analogies drawn from other ages, in metaphors of organic life as opposed to mechanical or rationalistic law, in the opposition of natural energy to the shallow artifices or gaudy show of a transient power system. The mythicizing of the French Revolution can be seen in Blake and Wordsworth, of the Wars of the Roses in Shakespeare's history plays.

The problem is to see the full imaginative structure within which the events of the poet's time are accommodated and given wider implication. In "Easter, 1916" (p. 307) Yeats recalls the Easter Rising whose Irish nationalist leaders were executed. In the poem he describes the transformation of various men—including one who seems a "drunken vainglorious lout"—and of their political cause into a "terrible beauty." The commonplace shallow life, a "casual comedy" or a scene "where motley is worn," and the fluid movement of organic life ("Minute by minute they live") are transformed into the unyielding stone of a single purpose, an "excess of love," a heroic (if possibly "bewildered") devotion. Yeats does not ignore the possibilities of error and of inhuman fanaticism, and he has deliberately heightened the opposition by equating the "casual comedy" of political indifference with the very process of natural life. For the "terrible beauty" must gain its full meaning from the sheer unchanging intensity of heroic commitment; it must be opposed to the suppleness of ordinary life just as the stone is opposed to stream, cloud, or moor-hen. The beauty is terrible in what it costs; but the condition of stone, harsh and inhuman as it is, achieves the splendor of that which transcends the conditions of life. Yeats's complex view of political commitment is caught in the image of stone and the myth that he has created around it.

Even where the poet does not address himself directly to a political event, his poem may express implicit social attitudes. In Ben Jonson's "To Penshurst" (pp. 113–15) the great English country house is celebrated for its warm hospitality, its owner's openness and sense of obligation, its mingling of classes in festivity. It is placed in opposition to the ambitious and ostentatiously fashionable buildings of those whose greatness comes not from inheritance and tradition but from displayed wealth and arrogance of station. "Their lords have built, but thy lord dwells." One can see the same theme at work in Pope's *To Burlington* (pp. 179–84), where the self-display of Timon's Villa, which is the very contradiction of true hospitality, finally crumbles before the natural vitality of cultivated fields, fields whose crops will nourish where formal terraces once impressed and stultified. In both poems there is a vision of an organic society, one of reciprocal duties and loyalties, and it is opposed to private ambition and its typical symbol, the effrontery of building in opposition to nature.

Recent Critical Approaches

Myth and Archetype

The mythical forms by which historical events are imaginatively transformed have long been the material of poets and a matter of interest to critics, but they have become a peculiar obsession of our own age. This is in part the result of such encyclopedic works of anthropology as Sir James Frazer's *The Golden Bough*, which in turn held a fascination for such poets as T. S. Eliot. It is in part also the result of what has been called "the disappearance of God," that is, the replacement, for many, of orthodox religious beliefs by a psychological secularism that stresses man's myth-making power and sees in all religious myths the expression of man's needs. Recent tendencies in criticism reflect this new view, and a few of them may be briefly sketched.

Archetypal criticism arises from the fusion of depth psychology and anthropology. The deepest impulses within the self are seen most clearly in primitive versions of social and artistic structures, perhaps most clearly of all in those myths which underlie both. For here the impulses are directly embodied, often with their internal conflicts and tensions, in narrative forms and social rituals. These commanding myths record impulses that reappear at all levels of civilized life, but their reappearance may take disguised forms that are woven into the complex customs of a particular society. To take a simple and familiar example, behind the "private eye" of much detective fiction there is often visible a scapegoat figure, asked to take on the burden of uncovering the guilt of others, finding himself more and more burdened with a guilt comparable to that which he reveals—he may be sympathetic with the murderer, he may be required to use methods no better than the crimes he exposes, he may be regarded as an outlaw by the police and a dangerous man by the very people who have hired him, he becomes a lonely and disillusioned man outside the pattern of respectability that others conspire to maintain, and he is often rejected by all those who cannot bear to face the truth he exposes. Not every tough detective reveals these traits, but one can find in much popular literature myths that survive in simple form and embody deep feeling. Such a critic as Maud Bodkin, following the archetypal psychology of Carl Jung, traces recurrent patterns, for example, of a rebirth archetype: a descent into darkness and chaos like that of the sea, which might be seen as the womb, and a temporary achievement of calm that may be felt as stagnation but is the necessary condition of a return to life and to fresh energy. She traces this pattern of regressive withdrawal and return in tribal customs, in psychological needs, and in a variety of poetic structures, most notably Coleridge's *The Rime of the Ancient Mariner*.

The effect of such criticism is to see in the finished literary work a power to evoke universal experience at a deeper level of consciousness than may at first appear. In this view, the poem alludes to myths which have enormous power in shaping our thoughts and feelings and which, like dreams, often survive in our waking life only as fragmentary memories. The poem connects the immediate or the commonplace with those myths that are implicit in the commonplace but are not readily seen consciously, and the poem can be taken as an act of homage or awe, an invocation of that realm of meaning which, like some sacred deity, we cannot face directly.

The most celebrated archetypal critic of our time is Northrop Frye, and Frye departs from the more psychological critics in finding the archetype in the myth itself rather than in some pattern of feeling that underlies the myth and can be studied directly. Works like Frazer's *The Golden Bough* or Jung's studies of psychological symbols become for Frye "primarily studies in literary criticism," that is, explorations of those great archetypal myths that are the starting point of literary study. Literature, throughout its history, tends to move from narrative toward thematic structure, from the great story-telling myths to more self-conscious and analytic works. The primal myths undergo more and more immersion in actuality, and the heroes of these myths become less and less heroic. They descend from gods to mortal heroes, from heroes to ordinary responsible men, and finally to the passive or limited creatures of a fragmentary, naturalistic world. But if literature moves toward realism in its later stages, it still recalls those unfragmented myths which once embodied the full range of experience and feeling. Each of the major literary genres—tragedy, comedy, satire, romance—catches one aspect of that comprehensive vision, and we are constantly reminded by Frye of the interrelationship of these aspects and genres. Therefore, any work of literature can be seen, if it is placed in its full context of related and opposed works, to carry rich implications of what it has been and has lost, namely the systematic and total myth of which each literary work is a derivative and limited product.

The "displacement" of myth, that is, the substitution of altered or reduced forms for the original, arises from the effort to relate myth to the immediate and credible, to give it plausibility and "realistic" order. A novel like James Joyce's *Ulysses* finds realistic counterparts to the adventures of Odysseus, so that Circe's island becomes a Dublin brothel and the princess Nausicaa a very conventional young Gertie MacDowell. But such displacement is always an alteration of a fiction that defies conventional plausibility, and our interest is held by the strain between the surface credibility and the deeper meaningfulness. The meaningful forms are mythical, formal versions of reality that make it accord with human need and desire. Myths are most transparently exposed in the stylized patterns of popular literature—the Western movie, the comic strip, science fiction; the transparent versions are scarcely the most compelling or complex, but they may serve to remind us of an element we should recognize in works of mature art as well.

Myth criticism, as Frye puts it, "pulls us away from 'life' toward a self-contained and autonomous literary universe." But this universe, which includes all kinds of literature and their archetypal embodiment in myth, is itself the total scheme of man's imaginative vision of himself and his world. In a study of Milton's *Lycidas*, Frye states that to ask questions about literary analogies and sources is to build up "a wider comprehension of literature and a deeper knowledge of its structural principles and recurring themes," whereas to ask questions about the occasion outside the poem (such as the nature of Edward King, whose death Milton treats in *Lycidas*, or of Milton's relation to him) takes us away from literary contexts and therefore away from relevant meaning. "Every poem," Frye says, "must be examined as a unity, but no poem is an isolatable unity. Every poem is inherently connected with other poems of its kind, whether explicitly, as *Lycidas* is with Theocritus and Virgil, or implicitly, . . . or by anticipation, as *Lycidas* is with later pastoral elegies." The full context of each poem becomes, therefore, all of literature, and the pressure of archetypal criticism is to seek unifying principles in that full context.

Poetry and Phenomenology

What Northrop Frye accomplishes by starting with literary myths rather than with the psychological and social forces that may create them is much like what the phenomenologist does. For the phenomenological critic is not interested in the biographical facts about the poet that may explain the origin of his feelings or the way in which they force themselves into expression. He is interested instead in the imaginative world the poet creates, or, as the psychoanalytic critic might say, projects. The projection is the starting point, and the question of its "truth to" actuality is set aside or (in the word of the philosopher Edmund Husserl) "bracketed." Each poet is seen as the creator of the imagined world which he inhabits, and its internal coherence is what the critic studies. Such a world may be revealed only fragmentarily in any given work, and yet the critic may be able to reconstruct it from the total body of the poet's writing, whether

in finished poems or in letters, diaries, or notebooks. The American critic
J. Hillis Miller claims that this method treats the writer's work "not as
the mere symptom or product of a pre-existent psychological condition,
but as the very means by which a writer apprehends and, in some measure,
creates himself."

The typical program of the phenomenological critic, then, is to trace in
all the writings of a given author the fundamental and distinctive imaginative patterns that shape his world and (in the process) his conception of
himself. The Swiss critic Georges Poulet finds in Emily Dickinson "the
apparition, in closest succession, of . . . two moments, in one of which
everything is given, and in the other everything taken away." Rather than
indulge herself in regret for the loss, Emily Dickinson chooses renunciation
and the "patient continuity of pain." Her thought relinquishes the future
to dwell on her present grief:

Pain Has an Element of Blank

Pain has an element of blank—
It cannot recollect
When it begun, or if there were
A time when it was not.

It has no future but itself—
Its infinite contain
Its past—enlightened to perceive
New periods of pain.

EMILY DICKINSON

As the critic Charles R. Anderson asserts: "Extreme suffering even changes
the very nature of time. . . . It makes clock and calendar time meaningless and annihilates the very idea of eternity. . . . It absorbs the whole of
consciousness, condensed to a measureless, momentless point."

The critic is here concerned with perceptual patterns that are taken as
the most fundamental movements of the poet's mind. Poulet's treatment
of Emily Dickinson is a brief section in an appendix to a work that re-
views the changing conceptions of time from Montaigne to Proust. His
work defines "period" conceptions of time. In tracing the shifting imaginative structures through which men perceive their world, the phenomenological critic becomes a historian of consciousness. But he is less concerned
with the responses to particular external events than with the gradual
changes in the fundamental metaphors by which the mind construes the
world. We can see this method carried out in two books, *The Disappearance of God* (1963) and *Poets of Reality* (1965), in which J. Hillis Miller
traces a "spiritual history" through a series of individual studies. In his
studies he moves from the inability of such Victorians as Thomas De
Quincey and Robert Browning to experience the presence of a transcen-

dental God to the recovery of a sense of immanent reality present in "the thing itself" by such recent poets as William Carlos Williams.

The phenomenological critic tends to slight the internal structure of the individual poem, like Frye distrusting its "isolatable unity," and has often woven a new imaginative pattern of the poet's consciousness from scattered fragments of his work. The critic relates these fragments through central patterns the critic himself emphasizes, whether or not the poet would have recognized these patterns himself. There is still a search for unity through context, but the context chosen is less distinctively literary and less concerned with literary genre and traditions than is the archetypal critic's. The unity sought by the phenomenological critic is less ambitious and extensive than Frye's total structure of the human imagination; it tends to fall more narrowly into historical epochs, each with its own total consciousness, of which literature is but one, although perhaps the best, expression.

Structuralism

In a system like that of Northrop Frye, which embraces all modes and genres of literature and studies their interrelationship, we can say that no one work achieves its full meaning except as it takes its place within the total system. If, for example, we follow Frye in charting the central mythical structures of literature so that each accords with a season of the year —comedy and spring, romance and summer, tragedy and autumn, irony or satire and winter—any new work must find its place within this calendar and gain its full meaning within it. In this system, the comic hero gains his full meaning when he is seen in contrast to the tragic hero: his resourcefulness and flexibility are seen as the other side of the integrity and stubbornness of his tragic counterpart; his power of survival is based on his skill in avoiding those confrontations that are the source of tragic catastrophe and dignity. By means such as these, Frye has elaborated and systematized the extension of genres into fully elaborated worlds, distinct but interrelated.

For the structuralist critic, systems become crucial, both for the conception of literature as a whole and for the analysis of individual works. Every system is seen as a language, that is, as an orderly structure that obeys rules of combination, which are unconsciously accepted by those who use it and may be based on innate patterns of human thought. Each new element in the structure is conceived according to rules of combination, and each element can be understood only as it participates in the systematic structure of the whole. This can be seen in the French anthropologist Claude Lévi-Strauss's discussion of proper names. In naming a dog, we classify the dog according to his characteristics, or, if we choose a name "freely" and without regard to the qualities of the dog, we classify ourselves by the kind of name we choose. We may call the dog Spot or Taffy for his coat and color, Bismarck or Fifi for the origin of the breed; or we may use expressive names, Butch or Fido or Cassandra. These may be explicit dog names, or they may be fanciful expressions of taste, and the latter will fall into one or another class (friendly, literary, whimsical, etc.). The point is that each name gains significance from the systems of names that are available, just as the names of children may reveal family tradition, social aspiration, national or ethnic origin, current fashions of hero-worship, and so on. What has been said of names can be said of the possessions we acquire, our furniture or dress, or in fact all those elements that make up a lifestyle, not least a choice of vocation. There are, as the French critic Roland Barthes has observed, as many "languages" as there are cultural objects "which society has endowed with a signifying power: for example, food is to be eaten, but it also serves to *signify*," as we can see by glancing at a fashionable homemaker's magazine, at our television advertising, or more directly at what our own tastes may mean to us and to our neighbors.

Clearly our feelings are private, personal, and individual, but we express them through a series of choices that are in large part set by our society. Each of these choices can be seen on the analogy of our use of a language. Our private thoughts must be communicated in a public language, and it is a question whether we can form thoughts at all without such a language. We may adapt a language and vary it; but each variation will gain its significance from the system it alters, and most alterations become systematic in turn, as do current slang or current fashions in dress.

The structuralist is interested in all those "languages" that make up our world, of which literature is only one part. Poetry is a peculiarly complex kind of structure, creating meaning by its variations upon an existing public language and employing all the possibilities of words—their sound, their historical as well as their current meanings, their dignity or lowness of tone, etc. The structuralist is interested most of all in the systematic relationships by which meanings are created, that is, the juxtapositions, oppositions, and repetitions which serve to build meaning. The structuralist attempts a rigorous and empirical approach to all the kinds of structure that a poem exhibits, refusing to exclude any, and seeking only at the close of such an examination, if at all, to consider how these different levels of "signifying" can be seen to form a unified thematic assertion. Structuralism seeks, in Barthes's words, "less to assign completed meanings to the objects it discovers than to know how meaning is possible, at what cost and by what means."

In the discussion of a sonnet by W. H. Auden which follows, we have tried to indicate some of the kinds of analyses a structuralist critic might pursue. We have concentrated on the semantic dimension and therefore much simplified a method that has sometimes been accused of collecting evidence that cannot in fact be perceived in the process of reading and cannot be shown to create meaning.

Sonnets from China, XVIII

Chilled by the Present, its gloom and its noise,
On waking we sigh for an ancient South,
A warm nude age of instinctive poise,
A taste of joy in an innocent mouth.

At night in our huts we dream of a part
In the balls of the Future: each ritual maze
Has a musical plan, and a musical heart
Can faultlessly follow its faultless ways.

We envy streams and houses that are sure,
But, doubtful, articled to error, we
Were never nude and calm as a great door,

And never will be faultless like our fountains:
We live in freedom by necessity,
A mountain people dwelling among mountains.

W. H. AUDEN

In the first two quatrains, we have an apparent contrast between the natural and spontaneous (associated with the past) and the elaborately planned (associated with the future). The "ancient South" suggests the pagan Mediterranean, the "warm nude age of instinctive poise" the grace of classical sculpture or vase-painting, and the "taste of joy" the wine and "sunburnt mirth" of Keats's "Ode to a Nightingale" (p. 250).

O for a beaker full of the warm South,
    Full of the true, the blushful Hippocrene,
        With beaded bubbles winking at the brim,
            And purple-stainèd mouth.

(ll. 15–18)

In contrast, "the balls of the Future" suggest a splendid dance, perhaps in an indoor and man-made structure, such as a palace. Whereas the first quatrain stresses the spontaneous and outward, the second moves to the "heart" and its passions, controlled by the ritualized patterns of a dance and the measures of a musical plan, contained within "faultless ways." In a sense the human passions are reduced to an order like that which Milton finds in the "mystical dance" of the heavens, which

Resembles nearest mazes intricate,
Eccentric, intervolved, yet regular
Then most, when most irregular they seem.

(*Paradise Lost*, Book V, ll. 622–24)

The contrast between past and future, between natural and man-made, gives way as we move to the last six lines. The "instinctive poise" and "faultless ways" draw together. They both become instances of sureness in a new contrast with a capacity for error. The "sigh" and "dream" of the first two quatrains are fused in the word "envy," and the envy is directed to "streams and houses." These present once more the contrasting terms of the natural and the man-made, but it is their common element—their "sureness"—that is now asserted. In contrast, "we," as humans, are "doubtful" and, even more, "articled to error." Once this new contrast between sureness and doubt is established, the older contrast between natural and man-made breaks down. The terms "nude and calm" are transferred to a "great door." This may suggest the door of a classical temple, but it has lost the organic vitality of "instinctive poise." On the other hand, the perfection of the intricate dance is now embodied in the movement of a natural object, water. But the movement of water is that of fountains, artificial structures, although outdoors and hence "in nature." (The fountains, like the balls, may be associated with a palace like Versailles.) Thus the old opposition—natural, simple, outdoors against artificial, complex, indoors—has collapsed and a new one has taken its place.

The shift has taken place because a more central and fundamental opposition has been introduced by "we are articled to error." This is the opposition of erratic to sure. The sureness or faultlessness that has been sighed for, dreamed of, and envied in inanimate objects now proves illusory. Man never has been nor ever will be free of error, and, as the poem makes clear, this is the source of his freedom. The phrase "articled to error" means "bound by contract to error." The articles of apprenticeship, for example, set forth the conditions under which the apprentice is given training in return for a term of service, and such "articles" imply a contractual legal structure, a distinctively human form of constraint.

The element of constraint is repeated in the next-to-last line, "We live in freedom by necessity." The necessity, like the articles that create it, is seen in contrast to wishful fantasies of sureness. It is necessary, in other words, that our lives be free and not reduced to the causal necessity that governs things. We cannot escape our freedom to choose, which makes us both "doubtful" and human. We have no alternative but to dwell among mountains (in an earlier version of the poem, they were "mountains of our choice"), for we are a "mountain people," destined to live a life of choice rather than a life of faultless certainty. The life of choice is an actual life in time present rather than an imagined life in time past or future. The elaborate set of oppositions in the first two quatrains collapses before a new opposition, as the poem moves toward a definition of a distinctively human condition, full of possible error, caught in the rigors of omnipresent choice, and more complex than the visions of mere nature or art.

The Problem of Evaluation

"The best poetry is what we want; the best poetry will be found to have a power of forming, sustaining, and delighting us, as nothing else can." So wrote the Victorian poet and critic Matthew Arnold in "The Study of Poetry," and he went on to warn that "a sense for the best, the really excellent . . . should be present in our minds and should govern our estimate of what we read. But this real estimate, the only true one, is likely to be superseded, if we are not watchful, by two other kinds of estimate, the historic estimate and the personal estimate, both of which are fallacious." By the historic estimate Arnold means our tendency to overrate a work because of its historical importance, its influence on other works that follow or its significance as a turning point in poetic development. By the personal estimate, he means the power of our personal likings or affinities— our gratitude to an author for his role in our own development—to distort our judgment of his value. Yet what is the "real" estimate? Arnold offers us great passages that we may carry as touchstones in our minds, but these brief passages do not define the nature of their greatness. They have only the negative value of being incomparably the best.

Arnold's remarks are useful in reminding us of how various are the kinds of judgment we make and how susceptible they are to conflict. We may recognize the courage of a poet's statement and find in his boldness the force of a culture-hero, but not all courageous poetry is great or even good poetry. Again, we may recognize the powerful influence of a poet over a whole age and continent—as was the case with Byron—and yet find poets we can admire more. Shall we rate a poet very high for his originality or recognize that his followers were able to write greater poems? Quite apart from the kinds of judgment Arnold deems "fallacious," there are others that seem to us partial and insufficient in themselves. We may find a memorable pictorial vividness in the imagery of one poet, a brilliant epigrammatic lucidity in another, a subtle musicality in a third—and yet we must decide whether any of these virtues outweigh others that may be missing.

Rather than ask ourselves what is the basis of the "real estimate" of a poem, we might better ask what poetry can do. We have already explored many of the possible answers, and it may be useful to review these:

(1) Poetry gives us density or concentration of meaning. It creates a structure of words that satisfy at the same time a number of functions, and this process of simultaneous fulfillment of patterns of sound, syntax, and symbolic meaning creates the effect of inevitability. That is, certain words seem to be required to fulfill one pattern and surprise us all the more by fulfilling several. There is the pleasure of a complex problem solved ele-

gantly and with economy, and there is also the recognition that no one element of the poetic structure can be changed without precipitating a series of changes in each dimension of the structure. This kind of inter-penetration of parts distinguishes the language of poetry from simpler dis-cursive uses of language.

(2) Through its use of metaphor, by juxtaposing two concrete images in order to suggest some implicit elements present in both, poetry may achieve great vividness of concrete detail. It often presents objects in rich detail in order to generate metaphors from these images; the sensuous vividness is a means to a further end, therefore, and it carries a suggestion of potential meaningfulness that may, at any moment, be exploited by the poet. Let us consider two instances. In Andrew Marvell's "The Gar-den" (p. 149) we find an image of the soul detaching itself from the world, enjoying its new freedom and fullness of being, still contemplating the world it is now poised to leave:

> Casting the body's vest aside,
> My soul into the boughs does glide:
> There, like a bird, it sits and sings,
> Then whets and combs its silver wings,
> And, till prepared for longer flight,
> Waves in its plumes the various light.
>
> (ll. 51–56)

Marvell fuses the vitality of the bird's movement with a state of the spirit. The "silver wings" hover between physical and spiritual, and the "longer flight" carries the suggestion of a new life of the spirit. The "various light" suggests the iridescence of refracted light that colors a bird's wings but also the reflection in "silver wings" of the colors of the world, in which the spirit seems to bathe before it departs.

In Wordsworth's famous lyric we find a different use of language.

She Dwelt Among the Untrodden Ways

> She dwelt among the untrodden ways
>   Beside the springs of Dove,
> A Maid whom there were none to praise
>   And very few to love:
>
> A violet by a mossy stone
>   Half hidden from the eye!
> —Fair as a star, when only one
>   Is shining in the sky.
>
> She lived unknown, and few could know
>   When Lucy ceased to be;
> But she is in her grave, and, oh,
>   The difference to me!

In the second of Wordsworth's stanzas, the poem undergoes a sudden change. The violet catches Lucy's obscurity in an image which also carries implications of her beauty. Then suddenly through a simile Wordsworth overturns the proportions of his metaphor. Now the beauty is dominant, and the isolation (for it is no longer mere obscurity) of the star becomes the means of realizing its beauty more fully. It is the only point of brilliance in the vast spaces of the sky. The third stanza repeats this pattern of change. The obscurity is emphasized again, and the isolation is caught in the phrase that marks the few mourners' rather detached awareness, "When Lucy ceased to be." But now we shift. Instead of the sudden brilliance of the star, we have the sudden intensity of deep personal grief. For the poet, Lucy is "in her grave"—the words are far more immediate and concrete than "ceased to be"—and the "oh," with which the third line ends, becomes, as a single cry of feeling, comparable to the single star in the sky. The final line—through its very understatement—becomes a tribute to emotion felt too deeply to permit elaboration.

(3) Poetry gives us the double effect of something seen and something interpreted, of both image and idea; and the idea may carry with it a considerable weight of feeling. The emergence of the idea governs the structure of the poem, for in its full statement the form of the poem completes itself. Wordsworth's lyric is a tribute to Lucy and also an implicit treatment of the way in which isolation and intensity reinforce each other and create a purity of feeling that the world at large tends to diffuse and attenuate. It is in this way that poetry approaches a form of knowledge, heightening our awareness of experience and exploring attitudes toward it.

(4) The most compelling assertions of what poetry can do emphasize its inclusiveness. Perhaps the best known is Coleridge's account of the "poet described in *ideal* perfection." In the *Biographia Literaria* Coleridge sees him bringing "the whole soul of man into activity." The poet's imaginative power reveals itself in "the balance or reconciliation of opposite or discordant qualities: of sameness, with difference . . . the individual, with the representative; the sense of novelty and freshness, with old and familiar objects; a more than usual state of emotion, with more than usual order; judgment ever awake and steady self-possession, with enthusiasm and feeling profound or vehement; and while it blends and harmonizes the natural and the artificial, still subordinates art to nature; the manner to the matter; and our admiration of the poet to our sympathy with the poetry."

Poems vary in both the form of the reconciliation they achieve and in the kind of opposites they reconcile. There are many differences in the balances that Marvell and Wordsworth create. To choose between these passages may be to choose between a poetry of wit and a poetry of feeling (although each has elements of both), between richly expansive language and the simplicity that suggests the ineffable. Such choices are rarely based upon some universal standard. They tend instead to reflect temperamental differences in the reader. If we think of the faults that might correspond to the different virtues of these poems, Marvell's method could lead to ostentatious ingenuity, somewhat frigid and playful intellectual riddling; Wordsworth's could lead to an unthinking sentimentality, feeling offered for its own sake or as a sign of nobility of heart, couched in conventionally pretty images. Judgments begin at this point to cross the line between the aesthetic and the moral. We may value a poem for its celebration of spontaneous feeling or for its power to resist and complicate it. A similar conflict may arise between those who prize poetry for its power to transcend the actual world in visionary images and those who feel that the truly imaginative lies less in the imaginary, more in the fresh interpretation of the familiar.

In short, literary choice and judgment are hard to separate from other kinds of choice which lie deeper in our consciousness. These may be moral choices, or they may be more fundamental still—choices of style that affect our vision of the world in all its aspects. If we consider the question of inclusiveness, we may agree that a great poem achieves with economy a great range of awareness. But how is the range to be judged? A term like "complexity" or "maturity" implies taking into account and holding together significantly opposed attitudes. But which oppositions are genuinely significant? What Marvell sees as transcendence may seem like escapism to some; what Wordsworth sees as intensity may seem like self-indulgence to others. We may seem to be faced with utter relativism, but in fact the conflict a poet embodies in his work may open up to suggest others. We may read Marvell's account of transcendence and contemplation in terms that are not strictly religious; we may recognize in Wordsworth's account of deep and personal loss a celebration of the value of the unheroic and unhistoric, like that of Thomas Hardy's "In the Time of the Breaking of Nations" (p. 295).

The openness of the literary work, its capacity for surprising us into new awareness, is one of its sources of power. This openness might be better called resonance, a power to echo through a far vaster range of experience than it at first seems to offer. We can see this in the wonderfully ironic poem that follows.

A High-Toned Old Christian Woman

Poetry is the supreme fiction, madame.
Take the moral law and make a nave of it
And from the nave build haunted heaven. Thus,
The conscience is converted into palms,
Like windy citherns hankering for hymns.
We agree in principle. That's clear. But take

The opposing law and make a peristyle,
And from the peristyle project a masque
Beyond the planets. Thus, our bawdiness,
Unpurged by epitaph, indulged at last,
Is equally converted into palms,
Squiggling like saxophones. And palm for palm,
Madame, we are where we began. Allow,
Therefore, that in the planetary scene
Your disaffected flagellants, well-stuffed,
Smacking their muzzy bellies in parade,
Proud of such novelties of the sublime,
Such tink and tank and tunk-a-tunk-tunk,
May, merely may, madame, whip from themselves
A jovial hullabaloo among the spheres.
This will make widows wince. But fictive things
Wink as they will. Wink most when widows wince.

WALLACE STEVENS

The widow expects poetry to celebrate the moral law, to embody it in a structure of worship, and lead us thence to a heavenly vision. But poetry may start just as well with the peristyle, the classical pagan temple, and build upon a law of pleasure. It can release our earthiness and create a heaven in its image, where the palm trees show jazzy movement, where the former flagellants, instead of punishing their bodies with whips, enjoy the flesh in new freedom and intensity. Poetry can undo our expectations, overturn our values, lead us where we had not expected to be. We may judge poems, but poems judge us as well.

A Note on Chaucer's Pronunciation and Metrics

A. *Pronunciation*

1. Consonants in Chaucer are pronounced more or less as they are today, with the following major exceptions:

> K and g are pronounced (e.g., *knight* and *gnawen*). The g in *ng* combinations is pronounced as in modern "finger" when stressed (e.g. *singen*), but is silent when unstressed as in *-ing* endings. L is pronounced before f, k, and m (e.g., *folk*, *palmer*). R is trilled or rolled. *Gh* is pronounced, as in Scottish "loch" or German "ach." *Ch* is pronounced as in modern "church."

2. Vowels, as in modern English, are either long or short. Modern examples are fate–fat, beet–bet, fight–fit, cope–cop, mute–mutt. It is often possible to tell whether a Chaucerian vowel is long or short from its modern equivalent, though the sounds differ. When in doubt, use the vowel sounds of modern French or German.

> a. Chaucerian *a* is pronounced "ah" as in modern "father." Long *a* (as in Chaucerian *bathed*) prolongs the basic *a* sound; short *a* (as in Chaucerian *whan*) clips it.
> b. Long *i* or *y*, has the "ee" sound of "i" in modern "machine." Short *i* is pronounced as it is today.
> c. Chaucerian *u* is similar in sound to modern "u," both long and short.
> d. Long *e* (as in *sweete*) is pronounced like modern long "a" (as in "mate"). Short *e* (as in *tendre*) is pronounced as it is today. Final *e* (as in *sonne*) is pronounced "uh." To complicate matters, however, Chaucerian *e* has a third sound, which resembles that in modern "when": this sound occurs in many words now spelled with "ea," like "sweat" and "teach," but it is not limited to such words.
> e. Long and short *o* are pronounced as they are today, but there is a third *o* sound, pronounced like the "oa" in modern "broad." Some examples are *aloon*, *cold*, *goost*, *hopen*, *ooth*, *so*, *sold*, *spoken*, *throte*, *throwen*. In other words, now spelled with a "u," such as *yonge* and *sonne*, the "o" is pronounced like "u" in modern "pull."

3. Diphthongs, where they differ from modern pronunciation, are sounded as follows: *ei* or *ey* or *ay*, like "ay" in modern "day"; *au* or *ou*, like "ou" in modern "house"; *ou* or *ow*, and also *o* before gh, like "ou" in modern "you"; *eu* or *ew*, like "u" in modern "mule."

B. *Metrics*

1. The General Prologue to *The Canterbury Tales* is written in iambic pentameter couplets, which means that most lines have ten syllables. One common exception is an unstressed *e* or *ed* or *es* at the end of a line (*sonne*–l. 7; *corages*

—l. 11), which adds an eleventh syllable. But many of the metrical variations frequent in modern English also occur here:

a. Omission of the first unstressed syllable, as in

$$\text{Whán}/\text{that Áp}/\text{ríl with}/\text{his shów}/\text{res soot}/\text{e} \quad (1.\ 1)$$

b. Trochaic inversion, as in the first foot of

$$\text{Rédy}/\text{to wén}/\text{den on}/\text{my pil}/\text{grim a}/\text{ge} \quad (1.\ 21)$$

c. Extra unstressed syllables, as in the fourth foot of

$$\text{Is lik}/\text{ned til}/\text{a fish}/\text{that is wat}/\text{er lees} \quad (1.\ 180)$$

d. Elision of extra syllables, as in the first and second feet of

$$\text{Grehound(es)}/\text{he hadd(e)}/\text{as swifte}/\text{as fowel}/\text{in flight} \quad (1.\ 190)$$

2. As a rule, the iambic rhythm is the best guide both to elision and to the pronunciation of words whose stress has changed (e.g., *vertu*, accented on the second syllable, rather than modern "virtue"). Though some words or syllables are invariable in sound, like *-ioun* which has two syllables (e.g., *naciouns*— l. 53), in many cases pronunciation must be worked out instance by instance. A good example is

$$\text{Of Englelond to Caunterbury they wende} \quad (1.\ 16)$$

where *Englelond* must be given three syllables, and *Caunterbury* pronounced "Caunterbry" for the line to scan. In contrast, in

$$\text{That toward Caunterbury wolden ride} \quad (1.\ 27)$$

toward must be given two syllables, and *Caunterbury* four, for the line to scan. Mainly this problem occurs with *e* or *es* or *ed* when they occur as endings to a word within the line, as in line 190 cited above, but with a little practice the reader learns to pronounce or elide these syllables in conformity with the iambic rhythm.

Geoffrey Chaucer   (1340?–1400)

The Canterbury Tales
from The General Prologue

Whan that April with his° showres soote°	*its / sweet*
The droghte of March hath perced to the roote,	
And bathed every vein in swich° licour°	*such / moisture*
Of which vertu° engendred is the flour;	*power*
Whan Zephirus eek° with his sweete breeth 5	*also*
Inspired hath in every holt° and heeth°	*wood / field*
The tendre croppes, and the yonge sonne	
Hath in the Ram his halve cours yronne;	
And smale fowles° maken melodye	*birds*
That slepen al the night with open yë° 10	*eye*
(So priketh hem nature in hir corages);	
Than longen folk to goon on pilgrimages	
(And palmers° for to seken straunge strondes)	*pilgrims*
To ferne halwes, couth° in sondry londes;	*known*
And specially, from every shires ende 15	
Of Englelond to Caunterbury they wende,	
The hooly blisful martyr for to seeke	
That hem hath holpen,° whan that they were seke.°	*helped / sick*
Befil that in that seson on a day,	
In Southwerk at the Tabard as I lay 20	
Redy to wenden on my pilgrimage	
To Caunterbury with ful devout corage,	
At night was come into that hostelrye	
Wel nine and twenty in a companye	
Of sondry folk, by aventure yfalle 25	
In felawshipe, and pilgrims were they alle	
That toward Caunterbury wolden ride;	
The chambres and the stables weren wide,	
And wel we weren esed atte beste.	
And shortly, whan the sonne was to reste, 30	
So hadde I spoken with hem° everichon°	*them / every one*
That I was of hir° felawshipe anon,°	*their / immediately*
And made forward erly for to rise	

GENERAL PROLOGUE   **5. Zephirus:** the west wind. **7–8. yonge . . . yronne:** the sun supposedly started the year at the vernal equinox. It now had progressed halfway through the sign of the Ram (Aries). **11. priketh hem:** goads them. **hir corages:** their hearts, instincts. **13. straunge strondes:** foreign shores. **14. ferne halwes:** distant shrines. **17. blisful martyr:** St. Thomas à Becket, Archbishop of Canterbury, who had been murdered there by knights of King Henry II in 1170. **20. Southwerk . . . Tabard:** the Tabard was an inn in the London suburb of Southwark, south of the Thames. **25. by aventure yfalle:** met together by chance. **29. esed atte beste:** well taken care of. **33. made forward:** agreed.

To take oure way ther as I yow devise.
　　But nathelees,° whil I have time and space,　　35　　*nevertheless*
Er that I ferther in this tale pace,°　　　　　　　　　　　　*proceed*
Me thinketh it accordaunt to resoun
To telle you al the condicioun
Of eech of hem, so as it seemed me,
And whiche they weren, and of what degree,　　40
And eek in what array that they were inne:
And at a knight than wol I first biginne.
　　A Knight ther was, and that a worthy man,
That fro the time that he first bigan
To riden out, he loved chivalrye,　　45
Trouthe and honour, fredom and curteisye.
Ful worthy was he in his lordes werre,
And therto hadde he riden, no man ferre,°　　　　　　　　　*farther*
As wel in Cristendom as hethenesse,
And ever honoured for his worthinesse.　　50
　　At Alisaundre he was, whan it was wonne;
Ful ofte time he hadde the bord bigonne
Above alle naciouns in Pruce.
In Lettow hadde he reysed,° and in Ruce,　　　　　　　　*campaigned*
No Cristen man so ofte of his degree;　　55
In Gernade at the sege eek hadde he be
Of Algezir, and riden in Belmarye;
At Lyeis was he, and at Satalye,
Whan they were wonne; and in the Grete See
At many a noble armee hadde he be.　　60
At mortal batailles had he been fiftcene,
And foughten for our faith at Tramissene
In listes thries, and ay° slain his fo.　　　　　　　　　　　　*always*
This ilke° worthy knight had been also　　　　　　　　　　　*same*
Sometime with the lord of Patalye　　65
Agayn° another hethen in Turkye;　　　　　　　　　　　　*against*
And everemore he hadde a sovereign pris.°　　　　　　　*reputation*
And though that he were worthy,° he was wis,°　　*brave / prudent*
And of his port° as meeke as is a maide.　　　　　　　　　*behavior*
He never yet no vilainye ne saide　　70
In al his lif unto no manere wight:
He was a verray,° parfit, gentil° knight.　　　　　　*true / courteous*
But for to tellen yow of his array:
His hors° were goode, but he was nat gay.　　　　　　　　*horses*
Of fustian° he wered a gipoun°　　75　　　　　*coarse cloth / tunic*
Al bismotered with his haubergeoun;°　　　　　　　*coat of mail*

45. riden out: go on military expeditions. **46. fredom:** a generous spirit. **47. his lordes werre:** wars of his overlord. **51–58. Alisaundre:** Alexandria (1365). **Pruce:** Prussia. **Lettow:** Lithuania. **Gernade:** Granada. **Algezir:** Algeciras (1343). **Belmarye:** Benmarin, in Morocco. **Lyeis:** Ayas, near Antioch. **Satalye:** Adalia, in Asia Minor. **52. bord bigonne:** given the place of honor at the head of the table. **59. Grete See:** Mediterranean. **62. Tramissene:** Tlemçen, in Algeria. **63. listes thries:** three single encounters at tournaments. **65. Patalye:** Balat, in Asia Minor. **71. no manere wight:** no kind of person. **76. bismotered with:** rust-stained from.

For he was late ycome from his viage,°   *expedition*
And wente for to doon his pilgrimage.
   With him ther was his sone, a yong Squier,
A lovere and a lusty bacheler,   80
With lokkes crulle,° as they were laid in presse.   *curly*
Of twenty year of age he was, I gesse.
Of his stature he was of evene lengthe,
And wonderly delivere, and of greet strengthe.
And he had been somtime in chivachye,   85
In Flaundres, in Artois, and Picardye,
And born him wel, as of so litel space,
In hope to stonden in his lady° grace.   *lady's*
Embrouded was he, as it were a mede
Al ful of fresshe flowres, white and rede;   90
Singing he was, or floiting, al the day:
He was as fresshe as is the month of May.
Short was his gowne, with sleeves longe and wide;
Wel coude he sitte on hors, and faire ride;
He coude songes make, and well endite,°   95   *compose lyrics*
Juste° and eek daunce, and wel purtraye° and write.   *joust / draw*
So hote he lovede, that by nightertale
He slepte namore than dooth a nightingale.
Curteis he was, lowly, and servisable,
And carf° biforn his fader at the table.   100   *carved*
   A Yeman hadde he, and servaunts namo
At that time, for him liste ride so;
And he was clad in cote and hood of greene;
A sheef of pecok arwes brighte and kene
Under his belt he bar° ful thriftily;°   105   *bore / carefully*
Wel coude he dresse his takel yemanly:
His arwes drouped nought with fetheres lowe,
And in his hand he bar a mighty bowe.
A not-heed° hadde he, with a brown visage.   *close-cropped head*
Of wodecraft wel coude° he al the usage.   110   *knew*
Upon his arm he bar a gay bracer,
And by his side a swerd and a bokeler,
And on that other side a gay daggere,
Harneised° wel, and sharp as point of spere;   *mounted*
A Cristofre on his brest of silver shene.°   115   *bright*
An horn he bar, the baudrik was of greene.
A forster was he, soothly,° as I gesse.   *truly*
   There was also a Nonne, a Prioresse,
That of her smiling was ful simple and coy;

80. **bacheler:** candidate for knighthood. 83. **evene lengthe:** average height. 84. **delivere:** agile, active. 85. **chivachye:** cavalry expedition. 87. **as . . . space:** in such a brief period. 89. **mede:** mead, meadow. 91. **floiting:** whistling; playing the flute. 97. **by nightertale:** by night. 99. **lowly:** modest in bearing. 101. **he:** the Knight. 102. **him liste ride:** it pleased him to ride. 106. **dresse . . . yemanly:** tend to his gear in a workmanlike fashion. 111. **bracer:** archer's wristguard. 115. **Cristofre:** medal of patron saint of foresters. 116. **baudrik:** shoulder strap (for his horn). 119. **simple and coy:** sincere and modest.

Hir gretteste ooth was but by sainte Loy;   120
And she was cleped° Madame Eglentyne.   *named*
Ful wel she soong the service divine,
Entuned in hir nose full semely;°   *decently*
And Frenssh she spak ful faire and fetisly,°   *elegantly*
After the scole of Stratford atte Bowe,   125
For Frenssh of Paris was to hir unknowe.
At mete° wel ytaught was she withalle:°   *meals / besides*
She leet no morsel from hir lippes falle,
Ne wette hir fingres in hir sauce deepe;
Wel coude she carye a morsel, and wel keepe°   130   *take care*
That no drope ne fille upon hir brest.
In curteisye was set ful muchel hir lest.
Hir overlippe wiped she so clene
That in her coppe° was no ferthing° seene   *cup / bit*
Of grece, when she dronken hadde hir draughte.   135
Ful semely after hir mete she raughte,°   *reached*
And sikerly° she was of greet disport,   *surely*
And ful pleasaunt, and amiable of port,
And pained hir to countrefete cheere
Of court, and been estatlich° of manere,   140   *dignified*
And to been holden digne of reverence.
But, for to speken of hir conscience,
She was so charitable and so pitous,
She wolde wepe, if that she sawe a mous
Caught in a trappe, if it were deed or bledde.   145
Of smale houndes had she, that she fedde
With rosted flessh, or milk and wastel-breed,°   *good bread*
But sore wepte she if oon of hem° were deed,   *one of them*
Or if men° smoot it with a yerde smerte: *someone*
And al was conscience and tendre herte.   150
Ful semely hir wimpel pinched° was;   *pleated*
Hir nose tretis;° hir eyen greye° as glas;   *well-proportioned / blue*
Hir mouth ful smal, and therto softe and reed;
But sikerly she had a fair forheed:
It was almost a spanne brood, I trowe;°   155   *believe*
For, hardily,° she was nat undergrowe.   *assuredly*
Ful fetis was hir cloke, as I was war.°   *aware*
Of smal coral aboute hir arm she bar
A paire of bedes, gauded al with greene,
And thereon heng a broche of gold ful sheene,   160
On which ther was first write a crowned A,
And after, *Amor vincit omnia.*
    Another Nonne with hir hadde she,

---

120. **sainte Loy**: St. Eligius (Eloi), patron of goldsmiths and carters. 125. **Stratford atte Bowe**: London suburb, where a convent was located. 132. **In . . . lest**: she was much concerned with manners. 137. **disport**: good nature, agreeableness. 139. **countrefete cheere**: imitate the manners. 141. **been holden digne**: thought worthy. 149. **yerde smerte**: rod sharply. 155. **spanne**: hand's breadth. 159. **paire of bedes**: rosary. **gauded**: ornamented (with special beads). 162. **Amor . . . omnia**: "Love conquers all."

That was hir chapelaine, and Preestes three.
   A Monk ther was, a fair for the maistrye,   165
An outridere, that lovede venerye,°   *hunting*
A manly man, to been an abbot able.
Ful many a daintee hors hadde he in stable:
And, whan he rood, men mighte his bridel heere
Ginglen in a whistling wind as clere,   170
And eek as loude as dooth the chapel belle.
Ther as this lord was keper of the celle,
The rule of Saint Maure or of Saint Beneit,
By cause that it was old and somdeel° strait,°   *somewhat / strict*
This ilke Monk leet olde thinges pace,°   175   *pass away*
And heeld after the newe world the space.°   *course*
He yaf° nat of that text a pulled° hen   *gave / plucked*
That saith, that hunters been nat holy men;
Ne that a monk, when he is recchelees,
Is likned til a fissh that is waterlees: 180
That is to sayn, a monk out of his cloistre;
But thilke° text heeld he nat worth an oistre;   *this*
And I saide his opinioun was good.
What° sholde he studie and make himselven wood,°   *why / mad*
Upon a book in cloistre alway to poure,   185
Or swinken° with his handes and laboure,   *work*
As Austin bit? How shal the world be served?
Lat Austin have his swink to him reserved!
Therfore he was a pricasour° aright: *hard rider*
Grehoundes he hadde, as swifte as fowel in flight;   190
Of priking° and of hunting for the hare   *tracking*
Was al his lust,° for no coste wolde he spare.   *pleasure*
I seigh° his sleves purfiled° at the hond   *saw / fur-lined*
With gris, and that the fineste of a lond;
And, for to festne his hood under his chin,   195
He hadde of gold ywroght a ful curious° pin: *elaborate*
A love-knotte in the gretter ende ther was.
His heed was balled, that shoon as any glas,
And eek his face, as he hadde been anoint.
He was a lord ful fat and in good point: 200
His eyen stepe, and rolling in his heed,
That stemed as a forneis of a leed;
His bootes souple,° his hors in great estat.°   *supple / condition*
Now certeinly he was a fair prelat.
He was nat pale as a forpined° gost.   205   *wasted away*
A fat swan loved he best of any rost.
His palfrey was as broun as is a berye.

164. **chapelaine:** assistant, secretary. 165. **fair . . . maistrye:** an excellent one. 166. **outridere:** a monk who supervised outlying monastic property. 170. **Ginglen:** jingling (with bells). 172. **celle:** subordinate monastery. 173. **Maure, Beneit:** St. Maurus and St. Benedict, authors of monastic "rules," or ordinances. 177. **text:** Biblical or other frequent quotation. 179. **recchelees:** reckless, careless of the "rule." 187. **Austin bit:** St. Augustine bids. 194. **gris:** an expensive gray fur. 200. **in good point:** in good shape, handsome, fat. 201. **stepe:** large, bright. 202. **That . . . leed:** that shone like a fire under a lead (pot).

A Frere ther was, a wantoune and a merye,
A limitour, a ful solempne man.
In all the ordres foure is noon that can°   210   *knows*
So muche of daliaunce and fair langage:
He hadde maad ful many a mariage
Of yonge wommen at his owne cost;
Unto his ordre he was a noble post.°   *pillar*
Ful wel biloved and famulier was he   215
With frankelains° over al in his contree,   *wealthy farmers*
And with worthy wommen of the toun:
For he hadde power of confessioun
As saide himself, more than a curat,°   *parish priest*
For of° his ordre he was licenciat.   220   *by*
Ful swetely herde he confessioun,
And plesaunt was his absolucioun;
He was an esy man to yeve° penaunce   *give*
Ther as he wiste to have a good pitaunce;°   *gift*
For unto a povre ordre for to yive   225
Is signe that a man is wel yshrive.°   *absolved*
For if he yaf,° he dorste make avaunt,   *gave*
He wiste° that a man was repentaunt.   *knew*
For many a man so hard is of his herte
He may not weepe although him sore smerte.   230
Therfore, in stede of weeping and prayeres,
Men moot° yeve silver to the povre freres.   *may*
His tipet° was ay farsed° ful of knives   *cape / packed*
And pinnes, for to yeven faire wives.
And certainly he hadde a merye note;   235
Wel coude he singe and playen on a rote.
Of yeddinges he bar utterly the pris.
His nekke whit was as the flour-de-lis;
Therto he strong was as a champioun.
He knew the tavernes wel in every toun,   240
And everich hostiler° and tappestere°   *innkeeper / barmaid*
Bet° than a lazar° or a beggestere;°   *better / leper / female beggar*
For unto swich a worthy man as he
Accorded nat, as by his facultee,
To have with seke lazars acquaintaunce: 245
It is nat honest,° it may nat avaunce°   *appropriate / profit*
For to delen with no swich poraille,°   *rabble*
But al with riche and sellers of vitaille;°   *victuals*
And over al ther as° profit sholde arise,   *wherever*
Curteis he was, and lowely of servise.   250
Ther nas° no man nowher so vertuous: *was not*

---

209. limitour: a friar granted a license to beg in a certain area. **solempne:** (1) distinguished; (2) festive. **210. ordres foure:** Dominicans, Franciscans, Carmelites, Augustinians. **220. licenciat:** empowered to hear confessions. **224. wiste to have:** knew he would have. **227. dorste make avaunt:** dared to boast. **230. him sore smerte:** he grieved greatly. **236. rote:** stringed instrument. **237. Of . . . pris:** he absolutely bore away the prize for songs or ballads. **244. facultee:** ability, position. **251. vertuous:** efficient, effective.

He was the beste beggere in his hous.
And yaf a certain ferme for the graunt;
Noon of his bretheren cam ther in his haunt;°   *assigned area*
For thogh a widwe° hadde noght a sho,°   255   *widow / shoe*
So plesaunt was his *In principio,*
Yet wolde he have a ferthing er he wente;
His purchas was wel bettre than his rente.°   *regular income*
And rage° he coude as it were right a whelpe.   *flirt*
In love-dayes ther coude he muchel helpe.   260
For ther he was nat lik a cloisterer,
With a thredbare cope, as is a povre scoler,
But he was like a maister° or a pope.   *learned man*
Of double worsted was his semicope,°   *short robe*
That rounded as a belle out of the presse.°   265   *bell-mold*
Somwhat he lisped, for his wantounesse,
To make his Englissh sweete upon his tonge;
And in his harping, when that he hadde songe,
His eyen twinkled in his heed aright
As doon the sterres in the frosty night.   270
This worthy limitour was cleped Huberd.

Anonymous Early Poems

Sir Patrick Spence

The king sits in Dumferling toune,
  Drinking the blude-reid wine:
"O whar will I get guid sailor,
  To sail this schip of mine?"

Up and spak an eldern knicht,   5
  Sat at the kings richt kne:
"Sir Patrick Spence is the best sailor,
  That sails upon the se."

The king has written a braid letter,
  And signd it wi' his hand,   10

253. **And . . . graunt:** and paid a certain amount for the grant (of his area) of begging. 256. **In principio:** "In the beginning," the first words of the Gospel of St. John, used as a friar's greeting. 258. **purchas:** proceeds of his begging. 259. **as . . . whelpe:** as if he were a puppy. 260. **love-dayes:** days fixed for settling lawsuits out of court. 266. **lisped . . . wantounesse:** lisped affectedly.
SIR PATRICK SPENCE   1. **Dumferling:** Dunfermline, capital of medieval Scotland, on the Firth of Forth. 9. **braid:** broad, i.e., a royal warrant.

And sent it to Sir Patrick Spence,
  Was walking on the sand.

The first line that Sir Patrick red,
  A loud lauch lauchèd he;
The next line that Sir Patrick red,   15
  The teir blinded his ee.

"O wha is this has don this deid,
  This ill deid don to me,
To send me out this time o' the yeir,
  To sail upon the se?   20

"Mak hast, mak hast, my mirry men all,
  Our guid schip sails the morne":
"O say na sae, my master deir,
  For I feir a deadlie storme.

"Late, late yestreen I saw the new moone,   25
  Wi' the auld moone in hir arme,
And I feir, I feir, my deir master,
  That we will cum to harme."

O our Scots nobles wer richt laith
  To weet their cork-heild schoone;   30
Bot lang owre a' the play wer playd,
  Thair hats they swam aboone.

O lang, lang may thair ladies sit,
  Wi' thair fans into their hand,
Or eir they se Sir Patrick Spence   35
  Cum sailing to the land.

O lang, lang may the ladies stand
  Wi' thair gold kems in their hair,
Waiting for thar ain deir lords,
  For they'll se thame na mair.   40

Haf owre, haf owre to Aberdour,
  It's fiftie fadom deip,
And thair lies guid Sir Patrick Spence,
  Wi' the Scots lords at his feit.

---

29. richt laith: right loath. **30. cork-heild schoone:** cork-heeled shoes. **31. owre:** before. **32. aboone:** above. **38. kems:** combs. **41. haf owre:** half way. **Aberdour:** port on the northeast coast of Scotland.

The Twa Corbies

As I was walking all alane,
I heard twa corbies making a mane;
The tane unto the t' other say,
"Where sall we gang and dine today?"

"In behint yon auld fail dyke,   5
I wot there lies a new-slain knight;
And naebody kens that he lies there,
But his hawk, his hound, and lady fair.

"His hound is to the hunting gane,
His hawk to fetch the wild-fowl hame,   10
His lady's ta'en another mate,
So we may mak our dinner sweet.

"Ye'll sit on his white hause-bane,
And I'll pike out his bonny blue een;
Wi' ae lock o' his gowden hair   15
We'll theek our nest when it grows bare.

"Mony a one for him makes mane,
But nane sall ken where he is gane;
O'er his white banes when they are bare,
The wind sall blaw for evermair."   20

Western Wind

Western wind, when will thou blow,
The small rain down can rain?
Christ, if my love were in my arms
And I in my bed again!

THE TWA CORBIES The two crows. **2.** mane: moan. **4.** gang: go. **5. fail dyke:** turf
wall. **6.** wot: know. **13. hause-bane:** neck bone. **14.** een: eyes. **15.** ae: one. **16. theek:**
thatch.

John Skelton   *(1460?–1529)*

To Mistress Margaret Hussey

Merry Margaret,
As midsummer flower,
Gentle as falcon
Or hawk of the tower;
 With solace and gladness,   5
Much mirth and no madness,
All good and no badness,
So joyously,
So maidenly,
So womanly   10
Her demeaning
In every thing,—
Far, far passing
That I can indite
Or suffice to write   15
Of merry Margaret,
As midsummer flower,
Gentle as falcon
Or hawk of the tower.
 As patient and as still   20
And as full of good will
As fair Isiphill,
Coliander,
Sweet pomander,
Good Cassaunder;   25
Steadfast of thought,
Well made, well wrought;
Far may be sought
Erst that ye can find
So courteous, so kind   30
As merry Margaret,
This midsummer flower,
Gentle as falcon
Or hawk of the tower.

TO MISTRESS MARGARET HUSSEY   3. **Gentle**: well bred; high spirited. 4. **hawk of the tower**: hawk trained to "tower" over (and swoop on) its prey. 5. **solace**: recreation, pleasure. 15. **suffice to write**: express adequately. 22. **Isiphill**: Hypsipyle, queen of Lemnos, was known for her devotion to her father and children. 23. **Coliander**: coriander, an aromatic herb used to relieve indigestion. 25. **Cassaunder**: Cassandra, sister of Hector of Troy, who refused to recant her accurate prophecies though she was beaten for them. 29. **Erst**: before.

Sir Thomas Wyatt *(1503–1542)*

My Galley Chargèd with Forgetfulness

My galley chargèd with forgetfulness
Thorough sharp seas, in winter nights, doth pass
'Tween rock and rock; and eke mine enemy, alas,
That is my lord, steereth with cruelness;
And every oar a thought in readiness,   5
As though that death were light in such a case.
An endless wind doth tear the sail apace,
Of forcèd sighs and trusty fearfulness;
A rain of tears, a cloud of dark disdain,
Have done the wearied cords great hinderance;   10
Wreathèd with error and eke with ignorance,
The stars be hid that led me to this pain;
Drownèd is reason, that should me comfort,
And I remain despairing of the port.

They Flee from Me

They flee from me, that sometime did me seek
With naked foot, stalking in my chamber.
I have seen them gentle, tame, and meek,
That now are wild, and do not remember
That sometime they put themselves in danger   5
To take bread at my hand; and now they range,
Busily seeking with a continual change.
    Thanked be fortune it hath been otherwise,
Twenty times better; but once in special,
In thin array, after a pleasant guise,   10
When her loose gown from her shoulders did fall,
And she me caught in her arms long and small,
Therewithal sweetly did me kiss,
And softly said, "Dear heart, how like you this?"
    It was no dream; I lay broad waking.   15
But all is turned thorough my gentleness,
Into a strange fashion of forsaking;
And I have leave to go, of her goodness,
And she also to use newfangleness.
But since that I so kindly am servèd,   20
I fain would know what she hath deservèd?

MY GALLEY   2. **Thorough:** through. 3. **eke:** also. 8. **trusty fearfulness:** fear that can be relied on to appear (?). 10. **hinderance:** damage. 11. **Wreathèd:** entangled.
THEY FLEE FROM ME   10. **guise:** manner. 12. **small:** thin. 16. **thorough:** through. 19. **use newfangleness:** act in a fashionable (i.e., fickle) way. 20. **kindly:** (1) according to nature; (2) generously, thoughtfully. Both meanings are, of course, ironic.

Edmund Spenser   (1552?–1599)

Prothalamion

1

Calme was the day, and through the trembling ayre
Sweete breathing *Zephyrus* did softly play,
A gentle spirit, that lightly did delay
Hot *Titans* beames, which then did glyster fayre:
When I whom sullein care,
Through discontent of my long fruitlesse stay
In Princes Court, and expectation vayne
Of idle hopes, which still doe fly away,
Like empty shaddowes, did afflict my brayne,
Walkt forth to ease my payne
Along the shoare of silver streaming *Themmes,*
Whose rutty Bancke, the which his River hemmes,
Was paynted all with variable flowers,
And all the meades adornd with daintie gemmes,
Fit to decke maydens bowres,   1
And crowne their Paramours,
Against the Brydale day, which is not long:
  Sweete *Themmes* runne softly, till I end my Song.

2

There, in a Meadow, by the Rivers side,
A Flocke of *Nymphes* I chaunced to espy,   20
All lovely Daughters of the Flood thereby,
With goodly greenish locks all loose untyde,
As each had bene a Bryde,
And each one had a little wicker basket,
Made of fine twigs entrayled curiously,   25
In which they gathered flowers to fill their flasket:
And with fine Fingers, cropt full feateously
The tender stalkes on hye.
Of every sort, which in that Meadow grew,
They gathered some; the Violet pallid blew,   30
The little Dazie, that at evening closes,
The virgin Lillie, and the Primrose trew,

PROTHALAMION   "Before the bridal chamber," a pre-marriage hymn which, as the
original title page says, was written in honor of the double marriage of the Ladies
Elizabeth and Katherine Somerset, daughters of the Earl of Worcester. **2. Zephyrus:**
the West Wind. **4. Titans:** Sun's. **12. rutty:** full of roots. **14. gemmes:** buds. **17. not
long:** not long distant. **22. greenish locks:** sea nymphs were supposed to have green
hair. **loose untyde:** brides let their hair hang loose. **25. entrayled curiously:** entwined
intricately or skillfully. **26. flasket:** basket. **27. feateously:** dextrously.

With store of vermeil Roses,
To decke their Bridegromes posies,
Against the Brydale day, which was not long: 35
   Sweete *Themmes* runne softly, till I end my Song.

3

With that, I saw two Swannes of goodly hewe
Come softly swimming downe along the Lee;
Two fairer Birds I yet did never see:
The snow which doth the top of *Pindus* strew   40
Did never whiter shew,
Nor *Jove* himselfe, when he a Swan would be
For love of *Leda*, whiter did appeare:
Yet *Leda* was, they say, as white as he,
Yet not so white as these, nor nothing neare;   45
So purely white they were,
That even the gentle streame, the which them bare,
Seem'd foule to them, and bad his billowes spare
To wet their silken feathers, least they might
Soyle their fayre plumes with water not so fayre,   50
And marre their beauties bright,
That shone as heavens light,
Against their Brydale day, which was not long:
   Sweete *Themmes* runne softly, till I end my Song.

4

Eftsoones the *Nymphes*, which now had Flowers their fill,   55
Ran all in haste, to see that silver brood,
As they came floating on the Christal Flood,
Whom when they sawe, they stood amazed still,
Their wondring eyes to fill.
Them seem'd they never saw a sight so fayre,   60
Of Fowles so lovely, that they sure did deeme
Them heavenly borne, or to be that same payre
Which through the Skie draw *Venus* silver Teeme,
For sure they did not seeme
To be begot of any earthly Seede,   65
But rather Angels or of Angels breede:
Yet were they bred of *Somers-heat* they say,
In sweetest Season, when each Flower and weede
The earth did fresh aray,
So fresh they seem'd as day,   70
Even as their Brydale day, which was not long:
   Sweete *Themmes* runne softly, till I end my Song.

---

34. **posies:** bunches of flowers, nosegays. 38. **Lee:** presumably the river Lea, which flows into the Thames. 40. **Pindus:** high mountain in Thessaly. 42–43. **Jove . . . Leda:** Jove, in the form of a swan, sexually possessed Leda; among the resulting children were the twins, Castor and Pollux (see 1. 173). 47. **bare:** bore. 49. **least:** lest. 55. **Eftsoones:** forthwith. 63. **Venus silver Teeme:** Venus's chariot drawn through the air by swans. 67. **Somers-heat:** a pun on "Somerset."

5

Then forth they all out of their baskets drew
Great store of Flowers, the honour of the field,
That to the sense did fragrant odours yield,   75
All which upon those goodly Birds they threw,
And all the Waves did strew,
That like old *Peneus* Waters they did seeme,
When downe along by pleasant *Tempes* shore
Scattred with Flowres, through *Thessaly* they streeme,   80
That they appeare through Lillies plenteous store,
Like a Brydes Chamber flore:
Two of those *Nymphes,* meane while, two Garlands bound,
Of freshest Flowres which in that Mead they found,
The which presenting all in trim Array,   85
Their snowie Foreheads therewithall they crownd,
Whil'st one did sing this Lay,
Prepar'd against that Day,
Against their Brydale day, which was not long:
     Sweete *Themmes* runne softly, till I end my Song.   90

6

"Ye gentle Birdes, the worlds faire ornament,
And heavens glorie, whom this happie hower
Doth leade unto your lovers blisfull bower,
Joy may you have and gentle hearts content
Of your loves couplement: 95
And let faire *Venus,* that is Queene of love,
With her heart-quelling Sonne upon you smile,
Whose smile, they say, hath vertue to remove
All Loves dislike, and friendships faultie guile
For ever to assoile.   100
Let endlesse Peace your steadfast hearts accord,
And blessed Plentie wait upon your bord,
And let your bed with pleasures chast abound,
That fruitfull issue may to you afford,
Which may your foes confound,   105
And make your joyes redound,
Upon your Brydale day, which is not long:
     Sweete *Themmes* run softlie, till I end my Song."

7

So ended she; and all the rest around
To her redoubled that her undersong,   110
Which said, their bridale daye should not be long.
And gentle Eccho from the neighbour ground,
Their accents did resound.

78–80. Peneus . . . Thessaly: the Peneus, chief river of Thessaly, flows through the Vale of Tempe. 97. her . . . Sonne: Cupid. 98. vertue: power. 100. assoile: clear up, forgive. 104. afford: provide. 106. redound: overflow; reverberate. 110. redoubled: repeated. undersong: refrain.

So forth those joyous Birdes did passe along,
Adowne the Lee, that to them murmurde low, 115
As he would speake, but that he lackt a tong,
Yet did by signes his glad affection show,
Making his streame run slow.
And all the foule which in his flood did dwell
Gan flock about these twaine, that did excell 120
The rest, so far, as *Cynthia* doth shend
The lesser starres. So they, enranged well,
Did on those two attend,
And their best service lend,
Against their wedding day, which was not long: 125
   Sweete *Themmes* run softly, till I end my Song.

8

At length they all to mery *London* came,
To mery London, my most kyndly Nurse,
That to me gave this Lifes first native sourse:
Though from another place I take my name, 130
An house of auncient fame.
There when they came, whereas those bricky towres,
The which on *Themmes* brode aged backe doe ryde,
Where now the studious Lawyers have their bowers,
There whylome wont the Templer Knights to byde, 135
Till they decayed through pride:
Next whereunto there standes a stately place,
Where oft I gayned giftes and goodly grace
Of that great Lord, which therein wont to dwell,
Whose want too well now feeles my freendless case: 140
But Ah here fits not well
Olde woes but joyes to tell
Against the bridale daye, which is not long:
   Sweete *Themmes* runne softly, till I end my Song.

9

Yet therein now doth lodge a noble Peer, 145
Great *Englands* glory and the Worlds wide wonder,
Whose dreadfull name, late through all *Spaine* did thunder,
And *Hercules* two pillors standing neere
Did make to quake and feare:
Faire branch of Honor, flower of Chevalrie, 150
That fillest *England* with thy triumphs fame,
Joy have thou of thy noble victorie,

120. Gan: began. 121. Cynthia: the moon. shend: surpass. 130–31. another place
. . . fame: an allusion to Spenser's relationship to the Spencers of Althorp, Northamp-
tonshire. 134–36. Where now . . . pride: the Inner and Middle Temples, where
lawyers still have their offices, once belonged to the Order of Knights Templars, suppressed in 1312. 134. bowers: halls. 135. whylome wont: once were accustomed. 137–
40. place . . . case: Leicester House, which belonged to the great Earl of Leicester,
Spenser's early patron. 145–49. Peer . . . feare: Robert Devereux, Earl of Essex, who
had just returned from sacking the Spanish port of Cadiz. 148. Hercules two pillors:
the Straits of Gibraltar.

And endlesse happinesse of thine owne name
That promiseth the same:
That through thy prowesse and victorious arms,   155
Thy country may be freed from forraine harmes:
And great *Elisaes* glorious name may ring
Through al the world, fil'd with thy wide Alarmes,
Which some brave muse may sing
To ages following,   160
Upon the Brydale day, which is not long:
  Sweete *Themmes* runne softly, till I end my Song.

10

From those high Towers, this noble Lord issuing,
Like Radiant *Hesper* when his golden hayre
In th'*Ocean* billowes he hath Bathed fayre,   165
Descended to the Rivers open vewing,
With a great traine ensuing.
Above the rest were goodly to bee seene
Two gentle Knights of lovely face and feature
Beseeming well the bower of anie Queene,   170
With gifts of wit and ornaments of nature,
Fit for so goodly stature:
That like the twins of *Jove* they seem'd in sight,
Which decke the Bauldricke of the Heavens bright.
They two, forth pacing to the Rivers side,   175
Received those two faire Brides, their Loves delight,
Which, at th'appointed tyde,
Each one did make his Bryde,
Against their Brydale day, which is not long:
  Sweete *Themmes* runne softly, till I end my Song.   180

The Faerie Queene
from Book I, Canto iv

16

Sudden upriseth from her stately place
  The royall Dame, and for her coche doth call:
All hurtlen forth, and she with Princely pace,
  As faire *Aurora* in her purple pall
Out of the East the dawning day doth call,   5

153–54. happinesse . . . same: Devereux — *deve* (*nir heu*)*reux* (French for "become happy"). 157. Elisaes: Queen Elizabeth's. 159. brave: gallant, splendid. 164. Hesper: the evening star. 169. gentle: well born. feature: form. 171. wit: intelligence. 173. twins of Jove: Castor and Pollux, who form the constellation Gemini (see note on ll. 42–43). 174. Bauldricke of the Heavens: the Zodiac. 177. tyde: time.

FAERIE QUEENE 1. place: throne. 2. royall Dame: Lucifera, or Pride. 3. hurtlen: rush confusedly. 4. Aurora: goddess of dawn.

So forth she comes: her brightnesse brode doth blaze;
The heapes of people thronging in the hall
Do ride each other, upon her to gaze:
Her glorious glittterand light doth all mens eyes amaze.

17

So forth she comes, and to her coche does clyme,   10
Adornèd all with gold, and girlonds gay,
That seemd as fresh as *Flora* in her prime,
And strove to match, in royall rich array,
Great *Junoes* golden chaire, the which they say
The Gods stand gazing on, when she does ride   15
To *Joves* high house through heavens bras-paved way
Drawne of faire Pecocks, that excell in pride,
And full of *Argus* eyes their tailes dispredden wide.

18

But this was drawne of six unequall beasts,
On which her six sage Counsellours did ryde,   20
Taught to obay their bestiall beheasts,
With like conditions to their kinds applyde:
Of which the first, that all the rest did guyde,
Was sluggish *Idlenesse*, the nourse of sin;
Upon a slouthfull Asse he chose to ryde,   25
Arayd in habit blacke, and amis thin,
Like to an holy Monck, the service to begin.

19

And in his hand his Portesse still he bare,
That much was worne, but therein little red,
For of devotion he had little care,   30
Still drownd in sleepe, and most of his dayes ded;
Scarse could he once uphold his heavie hed,
To looken, whether it were night or day:
May seeme the wayne was very evill led,
When such an one had guiding of the way,   35
That knew not, whether right he went, or else astray.

20

From worldly cares himselfe he did esloyne,
And greatly shunnèd manly exercise;
From every worke he chalengèd essoyne,
For contemplation sake: yet otherwise,   40
His life he led in lawlesse riotise;

---

12. **Flora**: goddess of flowers. 18. **Argus**: the mythical Argus was supposed to have a hundred eyes; at his death Juno transplanted his eyes into the peacock's tail. **21–22. Taught . . . applyde:** [the beasts were] taught to obey their riders' bestial orders, the riders being "applyde" (accommodated) to beasts who had similar natures to their own. 26. **amis**: a priest's vestment. 27. **the service**: the Mass. 28. **Portresse**: breviary. **still**: always. 34. **wayne**: wain, chariot. 37. **esloyne**: keep at a distance. 39. **essoyne**: excuse.

By which he grew to grievous malady;
For in his lustlesse limbs through evill guise
A shaking fever raignd continually:
Such one was *Idlenesse*, first of this company.   45

21

And by his side rode loathsome *Gluttony*,
Deformèd creature, on a filthie swyne,
His belly was up-blowne with luxury,
And eke with fatnesse swollen were his eyne,
And like a Crane his necke was long and fyne,   50
With which he swallowed up excessive feast,
For want whereof poore people oft did pyne;
And all the way, most like a brutish beast,
He spuèd up his gorge, that all did him deteast.

22

In greene vine leaves he was right fitly clad;   55
For other clothes he could not weare for heat,
And on his head an yvie girland had,
From under which fast trickled downe the sweat:
Still as he rode, he somewhat still did eat,
And in his hand did beare a bouzing can,   60
Of which he supt so oft, that on his seat
His dronken corse he scarse upholden can,
In shape and life more like a monster then a man.

23

Unfit he was for any worldly thing,
And eke unhable once to stirre or go,   65
Not meet to be of counsell to a king,
Whose mind in meat and drinke was drownèd so,
That from his friend he seldome knew his fo:
Full of diseases was his carcas blew,
And a dry dropsie through his flesh did flow,   70
Which by misdiet daily greater grew:
Such one was *Gluttony*, the second of that crew.

24

And next to him rode lustfull *Lechery*,
Upon a bearded Goat, whose rugged haire,
And whally eyes (the signe of gelosy)   75
Was like the person selfe, whom he did beare:
Who rough, and blacke, and filthy did appeare,
Unseemely man to please faire Ladies eye;

---

43. lustlesse: listless. **guise:** conduct. **49. eke:** also. **eyne:** eyes. **54. his gorge:** what he had swallowed. **55–57. greene . . . girland:** the outfit of Silenus, a mythological figure representing drunkenness. **60. can:** tankard. **61. supt:** tasted. **62. corse:** carcass. **63. then:** than. **65. unhable:** unskillful. **stirre or go:** move or walk. **70. dry:** thirsty. **75. whally:** discolored.

Yet he of Ladies oft was lovèd deare,
 When fairer faces were bid standen by: 80
O who does know the bent of womens fantasy?

25

In a greene gowne he clothèd was full faire,
 Which underneath did hide his filthinesse,
 And in his hand a burning hart he bare,
 Full of vaine follies, and new fanglenesse: 85
 For he was false, and fraught with ficklenesse,
 And learnèd had to love with secret lookes,
 And well could daunce, and sing with ruefulnesse,
 And fortunes tell, and read in loving bookes,
And thousand other wayes, to bait his fleshly hookes. 90

26

Inconstant man, that lovèd all he saw,
 And lusted after all that he did love,
 Ne would his looser life be tide to law,
 But joyd weake wemens hearts to tempt, and prove
 If from their loyall loves he might them move;   95
 Which lewdnesse fild him with reprochfull paine
 Of that fowle evill, which all men reprove,
 That rots the marrow, and consumes the braine:
Such one was *Lecherie*, the third of all this traine.

27

And greedy *Avarice* by him did ride,   100
 Upon a Camell loaden all with gold;
 Two iron coffers hong on either side,
 With precious mettall full as they might hold,
 And in his lap an heape of coine he told;
 For of his wicked pelfe his God he made,   105
 And unto hell him selfe for money sold;
 Accursèd usurie was all his trade,
And right and wrong ylike in equall ballaunce waide.

28

His life was nigh unto deaths doore yplast,
 And thred-bare cote, and cobled shoes he ware, 110
 Ne scarse good morsell all his life did tast,
 But both from backe and belly still did spare,
 To fill his bags, and richesse to compare;
 Yet chylde ne kinsman living had he none
 To leave them to; but thorough daily care   115

---

82. greene gowne: to give a woman a green gown meant "to copulate." **85. new fangle-nesse:** interest in changing fashions, i.e., infidelity. **88. ruefulnesse:** dolefulness, as was appropriate to the aspiring lover. **94. prove:** test. **97. fowle evill:** syphilis. **104. told:** counted. **105. pelfe:** dishonestly acquired wealth. **113. compare:** amass.

To get, and nightly feare to lose his owne,
He had a wretched life unto him selfe unknowne.

29

Most wretched wight, whom nothing might suffise,
  Whose greedy lust did lacke in greatest store,
  Whose need had end, but no end covetise,   120
  Whose wealth was want, whose plenty made him pore,
  Who had enough, yet wishèd ever more;
  A vile disease, and eke in foote and hand
  A grievous gout tormented him full sore,
  That well he could not touch, nor go, nor stand: 125
Such one was *Avarice*, the fourth of this faire band.

30

And next to him malicious *Envie* rode,
  Upon a ravenous wolfe, and still did chaw
  Betweene his cankred teeth a venemous tode,
  That all the poison ran about his chaw;   130
  But inwardly he chawèd his owne maw
  At neighbours wealth, that made him ever sad;
  For death it was, when any good he saw,
  And wept, that cause of weeping none he had,
But when he heard of harme, he wexèd wondrous glad.   135

31

All in a kirtle of discolourd say
  He clothèd was, ypainted full of eyes;
  And in his bosome secretly there lay
  An hatefull Snake, the which his taile uptyes
  In many folds, and mortall sting implyes.   140
  Still as he rode, he gnasht his teeth, to see
  Those heapes of gold with griple Covetyse,
  And grudgèd at the great felicitie
Of proud *Lucifera*, and his owne companie.

32

He hated all good workes and vertuous deeds,   145
  And him no lesse, that any like did use,
  And who with gracious bread the hungry feeds,
  His almes for want of faith he doth accuse;
  So every good to bad he doth abuse:
  And eke the verse of famous Poets witt   150
  He does backebite, and spightfull poison spues

---

118. **wight:** creature. 119. **lust . . . store:** appetite felt want [even] in the greatest abundance. 120. **covetise:** covetousness. 121. **want:** poverty. 130. **chaw:** jaw. 131. **maw:** insides (stomach, mouth, or gullet). 132. **wealth:** prosperity, welfare. 134. **he:** Envy's neighbor. 135. **wexèd:** waxed, grew. 136. **kirtle . . . say:** gown of many-colored fine, thin wool. 140. **implyes:** encloses. 142. **griple:** grasping. 146. **did use:** was accustomed to perform. 147–48. **who . . . accuse:** an allusion to the Calvinist doctrine that good works are useless without true faith.

From leprous mouth on all that ever writt:
Such one vile *Envie* was, that fifte in row did sitt.

33

And him beside rides fierce revenging Wrath,
   Upon a Lion, loth for to be led;   155
   And in his hand a burning brond he hath,
   The which he brandisheth about his hed;
   His eyes did hurle forth sparkles fiery red,
   And starèd sterne on all, that him beheld,
   As ashes pale of hew and seeming ded;   160
   And on his dagger still his hand he held,
Trembling through hasty rage, when choler in him sweld.

34

His ruffin raiment all was stained with blood,
   Which he had spilt, and all to rags yrent,
   Through unadvizèd rashnesse woxen wood;   165
   For of his hands he had no governement,
   Ne car'd for bloud in his avengèment:
   But when the furious fit was overpast,
   His cruell facts he often would repent;
   Yet wilfull man he never would forecast,   170
How many mischieves should ensue his heedlesse hast.

35

Full many mischiefes follow cruell Wrath;
   Abhorrèd bloudshed, and tumultuous strife,
   Unmanly murder, and unthrifty scath,
   Bitter despight, with rancours rusty knife,   175
   And fretting griefe, the enemy of life;
   All these, and many evils moe haunt ire,
   The swelling Splene, and Frenzy raging rife,
   The shaking Palsey, and Saint *Fraunces* fire:
Such one was Wrath, the last of this ungodly tire.   180

36

And after all, upon the wagon beame
   Rode *Sathan*, with a smarting whip in hand,
   With which he forward lasht the laesie teme,
   So oft as *Slowth* still in the mire did stand.
   Huge routs of people did about them band,   185
   Showting for joy, and still before their way
   A foggy mist had covered all the land;
   And underneath their feet, all scattered lay
Dead sculs and bones of men, whose life had gone astray.

---

156. **brond:** brand, wooden torch. 163. **ruffin:** disordered. 165. **woxen wood:** grown mad. 169. **facts:** deeds. 174. **unthrifty:** harmful. **scath:** destructiveness. 175. **despight:** malice. 178. **swelling Splene:** a swollen spleen was believed to be both a cause and symptom of anger. 179. **Saint Fraunces fire:** probably erysipelas, a disease of the skin or mucous membranes, characterized by inflammation. 180. **tire:** retinue.

Sir Walter Ralegh   (1552–1618)

Walsinghame

"As you came from the holy land
  Of Walsinghame,
Met you not with my true love
  By the way as you came?"

"How shall I know your true love,   5
  That have met many one
As I went to the holy land,
  That have come, that have gone?"

"She is neither white nor brown,
  But as the heavens fair: 10
There is none hath a form so divine
  In the earth or the air."

"Such an one did I meet, good sir,
  Such an angelic face,
Who like a queen, like a nymph, did appear   15
  By her gait, by her grace."

"She hath left me here all alone.
  All alone as unknown,
Who sometime did lead me with herself.
  And me loved as her own."   20

"What's the cause that she leaves you alone
  And a new way doth take,
Who loved you once as her own
  And her joy did you make?"

"I have loved her all my youth,   25
  But now, old, as you see;
Love likes not the falling fruit
  From the withered tree."

"Know that love is a careless child
  And forgets promise past;   30
He is blind, he is deaf when he list
  And in faith never fast.

WALSINGHAME Walsinghame Priory was a popular shrine for pilgrimages. **31. list:**
pleases. **32. fast:** steady.

"His desire is a dureless content
 And a trustless joy;
He is won with a world of despair   35
 And is lost with a toy.

"Of womenkind such indeed is the love,
 (Or the word, love, abused)
Under which many childish desires
 And conceits are excused.   40

"But true love is a durable fire
 In the mind ever burning—
Never sick, never old, never dead,
 From itself never turning."

The Nymph's Reply to the Shepherd

If all the world and love were young,
And truth in every shepherd's tongue,
These pretty pleasures might me move
To live with thee and be thy love.

Time drives the flocks from field to fold,   5
When rivers rage, and rocks grow cold,
And Philomel becometh dumb;
The rest complains of cares to come.

The flowers do fade, and wanton fields
To wayward winter reckoning yields;   10
A honey tongue, a heart of gall,
Is fancy's spring, but sorrow's fall.

Thy gowns, thy shoes, thy beds of roses,
Thy cap, thy kirtle, and thy posies
Soon break, soon wither, soon forgotten: 15
In folly ripe, in reason rotten.

Thy belt of straw and ivy buds,
Thy coral clasps and amber studs,
All these in me no means can move
To come to thee and be thy love.   20

But could youth last, and love still breed,
Had joys no date, nor age no need,
Then these delights my mind might move
To live with thee and be thy love.

---

33. **dureless:** transient. 40. **conceits:** fancies.
THE NYMPH'S REPLY See Christopher Marlowe, "The Passionate Shepherd," p. 94.
7. **Philomel:** the nightingale. 8. **rest complains:** "rest" is treated as a singular noun.
14. **kirtle:** gown. **posies:** nosegays. 21. **still:** always. 22. **date:** end.

Fulke Greville, Lord Brooke　*(1554–1628)*

Chorus Sacerdotum

Oh, wearisome condition of humanity,
Born under one law, to another bound;
Vainly begot, and yet forbidden vanity,
Created sick, commanded to be sound.
What meaneth nature by these diverse laws?　　　　5
Passion and reason self-division cause.
It is the mark or majesty of power
To make offenses that it may forgive.
Nature herself doth her own self deflower,
To hate those errors she herself doth give.　　　　10
For how should man think that he may not do,
If nature did not fail and punish too?
Tyrant to others, to herself unjust,
Only commands things difficult and hard,
Forbids us all things which it knows is lust,　　　　15
Makes easy pains, unpossible reward.
If nature did not take delight in blood,
She would have made more easy ways to good.
We that are bound by vows and by promotion,
With pomp of holy sacrifice and rites,　　　　20
To teach belief in God and still devotion,
To preach of heaven's wonders and delights—
Yet when each of us in his own heart looks
He finds the God there far unlike his books.

Sir Philip Sidney　*(1554–1586)*

With How Sad Steps, O Moon

With how sad steps, O moon, thou climb'st the skies!
　　How silently, and with how wan a face!
　　What! may it be that even in heavenly place
　　That busy archer his sharp arrows tries?
Sure, if that long-with-love-acquainted eyes　　　　5
　　Can judge of love, thou feel'st a lover's case;

CHORUS SACERDOTUM　Chorus of Priests. 11. that: that which. 15. lust: pleasure.
19. promotion: position. 21. still: instill.
WITH HOW SAD STEPS　4. archer: Cupid.

I read it in thy looks: thy languished grace
To me, that feel the like, thy state descries.
Then, even of fellowship, O moon, tell me,
  Is constant love deemed there but want of wit?   10
  Are beauties there as proud as here they be?
Do they above love to be loved, and yet
  Those lovers scorn whom that love doth possess?
  Do they call virtue there ungratefulness?

Come Sleep! O Sleep

Come sleep! O sleep, the certain knot of peace,
  The baiting place of wit, the balm of woe,
  The poor man's wealth, the prisoner's release,
  Th' indifferent judge between the high and low;
With shield of proof shield me from out the prease   5
  Of those fierce darts despair at me doth throw;
  O make in me those civil wars to cease;
  I will good tribute pay, if thou do so.
Take thou of me smooth pillows, sweetest bed,
  A chamber deaf to noise and blind to light,   10
  A rosy garland and a weary head;
And if these things, as being thine by right,
  Move not thy heavy grace, thou shalt in me,
  Livelier than elsewhere, Stella's image see.

Thou Blind Man's Mark

Thou blind man's mark, thou fool's self-chosen snare,
Fond fancy's scum, and dregs of scattered thought;
Band of all evils, cradle of causeless care;
Thou web of will, whose end is never wrought;
Desire, desire! I have too dearly bought,   5
With price of mangled mind, thy worthless ware;
Too long, too long, asleep thou hast me brought,
Who should my mind to higher things prepare.
But yet in vain thou hast my ruin sought;
In vain thou madest me to vain things aspire;   10
In vain thou kindlest all thy smoky fire;
For virtue hath this better lesson taught—
Within myself to seek my only hire,
Desiring nought but how to kill desire.

---

8. **descries:** proclaims. 14. **Do . . . ungratefulness:** In the moon do they call (the lady's) ungratefulness a virtue?

COME SLEEP! 2. **baiting place:** resting place on a journey. 5. **shield of proof:** strong, proven shield. **prease:** press, crowd. 11. **rosy garland:** garland of silence. 14. **Stella:** the lady addressed in the sequence from which this sonnet is taken.

THOU BLIND MAN'S MARK 1. **mark:** target. 2. **Fond:** foolish. 3. **Band:** swaddling band. 13. **hire:** payment, profit.

Leave Me, O Love

Leave me, O love, which reachest but to dust;
And thou, my mind, aspire to higher things;
Grow rich in that which never taketh rust;
Whatever fades but fading pleasure brings.
Draw in thy beams, and humble all thy might   5
To that sweet yoke where lasting freedoms be;
Which breaks the clouds and opens forth the light,
That doth both shine and give us sight to see.
O take fast hold; let that light be thy guide
In this small course which birth draws out to death,   10
And think how evil becometh him to slide,
Who seeketh heaven, and comes of heavenly breath.
  Then farewell, world; thy uttermost I see;
  Eternal Love, maintain thy life in me.

Christopher Marlowe (1564–1593)

The Passionate Shepherd to His Love

Come live with me and be my love,
And we will all the pleasures prove
That valleys, groves, hills, and fields,
Woods, or steepy mountain yields.

And we will sit upon the rocks,   5
Seeing the shepherds feed their flocks,
By shallow rivers, to whose falls
Melodious birds sing madrigals.

And I will make thee beds of roses
And a thousand fragrant posies,   10
A cap of flowers, and a kirtle
Embroidered all with leaves of myrtle;

A gown made of the finest wool
Which from our pretty lambs we pull;

LEAVE ME, O LOVE   5. beams: light of the eyes, eyebeams. 7. light: light of God. 11. evil: ill. slide: err, sin.
THE PASSIONATE SHEPHERD   2. prove: test. 11. kirtle: gown.

Fair linèd slippers for the cold,   15
With buckles of the purest gold;

A belt of straw and ivy buds,
With coral clasps and amber studs:
And if these pleasures may thee move,
Come live with me, and be my love.   20

The shepherds' swains shall dance and sing
For thy delight each May morning:
If these delights thy mind may move,
Then live with me and be my love.

William Shakespeare (1564–1616)

Sonnets

29

When, in disgrace with Fortune and men's eyes,
I all alone beweep my outcast state,
And trouble deaf heaven with my bootless cries,
And look upon myself and curse my fate,
Wishing me like to one more rich in hope,   5
Featured like him, like him with friends possessed,
Desiring this man's art, and that man's scope,
With what I most enjoy contented least;
Yet in these thoughts myself almost despising,
Haply I think on thee, and then my state,   10
Like to the lark at break of day arising
From sullen earth, sings hymns at heaven's gate;
    For thy sweet love remembered such wealth brings
    That then I scorn to change my state with kings.

30

When to the sessions of sweet silent thought
I summon up remembrance of things past,
I sigh the lack of many a thing I sought
And with old woes new wail my dear time's waste.
Then can I drown an eye (unused to flow)   5

SONNET 29   **3. bootless:** useless. **10. Haply:** by chance.
SONNET 30   **1. sessions:** originally, court or parliamentary meetings.

For precious friends hid in death's dateless night,
And weep afresh love's long since canceled woe,
And moan th' expense of many a vanished sight.
Then can I grieve at grievances foregone,
And heavily from woe to woe tell o'er   10
The sad account of fore-bemoanèd moan,
Which I new pay as if not paid before.
   But if the while I think on thee, dear friend,
   All losses are restored and sorrows end.

33

Full many a glorious morning have I seen
Flatter the mountain tops with sovereign eye,
Kissing with golden face the meadows green,
Gilding pale streams with heavenly alchemy;
Anon permit the basest clouds to ride   5
With ugly rack on his celestial face,
And from the forlorn world his visage hide,
Stealing unseen to west with this disgrace.
Even so my sun one early morn did shine
With all-triumphant splendor on my brow;   10
But, out alack! he was but one hour mine,
The region cloud hath masked him from me now.
   Yet him for this my love no whit disdaineth;
   Suns of the world may stain when heaven's sun staineth.

73

That time of year thou mayst in me behold
When yellow leaves, or none, or few, do hang
Upon those boughs which shake against the cold,
Bare ruined choirs where late the sweet birds sang.
In me thou see'st the twilight of such day   5
As after sunset fadeth in the west,
Which by-and-by black night doth take away,
Death's second self, that seals up all in rest.
In me thou see'st the glowing of such fire
That on the ashes of his youth doth lie,   10
As the deathbed whereon it must expire,

6. dateless: endless. 8. expense: loss. 9. foregone: past. 10. tell o'er: count, add up.
SONNET 33   5. Anon: immediately; soon. 6. rack: thin, floating clouds. 12. region: of the upper region. 14. stain: grow dim.
SONNET 73   7. by-and-by: quickly.

Consumed with that which it was nourished by.
  This thou perceiv'st, which makes thy love more strong,
  To love that well which thou must leave ere long.

94

They that have power to hurt and will do none,
That do not do the thing they most do show,
Who, moving others, are themselves as stone,
Unmovèd, cold, and to temptation slow—
They rightly do inherit heaven's graces   5
And husband nature's riches from expense;
They are the lords and owners of their faces,
Others but stewards of their excellence.
The summer's flower is to the summer sweet,
Though to itself it only live and die;   10
But if that flower with base infection meet,
The basest weed outbraves his dignity:
  For sweetest things turn sourest by their deeds;
  Lilies that fester smell far worse than weeds.

116

Let me not to the marriage of true minds
Admit impediments. Love is not love
Which alters when it alteration finds,
Or bends with the remover to remove.
O, no! it is an ever-fixèd mark   5
That looks on tempests and is never shaken;
It is the star to every wandering bark,
Whose worth's unknown, although his highth be taken.
Love's not Time's fool, though rosy lips and cheeks
Within his bending sickle's compass come.   10
Love alters not with his brief hours and weeks,
But bears it out even to the edge of doom.
  If this be error, and upon me proved,
  I never writ, nor no man ever loved.

SONNET 94 **2. show:** show that they could do (?); seem to do (?). **6. husband:** save up. **expense:** expenditure. **12. outbraves his dignity:** outdoes him in worth.

SONNET 116 **2. impediments:** an allusion to the marriage service: "if any of you know cause or just impediment why these persons should not be joined together . . . ." **4. bends . . . remove:** becomes inconstant when the other person is. **5. mark:** sea-mark, such as a buoy. **8. unknown:** incalculably great. **highth be taken:** altitude be calculated. **12. doom:** judgment (here, the Last Judgment).

129

Th' expense of spirit in a waste of shame
Is lust in action; and, till action, lust
Is perjured, murderous, bloody, full of blame,
Savage, extreme, rude, cruel, not to trust;
Enjoyed no sooner but despisèd straight;   5
Past reason hunted, and no sooner had,
Past reason hated, as a swallowed bait
On purpose laid to make the taker mad;
Mad in pursuit, and in possession so;
Had, having, and in quest to have, extreme;   10
A bliss in proof—and proved, a very woe;
Before, a joy proposed; behind, a dream.
    All this the world well knows; yet none knows well
    To shun the heaven that leads men to this hell.

130

My mistress' eyes are nothing like the sun;
Coral is far more red than her lips' red;
If snow be white, why then her breasts are dun;
If hairs be wires, black wires grow on her head.
I have seen roses damasked, red and white,   5
But no such roses see I in her cheeks;
And in some perfumes is there more delight
Than in the breath that from my mistress reeks.
I love to hear her speak; yet well I know
That music hath a far more pleasing sound.   10
I grant I never saw a goddess go:
My mistress, when she walks, treads on the ground.
    And yet, by heaven, I think my love as rare
    As any she belied with false compare.

138

When my love swears that she is made of truth
I do believe her, though I know she lies,
That she might think me some untutored youth,
Unlearnèd in the world's false subtilties.
Thus vainly thinking that she thinks me young,   5
Although she knows my days are past the best,

SONNET 129 1. Th' expense . . . waste: the expenditure of spirit (also, vitality) in a desert (also, "waist" as sexual region). 11. proof: experience.
SONNET 130 5. damasked: of mingled colors. 8. reeks: is exhaled. 11. go: walk. 14. she: woman. compare: comparison.

Simply I credit her false-speaking tongue:
On both sides thus is simple truth suppressed.
But wherefore says she not she is unjust?
And wherefore say not I that I am old?   10
O, love's best habit is in seeming trust,
And age in love loves not to have years told.
    Therefore I lie with her and she with me,
    And in our faults by lies we flattered be.

146

Poor soul, the center of my sinful earth,
My sinful earth these rebel powers that thee array,
Why dost thou pine within and suffer dearth,
Painting thy outward walls so costly gay?
Why so large cost, having so short a lease,   5
Dost thou upon thy fading mansion spend?
Shall worms, inheritors of this excess,
Eat up thy charge? Is this thy body's end?
Then, soul, live thou upon thy servant's loss,
And let that pine to aggravate thy store;   10
Buy terms divine in selling hours of dross;
Within be fed, without be rich no more.
    So shalt thou feed on Death, that feeds on men,
    And Death once dead, there's no more dying then.

Thomas Nashe   (1567–1601)

A Litany in Time of Plague

Adieu, farewell earth's bliss,
This world uncertain is;
Fond are life's lustful joys,

SONNET 138   7. **Simply:** at its face value. 9. **unjust:** unfaithful. 11. **habit:** dress, appearance, behavior. 13. **lie with:** (1) tell lies to; (2) have sexual intercourse with.
SONNET 146   2. **My sinful earth:** a printer's error. Emendations include "thrall to," "starved by," and "lord of." **array:** dress up; also possibly "besiege." 5. **cost:** expense. 8. **thy charge:** (1) your body; (2) your expenditure. 10. **aggravate:** increase. **store:** abundance. 11. **Buy terms divine:** acquire ages of immortality; also possibly "make a bargain with God."
A LITANY   3. **Fond:** foolish.

Death proves them all but toys,
None from his darts can fly.   5
I am sick, I must die.
       Lord, have mercy on us!

Rich men, trust not in wealth,
Gold cannot buy you health;
Physic himself must fade,   10
All things to end are made.
The plague full swift goes by;
I am sick, I must die.
       Lord, have mercy on us!

Beauty is but a flower   15
Which wrinkles will devour:
Brightness falls from the air,
Queens have died young and fair,
Dust hath closed Helen's eye.
I am sick, I must die.   20
       Lord, have mercy on us!

Strength stoops unto the grave,
Worms feed on Hector brave,
Swords may not fight with fate.
Earth still holds ope her gate;   25
Come! come! the bells do cry.
I am sick, I must die.
       Lord, have mercy on us!

Wit with his wantonness
Tasteth death's bitterness;   30
Hell's executioner
Hath no ears for to hear
What vain art can reply.
I am sick, I must die.
       Lord, have mercy on us!   35

Haste, therefore, each degree,
To welcome destiny.
Heaven is our heritage,
Earth but a player's stage;
Mount we unto the sky.   40
I am sick, I must die.
       Lord, have mercy on us!

---

10. Physic: medicine. **19. Helen:** Helen of Troy, a traditional example of beauty. **23. Hector:** the greatest Trojan hero. **26. bells:** funeral bells. **29. wantonness:** playfulness, heedlessness. **36. degree:** rank in society.

John Donne *(1572–1631)*

The Good-Morrow

I wonder by my troth, what thou and I
Did, till we loved? Were we not weaned till then,
But sucked on country pleasures, childishly?
Or snorted we in the seven sleepers' den?
'Twas so; but this, all pleasures fancies be.   5
If ever any beauty I did see,
Which I desired, and got, 'twas but a dream of thee.

And now good morrow to our waking souls,
Which watch not one another out of fear;
For love, all love of other sights controls,   10
And makes one little room an everywhere.
Let sea-discoverers to new worlds have gone,
Let maps to other, worlds on worlds have shown;
Let us possess one world, each hath one, and is one.

My face in thine eye, thine in mine appears,   15
And true plain hearts do in the faces rest;
Where can we find two better hemispheres
Without sharp north, without declining west?
Whatever dies was not mixed equally;
If our two loves be one, or thou and I   20
Love so alike that none do slacken, none can die.

The Sun Rising

Busy old fool, unruly sun,
Why dost thou thus
Through windows and through curtains call on us?
Must to thy motions lovers' seasons run?
Saucy pedantic wretch, go chide   5

THE GOOD-MORROW   The "good morning." **4. seven sleepers' den**: the cave at Ephesus
in which seven Christian youths escaped persecution by sleeping for almost two hundred years. **5. but**: except for. **12–13. Let . . . shown**: what do we care if explorers
have gone to new worlds. Or if maps have shown worlds upon worlds (perhaps maps
of the heavens showing new spheres) to other persons. **14. is one**: i.e., man is a
microcosm, a "little world." **19. Whatever . . . equally**: medieval philosophers thought
that matter would never decay if the elements in it were mixed equally.

THE SUN RISING   **5. pedantic**: schoolmasterly, officious.

Late schoolboys and sour prentices,
  Go tell court-huntsmen that the king will ride,
  Call country ants to harvest offices;
Love, all alike, no season knows, nor clime,
Nor hours, days, months, which are the rags of time.   10

Thy beams, so reverend and strong
  Why shouldst thou think?
I could eclipse and cloud them with a wink,
But that I would not lose her sight so long;
  If her eyes have not blinded thine,   15
  Look, and tomorrow late tell me
Whether both the Indias of spice and mine
Be where thou left'st them, or lie here with me.
Ask for those kings whom thou saw'st yesterday,
And thou shalt hear, all here in one bed lay.   20

She is all states, and all princes I;
  Nothing else is.
Princes do but play us; compared to this,
All honor's mimic, all wealth alchemy.
  Thou, sun, art half as happy as we,   25
  In that the world's contracted thus;
  Thine age asks ease, and since thy duties be
  To warm the world, that's done in warming us.
Shine here to us, and thou art everywhere;
This bed thy center is, these walls thy sphere.   30

The Canonization

For God sake hold your tongue, and let me love,
  Or childe my palsy or my gout,
My five grey hairs or ruined fortune flout;
With wealth your state, your mind with arts improve,
  Take you a course, get you a place,   5
  Observe his Honor or his Grace,
Or the King's real or his stampèd face
  Contemplate; what you will, approve,
    So you will let me love.

Alas, alas, who's injured by my love?   10
  What merchants' ships have my sighs drowned?

8. offices: tasks. 9. all alike: always unchanging. 17. the Indias . . . mine: the East and West Indies respectively. 24. alchemy: shining dross. 30. sphere: orbit.

THE CANONIZATION   5. course: course of action. place: government position. 6. Observe: (1) pay attention to; (2) serve. 7. stampèd face: face stamped on coins. 8. approve: test by experience.

Who says my tears have overflowed his ground?
When did my colds a forward spring remove?
   When did the heats which my veins fill
   Add one man to the plaguy bill?   15
Soldiers find wars, and lawyers find out still
   Litigious men which quarrels move,
      Though she and I do love.

Call us what you will, we are made such by love:
   Call her one, me another fly,   20
We are tapers too, and at our own cost die;
And we in us find the eagle and the dove.
   The phoenix riddle hath more wit
   By us; we two being one, are it:
So to one neutral thing both sexes fit.   25
   We die and rise the same, and prove
      Mysterious by this love.

We can die by it, if not live by love,
   And if unfit for tombs and hearse
Our legend be, it will be fit for verse;   30
And if no piece of chronicle we prove,
   We'll build in sonnets pretty rooms;
   As well a well-wrought urn becomes
The greatest ashes as half-acre tombs,
   And by these hymns all shall approve   35
      Us canonized for love.

And thus invoke us: "You whom reverend love
   Made one another's hermitage,
You to whom love was peace, that now is rage,
Who did the whole world's soul contract, and drove   40
   Into the glasses of your eyes
   (So made such mirrors and such spies
That they did all to you epitomize)
   Countries, towns, courts: beg from above
      A pattern of your love!"   45

---

13. remove: postpone. **15. plaguy bill:** list of victims of the plague, which usually struck in hot weather, issued weekly. **16. still:** continuously. **20. fly:** an example both of lechery and transitoriness. **21. die:** a secondary meaning of "die" is to have an orgasm. It was believed that each orgasm cost a day of life. **22. eagle and the dove:** symbols of male and female, with various connotations. **23. phoenix riddle:** the phoenix was a mysterious bird that merged both sexes into one. For its death and rebirth, see Carew, "A Song," note to l. 18. **wit:** sense. **29. hearse:** a canopy set over a tomb on which memorial inscriptions were hung. **30. legend:** (1) story; (2) biography of a saint. **31. chronicle:** the usual contemporary form of history, often the record of major political events. **32. sonnets:** stanzas; love poems. **rooms:** a pun, since one Italian word for "room" is *stanza*. **35. hymns:** these poems, which acquire a quasi-religious meaning. **37. You:** the lovers, now invoked as saints to intercede with God. **41. glasses:** mirrors.

A Valediction: Forbidding Mourning

As virtuous men pass mildly away,
    And whisper to their souls to go,
Whilst some of their sad friends do say,
    The breath goes now, and some say, no;

So let us melt, and make no noise,   5
    No tear-floods, nor sigh-tempests move;
'Twere profanation of our joys
    To tell the laity our love.

Moving of the earth brings harms and fears,
    Men reckon what it did and meant;   10
But trepidation of the spheres,
    Though greater far, is innocent.

Dull sublunary lovers' love,
    Whose soul is sense, cannot admit
Absence, because it doth remove   15
    Those things which elemented it.

But we by a love so much refined
    That our selves know not what it is,
Interassurèd of the mind,
    Care less eyes, lips, and hands to miss.   20

Our two souls therefore, which are one,
    Though I must go, endure not yet
A breach, but an expansion,
    Like gold to airy thinness beat.

If they be two, they are two so   25
    As stiff twin compasses are two;
Thy soul, the fixed foot, makes no show
    To move, but doth if th' other do.

And though it in the center sit,
    Yet when the other far doth roam,   30
It leans, and hearkens after it,
    And grows erect as that comes home.

A VALEDICTION **9. Moving of the earth:** earthquakes. **11. trepidation of the spheres:** the oscillation of the outermost of the heavenly spheres (see "Good Friday," note on ll. 1–2, p. 110), which in the Ptolemaic system causes the other spheres to vary from their regular paths. **12. innocent:** harmless. **13. sublunary:** beneath the moon, hence earthly and subject to change. **16. elemented it:** made it one substance. **26. twin compasses:** the two feet of a mathematical compass.

Such wilt thou be to me, who must
    Like th' other foot, obliquely run;
Thy firmness makes my circle just,   35
    And makes me end where I begun.

The Relic

When my grave is broke up again
Some second guest to entertain—
For graves have learned that woman-head
To be to more than one a bed—
    And he that digs it, spies   5
A bracelet of bright hair about the bone,
    Will he not let us alone,
And think that there a loving couple lies,
Who thought that this device might be some way
To make their souls, at the last busy day,   10
Meet at this grave, and make a little stay?

If this fall in a time or land
Where misdevotion doth command,
Then he that digs us up will bring
Us to the bishop and the king,   15
    To make us relics; then
Thou shalt be a Mary Magdalen, and I
    A something else thereby;
All women shall adore us, and some men;
And since at such times miracles are sought,   20
I would that age were by this paper taught
What miracles we harmless lovers wrought.

First, we loved well and faithfully,
Yet knew not what we loved, nor why;
Difference of sex no more we knew   25
Than our guardian angels do;
    Coming and going, we
Perchance might kiss, but not between those meals;
    Our hands ne'er touched the seals,
Which nature, injured by late law, sets free;   30

THE RELIC **1–2 When . . . entertain:** it was contemporary practice to use a grave for more than one body. **3. woman-head:** what is characteristic of woman. **10. last busy day:** the Day of Judgment. **17. Mary Magdalen:** the repentant prostitute whose sins were forgiven because she loved Jesus (Luke 7:37–50). **18. something else thereby:** Mary Magdalen was conventionally pictured as having long golden hair, so presumably the "bracelet of bright hair" (l. 6) would be thought to encircle the arm-bone of one of her lovers, perhaps even Jesus. **25–26. Difference . . . angels do:** angels were usually supposed to be incorporeal. **27–28. Coming . . . meals:** presumably an allusion to the common custom of kissing at meeting or parting from another person. **30. late law:** moral law, imposed on the amorality of nature.

These miracles we did; but now alas,
All measure and all language I should pass,
Should I tell what a miracle she was.

A Nocturnal upon Saint Lucy's Day

'Tis the year's midnight, and it is the day's,
Lucy's, who scarce seven hours herself unmasks;
    The sun is spent, and now his flasks
    Send forth light squibs, no constant rays;
        The world's whole sap is sunk;   5
The general balm th' hydroptic earth hath drunk,
Whither, as to the bed's feet, life is shrunk,
Dead and interred; yet all these seem to laugh,
Compared with me, who am their epitaph.

Study me then, you who shall lovers be   10
At the next world, that is, at the next spring;
    For I am every dead thing
    In whom Love wrought new alchemy.
        For his art did express
A quintessence even from nothingness,   15
From dull privations, and lean emptiness;
He ruined me, and I am re-begot
Of absence, darkness, death: things which are not.

All others, from all things, draw all that's good,
Life, soul, form, spirit, whence they being have;   20
    I, by Love's limbeck, am the grave
    Of all that's nothing. Oft a flood
        Have we two wept, and so
Drowned the whole world, us two; oft did we grow
To be two chaoses, when we did show   25
Care to aught else; and often absences
Withdrew our souls, and made us carcasses.

But I am by her death (which word wrongs her)
Of the first nothing the elixir grown;
    Were I a man, that I were one   30

A NOCTURNAL   **2. Lucy's:** St. Lucy's Day is December 13, regarded as the date of the
winter solstice (the shortest day of the year) under the Julian calendar. The name Lucy
means "light." **3. spent:** exhausted. **flasks:** the stars, which were thought to absorb
their light from the sun. **4. light squibs:** feeble sparks, as from fireworks. **6. balm:**
vital fluid. **hydroptic:** abnormally thirsty. **7. bed's feet . . . shrunk:** life sinks to the
foot of the bedstead, compared here to the roots of a plant. **14. express:** press out,
extract. **15. quintessence:** the fifth and highest essence or element, thought to compose the heavenly bodies and to be latent in the other four: earth, air, fire, and water.
21. limbeck: alembic, chemical flask. **29. first nothing:** the nothing from which the
world was created. **elixir:** quintessence.

I needs must know; I should prefer,
    If I were any beast,
Some ends, some means; yea plants, yea stones detest
And love; all, all some properties invest;
If I an ordinary nothing were,   35
As shadow, a light and body must be here.

But I am none; nor will my sun renew.
You lovers, for whose sake the lesser sun
    At this time to the Goat is run
      To fetch new lust, and give it you,   40
        Enjoy your summer all;
Since she enjoys her long night's festival,
Let me prepare towards her, and let me call
This hour her vigil, and her eve, since this
Both the year's and the day's deep midnight is.   45

Elegy 19. Going to Bed

Come, madam, come, all rest my powers defy,
Until I labor, I in labor lie.
The foe ofttimes having the foe in sight,
Is tired with standing though he never fight.
Off with that girdle, like heaven's zone glistering,   5
But a far fairer world encompassing.
Unpin that spangled breastplate which you wear,
That the eyes of busy fools may be stopped there.
Unlace yourself, for that harmonious chime
Tells me from you that now it is bed time.   10
Off with that happy busk, which I envy,
That still can be, and still can stand so nigh.
Your gown, going off, such beauteous state reveals,
As when from flowery meads the hill's shadow steals.
Off with that wiry coronet and show   15
The hairy diadem which on you doth grow:
Now off with those shoes, and then safely tread
In this love's hallowed temple, this soft bed.
In such white robes, heaven's angels used to be
Received by men; thou, Angel, bring'st with thee   20

---

31. prefer: select, pursue. **33–34. plants . . . love:** plants attract food and pollinators; even stones attract and repel. **34. some properties invest:** are endowed with some attributes. **39. Goat:** Capricorn, the sign of the zodiac which the sun entered, under the Julian calendar, on December 12. **42. festival:** day commemorating a saint. **44. vigil:** devotional watch, especially on the eve of a saint's day.

ELEGY 19 **5. heaven's zone:** the zone or girdle of Orion, or possibly the whole zone of fixed stars. **9. chime:** presumably, the sound of church bells. **11. busk:** corset. **15. coronet:** headband, crownlike ornament.

A heaven like Mahomet's Paradise; and though
Ill spirits walk in white, we easily know
By this these angels from an evil sprite:
Those set our hairs, but these our flesh upright.
    License my roving hands, and let them go   25
Before, behind, between, above, below.
O my America! my new-found-land,
My kingdom, safeliest when with one man manned,
My mine of precious stones, my empery,
How blest am I in this discovering thee!   30
To enter in these bonds is to be free;
Then where my hand is set, my seal shall be.
    Full nakedness!   All joys are due to thee,
As souls unbodied, bodies unclothed must be
To taste whole joys.   Gems which you women use   35
Are like Atlanta's balls, cast in men's views,
That when a fool's eye lighteth on a gem,
His earthly soul may covet theirs, not them.
Like pictures, or like books' gay coverings made
For laymen, are all women thus arrayed;   40
Themselves are mystic books, which only we
(Whom their imputed grace will dignify)
Must see revealed.   Then, since that I may know,
As liberally as to a midwife, show
Thyself: cast all, yea, this white linen hence,   45
Here is no penance, much less innocence.
    To teach thee, I am naked first; why than,
What needst thou have more covering than a man.

Holy Sonnets

7

At the round earth's imagined corners, blow
Your trumpets, angels, and arise, arise
From death, you numberless infinities
Of souls, and to your scattered bodies go,
All whom the Flood did, and fire shall o'erthrow,   5

---

21. **Mahomet's Paradise:** distinguished by its sensual pleasures. 29. **empery:** empire.
30. **discovering:** with a second meaning, "uncovering." 31. **in:** into. 36. **Atlanta's balls:**
to win the huntress Atalanta, a suitor had to outrun her in a race. One finally succeeded
by dropping three golden apples, one after the other, which she stopped to pick up.
42. **imputed grace:** the grace conferred on man by Christ's dying for him. 46. **penance
. . . innocence:** both symbolized by white. 47. **than:** then. 48. **covering:** (1) protection; (2) concealment.
SONNET 7 1. **imagined corners:** "I saw four angels standing on the four corners of
the earth" (Revelation 7:1). 1–2. **blow . . . angels:** the blowing of trumpets will announce the coming of the Last Judgment (Revelation 8–9). 5. **fire shall o'erthrow:**
at the earth's end (see II Peter 3:10).

All whom war, dearth, age, agues, tyrannies,
Despair, law, chance, hath slain, and you whose eyes
Shall behold God and never taste death's woe.
But let them sleep, Lord, and me mourn a space,
For if above all these my sins abound,   10
'Tis late to ask abundance of thy grace
When we are there; here on this lowly ground,
Teach me how to repent; for that's as good
As if thou hadst sealed my pardon with thy blood.

9

If poisonous minerals, and if that tree
Whose fruit threw death on else immortal us,
If lecherous goats, if serpents envious
Cannot be damned; alas! why should I be?
Why should intent or reason, born in me,   5
Make sins, else equal, in me more heinous?
And mercy being easy, and glorious
To God, in his stern wrath why threatens he?
But who am I that dare dispute with thee?
O God, oh! of thine only worthy blood,   10
And my tears, make a heavenly Lethean flood,
And drown in it my sins' black memory.
That thou remember them, some claim as debt;
I think it mercy, if thou wilt forget.

10

Death be not proud, though some have called thee
Mighty and dreadful, for thou art not so;
For those whom thou think'st thou dost overthrow
Die not, poor Death, nor yet canst thou kill me.
From rest and sleep, which but thy pictures be,   5
Much pleasure; then from thee much more must flow,
And soonest our best men with thee do go,
Rest of their bones, and soul's delivery.
Thou art slave to fate, chance, kings, and desperate men,
And dost with poison, war, and sickness dwell;   10

---

6. **dearth:** famine. **7–8. you . . . woe:** "there be some standing here, which shall not taste of death, till they see the Son of man coming in his kingdom" (Matthew 16:28). SONNET 9 **1–2. tree . . . fruit:** the Tree of Knowledge of Good and Evil (Genesis 2–3). **5. intent:** will. **11. Lethean flood:** Lethe, the river of forgetfulness in Hades. SONNET 10 **8. delivery:** (1) deliverance; (2) birth.

And poppy or charms can make us sleep as well,
And better than thy stroke; why swell'st thou then?
One short sleep past, we wake eternally,
And death shall be no more: Death, thou shalt die.

14

Batter my heart, three-personed God; for you
As yet but knock, breathe, shine, and seek to mend;
That I may rise and stand, o'erthrow me, and bend
Your force, to break, blow, burn, and make me new.
I, like an usurped town, to another due,   5
Labor to admit you, but oh, to no end!
Reason, your viceroy in me, me should defend,
But is captived, and proves weak or untrue.
Yet dearly I love you, and would be loved fain,
But am betrothed unto your enemy: 10
Divorce me, untie or break that knot again,
Take me to you, imprison me, for I,
Except you enthrall me, never shall be free,
Nor ever chaste, except you ravish me.

Good Friday, 1613. Riding Westward

Let man's soul be a sphere, and then in this
The intelligence that moves, devotion is;
And as the other spheres, by being grown
Subject to foreign motions, lose their own,
And being by others hurried every day   5
Scarce in a year their natural form obey,
Pleasure or business, so, our souls admit
For their first mover, and are whirled by it
Hence is't that I am carried towards the west
This day, when my soul's form bends toward the east.   10
There I should see a sun, by rising set,
And by that setting, endless day beget;
But that Christ on this cross did rise and fall,
Sin had eternally benighted all.
Yet dare I almost be glad I do not see   15
That spectacle of too much weight for me.

---

11. **poppy:** source of opium and other sedatives **charms:** magic or other potions;
spells. 12. **swell'st:** swell up (with pride).

SONNET 14 9. **fain:** gladly. 11. **knot:** union, tie. **again:** the knot was first broken
when Christ redeemed mankind.

GOOD FRIDAY, 1613 The Friday of the Crucifixion, called "good" because Christ's
sacrifice redeemed mankind. 1–2. **sphere . . . moves:** in the Ptolemaic system, the
sun, moon, each planet, and the fixed stars taken together were supposed to be carried
in concentric hollow globes (spheres), each guided by an intelligence (angel). These
spheres were in turn moved by an outer sphere called the "first mover" (l. 8). 6.
form: essential principle. 11. **sun:** Christ, as Son of God.

Who sees God's face, that is self life, must die;
What a death were it then to see God die!
It made his own lieutenant, Nature, shrink;
It made his footstool crack, and the sun wink. 20
Could I behold those hands which span the poles
And tune all spheres at once, pierced with those holes?
Could I behold that endless height, which is
Zenith to us and to' our antipodes,
Humbled below us? or that blood which is 25
The seat of all our souls, if not of his,
Make dirt of dust, or that flesh which was worn
By God for his apparel, ragged and torn?
If on these things I durst not look, durst I
Upon his miserable mother cast mine eye, 30
Who was God's partner here, and furnished thus
Half of that sacrifice which ransomed us?
Though these things, as I ride, be from mine eye,
They are present yet unto my memory,
For that looks towards them; and thou look'st towards me, 35
O Savior, as thou hang'st upon the tree;
I turn my back to thee but to receive
Corrections, till thy mercies bid thee leave.
Oh, think me worth thine anger, punish me,
Burn off my rusts, and my deformity; 40
Restore thine image, so much, by thy grace,
That thou mayst know me, and I'll turn my face.

Hymn to God, My God, in My Sickness

Since I am coming to that holy room
   Where, with thy choir of saints for evermore,
I shall be made thy music, as I come
   I tune the instrument here at the door,
   And what I must do then, think now before. 5

Whilst my physicians by their love are grown
   Cosmographers, and I their map, who lie
Flat on this bed, that by them may be shown

---

17. Who . . . die: Exodus 33:20. **20. footstool . . . wink:** supposedly an earthquake and an eclipse occurred at the time of the Crucifixion (Matthew 27:51–54; Luke 23:44–45). For earth as "footstool," see Isaiah 66:1. **21. poles:** of the universe. **22. tune all spheres:** contemporary pictures show the spheres arranged as along the sounding board of a musical instrument; their harmonic movement was thought to produce "the music of the spheres," inaudible to men. **26. seat:** mystic residence. **27. dirt:** mud. **38. leave:** leave off, cease. **41. thine image:** "God created man in his own image" (Genesis 1:27).
HYMN TO GOD, MY GOD **2. saints:** any dead persons raised to Heaven. **7. map:** since every man was a "little world."

That this is my southwest discovery,
Per fretum febris, by these straits to die,   10

I joy, that in these straits I see my west;
For, though their currents yield return to none,
What shall my west hurt me? As west and east
In all flat maps, and I am one, are one,
So death doth touch the resurrection.   15

Is the Pacific sea my home? or are
The eastern riches? is Jerusalem?
Anyan and Magellan and Gibraltar,
All straits, and none but straits, are ways to them,
Whether where Japhet dwelt, or Cham, or Sem.   20

We think that Paradise and Calvary,
Christ's cross and Adam's tree, stood in one place;
Look, Lord, and find both Adams met in me:
As the first Adam's sweat surrounds my face,
May the last Adam's blood my soul embrace.   25

So, in his purple wrapped, receive me, Lord;
By these, his thorns, give me his other crown;
And as to others' souls I preached thy word,
Be this my text, my sermon to mine own:
Therefore that he may raise, the Lord throws down.   30

9. **southwest discovery:** sought-for passage southwest of the Americas, like the Straits of Magellan. 10. *Per fretum febris:* Latin for "through the straits of fever." *Fretum* also means "burning heat." **straits:** with the second meaning of "difficult circumstances." 11. **west:** where life ends. 17. **eastern riches:** of the East Indies, China, etc. Donne is asking the location of the terrestrial paradise. 18. **Anyan:** now called the Bering Straits. 20. **Japhet, Cham, Sem:** Noah's three sons, supposedly the ancestors of the inhabitants of Europe (Japhet), Africa (Ham), and Asia (Shem). 22. **place:** presumably, general region. 23. **both Adams:** Adam was thought to be a "type" (prefiguration) of Christ. 26. **purple:** (1) blood; (2) royal garment (see Mark 15:17). 27. **his other crown:** "I have kept the faith: henceforth there is laid up for me a crown of righteousness, which the Lord, the righteous judge, shall give me at that day" (II Timothy 4:7–8). 29. **text:** Biblical text used as subject for a sermon. 30. **Therefore . . . down:** see Psalms 146:8.

Ben Jonson (1573–1637)

To Penshurst

Thou art not, Penshurst, built to envious show
    Of touch or marble, nor canst boast a row
Of polished pillars, or a roof of gold;
    Thou hast no lantern whereof tales are told,
Or stair or courts; but stand'st an ancient pile,   5
    And, these grudged at, art reverenced the while.
Thou joy'st in better marks, of soil, of air,
    Of wood, of water; therein thou art fair.
Thou hast thy walks for health as well as sport;
    Thy Mount, to which the dryads do resort,   10
Where Pan and Bacchus their high feasts have made
    Beneath the broad beech, and the chestnut shade,
That taller tree, which of a nut was set
    At his great birth, where all the Muses met.
There in the writhèd bark are cut the names   15
    Of many a sylvan, taken with his flames;
And thence the ruddy satyrs oft provoke
    The lighter fauns to reach thy Lady's oak.
Thy copse too, named of Gamage, thou hast there,
    That never fails to serve thee seasoned deer   20
When thou wouldst feast, or exercise thy friends.
    The lower land, that to the river bends,
Thy sheep, thy bullocks, kine, and calves do feed;
    The middle grounds thy mares and horses breed.
Each bank doth yield thee conies; and the tops,   25
    Fertile of wood, Ashore and Sidney's copse,
To crown thy open table, doth provide
    The purpled pheasant with the speckled side;
The painted partridge lies in every field,
    And, for thy mess, is willing to be killed.   30

PENSHURST   The estate of the Sidney family in Kent. **1. envious show:** ostentation arousing envy. **2. touch:** a fine black variety of basalt. **4. lantern:** glassed-in cupola. **5. stair:** presumably, elaborate staircase. **courts:** courtyards. **6. these grudged at:** i.e., and while these expensive or striking aspects of other houses are envied . . . . **10. dryads:** wood nymphs. **11. Pan and Bacchus:** gods of the countryside and wine. **14. his great birth:** on the day of Sir Philip Sidney's birth in 1574, supposedly an oak tree was planted. **16. a sylvan . . . flames:** a rustic, possessed with love like Sidney, who was famous for his love-sonnet sequence, *Astrophel and Stella*. **17. provoke:** incite (to a race). **18. thy Lady's oak:** according to tradition, named for a Lady Leicester. **19. copse . . . Gamage:** thicket, named after Barbara Gamage, wife of the contemporary owner of Penshurst, Viscount Lisle, who was Sir Philip's brother. **20. seasoned deer:** deer in season. **25. conies:** rabbits. **26. Ashore and Sidney's copse:** two small woods.

And if the high-swoln Medway fail thy dish,
   Thou hast thy ponds that pay thee tribute fish,
Fat agèd carps that run into thy net,
   And pikes, now weary their own kind to eat,
As loath the second draught or cast to stay,   35
   Officiously at first themselves betray;
Bright eels that emulate them, and leap on land
   Before the fisher, or into his hand.
Then hath thy orchard fruit, thy garden flowers
   Fresh as the air, and new as are the hours.   40
The early cherry, with the later plum,
   Fig, grape, and quince, each in his time doth come;
The blushing apricot and woolly peach
   Hang on thy walls, that every child may reach.
And though thy walls be of the country stone,   45
   They are reared with no man's ruin, no man's groan;
There's none that dwell about them wish them down,
   But all come in, the farmer and the clown,
And no one empty-handed, to salute
   Thy lord and lady, though they have no suit.   50
Some bring a capon, some a rural cake,
   Some nuts, some apples; some that think they make
The better cheeses bring 'em, or else send
   By their ripe daughters whom they would commend
This way to husbands, and whose baskets bear   55
   An emblem of themselves in plum or pear.
But what can this (more than express their love)
   Add to thy free provisions, far above
The need of such? whose liberal board doth flow
   With all that hospitality doth know!   60
Where comes no guest but is allowed to eat
   Without his fear, and of thy lord's own meat;
Where the same beer and bread, and selfsame wine
   That is his lordship's shall be also mine,
And I not fain to sit, as some this day   65
   At great men's tables, and yet dine away.
Here no man tells my cups, nor, standing by,
   A waiter doth my gluttony envy,
But gives me what I call and lets me eat;
   He knows below he shall find plenty of meat.   70
Thy tables hoard not up for the next day,
   Nor when I take my lodging need I pray
For fire or lights or livery; all is there
   As if thou, then, wert mine, or I reigned here;

---

31. Medway: the nearby river. **35. stay:** await. **36. Officiously:** dutifully. **44. Hang . . . walls:** grow on trellised walls. **48. clown:** rustic. **50. suit:** request. **58. free:** generous. **62. Without his fear:** freely, without fearing to eat too much. **65. fain:** required. **66. dine away:** dine on different food than that served to the lord; or dine elsewhere. **67. tells:** counts. **72. take my lodging:** go to my bedroom. **73. livery:** food or drink. **74. As if . . . mine:** as if you, then, were my servant or vassal.

There's nothing I can wish, for which I stay. 75
    That found King James, when hunting late this way
With his brave son, the Prince, they saw thy fires
    Shine bright on every hearth as the desires
Of thy Penates had been set on flame
    To entertain them, or the country came 80
With all their zeal to warm their welcome here.
    What (great I will not say, but) sudden cheer
Didst thou then make 'em! and what praise was heaped
    On thy good lady then! who therein reaped
The just reward of her high huswifery; 85
    To have her linen, plate, and all things nigh
When she was far, and not a room but dressed
    As if it had expected such a guest!
These, Penshurst, are thy praise, and yet not all.
    Thy lady's noble, fruitful, chaste withal; 90
His children thy great lord may call his own,
    A fortune in this age but rarely known.
They are and have been taught religion; thence
    Their gentler spirits have sucked innocence.
Each morn and even, they are taught to pray 95
    With the whole household, and may every day
Read, in their virtuous parents' noble parts,
    The mysteries of manners, arms, and arts.
Now, Penshurst, they that will proportion thee
    With other edifices, when they see 100
Those proud, ambitious heaps and nothing else,
    May say, their lords have built, but thy lord dwells.

Epitaph on S. P. a Child of Queen Elizabeth's Chapel

Weep with me, all you that read
    This little story,
And know, for whom a tear you shed,
    Death's self is sorry.
'Twas a child, that so did thrive 5
    In grace and feature,
As Heaven and Nature seemed to strive
    Which owned the creature.
Years he numbered scarce thirteen
    When Fates turned cruel, 10

76–77. King James . . . Prince: James I (1603–25) and his eldest son, Prince Henry, who died in 1612. **76. late:** recently. **79. Penates:** household gods. **82. sudden:** unpremeditated. **85. high huswifery:** fine household management. **90. chaste withal:** yet faithful. **97. parts:** attributes. **98. mysteries:** kinds of knowledge or action requiring apprenticeship or initiation. **manners:** general modes of behavior (a wider meaning than our modern one). **99. proportion:** compare.
EPITAPH ON S. P. Salomon Pavy (S. P.) was a child actor.

Yet three filled zodiacs had he been
   The stage's jewel,
And did act (what now we moan)
   Old men so duly,
As, sooth, the Parcae thought him one,   15
   He played so truly.
So, by error, to his fate
   They all consented;
But viewing him since (alas, too late)
   They have repented.   20
And have sought, to give new birth,
   In baths to steep him;
But, being so much too good for earth,
   Heaven vows to keep him.

Clerimont's Song

Still to be neat, still to be dressed
As you were going to a feast;
Still to be powdered, still perfumed—
Lady, it is to be presumed,
Though art's hid causes are not found,   5
All is not sweet, all is not sound.

Give me a look, give me a face,
That makes simplicity a grace;
Robes loosely flowing, hair as free:
Such sweet neglect more taketh me   10
Than all the adulteries of art;
They strike mine eyes, but not my heart.

Inviting a Friend to Supper

Tonight, grave sir, both my poor house and I
   Do equally desire your company;
Not that we think us worthy such a guest,
   But that your worth will dignify our feast
With those that come, whose grace may make that seem   5
   Something, which else could hope for no esteem.
It is the fair acceptance, sir, creates
   The entertainment perfect, not the cates.

---

11. **three filled zodiacs:** three years. 15. **sooth:** truly. **Parcae:** Fates. 22. **baths:** magical restorative baths.

CLERIMONT'S SONG   From *Epicoene, or The Silent Woman.* 11. **adulteries:** adulterations.

INVITING A FRIEND   5. **grace:** favor, condescension. 8. **cates:** delicacies.

Yet shall you have, to rectify your palate,
    An olive, capers, or some better salad   10
Ushering the mutton; with a short-legged hen,
    If we can get her, full of eggs, and then
Lemons, and wine for sauce; to these, a coney
    Is not to be despaired of, for our money;
And, though fowl now be scarce, yet there are clerks,   15
    The sky not falling, think we may have larks.
I'll tell you of more, and lie, so you will come:
    Of partridge, pheasant, woodcock, of which some
May yet be there, and godwit, if we can;
    Knat, rail, and ruff too. Howsoe'r, my man   20
Shall read a piece of Virgil, Tacitus,
    Livy, or of some better book to us,
Of which we'll speak our minds, amidst our meat;
    And I'll profess no verses to repeat.
To this, if aught appear which I not know of,   25
    That will the pastry, not my paper, show of.
Digestive cheese and fruit there sure will be;
    But that which most doth take my Muse and me,
Is a pure cup of rich Canary wine,
    Which is the Mermaid's now, but shall be mine;   30
Of which had Horace, or Anacreon tasted,
    Their lives, as do their lines, till now had lasted.
Tobacco, nectar, or the Thespian spring,
    Are all but Luther's beer to this I sing.
Of this we will sup free, but moderately,   35
    And we will have no Pooley, or Parrot by,
Nor shall our cups make any guilty men;
    But, at our parting we will be as when
We innocently met. No simple word
    That shall be uttered at our mirthful board,   40
Shall make us sad next morning or affright
    The liberty that we'll enjoy tonight.

---

9. **rectify:** restore, set right. 13. **coney:** rabbit. 15. **clerks:** scholars. 19–20. **godwit, knat, rail, ruff:** various game birds. 21. **Virgil:** Roman author of the epic poem, *The Aeneid*. 21–22. **Tacitus, Livy:** Roman historians. 23. **meat:** meal. 24. **profess . . . repeat:** claim I won't read any poetry. 25–26. **To this . . . show of:** in addition to this, if anything appears that I know nothing about, it will be shown by the pastry not this invitation. 28. **take:** please. 30. **Mermaid's . . . mine:** i.e., the wine will be ordered from the Mermaid Tavern. 31. **Horace, Anacreon:** Roman and Greek poets, respectively, who wrote in praise of wine. 33. **Thespian spring:** fountain of the Muses. 34. **Luther's beer:** bad German beer. 36. **Pooley . . . Parrot:** well-known government informers.

Robert Herrick   *(1591–1674)*

Corinna's Going A-Maying

Get up, get up for shame, the blooming morn
Upon her wings presents the god unshorn.
   See how Aurora throws her fair
   Fresh-quilted colors through the air;
   Get up, sweet slugabed, and see   5
   The dew-bespangling herb and tree.
Each flower has wept and bowed toward the east
Above an hour since; yet you not dressed,
   Nay, not so much as out of bed?
   When all the birds have matins said,   10
   And sung their thankful hymns, 'tis sin,
   Nay, profanation to keep in,
Whenas a thousand virgins on this day
Spring, sooner than the lark, to fetch in May.

Rise, and put on your foliage, and be seen   15
To come forth like the springtime, fresh and green,
   And sweet as Flora. Take no care
   For jewels for your gown or hair;
   Fear not, the leaves will strew
   Gems in abundance upon you;   20
Besides, the childhood of the day has kept,
Against you come, some orient pearls unwept;
   Come, and receive them while the light
   Hangs on the dew-locks of the night,
   And Titan on the eastern hill   25
   Retires himself, or else stands still,
Till you come forth. Wash, dress, be brief in praying:
Few beads are best when once we go a-maying.

Come, my Corinna, come; and coming, mark
How each field turns a street, each street a park   30
   Made green and trimmed with trees; see how
   Devotion gives each house a bough
   Or branch: each porch, each door, ere this,
   An ark, a tabernacle is,

CORINNA'S GOING A MAYING   **2. the god unshorn:** the sun imagined as Apollo, with hair flowing like rays of light. **3. Aurora:** goddess of dawn. **10. matins:** morning prayers. **12. profanation:** disparagement of the sacred. **14. fetch in May:** bring in flowers, especially the white hawthorn ("may") to decorate the house. **17. Flora:** goddess of flowers and, here, fertility. **22. Against:** until. **25. Titan:** the sun. **28. beads:** rosary beads, prayers. **34. An ark, a tabernacle:** sacred repositories. For the Hebrew custom of gathering boughs and palm branches for the Feast of Tabernacles, see Leviticus 23:33–43.

Made up of whitethorn neatly interwove, 35
As if here were those cooler shades of love.
 Can such delights be in the street
 And open fields, and we not see't?
 Come, we'll abroad, and let's obey
 The proclamation made for May, 40
And sin no more, as we have done, by staying;
But, my Corinna, come, let's go a-maying.

There's not a budding boy or girl this day
But is got up, and gone to bring in May.
 A deal of youth, ere this, is come 45
 Back, and with whitethorn laden, home.
 Some have despatched their cakes and cream
 Before that we have left to dream;
And some have wept, and wooed, and plighted troth,
And chose their priest, ere we can cast off sloth; 50
 Many a green-gown has been given,
 Many a kiss, both odd and even,
 Many a glance too has been sent
 From out the eye, love's firmament,
Many a jest told of the keys betraying 55
This night, and locks picked, yet we're not a-maying.

Come, let us go while we are in our prime,
And take the harmless folly of the time.
 We shall grow old apace, and die
 Before we know our liberty. 60
 Our life is short, and our days run
 As fast away as does the sun;
And as a vapor, or a drop of rain
Once lost, can ne'er be found again,
 So when or you or I are made 65
 A fable, song, or fleeting shade,
 All love, all liking, all delight
 Lies drowned with us in endless night.
Then while time serves, and we are but decaying,
Come, my Corinna, come, let's go a-maying. 70

To Daffodils

 Fair daffodils, we weep to see
  You haste away so soon;
 As yet the early-rising sun

---

40. proclamation . . . May: the general custom of "fetching in" May and, possibly, specific proclamations of Charles I permitting May games and the decorating of churches with rushes. **48. left to dream:** left off dreaming. **51. green-gown:** see Spenser, *Faerie Queene*, note on Bk. I, Canto iv, l. 82, p. 87. **52. odd and even:** both unsought and reciprocal (?).

Has not attained his noon.
                Stay, stay,   5
        Until the hasting day
                Has run
        But to the evensong,
And, having prayed together, we
        Will go with you along.   10

We have short time to stay as you,
    We have as short a spring;
As quick a growth to meet decay,
    As you or anything.
                We die   15
        As your hours do, and dry
                Away
        Like to the summer's rain,
Or as the pearls of morning's dew,
        Ne'er to be found again.   20

Upon Julia's Clothes

Whenas in silks my Julia goes,
Then, then (methinks) how sweetly flows
That liquefaction of her clothes.

Next, when I cast mine eyes and see
That brave vibration each way free,   5
Oh how that glittering taketh me!

Delight in Disorder

A sweet disorder in the dress
Kindles in clothes a wantonness;
A lawn about the shoulders thrown
Into a fine distraction;
An erring lace, which here and there   5
Enthralls the crimson stomacher;
A cuff neglectful, and thereby
Ribbands to flow confusedly;
A winning wave (deserving note)
In the tempestuous petticoat;   10
A careless shoestring, in whose tie

TO DAFFODILS **8. evensong:** vespers.
UPON JULIA'S CLOTHES **5. brave:** splendid.
DELIGHT IN DISORDER **3. lawn:** fine linen. **5. erring:** wandering. **6. stomacher:** garment worn under the bodice.

I see a wild civility:
Do more bewitch me, than when art
Is too precise in every part.

George Herbert *(1593–1633)*

Love (III)

Love bade me welcome, yet my soul drew back,
  Guilty of dust and sin.
But quick-eyed Love, observing me grow slack
  From my first entrance in,
Drew nearer to me, sweetly questioning   5
  If I lacked anything.

A guest, I answered, worthy to be here.
  Love said, "You shall be he."
"I, the unkind, ungrateful? ah, my dear,
  I cannot look on thee."   10
Love took my hand and smiling did reply,
  "Who made the eyes but I?"

"Truth, Lord, but I have marred them; let my shame
  Go where it doth deserve."
"And know you not," says Love, "who bore the blame?"   15
  "My dear, then I will serve."
"You must sit down," says Love, "and taste my meat."
  So I did sit and eat.

The Pulley

  When God at first made man,
Having a glass of blessings standing by,
"Let us," said He, "pour on him all we can.
Let the world's riches, which dispersèd lie,
  Contract into a span."   5

  So strength first made a way,
Then beauty flowed, then wisdom, honor, pleasure.

12. **civility:** elegance. 14. **precise:** (1) formal; (2) puritanical.
LOVE (III)   6. **lacked:** wanted (as a solicitous host might ask). 17. **meat:** meal (i.e.,
Holy Communion).
THE PULLEY   5. **span:** the span of a hand, about nine inches.

When almost all was out, God made a stay,
Perceiving that alone of all his treasure
　　Rest in the bottom lay.　　　　　　　　　10

"For if I should," said He,
"Bestow this jewel also on my creature,
He would adore my gifts instead of me,
And rest in nature, not the God of nature;
　　So both should losers be.　　　　　　　15

"Yet let him keep the rest,
But keep them with repining restlessness.
Let him be rich and weary, that at least,
If goodness lead him not, yet weariness
　　May toss him to my breast."　　　　　　20

Easter Wings

Lord, who createdst man in wealth and store,
　　Though foolishly he lost the same,
　　　　Decaying more and more
　　　　　　Till he became
　　　　　　　Most poor;　　　　　　　5
　　　　　　　With thee
　　　　　　Oh, let me rise
　　　　As　larks,　harmoniously,
And sing this day thy victories;
Then shall the fall further the flight in me.　　10

My　tender　age　in　sorrow　did　begin;
　　And still with sicknesses and shame
　　　　Thou didst so punish sin,
　　　　　　That I became
　　　　　　　Most thin.　　　　　　　15
　　　　　　　With thee
　　　　　　Let me combine,
　　　　And feel this day thy victory;
For if I imp my wing on thine,
Affliction shall advance the flight in me.　　20

Virtue

Sweet day, so cool, so calm, so bright,
　　The bridal of the earth and sky;

EASTER WINGS　1. store: abundance. 10. the fall: the Fall of Man. 19. imp: repair a
bird's wing by grafting.

The dew shall weep thy fall tonight,
　　For thou must die.

Sweet rose, whose hue angry and brave　　　　　5
Bids the rash gazer wipe his eye;
Thy root is ever in its grave,
　　And thou must die.

Sweet spring, full of sweet days and roses,
A box where sweets compacted lie;　　　　　　10
My music shows ye have your closes,
　　And all must die.

Only a sweet and virtuous soul,
Like seasoned timber, never gives;
But though the whole world turn to coal,　　　15
　　Then chiefly lives.

The Collar

I struck the board and cried, "No more!
　　I will abroad.
What? Shall I ever sigh and pine?
My lines and life are free, free as the road,
　　Loose as the wind, as large as store.　　　5
　　　　Shall I be still in suit?
Have I no harvest but a thorn
To let me blood, and not restore
What I have lost with cordial fruit?
　　　　Sure there was wine　　　　　　10
Before my sighs did dry it; there was corn
　　Before my tears did drown it.
Is the year only lost to me?
　　Have I no bays to crown it?
No flowers, no garlands gay? All blasted?　　15
　　　　All wasted?
Not so, my heart: but there is fruit,
　　And thou hast hands.
Recover all thy sigh-blown age
On double pleasures. Leave thy cold dispute　20
Of what is fit and not. Forsake thy cage,
　　　　Thy rope of sands,

VIRTUE **5. angry and brave:** red and defiant. **10. sweets:** sweet odors. **11. closes:** cadences. **14. gives:** breaks up. **15. coal:** cinders.

THE COLLAR (1) The priest's collar; (2) a yoke; (3) a suggestion of "choler" or rage. **1. board:** table, but with the suggestion of "God's board," the Communion table. **4. lines:** movements. **5. as store:** as abundance itself. **6. in suit:** in attendance on another. **9. cordial fruit:** fruit restoring the heart, a cordial or liqueur. **11. corn:** wheat. **14. bays:** the poet's wreath, exemplifying the secular life or fame or pleasure. **16. wasted:** blighted, destroyed. **22. rope of sands:** a proverbial expression meaning (1) a feeble hold, (2) an unending and profitless task.

Which petty thoughts have made, and made to thee
    Good cable, to enforce and draw,
            And be thy law,   25
    While thou didst wink and wouldst not see.
            Away; take heed:
            I will abroad.
Call in thy death's head there; tie up thy fears.
            He that forbears   30
        To suit and serve his need
            Deserves his load."
But as I raved and grew more fierce and wild
            At every word,
    Me thoughts I heard one calling, "Child!"   35
        And I replied, "My Lord!"

The Flower

    How fresh, O Lord, how sweet and clean
Are thy returns! Even as the flowers in spring,
    To which, besides their own demean,
The late-past frosts tributes of pleasure bring.
            Grief melts away   5
            Like snow in May,
        As if there were no such cold thing.

    Who would have thought my shriveled heart
Could have recovered greenness? It was gone
        Quite underground, as flowers depart   10
To see their mother-root when they have blown;
            Where they together
            All the hard weather,
        Dead to the world, keep house unknown.

    These are thy wonders, Lord of power,   15
Killing and quickening, bringing down to hell
        And up to heaven in an hour;
Making a chiming of a passing-bell.
            We say amiss
            This or that is;   20
        Thy word is all, if we could spell.

    Oh, that I once past changing were,

24. **enforce:** compel. 26. **wink:** close the eyes. 29. **death's head:** skull, as reminder of
death. 35. **Me thoughts:** I thought.

THE FLOWER   3. **demean:** (1) appearance; (2) demesne, estate. 11. **blown:** bloomed.
16. **quickening:** bringing to life. 18. **Making . . . passing-bell:** making a melodious
harmony of a funeral bell. 21. **spell:** comprehend (it).

Fast in thy paradise, where no flower can wither!
　　Many a spring I shoot up fair,
Offering at heaven, growing and groaning thither;　　25
　　　　Nor doth my flower
　　　　Want a spring shower,
　　My sins and I joining together.

But while I grow in a straight line,
　Still upwards bent, as if heaven were mine own,　　30
　　Thy anger comes, and I decline.
What frost to that? What pole is not the zone
　　　　Where all things burn,
　　　　When thou dost turn,
And the least frown of thine is shown?　　35

And now in age I bud again,
After so many deaths I live and write;
　I once more smell the dew and rain,
And relish versing: O my only light,
　　　　It cannot be　　40
　　　　That I am he
On whom thy tempests fell all night.

These are thy wonders, Lord of love,
To make us see we are but flowers that glide;
　Which when we once can find and prove,　　45
Thou hast a garden for us where to bide.
　　　　Who would be more,
　　　　Swelling through store,
Forfeit their paradise by their pride.

Jordan (I)

Who says that fictions only and false hair
Become a verse? Is there in truth no beauty?
Is all good structure in a winding stair?
May no lines pass except they do their duty
　Not to a true, but painted chair?　　5

Is it no verse except enchanted groves

23. **Fast:** firmly fixed. 25. **Offering at:** trying to reach. 27. **Want:** lack. 27–28. **spring . . . together:** my conscience becoming aware of my sins leads to tears of contrition. 30. **Still:** always. 44. **glide:** pass away silently. 45. **prove:** experience. 48. **store:** abundance, wealth.

JORDAN (I)　The Jordan is the river of baptism, and thus of cleansing. 1. **fictions:** artificial stories, here seen as close to lies. 4–5. **May . . . chair?:** may no verses be good unless they imitate art rather than nature?

And sudden arbors shadow coarse-spun lines?
Must purling streams refresh a lover's loves?
Must all be veiled, while he that reads, divines,
    Catching the sense at two removes?   10

Shepherds are honest people; let them sing.
Riddle who list for me, and pull for prime;
I envy no man's nightingale or spring,
    Nor let them punish me with loss of rhyme,
      Who plainly say, "My God, my King."   15

Jordan (II)

When first my lines of heavenly joys made mention,
Such was their luster, they did so excel,
That I sought out quaint words and trim invention;
My thoughts began to burnish, sprout, and swell,
Curling with metaphors a plain intention,   5
Decking the sense as if it were to sell.

Thousands of notions in my brain did run,
Offering their service, if I were not sped.
I often blotted what I had begun:
This was not quick enough, and that was dead.   10
Nothing could seem too rich to clothe the sun,
Much less those joys which trample on his head.

As flames do work and wind when they ascend,
So did I weave myself into the sense.
But while I bustled, I might hear a friend   15
Whisper, "How wide is all this long pretense!
There is in love a sweetness ready penned,
Copy out only that, and save expense."

---

7. **sudden:** unexpectedly revealed (a fashionable landscape device); also, a feature in romances, like "enchanted groves" (1. 6). **shadow:** overshadow, conceal. 9. **divines:** guesses at mysteries. 10. **two removes:** an allusion to the Platonic concept that art imitates nature and that nature in turn only imperfectly suggests the essential qualities of things—their universal forms. 12. **Riddle . . . me:** for all I care, anyone can write obscure verses. **pull for prime:** pull a lucky card at a game called primero, i.e., make a lucky guess at a poem's meaning.

JORDAN (II) 3. **quaint:** elaborately contrived. 4. **burnish:** grow. 8. **sped:** successful. 10. **quick:** alive, lively. 11. **sun:** a pun on "Son" of God (Christ). 12. **trample on:** encircle (?). 16. **wide:** wide of the mark. **pretense:** striving.

James Shirley   (1596–1666)

The Glories of Our Blood and State

The glories of our blood and state
   Are shadows, not substantial things;
There is no armor against fate;
   Death lays his icy hand on kings.
      Scepter and crown   5
      Must tumble down,
And in the dust be equal made
With the poor crooked scythe and spade.

Some men with swords may reap the field,
   And plant fresh laurels where they kill;   10
But their strong nerves at last must yield,
   They tame but one another still.
      Early or late,
      They stoop to fate,
And must give up their murmuring breath,   15
When they, pale captives, creep to death.

The garlands wither on your brow,
   Then boast no more your mighty deeds;
Upon death's purple altar now,
   See where the victor-victim bleeds.   20
      Your heads must come
      To the cold tomb;
Only the actions of the just
Smell sweet and blossom in their dust.

Thomas Carew   (1598?–1639?)

A Song

Ask me no more where Jove bestows,
When June is past, the fading rose;
For in your beauty's orient deep
These flowers, as in their causes, sleep.

A SONG   **3. orient:** (1) oriental or eastern, seen as a source (of light, beauty, etc.);
(2) lustrous. **4. causes:** essences, seeds.

Ask me no more whither doth stray   5
The golden atoms of the day;
For in pure love heaven did prepare
Those powders to enrich your hair.

Ask me no more whither doth haste
The nightingale when May is past;   10
For in your sweet dividing throat
She winters, and keeps warm her note.

Ask me no more where those stars light
That downwards fall in dead of night;
For in your eyes they sit, and there   15
Fixèd become as in their sphere.

Ask me no more if east or west
The phoenix builds her spicy nest;
For unto you at last she flies,
And in your fragrant bosom dies.   20

John Milton   *(1608–1674)*

L'Allegro

Hence loathèd Melancholy
   Of Cerberus and blackest Midnight born,
In Stygian cave forlorn
   'Mongst horrid shapes, and shrieks, and sights unholy,
Find out some uncouth cell,   5
   Where brooding Darkness spreads his jealous wings,
And the night-raven sings;
   There under ebon shades and low-browed rocks,
As ragged as thy locks,
   In dark Cimmerian desert ever dwell.   10
But come thou Goddess fair and free,
In Heaven ycleaped Euphrosyne,

---

11. **dividing:** "division" is musical ornamentation produced by dividing a note into smaller values. 16. **Fixèd . . . sphere:** according to the Ptolemaic system, all the fixed stars revolved in one sphere. 18–20. **phoenix . . . dies:** a fabulous bird supposed to consume itself by fire in its "spicy nest" every five hundred years and to rise again from its ashes.

L'ALLEGRO The gay, joyful man (Italian). 1–2. **loathèd . . . born:** a humorous genealogy. Cerberus is the three-headed dog of classical myth who guarded Hades on the banks of the river Styx. 5. **uncouth:** unknown; desolate. 10. **Cimmerian desert:** in classical geography, a barbarous, gloomy, remote region. 12. **ycleaped:** called.

And by men, heart-easing Mirth,
Whom lovely Venus at a birth
With two sister Graces more   15
To ivy-crownèd Bacchus bore;
Or whether (as some sager sing)
The frolic wind that breathes the spring,
Zephyr with Aurora playing,
As he met her once a-Maying,   20
There on beds of violets blue,
And fresh-blown roses washed in dew,
Filled her with thee, a daughter fair,
So buxom, blithe, and debonair.
Haste thee Nymph, and bring with thee   25
Jest and youthful jollity,
Quips and cranks, and wanton wiles,
Nods, and becks, and wreathèd smiles,
Such as hang on Hebe's cheek,
And love to live in dimple sleek;   30
Sport that wrinkled Care derides,
And Laughter holding both his sides.
Come, and trip it as ye go
On the light fantastic toe,
And in thy right hand lead with thee,   35
The mountain nymph, sweet Liberty;
And if I give thee honor due,
Mirth, admit me of thy crew
To live with her, and live with thee,
In unreprovèd pleasures free: 40
To hear the lark begin his flight,
And singing startle the dull night,
From his watchtower in the skies,
Till the dappled dawn doth rise;
Then to come in spite of sorrow,   45
And at my window bid good morrow,
Through the sweetbrier, or the vine,
Or the twisted eglantine;
While the cock with lively din,
Scatters the rear of darkness thin,   50
And to the stack or the barn door,
Stoutly struts his dames before;
Oft listening how the hounds and horn
Cheerly rouse the slumbering morn,
From the side of some hoar hill,   55
Through the high wood echoing shrill.
Some time walking not unseen

---

16. **ivy-crownèd Bacchus:** god of wine, traditionally wreathed with ivy. 18. **breathes:** exhales. 19. **Zephyr with Aurora:** the west wind with the goddess of dawn. 24. **buxom:** compliant. 27. **cranks:** amusing or fantastic remarks. **wanton:** playful. 28. **becks:** bows, curtsies. 29. **Hebe:** goddess of youth. 33. **trip:** dance. 45. **spite:** despite, contempt. 55. **hoar:** white or gray with frost.

By hedgerow elms, on hillocks green,
Right against the eastern gate,
Where the great sun begins his state,   60
Robed in flames and amber light,
The clouds in thousand liveries dight;
While the ploughman near at hand
Whistles o'er the furrowed land,
And the milkmaid singeth blithe,   65
And the mower whets his scythe,
And every shepherd tells his tale
Under the hawthorn in the dale.
Straight mine eye hath caught new pleasures
Whilst the lantskip round it measures: 70
Russet lawns and fallows gray,
Where the nibbling flocks do stray,
Mountains on whose barren breast
The laboring clouds do often rest,
Meadows trim with daisies pied,   75
Shallow brooks and rivers wide.
Towers and battlements it sees
Bosomed high in tufted trees,
Where perhaps some beauty lies,
The cynosure of neighboring eyes.   80
Hard by, a cottage chimney smokes,
From betwixt two agèd oaks,
Where Corydon and Thyrsis met,
Are at their savory dinner set
Of herbs and other country messes,   85
Which the neat-handed Phyllis dresses;
And then in haste her bower she leaves,
With Thestylis to bind the sheaves;
Or if the earlier season lead,
To the tanned haycock in the mead.   90
Sometimes with secure delight
The upland hamlets will invite,
When the merry bells ring round,
And the jocund rebecks sound
To many a youth and many a maid,   95
Dancing in the chequered shade;
And young and old come forth to play
On a sunshine holiday,
Till the livelong daylight fail;
Then to the spicy nut-brown ale,   100
With stories told of many a feat,
How fairy Mab the junkets eat;

---

59. **eastern gate:** gate of dawn. 60. **state:** stately progress (across the sky) 62. **liveries dight:** clothed in gorgeous robes. 67. **tells his tale:** counts his tally (of sheep). 70. **lantskip:** landscape. 71. **lawns:** meadows. 75. **pied:** variegated. 83. **Corydon, Thyrsis:** conventional shepherds' names in pastoral poetry, like Phyllis (1. 86) and Thestylis (1. 88). 85. **messes:** dishes. 87. **bower:** cottage. 90. **tanned:** sunbrowned. 91. **secure:** carefree. 94. **rebecks:** primitive versions of the violin. 102. **Mab:** fairy queen. **eat:** ate.

She was pinched and pulled, she said,
And he, by friar's lanthorn led,
Tells how the drudging goblin sweat, 105
To earn his cream-bowl duly set,
When in one night, ere glimpse of morn,
His shadowy flail hath threshed the corn
That ten day-laborers could not end;
Then lies him down the lubber fend, 110
And stretched out all the chimney's length,
Basks at the fire his hairy strength;
And crop-full out of doors he flings,
Ere the first cock his matin rings.
Thus done the tales, to bed they creep, 115
By whispering winds soon lulled asleep.
Towered cities please us then,
And the busy hum of men,
Where throngs of knights and barons bold
In weeds of peace high triumphs hold, 120
With store of ladies, whose bright eyes
Rain influence, and judge the prize
Of wit or arms, while both contend
To win her grace whom all commend.
There let Hymen oft appear 125
In saffron robe, with taper clear,
And pomp, and feast, and revelry,
With masque and antique pageantry:
Such sights as youthful poets dream
On summer eves by haunted stream. 130
Then to the well-trod stage anon,
If Jonson's learnèd sock be on,
Or sweetest Shakespeare, Fancy's child,
Warble his native wood-notes wild;
And ever against eating cares, 135
Lap me in soft Lydian airs,
Married to immortal verse,
Such as the meeting soul may pierce
In notes with many a winding bout
Of linkèd sweetness long drawn out, 140
With wanton heed and giddy cunning,

---

104. friar's lanthorn: will-o'-the-wisp. **105. drudging goblin:** Robin Goodfellow or Puck, who supposedly was fed for doing tasks. **110. lubber fend:** big, clumsy fiend (goblin). **111. chimney's:** fireplace's. **113. crop-full:** belly-full. **114. matin:** usually, morning prayer, but here something like morning bell. Traditionally spirits had to return to their resting places before cockcrow. **120. weeds:** clothes. **triumphs:** festivals. **121. store:** abundance, wealth. **122. Rain influence:** shine with power (like the stars). **125. Hymen:** god of marriage. **132. sock:** the light shoe worn by Greek comic actors, here standing for the learned comedies of Ben Jonson. **136. Lydian:** one of the Greek musical "modes," characterized as sweet and appropriate to love songs. **138. meeting:** responsive. **139. bout:** performance, turn.

The melting voice through mazes running,
Untwisting all the chains that tie
The hidden soul of harmony;
That Orpheus' self may heave his head   145
From golden slumber on a bed
Of heaped Elysian flowers, and hear
Such strains as would have won the ear
Of Pluto, to have quite set free
His half-regained Eurydice.   150
These delights if thou canst give,
Mirth, with thee I mean to live.

Il Penseroso

Hence vain deluding Joys,
    The brood of Folly without father bred,
How little you bestead,
    Or fill the fixèd mind with all your toys;
Dwell in some idle brain,   5
    And fancies fond with gaudy shapes possess,
As thick and numberless
    As the gay motes that people the sunbeams,
Or likest hovering dreams,
    The fickle pensioners of Morpheus' train.   10
But hail thou Goddess, sage and holy,
Hail divinest Melancholy,
Whose saintly visage is too bright
To hit the sense of human sight,
And therefore to our weaker view   15
O'erlaid with black, staid Wisdom's hue;
Black, but such as in esteem
Prince Memnon's sister might beseem,
Or that starred Ethiop queen that strove
To set her beauty's praise above   20
The sea nymphs, and their powers offended;
Yet thou art higher far descended:

---

142. **mazes:** interplay of melodic lines, as in a madrigal. **145–50. Orpheus . . . Eury-dice:** the music of Orpheus so charmed Pluto, the god of Hades, that he allowed Orpheus to lead his dead wife Eurydice back to earth on condition that Orpheus not look at her. When Orpheus glanced back, she vanished (see Milton, "Il Penseroso," ll. 105–08).

IL PENSEROSO   The contemplative man (Italian). **3. bestead:** profit. **5. idle:** diseased, as well as the usual meaning. **6. fancies . . . possess:** provide foolish fancies with showy shapes. **10. Morpheus:** god of dreams. **18. Prince Memnon's sister:** Hemera. Memnon was an extremely handsome Ethiopian prince. **19. starred Ethiop queen:** Cassiopeia was transformed into the constellation for boasting that her daughter Andromeda was more beautiful than the sea nymphs.

Thee bright-haired Vesta long of yore
To solitary Saturn bore;
His daughter she (in Saturn's reign   25
Such mixture was not held a stain).
Oft in glimmering bowers and glades
He met her, and in secret shades
Of woody Ida's inmost grove,
Whilst yet there was no fear of Jove.   30
Come pensive Nun, devout and pure,
Sober, steadfast, and demure,
All in a robe of darkest grain,
Flowing with majestic train,
And sable stole of cypress lawn,   35
Over thy decent shoulders drawn.
Come, but keep thy wonted state,
With even step and musing gait,
And looks commercing with the skies,
Thy rapt soul sitting in thine eyes;   40
There held in holy passion still,
Forget thyself to marble, till
With a sad leaden downward cast,
Thou fix them on the earth as fast.
And join with thee calm Peace and Quiet,   45
Spare Fast, that oft with gods doth diet,
And hears the Muses in a ring
Aye round above Jove's altar sing.
And add to these retired Leisure,
That in trim gardens takes his pleasure;   50
But first and chiefest, with thee bring
Him that yon soars on golden wing,
Guiding the fiery-wheelèd throne,
The Cherub Contemplation;
And the mute Silence hist along,   55
'Less Philomel will deign a song,
In her sweetest, saddest plight,
Smoothing the rugged brow of Night,
While Cynthia checks her dragon yoke,
Gently o'er th' accustomed oak;   60

23–24. Vesta . . . bore: Vesta, the chaste goddess of the hearth, conceived Melancholy
by her father Saturn, contemplative ruler of the gods before he was overthrown by his
son Jove (1. 30). As a planet, Saturn was supposed to govern melancholy or "saturnine"
persons. 25. Saturn's reign: the Golden Age. 29. Ida: mountain in Crete where Jove
was born. 33. grain: dye, color. 35. cypress lawn: a crepelike material, often worn for
mourning. 36. decent: modest. 37. wonted state: accustomed dignity. 39. commercing:
holding commerce, communicating. 43. sad: serious. 44. fast: steadily. 48. Aye: always.
51–54. first . . . Contemplation: the cherubim, the second highest order of angels,
were supposed to contemplate God directly. The imagery of their guiding God's throne
derives from Ezekiel, chs. 1 and 10. 55. hist: summon quietly. 56–57. Philomel . . .
plight: Philomela was raped by her brother-in-law Tereus, who tore out her tongue so
she could not reveal the deed. She was turned into a nightingale. 59. Cynthia . . .
yoke: goddess of the moon, pictured as driving a chariot.

Sweet bird that shunn'st the noise of folly,
Most musical, most melancholy!
Thee, chauntress, oft the woods among,
I woo to hear thy evensong;
And missing thee, I walk unseen   65
On the dry smooth-shaven green,
To behold the wandering moon,
Riding near her highest noon,
Like one that had been led astray
Through the heavens' wide pathless way;   70
And oft, as if her head she bowed,
Stooping through a fleecy cloud.
Oft on a plat of rising ground
I hear the far-off curfew sound,
Over some wide-watered shore,   75
Swinging slow with sullen roar;
Or if the air will not permit,
Some still, removèd place will fit,
Where glowing embers through the room
Teach light to counterfeit a gloom,   80
Far from all resort of mirth,
Save the cricket on the hearth,
Or the bellman's drowsy charm,
To bless the doors from nightly harm.
Or let my lamp at midnight hour   85
Be seen in some high lonely tower,
Where I may oft outwatch the Bear,
With thrice-great Hermes, or unsphere
The spirit of Plato to unfold
What worlds or what vast regions hold   90
Th' immortal mind that hath forsook
Her mansion in this fleshly nook;
And of those daemons that are found
In fire, air, flood, or under ground,
Whose power hath a true consent   95
With planet or with element.
Sometime let gorgeous Tragedy
In sceptered pall come sweeping by,
Presenting Thebes, or Pelops' line,
Or the tale of Troy divine,   100
Or what (though rare) of later age
Ennobled hath the buskined stage.

---

73. plat: small piece. **78. fit:** suit (me). **83. bellman's drowsy charm:** the night watch-man cried the hours. "Charm" means both song and spell. **87. the Bear:** the constellation Ursa Major, which never sets. **88. thrice-great Hermes:** Hermes Trismegistus, the Egyptian god Thoth, patron of magic; he was assimilated to the supposed author of various esoteric and mystical writings of the third and fourth centuries A.D. **88–89. unsphere . . . Plato:** recall the spirit of Plato from its heavenly sphere. **93. daemons:** spirits. **95. consent:** harmony. **96. element:** the four elements, listed in l. 94. **98. pall:** splendid cloak. **99–100. Thebes . . . Troy:** various subjects of Greek tragedy. **102. buskined stage:** tragic drama, since Greek actors wore the buskin or high boot.

But, O sad Virgin, that thy power
Might raise Musaeus from his bower,
Or bid the soul of Orpheus sing   105
Such notes as, warbled to the string,
Drew iron tears down Pluto's cheek,
And made Hell grant what love did seek;
Or call up him that left half told
The story of Cambuscan bold,   110
Of Camball, and of Algarsife,
And who had Canace to wife,
That owned the virtuous ring and glass,
And of the wondrous horse of brass,
On which the Tartar king did ride;   115
And if aught else great bards beside
In sage and solemn tunes have sung,
Of tourneys and of trophies hung,
Of forests and enchantments drear,
Where more is meant than meets the ear.   120
Thus Night oft see me in thy pale career,
Till civil-suited Morn appear,
Not tricked and frounced as she was wont
With the Attic boy to hunt,
But kerchiefed in a comely cloud,   125
While rocking winds are piping loud,
Or ushered with a shower still,
When the gust hath blown his fill,
Ending on the rustling leaves,
With minute-drops from off the eaves.   130
And when the sun begins to fling
His flaring beams, me Goddess bring
To archèd walks of twilight groves,
And shadows brown that Sylvan loves,
Of pine or monumental oak,   135
Where the rude axe with heavèd stroke
Was never heard the nymphs to daunt,
Or fright them from their hallowed haunt.
There in close covert by some brook,
Where no profaner eye may look,   140
Hide me from Day's garish eye,
While the bee with honied thigh,
That at her flowery work doth sing,
And the waters murmuring,
With such consort as they keep,   145

---

104. **Musaeus:** mythical Greek poet. 105–08. **Orpheus . . . seek:** see note to Milton, "L'Allegro," ll. 145–50. 110–15. **Cambuscan . . . king:** Milton recalls Chaucer's unfinished *Squire's Tale.* 116. **bards:** such as Spenser and the Italian romance writers, Ariosto and Tasso. 120. **Where . . . ear:** as in the allegorical aspects of Spenser's *Faerie Queene.* 121. **career:** course across the sky. 122. **civil-suited:** dressed as a civilian, i.e., soberly. 124. **Attic boy:** Cephalus of Attica, loved by Aurora, the dawn goddess. 130. **minute-drops:** drops falling at intervals of a minute. 134. **Sylvan:** god of the woods and fields. 145. **consort:** harmony.

Entice the dewy-feathered Sleep;
And let some strange mysterious dream
Wave at his wings in airy stream
Of lively portraiture displayed,
Softly on my eyelids laid.　　　　　　　　　　　　　　　150
And as I wake, sweet music breathe
Above, about, or underneath,
Sent by some spirit to mortals good,
Or th' unseen Genius of the wood.
But let my due feet never fail　　　　　　　　　　　　155
To walk the studious cloister's pale,
And love the high embowèd roof,
With antic pillars massy proof,
And storied windows richly dight,
Casting a dim, religious light.　　　　　　　　　　　160
There let the pealing organ blow
To the full-voiced choir below,
In service high and anthems clear,
As may with sweetness, through mine ear,
Dissolve me into ecstasies,　　　　　　　　　　　　165
And bring all Heaven before mine eyes.
And may at last my weary age
Find out the peaceful hermitage,
The hairy gown and mossy cell,
Where I may sit and rightly spell　　　　　　　　　170
Of every star that heaven doth show,
And every herb that sips the dew;
Till old experience do attain
To something like prophetic strain.
These pleasures Melancholy give,　　　　　　　　　175
And I with thee will choose to live.

Lycidas

Yet once more, O ye laurels, and once more,
Ye myrtles brown, with ivy never sere,
I come to pluck your berries harsh and crude,
And with forced fingers rude

146–50. Entice . . . laid: Milton combines the figure of Sleep with the dream Sleep is asked to bring, and pictures Sleep as looking at itself in the "stream" of its images. 154. Genius; guardian spirit. 155. due: respectful. 156. pale: enclosure. 158. antic: fantastically carved or ornamented. proof: proven strength. 159. dight: adorned. 170. spell: consider.

LYCIDAS "In this monody the author bewails a learned friend [Edward King], unfortunately drowned in his passage from Chester on the Irish seas, 1637. And by occasion foretells the ruin of our corrupted clergy then at their height" (Milton). 1. laurels: like myrtles and ivy (1. 2), used for wreaths for successful poets. 2. sere: withered.

Shatter your leaves before the mellowing year. 5
Bitter constraint, and sad occasion dear,
Compels me to disturb your season due;
For Lycidas is dead, dead ere his prime,
Young Lycidas, and hath not left his peer.
Who would not sing for Lycidas? he knew 10
Himself to sing, and build the lofty rhyme.
He must not float upon his watery bier
Unwept, and welter to the parching wind,
Without the meed of some melodious tear.
　　Begin, then, Sisters of the sacred well 15
That from beneath the seat of Jove doth spring;
Begin, and somewhat loudly sweep the string.
Hence with denial vain and coy excuse:
So may some gentle Muse
With lucky words favor my destined urn, 20
And, as he passes, turn
And bid fair peace be to my sable shroud!
　　For we were nursed upon the self-same hill,
Fed the same flock, by fountain, shade, and rill;
Together both, ere the high lawns appeared 25
Under the opening eyelids of the morn,
We drove afield, and both together heard
What time the gray-fly winds her sultry horn,
Battening our flocks with the fresh dews of night,
Oft till the star that rose at evening bright 30
Toward heaven's descent had sloped his westering wheel.
Meanwhile the rural ditties were not mute;
Tempered to the oaten flute,
Rough satyrs danced, and fauns with cloven heel
From the glad sound would not be absent long; 35
And old Damoetas loved to hear our song.
　　But, oh! the heavy change, now thou art gone,
Now thou art gone, and never must return!
Thee, Shepherd, thee the woods and desert caves,
With wild thyme and the gadding vine o'ergrown, 40
And all their echoes, mourn.
The willows, and the hazel copses green,
Shall now no more be seen
Fanning their joyous leaves to thy soft lays.
As killing as the canker to the rose, 45
Or taint-worm to the weanling herds that graze,
Or frost to flowers that their gay wardrop wear,
When first the whitethorn blows;

---

13. welter: roll and surge. **14. meed:** tribute. **15. Sisters . . . well:** the Muses, associated with the Pierian spring at the foot of Mt. Olympus. **18. coy:** modest; or possibly "disdainful." **23. nursed . . . hill:** i.e., attended the same university, Cambridge. **25. high lawns:** pastures. **29. Battening:** fattening. **36. Damoetas:** presumably an allusion to some real person, perhaps a tutor at Cambridge. **40. gadding:** wandering. **44. lays:** songs. **47. wardrop:** wardrobe. **48. blows:** blossoms.

Such, Lycidas, thy loss to shepherd's ear.
    Where were ye, Nymphs, when the remorseless deep   50
Closed o'er the head of your loved Lycidas?
For neither were ye playing on the steep
Where your old bards, the famous Druids, lie,
Nor on the shaggy top of Mona high,
Nor yet where Deva spreads her wizard stream.   55
Ay me, I fondly dream!
Had ye been there—for what could that have done?
What could the Muse herself that Orpheus bore,
The Muse herself, for her enchanting son,
Whom universal nature did lament,   60
When, by the rout that made the hideous roar,
His gory visage down the stream was sent,
Down the swift Hebrus to the Lesbian shore?
    Alas! what boots it with uncessant care
To tend the homely, slighted shepherd's trade,   65
And strictly meditate the thankless Muse?
Were it not better done, as others use,
To sport with Amaryllis in the shade,
Or with the tangles of Neaera's hair?
Fame is the spur that the clear spirit doth raise   70
(That last infirmity of noble mind)
To scorn delights and live laborious days;
But the fair guerdon when we hope to find,
And think to burst out into sudden blaze,
Comes the blind Fury with th' abhorrèd shears,   75
And slits the thin-spun life. But not the praise,
Phoebus replied, and touched my trembling ears:
Fame is no plant that grows on mortal soil,
Nor in the glistering foil
Set off to the world, nor in broad rumor lies,   80
But lives and spreads aloft by those pure eyes
And perfet witness of all-judging Jove;
As he pronounces lastly on each deed,
Of so much fame in heaven expect thy meed.
    O fountain Arethuse, and thou honored flood,   85
Smooth-sliding Mincius, crowned with vocal reeds,
That strain I heard was of a higher mood.
But now my oat proceeds,

---

54. Mona: the island of Anglesey, a Druid center, off the coast of Wales. **55. Deva:** the river Dee, which flows between England and Wales into the Irish Sea, supposedly foretold good or evil to either country by the shifting of its channel. **56. fondly:** foolishly. **58 63. Orpheus . . . shore:** the Thracian women, scorned by the bard Orpheus, tore him to pieces in a bacchanalian frenzy and threw his head into the river Hebrus to drift across the Aegean to the island of Lesbos. **59. enchanting:** Orpheus could move trees and rocks with his music. **64. boots:** profits. **66. meditate . . . Muse:** work seriously at being a poet. **67. use:** do. **73. guerdon:** reward. **75. blind . . . shears:** one of the three Fates, Atropos, who cuts the thread of life. **77. Phoebus:** Apollo, god of poetic inspiration. **79. glistering foil:** used to set off a gem. **80. rumor:** reputation, without regard to worth. **82. perfet:** perfect. **85. fountain Arethuse:** a Sicilian fountain which, like the river Mincius in northern Italy (1. 86), was associated with classical writers of pastoral. **88. oat:** oaten pipe.

And listens to the Herald of the Sea,
That came in Neptune's plea.   90
He asked the waves, and asked the felon winds,
What hard mishap hath doomed this gentle swain?
And questioned every gust of rugged wings
That blows from off each beakèd promontory.
They knew not of his story,   95
And sage Hippotades their answer brings,
That not a blast was from his dungeon strayed:
The air was calm, and on the level brine
Sleek Panope, with all her sisters, played.
It was that fatal and perfidious bark,   100
Built in th' eclipse, and rigged with curses dark,
That sunk so low that sacred head of thine.
    Next, Camus, reverend sire, went footing slow,
His mantle hairy, and his bonnet sedge,
Inwrought with figures dim, and on the edge   105
Like to that sanguine flower inscribed with woe.
"Ah, who hath reft," quoth he, "my dearest pledge?"
    Last came, and last did go,
The Pilot of the Galilean lake;
Two massy keys he bore of metals twain   110
(The golden opes, the iron shuts amain).
He shook his mitered locks, and stern bespake:
"How well could I have spared for thee, young swain,
Enow of such as, for their bellies' sake,
Creep, and intrude, and climb into the fold!   115
Of other care they little reckoning make
Than how to scramble at the shearers' feast,
And shove away the worthy bidden guest.
Blind mouths! that scarce themselves know how to hold
A sheep-hook, or have learned aught else the least   120
That to the faithful herdman's art belongs!
What recks it them? What need they? They are sped;
And when they list, their lean and flashy songs
Grate on their scrannel pipes of wretched straw;
The hungry sheep look up, and are not fed,   125
But, swoln with wind and the rank mist they draw,

89. listens . . . Sea: gives heed to Triton. 90. plea: behalf. 92. gentle swain: well-born youth. 96. Hippotades: Aeolus, god of the winds. 99. Panope: most important of the sea nymphs. 101. eclipse: eclipses were unlucky. 102. sacred: consecrated to God. 103. Camus: god of the river Cam, and so a symbol of the University. 106. sanguine . . . woe: Apollo killed his lover Hyacinthus accidentally when throwing the discus. The flower sprang from his blood with its petals marked "Ai! ai!" ("Woe, woe"). 107. reft: carried off forcibly. pledge: child considered as hostage to fortune. 109-12. Pilot . . . locks: St. Peter, since Jesus preached from his ship to the crowd at the Sea of Galilee (Luke 5:1-3). St. Peter's locks are "mitered" because he is represented as the first bishop; he carries the golden and iron keys which open the gates of Heaven and Hell respectively (see Matthew 16:19). 111. amain: forcefully. 114. Enow: enough. 115. fold: an allusion to the parable of the Good Shepherd (John 10:1-18). 119. Blind mouths: corrupt clergymen, whose sermons convey their blindness. 122. What . . . sped: what does it matter to them? What need have they? They have prospered. 123. list: choose. flashy: showy, empty, insipid. 124. scrannel: thin, harsh, feeble. 126. swoln . . . draw: swollen with empty and false doctrine.

Rot inwardly, and foul contagion spread;
Besides what the grim Wolf with privy paw
Daily devours apace, and nothing said.
But that two-handed engine at the door   130
Stands ready to smite once, and smite no more."
   Return, Alpheus; the dread voice is past
That shrunk thy streams; return, Sicilian Muse,
And call the vales, and bid them hither cast
Their bells and flowerets of a thousand hues.   135
Ye valleys low, where the mild whispers use,
Of shades and wanton winds and gushing brooks,
On whose fresh lap the swart star sparely looks,
Throw hither all your quaint enameled eyes,
That on the green turf suck the honeyed showers,   140
And purple all the ground with vernal flowers.
Bring the rathe primrose that forsaken dies,
The tufted crow-toe, and pale jessamine,
The white pink, and the pansy freaked with jet,
The glowing violet,   145
The musk-rose, and the well-attired woodbine,
With cowslips wan that hang the pensive head,
And every flower that sad embroidery wears;
Bid amaranthus all his beauty shed,
And daffadillies fill their cups with tears,   150
To strew the laureate hearse where Lycid lies.
For so, to interpose a little ease,
Let our frail thoughts dally with false surmise.
Ay me! whilst thee the shores and sounding seas
Wash far away, where'er thy bones are hurled;   155
Whether beyond the stormy Hebrides,
Where thou, perhaps, under the whelming tide
Visit'st the bottom of the monstrous world;
Or whether thou, to our moist vows denied,
Sleep'st by the fable of Bellerus old,   160
Where the great Vision of the guarded mount
Looks toward Namancos and Bayona's hold.
Look homeward, Angel, now, and melt with ruth:
And, O ye dolphins, waft the hapless youth.
   Weep no more, woeful shepherds, weep no more;   165

---

128. Wolf: perhaps both the Catholic and Anglican churches, or possibly Satan. **privy:** secret. **130. two-handed engine:** perhaps the two Houses of Parliament, but many interpretations have been suggested. **132. Alpheus:** the river god who loved Arethusa (l. 85), here a symbol of the return of the pastoral mode after the religious digression. **136. use:** frequent. **138. swart star:** Sirius, whose late summer rising was associated with the heat that burns the fields black. **142. rathe:** early. **149. amaranthus:** a never-fading flower. **157. whelming:** submerging. **158. monstrous:** filled with sea monsters. **159. moist vows:** tearful prayers. **160. Bellerus:** a legendary figure from whom Bellerium, the Roman name for Land's End in Cornwall, was derived. **161. guarded mount:** St. Michael's Mount at the tip of Land's End. **162. Namancos and Bayona's hold:** a mountainous region and stronghold in northern Spain. **163. Angel:** the Archangel Michael, **ruth:** pity. **164. waft:** convey safely by water.

For Lycidas, your sorrow, is not dead,
Sunk though he be beneath the watery floor.
So sinks the day-star in the ocean bed,
And yet anon repairs his drooping head,
And tricks his beams, and with new-spangled ore   170
Flames in the forehead of the morning sky:
So Lycidas sunk low, but mounted high,
Through the dear might of Him that walked the waves,
Where, other groves and other streams along,
With nectar pure his oozy locks he laves,   175
And hears the unexpressive nuptial song,
In the blest kingdoms meek of joy and love.
There entertain him all the saints above,
In solemn troops, and sweet societies
That sing, and singing in their glory move,   180
And wipe the tears forever from his eyes.
Now, Lycidas, the shepherds weep no more;
Henceforth thou art the Genius of the shore,
In thy large recompense, and shalt be good
To all that wander in that perilous flood.   185
    Thus sang the uncouth swain to th' oaks and rills,
While the still morn went out with sandals gray:
He touched the tender stops of various quills,
With eager thought warbling his Doric lay.
And now the sun had stretched out all the hills,   190
And now was dropped into the western bay;
At last he rose, and twitched his mantle blue:
Tomorrow to fresh woods, and pastures new.

On the Late Massacre in Piemont

Avenge, O Lord, thy slaughtered saints, whose bones
Lie scattered on the Alpine mountains cold;
Even them who kept thy truth so pure of old,
When all our fathers worshiped stocks and stones,
Forget not: in thy book record their groans   5
Who were thy sheep, and in their ancient fold
Slain by the bloody Piemontese, that rolled
Mother with infant down the rocks. Their moans
The vales redoubled to the hills, and they

168. **day-star:** sun. 169. **anon repairs:** soon renews. 170. **tricks:** arrays. 173. **Him** . . . **waves:** see Matthew 14:23–33. 176. **unexpressive nuptial song:** inexpressible song of the marriage of Christ and His Church (see Revelation 19:9). 178. **saints:** the saved. 181. **wipe the tears:** "God shall wipe away all tears from their eyes" (Revelation 21:4). 183. **Genius:** guardian spirit. 186. **uncouth:** unknown. 188. **quills:** reed pipes. 189. **Doric:** the dialect of Greek pastoral poets. 192. **twitched:** threw on.
ON THE LATE MASSACRE   In 1655, the Duke of Savoy massacred some 1700 Waldensians, members of a Protestant sect. 4. **stocks and stones:** graven images, whose worship is forbidden by the Ten Commandments.

To heaven. Their martyred blood and ashes sow   10
O'er all th' Italian fields, where still doth sway
The triple Tyrant; that from these may grow
A hundredfold, who, having learnt thy way,
Early may fly the Babylonian woe.

When I Consider . . .

When I consider how my light is spent
Ere half my days in this dark world and wide,
And that one talent which is death to hide
Lodged with me useless, though my soul more bent
To serve therewith my Maker, and present   5
My true account, lest he, returning, chide.
"Doth God exact day-labor, light denied?"
I fondly ask. But Patience, to prevent
That murmur, soon replies, "God doth not need
Either man's work or his own gifts. Who best   10
Bear his mild yoke, they serve him best. His state
Is kingly: thousands at his bidding speed,
And post o'er land and ocean without rest:
They also serve who only stand and wait."

Methought I Saw . . .

Methought I saw my late espousèd saint
Brought to me like Alcestis from the grave,
Whom Jove's great son to her glad husband gave,
Rescued from death by force, though pale and faint.
Mine, as whom washed from spot of childbed taint   5
Purification in the Old Law did save,
And such, as yet once more I trust to have
Full sight of her in heaven without restraint,
Came vested all in white, pure as her mind:
Her face was veiled; yet to my fancied sight   10

12. triple Tyrant: the Pope, identified with his triple-crowned tiara. 14. Babylonian
woe: the Catholic Church, often identified by Protestants with the whore of Babylon
(Revelation, chs. 17–18).

WHEN I CONSIDER   3. one talent: in the parable of the talents, the servant who buried
the one talent given him by his master instead of using it profitably was cast out on
his master's return (Matthew 25:14–30). 8. fondly: foolishly. 11. mild yoke: an allusion to Jesus's saying, "For my yoke is easy, and my burden is light" (Matthew 11:30).

METHOUGHT I SAW   1. saint: a soul in heaven. 2–4. Alcestis . . . faint: when Hercules
("Jove's great son") brought Alcestis back from the grave, her husband Admetus did
not at first recognize her veiled figure. 5–6. as whom . . . save: the Old (Mosaic)
Law prescribed a period of purification after childbirth (Leviticus, ch. 12). 9. vested:
clothed.

Love, sweetness, goodness, in her person shined
So clear as in no face with more delight.
But, oh! as to embrace me she inclined,
I waked, she fled, and day brought back my night.

Paradise Lost
from Book IV

Beneath him with new wonder now he views   205
To all delight of human sense exposed
In narrow room nature's whole wealth, yea more,
A heaven on earth, for blissful paradise
Of God the garden was, by him in the east
Of Eden planted; Eden stretched her line   210
From Auran eastward to the royal towers
Of great Seleucia, built by Grecian kings,
Or where the sons of Eden long before
Dwelt in Telassar: in this pleasant soil
His far more pleasant garden God ordained;   215
Out of the fertile ground he caused to grow
All trees of noblest kind for sight, smell, taste;
And all amid them stood the Tree of Life,
High-eminent, blooming ambrosial fruit
Of vegetable gold; and next to life   220
Our death, the Tree of Knowledge, grew fast by,
Knowledge of good bought dear by knowing ill.
Southward through Eden went a river large,
Nor changed his course, but through the shaggy hill
Passed underneath engulfed, for God had thrown   225
That mountain as his garden mold, high raised
Upon the rapid current, which through veins
Of porous earth with kindly thirst up drawn,
Rose a fresh fountain, and with many a rill
Watered the garden; thence united fell   230
Down the steep glade, and met the nether flood,
Which from his darksome passage now appears,
And now divided into four main streams,
Runs divers, wandering many a famous realm
And country whereof here needs no account;   235
But rather to tell how, if art could tell,
How from that sapphire fount the crispèd brooks,
Rolling on orient pearl and sands of gold,
With mazy error under pendent shades

PARADISE LOST   205. **he:** Satan, who sees the Garden of Eden stretched before him.
211–14. Auran . . . Seleucia . . . Telassar: all sites in ancient Mesopotamia. **214–35.
in this . . . account:** through this passage, Milton builds on Genesis 2:8–17. **219.
blooming:** bearing. **ambrosial fruit:** ambrosia was the food of the gods, as "nectar" (l.
240) was their drink. **228. kindly:** natural. **237. crispèd:** rippling. **238. orient:** (1)
eastern; (2) lustrous. **239. error:** from Latin *error*, wandering.

Ran nectar, visiting each plant, and fed   240
Flowers worthy of Paradise, which not nice art
In beds and curious knots, but nature boon
Poured forth profuse on hill and dale and plain,
Both where the morning sun first warmly smote
The open field, and where the unpierced shade   245
Imbrowned the noontide bowers: thus was this place,
A happy rural seat of various view;
Groves whose rich trees wept odorous gums and balm,
Others whose fruit burnished with golden rind
Hung amiable, Hesperian fables true,   250
If true, here only, and of delicious taste.
Betwixt them lawns, or level downs, and flocks
Grazing the tender herb, were interposed,
Or palmy hillock, or the flowery lap
Of some irriguous valley spread her store,   255
Flowers of all hue, and without thorn the rose;
Another side, umbrageous grots and caves
Of cool recess, o'er which the mantling vine
Lays forth her purple grape, and gently creeps
Luxuriant; meanwhile, murmuring waters fall   260
Down the slope hills, dispersed, or in a lake
That to the fringèd bank with myrtle crowned
Her crystal mirror holds, unite their streams.
The birds their choir apply; airs, vernal airs,
Breathing the smell of field and grove, attune   265
The trembling leaves, while universal Pan,
Knit with the Graces and the Hours in dance,
Led on th' eternal Spring.

Richard Lovelace   (1618–1656?)

The Grasshopper

To my noble friend, Mr. Charles Cotton

O thou that swing'st upon the waving hair
   Of some well-fillèd oaten beard,

241. **nice:** over-refined. 242. **beds . . . knots:** as in contemporary formal gardens.
boon: bounteous. 246. **Imbrowned:** darkened. 247. **various view:** varied aspect. 250.
amiable: from Latin *amabilis*, attractive. 250–51 **Hesperian . . . only:** if the fables
about the Garden of the Hesperides (with its golden apples) are true, they are true
only of Eden. 252. **lawns:** glades, meadows. 255. **irriguous:** watered. **store:** abundance
257. **umbrageous grots:** shady grottoes. 264. **apply:** from Latin *applicare*, join together.
266–68. **universal . . . Spring:** Milton suggests the encompassing nature of Eden by
joining Pan, the universal spirit of nature, with the Graces and Hours in dance, the
dance itself being a symbol of harmony.

THE GRASSHOPPER   2. **oaten beard:** tuft of oats.

Drunk every night with a delicious tear
    Dropped thee from heaven, where now th' art reared;

The joys of earth and air are thine entire,   5
    That with thy feet and wings dost hop and fly;
And when thy poppy works thou dost retire
    To thy carved acorn bed to lie.

Up with the day, the sun thou welcom'st then,
    Sport'st in the gilt-plats of his beams,   10
And all these merry days mak'st merry, men,
    Thyself, and melancholy streams.

But ah, the sickle! Golden ears are cropped;
    Ceres and Bacchus bid good night;
Sharp frosty fingers all your flowers have topped,   15
    And what scythes spared, winds shave off quite.

Poor verdant fool! and now green ice! thy joys
    Large and as lasting as thy perch of grass,
Bid us lay in 'gainst winter, rain, and poise
    Their floods with an o'erflowing glass.   20

Thou best of men and friends! we will create
    A genuine summer in each other's breast,
And spite of this cold time and frozen fate,
    Thaw us a warm seat to our rest.

Our sacred hearths shall burn eternally   25
    As vestal flames; the North Wind, he
Shall strike his frost-stretched wings, dissolve, and fly
    This Etna in epitome.

Dropping December shall come weeping in,
    Bewail th' usurping of his reign;   30
But when in showers of old Greek we begin,
    Shall cry, he hath his crown again!

Night as clear Hesper shall our tapers whip
    From the light casements where we play,
And the dark hag from her black mantle strip,   35
    And stick there everlasting day.

Thus richer than untempted kings are we,
    That asking nothing, nothing need:
Though lord of all what seas embrace, yet he
    That wants himself is poor indeed.   40

4. th': thou. **reared:** (1) nourished(?); (2) risen(?). **7. poppy:** opiate. **10. gilt-plats:** gilded meadows. **14. Ceres and Bacchus:** the grain and the grape. **16. quite:** completely. **19. poise:** balance. **26. As vestal flames:** as the eternal flame tended by the Vestal Virgins in ancient Rome. **27. strike:** contract(?). **28. Etna:** the volcano Mt. Etna. **in epitome:** in miniature. **31. old Greek:** old Greek wine. **32. crown:** garland worn by a drinker in ancient times. **33. Night . . . whip:** our tapers (candles) will drive away night just as clear Hesperus, the evening star, does. **40. wants:** lacks.

Andrew Marvell   *(1621–1678)*

A Dialogue Between the Soul and Body

SOUL

Oh, who shall from this dungeon raise
A soul enslaved so many ways?
With bolts of bones, that fettered stands
In feet, and manacled in hands.
Here blinded with an eye, and there   5
Deaf with the drumming of an ear.
A soul hung up, as 'twere, in chains
Of nerves and arteries and veins;
Tortured, besides each other part,
In a vain head and double heart.   10

BODY

Oh, who shall me deliver whole
From bonds of this tyrannic soul?
Which, stretched upright, impales me so
That mine own precipice I go;
And warms and moves this needless frame   15
(A fever could but do the same).
And, wanting where its spite to try,
Has made me live to let me die,
A body that could never rest,
Since this ill spirit it possessed.   20

SOUL

What magic could me thus confine
Within another's grief to pine?
Where whatsoever it complain,
I feel, that cannot feel, the pain.
And all my care itself employs,   25
That to preserve which me destroys;
Constrained not only to endure
Diseases, but, what's worse, the cure;
And ready oft the port to gain,
Am shipwrecked into health again.   30

BODY

But physic yet could never reach
The maladies thou me dost teach,

A DIALOGUE   **4. manacled:** from Latin *manus,* hand. **13–14. stretched . . . go:** man
walks erect because he has a soul, unlike the animals. But also he can fall to damnation because of his soul. **15. needless frame:** this body, which does not need (the soul).
20. ill: evil. **24. I feel . . . pain:** the soul sympathizes, though it cannot feel physical
pain. **29. port:** heaven. **31. physic:** medicine.

Whom first the cramp of hope does tear,
And then the palsy shakes of fear,
The pestilence of love does heat,   35
Or hatred's hidden ulcer eat.
Joy's cheerful madness does perplex,
Or sorrow's other madness vex;
Which knowledge forces me to know,
And memory will not forgo.   40
What but a soul could have the wit
To build me up for sin so fit?
So architects do square and hew
Green trees that in the forest grew.

To His Coy Mistress

Had we but world enough, and time,
This coyness, lady, were no crime.
We would sit down, and think which way
To walk, and pass our long love's day.
Thou by the Indian Ganges' side   5
Shouldst rubies find; I by the tide
Of Humber would complain. I would
Love you ten years before the Flood,
And you should, if you please, refuse
Till the conversion of the Jews.   10
My vegetable love should grow
Vaster than empires and more slow;
An hundred years should go to praise
Thine eyes, and on thy forehead gaze;
Two hundred to adore each breast,   15
But thirty thousand to the rest;
An age at least to every part,
And the last age should show your heart.
For, lady, you deserve this state,
Nor would I love at lower rate.   20
    But at my back I always hear
Time's wingèd chariot hurrying near;
And yonder all before us lie
Deserts of vast eternity.
Thy beauty shall no more be found,   25
Nor, in thy marble vault, shall sound
My echoing song; then worms shall try

41. wit: intelligence.
TO HIS COY MISTRESS   "Coy" means reserved, inaccessible; possibly also, disdainful. **6. rubies:** perhaps because they are associated with virginity. **7. Humber:** the river that runs through Marvell's native town, Hull, in Yorkshire. **complain:** sing of the cruelty or indifference of his mistress. **10. Till . . . Jews:** i.e., until just before the end of the world. **11. vegetable:** an allusion to the fact that vegetables have the power of growth but lack consciousness. Also vegetables were supposed to grow endlessly if they met no impediment. **19. state:** estimation.

That long-preserved virginity,
And your quaint honor turn to dust,
And into ashes all my lust: 30
The grave's a fine and private place,
But none, I think, do there embrace.
   Now therefore, while the youthful hue
Sits on thy skin like morning glew,
And while thy willing soul transpires   35
At every pore with instant fires,
Now let us sport us while we may,
And now, like amorous birds of prey,
Rather at once our time devour
Than languish in his slow-chapped power.   40
Let us roll all our strength and all
Our sweetness up into one ball,
And tear our pleasures with rough strife
Thorough the iron gates of life:
Thus, though we cannot make our sun   45
Stand still, yet we will make him run.

The Garden

   How vainly men themselves amaze
To win the palm, the oak, or bays,
And their uncessant labors see
Crowned from some single herb or tree,
Whose short and narrow-vergèd shade   5
Does prudently their toils upbraid;
While all flowers and all trees do close
To weave the garlands of repose.

   Fair Quiet, have I found thee here,
And Innocence, thy sister dear?   10
Mistaken long, I sought you then
In busy companies of men.
Your sacred plants, if here below,
Only among the plants will grow:
Society is all but rude   15
To this delicious solitude.

---

29. quaint honor: maidenhead; but "quaint" also suggests whimsical or overscrupulous, as well as a pun on "cunt," which derives from Middle English *queynte*. **34. glew:** sometimes emended to "dew," but glew seems to be a dialect form of "glow." **35. transpires:** breathes forth. **40. slow-chapped:** slow-jawed.

THE GARDEN **1. amaze:** bewilder. **2. palm . . . oak . . . bays:** garlands awarded for excellence in sports, military or civic duties, and poetry. **3. uncessant:** incessant. **5. short:** short-lived. **6. prudently:** wise in practical conduct. **toils:** (1) labors; (2) entanglements. **7. close:** unite. **15. rude:** rustic, barbaric. **16. To:** compared to.

No white nor red was ever seen
So amorous as this lovely green.
Fond lovers, cruel as their flame,
Cut in these trees their mistress' name: 20
Little, alas, they know or heed
How far these beauties hers exceed!
Fair trees, wherese'er your barks I wound,
No name shall but your own be found.

When we have run our passion's heat,   25
Love hither makes his best retreat.
The gods, that mortal beauty chase,
Still in a tree did end their race:
Apollo hunted Daphne so,
Only that she might laurel grow;   30
And Pan did after Syrinx speed,
Not as a nymph, but for a reed.

What wondrous life in this I lead!
Ripe apples drop about my head;
The luscious clusters of the vine   35
Upon my mouth do crush their wine;
The nectarine and curious peach
Into my hands themselves do reach;
Stumbling on melons, as I pass,
Ensnared with flowers, I fall on grass.   40

Meanwhile the mind, from pleasure less,
Withdraws into its happiness:
The mind, that ocean where each kind
Does straight its own resemblance find;
Yet it creates, transcending these,   45
Far other worlds and other seas,
Annihilating all that's made
To a green thought in a green shade.

Here at the fountain's sliding foot,
Or at some fruit-tree's mossy root,   50
Casting the body's vest aside,
My soul into the boughs does glide:
There, like a bird, it sits and sings,
Then whets and combs its silver wings,
And, till prepared for longer flight,   55
Waves in its plumes the various light.

---

17. **No white nor red:** the traditional colors of beauty. 19. **Fond:** foolish. 23. **wherese'er:** wheresoever. 25. **heat:** (1) ardor; (2) lap in a race, course. 28. **Still:** always. 29–32. **Apollo . . . reed:** two instances in which fleeing girls were saved from rape by transformation into plants. 37. **curious:** exquisite. 43–44. **mind . . . find:** traditionally, each land creature had its counterpart in the ocean. 51. **vest:** vesture, i.e., flesh. 54. **whets:** preens. 56. **various:** many-colored.

        Such was that happy garden-state,
        While man there walked without a mate:
        After a place so pure and sweet,
        What other help could yet be meet!   60
        But 'twas beyond a mortal's share
        To wander solitary there:
        Two paradises 'twere in one
        To live in paradise alone.

        How well the skillful gardener drew   65
        Of flowers and herbs this dial new,
        Where, from above, the milder sun
        Does through a fragrant zodiac run;
        And, as it works, th' industrious bee
        Computes its time as well as we: 70
        How could such sweet and wholesome hours
        Be reckoned but with herbs and flowers?

The Picture of Little T. C. in a Prospect of Flowers

        See with what simplicity
        This nymph begins her golden days!
        In the green grass she loves to lie,
        And there with her fair aspect tames
        The wilder flowers, and gives them names;   5
        But only with the roses plays,
                And them does tell
        What color best becomes them, and what smell.

        Who can foretell for what high cause
        This darling of the gods was born?   10
        Yet this is she whose chaster laws
        The wanton Love shall one day fear,
        And, under her command severe,
        See his bow broke and ensigns torn.
                Happy who can   15
        Appease this virtuous enemy of man!

        Oh, then let me in time compound
        And parley with those conquering eyes,

57. **garden-state:** Eden. **60. meet:** fitting. Eve was created as a "help meet" for Adam
(Genesis 2:18). **66–68. dial . . . zodiac:** possibly the garden is planted in the form
of a sundial complete with signs of the zodiac, but the expression may be totally metaphorical. The sun is "milder" because it moves through "a fragrant zodiac" rather than
in its own sphere of heat.
LITTLE T. C. "Prospect" in the title means (1) a scene, extended view; (2) a view
into the future. **4. aspect:** gaze, expression. **5. gives them names:** as Adam gave names
to all creatures, traditionally as a sign of his dominion over them (Genesis 1:26–28,
2:19–20). **12. Love:** Cupid.

Ere they have tried their force to wound;
Ere with their glancing wheels they drive 20
In triumph over hearts that strive,
And them that yield but more despise:
     Let me be laid
Where I may see thy glories from some shade.

Meantime, whilst every verdant thing 25
Itself does at thy beauty charm,
Reform the errors of the spring:
Make that the tulips may have share
Of sweetness, seeing they are fair;
And roses of their thorns disarm; 30
     But most procure
That violets may a longer age endure.

But, O young beauty of the woods,
Whom nature courts with fruits and flowers,
Gather the flowers, but spare the buds, 35
Lest Flora, angry at thy crime,
To kill her infants in their prime,
Do quickly make th' example yours;
     And, ere we see,
Nip in the blossom all our hopes and thee. 40

The Mower to the Glowworms

Ye living lamps, by whose dear light
The nightingale does sit so late,
And studying all the summer night,
Her matchless songs does meditate;

Ye country comets, that portend 5
No war nor prince's funeral,
Shining unto no higher end
Than to presage the grass's fall;

Ye glowworms, whose officious flame
To wandering mowers shows the way, 10
That in the night have lost their aim,
And after foolish fires do stray;

Your courteous lights in vain you waste,
Since Juliana here is come,

21. **strive:** contend with (her). 36. **Flora:** goddess of flowers. 39. **see:** i.e., see you mature.

TO THE GLOWWORMS 4. **meditate:** plan. 5. **comets:** popularly considered to portend disaster. 9. **officious:** kindly, eager. 12. **foolish fires:** *igni fatui*, shifting, elusive lights seen at night over marshes; often called "will-o'-the-wisps" and metaphorically extended to mean delusive hopes or goals.

For she my mind hath so displaced   15
That I shall never find my home.

The Mower's Song

My mind was once the true survey
Of all these meadows fresh and gay,
And in the greenness of the grass
Did see its hopes as in a glass;
When Juliana came, and she,   5
What I do to the grass, does to my thoughts and me.

But these, while I with sorrow pine,
Grew more luxuriant still and fine,
That not one blade of grass you spied
But had a flower on either side;   10
When Juliana came, and she,
What I do to the grass, does to my thoughts and me.

Unthankful meadows, could you so
A fellowship so true forgo?
And in your gaudy May-games meet   15
While I lay trodden under feet?
When Juliana came, and she,
What I do to the grass, does to my thoughts and me.

But what you in compassion ought,
Shall now by my revenge be wrought;   20
And flowers and grass and I and all
Will in one common ruin fall.
For Juliana comes, and she,
What I do to the grass, does to my thoughts and me.

And thus, ye meadows, which have been   25
Companions of my thoughts more green,
Shall now the heraldry become
With which I shall adorn my tomb;
For Juliana comes, and she,
What I do to the grass, does to my thoughts and me. 30

The Mower, Against Gardens

Luxurious man, to bring his vice in use,
     Did after him the world seduce,

THE MOWER'S SONG   **1. survey:** map, image. **15. gaudy:** festive, showy. **19. ought:** owed.

AGAINST GARDENS   **1. Luxurious:** licentious. **use:** common use.

And from the fields the flowers and plants allure,
    Where nature was most plain and pure.
He first enclosed within the garden's square   5
    A dead and standing pool of air,
And a more luscious earth for them did knead,
    Which stupefied them while it fed.
The pink grew then as double as his mind;
    The nutriment did change the kind.   10
With strange perfumes he did the roses taint;
    And flowers themselves were taught to paint.
The tulip white did for complexion seek,
    And learned to interline its cheek;
Its onion root they then so high did hold,   15
    That one was for a meadow sold:
Another world was searched, through oceans new,
    To find the Marvel of Peru;
And yet these rarities might be allowed
    To man, that sovereign thing and proud,   20
Had he not dealt between the bark and tree,
    Forbidden mixtures there to see.
No plant now knew the stock from which it came;
    He grafts upon the wild the tame,
That the uncertain and adulterate fruit   25
    Might put the palate in dispute.
His green seraglio has its eunuchs too,
    Lest any tyrant him outdo;
And in the cherry he does nature vex
    To procreate without a sex.   30
'Tis all enforced, the fountain and the grot,
    While the sweet fields do lie forgot,
Where willing nature does to all dispense
    A wild and fragrant innocence;
And fauns and fairies do the meadows till   35
    More by their presence than their skill.
Their statues, polished by some ancient hand,
    May to adorn the gardens stand;
But, howsoe'er the figures do excel,
    The gods themselves with us do dwell.   40

9. **pink . . . mind:** the double pink (carnation) is analogous to the "double" (hypocritical) mind. 12. **paint:** use cosmetics. 16. **one . . . sold:** tulip bulbs, then being introduced from Holland, sometimes brought extraordinary prices. 18. **Marvel of Peru:** a rare flower. 21–22. **Had he . . . see:** i.e., by grafting. 31. **enforced:** unnatural. **grot:** grotto. 39. **figures:** statues.

Henry Vaughan   *(1622–1695)*

The Retreat

Happy those early days! when I
Shined in my angel infancy;
Before I understood this place
Appointed for my second race,
Or taught my soul to fancy aught   5
But a white, celestial thought;
When yet I had not walked above
A mile or two from my first Love,
And looking back (at that short space)
Could see a glimpse of his bright face;   10
When on some gilded cloud or flower
My gazing soul would dwell an hour,
And in those weaker glories spy
Some shadows of eternity;
Before I taught my tongue to wound   15
My conscience with a sinful sound,
Or had the black art to dispense
A several sin to every sense,
But felt through all this fleshly dress
Bright shoots of everlastingness.   20
   Oh, how I long to travel back,
And tread again that ancient track!
That I might once more reach that plain
Where first I left my glorious train,
From whence th' enlightened spirit sees   25
That shady city of palm trees.
But, ah! my soul with too much stay
Is drunk, and staggers in the way.
Some men a forward motion love;
But I by backward steps would move,   30
And when this dust falls to the urn,
In that state I came, return.

THE RETREAT   **4. second race:** the "first race" was life spent in heaven before birth. **17. black art:** sinful magic. **18. several:** particular. **24. train:** course of action. **26. city . . . trees:** the Heavenly City, which the narrator sees as Moses saw the Promised Land, "the city of palm trees," he was destined not to enter (Deuteronomy 34:1–4). **27. stay:** hindrance, delay.

The World

I saw Eternity the other night
Like a great ring of pure and endless light,
    All calm, as it was bright;
And round beneath it, Time in hours, days, years,
        Driven by the spheres,   5
Like a vast shadow moved, in which the world
    And all her train were hurled:
The doting lover in his quaintest strain
        Did there complain;
Near him his lute, his fancy, and his flights,   10
        Wit's sour delights,
With gloves and knots, the silly snares of pleasure,
        Yet his dear treasure
All scattered lay, while he his eyes did pore
        Upon a flower.   15

The darksome statesman, hung with weights and woe,
Like a thick midnight fog moved there so slow
    He did not stay, nor go;
Condemning thoughts, like sad eclipses, scowl
        Upon his soul,   20
And clouds of crying witnesses without
    Pursued him with one shout;
Yet digged the mole, and lest his ways be found
        Worked under ground,
Where he did clutch his prey, but One did see   25
        That policy;
Churches and altars fed him; perjuries
        Were gnats and flies;
It rained about him blood and tears, but he
        Drank them as free.   30

The fearful miser on a heap of rust
Sat pining all his life there, did scarce trust
    His own hands with the dust,
Yet would not place one piece above, but lives
        In fear of thieves.   35
Thousands there were as frantic as himself,
    And hugged each one his pelf;

THE WORLD   **5. spheres:** see Donne, "Good Friday, 1613," note on ll. 1–2. **7. train:** retinue, peoples. **8. quaintest:** most ingenious. **9. complain:** sing about his hardhearted mistress. **10. flights:** extravagant words or moods. **12. knots:** decorative ribbons. **16. weights:** possibly, burdens or calculations. **26. policy:** cunning statecraft. **30. as free:** freely. **34. place . . . above:** invest one coin in heaven: "But lay up for yourselves treasures in heaven, where neither moth nor rust doth corrupt, and where thieves do not break through nor steal" (Matthew 6:20). **37. pelf:** ill-gotten wealth.

The downright epicure placed heaven in sense,
    And scorned pretense;
While others, slipped into a wide excess,   40
    Said little less;
The weaker sort slight trivial wares enslave,
    Who think them brave;
And poor despisèd truth sat counting by
    Their victory.   45

Yet some, who all this while did weep and sing,
And sing and weep, soared up into the ring;
    But most would use no wing.
"O fools," said I, "thus to prefer dark night
    Before true light,   50
To live in grots and caves, and hate the day
    Because it shows the way,
The way which from this dead and dark abode
    Leads up to God,
A way where you might tread the sun, and be   55
    More bright than he."
But as I did their madness so discuss,
    One whispered thus:
"This ring the bridegroom did for none provide
    But for his bride."   60

John Dryden   *(1631–1700)*

To the Memory of Mr. Oldham

Farewell, too little and too lately known,
Whom I began to think and call my own:
For sure our souls were near allied, and thine
Cast in the same poetic mold with mine.
One common note on either lyre did strike,   5
And knaves and fools we both abhorred alike.
To the same goal did both our studies drive;
The last set out the soonest did arrive.
Thus Nisus fell upon the slippery place,
While his young friend performed and won the race.   10

43. brave: splendid. **44. counting by:** reckoning. **51. grots:** grottoes. **55. tread:** tread
upon or above(?). **59–60. bridegroom . . . bride:** Christ and his Church (see Revelation 21:2).
TO MR. OLDHAM   John Oldham (1653–83) was the able, rough author of *Satires upon
the Jesuits.* **8. last . . . arrive:** though 22 years younger than Dryden, Oldham became
known earlier as a satirist. **9–10. Nisus . . . race:** when Nisus slipped during a race,
his young friend Euryalus won it (Virgil, *Aeneid*, Bk. V, ll. 315–39).

O early ripe! to thy abundant store
What could advancing age have added more?
It might (what nature never gives the young)
Have taught the numbers of thy native tongue.
But satire needs not those, and wit will shine   15
Through the harsh cadence of a rugged line:
A noble error, and but seldom made,
When poets are by too much force betrayed.
Thy generous fruits, though gathered ere their prime,
Still showed a quickness; and maturing time   20
But mellows what we write to the dull sweets of rhyme.
Once more, hail and farewell; farewell, thou young,
But ah! too short, Marcellus of our tongue;
Thy brows with ivy and with laurels bound;
But fate and gloomy night encompass thee around.   25

A Song for St. Cecilia's Day, 1687

I

From harmony, from heavenly harmony
        This universal frame began:
        When Nature underneath a heap
            Of jarring atoms lay,
        And could not heave her head,   5
    The tuneful voice was heard from high,
        "Arise, ye more than dead."
    Then cold, and hot, and moist, and dry,
    In order to their stations leap,
            And Music's power obey.   10
    From harmony, from heavenly harmony
        This universal frame began:
        From harmony to harmony
    Through all the compass of the notes it ran,
    The diapason closing full in man.   15

---

14. **numbers:** flow of verse. 16. **cadence:** rhythm. 18. **When:** but when. 20. **quickness:** vigor. 22. **hail and farewell:** the equivalent of the Latin elegiac phrase, *ave atque vale.* 23. **Marcellus:** the highly promising nephew and heir of the Emperor Augustus, who died at the age of 19 (see *Aeneid,* Bk. VI, ll. 860–86). The last line of this poem echoes the *Aeneid,* Bk. VI, 1. 866. 24. **ivy . . . laurels:** wreaths given to poets and heroes.

st. cecilia's day   A London music society annually celebrated the feast day of St. Cecilia, patroness of music and traditional inventor of the organ, with a religious service and concert. For the occasion an ode was commissioned and set to music. **1–4. From . . . lay:** Dryden builds on the idea that the universe was created by the harmonizing, through divine love, of the discordant elements: earth, fire, water, and air (whose major attributes are listed respectively in 1. 8). **14. compass of the notes:** the first seven notes of the octave. **15. diapason:** specifically, the consonance of the octave in music; generally, spiritual harmony throughout the Chain of Being from inanimate matter up to man.

II

What passion cannot Music raise and quell!
    When Jubal struck the corded shell,
    His listening brethren stood around,
    And, wondering, on their faces fell
    To worship that celestial sound.   20
Less than a god they thought there could not dwell
    Within the hollow of that shell
    That spoke so sweetly and so well.
What passion cannot Music raise and quell!

III

    The Trumpet's loud clangor   25
        Excites us to arms
    With shrill notes of anger
        And mortal alarms.
    The double double double beat
        Of the thundering Drum   30
Cries: "Hark! the foes come;
Charge, charge, 't is too late to retreat."

IV

    The soft complaining Flute
    In dying notes discovers
    The woes of hopeless lovers,   35
Whose dirge is whispered by the warbling Lute.

V

    Sharp Violins proclaim
Their jealous pangs, and desperation,
Fury, frantic indignation,
Depth of pains, and height of passion,   40
    For the fair, disdainful dame.

VI

    But oh! what art can teach,
    What human voice can reach,
The sacred Organ's praise?
    Notes inspiring holy love,   45
Notes that wing their heavenly ways
To mend the choirs above.

VII

Orpheus could lead the savage race;
And trees unrooted left their place,
    Sequacious of the lyre;   50

---

17. Jubal . . . shell: "father of all such as handle the harp and organ" (Genesis
4:21). Jubal is pictured as playing a primitive lyre made from a tortoise shell. **34. discovers:** reveals. **47. mend:** amend. **48–50. Orpheus . . . lyre:** see notes to Milton,
"L'Allegro," ll. 145–50, and "Il Penseroso," ll. 105–08. **50. Sequacious of:** following.

But bright Cecilia raised the wonder higher:
When to her Organ vocal breath was given,
An angel heard, and straight appeared,
    Mistaking earth for heaven.

GRAND CHORUS

As from the power of sacred lays   55
    The spheres began to move,
And sung the great Creator's praise
    To all the blessed above;
So, when the last and dreadful hour
This crumbling pageant shall devour,   60
The Trumpet shall be heard on high,
The dead shall live, the living die,
And Music shall untune the sky.

MacFlecknoe

All human things are subject to decay,
And, when Fate summons, monarchs must obey:
This Flecknoe found, who, like Augustus, young
Was called to empire and had governed long;
In prose and verse was owned, without dispute   5
Through all the realms of Nonsense, absolute.
This agèd prince, now flourishing in peace
And blessed with issue of a large increase,
Worn out with business, did at length debate
To settle the succession of the state;   10
And pondering which of all his sons was fit
To reign, and wage immortal war with wit,
Cried: " 'Tis resolved; for nature pleads that he
Should only rule who most resembles me:
Sh—— alone my perfect image bears,   15
Mature in dullness from his tender years.
Sh—— alone, of all my sons, is he
Who stands confirmed in full stupidity.
The rest to some faint meaning make pretense,
But Sh—— never deviates into sense.   20
Some beams of wit on other souls may fall,

---

55. sacred lays: angelic songs. **56. spheres**: see Donne, "Good Friday, 1613," notes on ll. 1–2, 22. **61. Trumpet**: which will announce the resurrection of the dead and the Last Judgment (I Corinthians 15:52).

MAC FLECKNOE "Son of Flecknoe." Richard Flecknoe was an Irish priest and bad poet. His "son" or spiritual heir is Thomas Shadwell, playwright and poet, who had attacked Dryden in the dedication to his comedy, *The Virtuoso* (1676). But Dryden may have had other reasons, now obscure, for attacking him. **8. with . . . increase**: with many children. **12. wit**: (1) intelligence, especially perceptiveness; (2) quickness of mind; (3) the poetic faculty.

Strike through and make a lucid inverval,
But Sh——'s genuine night admits no ray,
His rising fogs prevail upon the day;
Besides his goodly fabric fills the eye,   25
And seems designed for thoughtless majesty:
Thoughtless as monarch oaks that shade the plain
And, spread in solemn state, supinely reign.
Heywood and Shirley were but types of thee,
Thou last great prophet of tautology.   30
Even I, a dunce of more renown than they,
Was sent before but to prepare thy way;
And coarsely clad in Norwich drugget came
To teach the nations in thy greater name.
My warbling lute, the lute I whilom strung   35
When to King John of Portugal I sung,
Was but the prelude to that glorious day,
When thou on silver Thames didst cut thy way
With well-timed oars before the royal barge,
Swelled with the pride of thy celestial charge;   40
And big with hymn, commander of an host,
The like was ne'er in *Epsom* blankets tossed.
Methinks I see the new Arion sail,
The lute still trembling underneath thy nail;
At thy well-sharpened thumb from shore to shore   45
The treble squeaks for fear, the basses roar;
Echoes from Pissing-Alley Sh—— call,
And Sh—— they resound from A—— Hall.
About thy boat the little fishes throng
As at the morning toast that floats along.   50
Sometimes as prince of thy harmonious band
Thou wield'st thy papers in thy threshing hand.
St. André's feet ne'er kept more equal time,
Not even the feet of thy own *Psyche's* rhyme,
Though they in number as in sense excel;   55
So just, so like tautology they fell,
That, pale with envy, Singleton forswore
The lute and sword which he in triumph bore

25. goodly fabric: Shadwell was fat. **26. thoughtless:** (1) carefree; (2) stupid. **29. Heywood and Shirley:** two early seventeenth-century dramatists, derided in Dryden's day. **types:** prefigurations, as persons in the Old Testament are thought to prefigure those in the New. **30. tautology:** tedious repetition. **31–32. Even I . . . way:** as John the Baptist was a forerunner for Jesus. **33. Norwich drugget:** coarse woolen. John the Baptist was likewise poorly dressed (Mark 1:6). **34. teach . . . name:** as John the Baptist said, "There cometh one mightier than I after me" (Mark 1:7). **35. whilom:** formerly. **36. King John:** Flecknoe had lived in Lisbon, and apparently claimed King John as a patron. **42. *Epsom* blankets tossed:** a combined reference to Shadwell's comedy, *Epsom Wells,* and to a scene in his *Virtuoso* in which Sir Samuel Harty is tossed in a blanket. **43. Arion:** a legendary Greek poet and musician, rescued from drowning by a music-loving dolphin. **48. A—— Hall:** expanded in later editions to Aston Hall. The place is unidentified but the name, like Pissing Alley, suggests the quality of Shadwell's verse. **50. toast:** sewage. **53–54. St. André's . . . rhyme:** St. André, a dancing master, was choreographer for Shadwell's rhymed opera, *Psyche.* **57. Singleton:** a famous singer.

And vowed he ne'er would act Villerius more."
Here stopped the good old sire, and wept for joy   60
In silent raptures of the hopeful boy.
All arguments, but most his plays, persuade
That for anointed dullness he was made.
    Close to the walls which fair Augusta bind
(The fair Augusta much to fears inclined),   65
An ancient fabric, raised t' inform the sight,
There stood of yore and Barbican it hight.
A watchtower once; but now, so Fate ordains,
Of all the pile an empty name remains.
From its old ruins brothel-houses rise,   70
Scenes of lewd loves and of polluted joys.
Where their vast courts the mother-strumpets keep,
And, undisturbed by watch, in silence sleep.
Near these a Nursery erects its head,
Where queens are formed and future heroes bred;   75
Where unfledged actors learn to laugh and cry,
Where infant punks their tender voices try,
And little Maximins the gods defy.
Great Fletcher never treads in buskins here,
Nor greater Jonson dares in socks appear;   80
But gentle Simkin just reception finds
Amidst this monument of vanished minds;
Pure clinches the suburbian muse affords,
And Panton waging harmless war with words.
Here Flecknoe, as a place to fame well known,   85
Ambitiously designed his Sh——'s throne.
For ancient Dekker prophesied long since
That in this pile should reign a mighty prince,
Born for a scourge of wit and flail of sense;
To whom true dullness should some *Psyches* owe,   90
But worlds of *Misers* from his pen should flow;
Humorists and *Hypocrites* it should produce,
Whole Raymond families and tribes of Bruce.
    Now Empress Fame had published the renown
Of Sh——'s coronation through the town.   95
Roused by report of Fame, the nations meet

59. Villerius: a character in Sir William Davenant's opera, *The Siege of Rhodes.* **63. anointed:** an allusion to the anointing of the king with oil at his coronation. **64. Augusta:** poetic name for London. **65. fears:** of the "Popish Plot," if the poem can be dated as late as 1678. **66. fabric:** building. **inform:** animate, fill up. **67. Barbican it hight:** it was called Barbican (a watchtower). **73. watch:** constables. **74. Nursery:** a school for child actors. **77. punks:** whores. **78. Maximins:** Maximin is the bombastic hero of Dryden's own heroic play, *Tyrannic Love.* **79–80. Fletcher . . . appear:** John Fletcher, highly admired for his Elizabethan tragedies, represented by the buskin, or high boot, worn in ancient tragedy; Ben Jonson, noted for his comedies, represented by the sock, or light shoe, worn in ancient comedy. **81. Simkin:** character in contemporary farce. **83. clinches:** puns. **suburbian:** suburban. **84. Panton:** apparently another character in farce. **87. Dekker:** a minor Elizabethan dramatist, ridiculed in Jonson's *Poetaster.* **91–93. Misers . . . Bruce:** *The Miser, The Hypocrite,* and *The Humorists* are plays by Shadwell. Raymond appears in *The Humorists* and Bruce in *The Virtuoso.*

From near Bunhill and distant Watling Street.
No Persian carpets spread th' imperial way,
But scattered limbs of mangled poets lay;
From dusty shops neglected authors come,   100
Martyrs of pies and relics of the bum.
Much Heywood, Shirley, Ogleby there lay,
But loads of Sh—— almost choked the way.
Bilked stationers for yeomen stood prepared,
And H—— was Captain of the Guard.   105
The hoary Prince in majesty appeared,
High on a throne of his own labors reared.
At his right hand our young Ascanius sate,
Rome's other hope and pillar of the state.
His brows thick fogs, instead of glories, grace,   110
And lambent dullness played around his face.
As Hannibal did to the altars come,
Sworn by his sire a mortal foe to Rome;
So Sh—— swore, nor should his vow be vain,
That he till death true dullness would maintain,   115
And in his father's right and realm's defense
Ne'er to have peace with wit nor truce with sense.
The King himself the sacred unction made,
As king by office, and as priest by trade:
In his sinister hand instead of ball   120
He placed a mighty mug of potent ale;
Love's Kingdom to his right he did convey,
At once his scepter and his rule of sway,
Whose righteous lore the Prince had practiced young,
And from whose loins recorded *Psyche* sprung.   125
His temples last with poppies were o'erspread,
That nodding seemed to consecrate his head.
Just at that point of time, if fame not lie,
On his left hand twelve reverend owls did fly:
So Romulus, 'tis sung, by Tiber's brook   130

---

97. Bunhill . . . Watling Street: both Bunhill and Watling Street were near to the
Nursery, and restrict Shadwell's fame to the City of London, proverbially characterized
by its dull, vulgar merchants. **101. Martyrs . . . bum:** leftover paper was used in
bakeries and privies. "Bum" is English slang for "ass." **102. Ogleby:** a hack translator
of the classics. **104. Bilked stationers:** booksellers, cheated because they had stocked
Shadwell's badly selling works. **105. H——:** Herringman, publisher for both Dryden
and Shadwell. **107. labors:** works. **108-09. Ascanius . . . state:** son of Aeneas, Ascanius is "Rome's other hope" (Virgil, *Aeneid*, Bk. XII, l. 168). **111. lambent . . . face:**
at the fall of Troy, a tongue of flame played around Ascanius's face as a portent of
the gods' favor (*Aeneid*, Bk. II, ll. 680-84). **112-13. Hannibal . . . Rome:** his father
swore Hannibal as a child to eternal enmity to Rome (here seen as the symbol of
poetic value). **118. sacred unction:** holy oil, used in anointing a king. Dryden leaves
it to the reader to imagine *how* Flecknoe made the unction. **120. sinister:** (1) left; (2)
ominous. **120-23. ball . . . sway:** at his coronation, a British king holds an orb
("ball") in his left hand, and a scepter in his right. **122. Love's Kingdom:** a play by
Flecknoe. **125. from . . . sprung:** i.e., *Psyche* is the spiritual descendant of *Love's
Kingdom*. **recorded:** operatic. **126. poppies:** an allusion to Shadwell's fondness for
opium, as well as to the drowsiness his works inspired. **129. owls:** here symbols of dullness pretending to wisdom. **130. Romulus:** founder of Rome.

Presage of sway from twice six vultures took.
Th' admiring throng loud acclamations make,
And omens of his future empire take.
The sire then shook the honors of his head,
And from his brows damps of oblivion shed   135
Full on the filial dullness: long he stood
Repelling from his breast the raging god;
At length burst out in this prophetic mood:
"Heavens bless my son, from Ireland let him reign
To far Barbadoes on the western main;   140
Of his dominion may no end be known,
And greater than his father's be his throne.
Beyond *Love's Kingdom* let him stretch his pen."
He paused, and all the people cried, "Amen."
"Then thus," continued he, "my son, advance   145
Still in new impudence, new ignorance.
Success let others teach, learn thou from me
Pangs without birth and fruitless industry.
Let *Virtuosos* in five years be writ,
Yet not one thought accuse thy toil of wit.   150
Let gentle George in triumph tread the stage,
Make Dorimant betray, and Loveit rage;
Let Cully, Cockwood, Fopling, charm the pit,
And in their folly show the writer's wit.
Yet still thy fools shall stand in thy defense,   155
And justify their author's want of sense.
Let 'em be all by thy own model made
Of dullness, and desire no foreign aid,
That they to future ages may be known
Not copies drawn but issue of thy own.   160
Nay, let thy men of wit, too, be the same,
All full of thee and differing but in name;
But let no alien S—dl—y interpose
To lard with wit thy hungry *Epsom* prose.
And when false flowers of rhetoric thou wouldst cull,   165
Trust nature, do not labor to be dull; .
But write thy best, and top; and in each line
Sir Formal's oratory will be thine.

---

134. honors: ornaments, i.e., locks. **136. Full . . . dullness:** in Milton's *Paradise Lost*, the Father "on his Son with rays direct/Shone full" (Book VI, ll. 719–20). **136–38. long . . . mood:** at certain ancient oracles, the priestess had to be violently possessed by the god before she could prophesy; Dryden may be alluding in particular to Virgil's description of the Sibyl (*Aeneid*, Bk. VI, ll. 46–51, 77–82). Flecknoe, like the Biblical David, is priest, prophet, and king. **139–40. Ireland . . . main:** i.e., Shadwell's kingdom includes two savage lands and an empty ocean. **148. Pangs:** labor pains. **151. gentle:** well-born. **George:** Sir George Etherege, a fine contemporary comic dramatist. The following two lines name some of his best-known characters. **161. be the same:** i.e., as the fools. **163. S—dl—y:** Sir Charles Sedley, who Dryden suggests had contributed more than the prologue to *Epsom Wells*. **164. lard:** intersperse. **165. flowers of rhetoric:** figures of speech. **168. Sir Formal's oratory:** involved and ridiculous figures of speech used by Sir Formal Trifle in *The Virtuoso*.

Sir Formal, though unsought, attends thy quill
And does thy northern dedications fill.   170
Nor let false friends seduce thy mind to fame
By arrogating Jonson's hostile name.
Let Father Flecknoe fire thy mind with praise,
And Uncle Ogleby thy envy raise.
Thou art my blood, where Jonson has no part;   175
What share have we in nature or in art?
Where did his wit on learning fix a brand
And rail at arts he did not understand?
Where made he love in Prince Nicander's vein,
Or swept the dust in *Psyche's* humble strain?   180
Where sold he bargains, whip-stitch, kiss my arse,
Promised a play and dwindled to a farce?
When did his muse from Fletcher scenes purloin,
As thou whole Etherege dost transfuse to thine?
But so transfused as oil on waters flow,   185
His always floats above, thine sinks below.
This is thy province, this thy wondrous way,
New humors to invent for each new play;
This is that boasted bias of thy mind
By which one way, to dullness, 'tis inclined,   190
Which makes thy writings lean on one side still,
And in all changes that way bends thy will.
Nor let thy mountain belly make pretense
Of likeness; thine's a tympany of sense.
A tun of man in thy large bulk is writ,   195
But sure thou'rt but a kilderkin of wit.
Like mine thy gentle numbers feebly creep,
Thy tragic muse gives smiles, thy comic sleep.
With whate'er gall thou sett'st thyself to write,
Thy inoffensive satires never bite.   200
In thy felonious heart though venom lies,
It does but touch thy Irish pen, and dies.
Thy genius calls thee not to purchase fame

---

170. **northern dedications:** dedications to the Duke and Duchess of Newcastle, whose main estates and offices lay in the Midlands and North of England. Flecknoe had also dedicated works to the Duke, and Dryden himself had dedicated a play to him. 172. **Jonson's hostile name:** Shadwell admired and imitated Ben Jonson. 177–78. wit . . . understand: presumably a reference to the satire on scientific investigations in *The Virtuoso*. Jonson was noted for his classical learning. 179. **Prince Nicander:** a character in *Psyche*. 181. sold . . . arse: "selling bargains" was a game in which a presumably innocent question (e.g., "what is white and follows me?") was asked to evoke the answer, "my arse." "Whip-stitch" means "quick as a wink," and "whip-stitch, your nose in my breech" is a phrase used repeatedly by Sir Samuel Harty in *The Virtuoso*. 182. Promised . . . farce: as Shadwell did in *The Virtuoso*. 188. humors: characters focused on a basic eccentricity or "bias of . . . mind" (l. 189), a metaphor drawn from lawn bowls in which the ball is irregularly weighted and curves when thrown. 194. **tympany:** swelling caused by air. 195–96. **tun, kilderkin:** large and small casks. 197. **numbers:** verses. 201–02. In thy . . . dies: since there are no snakes in Ireland. (As Flecknoe was Irish, his "son" Shadwell would be also.) 203. **purchase:** earn by labor.

In keen iambics but mild anagram;
Leave writing plays, and choose for thy command   205
Some peaceful province in acrostic land.
There thou may'st wings display and altars raise,
And torture one poor word ten thousand ways.
Or, if thou wouldst thy different talents suit,
Set thy own songs and sing them to thy lute."   210
He said, but his last words were scarcely heard,
For Bruce and Longville had a trap prepared,
And down they sent the yet declaiming bard.
Sinking, he left his drugget robe behind,
Borne upwards by a subterranean wind.   215
The mantle fell to the young prophet's part,
With double portion of his father's art.

Absalom and Achitophel
from Part II

Next these, a troop of busy spirits press,   310
Of little fortunes, and of conscience less;
With them the tribe, whose luxury had drained
Their banks, in former sequestrations gained;
Who rich and great by past rebellions grew,
And long to fish the troubled streams anew.   315
Some future hopes, some present payment draws,
To sell their conscience and espouse the Cause.
Such stipends those vile hirelings best befit,
Priests without grace, and poets without wit.

204. iambics: verse form of Greek satire. **204–08. anagram . . . ways:** Dryden cites various overingenious verse forms or techniques. **212–13. Bruce . . . bard:** a trick played on Sir Formal Trifle in *The Virtuoso.* **216–17. mantle . . . art:** when the prophet Elijah was carried off on a whirlwind to heaven, his mantle fell to Elisha with a "double portion" of Elijah's spirit (II Kings 2:9–13). Prophets of dullness naturally *descend.*

ABSALOM AND ACHITOPHEL. Most of *Absalom and Achitophel*, Part II (1682), was written by Nahum Tate, a minor poet, but this section is by Dryden. Like Dryden's *Absalom and Achitophel*, Part I (1680), it comments on the contemporary political situation by building allegorically on the biblical story of Absalom's unsuccessful revolt (guided by Achitophel) against his father David (II Samuel, chs. 13–18). In 1680, England was divided into two political groups: Charles II (David) had repressed the Dissenting sects which had held power under Cromwell's Protectorate, and was thought to incline secretly to Roman Catholicism; his brother and heir, James, Duke of York, was a professed Roman Catholic. Some Anglicans and most of the Dissenters, one of whose leaders was the Earl of Shaftesbury (Achitophel), wanted to make Charles's illegitimate son, the Duke of Monmouth (Absalom), his heir. In the section of the poem printed here, Dryden attacks political, religious, and literary figures among Charles's opponents. **313. former sequestrations:** fines and confiscations, which many royalists had suffered under the Protectorate. **317. Cause:** the Good Old Cause, the name given to the Puritan and republican movement.

Shall that false Hebronite escape our curse,   320
Judas, that keeps the rebels' pension-purse;
Judas, that pays the treason-writer's fee,
Judas, that well deserves his namesake's tree;
Who at Jerusalem's own gates erects
His college for a nursery of sects;   325
Young prophets with an early care secures,
And with the dung of his own arts manures.
What have the men of Hebron here to do?
What part in Israel's promised land have you?
Here Phaleg, the lay Hebronite, is come,   330
'Cause like the rest he could not live at home;
Who from his own possessions could not drain
An omer even of Hebronitish grain,
Here struts it like a patriot, and talks high
Of injured subjects, altered property;   335
An emblem of that buzzing insect just,
That mounts the wheel, and thinks she raises dust.
Can dry bones live? or skeletons produce
The vital warmth of cuckoldizing juice?
Slim Phaleg could, and at the table fed,   340
Returned the grateful product to the bed.
A waiting-man to traveling nobles chose,
He his own laws would saucily impose,
Till bastinadoed back again he went,
To learn those manners he to teach was sent.   345
Chastised, he ought to have retreated home,
But he reads politics to Absalom;
For never Hebronite, though kicked and scorned,
To his own country willingly returned.
—But leaving famished Phaleg to be fed,   350
And to talk treason for his daily bread,
Let Hebron, nay, let hell produce a man
So made for mischief as Ben-Jochanan.
A Jew of humble parentage was he,
By trade a Levite, though of low degree: 355
His pride no higher than the desk aspired,

320. Hebronite: Scotsman. **321. Judas:** Robert Ferguson, a Dissenting preacher and pamphleteer, who kept a boys' school near London (ll. 324–25). **323. namesake's tree:** Judas Iscariot hanged himself (Matthew 27:5), according to tradition, on the tree that bears his name. **324. Jerusalem's:** London's. **328–29. men . . . you:** Scots interference in English affairs was bitterly resented. **330. Phaleg:** James Forbes, a Scotsman, sent as tutor with the Earl of Derby to Paris (ll. 342–45). Derby resented Forbes's attempts to control him and approved his being assaulted and wounded. **333. omer:** an ancient Hebrew dry measure, equal to less than one-tenth of a bushel. **338. Can . . . live:** an ironic allusion to Ezekiel 37:3, where God says to the prophet Ezekiel, "Son of man, can these bones live?" and Ezekiel answers, "O Lord God, thou knowest." **338–41. skeletons . . . bed:** this charge of seduction is unsubstantiated. **348–49. never . . . returned:** it was a common complaint of the English that the Scots lived parasitically on them. **353. Ben-Jochanan:** the Rev. Samuel Johnson, chaplain to one of the Dissenting noblemen. **354. Jew:** Englishman. **355. Levite:** clergyman.

But for the drudgery of priests was hired
To read and pray in linen ephod brave,
And pick up single shekels from the grave.
Married at last, and finding charge come faster, 360
He could not live by God, but changed his master;
Inspired by want, was made a factious tool,
They got a villain, and we lost a fool:
Still violent, whatever cause he took,
But most against the party he forsook; 365
For renegadoes, who ne'er turn by halves,
Are bound in conscience to be double knaves.
So this prose-prophet took most monstrous pains
To let his masters see he earned his gains.
But as the Devil owes all his imps a shame, 370
He chose th' Apostate for his proper theme;
With little pains he made the picture true,
And from reflection took the rogue he drew:
A wondrous work, to prove the Jewish nation
In every age a murmuring generation; 375
To trace 'em from their infancy of sinning,
And show 'em factious from their first beginning;
To prove they could rebel, and rail, and mock,
Much to the credit of the chosen flock;
A strong authority, which must convince, 380
That saints own no allegiance to their prince;
As 'tis a leading card to make a whore
To prove her mother had turned up before.
But, tell me, did the drunken patriarch bless
The son that showed his father's nakedness? 385
Such thanks the present Church thy pen will give,
Which proves rebellion was so primitive.
Must ancient failings be examples made?
Then murtherers from Cain may learn their trade.
As thou the heathen and the saint hast drawn, 390
Methinks th'Apostate was the better man;
And thy hot Father (waiving my respect)

---

358. **ephod brave:** showy vestment. 359. **pick up . . . grave:** do routine religious tasks for a pittance. 362. **factious tool:** tool of the faction opposed to Charles II. 370. **Devil . . . shame:** a proverbial phrase, meaning that the Devil owes his workers a disgrace 371. **th' Apostate . . . theme:** Johnson wrote a study of the Emperor Julian the Apostate, which implied that just as the early Christians had resisted a pagan emperor, contemporary Protestants would be justified in opposing a Catholic king. 373. **reflection:** introspection. 374. **the Jewish nation:** the English in the allegory, but the following lines also comment on Old Testament and Christian history. 381. **saints:** the Dissenters' term for themselves as "the elect" or saved. 382. **leading card:** trump card, since the first card led in certain card games designates trumps. 384–85. **drunken . . . nakedness:** Noah cursed his son Ham for this act (Genesis 9:20–25). 390. **the saint:** St. Gregory Nazianzus, a Father of the Church (l. 392), who attacked the memory of the Emperor Julian. 392. **waiving my respect:** "waiving *your* respect" was a polite phrase used to introduce disagreement with a superior.

Not of a mother church, but of a sect.
And such he needs must be of thy inditing;
This comes of drinking asses' milk and writing.   395
If Balak should be called to leave his place
(As profit is the loudest call of grace),
His temple, dispossessed of one, would be
Replenished with seven devils more by thee.
    Levi, thou art a load, I'll lay thee down,   400
And show rebellion bare, without a gown;
Poor slaves in meter, dull and addle-pated,
Who rhyme below even David's psalms translated;
Some in my speedy pace I must outrun,
As lame Mephibosheth the wizard's son;   405
To make quick way I'll leap o'er heavy blocks,
Shun rotten Uzza as I would the pox;
And hasten Og and Doeg to rehearse,
Two fools that crutch their feeble sense on verse;
Who, by my muse, to all succeeding times   410
Shall live, in spite of their own doggerel rhymes.
    Doeg, though without knowing how or why,
Made still a blundering kind of melody;
Spurred boldly on, and dashed through thick and thin,
Through sense and nonsense, never out nor in;   415
Free from all meaning, whether good or bad,
And, in one word, heroically mad:
He was too warm on picking-work to dwell,
But fagoted his notions as they fell,
And if they rhymed and rattled, all was well.   420
Spiteful he is not, though he wrote a satire,
For still there goes some *thinking* to ill-nature:
He needs no more than birds and beasts to think;
All his occasions are to eat and drink.
If he call rogue and rascal from a garret,   425
He means you no more mischief than a parrot;
The words for friend and foe alike were made,
To fetter 'em in verse is all his trade.
For almonds he'll cry whore to his own mother;

395. asses' milk: ordinarily a remedy for invalids. **396. Balak:** Gilbert Burnet, a celebrated preacher, whom Charles II had tried to deprive of his ministry at the Rolls Chapel. **400. Levi:** the priesthood, marked by its gown (l. 401). **403. David's psalms translated:** the English translation of the Psalms by Sternhold and Hopkins, often satirized. **405. lame . . . son:** Mephibosheth represents Samuel Pordage, a lawyer and poet, who had attacked Dryden in two poems. His father, a clergyman, had been accused of relations with evil spirits. **407. Uzza:** not certainly identified. **pox:** greatpox (syphilis). **408. Og:** Thomas Shadwell, the title-character of Dryden's *MacFlecknoe* (see note on its title), had recently attacked Dryden in a long, rancorous, and obscene poem. **Doeg:** Elkanah Settle, poet and dramatist, an old rival of Dryden who had just published *Absalom Senior, or Absalom Transprosed* (l. 444), in which Absalom is identified with the Duke of York (l. 430). **rehearse:** describe. **417. heroically mad:** ranting and excessive in phrase and action, like the protagonists in Settle's (and Dryden's) earlier heroic tragedies. **418. picking-work:** fastidious work. **419. fagoted:** bundled roughly together. **429. For . . . mother:** parrots were proverbially fond of almonds.

And call young Absalom King David's brother. 430
Let him be gallows-free by my consent,
And nothing suffer, since he nothing meant;
Hanging supposes human soul and reason,
This animal's below committing treason.
Shall he be hanged who never could rebel? 435
That's a preferment for Achitophel.
The woman that committed buggery,
Was rightly sentenced by the law to die;
But 'twas hard fate that to the gallows led
The dog that never heard the statute read. 440
Railing in other men may be a crime,
But ought to pass for mere instinct in him:
Instinct he follows, and no farther knows,
For to write verse with him is to *transprose*.
'Twere pity treason at his door to lay, 445
Who *makes heaven's gate a lock to its own key*:
Let him rail on, let his invective muse
Have four and twenty letters to abuse,
Which if he jumbles to one line of sense,
Indict him of a capital offense. 450
In fireworks give him leave to vent his spite,
Those are the only serpents he can write;
The height of his ambition is, we know,
But to be master of a puppet show:
On that one stage his works may yet appear, 455
And a month's harvest keeps him all the year.
    Now stop your noses, readers, all and some,
For here's a tun of midnight work to come,
Og, from a treason-tavern rolling home.
Round as a globe, and liquored every chink, 460
Goodly and great he sails behind his link.
With all this bulk there's nothing lost in Og,
For every inch that is not fool is rogue:
A monstrous mass of foul corrupted matter,
As all the devils had spewed to make the batter. 465
When wine has given him courage to blaspheme,
He curses God, but God before cursed him;
And if man could have reason, none has more,
That made his paunch so rich, and him so poor.
With wealth he was not trusted, for Heaven knew 470

---

436. preferment: (1) an advance in rank or public office; (2) elevation to the gallows. **442. mere:** pure. **446. makes . . . key:** Settle's *Absalom Senior* begins: "In gloomy times, when priestcraft bore the sway,/ And made heaven's gate a lock to their own key." **451. fireworks . . . spite:** Settle took an active part in anti-Catholic celebrations like Guy Fawkes Day. **452. serpents:** a kind of fireworks. **453–56. height . . . year:** presumably an allusion to Settle's connection with the puppeteers at Bartholomew and Southwark fairs; he later became an assistant to a booth-keeper. "Month's harvest" (l. 456) refers to the length of time the fairs were open. **458. tun:** a large cask, but perhaps also a barrel for collecting refuse. **461. link:** torch bearer. **468. reason:** i.e., to curse God.

What 't was of old to pamper up a Jew;
To what would he on quail and pheasant swell,
That even on tripe and carrion could rebel?
But though Heaven made him poor (with reverence speaking),
He never was a poet of God's making.   475
The midwife laid her hand on his thick skull,
With this prophetic blessing: *Be thou dull;*
Drink, swear, and roar, forbear no lewd delight
Fit for thy bulk, do anything but write:
Thou art of lasting make, like thoughtless men,   480
A strong nativity—but for the pen;
Eat opium, mingle arsenic in thy drink,
Still thou mayst live, avoiding pen and ink.
I see, I see, 'tis counsel given in vain,
For treason botched in rhyme will be thy bane;   485
Rhyme is the rock on which thou art to wreck,
'Tis fatal to thy fame and to thy neck:
Why should thy meter good King David blast?
A psalm of his will surely be thy last.
Dar'st thou presume in verse to meet thy foes,   490
Thou whom the penny pamphlet foiled in prose?
Doeg, whom God for mankind's mirth has made,
O'ertops thy talent in thy very trade;
Doeg to thee, thy paintings are so coarse,
A poet is, though he's the poets' horse.   495
A double noose thou on thy neck dost pull,
For writing treason, and for writing dull;
To die for faction is a common evil,
But to be hanged for nonsense is the devil.
Hadst thou the glories of thy king expressed,   500
Thy praises had been satire at the best;
But thou in clumsy verse, unlicked, unpointed,
Hast shamefully defied the Lord's anointed:
I will not rake the dunghill of thy crimes,
For who would read thy life that reads thy rhymes?   505
But of King David's foes, be this the doom,
May all be like the young man Absalom;
And for my foes may this their blessing be,
To talk like Doeg, and to write like thee.

---

478. roar: revel noisily. 481. nativity: astrological prediction. 482. Eat . . . drink: Shadwell took drugs. 485. bane: doom, particularly through poison. 488–89. meter . . . last: perhaps a reference to the burial service and to the biblical Psalms of David, as well as to King Charles as an object of Shadwell's attack. 502. unlicked: unformed. unpointed: (1) dull; (2) badly punctuated. 503. defied: the reading of the original, but "defiled" is a possible emendation. Lord's anointed: King Charles.

John Wilmot, Earl of Rochester *(1647–1680)*

The Disabled Debauchee

As some brave admiral, in former war
    Deprived of force, but pressed with courage still,
Two rival fleets appearing from afar,
    Crawls to the top of an adjacent hill;

From whence, with thoughts full of concern, he views   5
    The wise and daring conduct of the fight,
Whilst each bold action to his mind renews
    His present glory and his past delight;

From his fierce eyes flashes of fire he throws,
    As from black clouds when lightning breaks away;   10
Transported, thinks himself amidst the foes,
    And absent, yet enjoys the bloody day;

So, when my days of impotence approach,
    And I'm by pox and wine's unlucky chance
Forced from the pleasing billows of debauch   15
    On the dull shore of lazy temperance,

My pains at least some respite shall afford
    While I behold the battles you maintain
When fleets of glasses sail about the board,
    From whose broadsides volleys of wit shall rain.   20

Nor let the sight of honorable scars,
    Which my too forward valor did procure,
Frighten new-listed soldiers from the wars:
    Past joys have more than paid what I endure.

Should any youth (worth being drunk) prove nice,   25
    And from his fair inviter meanly shrink,
'Twill please the ghost of my departed vice
    If, at my counsel, he repent and drink.

Or should some cold-complexioned sot forbid,
    With his dull morals, our bold night-alarms,   30
I'll fire his blood by telling what I did
    When I was strong and able to bear arms.

THE DISABLED DEBAUCHEE   **14. pox:** greatpox (syphilis). **23. new-listed:** newly enlisted. **25. nice:** fastidious.

I'll tell of whores attacked, their lords at home;
    Bawds' quarters beaten up, and fortress won;
Windows demolished, watches overcome;   35
    And handsome ills by my contrivance done.

Nor shall our love-fits, Chloris, be forgot,
    When each the well-looked linkboy strove t' enjoy,
And the best kiss was the deciding lot
    Whether the boy fucked you, or I the boy.   40

With tales like these I will such thoughts inspire
    As to important mischief shall incline:
I'll make him long some ancient church to fire,
    And fear no lewdness he's called to by wine.

Thus, statesmanlike, I'll saucily impose,   45
    And safe from action, valiantly advise;
Sheltered in impotence, urge you to blows,
    And being good for nothing else, be wise.

Jonathan Swift   *(1667–1745)*

A Description of the Morning

Now hardly here and there an hackney coach
Appearing, showed the ruddy morn's approach.
Now Betty from her master's bed had flown,
And softly stole to discompose her own.
The slipshod 'prentice from his master's door   5
Had pared the dirt, and sprinkled round the floor.
Now Moll had whirled her mop with dexterous airs,
Prepared to scrub the entry and the stairs.
The youth with broomy stumps began to trace
The kennel-edge, where wheels had worn the place.   10
The small-coal man was heard with cadence deep,
Till drowned in shriller notes of chimney-sweep.
Duns at his lordship's gate began to meet;
And brick-dust Moll had screamed through half the street.
The turnkey now his flock returning sees,   15
Duly let out a-nights to steal for fees.

---

35. **watches:** night police patrols. 38. **linkboy:** torch bearer.
DESCRIPTION OF THE MORNING   10. **kennel-edge:** edge of the open sewer. 11. **small-coal man:** seller of small pieces of coal. 13. **Duns:** creditors demanding payment. 14. **brick-dust Moll:** seller of powdered brick, used for cleaning knives. 16. **fees:** jailor's perquisites.

The watchful bailiffs take their silent stands;
And schoolboys lag with satchels in their hands.

A Description of a City Shower

Careful observers may foretell the hour
(By sure prognostics) when to dread a shower.
While rain depends, the pensive cat gives o'er
Her frolics, and pursues her tail no more;
Returning home at night, you'll find the sink   5
Strike your offended sense with double stink.
If you be wise, then go not far to dine,
You'll spend in coach-hire more than save in wine.
A coming shower your shooting corns presage,
Old aches throb, your hollow tooth will rage.   10
Sauntering in coffee-house is Dulman seen;
He damns the climate, and complains of spleen.

Meanwhile the South, rising with dabbled wings,
A sable cloud athwart the welkin flings,
That swilled more liquor than it could contain,   15
And like a drunkard gives it up again.
Brisk Susan whips her linen from the rope,
While the first drizzling shower is born aslope;
Such is that sprinkling which some careless quean
Flirts on you from her mop, but not so clean.   20
You fly, invoke the gods; then turning, stop
To rail; she, singing, still whirls on her mop.
Not yet the dust had shunned th' unequal strife,
But aided by the wind, fought still for life,
And wafted with its foe by violent gust,   25
'Twas doubtful which was rain, and which was dust.
Ah! where must needy poet seek for aid,
When dust and rain at once his coat invade?
His only coat, where dust confused with rain
Roughen the nap, and leave a mingled stain.   30

Now in contiguous drops the flood comes down,
Threatening with deluge this devoted town.
To shops in crowds the daggled females fly,
Pretend to cheapen goods, but nothing buy.
The Templar spruce, while every spout's abroach,   35
Stays till 'tis fair, yet seems to call a coach.

DESCRIPTION OF A CITY SHOWER   **3. depends:** impends. **5. sink:** sewer, cesspool. **10. aches:** pronounced "aitches." **12. spleen:** depression, melancholy. **14. welkin:** sky. **18. born:** borne(?). **aslope:** obliquely. **19. quean:** wench. **32. devoted:** doomed. **33. daggled:** draggled. **34. cheapen:** bargain for. **35. Templar:** law student from the Inner or Middle Temple.

The tucked-up sempstress walks with hasty strides,
While streams run down her oiled umbrella's sides.
Here various kinds by various fortunes led,
Commence acquaintance underneath a shed.   40
Triumphant Tories, and desponding Whigs,
Forget their feuds, and join to save their wigs.
Boxed in a chair the beau impatient sits,
While spouts run clattering o'er the roof by fits;
And ever and anon, with frightful din   45
The leather sounds; he trembles from within.
So when Troy chairmen bore the wooden steed,
Pregnant with Greeks, impatient to be freed
(Those bully Greeks, who, as the moderns do,
Instead of paying chairmen, run them through),   50
Laocoon struck the outside with his spear,
And each imprisoned hero quaked for fear.

   Now from all parts the swelling kennels flow,
And bear their trophies with them as they go:
Filth of all hues and odors seem to tell   55
What street they sailed from, by their sight and smell.
They, as each torrent drives, with rapid force
From Smithfield, or St. Pulchre's shape their course,
And in huge confluent join at Snow Hill ridge,
Fall from the conduit prone to Holborn bridge.   60
Sweepings from butchers' stalls, dung, guts, and blood,
Drowned puppies, stinking sprats, all drenched in mud,
Dead cats, and turnip-tops, come tumbling down the flood.

The Day of Judgment

With a whirl of thought oppressed,
I sink from reverie to rest.
An horrid vision seized my head;
I saw the graves give up their dead.
Jove, armed with terrors, burst the skies,   5
And thunder roars and lightning flies!
Amazed, confused, its fate unknown,
The world stands trembling at his throne.
While each pale sinner hangs his head,
Jove, nodding, shook the heavens, and said: 10
"Offending race of human kind,

---

38. oiled: oiled silk. **39. kinds:** kinds of people. **40. shed:** covering. **41. Triumphant
. . . Whigs:** when this poem was published in 1710, the Tories had recently come
into power. **43. chair:** sedan chair, in which people were carried through the streets.
45. ever and anon: from time to time. **47–52. Troy . . . fear:** mistrusting the Trojan
Horse in which Greeks were concealed, the Trojan priest Laocoon struck it with his
spear. **53. kennels:** open sewers. **58. St. Pulchre's:** St. Sepulchre's Church, near to
Smithfield (a butchers' center) and Snow Hill. **62. sprats:** herrings.

By nature, reason, learning, blind;
You who, through frailty, stepped aside;
And you, who never fell—*through pride*;
You who in different sects have shammed,   15
And come to see each other damned;
(So some folks told you, but they knew
No more of Jove's designs than you).
The world's mad business now is o'er,
And I resent these pranks no more.   20
I to such blockheads set my wit!
I damn such fools!—Go, go, you're bit."

Cassinus and Peter

A Tragical Elegy

Two college sophs of Cambridge growth,
Both special wits and lovers both,
Conferring, as they used to meet,
On love and books, in rapture sweet;
(Muse, find me names to fix my meter,   5
Cassinus this, and t'other Peter).
Friend Peter to Cassinus goes,
To chat a while and warm his nose:
But such a sight was never seen,
The lad lay swallowed up in spleen.   10
He seemed as just crept out of bed;
One greasy stocking round his head,
The t'other he sat down to darn
With threads of different colored yarn;
His breeches torn, exposing wide   15
A ragged shirt and tawny hide;
Scorched were his shins, his legs were bare,
But well embrowned with dirt and hair.
A rug was o'er his shoulders thrown
(A rug, for nightgown he had none);   20
His jordan stood in manner fitting
Between his legs, to spew or spit in;
His ancient pipe, in sable dyed,
And half unsmoked, lay by his side.
Him thus accoutered Peter found,   25
With eyes in smoke and weeping drowned;
The leavings of his last night's pot
On embers placed, to drink it hot.

THE DAY OF JUDGMENT   21. set: apply. 22. bit: cheated.
CASSINUS AND PETER   10. spleen: melancholy, depression. 21. jordan: chamber pot.
27. pot: pot of wine.

"Why, Cassy, thou wilt doze thy pate:
What makes thee lie abed so late?   30
The finch, the linnet, and the thrush,
Their matins chant in every bush;
And I have heard thee oft salute
Aurora with thy early flute.
Heaven send thou hast not got the hyps!   35
How! not a word come from thy lips?"
    Then gave him some familiar thumps,
A college joke to cure the dumps.
    The swain at last, with grief oppressed,
Cried, "Celia!" thrice, and sighed the rest.   40
    "Dear Cassy, though to ask I dread,
Yet ask I must—is Celia dead?"
    "How happy I, were that the worst!
But I was fated to be cursed!"
    "Come, tell us, has she played the whore?"   45
    "O Peter, would it were no more!"
    "Why, plague confound her sandy locks!
Say, has the small or greater pox
Sunk down her nose, or seamed her face?
Be easy, 'tis a common case."   50
    "O Peter! beauty's but a varnish,
Which time and accidents will tarnish:
But Celia has contrived to blast
Those beauties that might ever last.
Nor can imagination guess,   55
Nor eloquence divine express,
How that ungrateful, charming maid
My purest passion has betrayed:
Conceive the most envenomed dart
To pierce an injured lover's heart."   60
    "Why, hang her; though she seemed so coy,
I know, she loves the barber's boy."
    "Friend Peter, this I could excuse,
For every nymph has leave to choose;
Nor have I reason to complain   65
She loves a more deserving swain.
But oh! how ill hast thou divined
A crime that shocks all humankind;
A deed unknown to female race,
At which the sun should hide his face: 70
Advice in vain you would apply—
Then leave me to despair and die.
Yet, kind Arcadians, on my urn

---

32. matins: morning songs. **34. Aurora:** goddess of dawn. **35. hyps:** hypochondria.
48–49. small . . . face: smallpox caused seaming, or pitting, of the face; the greatpox
(syphilis) in an advanced stage caused the bridge of the nose to collapse. **73. Arcadians:**
shepherds of pastoral Greece, often depicted as looking at a gravestone on which
Death has written, "Even in Arcadia I am."

These elegies and sonnets burn;
And on the marble grave these rhymes,   75
A monument to aftertimes—
'Here Cassy lies, by Celia slain,
And, dying, never told his pain.'
  "Vain empty world, farewell. But hark,
The loud Cerberian triple bark;   80
And there—behold Alecto stand,
A whip of scorpions in her hand;
Lo, Charon from his leaky wherry
Beckoning to waft me o'er the ferry;
I come! I come! Medusa see,   85
Her serpents hiss direct at me.
Begone; unhand me, hellish fry:
Avaunt—ye cannot say 'twas I."
  "Dear Cassy, thou must purge and bleed;
I fear thou wilt be mad indeed.   90
But now, by friendship's sacred laws,
I here conjure thee, tell the cause;
And Celia's horrid fact relate:
Thy friend would gladly share thy fate."
  "To force it out, my heart must rend;   95
Yet when conjured by such a friend—
Think, Peter, how my soul is racked!
These eyes, these eyes, beheld the fact.
Now bend thine ear, since out it must;
But, when thou seest me laid in dust,   100
The secret thou shalt ne'er impart,
Not to the nymph that keeps thy heart;
(How would her virgin soul bemoan
A crime to all her sex unknown!)
Nor whisper to the tattling reeds   105
The blackest of all female deeds;
Nor blab it on the lonely rocks,
Where Echo sits, and listening mocks;
Nor let the zephyr's treacherous gale
Through Cambridge waft the direful tale;   110
Nor to the chattering feathered race
Discover Celia's foul disgrace.

---

80. Cerberian triple bark: Cerberus, a triple-headed watchdog, is stationed at the threshold of Hades, the classical underworld. **81. Alecto:** one of the Furies, who can drive guilty men mad. **83. Charon:** the ferryman who carries the dead across the River Styx. **85. Medusa:** the Gorgon, whose locks are snakes and whose gaze turns men to stone. **87. fry:** offspring. **88. Avaunt . . . 'twas I:** "see *Macbeth*" (Swift). The line condenses two of Macbeth's cries on seeing Banquo's ghost: "Thou canst not say I did it" and "Avaunt! and quit my sight" (III. iv. 50, 93). **89. purge and bleed:** remedies for melancholy. **93. fact:** deed. **105. tattling reeds:** which betrayed the secret confided to them by King Midas's wife, that he had ass's ears. **108. Echo:** a nymph, whose incessant talking distracted Hera from discovering Zeus's adulterous affairs. She was punished by being restricted to repeating only the words of others. **111. chattering . . . race:** parrots. **112. Discover:** reveal.

But, if you fail, my specter dread,
Attending nightly round your bed—
And yet I dare confide in you;   115
So take my secret, and adieu:
  Nor wonder how I lost my wits;
Oh! Celia, Celia, Celia sh—!"

Alexander Pope   *(1688–1744)*

Epistle to Miss Blount, on Her Leaving the
Town, after the Coronation

As some fond virgin, whom her mother's care
Drags from the town to wholsome country air,
Just when she learns to roll a melting eye,
And hear a spark, yet think no danger nigh;
From the dear man unwilling she must sever,   5
Yet takes one kiss before she parts for ever:
Thus from the world fair Zephalinda flew,
Saw others happy, and with sighs withdrew;
Not that their pleasures caused her discontent,
She sighed not that they stayed, but that she went. 10
   She went, to plain-work, and to purling brooks,
Old-fashioned halls, dull aunts, and croaking rooks,
She went from opera, park, assembly, play,
To morning walks, and prayers three hours a day;
To pass her time 'twixt reading and bohea,   15
To muse, and spill her solitary tea,
Or o'er cold coffee trifle with the spoon,
Count the slow clock, and dine exact at noon;
Divert her eyes with pictures in the fire,
Hum half a tune, tell stories to the squire;   20
Up to her godly garret after seven,
There starve and pray, for that's the way to heaven.
   Some squire, perhaps, you take delight to rack;
Whose game is whisk, whose treat a toast in sack,
Who visits with a gun, presents you birds,   25
Then gives a smacking buss, and cries—"No words!"
Or with his hound comes hollowing from the stable,

EPISTLE TO MISS BLOUNT   Theresa Blount was a close friend of Pope. The coronation
was that of George I in 1714. **4. spark:** suitor, fop. **7. Zephalinda:** a fanciful name assumed by Miss Blount. **11. plain-work:** needlework. **13. assembly:** ball. **15. bohea:** a
kind of tea. **18. noon:** an unfashionably early hour for dinner. **22. starve:** i.e., go without
supper, a fashionable light meal that usually came just before bedtime. **24. whisk:** whist.
sack: Canary wine. **27. hollowing:** hallooing.

Makes love with nods, and knees beneath a table;
Whose laughs are hearty, though his jests are coarse,
And loves you best of all things—but his horse.   30
   In some fair evening, on your elbow laid,
You dream of triumphs in the rural shade;
In pensive thought recall the fancied scene,
See coronations rise on every green;
Before you pass th' imaginary sights   35
Of lords, and earls, and dukes, and gartered knights;
While the spread fan o'ershades your closing eyes;
Then give one flirt, and all the vision flies.
Thus vanish scepters, coronets, and balls,
And leave you in lone woods, or empty walls.   40
   So when your slave, at some dear, idle time
(Not plagued with headaches, or the want of rhyme),
Stands in the streets, abstracted from the crew,
And while he seems to study, thinks of you:
Just when his fancy points your sprightly eyes,   45
Or sees the blush of soft Parthenia rise,
Gay pats my shoulder, and you vanish quite;
Streets, chairs, and coxcombs rush upon my sight;
Vexed to be still in town, I knit my brow,
Look sour, and hum a tune—as you may now.   50

To Richard Boyle, Earl of Burlington:

Of the Use of Riches

'Tis strange, the miser should his cares employ
To gain those riches he can ne'er enjoy:
Is it less strange, the prodigal should waste
His wealth, to purchase what he ne'er can taste?
Not for himself he sees, or hears, or eats;   5
Artists must choose his pictures, music, meats:
He buys for Topham, drawings and designs,
For Pembroke, statues, dirty gods, and coins;
Rare monkish manuscripts for Hearne alone,
And books for Mead, and butterflies for Sloane.   10

---

36. gartered knights: the Order of the Garter carries knighthood with it. **38. flirt:** quick movement (of a fan). **44. study:** meditate. **46. Parthenia:** possibly Martha Blount, Theresa's sister. **47. Gay:** John Gay, poet and dramatist. **48. chairs:** sedan chairs, in which people were carried through the streets.

TO RICHARD BOYLE Richard Boyle, third Earl of Burlington, was an amateur architect and patron of architects. He favored a severe Roman classicism in opposition to the fashionable baroque, and spent large amounts of money on public buildings of such design. **6. meats:** food. **7. Topham:** "a gentleman famous for a judicious collection of drawings" (Pope). **8. Pembroke:** the eighth Earl of Pembroke, a well-known collector. **9. Hearne:** an eminent medievalist. **10. Mead . . . Sloane:** two doctors, one noted for his library and the other for his collection and natural curiosities.

Think we all these are for himself! no more
Than his fine wife, alas! or finer whore.
　　For what has Virro painted, built, and planted?
Only to show how many tastes he wanted.
What brought Sir Visto's ill-got wealth to waste?   15
Some demon whispered, "Visto! have a taste."
Heaven visits with a taste the wealthy fool,
And needs no rod but Ripley with a rule.
See! sportive fate, to punish awkward pride,
Bids Bubo build, and sends him such a guide: 20
A standing sermon, at each year's expense,
That never coxcomb reached magnificence!
　　You show us Rome was glorious, not profuse,
And pompous buildings once were things of use.
Yet shall (my Lord) your just, your noble rules   25
Fill half the land with imitating fools;
Who random drawings from your sheets shall take,
And of one beauty many blunders make;
Load some vain church with old theatric state,
Turn arcs of triumph to a garden gate;   30
Reverse your ornaments, and hang them all
On some patched dog-hole eked with ends of wall;
Then clap four slices of pilaster on't,
That, laced with bits of rustic, makes a front.
Shall call the winds through long arcades to roar,   35
Proud to catch cold at a Venetian door;
Conscious they act a true Palladian part,
And, if they starve, they starve by rules of art.
　　Oft have you hinted to your brother peer,
A certain truth, which many buy too dear: 40
Something there is more needful than expense,
And something previous even to taste—'tis sense:
Good sense, which only is the gift of Heaven,
And though no science, fairly worth the seven:
A light, which in yourself you must perceive;   45
Jones and Le Nôtre have it not to give.

---

14. wanted: lacked. **16. taste:** a sense for beauty, often considered indefinable. **18. Ripley:** a successful but mediocre architect. **rule:** (1) carpenter's rule, as a form of "rod"; (2) misapplied principle (see ll. 25–26). **20. Bubo:** Latin for "owl"; an allusion to Bubb Dodington, who spent £140,000 on his country house. **22. magnificence:** as well as splendor, "magnificence" suggests the Aristotelean virtue of expenditure on public objects rather than on oneself; tasteful generosity. **23–24. You . . . use:** Burlington published Palladio's *Classical Buildings* and the designs of Inigo Jones (see l. 46), whose "sheets" (1.27) could be plundered for details by those with no sense of "use" (1. 74) or the harmonic relationships of parts to whole. **30. arcs of triumph:** Roman triumphal arches. **33. pilaster:** column attached to a wall. **34. rustic:** stone used for an effect of rough strength. **front:** entrance. **36. Venetian door:** a kind of door invented by Palladio, unsuitable to the British climate. **38. starve:** suffer or die from cold. **44. science:** body of organized knowledge. **seven:** the seven liberal arts, first defined in the Middle Ages. **46. Jones:** Inigo Jones, great seventeenth-century English architect. **Le Nôtre:** noted French designer of formal gardens, including those at Versailles.

To build, to plant, whatever you intend,
To rear the column, or the arch to bend,
To swell the terrace, or to sink the grot;
In all, let Nature never be forgot.   50
But treat the goddess like a modest fair,
Nor overdress, nor leave her wholly bare;
Let not each beauty everywhere be spied,
Where half the skill is decently to hide.
He gains all points, who pleasingly confounds,   55
Surprises, varies, and conceals the bounds.
    Consult the genius of the place in all;
That tells the waters or to rise, or fall;
Or helps th' ambitious hill the heavens to scale,
Or scoops in circling theaters the vale;   60
Calls in the country, catches opening glades,
Joins willing woods, and varies shades from shades;
Now breaks, or now directs, th' intending lines;
Paints as you plant, and, as you work, designs.
    Still follow sense, of every art the soul,   65
Parts answering parts shall slide into a whole,
Spontaneous beauties all around advance,
Start even from difficulty, strike from chance;
Nature shall join you; time shall make it grow
A work to wonder at—perhaps a Stowe.   70
    Without it, proud Versailles! thy glory falls;
And Nero's terraces desert their walls:
The vast parterres a thousand hands shall make,
Lo! Cobham comes, and floats them with a lake:
Or cut wide views through mountains to the plains,   75
You'll wish your hill or sheltered seat again.
Even in an ornament its place remark,
Nor in an Hermitage set Dr. Clarke.
    Behold Villario's ten years' toil complete;
His quincunx darkens, his espaliers meet;   80
The wood supports the plain, the parts unite,
And strength of shade contends with strength of light;
A waving glow the bloomy beds display,

---

49. grot: grotto, artificial cave. **51. fair:** attractive woman. **54. decently:** (1) modestly;
(2) appropriately. **55–56. He . . . bounds:** Pope was influential in introducing the
"English" garden, which stressed naturalness in contrast to formal patterns. **57. genius
. . . place:** (1) character of the landscape; (2) guardian spirit of the place. **60. in
circling theaters:** as in the curves of classical amphitheaters. **63. th' intending lines:**
lines that lead the eye forward. **64. Paints:** (1) colors; (2) shapes picturesquely. **70.
Stowe:** the country estate of Lord Cobham, admired for its house and gardens. **72.
Nero's terraces:** Nero's elaborate gardens in Rome. **73. parterres:** formal terraces. **74.
Cobham . . . lake:** as he had done at Stowe. **floats:** inundates. **75. cut . . . plains:**
in a footnote, Pope cites an actual example of this procedure. **78. Hermitage . . .
Clarke:** Queen Caroline had placed a bust of the rationalistic, liberal theologian, Samuel
Clarke, in her Hermitage, an ornamental building in Richmond Park. Clarke was hardly
a hermit. **80. quincunx:** five trees planted so as to form a square with one in the center.
espaliers: trees or shrubs tied to a lattice.

Blushing in bright diversities of day,
With silver-quivering rills meandered o'er—   85
Enjoy them, you! Villario can no more;
Tired of the scene parterres and fountains yield,
He finds at last he better likes a field.
    Through his young woods how pleased Sabinus strayed,
Or sat delighted in the thickening shade,   90
With annual joy the reddening shoots to greet,
Or see the stretching branches long to meet!
His son's fine taste an opener vista loves,
Foe to the dryads of his father's groves;
One boundless green, or flourished carpet views,   95
With all the mournful family of yews;
The thriving plants ignoble broomsticks made,
Now sweep those alleys they were born to shade.
    At Timon's villa let us pass a day,
Where all cry out, "What sums are thrown away!"   100
So proud, so grand; of that stupendous air,
Soft and agreeable come never there.
Greatness, with Timon, dwells in such a draught
As brings all Brobdingnag before your thought.
To compass this, his building is a town,   105
His pond an ocean, his parterre a down:
Who but must laugh, the master when he sees,
A puny insect, shivering at a breeze!
Lo, what huge heaps of littleness around!
The whole, a labored quarry above ground.   110
Two cupids squirt before; a lake behind
Improves the keenness of the northern wind.
His gardens next your admiration call,
On every side you look, behold the wall!
No pleasing intricacies intervene,   115
No artful wildness to perplex the scene;
Grove nods at grove, each alley has a brother,
And half the platform just reflects the other.
The suffering eye inverted nature sees,
Trees cut to statues, statues thick as trees;   120
With here a fountain, never to be played,
And there a summerhouse, that knows no shade;
Here Amphitrite sails through myrtle bowers;
There gladiators fight, or die, in flowers;
Unwatered see the drooping sea-horse mourn,   125

---

94. **dryads:** wood nymphs. 95. **green . . . carpet:** opposite extremes of an open, naked lawn and elaborately patterned garden. 96. **yews:** the customary trees of cemeteries, here creating "pyramids of dark green continually repeated, not unlike a funeral procession" (Pope). 97. **thriving plants:** broom shrubs. 103. **draught:** design. 104. **Brobdingnag:** the land of giants in part two of Swift's *Gulliver's Travels*. 116. **perplex:** in its root meaning, to twist or plait together. 118. **platform:** terrace. 120. **Trees . . . trees:** in "Italian" gardens, trees or shrubs are cut into artificial shapes, and statues are common. 123. **Amphitrite:** a sea nymph.

And swallows roost in Nilus' dusty urn.
　My Lord advances with majestic mien,
Smit with the mighty pleasure, to be seen:
But soft—by regular approach—not yet—
First through the length of yon hot terrace sweat;　　　　　　130
And when up ten steep slopes you've dragged your thighs,
Just at his study door he'll bless your eyes.
　His study! with what authors is it stored?
In books, not authors, curious is my Lord;
To all their dated backs he turns you round:　　　　　　　135
These Aldus printed, those Duseuil has bound.
Lo, some are vellum, and the rest as good
For all his Lordship knows, but they are wood.
For Locke or Milton 'tis in vain to look,
These shelves admit not any modern book.　　　　　　　140
　And now the chapel's silver bell you hear,
That sumons you to all the pride of prayer:
Light quirks of music, broken and uneven,
Make the soul dance upon a jig to Heaven.
On painted ceilings you devoutly stare,　　　　　　　145
Where sprawl the saints of Verrio or Laguerre,
On gilded clouds in fair expansion lie,
And bring all Paradise before your eye.
To rest, the cushion and soft Dean invite,
Who never mentions Hell to ears polite.　　　　　　　150
　But hark! the chiming clocks to dinner call;
A hundred footsteps scrape the marble hall:
The rich buffet well-colored serpents grace,
And gaping tritons spew to wash your face.
Is this a dinner? this a genial room?　　　　　　　155
No, 'tis a temple, and a hecatomb;
A solemn sacrifice, performed in state,
You drink by measure, and to minutes eat.
So quick retires each flying course, you'd swear
Sancho's dread Doctor and his wand were there.　　　　　160
Between each act the trembling salvers ring,
From soup to sweet wine, and God bless the King.
In plenty starving, tantalized in state,

---

126. Nilus' dusty urn: river gods were commonly depicted with a flowing urn on their shoulders. 134. curious: discerning. 135. dated backs: early editions with dates stamped on their bindings. 136. Aldus: a fine Renaissance printer. Duseuil: a contemporary Parisian bookbinder. 138. wood: wood painted to look like books. 139. Locke: John Locke (1632–1704), great English philosopher. 146. Verrio or Laguerre: fashionable painters, here in baroque style. 149–50. Dean . . . polite: in a sermon, a Dean of Gloucester referred to "a place which he thought it not decent to name in so polite an assembly" (Pope). 153–54. serpents . . . tritons: incongruous ornamental figures. "Tritons" are attendants on a sea god. 155. genial room: room for feasting. 156. hecatomb: slaughter of a hundred oxen as an offering to the gods. 160. Sancho's . . . wand: in Cervantes' Don Quixote (part II, ch. 47), Sancho Panza's doctor has each dish taken away before Sancho can taste it, by touching it with his wand. 162. God . . . King: traditional toast drunk in port, at the end of a meal.

And complaisantly helped to all I hate,
Treated, caressed, and tired, I take my leave,   165
Sick of his civil pride from morn to eve;
I curse such lavish cost, and little skill,
And swear no day was ever passed so ill.

   Yet hence the poor are clothed, the hungry fed;
Health to himself, and to his infants bread   170
The laborer bears: what his hard heart denies,
His charitable vanity supplies.

   Another age shall see the golden ear
Embrown the slope, and nod on the parterre,
Deep harvests bury all his pride has planned,   175
And laughing Ceres reassume the land.

   Who then shall grace, or who improve the soil?
Who plants like Bathurst, or who builds like Boyle.
'Tis use alone that sanctifies expense,
And splendor borrows all her rays from sense.   180

   His father's acres who enjoys in peace,
Or makes his neighbors glad, if he increase:
Whose cheerful tenants bless their yearly toil,
Yet to their lord owe more than to the soil;
Whose ample lawns are not ashamed to feed   185
The milky heifer and deserving steed;
Whose rising forests, not for pride or show,
But future buildings, future navies, grow:
Let his plantations stretch from down to down,
First shade a country, and then raise a town.   190

   You too proceed! make falling arts your care,
Erect new wonders, and the old repair;
Jones and Palladio to themselves restore,
And be whate'er Vitruvius was before:
Till kings call forth the ideas of your mind,   195
Proud to accomplish what such hands designed,
Bid harbors open, public ways extend,
Bid temples, worthier of the god, ascend;
Bid the broad arch the dangerous flood contain,
The mole projected break the roaring main;   200
Back to his bounds their subject sea command,
And roll obedient rivers through the land:
These honors, peace to happy Britain brings,
These are imperial works, and worthy kings.

---

173. **ear:** of wheat. 176. **Ceres:** goddess of agriculture. 178. **Bathurst:** Pope's friend, Lord Bathurst, an enthusiastic landscaper. **Boyle:** to whom this poem is addressed. 191. **You:** Burlington. 194. **Vitruvius:** famous Roman writer on architecture. 198. **temples . . . ascend:** some recently erected churches, built on marshy ground, had sunk dangerously. 199. **broad arch:** the proposed Westminster Bridge, later built with Burlington as one of the directors of the project. Pope also refers in lines 197–202 to other specific projects.

The First Satire of the Second Book of Horace:

To Mr. Fortescue

P.   There are (I scarce can think it, but am told),
There are, to whom my satire seems too bold:
Scarce to wise Peter complaisant enough,
And something said of Chartres much too rough.
The lines are weak, another's pleased to say,   5
Lord Fanny spins a thousand such a day.
Timorous by nature, of the rich in awe,
I come to counsel learnèd in the law:
You'll give me, like a friend, both sage and free
Advice; and (as you use) without a fee.   10
   F.   I'd write no more.
   P.   Not write? but then I *think*,
And for my soul I cannot sleep a wink.
I nod in company, I wake at night,
Fools rush into my head, and so I write.
   F.   You could not do a worse thing for your life.   15
Why, if the nights seem tedious—take a wife;
Or rather truly, if your point be rest,
Lettuce and cowslip wine: *probatum est.*
But talk with Celsus, Celsus will advise
Hartshorn, or something that shall close your eyes.   20
Or, if you needs must write, write Caesar's praise:
You'll gain at least a knighthood, or the bays.
   P.   What? like Sir Richard, rumbling, rough, and fierce,
With Arms, and George, and Brunswick crowd the verse,
Rend with tremendous sound your ears asunder,   25
With gun, drum, trumpet, blunderbuss, and thunder?
Or nobly wild, with Budgell's fire and force,
Paint angels trembling round his falling horse?
   F.   Then all your Muse's softer art display,
Let Carolina smooth the tuneful lay,   30
Lull with Amelia's liquid name the Nine,

THE FIRST SATIRE   In this imitation of Horace, William Fortescue, a prominent lawyer and friend of Pope, replaces Horace's Trebatius. **3. Peter:** Peter Walter, a well-known moneylender and miser. **complaisant:** polite. **4. Chartres:** Francis Chartres, a notorious gambler, moneylender, and rake. **6. Lord Fanny:** Lord Hervey, an effeminate courtier, writer, and enemy of Pope. **9. free:** open, generous. **10. as you use:** as you are accustomed to do. **18. Lettuce . . . wine:** sedatives. *probatum est:* Latin, "it is approved"; i.e., these are proven remedies. **19. Celsus:** a Roman doctor. **20. Hartshorn:** ammonia (a joke). **21. Caesar:** George II. **22. bays:** garland of bay leaves, emblem of the poet laureate. **23. Sir Richard:** Sir Richard Blackmore, physician and author of several bad epic poems. **24. Brunswick:** one of the German principalities ruled by George II. **27. Budgell:** Eustace Budgell, author of an unintentionally ridiculous poem about George II. **30–31. Carolina . . . Amelia:** wife and daughter of George II. **31. Nine:** the nine Muses.

And sweetly flow through all the royal line.
    P.   Alas! few verses touch their nicer ear;
They scarce can bear their Laureate twice a year;
And justly Caesar scorns the poet's lays,   35
It is to history he trusts for praise.
    F.   Better be Cibber, I'll maintain it still,
Than ridicule all taste, blaspheme quadrille,
Abuse the City's best good men in meter,
And laugh at peers that put their trust in Peter.   40
Even those you touch not, hate you.
    P.   What should ail 'em?
    F.   A hundred smart in Timon and in Balaam.
The fewer still you name, you wound the more;
Bond is but one, but Harpax is a score.
    P.   Each mortal has his pleasure: none deny   45
Scarsdale his bottle, Darty his ham-pie;
Ridotta sips and dances, till she see
The doubling lusters dance as fast as she;
F— loves the Senate, Hockley Hole his brother,
Like in all else, as one egg to another.   50
I love to pour out all my self, as plain
As downright Shippen or as old Montaigne:
In them, as certain to be loved as seen,
The soul stood forth, nor kept a thought within;
In me what spots (for spots I have) appear,   55
Will prove at least the medium must be clear.
In this impartial glass, my Muse intends
Fair to expose myself, my foes, my friends;
Publish the present age; but where my text
Is vice too high, reserve it for the next: 60
My foes shall wish my life a longer date,
And every friend the less lament my fate.
    My head and heart thus flowing through my quill,
Verse-man or prose-man, term me which you will,
Papist or Protestant, or both between,   65
Like good Erasmus in an honest mean,
In moderation placing all my glory,

---

33. **nicer:** more delicate. 34. **Laureate . . . year:** the poet laureate, at this time Pope's enemy Colley Cibber, was supposed to celebrate the New Year and the King's birthday with odes. George II, who disliked poetry, is supposed to have remarked: "Who is this Pope? . . . Why will not my subjects write in prose?" 38. **quadrille:** a card game. 39. **City's . . . men:** London merchants. 42. **Timon . . . Balaam:** fictional characters in other poems by Pope. 43. **name:** identify by a real name. 44. **Bond . . . Harpax:** Denis Bond, director of a corporation for relief of the poor, is reported to have said, "Damn the poor." Pope attacked him in *To Bathurst*. Harpax is a fictitious name from the Greek for "robber." 47. **Ridotta:** from the Italian *ridotto*, an assembly for music and dancing. 48. **lusters:** glass chandeliers. 49. **F—— . . . brother:** Stephen and Henry Fox. The Senate is the House of Commons, while Hockley Hole was a bear-baiting garden. 52. **Shippen:** an outspoken and incorruptible member of the Commons. **Montaigne:** noted for his self-revelatory *Essays*. 59. **text:** literally, subject for a sermon. 66. **Erasmus:** criticized for being neither wholeheartedly Catholic nor Protestant. **mean:** an allusion to the golden mean.

While Tories call me Whig, and Whigs a Tory.
   Satire's my weapon, but I'm too discreet
To run amuck, and tilt at all I meet; 70
I only wear it in a land of hectors,
Thieves, supercargoes, sharpers, and directors.
Save but our army! and let Jove encrust
Swords, pikes, and guns, with everlasting rust!
Peace is my dear delight—not Fleury's more: 75
But touch me, and no Minister so sore.
Whoe'er offends, at some unlucky time
Slides into verse, and hitches in a rhyme,
Sacred to ridicule his whole life long,
And the sad burthen of some merry song. 80
   Slander or poison dread from Delia's rage,
Hard words or hanging, if your judge be Page.
From furious Sappho scarce a milder fate,
P—xed by her love, or libeled by her hate.
Its proper power to hurt, each creature feels; 85
Bulls aim their horns, and asses lift their heels;
'Tis a bear's talent not to kick, but hug;
And no man wonders he's not stung by Pug.
So drink with Walters, or with Chartres eat,
They'll never poison you, they'll only cheat. 90
   Then, learnèd sir! (to cut the matter short)
Whate'er my fate, or well or ill at Court,
Whether old age, with faint but cheerful ray,
Attends to gild the evening of my day,
Or death's black wing already be displayed, 95
To wrap me in the universal shade;
Whether the darkened room to muse invite,
Or whitened wall provoke the skewer to write:
In durance, exile, Bedlam, or the Mint,
Like Lee or Budgell, I will rhyme and print. 100
   F.   Alas, young man! your days can ne'er be long,
In flower of age you perish for a song!
Plums and directors, Shylock and his wife,
Will club their testers, now, to take your life!
   P.   What? armed for virtue when I point the pen, 105

---

71. **hectors:** bullies. 72. **supercargoes:** supervisors of cargoes and trade on merchant ships, who were proverbial for their wealth. **directors:** particularly those of the South Sea Company, notorious for fraud. 73–74. **Save . . . rust:** the Tories opposed a standing army. 75. **Fleury:** the French prime minister, who favored a peace policy. 78. **hitches:** becomes entangled. 80. **burthen:** burden, bass accompaniment or refrain. 83. **Sappho:** Lady Mary Wortley Montagu, who combined with Lord Hervey to attack Pope. 84. **P—xed:** infected with the greatpox (syphilis). 88. **Pug:** a pet dog. 97–99. **Whether . . . Mint:** whether confined to jail or a mental hospital. Bedlam (Bethlehem Hospital) housed the insane; the Mint was a sanctuary for debtors. 100. **Lee or Budgell:** Nathaniel Lee was a late seventeenth-century dramatist. Both he and Budgell were insane for a time. 103. **Plums:** sums of £100,000, acquired by plundering the nation. **Shylock:** the Earl of Selkirk. 104. **club their testers:** pool their sixpences.

Brand the bold front of shameless guilty men;
Dash the proud gamester in his gilded car;
Bare the mean heart that lurks beneath a Star;
Can there be wanting, to defend her cause,
Lights of the Church, or guardians of the laws?   110
Could pensioned Boileau lash in honest strain
Flatterers and bigots even in Louis' reign?
Could laureate Dryden pimp and friar engage,
Yet neither Charles nor James be in a rage?
And I not strip the gilding off a knave,   115
Unplaced, unpensioned, no man's heir, or slave?
I will, or perish in the generous cause:
Hear this, and tremble! you who 'scape the laws.
Yes, while I live, no rich or noble knave
Shall walk the world, in credit, to his grave.   120
To VIRTUE ONLY AND HER FRIENDS, A FRIEND,
The world beside may murmur, or commend.
Know, all the distant din that world can keep,
Rolls o'er my grotto, and but soothes my sleep.
There, my retreat the best companions grace,   125
Chiefs out of war, and statesmen out of place.
There St. John mingles with my friendly bowl
The feast of reason and the flow of soul;
And he, whose lightning pierced th' Iberian lines,
Now forms my quincunx, and now ranks my vines,   130
Or tames the genius of the stubborn plain,
Almost as quickly as he conquered Spain.
    Envy must own, I live among the Great,
No pimp of pleasure, and no spy of state,
With eyes that pry not, tongue that ne'er repeats,   135
Fond to spread friendships, but to cover heats;
To help who want, to forward who excel;
This, all who know me, know; who love me, tell;
And who unknown defame me, let them be
Scribblers or peers, alike are Mob to me.   140
This is my plea, on this I rest my cause—
What saith my counsel, learnèd in the laws?
    F.   Your plea is good; but still I say, beware!
Laws are explained by men—so have a care.

---

106. **front:** forehead. 107 **car:** chariot. 108. **Star:** decoration of the Order of the Garter or other order. 111. **Boileau:** French poet noted for his satires. 112. **Louis' reign:** the absolute monarchy of Louis XIV. 113. **pimp and friar:** combined in Friar Dominick of Dryden's play *The Spanish Friar*. 114. **Charles nor James:** Charles II and his successor, James II. James did in fact ban the play for its satire on the Catholic clergy. 116. **Unplaced:** without a government position. 117. **generous:** noble, public spirited. 124. **grotto:** a cave decorated by Pope. 127. **St. John:** Viscount Bolingbroke, a leading Government minister under Queen Anne. 129. **he . . . lines:** the Earl of Peterborough, successful in the Spanish campaign of 1705–06. 130. **quincunx:** five trees planted in a square with one in the center. 131. **genius:** inherent nature. 136. **cover heats:** dampen quarrels. 140. **Mob:** from the Latin, *mobile vulgus*, the fickle crowd.

It stands on record, that in Richard's times   145
A man was hanged for very honest rhymes.
Consult the statute: *quart.* I think it is,
Edwardi sext. or *prim. et quint. Eliz.*
See Libels, Satires—here you have it—read.
    P.   Libels and satires! lawless things indeed!   150
But grave epistles, bringing vice to light,
Such as a king might read, a bishop write,
Such as Sir Robert would approve—
    F.   Indeed?
The case is altered—you may then proceed;
In such a cause the plaintiff will be hissed,   155
My Lords the Judges laugh, and you're dismissed.

Samuel Johnson   *(1709–1784)*

On the Death of Dr. Robert Levet

Condemned to hope's delusive mine,
    As on we toil from day to day,
By sudden blasts, or slow decline,
    Our social comforts drop away.

Well tried through many a varying year,   5
    See Levet to the grave descend;
Officious, innocent, sincere,
    Of every friendless name the friend.

Yet still he fills affection's eye,
    Obscurely wise, and coarsely kind;   10
Nor, lettered arrogance, deny
    Thy praise to merit unrefined.

When fainting nature called for aid,
    And hovering death prepared the blow,
His vigorous remedy displayed   15
    The power of art without the show.

145–46. It . . . rhymes: the poet Collingbourne, hanged under Richard III. 147–48. quart. . . . . Eliz.: actual statutes dating from the reigns of Edward VI and Elizabeth I. 153. Sir Robert: Sir Robert Walpole, the prime minister, whom Pope opposed.

DR. ROBERT LEVET   Robert Levet, a self-taught doctor, lived in Johnson's household for many years. Boswell described him as "an obscure practicer in physic [medicine] amongst the lower people." 7. Officious: eager to be helpful.

In misery's darkest caverns known,
    His useful care was ever nigh,
Where hopeless anguish poured his groan,
    And lonely want retired to die.   20

No summons mocked by chill delay,
    No petty gain disdained by pride,
The modest wants of every day
    The toil of every day supplied.

His virtues walked their narrow round,   25
    Nor made a pause, nor left a void;
And sure th' Eternal Master found
    The single talent well employed.

The busy day, the peaceful night,
    Unfelt, uncounted, glided by;   30
His frame was firm, his powers were bright,
    Though now his eightieth year was nigh.

Then with no throbbing fiery pain,
    No cold gradations of decay,
Death broke at once the vital chain,   35
    And freed his soul the nearest way.

Thomas Gray   *(1716–1771)*

Elegy Written in a Country Churchyard

The curfew tolls the knoll of parting day,
    The lowing herd wind slowly o'er the lea,
The ploughman homeward plods his weary way,
    And leaves the world to darkness and to me.

Now fades the glimmering landscape on the sight,   5
    And all the air a solemn stillness holds,
Save where the beetle wheels his droning flight,
    And drowsy tinklings lull the distant folds;

Save that from yonder ivy-mantled tower
    The moping owl does to the moon complain   10
Of such as, wandering near her secret bower,
    Molest her ancient solitary reign.

28. **single talent:** single ability, with reference to the parable of the talents (Matthew 25:14–30).

Beneath those rugged elms, that yew-tree's shade,
   Where heaves the turf in many a moldering heap,
Each in his narrow cell forever laid,   15
   The rude forefathers of the hamlet sleep.

The breezy call of incense-breathing morn,
   The swallow twittering from the straw-built shed,
The cock's shrill clarion, or the echoing horn,
   No more shall rouse them from their lowly bed.   20

For them no more the blazing hearth shall burn,
   Or busy housewife ply her evening care;
No children run to lisp their sire's return,
   Or climb his knees the envied kiss to share.

Oft did the harvest to their sickle yield,   25
   Their furrow oft the stubborn glebe has broke;
How jocund did they drive their team afield!
   How bowed the woods beneath their sturdy stroke!

Let not Ambition mock their useful toil,
   Their homely joys, and destiny obscure;   30
Nor Grandeur hear, with a disdainful smile,
   The short and simple annals of the poor.

The boast of heraldry, the pomp of power,
   And all that beauty, all that wealth e'er gave,
Awaits alike th' inevitable hour:
   The paths of glory lead but to the grave.   35

Nor you, ye Proud, impute to these the fault,
   If Memory o'er their tomb no trophies raise,
Where through the long-drawn aisle and fretted vault
   The pealing anthem swells the note of praise.   40

Can storied urn or animated bust
   Back to its mansion call the fleeting breath?
Can Honor's voice provoke the silent dust,
   Or Flattery soothe the dull cold ear of Death?

Perhaps in this neglected spot is laid   45
   Some heart once pregnant with celestial fire;
Hands that the rod of empire might have swayed,
   Or waked to ecstasy the living lyre.

ELEGY **16. rude:** rustic. **19. horn:** hunter's horn. **26. glebe:** soil. **41. storied . . .
bust:** an urn giving a person's history, or a lifelike bust. **43. provoke:** call forth.

But Knowledge to their eyes her ample page,
  Rich with the spoils of time, did ne'er unroll;   50
Chill Penury repressed their noble rage,
  And froze the genial current of the soul.

Full many a gem of purest ray serene
  The dark unfathomed caves of ocean bear;
Full many a flower is born to blush unseen   55
  And waste its sweetness on the desert air.

Some village Hampden, that with dauntless breast
  The little tyrant of his fields withstood;
Some mute inglorious Milton here may rest,
  Some Cromwell, guiltless of his country's blood.   60

Th' applause of listening senates to command,
  The threats of pain and ruin to despise,
To scatter plenty o'er a smiling land,
  And read their history in a nation's eyes,

Their lot forbade; nor circumscribed alone   65
  Their growing virtues, but their crimes confined;
Forbade to wade through slaughter to a throne,
  And shut the gates of mercy on mankind;

The struggling pangs of conscious truth to hide,
  ' To quench the blushes of ingenuous shame,   70
Or heap the shrine of Luxury and Pride
  With incense kindled at the Muse's flame.

Far from the madding crowd's ignoble strife,
  Their sober wishes never learned to stray;
Along the cool sequestered vale of life   75
  They kept the noiseless tenor of their way.

Yet even these bones from insult to protect
  Some frail memorial still erected nigh,
With uncouth rhymes and shapeless sculpture decked,
  Implores the passing tribute of a sigh.   80

Their name, their years, spelt by th' unlettered muse,
  The place of fame and elegy supply;
And many a holy text around she strews,
  That teach the rustic moralist to die.

For who, to dumb Forgetfulness a prey,   85
  This pleasing, anxious being e'er resigned,

---

51. **rage**: ardor. 52. **genial current**: natural potentialities. 57. **Hampden**: John Hampden
refused to pay a special tax levied by Charles I in 1636, one of the events leading to
the Civil Wars. 70. **ingenuous shame**: innate innocence. 79. **uncouth**: unpolished.

Left the warm precincts of the cheerful day,
    Nor cast one longing lingering look behind?

On some fond breast the parting soul relies,
    Some pious drops the closing eye requires;   90
Even from the tomb the voice of nature cries,
    Even in our ashes live their wonted fires.

For thee, who mindful of th' unhonored dead,
    Dost in these lines their artless tale relate;
If chance, by lonely contemplation led,   95
    Some kindred spirit shall inquire thy fate,

Haply some hoary-headed swain may say,
    "Oft have we seen him at the peep of dawn
Brushing with hasty steps the dews away
    To meet the sun upon the upland lawn.   100

"There at the foot of yonder nodding beech
    That wreathes its old fantastic roots so high,
His listless length at noontide would he stretch,
    And pore upon the brook that babbles by.

"Hard by yon wood, now smiling as in scorn,   105
    Muttering his wayward fancies he would rove;
Now drooping, woeful-wan, like one forlorn,
    Or crazed with care, or crossed in hopeless love.

"One morn I missed him on the customed hill,
    Along the heath, and near his favorite tree;   110
Another came; nor yet beside the rill,
    Nor up the lawn, nor at the wood was he;

"The next, with dirges due, in sad array,
    Slow through the church-way path we saw him borne.
Approach and read (for thou canst read) the lay,   115
    Graved on the stone beneath yon agèd thorn."

THE EPITAPH

Here rests his head upon the lap of earth,
    A youth to fortune and to fame unknown;
Fair Science frowned not on his humble birth,
    And Melancholy marked him for her own.   120

---

90. **pious:** careful of duties to family or friends. 92. **wonted:** accustomed. 100. **lawn:** glade, meadow. 119. **Science:** learning in general. 120. **Melancholy:** a broad concept, including thoughtfulness and feeling for others.

Large was his bounty, and his soul sincere;
   Heaven did a recompense as largely send:
He gave to Misery all he had, a tear;
   He gained from Heaven ('twas all he wished) a friend.

No farther seek his merits to disclose,   125
   Or draw his frailties from their dread abode,
(There they alike in trembling hope repose)
   The bosom of his Father and his God.

Ode on the Death of a Favorite Cat,
Drowned in a Tub of Goldfishes

'Twas on a lofty vase's side,
Where China's gayest art had dyed
   The azure flowers that blow;
Demurest of the tabby kind,
The pensive Selima reclined,   5
   Gazed on the lake below.

Her conscious tail her joy declared;
The fair round face, the snowy beard,
   The velvet of her paws,
Her coat that with the tortoise vies,   10
Her ears of jet, and emerald eyes,
   She saw; and purred applause.

Still had she gazed; but midst the tide
Two angel forms were seen to glide,
   The genii of the stream: 15
Their scaly armor's Tyrian hue
Through richest purple to the view
   Betrayed a golden gleam.

The hapless nymph with wonder saw:
A whisker first and then a claw,   20
   With many an ardent wish,
She stretched in vain to reach the prize.
What female heart can gold despise?
   What cat's averse to fish?

Presumptuous maid! with looks intent   25
Again she stretched, again she bent,
   Nor knew the gulf between.
(Malignant Fate sat by and smiled)

ODE ON A FAVORITE CAT   3. **blow:** bloom. **15. genii:** guardian spirits. **16. Tyrian hue:**
ancient Tyre was famous for its purple dye.

The slippery verge her feet beguiled,
  She tumbled headlong in.   30

Eight times emerging from the flood
She mewed to every watery god,
  Some speedy aid to send.
No dolphin came, no nereid stirred;
Nor cruel Tom nor Susan heard.   35
  A favorite has no friend!

From hence, ye beauties, undeceived,
Know, one false step is ne'er retrieved,
  And be with caution bold.
Not all that tempts your wandering eyes   40
And heedless hearts is lawful prize.
  Nor all that glisters, gold.

The Candidate

When sly Jemmy Twicher had smugged up his face
With a lick of Court whitewash, and pious grimace,
A-wooing he went, where three sisters of old
In harmless society guttle and scold.
  "Lord! Sister," says Physic to Law, "I declare   5
Such a sheep-biting look, such a pickpocket air!
Not I, for the Indies! you know I'm no prude;
But his nose is a shame, and his eyes are so lewd!
Then he shambles and straddles so oddly, I fear—
No; at our time of life, 'twould be silly, my dear."   10
  "I don't know," says Law, "now methinks, for his look,
'Tis just like the picture in Rochester's book.
But his character, Phyzzy, his morals, his life!
When she died, I can't tell, but he once had a wife.
They say he's no Christian, loves drinking and whoring,   15

34. **dolphin**: a dolphin rescued the legendary Greek poet and musician Arion from drowning. **nereid**: sea nymph. 35. **Tom . . . Susan**: servants.

THE CANDIDATE This poem deals with the unsuccessful effort of the Earl of Sandwich to be elected High Steward of Cambridge University in 1764. He was backed by the "Court party." 1. **Jemmy Twicher**: the informer in Gay's play *The Beggar's Opera*. Sandwich had acquired this nickname when, shortly before, he had attacked John Wilkes for his obscene poem, *An Essay on Woman*; it was well known that he and Wilkes had been active members in a group devoted to obscenity. **smugged**: smartened. 2. **whitewash**: a cosmetic. 3. **three sisters**: the Faculties of Medicine ("Physic," l. 5), Law, and Divinity. 4. **guttle**: eat greedily. 6. **sheep-biting**: sneaking, thievish. 8. **his . . . shame**: possibly as the result of syphilis. 9. **straddles**: walks with his legs wide apart, with possibly an allusion to Sandwich's political opportunism. He was notoriously ugly and ungainly. 12. **picture . . . book**: presumably the portrait reproduced in early editions of Rochester's poems. Sandwich also resembled Rochester, his ancestor, in being a libertine. 14. **wife**: Lady Sandwich was confined as insane, but Sandwich's enemies asserted that she remained shut up after she had recovered her sanity.

And all the town rings of his swearing and roaring,
His lying, and filching, and Newgate-bird tricks:—
Not I, for a coronet, chariot and six!"
    Divinity heard, between waking and dozing,
Her sisters denying and Jemmy proposing;   20
From dinner she rose with her bumper in hand,
She stroked up her belly, and stroked down her band.
    "What a pother is here about wenching and roaring!
Why David loved catches, and Solomon whoring.
Did not Israel filch from th' Egyptians of old   25
Their jewels of silver, and jewels of gold?
The prophet of Bethel, we read, told a lie;
He drinks: so did Noah; he swears: so do I.
To refuse him for such peccadilloes were odd;
Besides, he repents, and he talks about God.   30
    "Never hang down your head, you poor penitent elf;
Come buss me, I'll be Mrs. Twitcher myself.
Damn you both for a couple of Puritan bitches!
He's Christian enough that repents, and that stitches."

William Collins *(1721–1759)*

Ode to Evening

If aught of oaten stop or pastoral song
May hope, chaste Eve, to soothe thy modest ear,
    Like thy own solemn springs,
    Thy springs and dying gales,

O nymph reserved, while now the bright-haired sun   5
Sits in yon western tent, whose cloudy skirts,
    With brede ethereal wove,
    O'erhang his wavy bed—

Now air is hushed, save where the weak-eyed bat,
With short shrill shriek, flits by on leathern wing;   10

16. **roaring:** riotous behavior. 17. **Newgate-bird tricks:** cheating, theft (from Newgate Prison). 19. **Divinity heard:** the Divinity faculty's support of Sandwich presumably resulted from his being the Ministerial candidate, since the Ministry distributed clerical appointments. 22. **band:** part of clerical dress. 24. **David . . . catches:** catches are musical "rounds", Gray alludes to the biblical Psalms of David. 25 26. **Israel . . . gold:** this story is told in Exodus 12:35–36. 27. **prophet of Bethel:** he tricked a fellow prophet with a lie (I Kings 13:11–19). 28. **drinks . . . Noah:** Noah got drunk on the wine he made (Genesis 9:20–21). 32. **buss:** kiss. 34. **stitches:** has sexual relations.
ODE TO EVENING 1. **oaten stop:** shepherd's reed pipe. 6. **skirts:** edges. 7. **brede:** braid, usually of interwoven colors.

Or where the beetle winds
His small but sullen horn,

As oft he rises midst the twilight path,
Against the pilgrim borne in heedless hum—
    Now teach me, maid composed,   15
    To breathe some softened strain,

Whose numbers, stealing through thy darkening vale,
May not unseemly with its stillness suit,
    As musing slow, I hail
    Thy genial loved return!   20

For when thy folding-star arising shows
His paly circlet, at his warning lamp
    The fragrant Hours, and elves
    Who slept in flowers the day,

And many a nymph who wreathes her brows with sedge, 25
And sheds the freshening dew, and, lovelier still,
    The pensive Pleasures sweet
    Prepare thy shadowy car.

Then lead, calm votaress, where some sheety lake
Cheers the lone heath, or some time-hallowed pile   30
    Or upland fallows gray
    Reflect its last cool gleam.

But when chill blustering winds or driving rain
Forbid my willing feet, be mine the hut
    That from the mountain's side   35
    Views wilds, and swelling floods,

And hamlets brown, and dim-discovered spires,
And hears their simple bell, and marks o'er all
    Thy dewy fingers draw
    The gradual dusky veil.   40

While Spring shall pour his showers, as oft he wont,
And bathe thy breathing tresses, meekest Eve!
    While Summer loves to sport
    Beneath thy lingering light;

While sallow Autumn fills thy lap with leaves;   45
Or Winter, yelling through the troublous air,
    Affrights thy shrinking train,
    And rudely rends thy robes;

11. **winds**: blows. 14. **pilgrim**: traveler. 17. **numbers**: verses. 21. **folding-star**: star arising at the time for folding or penning sheep; evening star. 28. **car**: chariot. 29. **votaress**: woman devoted to worship. 32. **its**: presumably referring to "lake" (l. 29). 41. **wont**: is accustomed to. 42. **breathing**: emitting fragrance. 47. **train**: attendants.

So long, sure-found beneath the sylvan shed,
Shall Fancy, Friendship, Science, rose-lipped Health,   50
    Thy gentlest influence own,
    And hymn thy favorite name!

Christopher Smart *(1722–1771)*

Jubilate Agno

from Fragment B₂

For I will consider my Cat Jeoffry.   697

For he is the servant of the Living God duly and daily serving him.

For at the first glance of the glory of God in the East he worships in his way.

For is this done by wreathing his body seven times round with elegant quickness.   700

For then he leaps up to catch the musk, which is the blessing of God upon his prayer.

For he rolls upon prank to work it in.

For having done duty and received blessing he begins to consider himself.

For this he performs in ten degrees.

For first he looks upon his forepaws to see if they are clean.   705

For secondly he kicks up behind to clear away there.

For thirdly he works it upon stretch with the forepaws extended.

For fourthly he sharpens his paws by wood.

For fifthly he washes himself.

49. **sylvan shed:** forest shelter. 50. **Science:** Knowledge.
JUBILATE AGNO "Rejoice in the Lamb" of God, i.e., Christ. Smart wrote this unfinished poem while in a mental hospital; it attempts to imitate the antiphonal character
of Biblical poetry in which two choirs alternately sing a verse. Much of *Jubilate Agno*
is divided into alternate "let" and "for" sections, but in this part the "let" verses are
lacking. 699. **glance . . . East:** sunrise. 701. **musk:** Smart apparently thought of
"musk" as Johnson's *Dictionary* defines it: "a dry, light, and friable substance of a dark
blackish color . . . feeling somewhat smooth or unctuous." 702. **upon prank:** in play.

For sixthly he rolls upon wash. 710

For seventhly he fleas himself, that he may not be interrupted upon the beat.

For eighthly he rubs himself against a post.

For ninthly he looks up for his instructions.

For tenthly he goes in quest of food.

For having considered God and himself he will consider his neighbor. 715

For if he meets another cat he will kiss her in kindness.

For when he takes his prey he plays with it to give it a chance.

For one mouse in seven escapes by his dallying.

For when his day's work is done his business more properly begins.

For he keeps the Lord's watch in the night against the adversary. 720

For he counteracts the powers of darkness by his electrical skin and glaring eyes.

For he counteracts the Devil, who is death, by brisking about the life.

For in his morning orisons he loves the sun and the sun loves him.

For he is of the tribe of Tiger.

For the Cherub Cat is a term of the Angel Tiger. 725

For he has the subtlety and hissing of a serpent, which in goodness he suppresses.

For he will not do destruction if he is well-fed, neither will he spit without provocation.

For he purrs in thankfulness, when God tells him he's a good Cat.

For he is an instrument for the children to learn benevolence upon.

For every house is incomplete without him and a blessing is lacking in the spirit. 730

For the Lord commanded Moses concerning the cats at the departure of the Children of Israel from Egypt.

---

711. **upon the beat:** in his activities. 720. **adversary:** the Devil. 723. **orisons:** prayers. 725. **term:** (diminutive) form. 731. **For the Lord . . . Egypt:** possibly a reference to the money, animals, etc., that the Israelites took with them, but the cats must be Smart's addition.

For every family had one cat at least in the bag.

For the English Cats are the best in Europe.

For he is the cleanest in the use of his forepaws of any quadruped.

For the dexterity of his defense is an instance of the love of God to him

exceedingly.   735

For he is the quickest to his mark of any creature.

For he is tenacious of his point.

For he is a mixture of gravity and waggery.

For he knows that God is his Savior.

For there is nothing sweeter than his peace when at rest.   740

For there is nothing brisker than his life when in motion.

For he is of the Lord's poor and so indeed is he called by benevolence

perpetually—Poor Jeoffry! poor Jeoffry! the rat has bit thy throat.

For I bless the name of the Lord Jesus that Jeoffry is better.

For the divine spirit comes about his body to sustain it in complete cat.

For his tongue is exceeding pure so that it has in purity what it wants in

music.   745

For he is docile and can learn certain things.

For he can set up with gravity, which is patience upon approbation.

For he can fetch and carry, which is patience in employment.

For he can jump over a stick, which is patience upon proof positive.

For he can spraggle upon waggle at the word of command.   750

For he can jump from an eminence into his master's bosom.

For he can catch the cork and toss it again.

For he is hated by the hypocrite and miser.

For the former is afraid of detection.

For the latter refuses the charge.   755

---

742. **For he is . . . perpetually:** possibly a reference to one of the Beatitudes: "blessed are the poor in spirit: for theirs is the kingdom of heaven" (Matthew 5:3). 747. **set:** sit. 749. **patience . . . positive:** positive proof of patience. 755. **charge:** cost (of keeping a cat).

For he camels his back to bear the first notion of business.

For he is good to think on, if a man would express himself neatly.

For he made a great figure in Egypt for his signal services.

For he killed the Icneumon-rat very pernicious by land.

For his ears are so acute that they sting again.   760

For from this proceeds the passing quickness of his attention.

For by stroking of him I have found out electricity.

For I perceived God's light about him both wax and fire.

For the Electrical fire is the spiritual substance, which God sends from heaven to sustain the bodies both of man and beast.

For God has blessed him in the variety of his movements.   765

For, though he cannot fly, he is an excellent clamberer.

For his motions upon the face of the earth are more than any other quadruped.

For he can tread to all the measures upon the music.

For he can swim for life.

For he can creep.   770

William Cowper   (1731–1800)

Lines Written During a Period of Insanity

Hatred and vengeance, my eternal portion,
Scarce can endure delay of execution,
Wait with impatient readiness to seize my
    Soul in a moment.

Damned below Judas; more abhorred than he was,   5
Who for a few pence sold his holy Master.
Twice-betrayed Jesus me, the last delinquent,
    Deems the profanest.

756. **bear:** bear (like a camel) seems to suggest "bare" (reveal). **758–59. great . . . land:** The cat was worshiped in ancient Egypt. The "Ichneumon-rat" is a mongoose. **761. passing:** exceeding. **768. tread:** dance.
LINES In part Cowper's intermittent insanity took the form of believing he was damned for eternity. **5–6. Judas . . . Master:** see Matthew 26:47–50 and 27:3–5.

Man disavows, and Deity disowns me;
Hell might afford my miseries a shelter;   10
Therefore Hell keeps her ever-hungry mouths all
         Bolted against me.

Hard lot! encompassed with a thousand dangers,
Weary, faint, trembling with a thousand terrors,
I'm called, if vanquished, to receive a sentence   15
         Worse than Abiram's.

Him the vindictive rod of angry justice
Sent quick and howling to the center headlong;
I, fed with judgment, in a fleshly tomb, am
         Buried above ground.   20

On the Death of Mrs. Throckmorton's Bullfinch

Ye nymphs! if e'er your eyes were red
With tears o'er hapless favorites shed,
   O share Maria's grief!
Her favorite, even in his cage,
(What will not hunger's cruel rage?)   5
   Assassined by a thief.

Where Rhenus strays his vines among,
The egg was laid from which he sprung,
   And though by nature mute,
Or only with a whistle blessed,
Well-taught, he all the sounds expressed   10
   Of flageolet or flute.

The honors of his ebon poll
Were brighter than the sleekest mole;
   His bosom of the hue   15
With which Aurora decks the skies,
When piping winds shall soon arise
   To sweep up all the dew.

Above, below, in all the house,
Dire foe, alike to bird and mouse,   20
   No cat had leave to dwell;

---

16. **Abiram:** when Korah, Dathan, and Abiram rebelled against Moses, they and their followers were swallowed up by the earth (Numbers 16:1–35). 18. **quick:** alive. 19. **fed with judgment:** the wicked leaders of the flock will be fed with God's judgment (that is, suffer divine punishment), according to Ezekiel (34:7–16).

MRS. THROCKMORTON'S BULLFINCH 7. **Rhenus:** the Rhine. 13. **honors:** ornamental hair. 16. **Aurora:** goddess of the dawn.

And Bully's cage supported stood,
On props of smoothest-shaven wood,
　　Large built and latticed well.

Well-latticed—but the grate, alas!　　　　　　　25
Not rough with wire of steel or brass,
　　For Bully's plumage sake,
But smooth with wands from Ouse's side,
With which, when neatly peeled and dried,
　　The swains their baskets make.　　　　　　30

Night veiled the pole; all seemed secure;
When led by instinct sharp and sure,
　　Subsistence to provide,
A beast forth sallied on the scout,
Long backed, long tailed, with whiskered snout,　　35
　　And badger-colored hide.

He, entering at the study door,
Its ample area 'gan explore;
　　And something in the wind
Conjectured, sniffing round and round,　　　　40
Better than all the books he found,
　　Food, chiefly, for the mind.

Just then, by adverse fate impressed,
A dream disturbed poor Bully's rest;
　　In sleep he seemed to view　　　　　　45
A rat, fast-clinging to the cage,
And, screaming at the sad presage,
　　Awoke and found it true.

For, aided both by ear and scent,
Right to his mark the monster went—　　　　50
　　Ah, Muse! forbear to speak
Minute the horrors that ensued;
His teeth were strong, the cage was wood—
　　He left poor Bully's beak.

He left it—but he should have ta'en　　　　55
That beak, whence issued many a strain
　　Of such mellifluous tone,
Might have repaid him well, I wote,
For silencing so sweet a throat,
　　Fast set within his own.　　　　　　60

28. Ouse: the nearby river. **51–52: speak minute:** speak in detail of. **58. wote:** know.

Maria weeps—the Muses mourn—
So, when by Bacchanalians torn,
　　On Thracian Hebrus' side
The tree-enchanter Orpheus fell,
His head alone remained to tell　　　　　　　　　65
　　The cruel death he died.

The Castaway

Obscurest night involved the sky,
　　Th' Atlantic billows roared,
When such a destined wretch as I,
　　Washed headlong from on board,
Of friends, of hope, of all bereft,　　　　　　　5
His floating home for ever left.

No braver chief could Albion boast
　　Than he with whom he went,
Nor ever ship left Albion's coast,
　　With warmer wishes sent.　　　　　　　　10
He loved them both, but both in vain,
Nor him behold, nor her again.

Not long beneath the whelming brine,
　　Expert to swim, he lay;
Nor soon he felt his strength decline,　　　　　15
　　Or courage die away;
But waged with death a lasting strife,
Supported by despair of life.

He shouted: nor his friends had failed
　　To check the vessel's course,　　　　　　　20
But so the furious blast prevailed
　　That, pitiless perforce,
They left their outcast mate behind,
And scudded still before the wind.

Some succour yet they could afford;　　　　　25
　　And, such as storms allow,
The cask, the coop, the floated cord,
　　Delayed not to bestow.
But he (they knew) nor ship nor shore,
Whate'er they gave, should visit more.　　　　30

62–66. Bacchanalians . . . he died: see Milton, "Lycidas," notes on ll. 58–63.
THE CASTAWAY This poem is based on an incident that occurred as a British expedition led by Captain George Anson against the Spanish was rounding Cape Horn during a storm. 7. chief: Anson. Albion: a literary name for England. 13. whelming: submerging. 27. coop: wicker basket for catching fish.

Nor, cruel as it seemed, could he
　　Their haste himself condemn,
Aware that flight, in such a sea,
　　Alone could rescue them;
Yet bitter felt it still to die　　　　　　　　　　35
Deserted, and his friends so nigh.

He long survives, who lives an hour
　　In ocean, self-upheld;
And so long he, with unspent power,
　　His destiny repelled;　　　　　　　　　　　40
And ever, as the minutes flew,
Entreated help, or cried, "Adieu!"

At length, his transient respite past,
　　His comrades, who before
Had heard his voice in every blast,　　　　　45
　　Could catch the sound no more.
For then, by toil subdued, he drank
The stifling wave, and then he sank.

No poet wept him: but the page
　　Of narrative sincere,　　　　　　　　　　50
That tells his name, his worth, his age,
　　Is wet with Anson's tear:
And tears by bards or heroes shed
Alike immortalize the dead.

I therefore purpose not, or dream,　　　　　55
　　Descanting on his fate,
To give the melancholy theme
　　A more enduring date:
But misery still delights to trace
Its semblance in another's case.　　　　　　60

No voice divine the storm allayed,
　　No light propitious shone,
When, snatched from all effectual aid,
　　We perished, each alone:
But I beneath a rougher sea,　　　　　　　　65
And whelmed in deeper gulfs than he.

49–50. page . . . sincere: Cowper's source was Richard Walter's *A Voyage Round the World by George Anson* (1748).

William Blake *(1757–1827)*

To Spring

O thou, with dewy locks, who lookest down
Through the clear windows of the morning; turn
Thine angel eyes upon our western isle,
Which in full choir hails thy approach, O Spring!

The hills tell each other, and the listening   5
Valleys hear; all our longing eyes are turned
Up to thy bright pavilions: issue forth,
And let thy holy feet visit our clime.

Come o'er the eastern hills, and let our winds
Kiss thy perfumed garments; let us taste   10
Thy morn and evening breath; scatter thy pearls
Upon our lovesick land that mourns for thee.

O deck her forth with thy fair fingers; pour
Thy soft kisses on her bosom; and put
Thy golden crown upon her languished head,   15
Whose modest tresses were bound up for thee!

To the Evening Star

Thou fair-haired angel of the evening,
Now, while the sun rests on the mountains, light
Thy bright torch of love; thy radiant crown
Put on, and smile upon our evening bed!
Smile on our loves; and, while thou drawest the   5
Blue curtains of the sky, scatter thy silver dew
On every flower that shuts its sweet eyes
In timely sleep. Let thy west wind sleep on
The lake; speak silence with thy glimmering eyes,
And wash the dusk with silver. Soon, full soon,   10
Dost thou withdraw; then the wolf rages wide,
And the lion glares through the dun forest:
The fleeces of our flocks are covered with
Thy sacred dew: protect them with thine influence.

TO THE EVENING STAR 14. **influence:** the astrological term for the star's power over
the world.

The Chimney Sweeper (Innocence)

When my mother died I was very young,
And my father sold me while yet my tongue,
Could scarcely cry, " 'weep, 'weep, 'weep, 'weep."
So your chimneys I sweep and in soot I sleep.

There's little Tom Dacre, who cried when his head   5
That curled like a lamb's back, was shaved, so I said,
"Hush, Tom, never mind it, for when your head's bare,
You know that the soot cannot spoil your white hair."

And so he was quiet, and that very night,
As Tom was a-sleeping he had such a sight,   10
That thousands of sweepers, Dick, Joe, Ned, and Jack
Were all of them locked up in coffins of black.

And by came an Angel who had a bright key,
And he opened the coffins and set them all free.
Then down a green plain leaping, laughing, they run   15
And wash in a river and shine in the sun.

Then naked and white, all their bags left behind,
They rise upon clouds, and sport in the wind.
And the Angel told Tom if he'd be a good boy,
He'd have God for his father and never want joy.   20

And so Tom awoke and we rose in the dark
And got with our bags and our brushes to work.
Though the morning was cold, Tom was happy and warm,
So if all do their duty, they need not fear harm.

The Chimney Sweeper (Experience)

A little black thing among the snow:
Crying 'weep, 'weep, in notes of woe!
Where are thy father and mother, say?
They are both gone up to the church to pray.

Because I was happy upon the heath,   5
And smiled among the winter's snow:

THE CHIMNEY SWEEPER (INNOCENCE)   **3. 'weep:** the child's version of the street cry,
"sweep!" **6. shaved:** to facilitate his climbing inside the chimneys.

They clothed me in the clothes of death,
And taught me to sing the notes of woe.

And because I am happy, and dance and sing,
They think they have done me no injury: 10
And are gone to praise God and his Priest and King,
Who make up a heaven of our misery.

The Sick Rose

O Rose, thou art sick.
The invisible worm
That flies in the night
In the howling storm:

Has found out thy bed   5
Of crimson joy;
And his dark secret love
Does thy life destroy.

The Divine Image (Innocence)

To Mercy, Pity, Peace, and Love,
All pray in their distress:
And to these virtues of delight
Return their thankfulness.

For Mercy, Pity, Peace, and Love,   5
Is God, our Father dear:
And Mercy, Pity, Peace, and Love,
Is Man, his child and care.

For Mercy has a human heart,
Pity, a human face;   10
And Love, the human form divine,
And Peace, the human dress.

Then every man of every clime,
That prays in his distress,
Prays to the human form divine: 15
Love, Mercy, Pity, Peace.

And all must love the human form,
In heathen, Turk, or Jew.
Where Mercy, Love, and Pity dwell
There God is dwelling too.   20

The Human Abstract (Experience)

Pity would be no more,
If we did not make somebody poor;
And Mercy no more could be,
If all were as happy as we;

And mutual fear brings peace,   5
Till the selfish loves increase.
Then Cruelty knits a snare,
And spreads his baits with care.

He sits down with holy fears,
And waters the ground with tears: 10
Then Humility takes its root
Underneath his foot.

Soon spreads the dismal shade
Of Mystery over his head;
And the caterpillar and fly   15
Feed on the Mystery.

And it bears the fruit of Deceit,
Ruddy and sweet to eat;
And the raven his nest has made
In its thickest shade.   20

The Gods of the earth and sea
Sought through Nature to find this Tree;
But their search was all in vain:
There grows one in the human brain.

The Tyger

Tyger, Tyger, burning bright,
In the forests of the night:
What immortal hand or eye
Could frame thy fearful symmetry?

In what distant deeps or skies   5
Burnt the fire of thine eyes!
On what wings dare he aspire?
What the hand, dare seize the fire?

THE HUMAN ABSTRACT (EXPERIENCE) **14. Mystery:** institutionalized religion, which obscures and distorts the true view of life, according to Blake. **19. raven:** as symbol of death. **22. Tree:** the Tree of Mystery is identified with the Tree of the Knowledge of Good and Evil.

And what shoulder, and what art,
Could twist the sinews of thy heart?　　　　10
And when thy heart began to beat,
What dread hand? and what dread feet?

What the hammer? what the chain,
In what furnace was thy brain?
What the anvil? what dread grasp,　　　　15
Dare its deadly terrors clasp?

When the stars threw down their spears
And watered heaven with their tears:
Did he smile his work to see?
Did he who made the Lamb make thee?　　　　20

Tyger, Tyger, burning bright,
In the forests of the night:
What immortal hand or eye
Dare frame thy fearful symmetry?

Ah! Sunflower

Ah Sunflower! weary of time,
Who countest the steps of the sun:
Seeking after that sweet golden clime
Where the traveler's journey is done.

Where the youth pined away with desire,　　　　5
And the pale virgin shrouded in snow,
Arise from their graves and aspire,
Where my Sunflower wishes to go.

Mock On, Mock On

Mock on, mock on, Voltaire, Rousseau,
Mock on, mock on, 'tis all in vain;
You throw the sand against the wind,
And the wind blows it back again.

And every sand becomes a gem　　　　5
Reflected in the beams divine,
Blown back they blind the mocking eye,
But still in Israel's paths they shine.

MOCK ON, MOCK ON 1. **Voltaire, Rousseau:** Blake interpreted both Voltaire and Rousseau as worshipers of Nature, or the world of objects, and mockers of human faith and imagination. 8. **Israel's paths:** the paths taken by the Jews, here representing those who believe in the spiritual imagination, in their flight from Egypt.

The atoms of Democritus,
And Newton's particles of light,   10
Are sands upon the Red Sea shore,
Where Israel's tents do shine so bright.

Robert Burns   (1759–1796)

Holy Willie's Prayer

And send the Godly in a pet to pray—
                                                  POPE.

O thou that in the heavens does dwell!
Wha, as it pleases best thysel,
Sends ane to heaven and ten to h–ll,
          A' for thy glory!
And no for ony gude or ill   5
          They've done before thee.—

I bless and praise thy matchless might,
When thousands thou has left in night,
That I am here before thy sight,
          For gifts and grace,   10
A burning and a shining light
          To a' this place.—

What was I, or my generation,
That I should get such exaltation?
I, wha deserv'd most just damnation,   15
          For broken laws
Sax thousand years ere my creation,
          Thro' Adam's cause!

When from my mother's womb I fell,
Thou might hae plunged me deep in hell,   20

9–10. atoms . . . light: classical and modern theories of the nature of matter.
HOLY WILLIE'S PRAYER   Burns explains in the "argument" to the poem that Holy
Willie (William Fisher) was an elder of the Presbyterian parish of Mauchline, who together with the parish minister, William Auld, brought a complaint against a local
lawyer, Gavin Hamilton, in the ecclesiastical courts. Hamilton, incide lly Burn's landlord and patron, was accused of not worshiping regularly and traveling on Sunday.
Epigraph: Pope's *Rape of the Lock*, iv. 64. 1–6. O thou . . . thee: according to the
Calvinist doctrine of predestination, salvation and damnation were unalterably determined from eternity. Willie, of course, regards himself as one of the "elect," or saved.
4. A': all. 10. gifts: abilities. 11. burning . . . light: John the Baptist, to whom Willie
is comparing himself, was "a burning and a shining light" (John 5:35). 13. generation:
begetting (?); class of person (?). 17. Sax: six. According to accepted chronology the
world was created in 4004 B.C.

To gnash my gooms, and weep, and wail,
                In burning lakes,
Where damnèd devils roar and yell
                Chain'd to their stakes.—

Yet I am here, a chosen sample,   25
To shew thy grace is great and ample:
I'm here, a pillar o' thy temple
                Strong as a rock,
A guide, a ruler, and example
                To a' thy flock.—   30

O L—d thou kens what zeal I bear,
When drinkers drink, and swearers swear,
And singin' there, and dancin' here,
                Wi' great an' sma';
For I am keepet by thy fear,   35
                Free frae them a'.—

But yet—O L—d—confess I must—
At times I'm fash'd wi' fleshly lust;
And sometimes too, in warldly trust
                Vile Self gets in;   40
But thou remembers we are dust,
                Defil'd wi' sin.—

O L—d—yestreen—thou kens—wi' Meg—
Thy pardon I sincerely beg!
O may 't ne'er be a living plague,   45
                To my dishonor!
And I'll ne'er lift a lawless leg
                Again upon her.—

Besides, I farther maun avow,
Wi' Leezie's lass, three times—I trow—   50
But L—d, that friday I was fou
                When I cam near her;
Or else, thou kens, thy servant true
                Wad never steer her.—

Maybe thou lets this fleshy thorn   55
Buffet thy servant e'en and morn,
Lest he o'er proud and high should turn,
                That he's sae gifted;
If sae, thy hand maun e'en be borne
                Untill thou lift it —   60

---

27. pillar . . . temple: "Him that overcometh will I make a pillar in the temple of my God" (Revelation 3:12). **31. kens:** knows. **38. fash'd:** troubled. **39–40. sometimes . . . gets in:** Willie was reported to have helped himself to the church collection. **43. yestreen:** last night. **49. maun:** must. **50. trow:** believe. **51. fou:** drunk. **54. steer:** stir, meddle with.

L—d bless thy Chosen in this place,
For here thou has a chosen race:
But G—d, confound their stubborn face,
   And blast their name,
Wha bring thy rulers to disgrace 65
   And open shame.—

L—d mind Gaun Hamilton's deserts!
He drinks, and swears, and plays at cartes,
Yet has sae mony taking arts
   Wi' Great and Sma', 70
Frae G—d's ain priest the people's hearts
   He steals awa.—

And when we chasten'd him therefore,
Thou kens how he bred sic a splore,
And set the warld in a roar 75
   O' laughin at us:
Curse thou his basket and his store,
   Kail and potatoes.—

L—d hear my earnest cry and prayer
Against that Presbytry of Ayr! 80
Thy strong right hand, L—d, make it bare
   Upon their heads!
L—d visit them, and dinna spare,
   For their misdeeds!

O L—d my G—d, that glib-tongu'd Aiken! 85
My very heart and flesh are quaking
To think how I sat, sweating, shaking,
   And p—ss'd wi' dread,
While he, wi' hingin lips and snakin,
   Held up his head. 90

L—d, in thy day o' vengeance try him!
L—d visit him that did employ him!
And pass not in thy mercy by them,
   Nor hear their prayer;
But for thy people's sake destroy them, 95
   And dinna spare!

But L—d, remember me and mine
Wi' mercies temporal and divine!

74. sic a splore: such a riot. **77. store:** abundance, goods. Willie echoes the curse of Deuteronomy 28:17, "Cursed shall be thy basket and thy store." **78. Kail:** cabbage. **79. earnest . . . prayer:** a cant Presbyterian phrase. **80. Presbytry of Ayr:** an ecclesiastical court. **85. Aiken:** Robert Aiken, Hamilton's lawyer. **89. hingin:** hanging. **snakin:** sneaking. **92. visit:** punish.

That I for grace and gear may shine,
              Excell'd by nane!
And a' the glory shall be thine!
              AMEN! AMEN!

100

To a Mouse, On Turning Her Up in Her Nest, with the Plough, November 1785

WEE, sleeket, cowran, tim'rous beastie,
O, what a panic 's in thy breastie!
Thou need na start awa sae hasty,
              Wi' bickering brattle!
I wad be laith to rin an' chase thee,
              Wi' murd'ring pattle!

5

I'm truly sorry Man's dominion
Has broken Nature's social union,
An' justifies that ill opinion,
              Which makes thee startle,
At me, thy poor, earth-born companion,
              An' fellow-mortal!

10

I doubt na, whyles, but thou may thieve;
What then? poor beastie, thou maun live!
A daimen-icker in a thrave
              'S a sma' request:
I'll get a blessin wi' the lave,
              An' never miss 't!

15

Thy wee-bit housie, too, in ruin!
It's silly wa's the win's are strewin!
An' naething, now, to big a new ane,
              O' foggage green!
An' bleak December's winds ensuin,
              Baith snell an' keen!

20

Thou saw the fields laid bare an' wast,
An' weary Winter comin fast,
An' cozie here, beneath the blast,
              Thou thought to dwell,
Till crash! the cruel coulter past
              Out thro' thy cell.

25

30

---

99. gear: worldly goods.
TO A MOUSE 1. sleeket: sleek. 4. bickering brattle: noisy scamper. 5. laith to rin:
loath to run. 6. pattle: plowstaff. 13. whyles: sometimes. 14. maun: must. 15. daimen-
icker in a thrave: an occasional ear in twenty-four sheaves. 17. lave: leave (i.e. rest).
20. silly wa's: feeble walls. 21. big: build. 22. foggage green: rank grass. 24. snell:
sharp.

That wee-bit heap o' leaves an' stibble,
Has cost thee monie a weary nibble!
Now thou's turn'd out, for a' thy trouble,
　　　But house or hald,
To thole the Winter's sleety dribble, 35
　　　An' cranreuch cauld!

But Mousie, thou are no thy-lane,
In proving foresight may be vain:
The best laid schemes o' Mice an' Men,
　　　Gang aft agley, 40
An' lea'e us nought but grief an' pain,
　　　For promis'd joy!

Still, thou art blest, compar'd wi' me!
The present only toucheth thee:
But Och! I backward cast my e'e, 45
　　　On prospects drear!
An' forward, tho' I canna see,
　　　I guess an' fear!

The Rantin Dog the Daddie O't

O Wha my babie-clouts will buy,
O Wha will tent me when I cry;
Wha will kiss me where I lie,
The rantin dog the daddie o't.

O Wha will own he did the faut, 5
O Wha will buy the groanin maut,
O Wha will tell me how to ca't,
The rantin dog the daddie o't.

When I mount the Creepie-chair,
Wha will sit beside me there, 10
Gie me Rob, I'll seek nae mair,
The rantin dog the Daddie o't.

---

31. stibble: stubble. **34. But . . . hald:** without house or home. **35. thole:** endure.
36. cranreuch: hoarfrost. **37. no thy-lane:** not alone. **40. Gang aft agley:** go often awry.
45. e'e: eye.
THE RANTIN DOG "Ranting" means "rollicking." **1. babie-clouts:** baby clothes. **2. tent:**
comfort. **5. faut:** fault. **6. groanin maut:** malt ale for the midwives at the birth. **7. how
to ca't:** what to name it. **9. Creepie-chair:** the stool of repentance in the church. The
"kirk session" (parish court) had the power to punish moral lapses. **11. Gie me Rob:**
give me Robert Burns.

Wha will crack to me my lane;
Wha will mak me fidgin fain;
Wha will kiss me o'er again   15
The rantin dog the Daddie o't.

Ae Fond Kiss

Ae fond kiss, and then we sever;
Ae fareweel, and then for ever!
Deep in heart-wrung tears I'll pledge thee,
Warring sighs and groans I'll wage thee.—

Who shall say that Fortune grieves him,   5
While the star of hope she leaves him:
Me, nae chearful twinkle lights me;
Dark despair around benights me.—

I'll ne'er blame my partial fancy,
Naething could resist my Nancy: 10
But to see her, was to love her;
Love but her, and love for ever.—

Had we never lov'd sae kindly,
Had we never lov'd sae blindly!
Never met—or never parted,   15
We had ne'er been broken-hearted.—

Fare-thee-weel, thou first and fairest!
Fare-thee-weel, thou best and dearest!
Thine be ilka joy and treasure,
Peace, Enjoyment, Love and Pleasure!—   20

Ae fond kiss, and then we sever!
Ae fareweel, Alas, for ever!
Deep in heart-wrung tears I'll pledge thee,
Warring sighs and groans I'll wage thee.—

Green Grow the Rashes, O

CHORUS

Green grow the rashes, O;
Green grow the rashes, O,
The sweetest hours that e'er I spend,
Are spent amang the lasses, O.

---

13. crack . . . lane: talk to me alone. 15. fidgin fain: sexually excited.
AE FOND KISS "Ae" means "one." 4. wage: pledge. 19. ilka: every.

I

THERE's nought but care on ev'ry han',
 In ev'ry hour that passes, O:
What signifies the life o' man,
 An' 'twere na for the lasses, O.

      Green grow, etc.

II

The warly race may riches chase,   5
 An' riches still may fly them, O;
An' tho' at last they catch them fast,
 Their hearts can ne'er enjoy them, O.

      Green grow, etc.

III

But gie me a canny hour at e'en,
 My arms about my Dearie, O;   10
An' warly cares, an' warly men,
 May a' gae tapsalteerie, O!

      Green grow, etc.

IV

For you sae douse, ye sneer at this,
 Ye're nought but senseless asses, O:
The wisest Man the warl' e'er saw,   15
 He dearly lov'd the lasses, O.

      Green grow, etc.

V

Auld Nature swears, the lovely Dears
 Her noblest work she classes, O:
Her prentice han' she try'd on man,
 An' then she made the lasses, O.   20

      Green grow, etc.

William Wordsworth (1770–1850)

It Is a Beauteous Evening

It is a beauteous evening, calm and free,
The holy time is quiet as a nun
Breathless with adoration; the broad sun
Is sinking down in its tranquillity;

GREEN GROW THE RASHES, O   "Rashes" means "rushes." This is Burns's version of an old song. **5. warly:** wordly. **9. gie . . . canny:** give me a pleasant. **12. a' gae tapsalteerie:** all go topsy-turvy. **13. sae douse:** so prim. **15. wisest Man:** King Solomon.

The gentleness of heaven broods o'er the sea: 5
Listen! the mighty being is awake,
And doth with his eternal motion make
A sound like thunder—everlastingly.
Dear Child! dear Girl! that walkest with me here,
If thou appear untouched by solemn thought,   10
Thy nature is not therefore less divine:
Thou liest in Abraham's bosom all the year;
And worship'st at the Temple's inner shrine,
God being with thee when we know it not.

The World Is Too Much with Us

The world is too much with us; late and soon,
Getting and spending, we lay waste our powers:
Little we see in nature that is ours;
We have given our hearts away, a sordid boon!
This sea that bares her bosom to the moon,   5
The winds that will be howling at all hours,
And are upgathered now like sleeping flowers,
For this, for everything, we are out of tune;
It moves us not.—Great God! I'd rather be
A pagan suckled in a creed outworn;   10
So might I, standing on this pleasant lea,
Have glimpses that would make me less forlorn;
Have sight of Proteus rising from the sea;
Or hear old Triton blow his wreathèd horn.

Composed upon Westminster Bridge

September 3, 1802

Earth has not anything to show more fair:
Dull would he be of soul who could pass by
A sight so touching in its majesty:
This city now doth, like a garment, wear
The beauty of the morning; silent, bare,   5
Ships, towers, domes, theaters, and temples lie
Open unto the fields, and to the sky;
All bright and glittering in the smokeless air.
Never did sun more beautifully steep
In his first splendor, valley, rock, or hill;   10

IT IS A BEAUTEOUS EVENING   **12. Abraham's bosom:** where those in heaven rest after
death (Luke 16:22). **13. Temple's . . . shrine:** perhaps a reference to the sanctuary
(the Holy of Holies) of the Temple of Solomon, which contained the Ark of the Covenant.

THE WORLD IS TOO MUCH WITH US   **13–14. Proteus . . . Triton:** two classical sea
gods; Triton was often represented as blowing on a conch shell.

Ne'er saw I, never felt, a calm so deep!
The river glideth at his own sweet will:
Dear God! the very houses seem asleep;
And all that mighty heart is lying still!

To Toussaint L'Ouverture

Toussaint, the most unhappy man of men!
Whether the whistling rustic tend his plough
Within thy hearing, or thy head be now
Pillowed in some deep dungeon's earless den—
O miserable chieftain! where and when   5
Wilt thou find patience! Yet die not; do thou
Wear rather in thy bonds a cheerful brow:
Though fallen thyself, never to rise again,
Live, and take comfort. Thou hast left behind
Powers that will work for thee; air, earth, and skies;   10
There's not a breathing of the common wind
That will forget thee; thou hast great allies;
Thy friends are exultations, agonies,
And love, and man's unconquerable mind.

Resolution and Independence

There was a roaring in the wind all night;
The rain came heavily and fell in floods;
But now the sun is rising calm and bright;
The birds are singing in the distant woods;
Over his own sweet voice the stockdove broods;   5
The jay makes answer as the magpie chatters;
And all the air is filled with pleasant noise of waters.

All things that love the sun are out of doors;
The sky rejoices in the morning's birth;
The grass is bright with raindrops;—on the moors   10
The hare is running races in her mirth;
And with her feet she from the plashy earth
Raises a mist, that, glittering in the sun,
Runs with her all the way, wherever she doth run.

I was a traveler then upon the moor;   15
I saw the hare that raced about with joy;
I heard the woods and distant waters roar;
Or heard them not, as happy as a boy:

TO TOUSSAINT L'OUVERTURE   Toussaint L'Ouverture led a slave revolt against the
French in Haiti and Santo Domingo, which was suppressed by Napoleon in 1802.
Toussaint died the following year in a French dungeon. This sonnet was composed in
August 1802.

The pleasant season did my heart employ:
My old remembrances went from me wholly;   20
And all the ways of men, so vain and melancholy.

But, as it sometimes chanceth, from the might
Of joy in minds that can no further go,
As high as we have mounted in delight
In our dejection do we sink as low;   25
To me that morning did it happen so;
And fears and fancies thick upon me came;
Dim sadness—and blind thoughts, I knew not, nor could name.

I heard the skylark warbling in the sky;
And I bethought me of the playful hare: 30
Even such a happy child of earth am I;
Even as these blissful creatures do I fare;
Far from the world I walk, and from all care;
But there may come another day to me—
Solitude, pain of heart, distress, and poverty.   35

My whole life I have lived in pleasant thought,
As if life's business were a summer mood;
As if all needful things would come unsought
To genial faith, still rich in genial good;
But how can he expect that others should   40
Build for him, sow for him, and at his call
Love him, who for himself will take no heed at all?

I thought of Chatterton, the marvelous boy,
The sleepless soul that perished in his pride;
Of him who walked in glory and in joy   45
Following his plough, along the mountainside:
By our own spirits are we deified:
We poets in our youth begin in gladness,
But thereof come in the end despondency and madness.

Now, whether it were by peculiar grace,   50
A leading from above, a something given,
Yet it befell that, in this lonely place,
When I with these untoward thoughts had striven,
Beside a pool bare to the eye of heaven
I saw a man before me unawares: 55
The oldest man he seemed that ever wore gray hairs.

As a huge stone is sometimes seen to lie
Couched on the bald top of an eminence;

RESOLUTION AND INDEPENDENCE   **39. genial:** innate. **43–44. Chatterton . . . pride:**
a precocious poet of considerable ability, who died at the age of 17, presumably from
self-administered poison. **45. him:** Robert Burns, regarded as a self-taught poet, who
died harassed and unhappy. **50. peculiar:** special.

Wonder to all who do the same espy,
By what means it could thither come, and whence; 60
So that it seems a thing endued with sense:
Like a sea-beast crawled forth, that on a shelf
Of rock or sand reposeth, there to sun itself;

Such seemed this man, not all alive nor dead,
Nor all asleep—in his extreme old age: 65
His body was bent double, feet and head
Coming together in life's pilgrimage;
As if some dire constraint of pain, or rage
Of sickness felt by him in times long past,
A more than human weight upon his frame had cast. 70

Himself he propped, limbs, body, and pale face,
Upon a long gray staff of shaven wood;
And, still as I drew near with gentle pace,
Upon the margin of that moorish flood
Motionless as a cloud the old man stood, 75
That heareth not the loud winds when they call,
And moveth all together, if it move at all.

At length, himself unsettling, he the pond
Stirred with his staff, and fixedly did look
Upon the muddy water, which he conned, 80
As if he had been reading in a book;
And now a stranger's privilege I took,
And, drawing to his side, to him did say,
"This morning gives us promise of a glorious day."

A gentle answer did the old man make, 85
In courteous speech which forth he slowly drew:
And him with further words I thus bespake,
"What occupation do you there pursue?
This is a lonesome place for one like you."
Ere he replied, a flash of mild surprise 90
Broke from the sable orbs of his yet-vivid eyes.

His words came feebly, from a feeble chest,
But each in solemn order followed each,
With something of a lofty utterance dressed—
Choice word and measured phrase, above the reach 95
Of ordinary men; a stately speech;
Such as grave Livers do in Scotland use,
Religious men, who give to God and man their dues.

He told that to these waters he had come
To gather leeches, being old and poor: 100

97. **grave Livers**: serious-minded men. 100. **leeches**: then used medically to suck blood.

Employment hazardous and wearisome!
And he had many hardships to endure:
From pond to pond he roamed, from moor to moor;
Housing, with God's good help, by choice or chance;
And in this way he gained an honest maintenance.   105

The old man still stood talking by my side;
But now his voice to me was like a stream
Scarce heard; nor word from word could I divide;
And the whole body of the man did seem
Like one whom I had met with in a dream;   110
Or like a man from some far region sent,
To give me human strength, by apt admonishment.

My former thoughts returned: the fear that kills;
And hope that is unwilling to be fed;
Cold, pain, and labor, and all fleshly ills;   115
And mighty poets in their misery dead.
—Perplexed, and longing to be comforted,
My question eagerly did I renew,
"How is it that you live, and what is it you do?"

He with a smile did then his words repeat;   120
And said that, gathering leeches, far and wide
He traveled; stirring thus about his feet
The waters of the pools where they abide.
"Once I could meet with them on every side,
But they have dwindled long by slow decay;   125
Yet still I persevere, and find them where I may."

While he was talking thus, the lonely place,
The old man's shape, and speech—all troubled me:
In my mind's eye I seemed to see him pace
About the weary moors continually,   130
Wandering about alone and silently.
While I these thoughts within myself pursued,
He, having made a pause, the same discourse renewed.

And soon with this he other matter blended,
Cheerfully uttered, with demeanor kind,   135
But stately in the main; and, when he ended,
I could have laughed myself to scorn to find
In that decrepit man so firm a mind.
"God," said I, "be my help and stay secure;
I'll think of the leech-gatherer on the lonely moor!"   140

139. stay: support.

The Solitary Reaper

Behold her, single in the field,
Yon solitary Highland Lass!
Reaping and singing by herself;
Stop here, or gently pass!
Alone she cuts and binds the grain,   5
And signs a melancholy strain;
O listen! for the vale profound
Is overflowing with the sound.

No nightingale did ever chaunt
More welcome notes to weary bands   10
Of travelers in some shady haunt,
Among Arabian sands;
A voice so thrilling ne'er was heard
In spring-time from the cuckoo-bird,
Breaking the silence of the seas   15
Among the farthest Hebrides.

Will no one tell me what she sings?—
Perhaps the plaintive numbers flow
For old, unhappy, far-off things,
And battles long ago;   20
Or is it some more humble lay,
Familiar matter of today?
Some natural sorrow, loss, or pain,
That has been, and may be again?

Whate'er the theme, the Maiden sang   25
As if her song could have no ending;
I saw her singing at her work,
And o'er the sickle bending;—
I listened, motionless and still;
And, as I mounted up the hill,   30
The music in my heart I bore,
Long after it was heard no more.

Strange Fits of Passion

Strange fits of passion have I known:
And I will dare to tell,
But in the lover's ear alone,
What once to me befell.

THE SOLITARY REAPER **17. Will . . . sings:** Highlanders mainly still spoke Gaelic.
18. numbers: stanzas. **21. lay:** song.

When she I loved looked every day   5
Fresh as a rose in June,
I to her cottage bent my way,
Beneath an evening moon.

Upon the moon I fixed my eye,
All over the wide lea;   10
With quickening pace my horse drew nigh
Those paths so dear to me.

And now we reached the orchard-plot;
And, as we climbed the hill,
The sinking moon to Lucy's cot   15
Came near, and nearer still.

In one of those sweet dreams I slept,
Kind Nature's gentlest boon!
And all the while my eyes I kept
On the descending moon.   20

My horse moved on; hoof after hoof
He raised, and never stopped:
When down behind the cottage roof,
At once, the bright moon dropped.

What fond and wayward thoughts will slide   25
Into a lover's head!
"O mercy!" to myself I cried,
"If Lucy should be dead!"

A Slumber Did My Spirit Seal

A slumber did my spirit seal;
  I had no human fears:
She seemed a thing that could not feel
  The touch of earthly years.

No motion has she now, no force;   5
  She neither hears nor sees;
Rolled round in earth's diurnal course,
  With rocks, and stones, and trees.

STRANGE FITS OF PASSION   **15. cot:** cottage. **25. fond:** foolish; tender.

Lines Composed a Few Miles Above Tintern Abbey

On Revisiting the Banks of the Wye
During a Tour. July 13, 1798

[handwritten margin note: Contrast bet. where he was there before + now that he's come back.]

Five years have passed; five summers, with the length
Of five long winters! and again I hear
These waters, rolling from their mountain springs
With a soft inland murmur.—Once again
Do I behold these steep and lofty cliffs,   5
That on a wild secluded scene impress
Thoughts of more deep seclusion; and connect
The landscape with the quiet of the sky.
The day is come when I again repose
Here, under this dark sycamore, and view   10
These plots of cottage-ground, these orchard-tufts,
Which at this season, with their unripe fruits,
Are clad in one green hue, and lose themselves
'Mid groves and copses. Once again I see
These hedgerows, hardly hedgerows, little lines   15
Of sportive wood run wild; these pastoral farms,
Green to the very door; and wreaths of smoke
Sent up, in silence from among the trees!
With some uncertain notice, as might seem
Of vagrant dwellers in the houseless woods,   20
Or of some hermit's cave, where by his fire
The hermit sits alone.

                These beauteous forms
Through a long absence, have not been to me
As is a landscape to a blind man's eye:
But oft, in lonely rooms, and 'mid the din   25
Of towns and cities, I have owed to them
In hours of weariness, sensations sweet,
Felt in the blood, and felt along the heart;
And passing even into my purer mind,
With tranquil restoration:—feelings too   30
Of unremembered pleasure; such, perhaps,
As have no slight or trivial influence
On that best portion of a good man's life,
His little, nameless, unremembered acts
Of kindness and of love. Nor less, I trust,   35
To them I may have owed another gift,
Of aspect more sublime; that blessèd mood,
In which the burthen of the mystery,
In which the heavy and the weary weight

TINTERN ABBEY   The ruins of Tintern Abbey lie in Monmouthshire on the Welsh border. **11. orchard-tufts:** clumps of trees. **14. copses:** thickets of shrubbery or small trees.

Of all this unintelligible world,   40
Is lightened—that serene and blessèd mood,
In which the affections gently lead us on—
Until, the breath of this corporeal frame
And even the motion of our human blood
Almost suspended, we are laid asleep   45
In body, and become a living soul:
While with an eye made quiet by the power
Of harmony, and the deep power of joy,
We see into the life of things.
                              If this
Be but a vain belief, yet, oh! how oft—   50
In darkness and amid the many shapes
Of joyless daylight; when the fretful stir
Unprofitable, and the fever of the world,
Have hung upon the beatings of my heart—
How oft, in spirit, have I turned to thee,   55
O sylvan Wye! thou wanderer through the woods,
How often has my spirit turned to thee!

    And now, with gleams of half-extinguished thought,
With many recognitions dim and faint,
And somewhat of a sad perplexity,   60
The picture of the mind revives again:
While here I stand, not only with the sense
Of present pleasure, but with pleasing thoughts
That in this moment there is life and food
For future years. And so I dare to hope,   65
Though changed, no doubt, from what I was when first
I came among these hills; when like a roe
I bounded o'er the mountains, by the sides
Of the deep rivers, and the lonely streams,
Wherever nature led—more like a man   70
Flying from something that he dreads, than one
Who sought the thing he loved. For nature then
(The coarser pleasures of my boyish days,
And their glad animal movements all gone by)
To me was all in all.—I cannot paint   75
What then I was. The sounding cataract
Haunted me like a passion; the tall rock,
The mountain, and the deep and gloomy wood,
Their colors and their forms, were then to me
An appetite; a feeling and a love   80
That had no need of a remoter charm
By thought supplied, nor any interest
Unborrowed from the eye.—That time is past,
And all its aching joys are now no more,
And all its dizzy raptures. Not for this   85
Faint I, nor mourn nor murmur; other gifts
Have followed; for such loss, I would believe,

Abundant recompense. For I have learned
To look on nature, not as in the hour
Of thoughtless youth; but hearing oftentimes   90
The still, sad music of humanity,
Nor harsh nor grating, though of ample power
To chasten and subdue. And I have felt
A presence that disturbs me with the joy
Of elevated thoughts; a sense sublime   95
Of something far more deeply interfused,
Whose dwelling is the light of setting suns,
And the round ocean and the living air,
And the blue sky, and in the mind of man;
A motion and a spirit, that impels   100
All thinking things, all objects of all thought,
And rolls through all things. Therefore am I still
A lover of the meadows and the woods,
And mountains; and of all that we behold
From this green earth; of all the mighty world   105
Of eye, and ear—both what they half create,
And what perceive; well pleased to recognize
In nature and the language of the sense,
The anchor of my purest thoughts, the nurse,
The guide, the guardian of my heart, and soul   110
Of all my moral being.
                    Nor perchance,
If I were not thus taught, should I the more
Suffer my genial spirits to decay:
For thou art with me here upon the banks
Of this fair river; thou my dearest friend,   115
My dear, dear friend; and in thy voice I catch
The language of my former heart, and read
My former pleasures in the shooting lights
Of thy wild eyes. Oh! yet a little while
May I behold in thee what I was once,   120
My dear, dear sister! and this prayer I make,
Knowing that nature never did betray
The heart that loved her; 'tis her privilege,
Through all the years of this our life, to lead
From joy to joy: for she can so inform   125
The mind that is within us, so impress
With quietness and beauty, and so feed
With lofty thoughts, that neither evil tongues,
Rash judgments, nor the sneers of selfish men,
Nor greetings where no kindness is, nor all   130
The dreary intercourse of daily life,
Shall e'er prevail against us, or disturb
Our cheerful faith, that all which we behold

---

108. sense: senses. 113. genial spirits: innate feelings, attributes, or powers. 115. friend: the sister of l. 121. 125. inform: give form to.

Is full of blessings. Therefore let the moon
Shine on thee in thy solitary walk;   135
And let the misty mountain winds be free
To blow against thee: and, in after years,
When these wild ecstasies shall be matured
Into a sober pleasure; when thy mind
Shall be a mansion for all lovely forms,   140
Thy memory be as a dwelling place
For all sweet sounds and harmonies; oh! then,
If solitude, or fear, or pain, or grief,
Should be thy portion, with what healing thoughts
Of tender joy wilt thou remember me,   145
And these my exhortations! Nor, perchance—
If I should be where I no more can hear
Thy voice, nor catch from thy wild eyes these gleams
Of past existence—wilt thou then forget
That on the banks of this delightful stream   150
We stood together, and that I, so long
A worshiper of nature, hither came
Unwearied in that service; rather say
With warmer love—oh! with far deeper zeal
Of holier love. Nor wilt thou then forget   155
That after many wanderings, many years
Of absence, these steep woods and lofty cliffs,
And this green pastoral landscape, were to me
More dear, both for themselves and for thy sake!

Ode: Intimations of Immortality
from Recollections of Early Childhood

The child is father of the man;
And I could wish my days to be
Bound each to each by natural piety.

There was a time when meadow, grove, and stream,
The earth, and every common sight,
    To me did seem
    Appareled in celestial light,
The glory and the freshness of a dream.   5
It is not now as it hath been of yore—
    Turn wheresoe'er I may,
    By night or day,
The things which I have seen I now can see no more.

---

140. forms: see l. 22.

ODE: INTIMATIONS   Wordsworth commented that he was not advocating the Platonic doctrine of the pre-existence of the soul as a religious belief, but taking this doctrine as a credible postulate for this poem. **Epigraph:** the last lines of Wordsworth's poem, "My Heart Leaps Up." **5. glory:** almost with its root meaning of "radiance" or "splendor."

The rainbow comes and goes, 10
And lovely is the rose,
The moon doth with delight
Look round her when the heavens are bare,
Waters on a starry night
Are beautiful and fair; 15
The sunshine is a glorious birth;
But yet I know, where'er I go,
That there hath passed away a glory from the earth.

Now, while the birds thus sing a joyous song,
And while the young lambs bound 20
As to the tabor's sound,
To me alone there came a thought of grief:
A timely utterance gave that thought relief,
And I again am strong:
The cataracts blow their trumpets from the steep; 25
No more shall grief of mine the season wrong;
I hear the echoes through the mountains throng,
The winds come to me from the fields of sleep.
And all the earth is gay;
Land and sea 30
Give themselves up to jollity,
And with the heart of May
Doth every beast keep holiday—
Thou Child of joy,
Shout round me, let me hear thy shouts, thou happy
Shepherd-boy! 35

Ye blessèd creatures, I have heard the call
Ye to each other make; I see
The heavens laugh with you in your jubilee;
My heart is at your festival,
My head hath its coronal, 40
The fullness of your bliss, I feel—I feel it all.
Oh evil day! if I were sullen
While earth herself is adorning,
This sweet May morning,
And the children are culling
On every side,
In a thousand valleys far and wide,
Fresh flowers; while the sun shines warm,
And the babe leaps up on his mother's arm— 50
I hear, I hear, with joy I hear!
—But there's a tree, of many, one,
A single field which I have looked upon,
Both of them speak of something that is gone:

21. tabor: a small drum. 40. coronal: coronet of flowers to celebrate May.

The pansy at my feet   55
Doth the same tale repeat:
Whither is fled the visionary gleam?
Where is it now, the glory and the dream?

Our birth is but a sleep and a forgetting:
The soul that rises with us, our life's star,   60
    Hath had elsewhere its setting,
        And cometh from afar:
    Not in entire forgetfulness,
    And not in utter nakedness,
But trailing clouds of glory do we come   65
        From God, who is our home:
Heaven lies about us in our infancy!
Shades of the prison-house begin to close
        Upon the growing boy,
But he beholds the light, and whence it flows,   70
        He sees it in his joy;
The youth, who daily farther from the east
        Must travel, still is nature's priest,
        And by the vision splendid
        Is on his way attended;   75
At length the man perceives it die away,
And fade into the light of common day.

Earth fills her lap with pleasures of her own;
Yearnings she hath in her own natural kind,
And, even with something of a mother's mind,   80
        And no unworthy aim,
        The homely nurse doth all she can
To make her foster child, her inmate man,
        Forget the glories he hath known,
And that imperial palace whence he came.   85

Behold the Child among his newborn blisses,
A six-years' darling of a pigmy size!
See, where 'mid work of his own hand he lies,
Fretted by sallies of his mother's kisses,
With light upon him from his father's eyes!   90
See, at his feet, some little plan or chart,
Some fragment from his dream of human life,
Shaped by himself with newly learnèd art;
        A wedding or a festival,
        A mourning or a funeral;   95
            And this hath now his heart,
        And unto this he frames his song;
            Then will he fit his tongue

---

61. Hath had . . . setting: i.e., pre-existed. **72. east:** where the soul, "our life's star" (l. 60), rises like the sun. **82. homely:** belonging to the home, domestic, familiar.

To dialogues of business, love, or strife;
　　　But it will not be long   100
　　　Ere this be thrown aside,
　　　And with new joy and pride
The little actor cons another part;
Filling from time to time his "humorous stage"
With all the persons, down to palsied age,   105
That life brings with her in her equipage;
　　　As if his whole vocation
　　　Were endless imitation.

Thou, whose exterior semblance doth belie
　　　Thy soul's immensity;   110
Thou best philosopher, who yet dost keep
Thy heritage, thou eye among the blind,
That, deaf and silent, read'st the eternal deep,
Haunted forever by the eternal mind—
　　　Mighty prophet! Seer blessed!   115
　　　On whom those truths do rest,
Which we are toiling all our lives to find,
In darkness lost, the darkness of the grave;
Thou, over whom thy immortality
Broods like the day, a master o'er a slave,   120
A presence which is not to be put by;
Thou little Child, yet glorious in the might
Of heaven-born freedom on thy being's height,
Why with such earnest pains dost thou provoke
The years to bring the inevitable yoke,   125
Thus blindly with thy blessedness at strife?
Full soon thy soul shall have her earthly freight,
And custom lie upon thee with a weight,
Heavy as frost, and deep almost as life!

　　　O joy! that in our embers   130
　　　Is something that doth live,
　　　That nature yet remembers
　　　What was so fugitive!
The thought of our past years in me doth breed
Perpetual benediction: not indeed   135
For that which is most worthy to be blessed;
Delight and liberty, the simple creed
Of childhood, whether busy or at rest,
With new-fledged hope still fluttering in his breast—
　　　Not for these I raise   140
　　　The song of thanks and praise;
　　　But for those obstinate questionings

---

103. **cons**: studies. 104. **"humorous stage"**: this phrase from a sonnet by the Elizabethan poet Samuel Daniel refers to the human "drama" in which we are marked by our distinctive "humor" or basic character and temperament. 106. **equipage**: train of attendants. 109. **Thou**: the Child (l. 86). 124. **provoke**: call forth.

Of sense and outward things,
Fallings from us, vanishings;
  Blank misgivings of a creature   145
Moving about in worlds not realized,
High instincts before which our mortal nature
Did tremble like a guilty thing surprised;
    But for those first affections,
    Those shadowy recollections,   150
    Which, be they what they may,
Are yet the fountain light of all our day,
Are yet a master light of all our seeing;
    Uphold us, cherish, and have power to make
Our noisy years seem moments in the being   155
Of the eternal silence: truths that wake
        To perish never;
Which neither listlessness, nor mad endeavor,
        Nor man nor boy,
Nor all that is at enmity with joy,   160
Can utterly abolish or destroy.
        Hence in a season of calm weather
        Though inland far we be,
Our souls have sight of that immortal sea
        Which brought us hither,   165
        Can in a moment travel thither,
And see the children sport upon the shore,
And hear the mighty waters rolling evermore.

Then sing, ye birds, sing, sing a joyous song!
        And let the young lambs bound   170
        As to the tabor's sound!
We in thought will join your throng,
        Ye that pipe and ye that play,
        Ye that through your hearts today
        Feel the gladness of the May!   175
What though the radiance which was once so bright
Be now forever taken from my sight,
        Though nothing can bring back the hour
Of splendor in the grass, of glory in the flower:
        We will grieve not, rather find   180
        Strength in what remains behind;
        In the primal sympathy
        Which having been must ever be;
        In the soothing thoughts that spring
        Out of human suffering;   185
        In the faith that looks through death,
In years that bring the philosophic mind.

146. not realized: not made real. **182. primal sympathy:** basic connection, either
between pre-existing and existing things, or between child and man.

And O, ye fountains, meadows, hills, and groves,
Forebode not any severing of our loves!
Yet in my heart of hearts I feel your might;   190
I only have relinquished one delight
To live beneath your more habitual sway.
I love the brooks which down their channels fret,
Even more than when I tripped lightly as they;
The innocent brightness of a newborn day   195
          Is lovely yet;
The clouds that gather round the setting sun
Do take a sober coloring from an eye
That hath kept watch o'er man's mortality;
Another race hath been, and other palms are won.   200
Thanks to the human heart by which we live,
Thanks to its tenderness, its joys, and fears,
To me the meanest flower that blows can give
Thoughts that do often lie too deep for tears.

Samuel Taylor Coleridge   *(1772–1834)*

Dejection: An Ode

Late, late yestreen I saw the new moon,
With the old moon in her arms:
And I fear, I fear, my master dear!
We shall have a deadly storm.
         Ballad of Sir Patrick Spence

Well! If the bard was weather-wise, who made
  The grand old ballad of Sir Patrick Spence,
  This night, so tranquil now, will not go hence
Unroused by winds, that ply a busier trade
Than those which mold yon cloud in lazy flakes,   5
Or the dull sobbing draft, that moans and rakes
Upon the strings of this Aeolian lute,
    Which better far were mute.
For lo! the new-moon winter-bright!
And overspread with phantom light,   10
(With swimming phantom light o'erspread
But rimmed and circled by a silver thread)

---

200. palms: prizes. **203. meanest:** most humble. **203. blows:** blossoms.
DEJECTION **2. ballad . . . Spence:** See pp. 75–76. **7. Aeolian lute:** a soundbox with strings or wires stretched over it that makes musical sounds when the wind blows across it.

I see the old moon in her lap, foretelling
　　The coming-on of rain and squally blast.
And oh! that even now the gust were swelling,　　　　　　　　15
　　And the slant night-shower driving loud and fast!
Those sounds which oft have raised me, whilst they awed,
　　　　And sent my soul abroad,
Might now perhaps their wonted impulse give,
Might startle this dull pain, and make it move and live!　　20

A grief without a pang, void, dark, and drear,
　　A stifled, drowsy, unimpassioned grief,
　　Which finds no natural outlet, no relief,
　　　　In word, or sigh, or tear—
O Lady! in this wan and heartless mood,　　　　　　　　25
To other thoughts by yonder throstle wooed,
　　All this long eve, so balmy and serene,
Have I been gazing on the western sky,
　　And its peculiar tint of yellow green:
And still I gaze—and with how blank an eye!　　　　　　30
And those thin clouds above, in flakes and bars,
That give away their motion to the stars;
Those stars, that glide behind them or between,
Now sparkling, now bedimmed, but always seen;
Yon crescent moon, as fixed as if it grew　　　　　　　35
In its own cloudless, starless lake of blue;
I see them all so excellently fair,
I see, not feel, how beautiful they are!

　　My genial spirits fail;
　　And what can these avail　　　　　　　　　　　40
To lift the smothering weight from off my breast?
　　It were a vain endeavor,
　　Though I should gaze forever
On that green light that lingers in the west:
I may not hope from outward forms to win　　　　　　45
The passion and the life whose fountains are within.

O Lady! we receive but what we give,
And in our life alone does Nature live:
Ours is her wedding garment, ours her shroud!
　　And would we aught behold, of higher worth,　　　　50
Than that inanimate cold world allowed
To the poor, loveless, ever-anxious crowd,
　　Ah! from the soul itself must issue forth
A light, a glory, a fair luminous cloud
　　Enveloping the earth—　　　　　　　　　　　55

---

19. wonted: customary. **26. throstle:** thrush. **39. genial spirits:** natural powers. **54. glory:** halo.

And from the soul itself must there be sent
   A sweet and potent voice, of its own birth,
Of all sweet sounds the life and element!

O pure of heart! thou need'st not ask of me
What this strong music in the soul may be!   60
What, and wherein it doth exist,
This light, this glory, this fair luminous mist,
This beautiful and beauty-making power.
   Joy, virtuous Lady! Joy that ne'er was given,
Save to the pure, and in their purest hour,   65
Life, and life's effluence, cloud at once and shower,
Joy, Lady! is the spirit and the power,
Which wedding Nature to us gives in dower
   A new earth and new heaven,
Undreamt of by the sensual and the proud—   70
Joy is the sweet voice, Joy the luminous cloud—
   We in ourselves rejoice!
And thence flows all that charms or ear or sight,
   All melodies the echoes of that voice,
All colors a suffusion from that light.   75

There was a time when, though my path was rough,
   This joy within me dallied with distress,
And all misfortunes were but as the stuff
   Whence Fancy made me dreams of happiness:
For hope grew round me, like the twining vine,   80
And fruits, and foliage, not my own, seemed mine.
But now afflictions bow me down to earth:
Nor care I that they rob me of my mirth;
   But oh! each visitation
Suspends what Nature gave me at my birth,   85
   My shaping spirit of Imagination.
For not to think of what I needs must feel,
   But to be still and patient, all I can;
And haply by abstruse research to steal
   From my own nature all the natural man—   90
   This was my sole resource, my only plan:
Till that which suits a part infects the whole,
And now is almost grown the habit of my soul.

Hence, viper thoughts, that coil around my mind,
     Reality's dark dream!   95
I turn from you, and listen to the wind,
   Which long has raved unnoticed. What a scream
Of agony by torture lengthened out
That lute sent forth! Thou wind, that rav'st without,

58. element: fundamental constituent. 67–69. Joy . . . heaven: Joy unites us to
Nature, and gives us as dowry a new view of earth and heaven. 89. haply: perhaps.

Bare crag, or mountain-tairn, or blasted tree,   100
Or pine grove whither woodman never clomb,
Or lonely house, long held the witches' home,
    Methinks were fitter instruments for thee,
Mad lutanist! who in this month of showers,
Of dark-brown gardens, and of peeping flowers,   105
Mak'st devils' yule, with worse than wintry song,
The blossoms, buds, and timorous leaves among.
    Thou actor, perfect in all tragic sounds!
Thou mighty poet, e'en to frenzy bold!
        What tell'st thou now about?   110
        'Tis of the rushing of an host in rout,
    With groans, of trampled men, with smarting wounds—
At once they groan with pain, and shudder with the cold!
But hush! there is a pause of deepest silence!
And all that noise, as of a rushing crowd,   115
With groans, and tremulous shudderings—all is over—
    It tells another tale, with sounds less deep and loud!
        A tale of less affright,
        And tempered with delight,
As Otway's self had framed the tender lay—   120
        'Tis of a little child
        Upon a lonesome wild,
Not far from home, but she hath lost her way:
And now moans low in bitter grief and fear,
And now screams loud, and hopes to make her mother hear.   125

'Tis midnight, but small thoughts have I of sleep:
Full seldom may my friend such vigils keep!
Visit her, gentle sleep! with wings of healing,
    And may this storm be but a mountain birth,
May all the stars hang bright above her dwelling,   130
    Silent as though they watched the sleeping earth!
        With light heart may she rise,
        Gay fancy, cheerful eyes,
Joy lift her spirit, joy attune her voice;
To her may all things live, from pole to pole,   135
Their life the eddying of her living soul!
    O simple spirit, guided from above,
Dear Lady! friend devoutest of my choice,
Thus mayest thou ever, evermore rejoice.

---

100. **mountain-tairn:** small mountain lake. 101. **clomb:** climbed. 104. **month:** the poem was written in April. 106. **yule:** Christmas. 120. **Otway's self:** Thomas Otway, a 17th-century dramatist, noted for his command of the pathetic. **lay:** ballad. 137. **simple:** pure.

Frost at Midnight

The frost performs its secret ministry,
Unhelped by any wind. The owlet's cry
Came loud—and hark, again! loud as before.
The inmates of my cottage, all at rest,
Have left me to that solitude, which suits   5
Abstruser musings: save that at my side
My cradled infant slumbers peacefully.
'Tis calm indeed! so calm that it disturbs
And vexes meditation with its strange
And extreme silentness. Sea, hill, and wood,   10
This populous village! Sea, and hill, and wood,
With all the numberless goings-on of life,
Inaudible as dreams! the thin blue flame
Lies on my low-burnt fire, and quivers not;
Only that film, which fluttered on the grate,   15
Still flutters there, the sole unquiet thing.
Methinks its motion in this hush of nature
Gives it dim sympathies with me who live,
Making it a companionable form,
Whose puny flaps and freaks the idling spirit   20
By its own moods interprets, everywhere
Echo or mirror seeking of itself,
And makes a toy of thought.

                              But oh! how oft,
How oft, at school, with most believing mind,   25
Presageful, have I gazed upon the bars,
To watch that fluttering *stranger!* and as oft
With unclosed lids, already had I dreamt
Of my sweet birthplace, and the old church tower,
Whose bells, the poor man's only music, rang
From morn to evening, all the hot fair-day,   30
So sweetly, that they stirred and haunted me
With a wild pleasure, falling on mine ear
Most like articulate sounds of things to come!
So gazed I, till the soothing things I dreamt
Lulled me to sleep, and sleep prolonged my dreams!   35
And so I brooded all the following morn,
Awed by the stern preceptor's face, mine eye

FROST AT MIDNIGHT   **15. film:** "These films are called *strangers* and supposed to portend the arrival of some absent friend" (Coleridge). **25. school:** Christ's Hospital in London, where Coleridge started school at the age of nine. He was born in Devonshire. **30. fair-day:** market day.

Fixed with mock study on my swimming book:
Save if the door half opened, and I snatched
A hasty glance, and still my heart leaped up,   40
For still I hoped to see the *stranger's* face,
Townsman, or aunt, or sister more beloved,
My playmate when we both were clothed alike!

Dear babe, that sleepest cradled by my side,
Whose gentle breathings, heard in this deep calm,   45
Fill up the interspersèd vacancies
And momentary pauses of the thought!
My babe so beautiful! it thrills my heart
With tender gladness thus to look at thee,
And think that thou shalt learn far other lore,   50
And in far other scenes! For I was reared
In the great city, pent mid cloisters dim,
And saw nought lovely but the sky and stars.
But *thou*, my babe! shalt wander like a breeze
By lakes and sandy shores, beneath the crags   55
Of ancient mountain, and beneath the clouds,
Which image in their bulk both lakes and shores
And mountain crags: so shalt thou see and hear
The lovely shapes and sounds intelligible
Of that eternal language, which thy God   60
Utters, who from eternity doth teach
Himself in all, and all things in himself.
Great universal teacher! he shall mold
Thy spirit, and by giving make it ask.

Therefore all seasons shall be sweet to thee,   65
Whether the summer clothe the general earth
With greenness, or the redbreast sit and sing
Betwixt the tufts of snow on the bare branch
Of mossy apple tree, while the nigh thatch
Smokes in the sun-thaw; whether the eave-drops fall   70
Heard only in the trances of the blast,
Or if the secret ministry of frost
Shall hang them up in silent icicles,
Quietly shining to the quiet moon.

---

43. we . . . alike: i.e., when they both were very small children. **69. nigh thatch:** short side of a thatch roof.

George Gordon, Lord Byron   *(1788–1824)*

Don Juan

from Canto I

CIII

'Twas on a summer's day—the sixth of June:
  I like to be particular in dates,
Not only of the age, and year, but moon;
    They are a sort of posthouse, where the Fates
Change horses, making history change its tune,   5
    Then spur away o'er empires and o'er states,
Leaving at last not much besides chronology,
Excepting the post-obits of theology.

CIV

'Twas on the sixth of June, about the hour
  Of half-past six—perhaps still nearer seven—   10
When Julia sate within as pretty a bower
    As e'er held houri in that heathenish heaven
Described by Mahomet, and Anacreon Moore,
    To whom the lyre and laurels have been given,
With all the trophies of triumphant song—   15
He won them well, and may he wear them long!

CV

She sate, but not alone; I know not well
  How this same interview had taken place,
And even if I knew, I shall not tell—
    People should hold their tongues in any case;   20
No matter how or why the thing befell,
    But there were she and Juan, face to face—
When two such faces are so, 'twould be wise,
But very difficult, to shut their eyes.

CVI

How beautiful she looked! her conscious heart   25
  Glowed in her cheek, and yet she felt no wrong:

DON JUAN   **4. posthouse:** station for changing horses. **8. post-obits:** settling of moral "accounts" after death. **11. Julia:** "married, charming, chaste, and twenty-three" (stanza LIX). **12–13. houri . . . Mahomet:** a beautiful nymph in the sensual Paradise promised by Mohammed to the faithful. **13. Anacreon Moore:** Thomas Moore had translated the love and drinking songs of the Greek poet, Anacreon; he had also written an Oriental tale called *Paradise and the Peri*. **22. Juan:** aged sixteen. **25. conscious heart:** heart aware of its feelings.

O Love! how perfect is thy mystic art,
    Strengthening the weak, and trampling on the strong!
How self-deceitful is the sagest part
    Of mortals whom thy lure hath led along!—
The precipice she stood on was immense,
So was her creed in her own innocence.

CVII

She thought of her own strength, and Juan's youth,
    And of the folly of all prudish fears,
Victorious virtue, and domestic truth,
    And then of Don Alfonso's fifty years:
I wish these last had not occurred, in sooth,
    Because that number rarely much endears,
And through all climes, the snowy and the sunny,
Sounds ill in love, whate'er it may in money.

CVIII

When people say, "I've told you *fifty* times,"
    They mean to scold, and very often do;
When poets say, "I've written *fifty* rhymes,"
    They make you dread that they'll recite them too;
In gangs of *fifty*, thieves commit their crimes;
    At *fifty* love for love is rare, 'tis true,
But then, no doubt, it equally as true is,
A good deal may be bought for *fifty* louis.

CIX

Julia had honor, virtue, truth, and love
    For Don Alfonso; and she inly swore,
By all the vows below to powers above,
    She never would disgrace the ring she wore,
Nor leave a wish which wisdom might reprove;
    And while she pondered this, besides much more,
One hand on Juan's carelessly was thrown,
Quite by mistake—she thought it was her own;

CX

Unconsciously she leaned upon the other,
    Which played within the tangles of her hair;
And to contend with thoughts she could not smother
    She seemed, by the distraction of her air.
'Twas surely very wrong in Juan's mother
    To leave together this imprudent pair,
She who for many years had watched her son so—
I'm very certain *mine* would not have done so.

30

35

40

45

50

55

60

---

32. **creed:** belief. 36. **Don Alfonso's:** Don Alfonso is Julia's husband. 37. **in sooth:** in truth. 48. **louis:** a French coin worth twenty francs. 50. **inly:** inwardly.

CXI

The hand which still held Juan's, by degrees,   65
   Gently but palpably confirmed its grasp,
As if it said, "Detain me, if you please";
   Yet there's no doubt she only meant to clasp
His fingers with a pure Platonic squeeze;
   She would have shrunk as from a toad, or asp,   70
Had she imagined such a thing could rouse
A feeling dangerous to a prudent spouse.

CXII

I cannot know what Juan thought of this,
   But what he did, is much what you would do;
His young lip thanked it with a grateful kiss,   75
   And then, abashed at its own joy, withdrew
In deep despair, lest he had done amiss—
   Love is so very timid when 'tis new:
She blushed, and frowned not, but she strove to speak,
And held her tongue, her voice was grown so weak.   80

CXIII

The sun set, and up rose the yellow moon:
   The devil's in the moon for mischief; they
Who called her CHASTE, methinks, began too soon
   Their nomenclature; there is not a day,
The longest, not the twenty-first of June,   85
   Sees half the business in a wicked way
On which three single hours of moonshine smile—
And then she looks so modest all the while!

CXIV

There is a dangerous silence in that hour,
   A stillness, which leaves room for the full soul   90
To open all itself, without the power
   Of calling wholly back its self-control;
The silver light which, hallowing tree and tower,
   Sheds beauty and deep softness o'er the whole,
Breathes also to the heart, and o'er it throws   95
A loving languor, which is not repose.

CXV

And Julia sate with Juan, half embraced
   And half retiring from the glowing arm,
Which trembled like the bosom where 'twas placed;
   Yet still she must have thought there was no harm,   100
Or else 'twere easy to withdraw her waist;
   But then the situation had its charm,
And then—God knows what next—I can't go on;
   I'm almost sorry that I e'er begun.

69. **Platonic:** indicating "ideal" rather than sexual feeling.

CXVI

Oh Plato! Plato! you have paved the way,   105
    With your confounded fantasies, to more
Immoral conduct by the fancied sway
    Your system feigns o'er the controlless core
Of human hearts, than all the long array
    Of poets and romancers:—You're a bore,   110
A charlatan, a coxcomb—and have been,
At best, no better than a go-between.

CXVII

And Julia's voice was lost, except in sighs,
    Until too late for useful conversation;
The tears were gushing from her gentle eyes;   115
    I wish, indeed, they had not had occasion;
But who, alas! can love, and then be wise?
    Not that remorse did not oppose temptation;
A little still she strove, and much repented,
And whispering "I will ne'er consent"—consented.   120

CXVIII

'Tis said that Xerxes offered a reward
    To those who could invent him a new pleasure:
Methinks the requisition's rather hard,
    And must have cost his Majesty a treasure:
For my part, I'm a moderate-minded bard,   125
    Fond of a little love (which I call leisure);
I care not for new pleasures, as the old
Are quite enough for me, so they but hold.

CXIX

O Pleasure! you're indeed a pleasant thing,
    Although one must be damned for you, no doubt: 130
I make a resolution every spring
    Of reformation, ere the year run out,
But somehow, this my vestal vow takes wing,
    Yet still, I trust, it may be kept throughout:
I'm very sorry, very much ashamed,   135
And mean, next winter, to be quite reclaimed.

CXX

Here my chaste Muse a liberty must take—
    Start not! still chaster reader—she'll be nice hence-
Forward, and there is no great cause to quake;
    This liberty is a poetic license,   140

---

105. Plato: in such works as the *Symposium,* where he traces the ascent from physical desire to spiritual love, Plato was popularly supposed to have asserted that man could transcend the sexual. **112. go-between:** pimp. **128. hold:** survive. **133. vestal:** chaste. **140. poetic license:** deviation from the facts or rules permissible to poets.

Which some irregularity may make
    In the design, and as I have a high sense
Of Aristotle and the Rules, 'tis fit
    To beg his pardon when I err a bit.

CXXI

This license is to hope the reader will   145
    Suppose from June the sixth (the fatal day,
Without whose epoch my poetic skill
    For want of facts would all be thrown away),
But keeping Julia and Don Juan still
    In sight, that several months have passed; we'll say   150
'Twas in November, but I'm not so sure
About the day—the era's most obscure.

CXXII

We'll talk of that anon.—'Tis sweet to hear
    At midnight on the blue and moonlit deep
The song and oar of Adria's gondolier,   155
    By distance mellowed, o'er the waters sweep;
'Tis sweet to see the evening star appear;
    'Tis sweet to listen as the night winds creep
From leaf to leaf; 'tis sweet to view on high
The rainbow, based on ocean, span the sky.   160

CXXIII

'Tis sweet to hear the watchdog's honest bark
    Bay deep-mouthed welcome as we draw near home;
'Tis sweet to know there is an eye will mark
    Our coming, and look brighter when we come;
'Tis sweet to be awakened by the lark,   165
    Or lulled by falling waters; sweet the hum
Of bees, the voice of girls, the song of birds,
The lisp of children, and their earliest words.

CXXIV

Sweet is the vintage, when the showering grapes
    In Bacchanal profusion reel to earth,   170
Purple and gushing: sweet are our escapes
    From civic revelry to rural mirth;
Sweet to the miser are his glittering heaps,
    Sweet to the father is his first-born's birth,
Sweet is revenge—especially to women—   175
Pillage to soldiers, prize-money to seamen.

---

143. Aristotle and the Rules: in the *Poetics*, Aristotle set down certain "rules," elaborated in the Renaissance, governing the unities of action, time, and place in drama. **144. err:** wander. **148. facts:** deeds. **155. Adria's gondolier:** in Venice on the Adriatic. **170. Bacchanal:** riotous. **172. civic:** urban.

CXXV

Sweet is a legacy, and passing sweet
   The unexpected death of some old lady
Or gentleman of seventy years complete,
   Who've made "us youth" wait too—too long already,   180
For an estate, or cash, or country seat,
   Still breaking, but with stamina so steady,
That all the Israelites are fit to mob its
Next owner for their double-damned post-obits.

CXXVI

'Tis sweet to win, no matter how, one's laurels,   185
   By blood or ink; 'tis sweet to put an end
To strife; 'tis sometimes sweet to have our quarrels,
   Particularly with a tiresome friend:
Sweet is old wine in bottles, ale in barrels;
   Dear is the helpless creature we defend   190
Against the world; and dear the schoolboy spot
We ne'er forget, though there we are forgot.

CXXVII

But sweeter still than this, than these, than all,
   Is first and passionate love—it stands alone,
Like Adam's recollection of his fall;   195
   The Tree of Knowledge has been plucked—all's known—
And life yields nothing further to recall
   Worthy of this ambrosial sin, so shown,
No doubt in fable, as the unforgiven
Fire which Prometheus filched for us from Heaven.   200

Percy Bysshe Shelley   (1792–1822)

Ode to the West Wind

I

O wild West Wind, thou breath of Autumn's being,
Thou, from whose unseen presence the leaves dead
Are driven, like ghosts from an enchanter fleeing,

---

177. passing: extremely 180. "us youth"; "They hate us youth," says the old Falstaff, "young men must live" (Shakespeare, *I Henry IV*, II.ii. 85, 90). 182. Still breaking: always growing feebler. 183. Israelites: traditionally, English moneylenders were Jewish. 184. post-obits: here, loans which fall due after an heir has come into his estate. 185. one's laurels: fame. 200. Prometheus: the Titan who aroused the anger of Zeus by stealing fire from heaven for man.

ODE TO THE WEST WIND   1. breath: animating power, soul.

Yellow, and black, and pale, and hectic red,
Pestilence-stricken multitudes: O thou, 5
Who chariotest to their dark wintry bed

The wingèd seeds, where they lie cold and low,
Each like a corpse within its grave, until
Thine azure sister of the Spring shall blow

Her clarion o'er the dreaming earth, and fill 10
(Driving sweet buds like flocks to feed in air)
With living hues and odors, plain and hill:

Wild Spirit, which art moving everywhere;
Destroyer and preserver; hear, oh, hear!

II

Thou on whose stream, mid the steep sky's commotion, 15
Loose clouds like earth's decaying leaves are shed,
Shook from the tangled boughs of heaven and ocean,

Angels of rain and lightning: there are spread
On the blue surface of thine aëry surge,
Like the bright hair uplifted from the head 20

Of some fierce Maenad, even from the dim verge
Of the horizon to the zenith's height,
The locks of the approaching storm. Thou dirge

Of the dying year, to which this closing night
Will be the dome of a vast sepulcher, 25
Vaulted with all thy congregated might

Of vapors, from whose solid atmosphere
Black rain, and fire, and hail will burst: oh, hear!

III

Thou who didst waken from his summer dreams
The blue Mediterranean, where he lay, 30
Lulled by the coil of his crystàlline streams,

Beside a pumice isle in Baiae's bay,
And saw in sleep old palaces and towers
Quivering within the wave's intenser day,

16–17. **Loose clouds . . . ocean:** smaller clouds, like leaves, are torn from the large
cloud masses formed by the union of air and water vapor. **18. Angels:** as in Latin
angelus, messenger. **21. Maenad:** the frenzied, female worshiper of Dionysus, the
vegetation god who dies in the fall and is reborn in the spring. **31. coil . . . streams:**
the currents of the Mediterranean. **32. Baiae's bay:** near Naples, which contains, rather
than reflects, the ruins of "old palaces and towers" (l. 33).

All overgrown with azure moss and flowers   35
So sweet, the sense faints picturing them! Thou

For whose path the Atlantic's level powers
Cleave themselves into chasms, while far below
The sea-blooms and the oozy woods which wear
The sapless foliage of the ocean, know   40

Thy voice, and suddenly grow gray with fear,
And tremble and despoil themselves: oh, hear!

IV

If I were a dead leaf thou mightest bear;
If I were a swift cloud to fly with thee;
A wave to pant beneath thy power, and share   45

The impulse of thy strength, only less free
Than thou, O uncontrollable! If even
I were as in my boyhood, and could be

The comrade of thy wanderings over heaven,
As then, when to outstrip thy skyey speed   50
Scarce seemed a vision; I would ne'er have striven

As thus with thee in prayer in my sore need.
Oh, lift me as a wave, a leaf, a cloud!
I fall upon the thorns of life! I bleed!

A heavy weight of hours has chained and bowed   55
One too like thee: tameless, and swift, and proud.

V

Make me thy lyre, even as the forest is:
What if my leaves are falling like its own!
The tumult of thy mighty harmonies

Will take from both a deep, autumnal tone,   60
Sweet though in sadness. Be thou, Spirit fierce,
My spirit! Be thou me, impetuous one!

Drive my dead thoughts over the universe
Like withered leaves to quicken a new birth!
And, by the incantation of this verse,   65

39–42. sea-blooms . . . themselves: "The vegetation at the bottom of the sea . . . sympathizes with that of the land in the change of seasons" (Shelley). **57. lyre:** Aeolian lyre (see note to Coleridge's "Dejection: An Ode," l. 7). **64. quicken:** vitalize.

Scatter, as from an unextinguished hearth
Ashes and sparks, my words among mankind!
Be through my lips to unawakened earth

The trumpet of a prophecy! O Wind,
If Winter comes, can Spring be far behind?   70

When the Lamp Is Shattered

When the lamp is shattered,
The light in the dust lies dead;
When the cloud is scattered,
The rainbow's glory is shed;
When the lute is broken,   5
Sweet tones are remembered not;
When the lips have spoken,
Loved accents are soon forgot.

As music and splendor
Survive not the lamp and the lute,   10
The heart's echoes render
No song when the spirit is mute:
No song but sad dirges,
Like the wind through a ruined cell,
Or the mournful surges   15
That ring the dead seaman's knell.

When hearts have once mingled,
Love first leaves the well-built nest;
The weak one is singled
To endure what it once possessed.   20
O Love! who bewailest
The frailty of all things here,
Why choose you the frailest
For your cradle, your home, and your bier?

Its passions will rock thee,   25
As the storms rock the ravens on high;
Bright reason will mock thee,
Like the sun from a wintry sky.
From thy nest every rafter
Will rot, and thine eagle home   30
Leave thee naked to laughter,
When leaves fall and cold winds come.

WHEN THE LAMP IS SHATTERED   **18. the well-built nest:** the stronger heart.

Sonnet: England in 1819

An old, mad, blind, despised, and dying king—
Princes, the dregs of their dull race, who flow
Through public scorn—mud from a muddy spring—
Rulers who neither see, nor feel, nor know,
But leechlike to their fainting country cling,   5
Till they drop, blind in blood, without a blow—
A people starved and stabbed in the untilled field—
An army, which liberticide and prey
Makes as a two-edged sword to all who wield—
Golden and sanguine laws which tempt and slay;   10
Religion Christless, Godless—a book sealed;
A Senate—Time's worst statute unrepealed—
Are graves, from which a glorious Phantom may
Burst, to illumine our tempestuous day.

To ———

One word is too often profaned
 For me to profane it,
One feeling too falsely disdained
 For thee to disdain it;
One hope is too like despair   5
 For prudence to smother,
And pity from thee more dear
 Than that from another.

I can give not what men call love,
 But wilt thou accept not   10
The worship the heart lifts above
 And the heavens reject not—
The desire of the moth for the star,
 Of the night for the morrow,
The devotion to something afar   15
 From the sphere of our sorrow?

ENGLAND IN 1819   **1. An old . . . king:** George III, aged 81, blind and incurably mad.
2–3. Princes . . . scorn: sons of George III, variously frivolous, clownish, and sinister.
7. people . . . field: in 1819, at Peterloo near Manchester, troops charged a large mass
of peaceful political demonstrators, killing eleven and injuring hundreds. **8. liberticide:**
murder of liberty. **10. Golden . . . laws:** laws established by corruption and the cause
of bloodshed. **12. Senate . . . unrepealed:** Parliament. (The House of Commons was
grotesquely unrepresentative of the electorate.) **13. glorious Phantom:** revolution, with
a possible allusion to the Glorious Revolution of 1688.

To the Moon (1820)

Art thou pale for weariness
Of climbing heaven and gazing on the earth,
   Wandering companionless
Among the stars that have a different birth—
And ever changing, like a joyless eye   5
That finds no object worth its constancy?

John Clare *(1793–1864)*

A Vision

I lost the love of heaven above,
   I spurned the lust of earth below,
I felt the sweets of fancied love,
   And hell itself my only foe.

I lost earth's joys, but felt the glow   5
   Of heaven's flame abound in me
Till loveliness and I did grow
   The bard of immortality.

I loved but woman fell away,
I hid me from her faded fame,   10
I snatched the sun's eternal ray,
   And wrote till earth was but a name.

In every language upon earth
   On every shore, o'er every sea,
I gave my name immortal birth   15
   And kept my spirit with the free.

A Sea Boy on the Giddy Mast

A sea boy on the giddy mast
Sees nought but ocean waves,
And hears the wild inconstant blast
Where loud the tempest raves.

My life is like the ocean wave,   5
And like th' inconstant sea:
In every hope appears a grave
And leaves no hope for me.

John Keats   *(1795–1821)*

Bright Star

Bright star! would I were steadfast as thou art—
    Not in lone splendor hung aloft the night
And watching, with eternal lids apart,
    Like nature's patient, sleepless eremite,
The moving waters at their priestlike task   5
    Of pure ablution round earth's human shores,
Or gazing on the new soft-fallen mask
    Of snow upon the mountains and the moors—
No—yet still steadfast, still unchangeable,
    Pillowed upon my fair love's ripening breast,   10
To feel forever its soft fall and swell,
    Awake forever in a sweet unrest,
Still, still to hear her tender-taken breath,
And so live ever—or else swoon to death.

Ode to a Nightingale

My heart aches, and a drowsy numbness pains
    My sense, as though of hemlock I had drunk,
Or emptied some dull opiate to the drains
    One minute past, and Lethe-wards had sunk:
'Tis not through envy of thy happy lot,   5
    But being too happy in thy happiness—
        That thou, light-wingèd dryad of the trees,
            In some melodious plot
Of beechen green, and shadows numberless,
    Singest of summer in full-throated ease.   10

O, for a draught of vintage! that hath been
    Cooled a long age in the deep delvèd earth,

BRIGHT STAR   **4. eremite:** hermit.

ODE TO A NIGHTINGALE   **2. hemlock:** an opiate, poisonous in large quantities. **3. drains:** dregs. **4. Lethe-wards:** towards Lethe, in classical mythology the river of forgetfulness. **5. thy:** the nightingale's. **7. dryad:** tree nymph.

Tasting of Flora and the country green,
　　Dance, and Provençal song, and sunburnt mirth!
O for a beaker full of the warm South,　　　　　　　　15
　　Full of the true, the blushful Hippocrene,
　　　　With beaded bubbles winking at the brim,
　　　　　　And purple-stainèd mouth;
　　That I might drink, and leave the world unseen,
　　　　And with thee fade away into the forest dim:　　20

Fade far away, dissolve, and quite forget
　　What thou among the leaves hast never known,
The weariness, the fever, and the fret
　　Here, where men sit and hear each other groan;
Where palsy shakes a few, sad, last gray hairs,　　　25
　　Where youth grows pale, and specter-thin, and dies;
　　　　Where but to think is to be full of sorrow
　　　　　　And leaden-eyed despairs,
　　Where Beauty cannot keep her lustrous eyes,
　　　　Or new Love pine at them beyond tomorrow.　　30

Away! away! for I will fly to thee,
　　Not charioted by Bacchus and his pards,
But on the viewless wings of Poesy,
　　Though the dull brain perplexes and retards:
Already with thee! tender is the night,　　　　　　35
　　And haply the Queen-Moon is on her throne,
　　　　Clustered around by all her starry Fays;
　　　　　　But here there is no light,
　　Save what from heaven is with the breezes blown
　　　　Through verdurous glooms and winding mossy ways.　40

I cannot see what flowers are at my feet,
　　Nor what soft incense hangs upon the boughs,
But, in embalmèd darkness, guess each sweet
　　Wherewith the seasonable month endows
The grass, the thicket, and the fruit tree wild;　　　45
　　White hawthorn, and the pastoral eglantine;
　　　　Fast fading violets covered up in leaves;
　　　　　　And mid-May's eldest child,
　　The coming musk rose, full of dewy wine,
　　　　The murmurous haunt of flies on summer eves.　　50

Darkling I listen; and, for many a time
　　I have been half in love with easeful Death,

---

13. Flora: the goddess of flowers. **14. Provençal song:** song of Provence, a region in southern France, and home of the medieval troubadours. **15. warm South:** the south of France, or in general the Mediterranean region. **16. true . . . Hippocrene:** wine. The Hippocrene was a fountain on Mt. Helicon whose water supposedly inspired poets. **32. Bacchus . . . pards:** the god of wine and the leopards who drew his chariot. **33. viewless:** invisible. **36. haply:** perhaps. **37. Fays:** fairies. **43. embalmèd:** scented. **51. darkling:** in the dark.

Called him soft names in many a musèd rhyme,
    To take into the air my quiet breath;
Now more than ever seems it rich to die,   55
    To cease upon the midnight with no pain,
        While thou art pouring forth thy soul abroad
           In such an ecstasy!
Still wouldst thou sing, and I have ears in vain—
    To thy high requiem become a sod.   60

Thou wast not born for death, immortal bird!
    No hungry generations tread thee down;
The voice I hear this passing night was heard
    In ancient days by emperor and clown:
Perhaps the selfsame song that found a path   65
    Through the sad heart of Ruth, when, sick for home,
        She stood in tears amid the alien corn;
           The same that ofttimes hath
Charmed magic casements, opening on the foam
    Of perilous seas, in faery lands forlorn.   70

Forlorn! the very word is like a bell
    To toll me back from thee to my sole self!
Adieu! the fancy cannot cheat so well
    As she is famed to do, deceiving elf.
Adieu! adieu! thy plaintive anthem fades   75
    Past the near meadows, over the still stream,
        Up the hillside; and now 'tis buried deep
           In the next valley-glades:
Was it a vision, or a waking dream?
    Fled is that music:—Do I wake or sleep?   80

Ode on a Grecian Urn

Thou still unravished bride of quietness,
    Thou foster child of silence and slow time,
Sylvan historian, who canst thus express
    A flowery tale more sweetly than our rhyme:
What leaf-fringed legend haunts about thy shape   5
    Of deities or mortals, or of both,

---

53. musèd: literally, inspired by the Muses, but also, pondered. **66–67. sad heart . . . corn:** in the Bible, Ruth was a Moabite who worked in the harvest fields near Bethlehem. **73. fancy:** the poetic imagination (see l. 33).

ODE ON A GRECIAN URN **3. Sylvan:** woodland. **5. legend:** (1) tale; (2) caption that explains a picture, map, etc.

In Tempe or the dales of Arcady?
   What men or gods are these? What maidens loath?
What mad pursuit? What struggle to escape?
   What pipes and timbrels? What wild ecstasy?   10

Heard melodies are sweet, but those unheard
   Are sweeter; therefore, ye soft pipes, play on;
Not to the sensual ear, but, more endeared,
   Pipe to the spirit ditties of no tone:
Fair youth, beneath the trees, thou canst not leave   15
   Thy song, nor ever can those trees be bare;
      Bold lover, never, never canst thou kiss,
Though winning near the goal—yet, do not grieve;
   She cannot fade, though thou hast not thy bliss,
      Forever wilt thou love, and she be fair!   20

Ah, happy, happy boughs! that cannot shed
   Your leaves, nor ever bid the spring adieu;
And, happy melodist, unwearièd,
   Forever piping songs forever new;
More happy love! more happy, happy love!   25
   Forever warm and still to be enjoyed,
      Forever panting, and forever young;
All breathing human passion far above,
   That leaves a heart high-sorrowful and cloyed,
      A burning forehead, and a parching tongue.   30

Who are these coming to the sacrifice?
   To what green altar, O mysterious priest,
Lead'st thou that heifer lowing at the skies,
   And all her silken flanks with garlands dressed?
What little town by river or sea shore,   35
   Or mountain-built with peaceful citadel,
      Is emptied of this folk, this pious morn?
And, little town, thy streets forevermore
   Will silent be; and not a soul to tell
      Why thou art desolate, can e'er return.   40

O Attic shape! Fair attitude! with brede
   Of marble men and maidens overwrought,
With forest branches and the trodden weed;
   Thou, silent form, dost tease us out of thought
As doth eternity: cold pastoral!   45
   When old age shall this generation waste,
      Thou shalt remain, in midst of other woe
Than ours, a friend to man, to whom thou say'st,

---

7. Tempe . . . Arcady: beautiful rural regions in Greece, symbolizing the pastoral. **10. timbrels:** ancient tambourines. **14. ditties . . . tone:** songs audible to the spirit but not to the ear. **41. Attic:** Attica is the region around Athens. **brede:** braid, interwoven pattern. **42. overwrought:** ornamented.

"Beauty is truth, truth beauty,"—that is all
    Ye know on earth, and all ye need to know.   50

Ode to Psyche

O Goddess! hear these tuneless numbers, wrung
    By sweet enforcement and remembrance dear,
And pardon that thy secrets should be sung
    Even into thine own soft-conchèd ear:
Surely I dreamt today, or did I see   5
    The wingèd Psyche with awakened eyes?
I wandered in a forest thoughtlessly,
    And, on the sudden, fainting with surprise,
Saw two fair creatures, couchèd side by side
    In deepest grass, beneath the whispering roof   10
    Of leaves and trembled blossoms, where there ran
        A brooklet, scarce espied:

Mid hushed, cool-rooted flowers, fragrant-eyed,
    Blue, silver-white, and budded Tyrian,
They lay calm-breathing, on the bedded grass;   15
    Their arms embracèd, and their pinions too;
    Their lips touched not, but had not bade adieu,
As if disjoinèd by soft-handed slumber,
And ready still past kisses to outnumber
    At tender eye-dawn of aurorean love: 20
        The wingèd boy I knew;
    But who wast thou, O happy, happy dove?
        His Psyche true!

O latest born and loveliest vision far
    Of all Olympus' faded hierarchy!   25
Fairer than Phoebe's sapphire-regioned star,
    Or Vesper, amorous glowworm of the sky;
Fairer than these, though temple thou hast none,
    Nor altar heaped with flowers;
Nor virgin choir to make delicious moan   30
    Upon the midnight hours;
No voice, no lute, no pipe, no incense sweet
    From chain-swung censer teeming;

---

49. **"Beauty . . . beauty"**: in some early transcripts of the poem, the quotation marks are missing.
ODE TO PSYCHE According to the *Cupid and Psyche* of Apuleius (2nd century A.D.), Cupid fell in love with Psyche, a mortal; after various difficulties caused by the jealousy of his mother, Venus, the two were married and Psyche became an immortal to live with the other gods on Olympus. 1. **tuneless numbers**: unmelodious lines. 4. **soft-conchèd**: soft and shaped like a conch (seashell). 14. **Tyrian**: purple, the famous dye of ancient Tyre. 20. **aurorean**: morning, from Aurora, goddess of dawn. 26. **Phoebe's . . . star**: the moon, governed by Phoebe (Diana). 27. **Vesper**: the evening star.

No shrine, no grove, no oracle, no heat
    Of pale-mouthed prophet dreaming.   35

O brightest! though too late for antique vows,
    Too, too late for the fond believing lyre,
When holy were the haunted forest boughs,
    Holy the air, the water, and the fire;
Yet even in these days so far retired   40
    From happy pieties, thy lucent fans,
    Fluttering among the faint Olympians,
I see, and sing, by my own eyes inspired.
So let me be thy choir, and make a moan
        Upon the midnight hours;   45
Thy voice, thy lute, thy pipe, thy incense sweet
    From swingèd censer teeming;
Thy shrine, thy grove, thy oracle, thy heat
    Of pale-mouthed prophet dreaming.

Yes, I will be thy priest, and build a fane   50
    In some untrodden region of my mind,
Where branchèd thoughts, new grown with pleasant pain
    Instead of pines shall murmur in the wind:
Far, far around shall those dark-clustered trees
    Fledge the wild-ridged mountains steep by steep;   55
And there by zephyrs, streams, and birds, and bees,
    The moss-lain dryads shall be lulled to sleep;
And in the midst of this wide quietness
A rosy sanctuary will I dress
With the wreathed trellis of a working brain,   60
    With buds, and bells, and stars without a name,
With all the gardener Fancy e'er could feign,
    Who, breeding flowers, will never breed the same:
And there shall be for thee all soft delight
    That shadowy thought can win,   65
A bright torch, and a casement ope at night,
    To let the warm Love in!

To Autumn

Season of mists and mellow fruitfulness,
    Close bosom-friend of the maturing sun;
Conspiring with him how to load and bless
    With fruit the vines that round the thatch-eaves run;
To bend with apples the mossed cottage trees,   5

34–35. oracle . . . dreaming: prophets of the gods often gave oracular responses in a trance induced by vapors. **37. fond:** also has the obsolete sense of foolish. **40. retired:** removed. **41. lucent fans:** shining wings. **50. fane:** shrine. **55. Fledge:** to cover thickly, as with rows of feathers. **57. dryads:** tree nymphs. **62. Fancy:** the poetic imagination. **67. Love:** Cupid. In Apuleius's tale, Cupid visited Psyche secretly at night by flying in her bedroom window.

And fill all fruit with ripeness to the core;
        To swell the gourd, and plump the hazel shells
With a sweet kernel; to set budding more,
And still more, later flowers for the bees,
Until they think warm days will never cease,   10
        For Summer has o'er-brimmed their clammy cells.

Who hath not seen thee oft amid thy store?
        Sometimes whoever seeks abroad may find
Thee sitting careless on a granary floor,
        Thy hair soft-lifted by the winnowing wind;   15
Or on a half-reaped furrow sound asleep,
        Drowsed with the fume of poppies, while thy hook
        Spares the next swath and all its twinèd flowers:
And sometimes like a gleaner thou dost keep
        Steady thy laden head across a brook;   20
Or by a cider press, with patient look,
        Thou watchest the last oozings hours by hours.

Where are the songs of Spring? Aye, where are they?
        Think not of them, thou hast thy music too—
While barrèd clouds bloom the soft-dying day,   25
        And touch the stubble-plains with rosy hue;
Then in a wailful choir the small gnats mourn
        Among the river sallows, borne aloft
        Or sinking as the light wind lives or dies;
And full-grown lambs loud bleat from hilly bourn;   30
        Hedge-crickets sing; and now with treble soft
The redbreast whistles from a garden croft;
        And gathering swallows twitter in the skies.

Ode on Melancholy

No, no, go not to Lethe, neither twist
        Wolfsbane, tight-rooted, for its poisonous wine;
Nor suffer thy pale forehead to be kissed
        By nightshade, ruby grape of Proserpine,
Make not your rosary of yew-berries,   5
        Nor let the beetle, nor the death-moth be
        Your mournful Psyche, nor the downy owl

TO AUTUMN   12. **store:** abundance. 17. **hook:** reaper's hook. 28. **sallows:** willows. 30.
bourn: brook. 32. **croft:** small cultivated piece of land.
ODE ON MELANCHOLY   1. **Lethe:** the river of forgetfulness in Hades. 2. **Wolfsbane:** a
plant that produces a narcotic and poison. 4. **nightshade . . . Proserpine:** another plant,
with large black berries, that produces a poisonous narcotic; here seen as sacred to
Proserpine, queen of Hades. 5. **yew-berries:** yews, a customary planting in graveyards,
have poisonous berries. 6. **beetle . . . death-moth:** insects symbolizing death. 7.
Psyche: the soul, sometimes thought in classical times to issue as a butterfly from the
mouth at the moment of death. **owl:** another graveyard emblem.

A partner in your sorrow's mysteries;
   For shade to shade will come too drowsily,
      And drown the wakeful anguish of the soul.   10

But when the melancholy fit shall fall
   Sudden from heaven like a weeping cloud,
That fosters the droop-headed flowers all,
   And hides the green hill in an April shroud;
Then glut thy sorrow on a morning rose,   15
   Or on the rainbow of the salt sand-wave,
      Or on the wealth of globèd peonies;
Or if thy mistress some rich anger shows,
   Imprison her soft hand, and let her rave,
    And feed deep, deep upon her peerless eyes.   20

She dwells with Beauty—Beauty that must die;
   And Joy, whose hand is ever at his lips
Bidding adieu; and aching Pleasure nigh,
   Turning to poison while the bee-mouth sips:
Ay, in the very temple of Delight   25
   Veiled Melancholy has her sovereign shrine,
      Though seen of none save him whose strenuous
      tongue
Can burst Joy's grape against his palate fine;
His soul shall taste the sadness of her might,
   And be among her cloudy trophies hung.   30

Alfred, Lord Tennyson   (1809–1892)

Ulysses

It little profits that an idle king,
By this still hearth, among these barren crags,
Matched with an agèd wife, I mete and dole
Unequal laws unto a savage race,
That hoard, and sleep, and feed, and know not me.   5
I cannot rest from travel; I will drink

8. **mysteries:** secret rites. 9. **shade . . . drowsily:** if dulled by narcotics or fascinated
by conventional "properties" of death (ll. 1–8), the "shade" (ghost) will advance too
imperceptibly toward "shade" (death). 21. **She:** Melancholy. 28. **fine:** discriminating.
30. **trophies:** in classical times, trophies were hung as offerings in temples.
ULYSSES In Dante's version of the story (*Inferno*, canto 26), Ulysses became restless
after returning to his island kingdom of Ithaca, and in old age persuaded a band of
followers to accompany him on a western voyage of exploration in search of virtue and
knowledge. 3–4. **mete . . . laws:** measure and distribute rewards and punishments.

Life to the lees: all times I have enjoyed
Greatly, have suffered greatly, both with those
That loved me, and alone; on shore, and when
Through scudding drifts the rainy Hyades   10
Vexed the dim sea. I am become a name:
For always roaming with a hungry heart
Much have I seen and known—cities of men
And manners, climates, councils, governments,
Myself not least, but honored of them all—   15
And drunk delight of battle with my peers,
Far on the ringing plains of windy Troy.
I am a part of all that I have met;
Yet all experience is an arch wherethrough
Gleams that untraveled world, whose margin fades   20
Forever and forever when I move.
How dull it is to pause, to make an end,
To rust unburnished, not to shine in use!
As though to breathe were life! Life piled on life
Were all too little, and of one to me   25
Little remains: but every hour is saved
From that eternal silence, something more,
A bringer of new things; and vile it were
For some three suns to store and hoard myself,
And this gray spirit yearning in desire   30
To follow knowledge like a sinking star,
Beyond the utmost bound of human thought.
    This is my son, mine own Telemachus,
To whom I leave the scepter and the isle—
Well-loved of me, discerning to fulfill   35
This labor, by slow prudence to make mild
A rugged people, and through soft degrees
Subdue them to the useful and the good.
Most blameless is he, centered in the sphere
Of common duties, decent not to fail   40
In offices of tenderness, and pay
Meet adoration to my household gods,
When I am gone. He works his work, I mine.
    There lies the port: the vessel puffs her sail;
There gloom the dark broad seas. My mariners,   45
Souls that have toiled, and wrought, and thought with me—
That ever with a frolic welcome took
The thunder and the sunshine, and opposed
Free hearts, free foreheads—you and I are old;
Old age hath yet his honor and his toil;   50
Death closes all: but something ere the end,
Some work of noble note, may yet be done,

---

10. **Hyades:** a group of stars whose rising forecasts rain. 14. **manners:** customs, modes of behavior. 40. **decent:** properly careful. 41. **offices:** duties. 42. **Meet:** proper. 48. **opposed:** i.e., to the thunder and sunshine.

Not unbecoming men that strove with gods.
The lights begin to twinkle from the rocks;
The long day wanes; the slow moon climbs; the deep 55
Moans round with many voices. Come, my friends,
'Tis not too late to seek a newer world.
Push off, and sitting well in order smite
The sounding furrows; for my purpose holds
To sail beyond the sunset, and the baths 60
Of all the western stars, until I die.
It may be that the gulfs will wash us down:
It may be we shall touch the Happy Isles,
And see the great Achilles, whom we knew.
Though much is taken, much abides; and though 65
We are not now that strength which in old days
Moved earth and heaven; that which we are, we are;
One equal temper of heroic hearts,
Made weak by time and fate, but strong in will
To strive, to seek, to find, and not to yield. 70

Tears, Idle Tears

Tears, idle tears, I know not what they mean,
Tears from the depth of some divine despair
Rise in the heart, and gather to the eyes,
In looking on the happy autumn-fields,
And thinking of the days that are no more. 5

Fresh as the first beam glittering on a sail,
That brings our friends up from the underworld,
Sad as the last which reddens over one
That sinks with all we love below the verge;
So sad, so fresh, the days that are no more. 10

Ah, sad and strange as in dark summer dawns
The earliest pipe of half-awakened birds
To dying ears, when unto dying eyes
The casement slowly grows a glimmering square;
So sad, so strange, the days that are no more. 15

Dear as remembered kisses after death,
And sweet as those by hopeless fancy feigned
On lips that are for others; deep as love,
Deep as first love, and wild with all regret;
O Death in Life, the days that are no more. 20

---

53. men . . . gods: Ulysses' men had fought with gods in the Trojan War. **60–61. baths . . . stars:** the outer ocean surrounding the known world. **62. gulfs . . . down:** in Dante's account, a waterspout destroyed Ulysses' ship. **63. Happy Isles:** the Islands of the Blest (Elysian Fields, Hesperides) far in the western ocean, where heroes like Achilles lived after death. **68. equal temper:** uniform mixture.

Now Sleeps the Crimson Petal

Now sleeps the crimson petal, now the white;
Nor waves the cypress in the palace walk;
Nor winks the gold fin in the porphyry font;
The firefly wakens; waken thou with me.

Now droops the milk-white peacock like a ghost,   5
And like a ghost she glimmers on to me.

Now lies the earth all Danaë to the stars,
And all thy heart lies open unto me.

Now slides the silent meteor on, and leaves
A shining furrow, as thy thoughts in me.   10

Now folds the lily all her sweetness up,
And slips into the bosom of the lake:
So fold thyself, my dearest, thou, and slip
Into my bosom and be lost in me.

Tithonus

The woods decay, the woods decay and fall,
The vapors weep their burthen to the ground,
Man comes and tills the field and lies beneath,
And after many a summer dies the swan.
Me only cruel immortality   5
Consumes: I wither slowly in thine arms,
Here at the quiet limit of the world,
A white-haired shadow roaming like a dream
The ever silent spaces of the East,
Far-folded mists, and gleaming halls of morn.   10
   Alas! for this gray shadow, once a man—
So glorious in his beauty and thy choice,
Who madest him thy chosen, that he seemed
To his great heart none other than a god!
I asked thee, "Give me immortality."   15
Then didst thou grant mine asking with a smile,
Like wealthy men who care not how they give.
But thy strong Hours indignant worked their wills,

NOW SLEEPS THE CRIMSON PETAL   7. **Danaë:** a Greek princess who, confined by her father in a tower, was seduced by Zeus in the form of a shower of gold.

TITHONUS   Tithonus, a Trojan prince loved by the dawn-goddess Eos, asked her for immortality but forgot to ask for eternal youth. **4. swan:** some species of swan are very long lived. **18. Hours:** the attendants of Eos.

And beat me down and marred and wasted me,
And though they could not end me, left me maimed   20
To dwell in presence of immortal youth.
Immortal age beside immortal youth,
And all I was, in ashes. Can thy love,
Thy beauty, make amends, though even now,
Close over us, the silver star, thy guide,   25
Shines in those tremulous eyes that fill with tears
To hear me? Let me go; take back thy gift:
Why should a man desire in any way
To vary from the kindly race of men,
Or pass beyond the goal of ordinance   30
Where all should pause, as is most meet for all?
    A soft air fans the cloud apart; there comes
A glimpse of that dark world where I was born.
Once more the old mysterious glimmer steals
From thy pure brows, and from thy shoulders pure,   35
And bosom beating with a heart renewed.
Thy cheek begins to redden through the gloom,
Thy sweet eyes brighten slowly close to mine,
Ere yet they blind the stars, and the wild team
Which love thee, yearning for thy yoke, arise,   40
And shake the darkness from their loosened manes,
And beat the twilight into flakes of fire.
    Lo! ever thus thou growest beautiful
In silence, then before thine answer given
Departest, and thy tears are on my check.   45
    Why wilt thou ever scare me with thy tears,
And make me tremble lest a saying learnt,
In days far-off, on the dark earth, be true?
"The gods themselves cannot recall their gifts."
    Ay me! ay me! with what another heart   50
In days far-off, and with what other eyes
I used to watch—if I be he that watched—
The lucid outline forming round thee; saw
The dim curls kindle into sunny rings;
Changed with thy mystic change, and felt my blood   55
Glow with the glow that slowly crimsoned all
Thy presence and thy portals, while I lay,
Mouth, forehead, eyelids, growing dewy-warm
With kisses balmier than half-opening buds
Of April, and could hear the lips that kissed   60
Whispering I knew not what of wild and sweet,
Like that strange song I heard Apollo sing,
While Ilion like a mist rose into towers.
    Yet hold me not for ever in thine East:

---

25. star: the morning star. **29. kindly:** natural. **30. goal of ordinance:** ordained goal of human destiny. **31. meet:** fitting. **39. team:** team of horses that draws the chariot of Eos through the sky. **62–63. strange . . . towers:** the walls of Troy (Ilion) rose to the music of Apollo.

How can my nature longer mix with thine? 65
Coldly thy rosy shadows bathe me, cold
Are all thy lights, and cold my wrinkled feet
Upon thy glimmering thresholds, when the steam
Floats up from those dim fields about the homes
Of happy men that have the power to die, 70
And grassy barrows of the happier dead.
Release me, and restore me to the ground:
Thou seëst all things, thou wilt see my grave;
Thou wilt renew thy beauty morn by morn;
I earth in earth forget these empty courts, 75
And thee returning on thy silver wheels.

Robert Browning   *(1812–1889)*

The Bishop Orders His Tomb
at Saint Praxed's Church

Rome, 15—

Vanity, saith the preacher, vanity!
Draw round my bed: is Anselm keeping back?
Nephews—sons mine . . . ah God, I know not! Well—
She, men would have to be your mother once,
Old Gandolf envied me, so fair she was! 5
What's done is done, and she is dead beside,
Dead long ago, and I am Bishop since,
And as she died so must we die ourselves,
And thence ye may perceive the world's a dream
Life, how and what is it? As here I lie 10
In this state-chamber, dying by degrees,
Hours and long hours in the dead night, I ask
"Do I live, am I dead?" Peace, peace seems all.
Saint Praxed's ever was the church for peace;
And so, about this tomb of mine. I fought 15
With tooth and nail to save my niche, ye know:
—Old Gandolf cozened me, despite my care;
Shrewd was that snatch from out the corner south
He graced his carrion with, God curse the same!
Yet still my niche is not so cramped but thence 20

THE BISHOP ORDERS HIS TOMB   St. Praxed's is a small church in Rome named for a second-century virgin who gave her wealth to the poor. **1. Vanity . . . vanity:** The Bishop remembers loosely Ecclesiastes 1:2, "vanity of vanities, saith the Preacher, vanity of vanities; all is vanity." **8. we:** the episcopal "we." **17. cozened:** cheated.

One sees the pulpit o' the epistle side,
And somewhat of the choir, those silent seats,
And up into the airy dome where live
The angels, and a sunbeam's sure to lurk:
And I shall fill my slab of basalt there,   25
And 'neath my tabernacle take my rest,
With those nine columns round me, two and two,
The odd one at my feet where Anselm stands:
Peach-blossom marble all, the rare, the ripe
As fresh-poured red wine of a mighty pulse.   30
—Old Gandolf with his paltry onion-stone,
Put me where I may look at him! True peach,
Rosy and flawless: how I earned the prize!
Draw close: that conflagration of my church
—What then? So much was saved if aught were missed!   35
My sons, ye would not be my death? Go dig
The white-grape vineyard where the oil-press stood,
Drop water gently till the surface sink,
And if ye find . . . Ah God, I know not, I! . . .
Bedded in store of rotten fig leaves soft,   40
And corded up in a tight olive-frail,
Some lump, ah God, of *lapis lazuli*,
Big as a Jew's head cut off at the nape,
Blue as a vein o'er the Madonna's breast . . .
Sons, all have I bequeathed you, villas, all,   45
That brave Frascati villa with its bath,
So, let the blue lump poise between my knees,
Like God the Father's globe on both his hands
Ye worship in the Jesu Church so gay,
For Gandolf shall not choose but see and burst!   50
Swift as a weaver's shuttle fleet our years:
Man goeth to the grave, and where is he?
Did I say basalt for my slab, sons? Black—
'Twas ever antique-black I meant! How else
Shall ye contrast my frieze to come beneath?   55
The bas-relief in bronze ye promised me,
Those Pans and Nymphs ye wot of, and perchance
Some tripod, thyrsus, with a vase or so,
The Saviour at his Sermon on the Mount,
Saint Praxed in a glory, and one Pan   60
Ready to twitch the Nymph's last garment off,
And Moses with the tables . . . but I know

21. **epistle side:** right-hand side of the altar as one faces it, where the epistle is read during the Mass. 26. **tabernacle:** canopy of the tomb under which the Bishop's effigy would lie. 31. **onion-stone:** an inferior kind of marble. 41. **olive-frail:** basket for olives. 42. **lapis lazuli:** a semi-precious stone, rich blue in color. 46. **brave:** splendid. **Frascati:** a Roman resort suburb. 49. **Jesu Church:** the splendid church of the Jesuits called Il Jesù, built 1568–77. The globe (l. 48) has been said to be the largest block of lapis lazuli in existence. 51. **Swift . . . years:** "My days are swifter than a weaver's shuttle, and are spent without hope" (Job 7:6). 53. **Black:** black marble. 57. **wot:** know. 60. **glory:** halo. 62. **tables:** stone tablets inscribed with the Ten Commandments.

Ye mark me not! What do they whisper thee,
Child of my bowels, Anselm? Ah, ye hope
To revel down my villas while I gasp   65
Bricked o'er with beggar's moldy travertine
Which Gandolf from his tomb-top chuckles at!
Nay, boys, ye love me—all of jasper, then!
'Tis jasper ye stand pledged to, lest I grieve
My bath must needs be left behind, alas!   70
One block, pure green as a pistachio nut,
There's plenty jasper somewhere in the world—
And have I not Saint Praxed's ear to pray
Horses for ye, and brown Greek manuscripts,
And mistresses with great smooth marbly limbs?   75
—That's if ye carve my epitaph aright,
Choice Latin, picked phrase, Tully's every word,
No gaudy ware like Gandolf's second line—
Tully, my masters? Ulpian serves his need!
And then how I shall lie through centuries,   80
And hear the blessèd mutter of the mass,
And see God made and eaten all day long,
And feel the steady candle flame, and taste
Good strong thick stupefying incense-smoke!
For as I lie here, hours of the dead night,   85
Dying in state and by such slow degrees,
I fold my arms as if they clasped a crook,
And stretch my feet forth straight as stone can point,
And let the bedclothes, for a mortcloth, drop
Into great laps and folds of sculptor's-work: 90
And as yon tapers dwindle, and strange thoughts
Grow, with a certain humming in my ears,
About the life before I lived this life,
And this life too, popes, cardinals, and priests,
Saint Praxed at his sermon on the mount,   95
Your tall pale mother with her talking eyes,
And new-found agate urns as fresh as day,
And marble's language, Latin pure, discreet,
—Aha, ELUCESCEBAT quoth our friend?
No Tully, said I, Ulpian at the best!   100
Evil and brief hath been my pilgrimage.
All *lapis*, all, sons! Else I give the Pope
My villas! Will ye ever eat my heart?
Ever your eyes were as a lizard's quick,
They glitter like your mother's for my soul,   105
Or ye would heighten my impoverished frieze,
Piece out its starved design, and fill my vase

---

64. Child . . . bowels: beloved child (in Biblical phrasing). **66. travertine:** ordinary limestone. **77. Tully's:** Marcus Tullius Cicero's. **79. Ulpian:** a later Roman lawyer, who wrote less pure Latin than Cicero. **87. crook:** bishop's staff. **89. mortcloth:** funeral pall. The Bishop anticipates his effigy. **99. elucescebat:** "he was illustrious." In Cicero's Latin the form is *elucebat*.

With grapes, and add a vizor and a Term,
And to the tripod ye would tie a lynx
That in his struggle throws the thyrsus down,   110
To comfort me on my entablature
Whereon I am to lie till I must ask
"Do I live, am I dead?" There, leave me, there!
For ye have stabbed me with ingratitude
To death—ye wish it—God, ye wish it! Stone—   115
Gritstone, a-crumble! Clammy squares which sweat
As if the corpse they keep were oozing through—
And no more *lapis* to delight the world!
Well go! I bless ye. Fewer tapers there,
But in a row: and, going, turn your backs   120
—Ay, like departing altar-ministrants,
And leave me in my church, the church for peace,
That I may watch at leisure if he leers—
Old Gandolf—at me, from his onion-stone,
As still he envied me, so fair she was!

"Childe Roland to the Dark Tower Came"

(See Edgar's song in *Lear*)

I

My first thought was, he lied in every word,
    That hoary cripple, with malicious eye
    Askance to watch the working of his lie
On mine, and mouth scarce able to afford
Suppression of the glee, that pursed and scored   5
    Its edge, at one more victim gained thereby.

II

What else should he be set for, with his staff?
    What, save to waylay with his lies, ensnare
    All travelers who might find him posted there,
And ask the road? I guessed what skull-like laugh   10
Would break, what crutch 'gin write my epitaph
    For pastime in the dusty thoroughfare,

III

If at his counsel I should turn aside
    Into that ominous tract which, all agree,
    Hides the Dark Tower. Yet acquiescingly   15

108. **vizor . . . Term:** a mask and a statue of Terminus, god of boundaries. **111. entablature:** surface supporting the effigy. **116. Gritstone:** cheap sandstone.
CHILDE RONALD "Childe" means young man of noble birth. In Shakespeare's *King Lear* (III. iv.), Edgar, pretending madness, sings on the heath, "Child Rowland to the dark tower came;/His word was still/Fie, foh, and fum!/I smell the blood of a British man." **3. Askance:** oblique and suspicious. **4. afford:** manage. **5. scored:** marked.

I did turn as he pointed: neither pride
Nor hope rekindling at the end descried,
    So much as gladness that some end might be.

IV

For, what with my whole worldwide wandering,
    What with my search drawn out through years, my hope   20
    Dwindled into a ghost not fit to cope
With that obstreperous joy success would bring—
I hardly tried now to rebuke the spring
    My heart made, finding failure in its scope.

V

As when a sick man very near to death   25
    Seems dead indeed, and feels begin and end
    The tears, and takes the farewell of each friend,
And hears one bid the other go, draw breath
Freelier outside ("since all is o'er," he saith,
    "And the blow fallen no grieving can amend");   30

VI

While some discuss if near the other graves
    Be room enough for this, and when a day
    Suits best for carrying the corpse away,
With care about the banners, scarves, and staves:
And still the man hears all, and only craves   35
    He may not shame such tender love and stay.

VII

Thus, I had so long suffered in this quest,
    Heard failure prophesied so oft, been writ
    So many times among "The Band"—to wit,
The knights who to the Dark Tower's search addressed   40
Their steps—that just to fail as they, seemed best,
    And all the doubt was now—should I be fit?

VIII

So, quiet as despair, I turned from him,
    That hateful cripple, out of his highway
    Into the path he pointed. All the day   45
Had been a dreary one at best, and dim
Was settling to its close, yet shot one grim
    Red leer to see the plain catch its estray.

IX

For mark! no sooner was I fairly found
    Pledged to the plain, after a pace or two,   50

34. banners . . . staves: funeral ornaments. **48. estray:** stray domestic animal.

Than, pausing to throw backward a last view
O'er the safe road, 'twas gone; gray plain all round:
Nothing but plain to the horizon's bound.
    I might go on; naught else remained to do.

X

So, on I went. I think I never saw   55
    Such starved ignoble nature; nothing throve:
    For flowers—as well expect a cedar grove!
But cockle, spurge, according to their law
Might propagate their kind, with none to awe:
    You'd think a burr had been a treasure-trove.   60

XI

No! penury, inertness, and grimace,
    In some strange sort, were the land's portion. "See
    Or shut your eyes," said Nature peevishly,
"It nothing skills: I cannot help my case:
'Tis the Last Judgment's fire must cure this place,   65
    Calcine its clods and set my prisoners free."

XII

If there pushed any ragged thistle-stalk
    Above its mates, the head was chopped; the bents
    Were jealous else. What made those holes and rents
In the dock's harsh swarth leaves, bruised as to balk   70
All hope of greenness? 'tis a brute must walk
    Pashing their life out, with a brute's intents.

XIII

As for the grass, it grew as scant as hair
    In leprosy; thin dry blades pricked the mud
    Which underneath looked kneaded up with blood.
One stiff blind horse, his every bone a-stare,   75
Stood stupefied, however he came there:
    Thrust out past service from the devil's stud!

XIV

Alive? he might be dead for aught I know,
    With that red gaunt and colloped neck a-strain,   80
    And shut eyes underneath the rusty mane;
Seldom went such grotesqueness with such woe;
I never saw a brute I hated so;
    He must be wicked to deserve such pain.

XV

I shut my eyes and turned them on my heart.   85
    As a man calls for wine before he fights,

58. cockle, spurge: weeds. Cockles have burrs. 60. had been: was. 64. It . . . skills: it makes no difference. 66. Calcine: turn to powder by heating. 68. bents: coarse grasses. 70. dock: weedy plant. 80. colloped: ridged.

I asked one draught of earlier, happier sights,
Ere fitly I could hope to play my part.
Think first, fight afterwards—the soldier's art:
    One taste of the old time sets all to rights.   90

XVI

Not it! I fancied Cuthbert's reddening face
    Beneath its garniture of curly gold,
    Dear fellow, till I almost felt him fold
An arm in mine to fix me to the place,
That way he used. Alas, one night's disgrace!   95
    Out went my heart's new fire and left it cold.

XVII

Giles then, the soul of honor—there he stands
    Frank as ten years ago when knighted first.
    What honest man should dare (he said) he durst.
Good—but the scene shifts—faugh! what hangman hands   100
Pin to his breast a parchment? His own bands
    Read it. Poor traitor, spit upon and cursed!

XVIII

Better this present than a past like that;
    Back therefore to my darkening path again!
    No sound, no sight as far as eye could strain.   105
Will the night send a howlet or a bat?
I asked: when something on the dismal flat
    Came to arrest my thoughts and change their train.

XIX

A sudden little river crossed my path
    As unexpected as a serpent comes.   110
    No sluggish tide congenial to the glooms;
This, as it frothed by, might have been a bath
For the fiend's glowing hoof—to see the wrath
    Of its black eddy bespate with flakes and spumes.

XX

So petty yet so spiteful! All along,   115
    Low scrubby alders kneeled down over it;
    Drenched willows flung them headlong in a fit
Of mute despair, a suicidal throng:
The river which had done them all the wrong,
    Whate'er that was, rolled by, deterred no whit.   120

XXI

Which, while I forded—good saints, how I feared
    To set my foot upon a dead man's cheek,

---

92. garniture: garnishing. **95. used:** was accustomed to do. **106. howlet:** owl, owlet.
114. bespate: bespattered.

Each step, or feel the spear I thrust to seek
For hollows, tangled in his hair or beard!
—It may have been a water-rat I speared,   125
    But, ugh! it sounded like a baby's shriek.

XXII

Glad was I when I reached the other bank.
    Now for a better country. Vain presage!
    Who were the strugglers, what war did they wage,
Whose savage trample thus could pad the dank   130
Soil to a plash? Toads in a poisoned tank,
    Or wild cats in a red-hot iron cage—

XXIII

The fight must so have seemed in that fell cirque.
    What penned them there, with all the plain to choose?
    No footprint leading to that horrid mews,   135
None out of it. Mad brewage set to work
Their brains, no doubt, like galley slaves the Turk
    Pits for his pastime, Christians against Jews.

XXIV

And more than that—a furlong on—why, there!
    What bad use was that engine for, that wheel,   140
    Or brake, not wheel—that harrow fit to reel
Men's bodies out like silk? with all the air
Of Tophet's tool, on earth left unaware,
    Or brought to sharpen its rusty teeth of steel.

XXV

Then came a bit of stubbed ground, once a wood,   145
    Next a marsh, it would seem, and now mere earth
    Desperate and done with; (so a fool finds mirth,
Makes a thing and then mars it, till his mood
Changes and off he goes!) within a rood—
    Bog, clay and rubble, sand and stark black dearth.   150

XXVI

Now blotches rankling, colored gay and grim,
    Now patches where some leanness of the soil's
    Broke into moss or substances like boils;
Then came some palsied oak, a cleft in him
Like a distorted mouth that splits its rim   155
    Gaping at death, and dies while it recoils.

---

133. fell cirque: deadly arena. **135. mews:** originally, a back street for stables; here, a blind alley. **141. brake:** (1) a device for separating flax or hemp fibers; (2) an instrument of torture. **143. Tophet's:** Hell's. **149. rood:** about six yards.

XXVII

And just as far as ever from the end!
    Naught in the distance but the evening, naught
    To point my footstep further! At the thought,
A great black bird, Apollyon's bosom-friend,   160
Sailed past, nor beat his wide wing dragon-penned
    That brushed my cap—perchance the guide I sought.

XXVIII

For, looking up, aware I somehow grew,
    'Spite of the dusk, the plain had given place
    All round to mountains—with such name to grace   165
Mere ugly heights and heaps now stolen in view.
How thus they had surprised me—solve it, you!
    How to get from them was no clearer case.

XXIX

Yet half I seemed to recognize some trick
    Of mischief happened to me, God knows when—   170
    In a bad dream perhaps. Here ended, then,
Progress this way. When, in the very nick
Of giving up, one time more, came a click
    As when a trap shuts—you're inside the den!

XXX

Burningly it came on me all at once,   175
    This was the place! those two hills on the right,
    Crouched like two bulls locked horn in horn in fight;
While to the left, a tall scalped mountain . . . dunce,
Dotard, a-dozing at the very nonce,
    After a life spent training for the sight!   180

XXXI

What in the midst lay but the Tower itself?
    The round squat turret, blind as the fool's heart,
    Built of brown stone, without a counterpart
In the whole world. The tempest's mocking elf
Points to the shipman thus the unseen shelf   185
    He strikes on, only when the timbers start.

XXXII

Not see? because of night perhaps?—why, day
    Came back again for that! before it left,
    The dying sunset kindled through a cleft:
The hills, like giants at a hunting, lay,   190
Chin upon hand, to see the game at bay—
    "Now stab and end the creature—to the heft!"

---

160. **Apollyon's:** the Devil's name, meaning "abyss," in the Book of Revelation (9:11).
161. **dragon-penned:** with dragon-like feathers. 179. **nonce:** particular moment. 186.
start: split. 192. **heft:** hilt.

XXXIII

Not hear? when noise was everywhere! it tolled
    Increasing like a bell. Names in my ears
    Of all the lost adventurers my peers— 195
How such a one was strong, and such was bold,
And such was fortunate, yet each of old
    Lost, lost! one moment knelled the woe of years.

XXXIV

There they stood, ranged along the hillsides, met
    To view the last of me, a living frame 200
    For one more picture! in a sheet of flame
I saw them and I knew them all. And yet
Dauntless the slug-horn to my lips I set,
    And blew. *"Childe Roland to the Dark Tower came."*

My Last Duchess

Ferrara

That's my last Duchess painted on the wall,
Looking as if she were alive. I call
That piece a wonder, now: Frà Pandolf's hands
Worked busily a day, and there she stands.
Will't please you sit and look at her? I said 5
"Frà Pandolf" by design, for never read
Strangers like you that pictured countenance,
The depth and passion of its earnest glance,
But to myself they turned (since none puts by
The curtain I have drawn for you, but I) 10
And seemed as they would ask me, if they durst,
How such a glance came there; so, not the first
Are you to turn and ask thus. Sir, 'twas not
Her husband's presence only, called that spot
Of joy into the Duchess' cheek: perhaps 15
Frà Pandolf chanced to say, "Her mantle laps
Over my Lady's wrist too much," or "Paint
Must never hope to reproduce the faint
Half-flush that dies along her throat"; such stuff
Was courtesy, she thought, and cause enough 20
For calling up that spot of joy. She had
A heart . . . how shall I say? . . . too soon made glad,
Too easily impressed; she liked whate'er
She looked on, and her looks went everywhere.
Sir, 'twas all one! My favor at her breast, 25

---

203. **slug-horn:** trumpet.
MY LAST DUCHESS Ferrara was a city-state in Renaissance Italy. **3. Frà Pandolf:** an
imaginary painter. **25. favor:** gift, token of affection.

The dropping of the daylight in the west,
The bough of cherries some officious fool
Broke in the orchard for her, the white mule
She rode with round the terrace—all and each
Would draw from her alike the approving speech,   30
Or blush, at least. She thanked men—good; but thanked
Somehow . . . I know not how . . . as if she ranked
My gift of a nine-hundred-years-old name
With anybody's gift. Who'd stoop to blame
This sort of trifling? Even had you skill   35
In speech—(which I have not)—to make your will
Quite clear to such an one, and say, "Just this
Or that in you disgusts me; here you miss,
Or there exceed the mark"—and if she let
Herself be lessoned so, nor plainly set   40
Her wits to yours, forsooth, and made excuse
—E'en then would be some stooping, and I choose
Never to stoop. Oh, Sir, she smiled, no doubt,
Whene'er I passed her; but who passed without
Much the same smile? This grew; I gave commands;   45
Then all smiles stopped together. There she stands
As if alive. Will't please you rise? We'll meet
The company below, then. I repeat,
The Count your master's known munificence
Is ample warrant that no just pretense   50
Of mine for dowry will be disallowed;
Though his fair daughter's self, as I avowed
At starting, is my object. Nay, we'll go
Together down, Sir. Notice Neptune, though,
Taming a sea horse, thought a rarity,   55
Which Claus of Innsbruck cast in bronze for me.

Up at a Villa—Down in the City

(As Distinguished by an Italian Person of Quality)

I

Had I but plenty of money, money enough and to spare,
The house for me, no doubt, were a house in the city square;
Ah, such a life, such a life, as one leads at the window there!

II

Something to see, by Bacchus, something to hear, at least!
There, the whole day long, one's life is a perfect feast;   5
While up at a villa one lives, I maintain it, no more than a beast.

III

Well now, look at our villa! stuck like the horn of a bull

---

56. Claus of Innsbruck: another imaginary artist.
UP AT A VILLA   "Person of quality" means one of the upper class, often a nobleman.

Just on a mountain edge as bare as the creature's skull,
Save a mere shag of a bush with hardly a leaf to pull!
—I scratch my own, sometimes, to see if the hair's turned wool.   10

IV

But the city, oh the city—the square with the houses! Why?
They are stone-faced, white as a curd, there's something to take the eye!
Houses in four straight lines, not a single front awry;
You watch who crosses and gossips, who saunters, who hurries by;
Green blinds, as a matter of course, to draw when the sun gets high;   15
And the shops with fanciful signs which are painted properly.

V

What of a villa? Though winter be over in March by rights,
'Tis May perhaps ere the snow shall have withered well off the heights:
You've the brown ploughed land before, where the oxen steam and
    wheeze,
And the hills over-smoked behind by the faint gray olive-trees.   20

VI

Is it better in May, I ask you? You've summer all at once;
In a day he leaps complete with a few strong April suns.
'Mid the sharp short emerald wheat, scarce risen three fingers well,
The wild tulip, at end of its tube, blows out its great red bell
Like a thin clear bubble of blood, for the children to pick and sell.   25

VII

Is it ever hot in the square? There's a fountain to spout and splash!
In the shade it sings and springs; in the shine such foam-bows flash
On the horses with curling fishtails, that prance and paddle and pash
Round the lady atop in her conch—fifty gazers do not abash,
Though all that she wears is some weeds round her waist in a sort of sash.   30

VIII

All the year long at the villa, nothing to see though you linger,
Except yon cypress that points like death's lean lifted forefinger.
Some think fireflies pretty, when they mix i' the corn and mingle,
Or thrid the stinking hemp till the stalks of it seem a-tingle.
Late August or early September, the stunning cicala is shrill,   35
And the bees keep their tiresome whine round the resinous firs on
    the hill.
Enough of the seasons—I spare you the months of the fever and chill.

IX

Ere you open your eyes in the city, the blessèd church bells begin:
No sooner the bells leave off than the diligence rattles in:
You get the pick of the news, and it costs you never a pin.   40
By and by there's the traveling doctor gives pills, lets blood, draws teeth;

---

33. corn and mingle: wheat and jumble (of plants). **34. thrid:** thread through. **39. diligence:** stagecoach.

Or the Pulcinello-trumpet breaks up the market beneath.
At the post office such a scene-picture—the new play, piping hot!
And a notice how, only this morning, three liberal thieves were shot.
Above it, behold the Archbishop's most fatherly of rebukes,   45
And beneath, with his crown and his lion, some little new law of the
    Duke's!
Or a sonnet with flowery marge, to the Reverend Don So-and-so
Who is Dante, Boccaccio, Petrarca, Saint Jerome, and Cicero,
"And moreover," (the sonnet goes rhyming) "the skirts of Saint Paul
    has reached,
Having preached us those six Lent-lectures more unctuous than ever
    he preached."   50
Noon strikes—here sweeps the procession! our Lady borne smiling and
    smart
With a pink gauze gown all spangles, and seven swords stuck in her
    heart!
Bang-whang-whang goes the drum, *tootle-te-tootle* the fife;
No keeping one's haunches still: it's the greatest pleasure in life.

x

But bless you, it's dear—it's dear! fowls, wine, at double the rate.   55
They have clapped a new tax upon salt, and what oil pays passing the
    gate
It's a horror to think of. And so, the villa for me, not the city!
Beggars can scarcely be choosers: but still—ah, the pity, the pity!
Look, two and two go the priests, then the monks with cowls and
    sandals,
And the penitents dressed in white shirts, a-holding the yellow candles;   60
One, he carries a flag up straight, and another a cross with handles,
And the Duke's guard brings up the rear, for the better prevention of
    scandals:
Bang-whang-whang goes the drum, *tootle-te-tootle* the fife.
Oh, a day in the city square, there is no such pleasure in life!

Arthur Hugh Clough   (1819–1861)

The Latest Decalogue

Thou shalt have one God only; who
Would be at the expense of two?
No graven images may be
Worshiped, except the currency;

---

42. **Pulcinello-trumpet:** trumpet announcing Pulcinello the buffoon, and the rest of the puppet show. 43. **scene-picture:** playbill. 44. **liberal thieves:** revolutionaries. 49. **skirts . . . reached:** has acquired some of the eloquence of St. Paul. 52. **seven swords:** symbolizing the seven sorrows of the Virgin Mary. 56. **oil . . . gate:** goods brought into towns were taxed at the gates.

Swear not at all: for, for thy curse,   5
Thine enemy is none the worse;
At church on Sunday to attend
Will serve to keep the world thy friend;
Honor thy parents: that is, all
From whom advancement may befall;   10
Thou shalt not kill: but needst not strive
Officiously to keep alive;
Do not adultery commit:
Advantage rarely comes of it;
Thou shalt not steal: an empty feat,   15
When it's so lucrative to cheat;
Bear not false witness: let the lie
Have time on its own wings to fly;
Thou shalt not covet, but tradition
Approves all forms of competition.   20

Walt Whitman   *(1819–1892)*

When Lilacs Last in the Dooryard Bloomed

1

When lilacs last in the dooryard bloomed,
And the great star early drooped in the western sky in the night,
I mourned, and yet shall mourn with ever-returning spring.

Ever-returning spring, trinity sure to me you bring,
Lilac blooming perennial and drooping star in the west,   5
And thought of him I love.

2

O powerful western fallen star!
O shades of night—O moody, tearful night!
O great star disappeared—O the black murk that hides the star!
O cruel hands that hold me powerless—O helpless soul of me!   10
O harsh surrounding cloud that will not free my soul.

3

In the dooryard fronting an old farmhouse near the whitewashed palings,
Stands the lilac bush tall-growing with heart-shaped leaves of rich green,
With many a pointed blossom rising delicate, with the perfume strong
    I love,
With every leaf a miracle—and from this bush in the dooryard,   15
With delicate-colored blossoms and heart-shaped leaves of rich green,
A sprig with its flower I break.

WHEN LILACS LAST IN THE DOORYARD BLOOMED An elegy on the death of President Lincoln.

4

In the swamp in secluded recesses,
A shy and hidden bird is warbling a song.

Solitary the thrush,　　　　　　　　　　　　　　　　　　　　　　20
The hermit withdrawn to himself, avoiding the settlements,
Sings by himself a song.

Song of the bleeding throat,
Death's outlet song of life (for well dear brother I know,
If thou wast not granted to sing thou wouldst surely die).　　　25

5

Over the breast of the spring, the land, amid cities,
Amid lanes and through old woods, where lately the violets peeped from
　　　the ground, spotting the gray debris,
Amid the grass in the fields each side of the lanes, passing the endless
　　　grass,
Passing the yellow-speared wheat, every grain from its shroud in the dark-
　　　brown fields uprisen,
Passing the apple-tree blows of white and pink in the orchards,　　　30
Carrying a corpse to where it shall rest in the grave,
Night and day journeys a coffin.

6

Coffin that passes through lanes and streets,
Through day and night with the great cloud darkening the land,
With the pomp of the inlooped flags with the cities draped in black,　　　35
With the show of the States themselves as of crape-veiled women standing,
With processions long and winding and the flambeaus of the night,
With the countless torches lit, with the silent sea of faces and the unbared
　　　heads,
With the waiting depot, the arriving coffin, and the somber faces,
With dirges through the night, with the thousand voices rising strong and
　　　solemn,
　　　　　　　　　　　　　　　　　　　　　　　　　　　　　　40
With all the mournful voices of the dirges poured around the coffin,
The dim-lit churches and the shuddering organs—where amid these you
　　　journey,
With the tolling tolling bells' perpetual clang,
Here, coffin that slowly passes,
I give you my sprig of lilac.　　　　　　　　　　　　　　　　　　　　45

7

(Nor for you, for one alone,
Blossoms and branches green to coffins all I bring,

---

21. hermit: i.e., the hermit thrush, noted for its beautiful song. **26–32. Over
. . . coffin:** Lincoln's funeral train moved slowly from Washington, D.C., to Spring-
field, Illinois. **30. blows:** blossoms. **37. flambeaus:** torches.

For fresh as the morning, thus would I chant a song for you O sane and
    sacred death.

All over bouquets of roses,
O death, I cover you over with roses and early lilies,   50
But mostly and now the lilac that blooms the first,
Copious I break, I break the sprigs from the bushes,
With loaded arms I come, pouring for you,
For you and the coffins all of you O death.)

8

O western orb sailing the heaven,   55
Now I know what you must have meant as a month since I walked.
As I walked in silence the transparent shadowy night,
As I saw you had something to tell as you bent to me night after night,
As you drooped from the sky low down as if to my side (while the other
    stars all looked on),
As we wandered together the solemn night (for something I know not
    what kept me from sleep),   60
As the night advanced, and I saw on the rim of the west how full you were
    of woe,
As I stood on the rising ground in the breeze in the cool transparent night,
As I watched where you passed and was lost in the netherward black of
    the night,
As my soul in its trouble dissatisfied sank, as where you sad orb,
Concluded, dropped in the night, and was gone.   65

9

Sing on there in the swamp,
O singer bashful and tender, I hear your notes, I hear your call,
I hear, I come presently, I understand you,
But a moment I linger, for the lustrous star has detained me,
The star my departing comrade holds and detains me.   70

10

O how shall I warble myself for the dead one there I loved?
And how shall I deck my song for the large sweet soul that has gone?
And what shall my perfume be for the grave of him I love?

Sea-winds blown from east and west,
Blown from the Eastern sea and blown from the Western sea, till there
    on the prairies meeting,   75
These and with these and the breath of my chant,
I'll perfume the grave of him I love.

11

O what shall I hang on the chamber walls?
And what shall the pictures be that I hang on the walls,
To adorn the burial-house of him I love?   80

Pictures of growing spring and farms and homes,
With the Fourth-month eve at sundown, and the gray smoke lucid and
  bright,
With floods of the yellow gold of the gorgeous, indolent, sinking sun,
  burning, expanding the air,
With the fresh sweet herbage under foot, and the pale green leaves of the
  trees prolific,
In the distance the flowing glaze, the breast of the river, with a wind-
  dapple here and there,   85
With ranging hills on the banks, with many a line against the sky, and
  shadows,
And the city at hand with dwellings so dense, and stacks of chimneys,
And all the scenes of life and the workshops, and the workmen homeward
  returning.

                              12

Lo, body and soul—this land,
My own Manhattan with spires, and the sparkling and hurrying tides, and
  the ships,   90
The varied and ample land, the South and the North in the light, Ohio's
  shores and flashing Missouri,
And ever the far-spreading prairies covered with grass and corn.

Lo, the most excellent sun so calm and haughty,
The violet and purple morn with just-felt breezes,
The gentle soft-born measureless light,   95
The miracle spreading bathing all, the fulfilled noon,
The coming eve delicious, the welcome night and the stars,
Over my cities shining all, enveloping man and land.

                              13

Sing on, sing on you gray-brown bird,
Sing from the swamps, the recesses, pour your chant from the bushes, 100
Limitless out of the dusk, out of the cedars and pines.

Sing on dearest brother, warble your reedy song,
Loud human song, with voice of uttermost woe.

O liquid and free and tender!
O wild and loose to my soul—O wondrous singer!   105
You only I hear—yet the star holds me (but will soon depart),
Yet the lilac with mastering odor holds me.

                              14

Now while I sat in the day and looked forth,
In the close of the day with its light and the fields of spring, and the
  farmers preparing their crops,
In the large unconscious scenery of my land with its lakes and forests, 110
In the heavenly aerial beauty (after the perturbed winds and the storms),

Under the arching heavens of the afternoon swift passing, and the voices
    of children and women,
The many-moving sea-tides, and I saw the ships how they sailed,
And the summer approaching with richness, and the fields all busy with
    labor,
And the infinite separate houses, how they all went on, each with its meals
    and minutia of daily usages,   115
And the streets how their throbbings throbbed, and the cities pent—lo,
    then and there,
Falling upon them all and among them all, enveloping me with the rest,
Appeared the cloud, appeared the long black trail,
And I knew death, its thought, and the sacred knowledge of death.

Then with the knowledge of death as walking one side of me,   120
And the thought of death close-walking the other side of me,
And I in the middle as with companions, and as holding the hands of
    companions,
I fled forth to the hiding receiving night that talks not,
Down to the shores of the water, the path by the swamp in the dimness,
To the solemn shadowy cedars and ghostly pines so still.   125

And the singer so shy to the rest received me,
The gray-brown bird I know received us comrades three,
And he sang the carol of death, and a verse for him I love.

From deep secluded recesses,
From the fragrant cedars and the ghostly pines so still,   130
Came the carol of the bird.

And the charm of the carol rapt me,
As I held as if by their hands my comrades in the night,
And the voice of my spirit tallied the song of the bird.

Come lovely and soothing death,   135
Undulate round the world, serenely arriving, arriving,
In the day, in the night, to all, to each,
Sooner or later delicate death.

Praised be the fathomless universe,
For life and joy, and for objects and knowledge curious,   140
And for love, sweet love—but praise! praise! praise!
For the sure-enwinding arms of cool-enfolding death.

Dark mother always gliding near with soft feet,
Have none chanted for thee a chant of fullest welcome?
Then I chant it for thee, I glorify thee above all,   145
I bring thee a song that when thou must indeed come, come unfalteringly.

134. tallied: corresponded to.

Approach strong deliveress,
When it is so, when thou hast taken them I joyously sing the dead,
Lost in the loving floating ocean of thee,
Laved in the flood of thy bliss O death.   150

From me to thee glad serenades,
Dances for thee I propose saluting thee, adornments and feastings for
      thee,
And the sights of the open landscape and the high-spread sky are fitting,
And life and the fields, and the huge and thoughtful night.

The night in silence under many a star,   155
The ocean shore and the husky whispering wave whose voice I know,
And the soul turning to thee O vast and well-veiled death,
And the body gratefully nestling close to thee.

Over the tree-tops I float thee a song,
Over the rising and sinking waves, over the myriad fields and the prairies
      wide,   160
Over the dense-packed cities all and the teeming wharves and ways,
I float this carol with joy, with joy to thee O death.

15

To the tally of my soul,
Loud and strong kept up the gray-brown bird,
With pure deliberate notes spreading filling the night.   165

Loud in the pines and cedars dim,
Clear in the freshness moist and the swamp-perfume,
And I with my comrades there in the night.

While my sight that was bound in my eyes unclosed,
As to long panoramas of visions.   170

And I saw askant the armies,
I saw as in noiseless dreams hundreds of battle-flags,
Borne through the smoke of the battles and pierced with missiles I saw
      them,
And carried hither and yon through the smoke, and torn and bloody,
And at last but a few shreds left on the staffs (and all in silence),   175
And the staffs all splintered and broken.

I saw battle-corpses, myriads of them,
And the white skeletons of young men, I saw them,
I saw the debris and debris of all the slain soldiers of the war,
But I saw they were not as was thought,   180
They themselves were fully at rest, they suffered not,
The living remained and suffered, the mother suffered,
And the wife and the child and the musing comrade suffered,
And the armies that remained suffered.

163. **tally:** agreement. 171. **askant:** with a sidelong glance.

16

Passing the visions, passing the night,   185
Passing, unloosing the hold of my comrades' hands,
Passing the song of the hermit bird and the tallying song of my soul,
Victorious song, death's outlet song, yet varying ever-altering song,
As low and wailing, yet clear the notes, rising and falling, flooding the
    night,
Sadly sinking and fainting, as warning and warning, and yet again bursting
    with joy,   190
Covering the earth and filling the spread of the heaven,
As that powerful psalm in the night I heard from recesses,
Passing, I leave thee lilac with heart-shaped leaves,
I leave thee there in the dooryard, blooming, returning with spring.

I cease from my song for thee,   195
From my gaze on thee in the west, fronting the west, communing with
    thee,
O comrade lustrous with silver face in the night.

Yet each to keep and all, retrievements out of the night,
The song, the wondrous chant of the gray-brown bird,
And the tallying chant, the echo aroused in my soul,   200
With the lustrous and drooping star with the countenance full of woe,
With the holders holding my hand nearing the call of the bird,
Comrades mine and I in the midst, and their memory ever to keep, for
    the dead I loved so well,
For the sweetest, wisest soul of all my days and lands—and this for his
    dear sake,
Lilac and star and bird twined with the chant of my soul,   205
There in the fragrant pines and the cedars dusk and dim.

Come Up from the Fields Father

Come up from the fields father, here's a letter from our Pete,
And come to the front door mother, here's a letter from thy dear son.

Lo, 'tis autumn,
Lo, where the trees, deeper green, yellower and redder,
Cool and sweeten Ohio's villages with leaves fluttering in the moderate
    wind,   5
Where apples ripe in the orchards hang and grapes on the trellised vines,
(Smell you the smell of the grapes on the vines?
Smell you the buckwheat where the bees were lately buzzing?)
Above all, lo, the sky so calm, so transparent after the rain, and with
    wondrous clouds,
Below too, all calm, all vital and beautiful, and the farm prospers well.   10

Down in the fields all prospers well,
But now from the fields come father, come at the daughter's call,
And come to the entry mother, to the front door come right away.

Fast as she can she hurries, something ominous, her steps trembling,
She does not tarry to smooth her hair nor adjust her cap.   15

Open the envelope quickly,
O this is not our son's writing, yet his name is signed,
O a strange hand writes for our dear son, O stricken mother's soul!
All swims before her eyes, flashes with black, she catches the main words
    only,
Sentences broken, *gunshot wound in the breast, cavalry skirmish, taken
    to hospital,*   20
At present low, but will soon be better.

Ah now the single figure to me,
Amid all teeming and wealthy Ohio with all its cities and farms,
Sickly white in the face and dull in the head, very faint,
By the jamb of a door leans.   25

Grieve not so, dear mother (the just-grown daughter speaks through her
    sobs,
The little sisters huddle around speechless and dismayed),
See, dearest mother, the letter says Pete will soon be better.

Alas poor boy, he will never be better (nor may-be needs to be better,
    that brave and simple soul),
While they stand at home at the door he is dead already,   30
The only son is dead.

But the mother needs to be better,
She with thin form presently dressed in black,
By day her meals untouched, then at night fitfully sleeping, often waking,
In the midnight waking, weeping, longing with one deep longing,   35
O that she might withdraw unnoticed, silent from life escape and with-
    draw,
To follow, to seek, to be with her dear dead son.

The Dalliance of the Eagles

Skirting the river road (my forenoon walk, my rest),
Skyward in air a sudden muffled sound, the dalliance of the eagles,
The rushing amorous contact high in space together,
The clinching interlocking claws, a living, fierce, gyrating wheel,

Four beating wings, two beaks, a swirling mass tight grappling,　　5
In tumbling turning clustering loops, straight downward falling,
Till o'er the river poised, the twain yet one, a moment's lull,
A motionless still balance in the air, then parting, talons loosing,
Upward again on slow-firm pinions slanting, their separate diverse flight,
She hers, he his, pursuing.　　10

Are You the New Person Drawn Toward Me?

Are you the new person drawn toward me?
To begin with take warning, I am surely far different from what you
　　suppose;
Do you suppose you will find in me your ideal?
Do you think it so easy to have me become your lover?
Do you think the friendship of me would be unalloyed satisfaction?　　5
Do you think I am trusty and faithful?
Do you see no further than this façade, this smooth and tolerant manner
　　of me?
Do you suppose yourself advancing on real ground toward a real heroic
　　man?
Have you no thought O dreamer that it may be all maya, illusion?

I Hear It Was Charged Against Me

I hear it was charged against me that I sought to destroy institutions,
But really I am neither for nor against institutions,
(What indeed have I in common with them? or what with the destruc-
　　tion of them?)
Only I will establish in the Mannahatta and in every city of these States
　　inland and seaboard,
And in the fields and woods, and above every keel little or large that dents
　　the water,　　5
Without edifices or rules or trustees or any argument,
The institution of the dear love of comrades.

A Glimpse

A glimpse through an interstice caught,
Of a crowd of workmen and drivers in a barroom around the stove late of
　　a winter night, and I unremarked seated in a corner,

ARE YOU THE NEW PERSON　**9. maya:** a Hindu term for the veil of appearances that
hangs over reality.
I HEAR IT WAS CHARGED　**4. Mannahatta:** Manhattan, a separate city until 1898.

Of a youth who loves me and whom I love, silently approaching and
    seating himself near, that he may hold me by the hand,
A long while amid the noises of coming and going, of drinking and oath
    and smutty jest,
There we two, content, happy in being together, speaking little, perhaps
    not a word.   5

Matthew Arnold *(1822–1888)*

To Marguerite—Continued

Yes! in the sea of life enisled,
With echoing straits between us thrown,
Dotting the shoreless watery wild,
We mortal millions live *alone*.
The islands feel the enclasping flow,   5
And then their endless bounds they know.

But when the moon their hollows lights,
And they are swept by balms of spring,
And in their glens, on starry nights,
The nightingales divinely sing;   10
And lovely notes, from shore to shore,
Across the sounds and channels pour—

Oh! then a longing like despair
Is to their farthest caverns sent;
For surely once, they feel, we were   15
Parts of a single continent!
Now round us spreads the watery plain—
Oh might our marges meet again!

Who ordered, that their longing's fire
Should be, as soon as kindled, cooled?   20
Who renders vain their deep desire?—
A God, a God their severance ruled!
And bade betwixt their shores to be
The unplumbed, salt, estranging sea.

TO MARGUERITE—CONTINUED In a preceding poem addressed to Marguerite, a girl he
had once known, Arnold emphasizes human isolation despite any dreams of shared
love. **18. marges:** margins, edges.

Philomela

Hark! ah, the nightingale—
The tawny-throated!
Hark, from that moonlit cedar what a burst!
What triumph! hark—what pain!

O wanderer from a Grecian shore,   5
Still, after many years, in distant lands,
Still nourishing in thy bewildered brain
That wild, unquenched, deep-sunken, old-world pain—
Say, will it never heal?
And can this fragrant lawn   10
With its cool trees, and night,
And the sweet, tranquil Thames,
And moonshine, and the dew,
To thy racked heart and brain
Afford no balm?   15
Dost thou tonight behold,
Here, through the moonlight on this English grass,
The unfriendly palace in the Thracian wild?
Dost thou again peruse
With hot cheeks and seared eyes   20
The too clear web, and thy dumb sister's shame?
Dost thou once more assay
Thy flight, and feel come over thee,
Poor fugitive, the feathery change
Once more, and once more seem to make resound   25
With love and hate, triumph and agony,
Lone Daulis, and the high Cephissian vale?
Listen, Eugenia—
How thick the bursts come crowding through the leaves!
Again—thou hearest?   30
Eternal passion!
Eternal pain!

PHILOMELA   In Arnold's version of this legend, Tereus, a king of Thrace, was married
to Philomela but raped her sister, Procne. To prevent Procne from revealing this crime,
he cut out her tongue. Procne, however, wove a tapestry describing what had happened. In revenge, Philomela served up their son Itys to Tereus in a stew. Upon
discovering this, Tereus started to pursue the sisters, but before he could kill them,
they were changed into birds, Philomela into the nightingale. **27. Daulis:** Tereus's capital in Phocis. **Cephissian vale:** a valley in Phocis.

Dover Beach

The sea is calm tonight,
The tide is full, the moon lies fair
Upon the Straits;—on the French coast the light
Gleams, and is gone; the cliffs of England stand
Glimmering and vast, out in the tranquil bay.   5
Come to the window, sweet is the night air!
Only, from the long line of spray
Where the ebb meets the moon-blanched sand,
Listen! you hear the grating roar
Of pebbles which the waves suck back, and fling,   10
At their return, up the high strand,
Begin, and cease, and then again begin,
With tremulous cadence slow, and bring
The eternal note of sadness in.

Sophocles long ago   15
Heard it on the Aegean, and it brought
Into his mind the turbid ebb and flow
Of human misery; we
Find also in the sound a thought,
Hearing it by this distant northern sea.   20

The sea of faith
Was once, too, at the full, and round earth's shore
Lay like the folds of a bright girdle furled:
But now I only hear
Its melancholy, long, withdrawing roar,   25
Retreating to the breath
Of the night wind down the vast edges drear
And naked shingles of the world.

Ah, love, let us be true
To one another! for the world, which seems   30
To lie before us like a land of dreams,
So various, so beautiful, so new,
Hath really neither joy, nor love, nor light,
Nor certitude, nor peace, nor help for pain;
And we are here as on a darkling plain   35
Swept with confused alarms of struggle and flight,
Where ignorant armies clash by night,

DOVER BEACH   **15–18. Sophocles . . . misery:** in *Antigone,* Sophocles uses a similar image to describe the fate of the house of Oedipus (ll. 583ff.). **23. furled:** tightly clasping (the shore). **28. shingles:** gravel beaches.

Palladium

Set where the upper streams of Simois flow
Was the Palladium, high mid rock and wood;
And Hector was in Ilium, far below,
And fought, and saw it not—but there it stood!

It stood, and sun and moonshine rainéd their light   5
On the pure columns of its glen-built hall.
Backward and forward rolled the waves of fight
Round Troy—but while this stood, Troy could not fall.

So, in its lovely moonlight, lives the soul.
Mountains surround it, and sweet virgin air;   10
Cold plashing, past it, crystal waters roll;
We visit it by moments, ah, too rare!

We shall renew the battle in the plain
Tomorrow—red with blood will Xanthus be;
Hector and Ajax will be there again,   15
Helen will come upon the wall to see.

Then we shall rust in shade, or shine in strife,
And fluctuate 'twixt blind hopes and blind despairs,
And fancy that we put forth all our life,
And never know how with the soul it fares.   20

Still doth the soul, from its lone fastness high,
Upon our life a ruling effluence send.
And when it fails, fight as we will, we die;
And while it lasts, we cannot wholly end.

Emily Dickinson   (1830–1886)

There's a Certain Slant of Light

There's a certain slant of light,
Winter afternoons,

PALLADIUM   A statue of the goddess Pallas Athena that ensured the safety of Troy (Ilium) so long as it remained uncaptured. **1. Simois:** a river near Troy. **3. Hector:** the greatest of the Trojan heroes. **14. Xanthus:** a river. **15. Ajax:** next to Achilles, the greatest of the Grecian heroes. **16. Helen:** wife of Menelaus, king of Sparta. The Trojan War started when a Trojan prince, Paris, abducted the willing Helen.

That oppresses, like the heft
Of cathedral tunes.

Heavenly hurt it gives us;   5
We can find no scar,
But internal difference
Where the meanings are.

None may teach it any:
'Tis the seal, despair—   10
An imperial affliction
Sent us of the air.

When it comes, the landscape listens,
Shadows hold their breath;
When it goes, 'tis like the distance   15
On the look of death.

I Heard a Fly Buzz

I heard a fly buzz when I died—
The stillness in the room
Was like the stillness in the air
Between the heaves of storm.

The eyes around had wrung them dry   5
And breaths were gathering firm
For that last onset when the King
Be witnessed in the room.

I willed my keepsakes, signed away
What portion of me be   10
Assignable—and then it was
There interposed a fly,

With blue, uncertain, stumbling buzz,
Between the light and me.
And then the windows failed, and then   15
I could not see to see.

A Narrow Fellow in the Grass

A narrow fellow in the grass
Occasionally rides;
You may have met him? Did you not?
His notice sudden is.

The grass divides as with a comb,   5
A spotted shaft is seen;
And then it closes at your feet
And opens further on.

He likes a boggy acre,
A floor too cool for corn,   10
Yet when a boy, and barefoot,
I more than once, at noon

Have passed, I thought, a whiplash
Unbraiding in the sun—
When, stooping to secure it,   15
It wrinkled, and was gone.

Several of nature's people
I know, and they know me;
I feel for them a transport
Of cordiality;   20

But never met this fellow,
Attended or alone,
Without a tighter breathing,
And zero at the bone.

Apparently with No Surprise

Apparently with no surprise
To any happy flower,
The frost beheads it at its play
In accidental power.
The blond assassin passes on,   5
The sun proceeds unmoved
To measure off another day
For an approving God.

My Life Closed Twice

My life closed twice before its close;
It yet remains to see
If immortality unveil
A third event to me,

So huge, so hopeless to conceive,   5
As these that twice befell.
Parting is all we know of heaven,
And all we need of hell.

An Altered Look About the Hills

An altered look about the hills,
A Tyrian light the village fills,
A wider sunrise in the morn,
A deeper twilight on the lawn,
A print of a vermilion foot,   5
A purple finger on the slope,
A flippant fly upon the pane,
A spider at his trade again,
An added strut in Chanticleer,
A flower expected everywhere,   10
An axe shrill singing in the woods,
Fern odors on untraveled roads,
All this and more I cannot tell,
A furtive look you know as well:
And Nicodemus' mystery   15
Receives its annual reply!

The Heart Asks Pleasure—First

The heart asks pleasure first,
And then excuse from pain,
And then those little anodynes
That deaden suffering.

And then to go to sleep,   5
And then if it should be
The will of its Inquisitor
The privilege to die.

Crumbling Is Not an Instant's Act

Crumbling is not an instant's act,
A fundamental pause;
Dilapidation's processes
Are organized decays.

'Tis first a cobweb on the soul,   5
A cuticle of dust,

AN ALTERED LOOK   **2. Tyrian:** purple. **15. Nicodemus' mystery:** Nicodemus asked Jesus how man could be born again (see John 3:1–21).

A borer in the axis,
An elemental rust.

Ruin is formal—devil's work,
Consecutive and slow;   10
Fail in an instant, no man did;
Slipping—is crash's law.

Tell All the Truth

Tell all the truth but tell it slant—
Success in circuit lies;
Too bright for our infirm delight
The truth's superb surprise.
As lightning to the children eased   5
With explanation kind,
The truth must dazzle gradually
Or every man be blind.

While We Were Fearing It

While we were fearing it, it came—
But came with less of fear
Because that fearing it so long
Had almost made it fair.

There is a fitting—a dismay—   5
A fitting—a despair—
'Tis harder knowing it is due
Than knowing it is here.

The trying on the utmost
The morning it is new   10
Is terribler than wearing it
A whole existence through.

It Struck Me Every Day

It struck me every day
The lightning was as new
As if the cloud that instant slit
And let the fire through.

It burned me in the night,   5
It blistered to my dream,

CRUMBLING IS NOT AN INSTANT'S ACT **7. axis:** main stem or central part of a plant, tree, etc.

It sickened fresh upon my sight
With every morn that came.

I thought that storm was brief,
The maddest quickest by,   10
But Nature lost the date of this
And left it in the sky.

Lewis Carroll *(1832–1898)*

Jabberwocky

'Twas brillig, and the slithy toves
     Did gyre and gimble in the wabe:
All mimsy were the borogoves,
     And the mome raths outgrabe.

"Beware the Jabberwock, my son!   5
     The jaws that bite, the claws that catch!
Beware the Jubjub bird, and shun
     The frumious Bandersnatch!"

He took his vorpal sword in hand:
     Long time the manxome foe he sought—   10
So rested he by the Tumtum tree,
     And stood awhile in thought.

And, as in uffish thought he stood,
     The Jabberwock, with eyes of flame,
Came whiffling through the tulgey wood,   15
     And burbled as it came!

One, two! One, two! And through and through
     The vorpal blade went snicker-snack!
He left it dead, and with its head
     He went galumphing back.   20

JABBERWOCKY The poem appears in *Through the Looking-Glass*, where Humpty Dumpty and Alice explicate certain difficult words in the first stanza. **1. brillig:** Humpty Dumpty, deriving it from "*broiling* things for dinner," defines it as "four o'clock in the afternoon." **slithy:** a combination of "lithe" and "slimy." **toves:** animals resembling badgers, lizards, and corkscrews. **2. gyre.** revolve like a gyroscope. **gimble:** make holes like a gimlet. **wabe:** grass plot around a sundial. **3. mimsy:** "flimsy" and "miserable." **borogoves:** birds resembling a live mop. **4. mome:** possibly "from home," i.e., lost. **raths:** sort of green pigs. **outgrabe:** " 'outgribing' is something between bellowing and whistling, with a kind of sneeze in the middle" (Humpty Dumpty).

"And hast thou slain the Jabberwock?
  Come to my arms, my beamish boy!
O frabjous day! Callooh! Callay!"
  He chortled in his joy.

'Twas brillig, and the slithy toves   25
  Did gyre and gimble in the wabe:
All mimsy were the borogoves,
  And the mome raths outgrabe.

Thomas Hardy (1840–1928)

Hap

If but some vengeful god would call to me
From up the sky, and laugh: "Thou suffering thing,
Know that thy sorrow is my ecstasy,
That thy love's loss is my hate's profiting!"

Then would I bear it, clench myself, and die,   5
Steeled by the sense of ire unmerited;
Half-eased in that a Powerfuller than I
Had willed and meted me the tears I shed.

But not so. How arrives it joy lies slain,
And why unblooms the best hope ever sown?   10
—Crass Casualty obstructs the sun and rain,
And dicing Time for gladness casts a moan. . . .
These purblind Doomsters had as readily strown
Blisses about my pilgrimage as pain.

The Subalterns

I
"Poor wanderer," said the leaden sky,
  "I fain would lighten thee,
But there are laws in force on high
  Which say it must not be."

HAP Fortune or chance. **13. purblind:** nearly blind; dull.
THE SUBALTERNS Junior officers. **2. fain:** gladly.

II

—"I would not freeze thee, shorn one," cried   5
        The North, "knew I but how
To warm my breath, to slack my stride;
        But I am ruled as thou."

III

—"Tomorrow I attack thee, wight,"
        Said Sickness. "Yet I swear   10
I bear thy little ark no spite,
        But am bid enter there."

IV

—"Come hither, Son," I heard Death say;
        "I did not will a grave
Should end thy pilgrimage today,   15
        But I, too, am a slave!"

V

We smiled upon each other then,
        And life to me had less
Of that fell look it wore ere when
        They owned their passiveness.   20

Neutral Tones

We stood by a pond that winter day,
And the sun was white, as though chidden of God,
And a few leaves lay on the starving sod;
        —They had fallen from an ash, and were gray.

Your eyes on me were as eyes that rove   5
Over tedious riddles of years ago;
And some words played between us to and fro
        On which lost the more by our love.

The smile on your mouth was the deadest thing
Alive enough to have strength to die;   10
And a grin of bitterness swept thereby
        Like an ominous bird a-wing. . . .

Since then, keen lessons that love deceives,
And wrings with wrong, have shaped to me
Your face, and the God-cursed sun, and a tree,   15
        And a pond edged with grayish leaves.

9. **wight**: human being. 19. **fell**: cruel, sinister.

In Time of "The Breaking of Nations"

I

Only a man harrowing clods
    In a slow silent walk
With an old horse that stumbles and nods
    Half asleep as they stalk.

II

Only thin smoke without flame   5
    From the heaps of couch-grass;
Yet this will go onward the same
    Though Dynasties pass.

III

Yonder a maid and her wight
    Come whispering by: 10
War's annals will fade into night
    Ere their story die.

A Wet August

Nine drops of water bead the jessamine,
And nine-and-ninety smear the stones and tiles:
—'Twas not so in that August—full-rayed, fine—
When we lived out-of-doors, sang songs, strode miles.

Or was there then no noted radiancy   5
Of summer?   Were dun clouds, a dribbling bough,
Gilt over by the light I bore in me,
And was the waste world just the same as now?

It can have been so: yea, that threatenings
Of coming down-drip on the sunless gray,   10
By the then golden chances seen in things
Were wrought more bright than brightest skies today.

IN TIME OF "THE BREAKING OF NATIONS" The poem "contains a feeling that moved me in 1870, during the Franco-Prussian War, when I chanced to be looking at such an agricultural incident in Cornwall. But I did not write the verses till during the war with Germany of 1914 and onwards" (Hardy). The title refers to the words of God in Jeremiah 51:20, "Thou art my battle ax and weapons of war: for with thee will I break in pieces the nations, and with thee will I destroy kingdoms." 6. **couch-grass:** the weed that grows in cornfields. 9. **wight:** lad.

A Backward Spring

The trees are afraid to put forth buds,
And there is timidity in the grass;
The plots lie gray where gouged by spuds,
    And whether next week will pass
Free of sly sour winds is the fret of each bush   5
    Of barberry waiting to bloom.

Yet the snowdrop's face betrays no gloom,
And the primrose pants in its heedless push,
Though the myrtle asks if it's worth the fight
    This year with frost and rime   10
    To venture one more time
On delicate leaves and buttons of white
From the selfsame bough as at last year's prime,
And never to ruminate on or remember
What happened to it in mid-December.   15

Transformations

Portion of this yew
Is a man my grandsire knew,
Bosomed here at its foot:
This branch may be his wife,
A ruddy human life   5
Now turned to a green shoot.

These grasses must be made
Of her who often prayed,
Last century, for repose;
And the fair girl long ago   10
Whom I often tried to know
May be entering this rose.

So, they are not underground,
But as nerves and veins abound
In the growths of upper air,   15
And they feel the sun and rain,
And the energy again
That made them what they were!

A BACKWARD SPRING   **3. spuds:** digging forks or spades.

Snow in the Suburbs

Every branch big with it,
Bent every twig with it;
Every fork like a white web-foot;
Every street and pavement mute:
Some flakes have lost their way, and grope back upward, when   5
Meeting those meandering down they turn and descend again.
The palings are glued together like a wall,
And there is no waft of wind with the fleecy fall.

A sparrow enters the tree,
Whereon immediately   10
A snow-lump thrice his own slight size
Descends on him and showers his head and eyes,
And overturns him,
And near inurns him,
And lights on a nether twig, when its brush   15
Starts off a volley of other lodging lumps with a rush.

The steps are a blanched slope,
Up which, with feeble hope,
A black cat comes, wide-eyed and thin;
And we take him in.   20

The Darkling Thrush

I leant upon a coppice gate
   When Frost was specter-gray,
And Winter's dregs made desolate
   The weakening eye of day.
The tangled bine-stems scored the sky   5
   Like strings of broken lyres,
And all mankind that haunted nigh
   Had sought their household fires.

The land's sharp features seemed to be
   The Century's corpse outleant,   10
His crypt the cloudy canopy,

SNOW IN THE SUBURBS 7. **palings:** uprights (pickets) of a fence.
THE DARKLING THRUSH "Darkling" means shrouded in darkness. Cf. Milton, *Paradise Lost*, iii. 37–40, where the blind poet describes himself: "Then [I] feed on thoughts, that voluntary move/Harmonious numbers; as the wakeful bird/Sings darkling, and in shadiest covert hid/Tunes her nocturnal note." **1. coppice:** a small wood or thicket grown for cutting. **5. bine-stems:** shoots of a climbing plant or vine. **10. The Century's corpse:** the poem was written on December 31, 1900, and was originally titled "By the Century's Deathbed." **outleant:** stretched out.

The wind his death-lament.
The ancient pulse of germ and birth
    Was shrunken hard and dry,
And every spirit upon earth   15
    Seemed fervorless as I.

At once a voice arose among
    The bleak twigs overhead
In a full-hearted evensong
    Of joy illimited;   20
An agèd thrush, frail, gaunt, and small,
    In blast-beruffled plume,
Had chosen thus to fling his soul
    Upon the growing gloom.

So little cause for carolings   25
    Of such ecstatic sound
Was written on terrestrial things
    Afar or nigh around,
That I could think there trembled through
    His happy good-night air   30
Some blessèd Hope, whereof he knew
    And I was unaware.

The Oxen

Christmas Eve, and twelve of the clock.
    "Now they are all on their knees,"
An elder said as we sat in a flock
    By the embers in hearthside ease.

We pictured the meek mild creatures where   5
    They dwelt in their strawy pen,
Nor did it occur to one of us there
    To doubt they were kneeling then.

So fair a fancy few would weave
    In these years! Yet, I feel,   10
If someone said on Christmas Eve,
    "Come; see the oxen kneel,

"In the lonely barton by yonder coomb
    Our childhood used to know,"
I should go with him in the gloom,   15
    Hoping it might be so.

20. illimited: unbounded.
THE OXEN 1–2. Christmas . . . knees: according to legend, all creatures knelt in
prayer and adoration at midnight of Christmas Eve. 13. barton: farmyard. coomb:
valley.

During Wind and Rain

They sing their dearest songs—
He, she, all of them—yea,
Treble and tenor and bass,
   And one to play;
With the candles mooning each face. . . .   5
   Ah, no; the years O!
How the sick leaves reel down in throngs!

They clear the creeping moss—
Elders and juniors—aye,
Making the pathways neat   10
   And the garden gay;
And they build a shady seat. . . .
   Ah, no; the years, the years;
See, the white storm-birds wing across!

They are blithely breakfasting all—   15
Men and maidens—yea,
Under the summer tree,
   With a glimpse of the bay,
While pet fowl come to the knee. . . .
   Ah, no; the years O!   20
And the rotten rose is ripped from the wall.

They change to a high new house,
He, she, all of them—aye,
Clocks and carpets, and chairs
   On the lawn all day,   25
And brightest things that are theirs. . . .
   Ah, no; the years, the years;
Down their carved names the raindrop ploughs.

Gerard Manley Hopkins (1844–1889)

God's Grandeur

The world is charged with the grandeur of God.
  It will flame out, like shining from shook foil;
  It gathers to a greatness, like the ooze of oil
Crushed. Why do men then now not reck his rod?

GOD'S GRANDEUR 2. foil: gold or tinsel foil. 4. **Crushed:** as from olives: **reck:** pay attention to.

Generations have trod, have trod, have trod;   5
   And all is seared with trade; bleared, smeared with toil;
   And wears man's smudge and shares man's smell: the soil
Is bare now, nor can foot feel, being shod.

And for all this, nature is never spent;
   There lives the dearest freshness deep down things;   10
And though the last lights off the black West went
   Oh, morning, at the brown brink eastward, springs—
Because the Holy Ghost over the bent
   World broods with warm breast and with ah! bright wings.

The Starlight Night

Look at the stars! look, look up at the skies!
   O look at all the fire-folk sitting in the air!
   The bright boroughs, the circle-citadels there!
Down in dim woods the diamond delves! the elves'-eyes!
The gray lawns cold where gold, where quickgold lies!   5
   Wind-beat whitebeam! airy abeles set on a flare!
   Flake-doves sent floating forth at a farmyard scare!—
Ah well! it is all a purchase, all is a prize.

Buy then! bid then!—What?—Prayer, patience, alms, vows.
Look, look: May-mess, like on orchard boughs!   10
   Look! March-bloom, like on mealed-with-yellow sallows!
These are indeed the barn; withindoors house
The shocks. This piece-bright paling shuts the spouse
   Christ home, Christ and his mother and all his hallows.

The Windhover

To Christ Our Lord

I caught this morning morning's minion, king-
   dom of daylight's dauphin, dapple-dawn-drawn Falcon, in his riding
Of the rolling level underneath him steady air, and striding
High there, how he rung upon the rein of a wimpling wing

13–14. Holy Ghost . . . wings: cf. Milton's description of the Holy Ghost: "thou from the first/Wast present, and with mighty wings outspread/Dovelike satst brooding on the vast abyss/And mad'st it pregnant" (*Paradise Lost*, i. 19–22).
THE STARLIGHT NIGHT 4. delves: mines. 5. quickgold: dewdrops (compare *quicksilver*). 6. abeles: white poplars. 9. What?: What is the price? 11. mealed-with-yellow sallows: yellow-spotted willows. 12. barn: where Christ's harvest is gathered (Matthew 13:30). 13. shocks: wheat sheaves. piece-bright paling: coin-bright fencing. spouse: the Church, as the spouse of Christ. 14. hallows: saints.
THE WINDHOVER The windhover is a kestrel, a kind of falcon. 1. minion: favorite, darling. 2. dauphin: prince. 4. rung . . . rein: as a horse circles at the end of a long tether (a riding-school term). wimpling: rippling.

In his ecstasy! then off, off forth on swing,   5
    As a skate's heel sweeps smooth on a bow-bend: the hurl and gliding
    Rebuffed the big wind. My heart in hiding
Stirred for a bird,—the achieve of, the mastery of the thing!

Brute beauty and valor and act, oh, air, pride, plume, here
    Buckle! AND the fire that breaks from thee then, a billion   10
Times told lovelier, more dangerous, O my chevalier!

    No wonder of it: shéer plód makes plough down sillion
Shine, and blue-bleak embers, ah my dear,
    Fall, gall themselves, and gash gold-vermilion.

Pied Beauty

    Glory be to God for dappled things—
        For skies of couple-color as a brinded cow;
            For rose-moles all in stipple upon trout that swim;
    Fresh-firecoal chestnut-falls; finches' wings;
        Landscape plotted and pieced—fold, fallow, and plough;   5
        And áll trádes, their gear and tackle and trim.

    All things counter, original, spare, strange;
        Whatever is fickle, freckled (who knows how?)
        With swift, slow; sweet, sour; adazzle, dim;
    He fathers-forth whose beauty is past change: 10
                Praise him.

Carrion Comfort

Not, I'll not, carrion comfort, Despair, not feast on thee;
Not untwist—slack they may be—these last strands of man
In me ór, most weary, cry *I can no more*. I can;
Can something, hope, wish day come, not choose not to be.
But ah, but O thou terrible, why wouldst thou rude on me   5
Thy wring-world right foot rock? lay a lionlimb against me? scan
With darksome devouring eyes my bruisèd bones? and fan,

10. **Buckle:** variously interpreted as (1) join, (2) crumple, (3) prepare for action (as in "buckle down"). 11. **told:** perhaps, "accounted." **chevalier:** literally, knight or champion; figuratively, perhaps Christ. 12. **sillion:** furrow.

PIED BEAUTY "Pied" mean variegated. 2. **brinded:** brindled, streaked. 3. **stipple:** dots, flecks. 4. **chestnut-falls:** roasted chestnuts stripped of their husks. 6. **trim:** equipment. 7. **spare:** unusual.

CARRION COMFORT 5. **rude:** rudely, violently. 6. **scan:** with some of its archaic meaning, "criticize." 7. **fan:** winnow.

O in turns of tempest, me heaped there; me frantic to avoid thee and flee?
Why? That my chaff might fly; my grain lie, sheer and clear.
Nay in all that toil, that coil, since (seems) I kissed the rod,   10
Hand rather, my heart lo! lapped strength, stole joy, would laugh, chéer.
Cheer whom though? The hero whose heaven-handling flung me, fóot tród
Me? or me that fought him? O which one? is it each one? That night, that
    year
Of now done darkness I wretch lay wrestling with (my God!) my God.

No Worst, There Is None

No worst, there is none. Pitched past pitch of grief,
More pangs will, schooled at forepangs, wilder wring.
Comforter, where, where is your comforting?
Mary, mother of us, where is your relief?
My cries heave, herds-long; huddle in a main, a chief-   5
woe, world-sorrow; on an age-old anvil wince and sing—
Then lull, then leave off. Fury had shrieked "No ling-
ering! Let me be fell: force I must be brief."

  O the mind, mind has mountains; cliffs of fall
Frightful, sheer, no-man fathomed. Hold them cheap   10
May who ne'er hung there. Nor does long our small
Durance deal with that steep or deep. Here! creep,
Wretch, under a comfort serves in a whirlwind: all
Life death does end and each day dies with sleep.

I Wake and Feel the Fell of Dark

I wake and feel the fell of dark, not day.
What hours, O what black hoürs we have spent
This night! what sighs you, heart, saw; ways you went!
And more must, in yet longer light's delay.
With witness I speak this. But where I say   5
Hours I mean years, mean life. And my lament
Is cries countless, cries like dead letters sent
To dearest him that lives alas! away.
    I am gall, I am heartburn. God's most deep decree
Bitter would have me taste: my taste was me;   10
Bones built in me, flesh filled, blood brimmed the curse.

---

10. kissed the rod: submitted to correction.
NO WORST, THERE IS NONE   3. Comforter: the Holy Ghost. 5. herds-long: in herds.
8. fell: unsparing, cruel, deadly. force: perforce, necessarily. 12. Durance: endurance.
13. a comfort serves: such comfort as serves.
I WAKE AND FEEL THE FELL OF DARK   1. fell: cruelty, deadliness, bitterness. 5. With
witness: "With a witness" means "intensely."

Selfyeast of spirit a dull dough sours. I see
The lost are like this, and their scourge to be
As I am mine, their sweating selves; but worse.

Spring and Fall:

to a young child

Márgarét, áre you gríeving
Over Goldengrove unleaving?
Leáves, líke the things of man, you
With your fresh thoughts care for, can you?
Áh! ás the heart grows older   5
It will come to such sights colder
By and by, nor spare a sigh
Though worlds of wanwood leafmeal lie;
And yet you *will* weep and know why.
Now no matter, child, the name: 10
Sórrow's spríngs áre the same.
Nor mouth had, no nor mind, expressed
What heart heard of, ghost guessed:
It ís the blight man was born for,
It is Margaret you mourn for.   15

A. E. Housman (1859–1936)

The Street Sounds to the Soldiers' Tread

The street sounds to the soldiers' tread,
    And out we troop to see:
A single redcoat turns his head,
    He turns and looks at me.

My man, from sky to sky's so far,   5
    We never crossed before;
Such leagues apart the world's ends are,
    We're like to meet no more;

What thoughts at heart have you and I
    We cannot stop to tell;   10

---

12. **Selfyeast . . . sours:** early drafts suggest that "selfyeast" rather than "dough" is
the subject of "sours." 13. **The lost:** the damned.
SPRING AND FALL   8. **wanwood:** possibly, pale or dead wood that lies in fragments like
moldering leaves ("leafmeal"). 13. **ghost:** spirit (of the living).

But dead or living, drunk or dry,
Soldier, I wish you well.

Others, I Am Not the First

Others, I am not the first,
Have willed more mischief than they durst:
If in the breathless night I too
Shiver now, 'tis nothing new.

More than I, if truth were told,   5
Have stood and sweated hot and cold,
And through their reins in ice and fire
Fear contended with desire.

Agued once like me were they,
But I like them shall win my way   10
Lastly to the bed of mould
Where there's neither heat nor cold.

But from my grave across my brow
Plays no wind of healing now,
And fire and ice within me fight   15
Beneath the suffocating night.

Could Man Be Drunk For Ever

Could man be drunk for ever
    With liquor, love, or fights,
Lief should I rouse at morning
    And lief lie down of nights.

But men at whiles are sober   5
    And think by fits and starts,
And if they think, they fasten
    Their hands upon their hearts.

Epitaph on an Army of Mercenaries

These, in the day when heaven was falling,
    The hour when earth's foundations fled,

OTHERS   7. **reins:** loins.
COULD MAN BE DRUNK FOR EVER   3. **Lief:** gladly. **5. whiles:** times.

Followed their mercenary calling
    And took their wages and are dead.

Their shoulders held the sky suspended;   5
    They stood, and earth's foundations stay;
What God abandoned, these defended,
    And saved the sum of things for pay.

The Chestnut Casts His Flambeaux

The chestnut casts his flambeaux, and the flowers
    Stream from the hawthorn on the wind away,
The doors clap to, the pane is blind with showers.
    Pass me the can, lad; there's an end of May.

There's one spoilt spring to scant our mortal lot,   5
    One season ruined of our little store.
May will be fine next year as like as not:
    Oh ay, but then we shall be twenty-four.

We for a certainty are not the first
    Have sat in taverns while the tempest hurled   10
Their hopeful plans to emptiness, and cursed
    Whatever brute and blackguard made the world.

It is in truth iniquity on high
    To cheat our sentenced souls of aught they crave,
And mar the merriment as you and I   15
    Fare on our long fool's-errand to the grave.

Iniquity it is; but pass the can.
    My lad, no pair of kings our mothers bore;
Our only portion is the estate of man:
    We want the moon, but we shall get no more.   20

If here today the cloud of thunder lours
    Tomorrow it will hie on far behests;
The flesh will grieve on other bones than ours
    Soon, and the soul will mourn in other breasts.

The troubles of our proud and angry dust   25
    Are from eternity, and shall not fail.
Bear them we can, and if we can we must.
    Shoulder the sky, my lad, and drink your ale.

THE CHESTNUT   **1. flambeaux:** the torch-shaped blossoms of the horse chestnut. **4. can:** tankard. **19. portion:** inheritance, fortune. **22. hie . . . behests:** hasten on orders far away.

The Laws of God

The laws of God, the laws of man,
He may keep that will and can;
Not I: let God and man decree
Laws for themselves and not for me;
And if my ways are not as theirs   5
Let them mind their own affairs.
Their deeds I judge and much condemn,
Yet when did I make laws for them?
Please yourselves, say I, and they
Need only look the other way.   10
But no, they will not; they must still
Wrest their neighbor to their will,
And make me dance as they desire
With jail and gallows and hell-fire.
And how am I to face the odds   15
Of man's bedevilment and God's?
I, a stranger and afraid
In a world I never made.
They will be master, right or wrong;
Though both are foolish, both are strong.   20
And since, my soul, we cannot fly
To Saturn nor to Mercury,
Keep we must, if keep we can,
These foreign laws of God and man.

William Butler Yeats (1865–1939)

An Irish Airman Foresees His Death

I know that I shall meet my fate
Somewhere among the clouds above;
Those that I fight I do not hate,
Those that I guard I do not love;
My country is Kiltartan Cross,   5
My countrymen Kiltartan's poor,
No likely end could bring them loss
Or leave them happier than before.

AN IRISH AIRMAN   1. I: Major Robert Gregory, the son of Yeats's friend Lady Gregory, killed in action on the Italian front on January 23, 1918; he had been a man of various talents—painter, horseman, athlete—and had been honored for gallantry for his service in the Royal Flying Corps. 3. Those . . . fight: the Germans. 4. Those . . . guard: the English. 5. Kiltartan Cross: near Lady Gregory's estate at Coole.

Nor law, nor duty bade me fight,
Nor public men, nor cheering crowds,   10
A lonely impulse of delight
Drove to this tumult in the clouds;
I balanced all, brought all to mind,
The years to come seemed waste of breath,
A waste of breath the years behind   15
In balance with this life, this death.

After Long Silence

Speech after long silence; it is right,
All other lovers being estranged or dead,
Unfriendly lamplight hid under its shade,
The curtains drawn upon unfriendly night,
That we descant and yet again descant   5
Upon the supreme theme of Art and Song:
Bodily decrepitude is wisdom; young
We loved each other and were ignorant.

Easter 1916

I have met them at close of day
Coming with vivid faces
From counter or desk among grey
Eighteenth-century houses.
I have passed with a nod of the head   5
Or polite meaningless words,
Or have lingered awhile and said
Polite meaningless words,
And thought before I had done
Of a mocking tale or a gibe   10
To please a companion
Around the fire at the club,
Being certain that they and I
But lived where motley is worn:
All changed, changed utterly: 15
A terrible beauty is born.

That woman's days were spent
In ignorant good will,

EASTER 1916   The title refers to an insurrection of Irish nationalists on Easter Monday, 1916; fifteen of the leaders—including the four mentioned in the poem—were executed by the English. 4. **Eighteenth-century houses**: typical of Dublin and suggestive of its comparatively serene past. 14. **motley**: the costume of the fool or clown. 17. **That woman**: Constance Gore-Booth, Countess Marciewicz, took part in the Easter Rising and was sentenced to life imprisonment; she had been famous earlier as a beautiful horsewoman.

Her nights in argument
Until her voice grew shrill.   20
What voice more sweet than hers
When, young and beautiful,
She rode to harriers?
This man had kept a school
And rode our wingèd horse;   25
This other his helper and friend
Was coming into his force;
He might have won fame in the end,
So sensitive his nature seemed,
So daring and sweet his thought.   30
This other man I had dreamed
A drunken, vainglorious lout.
He had done most bitter wrong
To some who are near my heart,
Yet I number him in the song;   35
He, too, has resigned his part
In the casual comedy;
He, too, has been changed in his turn,
Transformed utterly:
A terrible beauty is born.   40

Hearts with one purpose alone
Through summer and winter seem
Enchanted to a stone
To trouble the living stream.
The horse that comes from the road,   45
The rider, the birds that range
From cloud to tumbling cloud,
Minute by minute they change;
A shadow of cloud on the stream
Changes minute by minute;   50
A horse-hoof slides on the brim,
And a horse plashes within it;
The long-legged moor-hens dive,
And hens to moor-cocks call;
Minute by minute they live: 55
The stone's in the midst of all.

Too long a sacrifice
Can make a stone of the heart.
O when may it suffice?
That is Heaven's part, our part   60
To murmur name upon name,
As a mother names her child

23. **harriers:** hounds. 24. **This man:** Patrick Pearse, commander of the insurrectionary forces, was a poet and the founder of a bilingual school where Gaelic was to be revived. 25. **wingèd horse:** Pegasus, symbol of poetry. 26. **This other:** Thomas MacDonagh, a promising writer. 31. **This other man:** Major John MacBride, husband of Maud Gonne.

When sleep at last has come
On limbs that had run wild.
What is it but nightfall?   65
No, no, not night but death;
Was it needless death after all?
For England may keep faith
For all that is done and said.
We know their dream; enough   70
To know they dreamed and are dead;
And what if excess of love
Bewildered them till they died?
I write it out in a verse—
MacDonagh and MacBride   75
And Connolly and Pearse
Now and in time to be,
Wherever green is worn,
Are changed, changed utterly:
A terrible beauty is born.   80

The Wild Swans at Coole

The trees are in their autumn beauty,
The woodland paths are dry,
Under the October twilight the water
Mirrors a still sky;
Upon the brimming water among the stones   5
Are nine-and-fifty swans.

The nineteenth autumn has come upon me
Since I first made my count;
I saw, before I had well finished,
All suddenly mount   10
And scatter wheeling in great broken rings
Upon their clamorous wings.

I have looked upon those brilliant creatures,
And now my heart is sore.
All's changed since I, hearing at twilight,   15
The first time on this shore,
The bell-beat of their wings above my head,
Trod with a lighter tread.

Unwearied still, lover by lover,
They paddle in the cold   20

---

76. **Connolly:** James Connolly, long an anti-English agitator and a leader of the Easter Rising.

THE WILD SWANS Coole Park was the estate in Western Ireland of Lady Augusta Gregory (1852–1932); Yeats stayed there first in 1897 and wrote this poem during a visit in 1916.

Companionable streams or climb the air;
Their hearts have not grown old;
Passion or conquest, wander where they will,
Attend upon them still.

But now they drift on the still water,   25
Mysterious, beautiful;
Among what rushes will they build,
By what lake's edge or pool
Delight men's eyes when I awake some day
To find they have flown away?   30

Coole Park and Ballylee, 1931

Under my window-ledge the waters race,
Otters below and moor-hens on the top,
Run for a mile undimmed in Heaven's face
Then darkening through "dark" Raftery's "cellar" drop,
Run underground, rise in a rocky place   5
In Coole demesne, and there to finish up
Spread to a lake and drop into a hole.
What's water but the generated soul?

Upon the border of that lake's a wood
Now all dry sticks under a wintry sun,   10
And in a copse of beeches there I stood,
For Nature's pulled her tragic buskin on
And all the rant's a mirror of my mood:
At sudden thunder of the mounting swan
I turned about and looked where branches break   15
The glittering reaches of the flooded lake.

Another emblem there! That stormy white
But seems a concentration of the sky;
And, like the soul, it sails into the sight
And in the morning's gone, no man knows why;   20
And is so lovely that it sets to right
What knowledge or its lack had set awry,
So arrogantly pure, a child might think
It can be murdered with a spot of ink.

COOLE PARK AND BALLYLEE   Coole Park was the estate of Yeats's friend Lady Gregory
(see "The Wild Swans at Coole"). Ballylee was a half-ruined tower near Coole Park
which Yeats bought in 1917 and fixed as a residence. 4. "dark" . . . drop: an opening
of limestone mentioned in a poem by Anthony Raftery (1784 1834), the blind Gaelic
poet; this is one of several underground rivers in the area. 8. generated soul: "Did not
the wise Porphyry think that all souls come to be born because of water, and that
'even the generation of images in the mind is from water'" (Yeats). Here water is an
"emblem" of the soul's career. Porphyry was a Neoplatonic philosopher of the third century A.D. 12. buskin: the boot worn by tragic actors in the ancient Greek theater.

Sound of a stick upon the floor, a sound   25
From somebody that toils from chair to chair;
Beloved books that famous hands have bound,
Old marble heads, old pictures everywhere;
Great rooms where traveled men and children found
Content or joy; a last inheritor   30
Where none has reigned that lacked a name and fame
Or out of folly into folly came.

A spot whereon the founders lived and died
Seemed once more dear than life; ancestral trees,
Or gardens rich in memory glorified   35
Marriages, alliances and families,
And every bride's ambition satisfied.
Where fashion or mere fantasy decrees
We shift about—all that great glory spent—
Like some poor Arab tribesman and his tent.   40

We were the last romantics—chose for theme
Traditional sanctity and loveliness;
Whatever's written in what poets name
The book of the people; whatever most can bless
The mind of man or elevate a rhyme;   45
But all is changed, that high horse riderless,
Though mounted in that saddle Homer rode
Where the swan drifts upon a darkening flood.

The Second Coming

Turning and turning in the widening gyre
The falcon cannot hear the falconer;
Things fall apart; the center cannot hold;
Mere anarchy is loosed upon the world,
The blood-dimmed tide is loosed, and everywhere   5
The ceremony of innocence is drowned;
The best lack all conviction, while the worst
Are full of passionate intensity.

Surely some revelation is at hand;
Surely the Second Coming is at hand.   10
The Second Coming! Hardly are those words out
When a vast image out of *Spiritus Mundi*

---

26. **somebody:** Lady Gregory, alone in the last year of her life, having lost her only child, Robert, in the First World War (see "An Irish Airman Foresees His Death"). 44. **book of the people:** legend or folktale (?). 46. **high horse:** Pegasus, the embodiment of poetry.

THE SECOND COMING The title fuses the prophecy by Jesus of his return (Matthew 24) with the account of the Great Beast of the Apocalypse in Revelation 13. 1. **gyre:** spiral. 12. **Spiritus Mundi:** "a general storehouse of images which have ceased to be a property of any personality or spirit" (Yeats).

Troubles my sight: somewhere in sands of the desert
A shape with lion body and the head of a man,
A gaze blank and pitiless as the sun, 15
Is moving its slow thighs, while all about it
Reel shadows of the indignant desert birds.
The darkness drops again; but now I know
That twenty centuries of stony sleep
Were vexed to nightmare by a rocking cradle, 20
And what rough beast, its hour come round at last,
Slouches towards Bethlehem to be born?

Two Songs from a Play

I

I saw a staring virgin stand
Where holy Dionysus died,
And tear the heart out of his side,
And lay the heart upon her hand
And bear that beating heart away; 5
And then did all the Muses sing
Of Magnus Annus at the spring,
As though God's death were but a play.

Another Troy must rise and set,
Another lineage feed the crow, 10
Another Argo's painted prow
Drive to a flashier bauble yet.
The Roman Empire stood appalled:
It dropped the reins of peace and war

14. shape . . . man: This sphinx-like creature is related, according to Yeats, to an image he had earlier described (in the Introduction to his play, *The Resurrection*): "a brazen winged beast that I associated with laughing, ecstatic destruction." **19. twenty centuries** i e the era of two thousand years that preceded the span of the Christian era (beginning with the birth of Christ in Bethlehem), itself a comparable period now drawing to its close.

TWO SONGS Sung by a Chorus of Musicians in *Resurrection* (1931). **1–2. staring virgin . . . died:** Both Christ and Dionysus died and were reborn in March, when the moon was beside the constellation Virgo, who carries the star Spica in her hand. Virgo represents Astraea (goddess of justice), who was the last goddess to leave the world after the golden age and, according to Virgil's prophecy, will return and bring it again; thus the story of Astraea was often taken as a prophecy of the coming of the Virgin Mary, and Spica identified with Mary's son, the Star of Bethlehem. But the myth of Dionysus presents a parallel, too: after he was torn to pieces by the Titans, Athene (the virgin goddess) brought his heart in her hand to Zeus, who swallowed the heart and begot Dionysus anew upon Semele. **5. beating heart:** still containing the life to be reborn. **7. Magnus Annus:** a new cycle of two thousand years (cf "The Second Coming," l. 19, above). **8. but a play:** part of a ritual cycle. **9. Another Troy:** In "The Adoration of the Magi" (1896), Yeats stated Virgil's prophecy (*Eclogue IV*) in these terms: "after you have bowed down the old things shall be again, and another Argo shall carry heroes over the sea, and another Achilles beleaguer another Troy." **12. flashier bauble:** than the Golden Fleece, which the Argonauts procured. **13. Roman Empire:** which fell, according to the historian Edward Gibbon, through the "triumph of barbarism and religion."

When that fierce virgin and her Star   15
Out of the fabulous darkness called.

II

In pity for man's darkening thought
He walked that room and issued thence
In Galilean turbulence;
The Babylonian starlight brought   20
A fabulous, formless darkness in;
Odor of blood when Christ was slain
Made all Platonic tolerance vain
And vain all Doric discipline.

Everything that man esteems   25
Endures a moment or a day.
Love's pleasure drives his love away,
The painter's brush consumes his dreams;
The herald's cry, the soldier's tread
Exhaust his glory and his might: 30
Whatever flames upon the night
Man's own resinous heart has fed.

Sailing to Byzantium

I

That is no country for old men. The young
In one another's arms, birds in the trees
—Those dying generations—at their song,
The salmon-falls, the mackerel-crowded seas,
Fish, flesh, or fowl, commend all summer long   5

16. **fabulous darkness**: Proclus (fourth century A.D.), a Neoplatonist philosopher, called Christianity a "fabulous, formless darkness" and reflects, in Yeats's view, the horror of an aristocratic, hierarchic culture at an irrational force that would blot out its order and light. 19. **Galilean turbulence**: the culmination of all the irrational tendencies in Greek and Roman thought; as reason gives way to miracle, so does man's mind to powers beyond his control or comprehension. "Night will fall upon man's wisdom now that man has been taught that he is nothing" (Yeats). 20. **Babylonian starlight**: Babylonian astronomy and astrology began to reduce man to featureless passivity before the abstractions of science. 22. **Odor of blood**: Christ's existence as man as well as god confounded the separation that once existed between natural and supernatural, and the consequent confidence of man in his own rational and imaginative powers. 28. **painter's brush . . . dreams**: In *The Trembling of the Veil* Yeats laments the transitoriness of all passion: "Our love letters wear out our love . . . every stroke of the brush exhausts the impulse. . . ." 32. **resinous**: creating a brilliant but short-lasting flame (like the pine torches carried by the women who worshiped Dionysus).

SAILING TO BYZANTIUM Byzantium (Constantinople) was the capital of the eastern Roman empire and the center of a great formalized art and architecture of late antiquity. "I think that in early Byzantium, maybe never before or since in recorded history, religion, aesthetic and practical life were one. . . . The painter, the mosaic worker, the worker in gold and silver, the illuminator of sacred books, were almost impersonal, almost perhaps without the consciousness of individual design, absorbed in their subject matter and that the vision of a whole people" (Yeats).

Whatever is begotten, born, and dies.
Caught in that sensual music all neglect
Monuments of unageing intellect.

II

An agèd man is but a paltry thing,
A tattered coat upon a stick, unless   10
Soul clap its hands and sing, and louder sing
For every tatter in its mortal dress,
Nor is there singing school but studying
Monuments of its own magnificence;
And therefore I have sailed the seas and come   15
To the holy city of Byzantium.

III

O sages standing in God's holy fire
As in the gold mosaic of a wall,
Come from the holy fire, perne in a gyre,
And be the singing-masters of my soul.   20
Consume my heart away; sick with desire
And fastened to a dying animal
It knows not what it is; and gather me
Into the artifice of eternity.

IV

Once out of nature I shall never take   25
My bodily form from any natural thing,
But such a form as Grecian goldsmiths make
Of hammered gold and gold enameling
To keep a drowsy Emperor awake;
Or set upon a golden bough to sing   30
To lords and ladies of Byzantium
Of what is past, or passing, or to come.

Byzantium

The unpurged images of day recede;
The Emperor's drunken soldiery are abed;

---

10. tattered coat . . . stick: Cf. the image of the scarecrow in "Among School Children" (1. 48, p. 318). 16. holy city: as the center of the Eastern or Orthodox Church, but as much the holy city of art. 17. God's holy fire: alluding to the splintered golden light of the mosaic background. 19. perne in a gyre: descend (from eternity) by winding yourselves with the changes of time as in a spiral. 30. to sing: "I have read somewhere that in the Emperor's palace at Byzantium was a tree made of gold and silver, and artificial birds that sang" (Yeats); here they sing in eternity of the passage of time (1. 32).

BYZANTIUM For the implications of Byzantium, see the notes to "Sailing to Byzantium." Here it becomes a place of passage from "life" to "death" or from unpurged human complexity to the artifice of eternity, with the golden birds, the flames, and the Emperor's smithies providing the means of passage.

Night resonance recedes, night-walkers' song
After great cathedral gong;
A starlit or a moonlit dome disdains 5
All that man is,
All mere complexities,
The fury and the mire of human veins.

Before me floats an image, man or shade,
Shade more than man, more image than a shade; 10
For Hades' bobbin bound in mummy-cloth
May unwind the winding path;
A mouth that has no moisture and no breath
Breathless mouths may summon;
I hail the superhuman; 15
I call it death-in-life and life-in-death.

Miracle, bird or golden handiwork,
More miracle than bird or handiwork,
Planted on the starlit golden bough,
Can like the cocks of Hades crow, 20
Or, by the moon embittered, scorn aloud
In glory of changeless metal
Common bird or petal
And all complexities of mire or blood.

At midnight on the Emperor's pavement flit 25
Flames that no faggot feeds, nor steel has lit,
Nor storm disturbs, flames begotten of flame,
Where blood-begotten spirits come
And all complexities of fury leave,
Dying into a dance, 30
An agony of trance,
An agony of flame that cannot singe a sleeve.

Astraddle on the dolphin's mire and blood,
Spirit after spirit! The smithies break the flood,
The golden smithies of the Emperor! 35
Marbles of the dancing floor
Break bitter furies of complexity,
Those images that yet
Fresh images beget,
That dolphin-torn, that gong-tormented sea. 40

5. **dome:** the night sky of Byzantium, seen as itself a work of artifice. 11. **Hades'**
bobbin: the winding cloth or mummy-bands may be unwound as the shade returns at a
human summons. 14. **Breathless mouths:** breathless with anticipation as they summon
the dead and the eternal. 20. **like . . . crow:** the golden bird (see "Sailing to Byzantium," ll. 27–32) now identified with the cock carved on Roman tombstones as an
emblem of rebirth. 26. **nor . . . lit:** that is, the sparks of the flint. 33. **dolphin's . . .**
blood: in Roman tomb decoration, dolphins served as an escort of the dead to the
Isles of the Blest; in legend, dolphins rescued Arion and other musicians by bearing
them to safety on their backs; here they seem to bear men into the realm where mortals
become "spirit." 34. **break the flood:** splinter its continuity, as the mosaics do a surface; tame it to artifice and form, as in Roman mosaic pavements of dolphins in the sea.

No Second Troy

Why should I blame her that she filled my days
With misery, or that she would of late
Have taught to ignorant men most violent ways,
Or hurled the little streets upon the great,
Had they but courage equal to desire?   5
What could have made her peaceful with a mind
That nobleness made simple as a fire,
With beauty like a tightened bow, a kind
That is not natural in an age like this,
Being high and solitary and most stern?   10
Why, what could she have done, being what she is?
Was there another Troy for her to burn?

Among School Children

I

I walk through the long schoolroom questioning;
A kind old nun in a white hood replies;
The children learn to cipher and to sing,
To study reading-books and history,
To cut and sew, be neat in everything   5
In the best modern way—the children's eyes
In momentary wonder stare upon
A sixty-year-old smiling public man.

II

I dream of a Ledaean body, bent
Above a sinking fire, a tale that she   10
Told of a harsh reproof, or trivial event
That changed some childish day to tragedy—
Told, and it seemed that our two natures blent
Into a sphere from youthful sympathy,
Or else, to alter Plato's parable,   15
Into the yolk and white of the one shell.

NO SECOND TROY 1. her: Maud Gonne, a woman of extraordinary beauty and deep commitment to Irish nationalism; Yeats fell in love with her in 1889 but never succeeded in his proposals. She later married Major John MacBride (see "Easter 1916," note to l. 31, p. 308), and died, still beautiful, in 1953. Her power for destruction is given emphasis in the reference to Helen of Troy.

AMONG SCHOOL CHILDREN 1. schoolroom: Yeats, then an Irish Senator, visited St. O'Heran's School, Waterford, in February 1926. 3. cipher: do calculations. 9. Ledaean: like that of Leda who, when raped by Zeus in the form of a swan, became the mother of Helen of Troy. Here "Ledaean body" recalls the young Maud Gonne (see "No Second Troy," above). 15. Plato's parable: in Plato's *Symposium*, Aristophanes says that humans were all once spherical until Zeus cut everyone in two (as men "cut eggs in two with a hair"); since then, each half seeks the other, and this is the origin of love.

III

And thinking of that fit of grief or rage
I look upon one child or t'other there
And wonder if she stood so at that age—
For even daughters of the swan can share   20
Something of every paddler's heritage—
And had that color upon cheek or hair,
And thereupon my heart is driven wild:
She stands before me as a living child.

IV

Her present image floats into the mind—   25
Did Quattrocento finger fashion it
Hollow of cheek as though it drank the wind
And took a mess of shadows for its meat?
And I though never of Ledaean kind
Had pretty plumage once—enough of that,   30
Better to smile on all that smile, and show
There is a comfortable kind of old scarecrow.

V

What youthful mother, a shape upon her lap
Honey of generation had betrayed,
And that must sleep, shriek, struggle to escape   35
As recollection or the drug decide,
Would think her son, did she but see that shape
With sixty or more winters on its head,
A compensation for the pang of his birth,
Or the uncertainty of his setting forth?   40

VI

Plato thought nature but a spume that plays
Upon a ghostly paradigm of things;
Solider Aristotle played the taws
Upon the bottom of a king of kings;
World-famous golden-thighed Pythagoras   45
Fingered upon a fiddle-stick or strings

26. Quattrocento: that is, of an Italian painter of the fifteenth century (e.g., Fra Lippo Lippi or Botticelli); in earlier versions of the poem, this appeared as "Quintocento" (sixteenth century) and, more specifically, "Da Vinci," who did a painting of Leda and the Swan. **34. Honey of generation:** Yeats draws on the Neoplatonist Porphyry (third century A.D.) for this image of the pleasure that seduces the soul into incarnate life; Yeats makes it also the "drug" that destroys the soul's recollection of its prenatal freedom. **42. ghostly paradigm:** spiritual model, the disembodied Forms of which natural forms are imperfect copies. **43. Solider Aristotle:** who denied any direct access to Platonic Forms but found them only as embodied in material objects. **taws:** birch rods or leather straps used to punish students. **44. king of kings:** Alexander the Great, who was Aristotle's pupil. **45. golden-thighed Pythagoras:** one of his supposed attributes was a golden hip or thigh bone. **46. fiddle-stick or strings:** on which Pythagoras marked the intervals between musical notes; he not only found mathematical correspondences to musical harmonies but, according to legend, could hear the music of the spheres (that is, the harmonies created by the movement of the heavenly bodies in their rotation around the earth).

What a star sang and careless Muses heard:
Old clothes upon old sticks to scare a bird.

VII

Both nuns and mothers worship images,
But those the candles light are not as those   50
That animate a mother's reveries,
But keep a marble or a bronze repose.
And yet they too break hearts—O Presences
That passion, piety or affection knows,
And that all heavenly glory symbolize—   55
O self-born mockers of man's enterprise;

VIII

Labor is blossoming or dancing where
The body is not bruised to pleasure soul,
Nor beauty born out of its own despair,
Nor blear-eyed wisdom out of midnight oil.   60
O chestnut-tree, great-rooted blossomer,
Are you the leaf, the blossom or the bole?
O body swayed to music, O brightening glance,
How can we know the dancer from the dance?

Crazy Jane Talks with the Bishop

I met the Bishop on the road
And much said he and I.
"Those breasts are flat and fallen now,
Those veins must soon be dry;
Live in a heavenly mansion,   5
Not in some foul sty."

"Fair and foul are near of kin,
And fair needs foul," I cried.
"My friends are gone, but that's a truth
Nor grave nor bed denied,   10
Learned in bodily lowliness
And in the heart's pride.

"A woman can be proud and stiff
When on love intent;
But Love has pitched his mansion in   15

48. **Old . . . bird:** but each of these philosophers and philosophies grew old, i.e., reached a scarecrow age. 56. **self-born:** independent of man.
CRAZY JANE The Crazy Jane who appears and speaks in a series of late poems by Yeats was founded on "Cracked Mary," an old woman who lived near Lady Gregory and was "the local satirist and a really terrible one" (Yeats).

The place of excrement;
For nothing can be sole or whole
That has not been rent."

Leda and the Swan

A sudden blow: the great wings beating still
Above the staggering girl, her thighs caressed
By the dark webs, her nape caught in his bill,
He holds her helpless breast upon his breast.

How can those terrified vague fingers push   5
The feathered glory from her loosening thighs?
And how can body, laid in that white rush,
But feel the strange heart beating where it lies?

A shudder in the loins engenders there
The broken wall, the burning roof and tower   10
And Agamemnon dead.
                              Being so caught up,
So mastered by the brute blood of the air,
Did she put on his knowledge with his power
Before the indifferent beak could let her drop?

Edwin Arlington Robinson (1869–1935)

Bewick Finzer

Time was when his half million drew
        The breath of six per cent;
But soon the worm of what-was-not
        Fed hard on his content;
And something crumbled in his brain   5
        When his half million went.

LEDA AND THE SWAN   Zeus, in the form of a swan, raped Leda, queen of Sparta. Their daughter Helen married Menelaus, king of Sparta, but later ran away with Paris, son of Priam, king of Troy. To get her back, Menelaus and his brother Agamemnon, king of Argos, led the Greeks in a ten-year siege of Troy. 10–11. broken . . . dead: The Greeks sacked Troy, after tricking the Trojans into breaking a hole in the city wall to drag in a large, hollow wooden horse, which was filled with Greek warriors. On his return to Argos, Agamemnon was murdered by his wife Clytemnestra, Helen's sister.

Time passed, and filled along with his
    The place of many more;
Time came, and hardly one of us
    Had credence to restore,   10
From what appeared one day, the man
    Whom we had known before.

The broken voice, the withered neck,
    The coat worn out with care,
The cleanliness of indigence,   15
    The brilliance of despair,
The fond imponderable dreams
    Of affluence—all were there.

Poor Finzer, with his dreams and schemes,
    Fares hard now in the race,   20
With heart and eye that have a task
    When he looks in the face
Of one who might so easily
    Have been in Finzer's place.

He comes unfailing for the loan   25
    We give and then forget;
He comes, and probably for years
    Will he be coming yet—
Familiar as an old mistake,
    And futile as regret.   30

Mr. Flood's Party

Old Eben Flood, climbing alone one night
Over the hill between the town below
And the forsaken upland hermitage
That held as much as he should ever know
On earth again of home, paused warily.   5
The road was his with not a native near;
And Eben, having leisure, said aloud,
For no man else in Tilbury Town to hear:

"Well, Mr. Flood, we have the harvest moon
Again, and we may not have many more;   10
The bird is on the wing, the poet says,
And you and I have said it here before.
Drink to the bird." He raised up to the light
The jug that he had gone so far to fill,

MR. FLOOD'S PARTY 8. **Tilbury Town:** fictional setting for various of Robinson's poems. 11. **The bird . . . says:** from Edward FitzGerald, *The Rubáiyát of Omar Khayyám*, stanza 7.

And answered huskily: "Well, Mr. Flood,　　　　　15
Since you propose it, I believe I will."

Alone, as if enduring to the end
A valiant armor of scarred hopes outworn,
He stood there in the middle of the road
Like Roland's ghost winding a silent horn.　　　　20
Below him, in the town among the trees,
Where friends of other days had honored him,
A phantom salutation of the dead
Rang thinly till old Eben's eyes were dim.

Then, as a mother lays her sleeping child　　　　25
Down tenderly, fearing it may awake,
He set the jug down slowly at his feet
With trembling care, knowing that most things break;
And only when assured that on firm earth
It stood, as the uncertain lives of men　　　　30
Assuredly did not, he paced away,
And with his hand extended paused again:

"Well, Mr. Flood, we have not met like this
In a long time; and many a change has come
To both of us, I fear, since last it was　　　　35
We had a drop together. Welcome home!"
Convivially returning with himself,
Again he raised the jug up to the light;
And with an acquiescent quaver said:
"Well, Mr. Flood, if you insist, I might.　　　　40

"Only a very little, Mr. Flood—
For auld lang syne. No more, sir; that will do."
So, for the time, apparently it did,
And Eben evidently thought so too;
For soon amid the silver loneliness　　　　45
Of night he lifted up his voice and sang,
Secure, with only two moons listening,
Until the whole harmonious landscape rang—

"For auld lang syne." The weary throat gave out,
The last word wavered, and the song was done.　　　　50
He raised again the jug regretfully
And shook his head, and was again alone.
There was not much that was ahead of him,
And there was nothing in the town below—
Where strangers would have shut the many doors　　　　55
That many friends had opened long ago.

20. **Roland's . . . horn:** in the medieval French epic *The Song of Roland,* Roland
blows his horn before he dies to warn his emperor, Charlemagne, of the Saracen attack
on the army's rear guard.

Robert Frost   *(1874–1963)*

After Apple-Picking

My long two-pointed ladder's sticking through a tree
Toward heaven still,
And there's a barrel that I didn't fill
Beside it, and there may be two or three
Apples I didn't pick upon some bough.   5
But I am done with apple-picking now.
Essence of winter sleep is on the night,
The scent of apples: I am drowsing off.
I cannot rub the strangeness from my sight
I got from looking through a pane of glass   10
I skimmed this morning from the drinking trough
And held against the world of hoary grass.
It melted, and I let it fall and break.
But I was well
Upon my way to sleep before it fell,   15
And I could tell
What form my dreaming was about to take.
Magnified apples appear and disappear,
Stem end and blossom end,
And every fleck of russet showing clear.   20
My instep arch not only keeps the ache,
It keeps the pressure of a ladder-round.
I feel the ladder sway as the boughs bend.
And I keep hearing from the cellar bin
The rumbling sound   25
Of load on load of apples coming in.
For I have had too much
Of apple-picking: I am overtired
Of the great harvest I myself desired.
There were ten thousand thousand fruit to touch,   30
Cherish in hand, lift down, and not let fall.
For all
That struck the earth,
No matter if not bruised or spiked with stubble,
Went surely to the cider-apple heap   35
As of no worth.
One can see what will trouble
This sleep of mine, whatever sleep it is.
Were he not gone,
The woodchuck could say whether it's like his   40

AFTER APPLE-PICKING   **10. pane of glass:** sheet of ice. **12. hoary:** white with hoar-frost.

Long sleep, as I describe its coming on,
Or just some human sleep.

Desert Places

Snow falling and night falling fast, oh, fast
In a field I looked into going past,
And the ground almost covered smooth in snow,
But a few weeds and stubble showing last.

The woods around it have it—it is theirs.   5
All animals are smothered in their lairs.
I am too absent-spirited to count;
The loneliness includes me unawares.

And lonely as it is, that loneliness
Will be more lonely ere it will be less—   10
A blanker whiteness of benighted snow
With no expression, nothing to express.

They cannot scare me with their empty spaces
Between stars—on stars where no human race is.
I have it in me so much nearer home   15
To scare myself with my own desert places.

The Oven Bird

There is a singer everyone has heard,
Loud, a mid-summer and a mid-wood bird,
Who makes the solid tree trunks sound again.
He says that leaves are old and that for flowers
Mid-summer is to spring as one to ten.   5
He says the early petal-fall is past,
When pear and cherry bloom went down in showers
On sunny days a moment overcast;
And comes that other fall we name the fall.
He says the highway dust is over all.   10
The bird would cease and be as other birds
But that he knows in singing not to sing.
The question that he frames in all but words
Is what to make of a diminished thing.

Mowing

There was never a sound beside the wood but one,
And that was my long scythe whispering to the ground.

What was it it whispered? I knew not well myself;
Perhaps it was something about the heat of the sun,
Something, perhaps, about the lack of sound—   5
And that was why it whispered and did not speak.
It was no dream of the gift of idle hours,
Or easy gold at the hand of fay or elf:
Anything more than the truth would have seemed too weak
To the earnest love that laid the swale in rows,   10
Not without feeble-pointed spikes of flowers
(Pale orchises), and scared a bright green snake.
The fact is the sweetest dream that labor knows.
My long scythe whispered and left the hay to make.

Design

I found a dimpled spider, fat and white,
On a white heal-all, holding up a moth
Like a white piece of rigid satin cloth—
Assorted characters of death and blight
Mixed ready to begin the morning right,   5
Like the ingredients of a witches' broth—
A snow-drop spider, a flower like a froth,
And dead wings carried like a paper kite.

What had that flower to do with being white,
The wayside blue and innocent heal-all?   10
What brought the kindred spider to that height,
Then steered the white moth thither in the night?
What but design of darkness to appall?—
If design govern in a thing so small.

Provide, Provide

The witch that came (the withered hag)
To wash the steps with pail and rag
Was once the beauty Abishag,

The picture pride of Hollywood.
Too many fall from great and good,   5
For you to doubt the likelihood.

MOWING   10. swale: marshy depression.
DESIGN   2. heal-all: a medicinal flower, usually blue (see ll. 9–10).
PROVIDE, PROVIDE   3. Abishag: In David's old age, a young virgin was sought to lie in
his bosom that he might "get heat"; "so they sought for a fair damsel throughout all
the coasts of Israel, and found Abishag a Shunammite. . . . And the damsel was
very fair, and cherished the king, and ministered to him: but the king knew her not" (I
Kings 1:2–4).

Die early and avoid the fate.
Or if predestined to die late,
Make up your mind to die in state.

Make the whole stock exchange your own!   10
If need be occupy a throne,
Where nobody can call *you* crone.

Some have relied on what they knew,
Others on being simply true.
What worked for them might work for you.   15

No memory of having starred
Atones for later disregard
Or keeps the end from being hard.

Better to go down dignified
With boughten friendship at your side   20
Than none at all. Provide, provide!

Directive

Back out of all this now too much for us,
Back in a time made simple by the loss
Of detail, burned, dissolved, and broken off
Like graveyard marble sculpture in the weather,
There is a house that is no more a house   5
Upon a farm that is no more a farm
And in a town that is no more a town.
The road there, if you'll let a guide direct you
Who only has at heart your getting lost,
May seem as if it should have been a quarry—   10
Great monolithic knees the former town
Long since gave up pretense of keeping covered.
And there's a story in a book about it:
Besides the wear of iron wagon wheels
The ledges show lines ruled southeast-northwest,   15
The chisel work of an enormous Glacier
That braced his feet against the Arctic Pole.
You must not mind a certain coolness from him
Still said to haunt this side of Panther Mountain.
Nor need you mind the serial ordeal   20
Of being watched from forty cellar holes
As if by eye pairs out of forty firkins.
As for the woods' excitement over you
That sends light rustle rushes to their leaves,

DIRECTIVE   **22. firkins:** small casks or jugs.

Charge that to upstart inexperience.   25
Where were they all not twenty years ago?
They think too much of having shaded out
A few old pecker-fretted apple trees.
Make yourself up a cheering song of how
Someone's road home from work this once was,   30
Who may be just ahead of you on foot
Or creaking with a buggy load of grain.
The height of the adventure is the height
Of country where two village cultures faded
Into each other. Both of them are lost.   35
And if you're lost enough to find yourself
By now, pull in your ladder road behind you
And put a sign up CLOSED to all but me.
Then make yourself at home. The only field
Now left's no bigger than a harness gall.   40
First there's the children's house of make-believe,
Some shattered dishes underneath a pine,
The playthings in the playhouse of the children.
Weep for what little things could make them glad.
Then for the house that is no more a house,   45
But only a belilaced cellar hole,
Now slowly closing like a dent in dough.
This was no playhouse but a house in earnest.
Your destination and your destiny's
A brook that was the water of the house,   50
Cold as a spring as yet so near its source,
Too lofty and original to rage.
(We know the valley streams that when aroused
Will leave their tatters hung on barb and thorn.)
I have kept hidden in the instep arch   55
Of an old cedar at the waterside
A broken drinking goblet like the Grail
Under a spell so the wrong ones can't find it,
So can't get saved, as Saint Mark says they mustn't,
(I stole the goblet from the children's playhouse.)   60
Here are your waters and your watering place.
Drink and be whole again beyond confusion.

There are Roughly Zones

We sit indoors and talk of the cold outside.
And every gust that gathers strength and heaves

---

28. **pecker-fretted:** drilled by woodpeckers. **40. harness gall:** a swelling or irritation, a place rubbed bare, on a horse. **57. Grail:** the object of quest by knights of romance; the cup (or platter) used at the Last Supper, in which Joseph of Arimathea later received Christ's blood at the Cross. **59. Saint . . . mustn't:** "He that believeth and is baptized shall be saved; but he that believeth not shall be damned" (Mark 16:16). Elsewhere Mark speaks of the Lord's mercy "for the elect's sake" (13:20).

Is a threat to the house. But the house has long been tried.
We think of the tree. If it never again has leaves,
We'll know, we say, that this was the night it died.   5
It is very far north, we admit, to have brought the peach.
What comes over a man, is it soul or mind—
That to no limits and bounds he can stay confined?
You would say his ambition was to extend the reach
Clear to the Arctic of every living kind.   10
Why is his nature forever so hard to teach
That though there is no fixed line between wrong and right,
There are roughly zones whose laws must be obeyed?
There is nothing much we can do for the tree tonight,
But we can't help feeling more than a little betrayed   15
That the northwest wind should rise to such a height
Just when the cold went down so many below.
The tree has no leaves and may never have them again.
We must wait till some months hence in the spring to know.
But if it is destined never again to grow,   20
It can blame this limitless trait in the hearts of men.

[handwritten margin note: over come. Man has almost thru. tech nature]

[handwritten note: Man has desire for technology.]

The Onset

Always the same, when on a fated night
At last the gathered snow lets down as white
As may be in dark woods, and with a song
It shall not make again all winter long
Of hissing on the yet uncovered ground,   5
I almost stumble looking up and round,
As one who overtaken by the end
Gives up his errand, and lets death descend
Upon him where he is, with nothing done
To evil, no important triumph won,   10
More than if life had never been begun.

Yet all the precedent is on my side:
I know that winter death has never tried
The earth but it has failed: the snow may heap
In long storms an undrifted four feet deep   15
As measured against maple, birch, and oak,
It cannot check the peeper's silver croak;
And I shall see the snow all go downhill
In water of a slender April rill
That flashes tail through last year's withered brake   20
And dead weeds, like a disappearing snake.
Nothing will be left white but here a birch,
And there a clump of houses with a church.

THE ONSET   17. peeper: frog, tree-toad. 20. brake: thicket.

A Considerable Speck

(*Microscopic*)

A speck that would have been beneath my sight
On any but a paper sheet so white
Set off across what I had written there.
And I had idly poised my pen in air
To stop it with a period of ink,   5
When something strange about it made me think.
This was no dust speck by my breathing blown,
But unmistakably a living mite
With inclinations it could call its own.
It paused as with suspicion of my pen,   10
And then came racing wildly on again
To where my manuscript was not yet dry;
Then paused again and either drank or smelt—
With loathing, for again it turned to fly.
Plainly with an intelligence I dealt.   15
It seemed too tiny to have room for feet,
Yet must have had a set of them complete
To express how much it didn't want to die.
It ran with terror and with cunning crept.
It faltered: I could see it hesitate;   20
Then in the middle of the open sheet
Cower down in desperation to accept
Whatever I accorded it of fate.
I have none of the tenderer-than-thou
Collectivistic regimenting love   25
With which the modern world is being swept.
But this poor microscopic item now!
Since it was nothing I knew evil of
I let it lie there till I hope it slept.

I have a mind myself and recognize   30
Mind when I meet with it in any guise.
No one can know how glad I am to find
On any sheet the least display of mind.

The Gift Outright

The land was ours before we were the land's.
She was our land more than a hundred years
Before we were her people. She was ours
In Massachusetts, in Virginia,
But we were England's, still colonials,   5
Possessing what we still were unpossessed by,

Possessed by what we now no more possessed.
Something we were withholding made us weak
Until we found out that it was ourselves
We were withholding from our land of living, 10
And forthwith found salvation in surrender.
Such as we were we gave ourselves outright
(The deed of gift was many deeds of war)
To the land vaguely realizing westward,
But still unstoried, artless, unenhanced, 15
Such as she was, such as she would become.

Acquainted with the Night

I have been one acquainted with the night.
I have walked out in rain—and back in rain.
I have outwalked the furthest city light.

I have looked down the saddest city lane.
I have passed by the watchman on his beat 5
And dropped my eyes, unwilling to explain.

I have stood still and stopped the sound of feet
When far away an interrupted cry
Came over houses from another street,

But not to call me back or say good-by; 10
And further still at an unearthly height
One luminary clock against the sky

Proclaimed the time was neither wrong nor right.
I have been one acquainted with the night.

Wallace Stevens *(1879–1955)*

Anecdote of the Jar

I placed a jar in Tennessee,
And round it was, upon a hill.
It made the slovenly wilderness
Surround that hill.

ACQUAINTED WITH THE NIGHT   **12. luminary:** lighted; with overtones of "like a heavenly body."

The wilderness rose up to it,   5
And sprawled around, no longer wild.
The jar was round upon the ground
And tall and of a port in air.

It took dominion everywhere.
The jar was gray and bare.   10
It did not give of bird or bush,
Like nothing else in Tennessee.

Peter Quince at the Clavier

I

Just as my fingers on these keys
Make music, so the selfsame sounds
On my spirit make a music, too.

Music is feeling, then, not sound;
And thus it is that what I feel,   5
Here in this room, desiring you,

Thinking of your blue-shadowed silk,
Is music. It is like the strain
Waked in the elders by Susanna.

Of a green evening, clear and warm,   10
She bathed in her still garden, while
The red-eyed elders watching, felt

The basses of their beings throb
In witching chords, and their thin blood
Pulse pizzicati of Hosanna.   15

II

In the green water, clear and warm,
Susanna lay.
She searched
The touch of springs,
And found   20
Concealed imaginings.

PETER QUINCE   The name Peter Quince is derived from the carpenter who directs the
ludicrous "tragedy" of Pyramus and Thisbe in Shakespeare's A *Midsummer-Night's
Dream*. 9. **Susanna**: A just woman (in the tale of the Apocrypha) was spied upon as
she bathed in the garden by two lustful old judges who threatened to defame her if she
did not submit to them. Refusing, she was accused of adultery with a young man and
condemned to death; but the prophet Daniel discovered the discrepancies in the old
men's stories, exposed them, and brought about their execution in place of Susanna.
15. pizzicati: notes plucked from strings.

She sighed,
For so much melody.

Upon the bank, she stood
In the cool   25
Of spent emotions.
She felt, among the leaves,
The dew
Of old devotions.

She walked upon the grass,   30
Still quavering.
The winds were like her maids,
On timid feet,
Fetching her woven scarves,
Yet wavering.   35

A breath upon her hand
Muted the night.
She turned—
A cymbal crashed,
And roaring horns.   40

III

Soon, with a noise like tambourines,
Came her attendant Byzantines.

They wondered why Susanna cried
Against the elders by her side;

And as they whispered, the refrain   45
Was like a willow swept by rain.

Anon, their lamps' uplifted flame
Revealed Susanna and her shame.

And then, the simpering Byzantines
Fled, with a noise like tambourines.   50

IV

Beauty is momentary in the mind—
The fitful tracing of a portal;
But in the flesh it is immortal.

The body dies; the body's beauty lives.
So evenings die, in their green going,   55
A wave, interminably flowing.
So gardens die, their meek breath scenting

42. **Byzantines:** "Somebody once called my attention to the fact that there were no Byzantines in Susanna's time. I hope that that bit of precious pedantry will seem as unimportant to you as it does to me" (Stevens).

The cowl of winter, done repenting.
So maidens die, to the auroral
Celebration of a maiden's choral.   60
Susanna's music touched the bawdy strings
Of those white elders; but, escaping,
Left only Death's ironic scraping.
Now, in its immortality, it plays
On the clear viol of her memory,   65
And makes a constant sacrament of praise.

The Idea of Order at Key West

She sang beyond the genius of the sea.
The water never formed to mind or voice,
Like a body wholly body, fluttering
Its empty sleeves; and yet its mimic motion
Made constant cry, caused constantly a cry,   5
That was not ours although we understood,
Inhuman, of the veritable ocean.

The sea was not a mask. No more was she.
The song and water were not medleyed sound
Even if what she sang was what she heard,   10
Since what she sang was uttered word by word.
It may be that in all her phrases stirred
The grinding water and the gasping wind;
But it was she and not the sea we heard.

For she was the maker of the song she sang.   15
The ever-hooded, tragic-gestured sea
Was merely a place by which she walked to sing.
Whose spirit is this? we said, because we knew
It was the spirit that we sought and knew
That we should ask this often as she sang.   20

If it was only the dark voice of the sea
That rose, or even colored by many waves;
If it was only the outer voice of sky
And cloud, of the sunken coral water-walled,
However clear, it would have been deep air,   25
The heaving speech of air, a summer sound
Repeated in a summer without end
And sound alone. But it was more than that,
More even than her voice, and ours, among
The meaningless plungings of water and the wind,   30
Theatrical distances, bronze shadows heaped
On high horizons, mountainous atmospheres
Of sky and sea.
                    It was her voice that made

The sky acutest at its vanishing.
She measured to the hour its solitude. 35
She was the single artificer of the world
In which she sang. And when she sang, the sea,
Whatever self it had, became the self
That was her song, for she was the maker. Then we,
As we beheld her striding there alone, 40
Knew that there never was a world for her
Except the one she sang and, singing, made.

Ramon Fernandez, tell me, if you know,
Why, when the singing ended and we turned
Toward the town, tell why the glassy lights, 45
The lights in the fishing boats at anchor there,
As the night descended, tilting in the air,
Mastered the night and portioned out the sea,
Fixing emblazoned zones and fiery poles,
Arranging, deepening, enchanting night. 50

Oh! Blessed rage for order, pale Ramon,
The maker's rage to order words of the sea,
Words of the fragrant portals, dimly-starred,
And of ourselves and of our origins,
In ghostlier demarcations, keener sounds. 55

The World as Meditation

*J'ai passé trop de temps à travailler
mon violon, à voyager. Mais l'exer-
cice essentiel du compositeur—la
méditation—rien ne l'a jamais sus-
pendu en moi . . . Je vis un rêve
permanent, qui ne s'arrête ni nuit
ni jour.*

—GEORGES ENESCO

Is it Ulysses that approaches from the east,
The interminable adventurer? The trees are mended.
That winter is washed away. Someone is moving

THE IDEA OF ORDER **36. single artificer:** In this poem, Stevens explained, "life has ceased to be a matter of chance. It may be that every man introduces his own order into the life about him and that the idea of order in general is simply what Bishop Berkeley might have called a fortuitous concourse of personal orders. But still there is order." **43. Ramon Fernandez:** "not intended to be anyone at all. I chose two everyday Spanish names. I knew of Ramon Fernandez, the critic, and had read some of his criticisms but I did not have him in mind" (Stevens). *Messages* by Ramon Fernandez (1894–1944) has sometimes been cited as analogous to the poem in its attitudes toward the ordering of the world.

THE WORLD AS MEDITATION **Epigraph:** "I have spent too much time practicing my violin to travel. But the essential exercise of the composer—meditation—nothing has ever stopped in me. . . . I live a permanent dream, which ceases neither night nor day." George Enesco (1881–1955) was a distinguished Romanian violinist and composer.

On the horizon and lifting himself up above it.
A form of fire approaches the cretonnes of Penelope,   5
Whose mere savage presence awakens the world in which she dwells.

She has composed, so long, a self with which to welcome him,
Companion to his self for her, which she imagined,
Two in a deep-founded sheltering, friend and dear friend.

The trees had been mended, as an essential exercise   10
In an inhuman meditation, larger than her own.
No winds like dogs watched over her at night.

She wanted nothing he could not bring her by coming alone.
She wanted no fetchings. His arms would be her necklace
And her belt, the final fortune of their desire.   15

But was it Ulysses? Or was it only the warmth of the sun
On her pillow? The thought kept beating in her like her heart.
The two kept beating together. It was only day.

It was Ulysses and it was not. Yet they had met,
Friend and dear friend and a planet's encouragement.   20
The barbarous strength within her would never fail.

She would talk a little to herself as she combed her hair,
Repeating his name with its patient syllables,
Never forgetting him that kept coming constantly so near.

Angel Surrounded by Paysans

One of the countrymen:
                                                    There is
        A welcome at the door to which no one comes?
The angel:
        I am the angel of reality,
        Seen for a moment standing in the door.

        I have neither ashen wing nor wear of ore   5

5. **Penelope:** the wife of Ulysses awaiting his return from Troy, besieged by suitors whom she resists with cunning and fidelity.

ANGEL SURROUNDED BY PAYSANS   In discussing a painting he had acquired, Stevens wrote: "Tal Coat is supposed to be a man of violence but one soon becomes accustomed to the present picture. I have even given it a title of my own: *Angel Surrounded by Peasants*. The angel is the Venetian glass bowl on the left with the little spray of leaves in it. The peasants are the terrines, bottles, and the glasses that surround it. This title alone tames it as a lump of sugar might tame a lion." Tal Coat is a French painter (1905–   ). 5. **nor wear of ore:** "I suppose that what I had in mind when I said that he had no wear of ore was that he had no crown or other symbol. I was definitely trying to think of an earthly figure, not a heavenly figure. The point of the poem is that there must be in the world about us things that solace us quite as fully as any heavenly visitation could" (Stevens).

And live without a tepid aureole,

Or stars that follow me, not to attend,
But, of my being and its knowing, part.

I am one of you and being one of you
Is being and knowing what I am and know.   10

Yet I am the necessary angel of earth,
Since, in my sight, you see the earth again,

Cleared of its stiff and stubborn, man-locked set,
And, in my hearing, you hear its tragic drone

Rise liquidly in liquid lingerings,   15
Like watery words awash; like meanings said

By repetitions of half-meanings. Am I not,
Myself, only half of a figure of a sort,

A figure half seen, or seen for a moment, a man
Of the mind, an apparition appareled in   20

Apparels of such lightest look that a turn
Of my shoulder and quickly, too quickly, I am gone?

William Carlos Williams *(1883–1963)*

Danse Russe

If I when my wife is sleeping
and the baby and Kathleen
are sleeping
and the sun is a flame-white disc
in silken mists   5
above shining trees,—
if I in my north room
dance naked, grotesquely
before my mirror
waving my shirt round my head   10
and singing softly to myself:

11. **necessary . . . earth:** "The angel is the angel of reality. This is clear only if the reader is of the idea that we live in a world of the imagination, in which reality and contact with it are the great blessings. For nine readers out of ten, the necessary angel will appear to be the angel of the imagination and for nine days out of ten that is true, although it is the tenth day that counts" (Stevens).

"I am lonely, lonely.
I was born to be lonely,
I am best so!"
If I admire my arms, my face   15
my shoulders, flanks, buttocks
against the yellow drawn shades,—

Who shall say I am not
the happy genius of my household?

The Poor

It's the anarchy of poverty
delights me, the old
yellow wooden house indented
among the new brick tenements

Or a cast-iron balcony   5
with panels showing oak branches
in full leaf. It fits
the dress of the children

reflecting every stage and
custom of necessity—
custom of necessity—   10
Chimneys, roofs, fences of
wood and metal in an unfenced

age and enclosing next to
nothing at all: the old man
in a sweater and soft black   15
hat who sweeps the sidewalk—

his own ten feet of it
in a wind that fitfully
turning his corner has
overwhelmed the entire city   20

The Yachts

contend in a sea which the land partly encloses
shielding them from the too heavy blows
of an ungoverned ocean which when it chooses

tortures the biggest hulls, the best man knows
to pit against its beatings, and sinks them pitilessly.   5
Mothlike in mists, scintillant in the minute

THE YACHTS   **6. scintillant:** sparkling, flashing.

brilliance of cloudless days, with broad bellying sails
they glide to the wind tossing green water
from their sharp prows while over them the crew crawls

ant like, solicitously grooming them, releasing,   10
making fast as they turn, lean far over and having
caught the wind again, side by side, head for the mark.

In a well guarded arena of open water surrounded by
lesser and greater craft which, sycophant, lumbering
and flittering follow them, they appear youthful, rare   15

as the light of a happy eye, live with the grace
of all that in the mind is feckless, free and
naturally to be desired. Now the sea which holds them

is moody, lapping their glossy sides, as if feeling
for some slightest flaw but fails completely.   20
Today no race. Then the wind comes again. The yachts

move, jockeying for a start, the signal is set and they
are off. Now the waves strike at them but they are too
well made, they slip through, though they take in canvas.

Arms with hands grasping seek to clutch at the prows.   25
Bodies thrown recklessly in the way are cut aside.
It is a sea of faces about them in agony, in despair

until the horror of the race dawns staggering the mind,
the whole sea become an entanglement of watery bodies
lost to the world bearing what they cannot hold. Broken,   30

beaten, desolate, reaching from the dead to be taken up
they cry out, failing, failing! their cries rising
in waves still as the skillful yachts pass over.

Pictures from Brueghel

II   Landscape with the Fall of Icarus

According to Brueghel
when Icarus fell
it was spring

a farmer was ploughing
his field   5
the whole pageantry

PICTURES FROM BRUEGHEL, II **Landscape . . . Icarus:** Compare W. H. Auden's use
of this picture in "Musée des Beaux Arts" (p. 382).

of the year was
awake tingling
near

the edge of the sea　　　　　　　　　10
concerned
with itself

sweating in the sun
that melted
the wings' wax　　　　　　　　　　15

unsignificantly
off the coast
there was

a splash quite unnoticed
this was　　　　　　　　　　　　　20
Icarus drowning

VII　The Corn Harvest

Summer!
the painting is organized
about a young

reaper enjoying his
noonday rest　　　　　　　　　　　5
completely

relaxed
from his morning labors
sprawled

in fact sleeping　　　　　　　　　　10
unbuttoned
on his back

the women
have brought him his lunch
perhaps　　　　　　　　　　　　　15

a spot of wine
they gather gossiping
under a tree

whose shade
carelessly　　　　　　　　　　　　20
he does not share the

resting
center of
their workaday world

D. H. Lawrence   *(1885–1930)*

The Elephant is Slow to Mate—

The elephant, the huge old beast,
     is slow to mate;
he finds a female, they show no haste,
     they wait

for the sympathy in their vast shy hearts   5
     slowly, slowly to rouse
as they loiter along the river-beds
     and drink and browse

and dash in panic through the brake
     of forest with the herd,   10
and sleep in massive silence, and wake
     together, without a word.

So slowly the great hot elephant hearts
     grow full of desire,
and the great beasts mate in secret at last,   15
     hiding their fire.

Oldest they are and the wisest of beasts
     so they know at last
how to wait for the loneliest of feasts
     for the full repast.   20

They do not snatch, they do not tear;
     their massive blood
moves as the moon-tides, near, more near,
     till they touch in flood.

Snake

A snake came to my water-trough
On a hot, hot day, and I in pajamas for the heat,
To drink there.

In the deep, strange-scented shade of the great dark carob tree
I came down the steps with my pitcher   5
And must wait, must stand and wait, for there he was at the trough before
    me.

He reached down from a fissure in the earth-wall in the gloom
And trailed his yellow-brown slackness soft-bellied down, over the edge of
    the stone trough
And rested his throat upon the stone bottom,
And where the water had dripped from the tap, in a small clearness,   10
He sipped with his straight mouth,
Softly drank through his straight gums, into his slack long body,
Silently.

Someone was before me at my water-trough,
And I, like a second comer, waiting.   15

He lifted his head from his drinking, as cattle do,
And looked at me vaguely, as drinking cattle do,
And flickered his two-forked tongue from his lips, and mused a moment,
And stooped and drank a little more,
Being earth-brown, earth-golden from the burning bowels of the earth   20
On the day of Sicilian July, with Etna smoking.

The voice of my education said to me
He must be killed,
For in Sicily the black, black snakes are innocent, the gold are venomous.

And voices in me said, If you were a man   25
You would take a stick and break him now, and finish him off.

But must I confess how I liked him,
How glad I was he had come like a guest in quiet, to drink at my water-
    trough
And depart peaceful, pacified, and thankless,
Into the burning bowels of this earth?   30

Was it cowardice, that I dared not kill him?
Was it perversity, that I longed to talk to him?
Was it humility, to feel so honored?
I felt so honored.

And yet those voices: 35
If you were not afraid, you would kill him!

And truly I was afraid, I was most afraid,
But even so, honored still more

That he should seek my hospitality
From out the dark door of the secret earth.   40

He drank enough
And lifted his head, dreamily, as one who has drunken,
And flickered his tongue like a forked night on the air, so black,
Seeming to lick his lips,
And looked around like a god, unseeing, into the air,   45
And slowly turned his head,
And slowly, very slowly, as if thrice adream,
Proceeded to draw his slow length curving round
And climb again the broken bank of my wall-face.

And as he put his head into that dreadful hole,   50
And as he slowly drew up, snake-easing his shoulders, and entered farther,
A sort of horror, a sort of protest against his withdrawing into that horrid
    black hole,
Deliberately going into the blackness, and slowly drawing himself after,
Overcame me now his back was turned.

I looked round, I put down my pitcher,   55
I picked up a clumsy log
And threw it at the water-trough with a clatter.

I think it did not hit him,
But suddenly that part of him that was left behind convulsed in undignified
    haste,
Writhed like lightning, and was gone   60
Into the black hole, the earth-lipped fissure in the wall-front,
At which, in the intense still noon, I stared with fascination.

And immediately I regretted it.
I thought how paltry, how vulgar, what a mean act!
I despised myself and the voices of my accursed human education.   65

And I thought of the albatross,
And I wished he would come back, my snake.

For he seemed to me again like a king,
Like a king in exile, uncrowned in the underworld,
Now due to be crowned again.   70

And so, I missed my chance with one of the lords
Of life.
And I have something to expiate;
A pettiness.

SNAKE 66. albatross: the great sea bird shot without motive by the Ancient Mariner
in Coleridge's poem.

Hummingbird

I can imagine, in some otherworld
Primeval-dumb, far back
In that most awful stillness, that only gasped and hummed,
Hummingbirds raced down the avenues.

Before anything had a soul,   5
While life was a heave of Matter, half inanimate,
This little bit chipped off in brilliance
And went whizzing through the slow, vast, succulent stems.

I believe there were no flowers then,
In the world where the hummingbird flashed ahead of creation.   10
I believe he pierced the slow vegetable veins with his long beak.

Probably he was big
As mosses, and little lizards, they say, were once big.
Probably he was a jabbing, terrifying monster.

We look at him through the wrong end of the long telescope of Time, 15
Luckily for us.

Ezra Pound   *(1885–1972)*

Portrait d'une Femme

Your mind and you are our Sargasso Sea,
London has swept about you this score years
And bright ships left you this or that in fee:
Ideas, old gossip, oddments of all things,
Strange spars of knowledge and dimmed wares of price.   5
Great minds have sought you—lacking someone else.
You have been second always. Tragical?
No. You preferred it to the usual thing:
One dull man, dulling and uxorious,
One average mind—with one thought less, each year.   10
Oh, you are patient, I have seen you sit
Hours, where something might have floated up.

PORTRAIT D'UNE FEMME   Portrait of a Lady. **1. Sargasso Sea:** a portion of the North Atlantic sea between the Azores and the West Indies, choked with gulf-weed and a place of frequent shipwrecks (here leaving debris as payment, "in fee," l. 3).

And now you pay one. Yes, you richly pay.
You are a person of some interest, one comes to you
And takes strange gain away: 15
Trophies fished up; some curious suggestion;
Fact that leads nowhere; and a tale or two,
Pregnant with mandrakes, or with something else
That might prove useful and yet never proves,
That never fits a corner or shows use, 20
Or finds its hour upon the loom of days:
The tarnished, gaudy, wonderful old work;
Idols and ambergris and rare inlays,
These are your riches, your great store; and yet
For all this sea-hoard of deciduous things, 25
Strange woods half sodden, and new brighter stuff:
In the slow float of differing light and deep,
No! there is nothing! In the whole and all,
Nothing that's quite your own.
             Yet this is you. 30

The River-Merchant's Wife: A Letter

While my hair was still cut straight across my forehead
I played about the front gate, pulling flowers.
You came by on bamboo stilts, playing horse,
You walked about my seat, playing with blue plums.
And we went on living in the village of Chokan: 5
Two small people, without dislike or suspicion.

At fourteen I married My Lord you.
I never laughed, being bashful.
Lowering my head, I looked at the wall.
Called to, a thousand times, I never looked back. 10

At fifteen I stopped scowling,
I desired my dust to be mingled with yours
Forever and forever and forever.
Why should I climb the look out?

18. **Pregnant with mandrakes:** Mandrakes have a forked root that resembles a human body and gave them their reputation as an aphrodisiac; they were also given human properties, such as screaming when torn up, and even (at least ironically) the capacity for becoming pregnant (as in John Donne's famous line, "Get with child a mandrake root"). **23. ambergris:** the precious, waxy substance derived from the sperm whale and used as a fixative in perfumes; found floating on the sea in large lumps. **25. deciduous:** falling, cast-off (used of trees that shed their leaves).
THE RIVER-MERCHANT'S WIFE The poem is derived from one by the Chinese poet Li Po (ca. A.D. 700–62).

At sixteen you departed,   15
You went into far Ku-to-yen, by the river of swirling eddies,
And you have been gone five months.
The monkeys make sorrowful noise overhead.

You dragged your feet when you went out.
By the gate now, the moss is grown, the different mosses,   20
Too deep to clear them away!
The leaves fall early this autumn, in wind.
The paired butterflies are already yellow with August
Over the grass in the West garden;
They hurt me.   I grow older.   25
If you are coming down through the narrows of the river Kiang,
Please let me know beforehand,
And I will come out to meet you
                    As far as Cho-fu-Sa.

The Garden

> *En robe de parade.*
>   Samain

Like a skein of loose silk blown against a wall
She walks by the railing of a path in Kensington Gardens,
And she is dying piecemeal
                    of a sort of emotional anemia.

And round about there is a rabble   5
Of the filthy, sturdy, unkillable infants of the very poor.
They shall inherit the earth.

In her is the end of breeding.
Her boredom is exquisite and excessive.
She would like some one to speak to her,   10
And is almost afraid that I
                    will commit that indiscretion.

---

29. Cho-fu-Sa: several hundred miles up the river from Nanking, in whose suburb the
wife is waiting.
THE GARDEN Epigraph: "[My soul is an infanta] in processional gown." Albert
Samain, *In the Garden of the Infanta* (1893). 7. They . . . earth: see Matthew 5:5,
"Blessed are the meek, for they shall inherit the earth."

Marianne Moore   *(1887–1972)*

The Mind Is an Enchanting Thing

is an enchanted thing
    like the glaze on a
katydid-wing
        subdivided by sun
           till the nettings are legion.   5
Like Gieseking playing Scarlatti;

like the apteryx-awl
    as a beak, or the
kiwi's rain-shawl
        of haired feathers, the mind   10
           feeling its way as though blind,
walks along with its eyes on the ground.

It has memory's ear
    that can hear without
having to hear.   15
        Like the gyroscope's fall,
           truly unequivocal
because trued by regnant certainty,

it is a power of
    strong enchantment. It   20
is like the dove-
        neck animated by
           sun; it is memory's eye;
it's conscientious inconsistency.

It tears off the veil; tears   25
    the temptation, the
mist the heart wears,
        from its eyes—if the heart
          has a face; it takes apart
dejection. It's fire in the dove-neck's   30

THE MIND IS   **6. Like . . . Scarlatti**: Walter Gieseking (1895–1956), one of the great pianists of his day, playing the keyboard works of Domenico Scarlatti (1683–1757), a baroque composer of great rhythmic and harmonic subtlety. Gieseking was notable for the clarity and delicacy with which he brought out Scarlatti's intricate patterns. **7. apteryx-awl**: the awl-like beak of the apteryx or kiwi, the hair-feathered bird of New Zealand with rudimentary wings and without tail for flight.

iridescence; in the
    inconsistencies
of Scarlatti.
    Unconfusion submits
      its confusion to proof; it's   35
not a Herod's oath that cannot change.

The Fox and the Crow

On his airy perch among the branches
    Master Crow was holding cheese in his beak.
Master Fox, whose pose suggested fragrances,
    Said in language which of course I cannot speak,
        "Aha, superb Sir Ebony, well met.   5
How black! who else boasts your metallic jet!
        If your warbling were unique,
        Rest assured, as you are sleek,
One would say that our wood had hatched nightingales."
All aglow, Master Crow tried to run a few scales,   10
        Risking trills and intervals,
Dropping the prize as his huge beak sang false.
The fox pounced on the cheese and remarked, "My dear sir,
        Learn that every flatterer
        Lives at the flattered listener's cost: 15
A lesson worth more than the cheese that you lost."
        The tardy learner, smarting under ridicule,
Swore he'd learned his last lesson as somebody's fool.

36. **Herod's oath:** Herod Antipas (prince of Galilee from 4 B.C. to A.D. 39) was so pleased with Salome's dancing upon his birthday that he "promised with an oath to give her whatsoever she would ask." Instructed by her mother, Herodias, she asked for the head of John the Baptist on a platter. Herod, although reluctant because the people regarded John as a prophet, felt bound by his oath and had John beheaded (Matthew 14:6–11).

THE FOX AND THE CROW   Translated from the *Fables choisies* of Jean de La Fontaine, published 1668–94. 6. **jet:** glossy black. 11. **intervals:** jumps from one note to another.

T. S. Eliot   *(1888–1965)*

[handwritten: Read Ash Weds. & Wasteland.]

The Love Song of J. Alfred Prufrock

S'io credesse che mia risposta fosse
a persona che mai tornasse al mondo,
questa fiamma staria senza più scosse.
Ma però che già mai di questo fondo
non tornò vivo alcun, s'i'odo il vero,
senza tema d'infamia ti rispondo.

Let us go then, you and I,
When the evening is spread out against the sky
Like a patient etherized upon a table;
Let us go, through certain half-deserted streets,
The muttering retreats   5
Of restless nights in one-night cheap hotels
And sawdust restaurants with oyster-shells:
Streets that follow like a tedious argument
Of insidious intent
To lead you to an overwhelming question . . .   10
Oh, do not ask, "What is it?"
Let us go and make our visit.

In the room the women come and go
Talking of Michelangelo.

The yellow fog that rubs its back upon the window-panes,   15
The yellow smoke that rubs its muzzle on the window-panes,
Licked its tongue into the corners of the evening,
Lingered upon the pools that stand in drains,
Let fall upon its back the soot that falls from chimneys,
Slipped by the terrace, made a sudden leap,   20
And seeing that it was a soft October night,
Curled once about the house, and fell asleep.

And indeed there will be time
For the yellow smoke that slides along the street,
Rubbing its back upon the window-panes;   25
There will be time, there will be time
To prepare a face to meet the faces that you meet;
There will be time to murder and create,

THE LOVE SONG   **Epigraph:** the words of Guido in Dante, *Inferno*, xxvii. 61–66, when asked to identify himself: "If I thought my answer were to one who could ever return to the world, this flame would shake no more; but since none ever did return above from this depth, if what I hear be true, without fear of infamy I answer thee."

And time for all the works and days of hands
That lift and drop a question on your plate;   30
Time for you and time for me,
And time yet for a hundred indecisions,
And for a hundred visions and revisions,
Before the taking of a toast and tea.

In the room the women come and go   35
Talking of Michelangelo.

And indeed there will be time
To wonder, "Do I dare?" and, "Do I dare?"
Time to turn back and descend the stair,
With a bald spot in the middle of my hair—   40
[They will say: "How his hair is growing thin!"]
My morning coat, my collar mounting firmly to the chin,
My necktie rich and modest, but asserted by a simple pin—
[They will say: "But how his arms and legs are thin!"]
Do I dare   45
Disturb the universe?
In a minute there is time
For decisions and revisions which a minute will reverse.

For I have known them all already, known them all—
Have known the evenings, mornings, afternoons,   50
I have measured out my life with coffee spoons;
I know the voices dying with a dying fall
Beneath the music from a farther room.
    So how should I presume?

And I have known the eyes already, known them all—   55
The eyes that fix you in a formulated phrase,
And when I am formulated, sprawling on a pin,
When I am pinned and wriggling on the wall,
Then how should I begin
To spit out all the butt-ends of my days and ways?   60
    And how should I presume?

And I have known the arms already, known them all—
Arms that are braceleted and white and bare
[But in the lamplight, downed with light brown hair!]
Is it perfume from a dress   65
That makes me so digress?
Arms that lie along a table, or wrap about a shawl.

29. **works and days.** the title of a poem by the Greek poet Hesiod (eighth century B.C.)
on the labors of the farmer's life. **51. coffee spoons:** the small spoons that accompany
demitasses. **52. dying fall:** a cadence, accompanied by a fall in volume or pitch;
also an allusion to the opening lines of Shakespeare's *Twelfth Night*, where the romantic young duke, Orsino, says, "If music be the food of love, play on/ . . . That
strain again! It had a dying fall. . . ."

And should I then presume?
And how should I begin?

.   .   .   .   .

Shall I say, I have gone at dusk through narrow streets   70
And watched the smoke that rises from the pipes
Of lonely men in shirt-sleeves, leaning out of windows? . . .

I should have been a pair of ragged claws
Scuttling across the floors of silent seas.

.   .   .   .   .

And the afternoon, the evening, sleeps so peacefully!   75
Smoothed by long fingers,
Asleep . . . tired . . . or it malingers,
Stretched on the floor, here beside you and me.
Should I, after tea and cakes and ices,
Have the strength to force the moment to its crisis?   80
But though I have wept and fasted, wept and prayed,
Though I have seen my head [grown slightly bald] brought in upon a
    platter,
I am no prophet—and here's no great matter;
I have seen the moment of my greatness flicker,
And I have seen the eternal Footman hold my coat, and snicker,   85
And in short, I was afraid.

And would it have been worth it, after all,
After the cups, the marmalade, the tea,
Among the porcelain, among some talk of you and me,
Would it have been worth while,   90
To have bitten off the matter with a smile,
To have squeezed the universe into a ball
To roll it toward some overwhelming question,
To say: "I am Lazarus, come from the dead,
Come back to tell you all, I shall tell you all"—   95
If one, settling a pillow by her head,
    Should say: "That is not what I meant at all.
    That is not it, at all."

And would it have been worth it, after all,
Would it have been worth while,   100
After the sunsets and the dooryards and the sprinkled streets,
After the novels, after the teacups, after the skirts that trail along the floor—

82. **brought in . . . platter:** like that of John the Baptist, beheaded by Herod to please his wife Herodias and to reward the dancing of her daughter Salome (Matthew 14:1–11). 85. **Footman:** Death. 92. **squeezed . . . ball:** Cf. Andrew Marvell, "To His Coy Mistress": "Let us roll all our strength and all/ Our sweetness up into one ball,/ And tear our pleasures with rough strife/ Thorough the iron gates of life" (ll. 41–44, p. 147). The vigor of Marvell's lover forms a constant contrast to Prufrock's hesitancy, as the lover's "Had we but world enough, and time" contrasts in its urgency with Prufrock's "There will be time." 94. **Lazarus:** Jesus raised him from the dead (John 11:1–44).

And this, and so much more?—
It is impossible to say just what I mean!
But as if a magic lantern threw the nerves in patterns on a screen: 105
Would it have been worth while
If one, settling a pillow or throwing off a shawl,
And turning toward the window, should say:
    "That is not it at all,
    That is not what I meant, at all."   110

               .   .   .   .   .

No! I am not Prince Hamlet, nor was meant to be;
Am an attendant lord, one that will do
To swell a progress, start a scene or two,
Advise the prince; no doubt, an easy tool,
Deferential, glad to be of use,   115
Politic, cautious, and meticulous;
Full of high sentence, but a bit obtuse;
At times, indeed, almost ridiculous—
Almost, at times, the Fool.

I grow old . . . I grow old . . .   120
I shall wear the bottoms of my trousers rolled.

Shall I part my hair behind? Do I dare to eat a peach?
I shall wear white flannel trousers, and walk upon the beach.
I have heard the mermaids singing, each to each.

I do not think that they will sing to me.   125

I have seen them riding seaward on the waves
Combing the white hair of the waves blown back
When the wind blows the water white and black.

We have lingered in the chambers of the sea
By sea-girls wreathed with seaweed red and brown   130
Till human voices wake us, and we drown.

Preludes

I

The winter evening settles down
With smell of steaks in passageways.
Six o'clock.
The burnt-out ends of smoky days.
And now a gusty shower wraps   5

---

113. **progress:** procession, journey of state. 117. **high sentence:** maxims or formal wisdom (from Latin *sententia*). 121. **rolled:** cuffed (as a younger man would at the time).

The grimy scraps
Of withered leaves about your feet
And newspapers from vacant lots;
The showers beat
On broken blinds and chimney-pots,　　　　10
And at the corner of the street
A lonely cab-horse steams and stamps.
And then the lighting of the lamps.

II

The morning comes to consciousness
Of faint stale smells of beer　　　　15
From the sawdust-trampled street
With all its muddy feet that press
To early coffee-stands.
With the other masquerades
That time resumes,　　　　20
One thinks of all the hands
That are raising dingy shades
In a thousand furnished rooms.

III

You tossed a blanket from the bed,
You lay upon your back, and waited;　　　　25
You dozed, and watched the night revealing
The thousand sordid images
Of which your soul was constituted;
They flickered against the ceiling.
And when all the world came back　　　　30
And the light crept up between the shutters
And you heard the sparrows in the gutters,
You had such a vision of the street
As the street hardly understands;
Sitting along the bed's edge, where　　　　35
You curled the papers from your hair,
Or clasped the yellow soles of feet
In the palms of both soiled hands.

IV

His soul stretched tight across the skies
That fade behind a city block,　　　　40
Or trampled by insistent feet
At four and five and six o'clock;
And short square fingers stuffing pipes,
And evening newspapers, and eyes
Assured of certain certainties,　　　　45
The conscience of a blackened street
Impatient to assume the world.

I am moved by fancies that are curled
Around these images, and cling:
The notion of some infinitely gentle   50
Infinitely suffering thing.

Wipe your hand across your mouth, and laugh;
The worlds revolve like ancient women
Gathering fuel in vacant lots.

Sweeney Among the Nightingales

ὤμοι, πέπληγμαι καιρίαν πληγὴν ἔσω.

Apeneck Sweeney spreads his knees
Letting his arms hang down to laugh,
The zebra stripes along his jaw
Swelling to maculate giraffe.

The circles of the stormy moon   5
Slide westward toward the River Plate,
Death and the Raven drift above
And Sweeney guards the hornèd gate.

Gloomy Orion and the Dog
Are veiled; and hushed the shrunken seas;   10
The person in the Spanish cape
Tries to sit on Sweeney's knees

Slips and pulls the table cloth
Overturns a coffee-cup,
Reorganized upon the floor   15
She yawns and draws a stocking up;

The silent man in mocha brown
Sprawls at the window-sill and gapes;
The waiter brings in oranges
Bananas figs and hothouse grapes;   20

The silent vertebrate in brown
Contracts and concentrates, withdraws;
Rachel *née* Rabinovitch
Tears at the grapes with murderous paws;

SWEENEY **Epigraph;** the cry of Agamemnon in Aeschylus's tragedy as he is murdered by his wife Clytemnestra: "Alas, I am smitten deep with a mortal blow." **4. maculate:** spotted. **6. River Plate:** the estuary between Argentina and Uruguay. **8. hornèd gate:** of the two gates in Hades, that of ivory admits false dreams and that of horn true dreams to the upper world (with possible play upon the horns of the cuckold). **9. Orion . . . Dog:** the constellations of the huntsman and his dog, as the Raven (1. 7) may refer to the constellation Corvo.

She and the lady in the cape 25
Are suspect, thought to be in league;
Therefore the man with heavy eyes
Declines the gambit, shows fatigue,

Leaves the room and reappears
Outside the window, leaning in, 30
Branches of wistaria
Circumscribe a golden grin;

The host with someone indistinct
Converses at the door apart,
The nightingales are singing near 35
The Convent of the Sacred Heart,

And sang within the bloody wood
When Agamemnon cried aloud,
And let their liquid siftings fall
To stain the stiff dishonored shroud. 40

Gerontion

Thou hast nor youth nor age
But as it were an after dinner sleep
Dreaming of both.

Here I am, an old man in a dry month,
Being read to by a boy, waiting for rain.
I was neither at the hot gates
Nor fought in the warm rain
Nor knee deep in the salt marsh, heaving a cutlass, 5
Bitten by flies, fought.
My house is a decayed house,
And the Jew squats on the window sill, the owner,
Spawned in some estaminet of Antwerp,
Blistered in Brussels, patched and peeled in London. 10
The goat coughs at night in the field overhead;
Rocks, moss, stonecrop, iron, merds.
The woman keeps the kitchen, makes tea,

---

37. bloody wood: the grove of the Furies described by Sophocles in *Oedipus at Colonus*, ll. 17–18. **39. liquid siftings:** droppings.
GERONTION From the Greek, "little old man." **Epigraph:** from the speech of the Duke in Shakespeare, *Measure for Measure*, III.i, stressing the vanity of man's life and here suggesting the dreamlike movement of the poem. **3. hot gates:** literal translation of Thermopylae, the battle at which Leonidas and the Spartans heroically yielded their lives in holding off the Persian invasion. **9. estaminet:** low café, "dive." **11. goat . . . overhead:** perhaps an allusion to the constellation Capricorn (goat). **12. stonecrop:** mosslike plant that grows among rocks. **merds:** excrement.

Sneezes at evening, poking the peevish gutter.
　　　　　　　　　　　I an old man,　　　　　　　　　15
A dull head among windy spaces.

Signs are taken for wonders. "We would see a sign!"
The word within a word, unable to speak a word,
Swaddled with darkness. In the juvescence of the year
Came Christ the tiger　　　　　　　　　　　　　　20

In depraved May, dogwood and chestnut, flowering judas,
To be eaten, to be divided, to be drunk
Among whispers; by Mr. Silvero
With caressing hands, at Limoges
Who walked all night in the next room;　　　　　　25

By Hakagawa, bowing among the Titians;
By Madame de Tornquist, in the dark room
Shifting the candles; Fräulein von Kulp
Who turned in the hall, one hand on the door. Vacant shuttles
Weave the wind. I have no ghosts,　　　　　　　　30
An old man in a draughty house
Under a windy knob.

After such knowledge, what forgiveness? Think now
History has many cunning passages, contrived corridors
And issues, deceives with whispering ambitions,　　35
Guides us by vanities. Think now
She gives when our attention is distracted
And what she gives, gives with such supple confusions

---

14. gutter: drain. 17. Signs . . . wonders: adapted from the Nativity Sermon (1618) of the Anglican preacher Lancelot Andrewes; after dealing with the nativity crêche as a sign of Christ ("Signs are taken for wonders. 'Master, we would fain see a sign,' that is, a miracle"), Andrewes goes on: "every word (here) is a wonder: . . . an Infant, Verbum Infans, the Word without a Word; the eternal word not able to speak a word; a wonder sure." We would . . . sign: Cf. Matthew 12:38–39, "Then certain of the scribes and of the Pharisees answered, saying, Master, we would see a sign from thee. But he answered and said unto them, An evil and adulterous generation seeketh after a sign; and there shall no sign be given to it." 18. word . . . speak a word: "Infant" derives from the Latin infans (unable to speak). See John 1:1, "In the beginning was the Word, and the Word was with God, and the Word was God." 19. juvescence: presumably "juvenescence," youth; greening. 20. Christ the tiger: Cf. "The Tyger" of William Blake (p. 209) for such an image of divinity. 21. In depraved . . . judas: adapted from the autobiographical The Education of Henry Adams (1918), where Adams describes spring in Washington: the "passionate depravity" of the Maryland May, "sensual, animal, elemental." Judas Iscariot is supposed to have hanged himself on the flowering shrub or tree which takes his name. 22–23. To be eaten . . . whispers: a parody of Communion, where the priest as he puts the wafer on the communicant's tongue says sotto voce, "Eat this in remembrance of me [Christ]"; "to be drunk" may allude to the Communion given in both forms (bread and wine) as practiced in some Christian churches. 29–30. Vacant . . . wind: See Job 7:6–7, "My days are swifter than a weaver's shuttle, and are spent without hope. O remember that my life is wind: mine eye shall no more see good." 32. knob: hill.

That the giving famishes the craving. Gives too late
What's not believed in, or if still believed, 40
In memory only, reconsidered passion. Gives too soon
Into weak hands, what's thought can be dispensed with
Till the refusal propagates a fear. Think
Neither fear nor courage saves us. Unnatural vices
Are fathered by our heroism. Virtues 45
Are forced upon us by our impudent crimes.
These tears are shaken from the wrath-bearing tree.

The tiger springs in the new year. Us he devours. Think at last
We have not reached conclusion, when I
Stiffen in a rented house. Think at last 50
I have not made this show purposelessly
And it is not by any concitation
Of the backward devils
I would meet you upon this honestly.
I that was near your heart was removed therefrom 55
To lose beauty in terror, terror in inquisition.
I have lost my passion: why should I need to keep it
Since what is kept must be adulterated?
I have lost my sight, smell, hearing, taste and touch:
How should I use them for your closer contact? 60

These with a thousand small deliberations
Protract the profit of their chilled delirium,
Excite the membrane, when the sense has cooled,
With pungent sauces, multiply variety
In a wilderness of mirrors. What will the spider do, 65
Suspend its operations, will the weevil
Delay? De Bailhache, Fresca, Mrs. Cammel, whirled
Beyond the circuit of the shuddering Bear
In fractured atoms. Gull against the wind, in the windy straits
Of Belle Isle, or running on the Horn, 70
White feathers in the snow, the Gulf claims,
And an old man driven by the Trades
To a sleepy corner.
                              Tenants of the house,
Thoughts of a dry brain in a dry season. 75

47. **wrath-bearing tree:** perhaps the Tree of the Knowledge of Good and Evil in Eden, perhaps the Cross. 52. **concitation:** instigation. 65. **wilderness of mirrors:** as used by some to intensify sexual excitement. 70. **Belle Isle:** between Newfoundland and Labrador.

East Coker

I

In my beginning is my end. In succession
Houses rise and fall, crumble, are extended,
Are removed, destroyed, restored, or in their place
Is an open field, or a factory, or a by-pass.
Old stone to new building, old timber to new fires,   5
Old fires to ashes, and ashes to the earth
Which is already flesh, fur and faeces,
Bone of man and beast, cornstalk and leaf.
Houses live and die: there is a time for building
And a time for living and for generation   10
And a time for the wind to break the loosened pane
And to shake the wainscot where the field-mouse trots
And to shake the tattered arras woven with a silent motto.

In my beginning is my end. Now the light falls
Across the open field, leaving the deep lane   15
Shuttered with branches, dark in the afternoon,
Where you lean against a bank while a van passes,
And the deep lane insists on the direction
Into the village, in the electric heat
Hypnotized. In a warm haze the sultry light   20
Is absorbed, not refracted, by gray stone.
The dahlias sleep in the empty silence.
Wait for the early owl.
            In that open field
If you do not come too close, if you do not come too close,   25
On a Summer midnight, you can hear the music
Of the weak pipe and the little drum
And see them dancing around the bonfire
The association of man and woman
In daunsinge, signifying matrimonie—   30
A dignified and commodious sacrament.

EAST COKER   East Coker is a village in Somerset where Eliot's ancestors lived for two centuries before Andrew Eliot emigrated to America in 1667. **1. In my beginning . . . end:** recalling the motto of Mary, Queen of Scots (1542–87), "In my end is my beginning" (which is the last line of the poem). The references here and below (to Sir Thomas Elyot) are to the sixteenth century, the beginning of both the Eliot family as a traceable unit and of modern England. The first line also recalls the saying of the pre-Socratic philosopher Heraclitus, "The beginning and the end are common." **9–13. there is . . . motto:** Cf. Ecclesiastes 3: "To everything there is a season, and a time to every purpose under the heaven: a time to be born, and a time to die, a time to plant, and a time to pluck up that which is planted; a time to kill, and a time to heal; a time to break down, and a time to build up. . . ." **13. silent motto:** recalling that of the Eliot family, *tace et fac,* "be silent and do." **17. van:** small delivery truck. **28. them:** the villagers of the past. **30. In daunsinge:** In the following passage are woven phrases from i.21 of *The Boke named The Gouvernour* (1531), a work on politics and moral philosophy by Sir Thomas Elyot (d. 1546), who was born in Coker.

[Handwritten marginal notes: "everything has a beginning & an end. all must live, die & be replaced. houses, fields, crops & humans"]

Two and two, necessarye coniunction,
Holding eche other by the hand or the arm
Whiche betokeneth concorde. Round and round the fire
Leaping through the flames, or joined in circles,   35
Rustically solemn or in rustic laughter
Lifting heavy feet in clumsy shoes,
Earth feet, loam feet, lifted in country mirth
Mirth of those long since under earth
Nourishing the corn. Keeping time,   40
Keeping the rhythm in their dancing
As in their living in the living seasons
The time of the seasons and the constellations
The time of milking and the time of harvest
The time of the coupling of man and woman   45
And that of beasts. Feet rising and falling.
Eating and drinking. Dung and death.

Dawn points, and another day
Prepares for heat and silence. Out at sea the dawn wind
Wrinkles and slides. I am here   50
Or there, or elsewhere. In my beginning.

                                    II

What is the late November doing
With the disturbance of the spring
And creatures of the summer heat,
And snowdrops writhing under feet   55
And hollyhocks that aim too high
Red into gray and tumble down
Late roses filled with early snow?
Thunder rolled by the rolling stars
Simulates triumphal cars   60
Deployed in constellated wars
Scorpion fights against the Sun
Until the Sun and Moon go down
Comets weep and Leonids fly
Hunt the heavens and the plains   65
Whirled in a vortex that shall bring
The world to that destructive fire
Which burns before the ice-cap reigns.

That was a way of putting it—not very satisfactory:
A periphrastic study in a worn-out poetical fashion,   70

---

40. corn: wheat or other grain. **62. Scorpion fights . . . Sun:** the constellation Scorpio, which might be seen as a Titan or a dragon warring against the governing deity and, unlike Satan (often identified with the dragon of evil), successful in destroying the order of the heavens. **64. Leonids:** the showering meteors that appear in mid-November three times a century. **70. periphrastic:** roundabout, making a statement in oblique form.

Leaving one still with the intolerable wrestle
With words and meanings. The poetry does not matter.
It was not (to start again) what one had expected.
What was to be the value of the long looked forward to,
Long hoped for calm, the autumnal serenity   75
And the wisdom of age? Had they deceived us
Or deceived themselves, the quiet-voiced elders,
Bequeathing us merely a receipt for deceit?
The serenity only a deliberate hebetude,
The wisdom only the knowledge of dead secrets   80
Useless in the darkness into which they peered
Or from which they turned their eyes. There is, it seems to us,
At best, only a limited value
In the knowledge derived from experience.
The knowledge imposes a pattern, and falsifies,   85
For the pattern is new in every moment
And every moment is a new and shocking
Valuation of all we have been. We are only undeceived
Of that which, deceiving, could no longer harm.
In the middle, not only in the middle of the way   90
But all the way, in a dark wood, in a bramble,
On the edge of a grimpen, where is no secure foothold,
And menaced by monsters, fancy lights,
Risking enchantment. Do not let me hear
Of the wisdom of old men, but rather of their folly,   95
Their fear of fear and frenzy, their fear of possession,
Of belonging to another, or to others, or to God.
The only wisdom we can hope to acquire
Is the wisdom of humility: humility is endless.

The houses are all gone under the sea.   100

The dancers are all gone under the hill.

III

O dark dark dark. They all go into the dark,
The vacant interstellar spaces, the vacant into the vacant,
The captains, merchant bankers, eminent men of letters,

78. **receipt:** recipe. 79. **hebetude:** lethargy, lassitude. 90. **In the . . . way:** recalling the opening of Dante's *Inferno:* "In the middle of the journey of our life/ I found myself in a dark wood,/ Having lost the straight path." 92. **grimpen:** a reference to Sir Conan Doyle's *The Hound of the Baskervilles,* where Dr. Watson describes "that great Grimpen Mire, with little green patches everywhere into which one may sink and with no guide to point the track" (the "fancy lights," l. 93, are the will-o'-the-wisps, produced by gases in a swamp or "mire," that mislead travelers). 100–101. **houses . . . hill:** Cf. Robert Louis Stevenson's "Requiem": "Home is the sailor, home from sea,/ And the hunter home from the hill." 102. **O dark:** Cf. John Milton, *Samson Agonistes* (ll. 80–82): "O dark, dark, dark, amid the blaze of noon,/ Irreoov erably dark, total eclipse/ Without all hope of day!" Beside the words of Samson, one can place Henry Vaughan's "Ascension Hymn": "They are all gone into the world of light!" 103. **vacant interstellar spaces:** This phrase recalls the darkness suggested by Milton's phrase "vacant interlunar cave" (*Samson Agonistes,* l. 89), just as "dark the Sun and Moon" (l. 108) recalls "The Sun to me is dark/ And silent as the Moon" (*Samson Agonistes,* ll. 86–87).

The generous patrons of art, the statesmen and the rulers,   105
Distinguished civil servants, chairmen of many committees,
Industrial lords and petty contractors, all go into the dark,
And dark the Sun and Moon, and the Almanach de Gotha
And the Stock Exchange Gazette, the Directory of Directors,
And cold the sense and lost the motive of action.   110
And we all go with them, into the silent funeral,
Nobody's funeral, for there is no one to bury.
I said to my soul, be still, and let the dark come upon you
Which shall be the darkness of God.   As, in a theatre,
The lights are extinguished, for the scene to be changed   115
With a hollow rumble of wings, with a movement of darkness on darkness,
And we know that the hills and the trees, the distant panorama
And the bold imposing façade are all being rolled away—
Or as, when an underground train, in the tube, stops too long between
     stations
And the conversation rises and slowly fades into silence   120
And you see behind every face the mental emptiness deepen
Leaving only the growing terror of nothing to think about;
Or when, under ether, the mind is conscious but conscious of nothing—
I said to my soul, be still, and wait without hope
For hope would be hope for the wrong thing; wait without love   125
For love would be love of the wrong thing; there is yet faith
But the faith and the love and the hope are all in the waiting.
Wait without thought, for you are not ready for thought:
So the darkness shall be the light, and the stillness the dancing.

Whisper of running streams, and winter lightning.   130
The wild thyme unseen and the wild strawberry,
The laughter in the garden, echoed ecstasy
Not lost, but requiring, pointing to the agony
Of death and birth.
                You say I am repeating
Something I have said before. I shall say it again.   135
Shall I say it again? In order to arrive there,
To arrive where you are, to get from where you are not,

108. Almanach de Gotha: the record of royal and noble families of Europe, as the works following are records of financial magnates and company directors. Cf. Eliot, *The Idea of a Christian Society* (1939), on the events of September 1938 (i.e., the Munich crisis and the appeasement of Adolf Hitler by Neville Chamberlain, the British Prime Minister): "Was our society, which had always been so assured of its superiority and rectitude, so confident of its unexamined premises, assembled round anything more permanent than a congeries of banks, insurance companies, and industries, and had it any beliefs more essential than a belief in compound interest and the maintenance of dividends?" **119. tube:** London subway. **124. I said to my soul:** Eliot evokes the "negative way" of the Spanish mystic St. John of the Cross (1542–91): "advice must be given to learn to abide attentively and to pay no heed either to the imagination or its workings; for here, as we may say, the faculties are at rest, and are working not actively but passively by receiving that which God works in them." **137. To arrive . . . are:** This and the following lines are an adaptation of St. John of the Cross: "In order to arrive at that which thou knowest not,/ Thou must go by a way that thou knowest not./ In order to arrive at that which thou possessest not,/ Thou must go by a way that thou possessest not./ In order to arrive at that which thou art not,/ Thou must go through that which thou art not."

You must go by a way wherein there is no ecstasy.
In order to arrive at what you do not know
    You must go by a way which is the way of ignorance.   140
In order to possess what you do not possess
    You must go by the way of dispossession.
In order to arrive at what you are not
    You must go through the way in which you are not.
And what you do not know is the only thing you know   145
And what you own is what you do not own
And where you are is where you are not.

IV

The wounded surgeon plies the steel
That questions the distempered part;
Beneath the bleeding hands we feel   150
The sharp compassion of the healer's art
Resolving the enigma of the fever chart.

Our only health is the disease
If we obey the dying nurse
Whose constant care is not to please   155
But to remind of our, and Adam's curse,
And that, to be restored, our sickness must grow worse.

The whole earth is our hospital
Endowed by the ruined millionaire,
Wherein, if we do well, we shall   160
Die of the absolute paternal care
That will not leave us, but prevents us everywhere.

The chill ascends from feet to knees,
The fever sings in mental wires.
If to be warmed, then I must freeze   165
And quake in frigid purgatorial fires
Of which the flame is roses, and the smoke is briars.

The dripping blood our only drink,
The bloody flesh our only food:
In spite of which we like to think   170

---

148. wounded surgeon: This theme of our cure by a suffering savior may echo a sermon by Lancelot Andrewes (1555–1626): "the Physician slain, and of His Flesh and Blood a receipt made, that the patient might recover." But the theme is familiar in devotional literature. **154. dying nurse:** the Church. **156. our . . . curse:** our participation in the sin and curse of Adam (the "ruined millionaire" of l. 159) and the consequent expulsion from Eden into a fallen world, which may also be the scene of redemption ("our hospital," l. 158). **162. prevents:** anticipates, comes before (as in prevenient grace, by which God gives us the power to seek His aid). **168. dripping blood:** the blood of the Eucharist or Communion, where it is found in the wine, as the "bloody flesh" (l. 169) is the bread.

That we are sound, substantial flesh and blood—   *crucifixion*
Again, in spite of that, we call this Friday good.

V

So here I am, in the middle way, having had twenty years—
Twenty years largely wasted, the years of *l'entre deux guerres*—
Trying to learn to use words, and every attempt   175
Is a wholly new start, and a different kind of failure
Because one has only learnt to get the better of words
For the thing one no longer has to say, or the way in which
One is no longer disposed to say it. And so each venture
Is a new beginning, a raid on the inarticulate   180
With shabby equipment always deteriorating
In the general mess of imprecision of feeling,
Undisciplined squads of emotion. And what there is to conquer
By strength and submission, has already been discovered
Once or twice, or several times, by men whom one cannot hope   185
To emulate—but there is no competition—
There is only the fight to recover what has been lost
And found and lost again and again: and now, under conditions
That seem unpropitious. But perhaps neither gain nor loss.
For us, there is only the trying. The rest is not our business.   190

Home is where one starts from. As we grow older
The world becomes stranger, the pattern more complicated
Of dead and living. Not the intense moment
Isolated, with no before and after,
But a lifetime burning in every moment   195
And not the lifetime of one man only
But of old stones that cannot be deciphered.
There is a time for the evening under starlight,
A time for the evening under lamplight
(The evening with the photograph album).   200
Love is most nearly itself
When here and now cease to matter.
Old men ought to be explorers
Here and there does not matter
We must be still and still moving   205
Into another intensity
For a further union, a deeper communion

---

172. **this Friday good**: the day of the Crucifixion is "good" (insofar as it brings redemption) and in contrast to the illusion of soundness or of our being "substantial" ("essentially" in one sense, and "solid" in another) "flesh and blood" (l. 171). **174. l'entre deux guerres**: the period between two years, the First World War of 1914–18 and the Second, which began in 1939, the year before the poem was published; see the note to l. 108. **190. The rest . . . business**: The achievement is not in our hands. **197. old stones**: gravestones, or even earlier and more mysterious artifacts, whose language we cannot read.

Through the dark cold and the empty desolation,
The wave cry, the wind cry, the vast waters
Of the petrel and the porpoise. In my end is my beginning.　　　　210

John Crowe Ransom *(1888–　　)*

Two in August

Two that could not have lived their single lives
As can some husbands and wives
Did something strange: they tensed their vocal cords
And attacked each other with silences and words
Like catapulted stones and arrowed knives.　　　　5

Dawn was not yet; night is for loving or sleeping,
Sweet dreams or safekeeping;
Yet he of the wide brows that were used to laurel
And she, the famed for gentleness, must quarrel.
Furious both of them, and scared, and weeping.·　　　　10

How sleepers groan, twitch, wake to such a mood
Is not well understood,
Nor why two entities grown almost one
Should rend and murder trying to get undone,
With individual tigers in their blood.　　　　15

She in terror fled from the marriage chamber
Circuiting the dark rooms like a string of amber
Round and round and back,
And would not light one lamp against the black,
And heard the clock that clanged: Remember, Remember.　　　　20

And he must tread barefooted the dim lawn,
Soon he was up and gone;
High in the trees the night-mastered birds were crying
With fear upon their tongues, no singing nor flying
Which are their lovely attitudes by dawn.　　　　25

Whether those bird cries were of heaven or hell
There is no way to tell;
In the long ditch of darkness the man walked
Under the hackberry trees where the birds talked
With words too sad and strange to syllable.　　　　30

TWO IN AUGUST　**8. laurel:** the crown of the poet.

The Equilibrists

Full of her long white arms and milky skin
He had a thousand times remembered sin.
Alone in the press of people traveled he,
Minding her jacinth, and myrrh, and ivory.

Mouth he remembered: the quaint orifice   5
From which came heat that flamed upon the kiss,
Till cold words came down spiral from the head,
Grey doves from the officious tower illsped.

Body: it was a white field ready for love,
On her body's field, with the gaunt tower above,   10
The lilies grew, beseeching him to take,
If he would pluck and wear them, bruise and break.

Eyes talking: Never mind the cruel words,
Embrace my flowers, but not embrace the swords.
But what they said, the doves came straightway flying   15
And unsaid: Honor, Honor, they came crying.

Importunate her doves. Too pure, too wise,
Clambering on his shoulder, saying, Arise,
Leave me now, and never let us meet,
Eternal distance now command thy feet.   20

Predicament indeed, which thus discovers
Honor among thieves, Honor between lovers.
O such a little word is Honor, they feel!
But the grey word is between them cold as steel.

At length I saw these lovers fully were come   25
Into their torture of equilibrium;
Dreadfully had forsworn each other, and yet
They were bound each to each, and they did not forget.

And rigid as two painful stars, and twirled
About the clustered night their prison world,   30
They burned with fierce love always to come near,
But Honor beat them back and kept them clear.

Ah, the strict lovers, they are ruined now!
I cried in anger. But with puddled brow

THE EQUILIBRISTS   **4. jacinth:** reddish-brown precious stone; here, like ivory and the perfume of myrrh, characterizing the woman's body. **24. between them . . . steel:** perhaps recalling the sword Tristan and Iseult placed between themselves. **34. puddled:**
wrinkled, pondering.

Devising for those gibbeted and brave   35
Came I descanting: Man, what would you have?

For spin your period out, and draw your breath,
A kinder saeculum begins with Death.
Would you ascend to Heaven and bodiless dwell?
Or take your bodies honorless to Hell?   40

In Heaven you have heard no marriage is,
No white flesh tinder to your lecheries,
Your male and female tissue sweetly shaped
Sublimed away, and furious blood escaped.

Great lovers lie in Hell, the stubborn ones   45
Infatuate of the flesh upon the bones;
Stuprate, they rend each other when they kiss,
The pieces kiss again, no end to this.

But still I watched them spinning, orbited nice.
Their flames were not more radiant than their ice.   50
I dug in the quiet earth and wrought the tomb
And made these lines to memorize their doom:—

EPITAPH

Equilibrists lie here; stranger, tread light;
Close, but untouching in each other's sight;
Moldered the lips and ashy the tall skull.   55
Let them lie perilous and beautiful.

Bells for John Whiteside's Daughter

There was such speed in her little body,
And such lightness in her footfall,
It is no wonder her brown study
Astonishes us all.

Her wars were bruited in our high window.   5
We looked among orchard trees and beyond
Where she took arms against her shadow,
Or harried unto the pond

---

35. gibbeted. trapped, sacrified, as on a gallows; subject to public scorn. **38. saeculum:** era. **41. In Heaven . . . no marriage is:** Cf. Mark 12:25, "for when they shall rise from the dead, they neither marry, nor are given in marriage; but are as the angels which are in heaven." **47. Stuprate:** ravaging, debauched. **49. nice:** with precision.
BELLS FOR JOHN WHITESIDE'S DAUGHTER **3. brown study:** appearance of mental abstraction, reverie. **5. bruited:** sounded.

The lazy geese, like a snow cloud
Dripping their snow on the green grass, 10
Tricking and stopping, sleepy and proud,
Who cried in goose, Alas,

For the tireless heart within the little
Lady with rod that made them rise
From their noon apple-dreams and scuttle 15
Goose-fashion under the skies!

But now go the bells, and we are ready,
In one house we are sternly stopped
To say we are vexed at her brown study,
Lying so primly propped. 20

Claude McKay *(1890–1948)*

If We Must Die

If we must die, let it not be like hogs
Hunted and penned in an inglorious spot,
While round us bark the mad and hungry dogs,
Making their mock at our accursèd lot.
If we must die, O let us nobly die, 5
So that our precious blood may not be shed
In vain; then even the monsters we defy
Shall be constrained to honor us though dead!
O kinsmen! we must meet the common foe!
Though far outnumbered let us show us brave, 10
And for their thousand blows deal one deathblow!
What though before us lies the open grave?
Like men we'll face the murderous, cowardly pack,
Pressed to the wall, dying, but fighting back!

Archibald MacLeish (1892–   )

You, Andrew Marvell

And here face down beneath the sun
And here upon earth's noonward height
To feel the always coming on
The always rising of the night:

To feel creep up the curving east   5
The earthly chill of dusk and slow
Upon those under lands the vast
And ever climbing shadow grow

And strange at Ecbatan the trees
Take leaf by leaf the evening strange   10
The flooding dark about their knees
The mountains over Persia change

And now at Kermanshah the gate
Dark empty and the withered grass
And through the twilight now the late   15
Few travelers in the westward pass

And Baghdad darken and the bridge
Across the silent river gone
And through Arabia the edge
Of evening widen and steal on   20

And deepen on Palmyra's street
The wheel rut in the ruined stone
And Lebanon fade out and Crete
High through the clouds and overblown

And over Sicily the air   25
Still flashing with the landward gulls
And loom and slowly disappear
The sails above the shadowy hulls

And Spain go under and the shore
Of Africa the gilded sand   30

YOU, ANDREW MARVELL See Marvell's "To His Coy Mistress" (pp. 147–48), especially the last two lines. **9. Ecbatan:** Ecbatana (modern Hamadan), summer capital of
the Persian Empire (sixth to fourth centuries B.C.). **13. Kermanshah:** city on the road
between Hamadan and Baghdad. **21. Palmyra:** Syrian capital of a powerful empire of
the third century A.D.

And evening vanish and no more
The low pale light across that land

Nor now the long light on the sea:

And here face downward in the sun
To feel how swift how secretly   35
The shadow of the night comes on . . .

Wilfred Owen   (1893–1918)

Dulce et Decorum Est

Bent double, like old beggars under sacks,
Knock-kneed, coughing like hags, we cursed through sludge,
Till on the haunting flares we turned our backs
And towards our distant rest began to trudge.
Men marched asleep. Many had lost their boots   5
But limped on, blood-shod. All went lame; all blind;
Drunk with fatigue; deaf even to the hoots
Of tired, outstripped Five-Nines that dropped behind.

Gas! Gas! Quick, boys!—An ecstasy of fumbling,
Fitting the clumsy helmets just in time;   10
But someone still was yelling out and stumbling
And floundering like a man in fire or lime . . .
Dim, through the misty panes and thick green light,
As under a green sea, I saw him drowning.

In all my dreams, before my helpless sight,   15
He plunges at me, guttering, choking, drowning.

If in some smothering dreams you too could pace
Behind the wagon that we flung him in,
And watch the white eyes writhing in his face,
His hanging face, like a devil's sick of sin;   20
If you could hear, at every jolt, the blood
Come gargling from the froth-corrupted lungs,
Obscene as cancer, bitter as the cud
Of vile, incurable sores on innocent tongues,—
My friend, you would not tell with such high zest   25
To children ardent for some desperate glory,

DULCE ET DECORUM EST   See note to ll. 27–28. **8. Five-Nines:** gas shells. **12. lime:** quicklime, which becomes very hot when exposed to air.

The old lie: *Dulce et decorum est*
Pro patria mori.

Anthem for Doomed Youth

What passing-bells for these who die as cattle?
   Only the monstrous anger of the guns.
   Only the stuttering rifles' rapid rattle
Can patter out their hasty orisons.
No mockeries now for them; no prayers nor bells,   5
   Nor any voice of mourning save the choirs,—
The shrill, demented choirs of wailing shells;
   And bugles calling for them from sad shires.

What candles may be held to speed them all?
   Not in the hands of boys, but in their eyes   10
Shall shine the holy glimmers of good-byes.
   The pallor of girls' brows shall be their pall;
Their flowers the tenderness of patient minds,
And each slow dusk a drawing-down of blinds.

E. E. Cummings   *(1894–1962)*

Pity This Busy Monster, Manunkind

pity this busy monster,manunkind,

not.   Progress is a comfortable disease:
your victim(death and life safely beyond)

plays with the bigness of his littleness
—electrons deify one razorblade   5
into a mountainrange;lenses extend

unwish through curving wherewhen till unwish
returns on its unself.
          A world of made
is not a world of born—pity poor flesh

27–28. Dulce . . . mori: "It is sweet and glorious to die for one's country" (Horace, *Odes,* III.ii.13).
ANTHEM **1. passing-bells:** bells rung for someone's death. **4. orisons:** prayers. **8. shires:** British regiments are often named for shires (e.g., Lincolnshire).

and trees,poor stars and stones,but never this   10
fine specimen of hypermagical

ultraomnipotence.   We doctors know

a hopeless case if—listen:there's a hell
of a good universe next door;let's go

My Sweet Old Etcetera

my sweet old etcetera
aunt lucy during the recent

war could and what
is more did tell you just
what everybody was fighting   5

for,
my sister

isabel created hundreds
(and
hundreds)of socks not to   10
mention shirts fleaproof earwarmers

etcetera wristers etcetera, my
mother hoped that

i would die etcetera
bravely of course my father used   15
to become hoarse talking about how it was
a privilege and if only he
could meanwhile my

self etcetera lay quietly
in the deep mud et   20

cetera
(dreaming,
et
    cetera, of
Your smile   25
eyes knees and of your Etcetera)

What If a Much of a Which of a Wind

what if a much of a which of a wind
gives the truth to summer's lie;

bloodies with dizzying leaves the sun
and yanks immortal stars awry?
Blow king to beggar and queen to seem   5
(blow friend to fiend:blow space to time)
—when skies are hanged and oceans drowned,
the single secret will still be man

what if a keen of a lean wind flays
screaming hills with sleet and snow: 10
strangles valleys by ropes of thing
and stifles forests in white ago?
Blow hope to terror;blow seeing to blind
(blow pity to envy and soul to mind)
—whose hearts are mountains,roots are trees,   15
it's they shall cry hello to the spring

what if a dawn of a doom of a dream
bites this universe in two,
peels forever out of his grave
and sprinkles nowhere with me and you?   20
Blow soon to never and never to twice
(blow life to isn't:blow death to was)
—all nothing's only our hugest home;
the most who die,the more we live

r-p-o-p-h-e-s-s-a-g-r

                   r-p-o-p-h-e-s-s-a-g-r
               who
a)s w(e loo)k
upnowgath
          PPEGORHRASS   5
                     eringint(o-
aThe):l
       eA
         !p:
S   a   10
                 (r
rIvInG   .gRrEaPsPhOs)
                             to
rea(be)rran(com)gi(e)ngly
,grasshopper;   15

Jean Toomer *(1894–1967)*

Reapers

Black reapers with the sound of steel on stones
Are sharpening scythes. I see them place the hones
In their hip-pockets as a thing that's done,
And start their silent swinging, one by one.
Black horses drive a mower through the weeds, 5
And there, a field rat, startled, squealing bleeds,
His belly close to ground. I see the blade,
Blood-stained, continue cutting weeds and shade.

Hart Crane *(1899–1932)*

Praise for an Urn

In Memoriam: Ernest Nelson

It was a kind and northern face
That mingled in such exile guise
The everlasting eyes of Pierrot
And, of Gargantua, the laughter.

His thoughts, delivered to me 5
From the white coverlet and pillow,
I see now, were inheritances—
Delicate riders of the storm.

The slant moon on the slanting hill
Once moved us toward presentiments 10
Of what the dead keep, living still,
And such assessments of the soul

PRAISE FOR AN URN   Ernest Nelson was a Norwegian immigrant, a poet and commercial artist, whom Crane met in Cleveland in 1921, shortly before Nelson's death: "One of the best-read people I ever met, wonderful kindliness and tolerance and a true Nietzschean. He was one of many broken against the stupidity of American life in such places as here" (Crane). **3. Pierrot:** the traditional feckless and ruefully sad clown of pantomine. **4. Gargantua:** the robust giant of Rabelais's romance.

As, perched in the crematory lobby,
The insistent clock commented on,
Touching as well upon our praise   15
Of glories proper to the time.

Still, having in mind gold hair,
I cannot see that broken brow
And miss the dry sound of bees
Stretching across a lucid space.   20

Scatter these well-meant idioms
Into the smoky spring that fills
The suburbs, where they will be lost.
They are no trophies of the sun.

Black Tambourine

The interests of a black man in a cellar
Mark tardy judgment on the world's closed door.
Gnats toss in the shadow of a bottle,
And a roach spans a crevice in the floor.

Aesop, driven to pondering, found   5
Heaven with the tortoise and the hare;
Fox brush and sow ear top his grave
And mingling incantations on the air.

The black man, forlorn in the cellar,
Wanders in some mid-kingdom, dark, that lies,   10
Between his tambourine, stuck on the wall,
And, in Africa, a carcass quick with flies.

Island Quarry

Square sheets—they saw the marble into
Flat slabs there at the marble quarry
At the turning of the road around the roots of the mountain

13. **crematory lobby:** Nelson was cremated.
BLACK TAMBOURINE   1. **in a cellar:** the poem was written when Crane was hired by
his father to replace a discharged black porter in the basement storeroom of his
restaurant; the "cellar" becomes metaphorical, as does the "closed door." 10. **mid-kingdom:** "The word 'mid-kingdom' is perhaps the key word to what ideas there are in
[the poem]. The poem is a description and bundle of insinuations, suggestions bearing
on the Negro's place somewhere between man and beast. That is why Aesop [the
author of beast fables] is brought in, etc.—the popular conception of Negro romance,
the tambourine on the wall. . . . My only declaration in it is that I find the Negro
(in the popular mind) sentimentally or brutally 'placed' in this mid-kingdom" (Crane).

Where the straight road would seem to ply below the stone, that fierce
Profile of marble spiked with yonder   5
Palms against the sunset's towering sea, and maybe
Against mankind. It is at times—

In dusk it is at times as though this island lifted, floated
In Indian baths. At Cuban dusk the eyes
Walking the straight road toward thunder—   10
This dry road silvering toward the shadow of the quarry
—It is at times as though the eyes burned hard and glad
And did not take the goat path quivering to the right,
Wide of the mountain—thence to tears and sleep—
But went on into marble that does not weep.   15

Voyages: II

And yet this great wink of eternity,
Of rimless floods, unfettered leewardings,
Samite sheeted and processioned where
Her undinal vast belly moonward bends,
Laughing the wrapt inflections of our love;   5

Take this Sea, whose diapason knells
On scrolls of silver snowy sentences,
The sceptred terror of whose sessions rends
As her demeanors motion well or ill,
All but the pieties of lovers' hands.   10

And onward, as bells off San Salvador
Salute the crocus lustres of the stars,
In these poinsettia meadows of her tides,—
Adagios of islands, O my Prodigal,
Complete the dark confessions her veins spell.   15

Mark how her turning shoulders wind the hours,
And hasten while her penniless rich palms
Pass superscription of bent foam and wave,—

VOYAGES: II 2. **leewardings:** movements away from the wind. 3. **Samite:** silk fabric interwoven with silver and gold. 4. **undinal:** from Undine, a water-goddess (with overtones of *unda*, Latin for "wave"). 5. **wrapt inflections:** finite or limited expressions. 6. **diapason:** concord of high and low notes. 7. **sentences:** judgments. 8. **sessions:** as of a court. 11. **bells . . . San Salvador:** possibly of legendary sunken cities. 13. **poinsettia meadows:** tropical islands. 14. **Adagios of islands:** "the motion of a boat through islands clustered thickly, the rhythm of the motion, etc." (Crane, "General Aims and Theories"), also invoking the "whole world of music." **Prodigal:** the generous, self-giving lover. 17. **penniless rich palms:** "literally penniless but emotionally rich" hands (R. W. B. Lewis). 18. **superscription:** with suggestion of a coin; cf. the words of Jesus in Luke 20:24, "Show me a penny. Whose image and superscription hath it? They answered and said, Caesar's" (J. W. Beach).

Hasten, while they are true,—sleep, death, desire,
Close round one instant in one floating flower.   20

Bind us in time, O Seasons clear, and awe.
O minstrel galleons of Carib fire,
Bequeath us to no earthly shore until
Is answered in the vortex of our grave
The seal's wide spindrift gaze toward paradise.   25

Stevie Smith   *(1902–1971)*

Not Waving But Drowning

Nobody heard him, the dead man,
But still he lay moaning:
I was much further out than you thought
And not waving but drowning.

Poor chap, he always loved larking   5
And now he's dead
It must have been too cold for him his heart gave way,
They said.

Oh, no no no, it was too cold always
(Still the dead one lay moaning)   10
I was much too far out all my life
And not waving but drowning.

Langston Hughes   *(1902–1967)*

Beale Street

The dream is vague
And all confused
With dice and women
And jazz and booze.

The dream is vague,   5
Without a name,

25. **spindrift**: like the driving of spray.

Yet warm and wavering
And sharp as flame.

The loss
Of the dream   10
Leaves nothing
The same.

Dream Deferred

What happens to a dream deferred?

Does it dry up
like a raisin in the sun?
Or fester like a sore—
And then run?   5
Does it stink like rotten meat?
Or crust and sugar over—
like a syrupy sweet?

Maybe it just sags
like a heavy load.   10

Or does it explode?

Harlem

Here on the edge of hell
Stands Harlem—
Remembering the old lies,
The old kicks in the back,
The old "Be patient"   5
They told us before.

Sure, we remember.
Now when the man at the corner store
Says sugar's gone up another two cents,
And bread one,   10
And there's a new tax on cigarettes—
We remember the job we never had,
Never could get,
And can't have now
Because we're colored.   15

So we stand here
On the edge of hell

In Harlem
And look out on the world
And wonder   20
What we're gonna do
In the face of what
We remember.

Robert Penn Warren *(1905–   )*

Pursuit

The hunchback on the corner, with gum and shoelaces,
Has his own wisdom and pleasures, and may not be lured
To divulge them to you, for he has merely endured
Your appeal for his sympathy and your kind purchases;
And wears infirmity but as the general who turns   5
Apart, in his famous old greatcoat there on the hill
At dusk when the rapture and cannonade are still,
To muse withdrawn from the dead, from his gorgeous subalterns;
Or stares from the thicket of his familiar pain, like a fawn
That meets you a moment, wheels, in imperious innocence is gone. 10

Go to the clinic. Wait in the outer room
Where like an old possum the snag-nailed hand will hump
On its knee in murderous patience, and the pomp
Of pain swells like the Indies, or a plum.
And there you will stand, as on the Roman hill,   15
Stunned by each withdrawn gaze and severe shape,
The first barbarian victor stood to gape
At the sacrificial fathers, white robed, still;
And even the feverish old Jew stares stern with authority
Till you feel like one who has come too late, or improperly clothed, to a
    party.   20

The doctor will take you now. He is burly and clean;
Listening, like lover or worshiper, bends at your heart.
He cannot make out just what it tries to impart,
So smiles; says you simply need a change of scene.
Of scene, of solace: therefore Florida,   25
Where Ponce de Leon clanked among the lilies,
Where white sails skit on blue and cavort like fillies,
And the shoulder gleams white in the moonlit corridor.

PURSUIT **15–18. Roman . . . still:** when the Gauls conquered Rome in the 4th
century B.C., the Roman senators sat impassively in their meeting place waiting for
death. **26. Ponce de Leon:** the discoverer of Florida (1460?–1521); tradition holds
that he was seeking the Fountain of Youth.

A change of love: if love is a groping Godward, though blind,
No matter what crevice, cranny, chink, bright in dark, the pale tentacle
    find.   30

In Florida consider the flamingo,
Its color passion but its neck a question.
Consider even that girl the other guests shun
On beach, at bar, in bed, for she may know
The secret you are seeking, after all;   35
Or the child you humbly sit by, excited and curly,
That screams on the shore at the sea's sunlit hurlyburly,
Till the mother calls its name, toward nightfall.
Till you sit alone: in the dire meridians, off Ireland, in fury
Of spume-tooth and dawnless sea-heave, salt rimes the lookout's devout
    eye.   40

Till you sit alone—which is the beginning of error—
Behind you the music and lights of the great hotel:
Solution, perhaps, is public, despair personal,
But history held to your breath clouds like a mirror.
There are many states, and towns in them, and faces,   45
But meanwhile, the little old lady in black, by the wall,
Admires all the dancers, and tells you how just last fall
Her husband died in Ohio, and damp mists her glasses;
She blinks and croaks, like a toad or a Norn, in the horrible light,
And rattles her crutch, which may put forth a small bloom, perhaps white. 50

Original Sin: A Short Story

Nodding, its great head rattling like a gourd,
And locks like seaweed strung on the stinking stone,
The nightmare stumbles past, and you have heard
It fumble your door before it whimpers and is gone:
It acts like the old hound that used to snuffle your door and moan.   5

You thought you had lost it when you left Omaha,
For it seemed connected then with your grandpa, who
Had a wen on his forehead and sat on the veranda
To finger the precious protuberance, as was his habit to do,
Which glinted in sun like rough garnet or the rich old brain bulging through.   10

But you met it in Harvard Yard as the historic steeple
Was confirming the midnight wth its hideous racket,
And you wondered how it had come, for it stood so imbecile,

---

49. Norn: one of the sisters who correspond in Norse mythology to the Greek Fates; a
dispenser of destiny.

With empty hands, humble, and surely nothing in pocket:
Riding the rods, perhaps— or Grandpa's will paid the ticket.   15

You were almost kindly then, in your first homesickness,
As it tortured its stiff face to speak, but scarcely mewed.
Since then you have outlived all your homesickness,
But have met it in many another distempered latitude:
Oh, nothing is lost, ever lost! at last you understood.   20

It never came in the quantum glare of sun
To shame you before your friends, and had nothing to do
With your public experience or private reformation:
But it thought no bed too narrow—it stood with lips askew
And shook its great head sadly like the abstract Jew.   25

Never met you in the lyric arsenical meadows
When children call and your heart goes stone in the bosom—
At the orchard anguish never, nor ovoid horror,
Which is furred like a peach or avid like the delicious plum.
It takes no part in your classic prudence or fondled axiom.   30

Not there when you exclaimed: "Hope is betrayed by
Disastrous glory of sea-capes, sun-torment of whitecaps
—There must be a new innocence for us to be stayed by."
But there it stood, after all the timetables, all the maps,
In the crepuscular clutter of *always, always,* or *perhaps.*   35

You have moved often and rarely left an address,
And hear of the deaths of friends with a sly pleasure,
A sense of cleansing and hope which blooms from distress;
But it has not died, it comes, its hand childish, unsure,
Clutching the bribe of chocolate or a toy you used to treasure.   40

It tries the lock. You hear, but simply drowse:
There is nothing remarkable in that sound at the door
Later you may hear it wander the dark house
Like a mother who rises at night to seek a childhood picture;
Or it goes to the backyard and stands like an old horse cold in the pasture. 45

Dragon Country: To Jacob Boehme

This is the dragon's country, and these his own streams.
The slime on the railroad rails is where he has crossed the track.
On a frosty morning, that field mist is where his great turd steams,
And there are those who have gone forth and not come back.

DRAGON COUNTRY: TO JACOB BOEHME   Jacob Boehme (1575–1624) was a German
mystic who believed in the dualism of God and the necessity of evil as one of two antithetical or dialectical principles in the divine nature. The dragon is a traditional symbol of evil.

I was only a boy when Jack Simms reported the first depredation,   5
What something had done to his hog pen. They called him a God-damn
   liar.
Then said it must be a bear, after some had viewed the location,
With fence rails, like matchwood, splintered, and earth a bloody mire.

But no bear had been seen in the county in fifty years, they knew.
It was something to say, merely that, for people compelled to explain   10
What, standing in natural daylight, they agreed couldn't be true;
And saying the words, a man felt in the chest a constrictive pain.

At least, some admitted this later, when things had got to the worst—
When, for instance, they found in the woods the wagon turned on its side,
Mules torn from trace chains, and you saw how the harness had burst.   15
Spectators averted the face from the spot where the teamster had died.

But that was long back, in my youth, just the first of case after case.
The great hunts fizzled. You followed the track of disrepair,
Ruined fence, blood-smear, brush broken, but came in the end to a place
With weed unbent and leaf calm—and nothing, nothing was there.   20

So what, in God's name, could men think when they couldn't bring to bay
That belly-dragging earth-evil, but found that it took to air?
Thirty-thirty or buckshot might fail, but then at least you could say
You had faced it—assuming, of course, that you had survived the affair.

We were promised troops, the Guard, but the Governor's skin got thin   25
When up in New York the papers called him Saint George of Kentucky.
Yes, even the Louisville reporters who came to Todd County would grin.
Reporters, though rarely, still come. No one talks. They think it unlucky.

If a man disappears—well, the fact is something to hide.
The family says, gone to Akron, or up to Ford, in Detroit.   30
When we found Jebb Johnson's boot, with the leg, what was left, inside,
His mother said, no, it's not his. So we took it out to destroy it.

Land values are falling, no longer do lovers in moonlight go.
The rabbit, thoughtless of air gun, in the nearest pasture cavorts.
Now certain fields go untended, the local birth rate goes low.   35
The coon dips his little black paw in the riffle where he nightly resorts.

Yes, other sections have problems somewhat different from ours.
Their crops may fail, bank rates rise, loans at rumor of war be called,
But we feel removed from maneuvers of Russia, or other great powers,
And from much ordinary hope we are now disenthralled.   40

The Catholics have sent in a mission, Baptists report new attendance.
All that's off the point! We are human, and the human heart
Demands language for reality that has not the slightest dependence
On desire, or need—and in church fools pray only that the Beast depart.

But if the Beast were withdrawn now, life might dwindle again   45
To the ennui, the pleasure, and the night sweat, known in the time before
Necessity of truth had trodden the land, and our hearts, to pain,
And left, in darkness, the fearful glimmer of joy, like a spoor.

A Real Question Calling for Solution

Don't bother a bit, you are only a dream you are having,
And if when you wake your symptoms are not relieved,
That is only because you harbor a morbid craving
For belief in the old delusion in which you have always believed.

Yes, there was the year when every morning you ran   5
. A mile before breakfast—yes, and the year you read
Virgil two hours just after lunch and began
Your practice of moral assessment, before the toothbrush and bed.

But love boiled down like porridge in a pot,
And beyond the far snow-fields westward, redder than hate,   10
The sun burned; and one night much better forgot,
Pity, like sputum, gleamed on the station floor-tiles, train late.

When you slept on a board you found your back much better.
When you took the mud baths you found that verse came easy.
When you slept with another woman you found that the letter   15
You owed your wife was a pleasure to write, gay now and teasy.

There once was a time when you thought you would understand
Many things, many things, including yourself, and learn Greek,
But light changes old landscape, and your own hand
Makes signs unseen in the dark, and lips move but do not speak,   20

For given that vulture and vector which is the stroke
Of the clock, absolute, on the bias of midnight, memory
Is nothing, is nothing, not even the memory of smoke
Dispersed on windless ease in the great fuddled head of the sky,

And all recollections are false, and all you suffer   25
Is only the punishment thought appropriate for guilt
You cuddle and kiss, and wish you had the crime for,
For the bitterest tears are those shed for milk—or blood—not spilt.

There is only one way, then, to make things hang together,
Which is to accept the logic of dream, and avoid   30
Night air, politics, French sauces, autumn weather,
And the thought that, on your awaking, identity may be destroyed.

A. D. Hope   *(1907–   )*

Circe

after the painting by Dosso Dossi

Behind her not the quivering of a leaf
Flutters the deep enchantment of the wood;
No ripple at her feet disturbs the well;
She sits among her lovers dazed with grief,
Bewildered by the charge of alien blood.   5
Herself transfigured by the hideous spell

She sits among her creatures motionless,
Sees the last human shadow of despair
Fade from the sad, inquisitive, animal eyes,
The naked body of the sorceress   10
Mocked by the light, sleek shapes of feather and hair.
And as on snout and beak and muzzle dies

The melancholy trace of human speech,
For the first time her heart is rich with words
And with her voice she disenchants the grove.   15
The lonely island and the sounding beach
Answer with barks and howls, the scream of birds,
Her uncontrollable, aching cry of love.

Coup de Grâce

Just at that moment the Wolf,
Shag jaws and slavering grin,
Steps from the property wood.
O, what a gorge, what a gulf
Opens to gobble her in,   5
Little Red Riding Hood!

O, what a face full of fangs!
Eyes like saucers at least

CIRCE   Circe is the enchantress in the *Odyssey* who changed her lovers into animals.
Subtitle: The late-Renaissance Italian painter Dosso Dossi (1479–1542) combined
pastoral with magical suggestions, notably in the *Circe* (in the Borghese Gallery,
Rome).
COUP DE GRÂCE   "Finishing stroke." **3. property:** like a stage set.

Roll to seduce and beguile.
Miss, with her dimples and bangs,   10
Thinks him a handsome beast;
Flashes the Riding Hood Smile;

Stands her ground like a queen,
Velvet red of the rose
Framing each little milk-tooth,   15
Pink tongue peeping between.
Then, wider than anyone knows,
Opens her minikin mouth,

Swallows up Wolf in a trice;
Tail going down gives a flick,   20
Caught as she closes her jaws.
Bows, all sugar and spice.
O, what a lady-like trick!
O, what a round of applause!

W. H. Auden (1907–1973)

Musée des Beaux Arts

About suffering they were never wrong,
The Old Masters: how well they understood
Its human position; how it takes place
While someone else is eating or opening a window or just walking dully
     along;
How, when the aged are reverently, passionately waiting   5
For the miraculous birth, there always must be
Children who did not specially want it to happen, skating
On a pond at the edge of the wood:
They never forgot
That even the dreadful martyrdom must run its course   10
Anyhow in a corner, some untidy spot
Where the dogs go on with their doggy life and the torturer's horse
Scratches its innocent behind on a tree.

---

18. **minikin:** small or affectedly dainty.

MUSÉE DES BEAUX ARTS   The title means "Museum of Fine Arts," with special reference to the Royal Museum in Brussels, where Auden saw the "Landscape with the Fall of Icarus" of Pieter Brueghel the Elder (1525–69). **2. Old Masters:** great painters of the past, especially of the Renaissance. **6. miraculous birth:** of a Messiah or Redeemer.

In Brueghel's *Icarus*, for instance: how everything turns away
Quite leisurely from the disaster; the ploughman may   15
Have heard the splash, the forsaken cry,
But for him it was not an important failure; the sun shone
As it had to on the white legs disappearing into the green
Water; and the expensive delicate ship that must have seen
Something amazing, a boy falling out of the sky,   20
Had somewhere to get to and sailed calmly on.

Lullaby

Lay your sleeping head, my love,
Human on my faithless arm;
Time and fevers burn away
Individual beauty from
Thoughtful children, and the grave   5
Proves the child ephemeral:
But in my arms till break of day
Let the living creature lie,
Mortal, guilty, but to me
The entirely beautiful.   10

Soul and body have no bounds:
To lovers as they lie upon
Her tolerant enchanted slope
In their ordinary swoon,
Grave the vision Venus sends   15
Of supernatural sympathy,
Universal love and hope;
While an abstract insight wakes
Among the glaciers and the rocks
The hermit's carnal ecstasy.   20

Certainty, fidelity
On the stroke of midnight pass
Like vibrations of a bell,
And fashionable madmen raise
Their pedantic boring cry: 25
Every farthing of the cost,
All the dreaded cards foretell,
Shall be paid, but from this night
Not a whisper, not a thought,
Not a kiss nor look be lost.   30

Beauty, midnight, vision dies:
Let the winds of dawn that blow

---

14. **Icarus:** in the Greek story, Icarus flew too high on the wax wings his father had
made for him; the sun melted the wings and he fell into the sea.

Softly round your dreaming head
Such a day of welcome show
Eye and knocking heart may bless,   35
Find our mortal world enough;
Noons of dryness find you fed
By the involuntary powers,
Nights of insult let you pass
Watched by every human love.   40

In Memory of W. B. Yeats

(d. Jan. 1939)

1

He disappeared in the dead of winter:
The brooks were frozen, the airports almost deserted,
And snow disfigured the public statues;
The mercury sank in the mouth of the dying day.
What instruments we have agree   5
The day of his death was a dark cold day.

Far from his illness
The wolves ran on through the evergreen forests,
The peasant river was untempted by the fashionable quays;
By mourning tongues   10
The death of the poet was kept from his poems.

But for him it was his last afternoon as himself,
An afternoon of nurses and rumors;
The provinces of his body revolted,
The squares of his mind were empty,   15
Silence invaded the suburbs,
The current of his feeling failed; he became his admirers.

Now he is scattered among a hundred cities
And wholly given over to unfamiliar affections,
To find his happiness in another kind of wood   20
And be punished under a foreign code of conscience.
The words of a dead man
Are modified in the guts of the living.

But in the importance and noise of tomorrow
When the brokers are roaring like beasts on the floor of the Bourse,   25

IN MEMORY OF W. B. YEATS   5. **What . . . agree:** a deliberate playing upon the form
of the pastoral elegy, where all nature mourns with man; here the sympathy is at most
coincidental and registered through "instruments." 25. **Bourse:** the Paris stock exchange.

And the poor have the sufferings to which they are fairly accustomed,
And each in the cell of himself is almost convinced of his freedom,
A few thousand will think of this day
As one thinks of a day when one did something slightly unusual.
What instruments we have agree   30
The day of his death was a dark cold day.

2

You were silly like us; your gift survived it all:
The parish of rich women, physical decay,
Yourself. Mad Ireland hurt you into poetry.
Now Ireland has her madness and her weather still,   35
For poetry makes nothing happen: it survives
In the valley of its making where executives
Would never want to tamper, flows on south
From ranches of isolation and the busy griefs,
Raw towns that we believe and die in; it survives,   40
A way of happening, a mouth.

3

Earth, receive an honored guest:
William Yeats is laid to rest.
Let the Irish vessel lie
Emptied of its poetry.   45

In the nightmare of the dark
All the dogs of Europe bark,
And the living nations wait,
Each sequestered in its hate;

Intellectual disgrace   50
Stares from every human face,
And the seas of pity lie
Locked and frozen in each eye.

Follow, poet, follow right
To the bottom of the night,   55
With your unconstraining voice
Still persuade us to rejoice;

With the farming of a verse
Make a vineyard of the curse,
Sing of human unsuccess   60
In a rapture of distress;

---

33. rich women: such friends and patrons as Lady Gregory and Olivia Shakespeare.
36. poetry . . . happen: or, as Auden puts it elsewhere, "art is a product of history, not a cause." **46. nightmare of the dark:** the poem was written on the eve of the Second World War, when its coming seemed inevitable.

In the deserts of the heart
Let the healing fountain start,
In the prison of his days
Teach the free man how to praise.   65

In Praise of Limestone

If it form the one landscape that we, the inconstant ones,
    Are consistently homesick for, this is chiefly
Because it dissolves in water. Mark these rounded slopes
    With their surface fragrance of thyme and, beneath,
A secret system of caves and conduits; hear the springs   5
    That spurt out everywhere with a chuckle,
Each filling a private pool for its fish and carving
    Its own little ravine whose cliffs entertain
The butterfly and the lizard; examine this region
    Of short distances and definite places: 10
What could be more like Mother or a fitter background
    For her son, the flirtatious male who lounges
Against the rock in the sunlight, never doubting
    That for all his faults he is loved; whose works are but
Extensions of his power to charm? From weathered outcrop   15
    To hill-top temple, from appearing waters to
Conspicuous fountains, from a wild to a formal vineyard,
    Are ingenious but short steps that a child's wish
To receive more attention than his brothers, whether
    By pleasing or teasing, can easily take.   20

Watch, then, the band of rivals as they climb up and down
    Their steep stone gennels in twos and threes, at times
Arm in arm, but never, thank God, in step; or engaged
    On the shady side of a square at midday in
Voluble discourse, knowing each other too well to think   25
    There are any important secrets, unable
To conceive a god whose temper-tantrums are moral
    And not to be pacified by a clever line
Or a good lay: for, accustomed to a stone that responds,
    They have never had to veil their faces in awe   30
Of a crater whose blazing fury could not be fixed;
    Adjusted to the local needs of valleys
Where everything can be touched or reached by walking,
    Their eyes have never looked into infinite space
Through the lattice-work of a nomad's comb, born lucky,   35
    Their legs have never encountered the fungi
And insects of the jungle, the monstrous forms and lives
    With which we have nothing, we like to hope, in common.

IN PRAISE OF LIMESTONE   **22. gennels:** narrow passages among the rocks.

So, when one of them goes to the bad, the way his mind works
    Remains comprehensible: to become a pimp   40
Or deal in fake jewelry or ruin a fine tenor voice
    For effects that bring down the house, could happen to all
But the best and the worst of us . . .
                             That is why, I suppose,
    The best and worst never stayed here long but sought
Immoderate soils where the beauty was not so external,   45
    The light less public and the meaning of life
Something more than a mad camp. "Come!" cried the granite wastes,
    "How evasive is your humor, how accidental
Your kindest kiss, how permanent is death." (Saints-to-be
    Slipped away sighing.) "Come!" purred the clays and gravels.   50
"On our plains there is room for armies to drill; rivers
    Wait to be tamed and slaves to construct you a tomb
In the grand manner: soft as the earth is mankind and both
    Need to be altered." (Intendant Caesars rose and
Left, slamming the door.) But the really reckless were fetched   55
    By an older colder voice, the oceanic whisper:
"I am the solitude that asks and promises nothing;
    That is how I shall set you free. There is no love;
There are only the various envies, all of them sad."
    They were right, my dear, all those voices were right   60
And still are; this land is not the sweet home that it looks,
    Nor its peace the historical calm of a site
Where something was settled once and for all: A backward
    And dilapidated province, connected
To the big busy world by a tunnel, with a certain   65
    Seedy appeal, is that all it is now? Not quite:
It has a worldly duty which in spite of itself
    It does not neglect, but calls into question
All the Great Powers assume; it disturbs our rights. The poet,
    Admired for his earnest habit of calling   70
The sun the sun, his mind Puzzle, is made uneasy
    By these marble statues which so obviously doubt
His antimythological myth; and these gamins,
    Pursuing the scientist down the tiled colonnade
With such lively offers, rebuke his concern for Nature's   75
    Remotest aspects: I, too, am reproached, for what
And how much you know. Not to lose time, not to get caught,
    Not to be left behind, not, please! to resemble
The beasts who repeat themselves, or a thing like water
    Or stone whose conduct can be predicted, these   80
Are our Common Prayer, whose greatest comfort is music
    Which can be made anywhere, is invisible,

---

47. **mad camp:** preposterous and amusing game. **55. slamming the door:** Joseph
Goebbels, the propaganda minister of Hitler's Germany, declared, "If we are defeated,
we shall slam the doors of history behind us." **81. Common Prayer:** an allusion to
the Book of Common Prayer, the prayer book used in Anglican services.

And does not smell. In so far as we have to look forward
   To death as a fact, no doubt we are right: But if
Sins can be forgiven, if bodies rise from the dead,   85
   These modifications of matter into
Innocent athletes and gesticulating fountains,
   Made solely for pleasure, make a further point:
The blessed will not care what angle they are regarded from,
   Having nothing to hide. Dear, I know nothing of   90
Either, but when I try to imagine a faultless love
   Or the life to come, what I hear is the murmur
Of underground streams, what I see is a limestone landscape.

Theodore Roethke   *(1908–1963)*

Root Cellar

Nothing would sleep in that cellar, dank as a ditch,
Bulbs broke out of boxes hunting for chinks in the dark,
Shoots dangled and drooped,
Lolling obscenely from mildewed crates,
Hung down long yellow evil necks, like tropical snakes.   5
And what a congress of stinks!—
Roots ripe as old bait,
Pulpy stems, rank, silo-rich,
Leaf-mold, manure, lime, piled against slippery planks.
Nothing would give up life: 10
Even the dirt kept breathing a small breath.

My Papa's Waltz

The whiskey on your breath
Could make a small boy dizzy;
But I hung on like death:
Such waltzing was not easy.

We romped until the pans   5
Slid from the kitchen shelf;
My mother's countenance
Could not unfrown itself.

The hand that held my wrist
Was battered on one knuckle;   10

At every step you missed
My right ear scraped a buckle.

You beat time on my head
With a palm caked hard by dirt,
Then waltzed me off to bed   15
Still clinging to your shirt.

The Waking

I wake to sleep, and take my waking slow.
I feel my fate in what I cannot fear.
I learn by going where I have to go.

We think by feeling. What is there to know?   5
I hear my being dance from ear to ear.
I wake to sleep, and take my waking slow.

Of those so close beside me, which are you?
God bless the Ground! I shall walk softly there,
And learn by going where I have to go.   10

Light takes the Tree; but who can tell us how?
The lowly worm climbs up a winding stair;
I wake to sleep, and take my waking slow.

Great Nature has another thing to do
To you and me; so take the lively air,   15
And, lovely, learn by going where to go.

This shaking keeps me steady. I should know.
What falls away is always. And is near.
I wake to sleep, and take my waking slow.
I learn by going where I have to go.   20

In a Dark Time

In a dark time, the eye begins to see,
I meet my shadow in the deepening shade;
I hear my echo in the echoing wood—
A lord of nature weeping to a tree.
I live between the heron and the wren,   5
Beasts of the hill and serpents of the den.

What's madness but nobility of soul
At odds with circumstance? The day's on fire!
I know the purity of pure despair,

My shadow pinned against a sweating wall.   10
That place among the rocks—is it a cave,
Or winding path? The edge is what I have.

A steady storm of correspondences!
A night flowing with birds, a ragged moon,
And in broad day the midnight come again!   15
A man goes far to find out what he is—
Death of the self in a long, tearless night,
All natural shapes blazing unnatural light.

Dark, dark my light, and darker my desire.
My soul, like some heat-maddened summer fly,   20
Keeps buzzing at the sill. Which I is *I?*
A fallen man, I climb out of my fear.
The mind enters itself, and God the mind,
And one is One, free in the tearing wind.

Charles Olson   *(1910–1970)*

The Songs of Maximus: 3

This morning of the small snow
I count the blessings, the leak in the faucet
which makes of the sink time, the drop
of the water on water as sweet
as the Seth Thomas   5
in the old kitchen
my father stood in his drawers to wind (always
he forgot the 30th day, as I don't want to remember
the rent
          a house these days   10
so much somebody else's,
especially,
Congoleum's

                 Or the plumbing,
that it doesn't work, this I like, have even used paper clips 15
as well as string to hold the ball up   And flush it
with my hand
               But that the car doesn't, that no moving thing moves

IN A DARK TIME   **13. correspondences:** symbolic equivalences between human values
and natural objects.
THE SONGS OF MAXIMUS: 3   **5. Seth Thomas:** a make of clock.

without that song I'd void my ear of, the musickracket
of all ownership . . .   20

        Holes
in my shoes, that's all right, my fly
gaping, me out
at the elbows, the blessing
           that difficulties are once more   25

      "In the midst of plenty, walk
      as close to
      bare
        In the face of sweetness,
      piss   30
          In the time of goodness,
      go side, go
      smashing, beat them, go as
      (as near as you can

      tear   35

      In the land of plenty, have
      nothing to do with it
            take the way of
      the lowest,
      including your legs, go   40
      contrary, go
      sing

Elizabeth Bishop *(1911–   )*

Seascape

This celestial seascape, with white herons got up as angels,
flying as high as they want and as far as they want sidewise
in tiers and tiers of immaculate reflections;
the whole region, from the highest heron
down to the weightless mangrove island   5
with bright green leaves edged neatly with bird-droppings
like illumination in silver,
and down to the suggestively Gothic arches of the mangrove roots
and the beautiful pea-green back-pasture
where occasionally a fish jumps, like a wild-flower   10
in an ornamental spray of spray;

this cartoon by Raphael for a tapestry for a Pope:
it does look like heaven.
But a skeletal lighthouse standing there
in black and white clerical dress,   15
who lives on his nerves, thinks he knows better.
He thinks that hell rages below his iron feet,
that that is why the shallow water is so warm,
and he knows that heaven is not like this.
Heaven is not like flying or swimming,   20
but has something to do with blackness and a strong glare
and when it gets dark he will remember something
strongly worded to say on the subject.

The Man-Moth

Here, above,
cracks in the building are filled with battered moonlight.
The whole shadow of Man is only as big as his hat.
It lies at his feet like a circle for a doll to stand on,
and he makes an inverted pin, the point magnetized to the moon.   5
He does not see the moon; he observes only her vast properties,
Feeling the queer light on his hands, neither warm nor cold,
of a temperature impossible to record in thermometers.

But when the Man-Moth
pays his rare, although occasional, visits to the surface,
the moon looks rather different to him. He emerges   10
from an opening under the edge of one of the sidewalks
and nervously begins to scale the faces of the buildings.
He thinks the moon is a small hole at the top of the sky,
proving the sky quite useless for protection.   15
He trembles, but must investigate as high as he can climb.

Up the façades,
his shadow dragging like a photographer's cloth behind him,
he climbs fearfully, thinking that this time he will manage
to push his small head through that round clean opening   20
and be forced through, as from a tube, in black scrolls on the light.
(Man, standing below him, has no such illusions.)
But what the Man-Moth fears most he must do, although
he fails, of course, and falls back scared but quite unhurt.

Then he returns   25
to the pale subways of cement he calls his home. He flits,

SEASCAPE **12. cartoon . . . tapestry:** a design (full-scale painting) for a tapestry by
the great Renaissance painter Raphael Sanzio (1483–1520); the "cartoons" are now in
the Victoria and Albert Museum, London.
THE MAN-MOTH "Newspaper misprint for 'mammoth'" (Bishop).

he flutters, and cannot get aboard the silent trains
fast enough to suit him. The doors close swiftly.
The Man-Moth always seats himself facing the wrong way
and the train starts at once at its full, terrible speed, 30
without a shift in gears or a gradation of any sort.
He cannot tell the rate at which he travels backwards.

Each night he must
be carried through artificial tunnels and dream recurrent dreams.
Just as the ties recur beneath his train, these underlie 35
his rushing brain. He does not dare look out the window,
for the third rail, the unbroken draught of poison,
runs there beside him. He regards it as a disease
he has inherited susceptibility to. He has to keep
his hands in pockets, as others must wear mufflers. 40

If you catch him,
hold up a flashlight to his eye. It's all dark pupil,
an entire night itself, whose haired horizon tightens
as he stares back, and closes up the eye. Then from the lids
one tear, his only possession, like the bee's sting, slips. 45
Slyly he palms it, and if you're not paying attention
he'll swallow it. However, if you watch, he'll hand it over,
cool as from underground springs and pure enough to drink.

The Prodigal

The brown enormous odor he lived by
was too close, with its breathing and thick hair,
for him to judge. The floor was rotten; the sty
was plastered halfway up with glass-smooth dung.
Light-lashed, self-righteous, above moving snouts, 5
the pigs' eyes followed him, a cheerful stare—
even to the sow that always ate her young—
till, sickening, he leaned to scratch her head.
But sometimes mornings after drinking bouts
(he hid the pints behind a two-by-four), 10
the sunrise glazed the barnyard mud with red;
the burning puddles seemed to reassure.
And then he thought he almost might endure
his exile yet another year or more.

THE PRODIGAL   For the parable of the Prodigal Son, see Luke 15:11–32, especially verses 16–19: "And he would fain have filled his belly with the husks that the swine did eat: and no man gave unto him. And when he came to himself, he said, How many hired servants of my father's have bread enough and to spare, and I perish with hunger! I will arise and go to my father, and will say unto him, Father, I have sinned against heaven, and before thee, and am no more worthy to be called thy son. . . ."

But evenings the first star came to warn.   15
The farmer whom he worked for came at dark
to shut the cows and horses in the barn
beneath their overhanging clouds of hay,
with pitchforks, faint forked lightnings, catching light,
safe and companionable as in the Ark.   20
The pigs stuck out their little feet and snored.
The lantern—like the sun, going away—
laid on the mud a pacing aureole.
Carrying a bucket along a slimy board,
he felt the bats' uncertain staggering flight,   25
his shuddering insights, beyond his control,
touching him. But it took him a long time
finally to make his mind up to go home.

Robert Hayden *(1913–   )*

Those Winter Sundays

Sundays too my father got up early
and put his clothes on in the blueblack cold,
then with cracked hands that ached
from labor in the weekday weather made
banked fires blaze. No one ever thanked him.   5

I'd wake and hear the cold splintering, breaking.
When the rooms were warm, he'd call,
and slowly I would rise and dress,
fearing the chronic angers of that house,

Speaking indifferently to him,   10
who had driven out the cold
and polished my good shoes as well.
What did I know, what did I know
of love's austere and lonely offices?

Tour 5

The road winds down through autumn hills
in blazonry of farewell scarlet
and recessional gold,
past cedar groves, through static villages

whose names are all that's left   5
of Choctaw, Chickasaw.

We stop a moment in a town
watched over by Confederate sentinels,
buy gas and ask directions of a rawboned man
whose eyes revile us as the enemy.   10

Shrill gorgon silence breathes behind
his taut civility
and in the ever-tautening air,
dark for us despite its Indian summer glow.
We drive on, following the route   15
of highwaymen and phantoms,

Of slaves and armies.
Children, wordless and remote,
wave at us from kindling porches.
And now the land is flat for miles,   20
the landscape lush, metallic, flayed,
its brightness harsh as bloodstained swords.

"Summertime and the Living . . ."

Nobody planted roses, he recalls,
but sunflowers gangled there sometimes,
tough-stalked and bold
and like the vivid children there unplanned.
There circus-poster horses curveted   5
in trees of heaven
above the quarrels and shattered glass,
and he was bareback rider of them all.

No roses there in summer—
oh, never roses except when people died—   10
and no vacations for his elders,
so harshened after each unrelenting day
that they were shouting-angry.
But summer was, they said, the poor folks' time
of year. And he remembers   15
how they would sit on broken steps amid

TOUR 5   **6. Choctaw, Chickasaw:** Indian tribes who lived in what is now Alabama and
Mississippi. **11. gorgon:** in Greek mythology, the Gorgons were three sisters (one of
them Medusa) whose faces when looked at directly turned the beholder to stone.
"SUMMERTIME AND THE LIVING . . ."   The title is taken from the first line of the
George Gershwin song "Summertime," from *Porgy and Bess*: "Summertime . . . and
the livin' is easy."

The fevered tossings of the dusk, the dark,
wafting hearsay with funeral-parlor fans
or making evening solemn by
their quietness. Feels their Mosaic eyes   20
upon him, though the florist roses
that only sorrow could afford
long since have bidden them Godspeed.

Oh, summer summer summertime—

Then grim street preachers shook   25
their tambourines and Bibles in the face
of tolerant wickedness;
then Elks parades and big splendiferous
Jack Johnson in his diamond limousine
set the ghetto burgeoning   30
with fantasies
of Ethiopia spreading her gorgeous wings.

Dylan Thomas   (1914–1953)

The Force That Through the Green Fuse Drives the Flower

The force that through the green fuse drives the flower
Drives my green age; that blasts the roots of trees
Is my destroyer.
And I am dumb to tell the crooked rose
My youth is bent by the same wintry fever.   5

The force that drives the water through the rocks
Drives my red blood; that dries the mouthing streams
Turns mine to wax.
And I am dumb to mouth unto my veins
How at the mountain spring the same mouth sucks.   10

The hand that whirls the water in the pool
Stirs the quicksand; that ropes the blowing wind
Hauls my shroud sail.
And I am dumb to tell the hanging man
How of my clay is made the hangman's lime.   15

---

29. Jack Johnson: the black heavyweight champion who lost his title to Jess Willard in 1915.

THE FORCE THAT THROUGH THE GREEK FUSE   **1. fuse:** the hollow stalk. **4. dumb:** mute, painfully unable to speak. **9. mouth:** tell. **13. shroud:** both rigging (ropes) and burial sheet. **15. hangman's lime:** quicklime, in which the bodies of those hanged were buried for quick dissolution.

The lips of time leech to the fountain head;
Love drips and gathers, but the fallen blood
Shall calm her sores.
And I am dumb to tell a weather's wind
How time has ticked a heaven round the stars.   20

And I am dumb to tell the lover's tomb
How at my sheet goes the same crooked worm.

Fern Hill

Now as I was young and easy under the apple boughs
About the lilting house and happy as the grass was green,
    The night above the dingle starry,
       Time let me hail and climb
    Golden in the heydays of his eyes,   5
And honored among wagons I was prince of the apple towns
And once below a time I lordly had the trees and leaves
       Trail with daisies and barley
    Down the rivers of the windfall light.

And as I was green and carefree, famous among the barns   10
About the happy yard and singing as the farm was home,
    In the sun that is young once only,
       Time let me play and be
    Golden in the mercy of his means,
And green and golden I was huntsman and herdsman, the calves 15
Sang to my horn, the foxes on the hills barked clear and cold,
       And the sabbath rang slowly
    In the pebbles of the holy streams.

All the sun long it was running, it was lovely, the hay
Fields high as the house, the tunes from the chimneys, it was air   20
    And playing, lovely and watery
       And fire green as grass.
    And nightly under the simple stars
As I rode to sleep the owls were bearing the farm away,
All the moon long I heard, blessed among stables, the nightjars   25
    Flying with the ricks, and the horses
       Flashing into the dark.

And then to awake, and the farm, like a wanderer white
With the dew, come back, the cock on his shoulder: it was all
    Shining, it was Adam and maiden,   30
       The sky gathered again

16. **leech**: cling sucking.
FERN HILL Fern Hill was the farm of Thomas's aunt, Ann Jones, where he went for
holidays. **3. dingle**: deep valley. **9. windfall**: falling like apples dropping from the
trees. **25. nightjars**: nocturnal birds like whippoorwills. **26. ricks**: haystacks.

And the sun grew round that very day.
So it must have been after the birth of the simple light
In the first, spinning place, the spellbound horses walking warm
    Out of the whinnying green stable   35
        On to the fields of praise.

And honored among foxes and pheasants by the gay house
Under the new made clouds and happy as the heart was long,
    In the sun born over and over,
        I ran my heedless ways,   40
    My wishes raced through the house high hay
And nothing I cared, at my sky blue trades, that time allows
In all his tuneful turning so few and such morning songs
    Before the children green and golden
        Follow him out of grace,   45

Nothing I cared, in the lamb white days, that time would take me
Up to the swallow thronged loft by the shadow of my hand,
    In the moon that is always rising,
        Nor that riding to sleep
    I should hear him fly with the high fields   50
And wake to the farm forever fled from the childless land.
Oh as I was young and easy in the mercy of his means,
        Time held me green and dying
    Though I sang in my chains like the sea.

Lament

    When I was a windy boy and a bit
    And the black spit of the chapel fold,
    (Sighed the old ram rod, dying of women),
    I tiptoed shy in the gooseberry wood,
    The rude owl cried like a telltale tit,   5
    I skipped in a blush as the big girls rolled
    Ninepin down on the donkeys' common,
    And on seesaw sunday nights I wooed
    Whoever I would with my wicked eyes,
    The whole of the moon I could love and leave   10
    All the green leaved little weddings' wives
    In the coal black bush and let them grieve.

    When I was a gusty man and a half
    And the black beast of the beetles' pews,

---

34. first . . . place: Eden in the time of the Creation. **35. Out . . . stable:** as Milton, in Book VII of *Paradise Lost*, shows the animals springing into life out of the earth. **42. sky blue trades:** innocent games. **45. out of grace:** out of a state of innocence and into a fallen world (cf. "childless land," l. 51).

LAMENT **2. spit:** likeness, as in "spit and image"; here a black rather than white sheep. **5. rude:** coarse. **tit:** small bird, e.g. titmouse. **7. Ninepin down:** down like ninepins.

(Sighed the old ram rod, dying of bitches), ·   15
Not a boy and a bit in the wick-
Dipping moon and drunk as a new dropped calf,
I whistled all night in the twisted flues,
Midwives grew in the midnight ditches,
And the sizzling beds of the town cried, Quick!—   20
Whenever I dove in a breast high shoal,
Wherever I ramped in the clover quilts,
Whatsoever I did in the coal-
Black night, I felt my quivering prints.

When I was a man you could call a man   25
And the black cross of the holy house,
(Sighed the old ram rod, dying of welcome),
Brandy and ripe in my bright, bass prime,
No springtailed tom in the red hot town
With every simmering woman his mouse   30
But a hillocky bull in the swelter
Of summer come in his great good time
To the sultry, biding herds, I said,
Oh, time enough when the blood creeps cold,
And I lie down but to sleep in bed,   35
For my sulking, skulking, coal black soul!

When I was a half of the man I was
And serve me right as the preachers warn,
(Sighed the old ram rod, dying of downfall),
No flailing calf or cat in a flame   40
Or hickory bull in milky grass
But a black sheep with a crumpled horn,
At last the soul from its foul mousehole
Slunk pouting out when the limp time came;
And I gave my soul a blind, slashed eye,   45
Gristle and rind, and a roarer's life,
And I shoved it into the coal black sky
To find a woman's soul for a wife.

Now I am a man no more no more
And a black reward for a roaring life,   50
(Sighed the old ram rod, dying of strangers),
Tidy and cursed in my dove cooed room
I lie down thin and hear the good bells jaw—
For, oh, my soul found a sunday wife
In the coal black sky and she bore angels!   55
Harpies around me out of her womb!
Chastity prays for me, piety sings,
Innocence sweetens my last black breath,
Modesty hides my thighs in her wings,
And all the deadly virtues plague my death!   60

---

29. **tom**: tomcat. 46. **roarer's**: rioter's, bully boy's. 57. **harpies**: in classical mythology,
foul monsters, half-woman and half-bird, who prey on humans.

Weldon Kees   *(1914–1955)*

River Song

By the public hook for the private eye,
Near the neutral river where the children were,
I was hung for the street, to watch the sky.

When they strung me there, I waved like a flag
Near the bright blue river where the children played,   5
And my smile became part of the cultural lag.

I named three martyrs. My mother came
To the grayish river where the children stared:
"My son, you have honored the family name."

I was happy. Then a parade went by   10
Near the shadowy river where the children waved,
And the uniforms made me shiver and cry.

I tried to get down. What I had learned
Near the sunless river where the children screamed
Was only pain. My ropemarks burned.   15

But I couldn't move. Had I been thrown
By the darkening river where the children failed,
Or had I come there quite alone?

The bands were playing when they cut me down
By the dirty river where the children cried,   20
And a man made a speech in a long black gown.

He called me a hero. I didn't care.
The river ran blood and the children died.
And I wanted to die, but they left me there.

Five

We had the notion it was dawn,
But it was only torches on the height.
The truce was signed, but the attack goes on.

FIVE   From "Five Villanelles."

The major fell down on the blackened lawn
And cried like a fool; his face was white.   5
We had the notion it was dawn.

On a bombed wall someone had drawn
A picture of a nude hermaphrodite.
The truce was signed, but the attack goes on.

Our food was rotten, all our water gone.   10
We had penicillin and dynamite,
And had the notion it was dawn

Because a cold gleam, fitful, gray, and wan,
Held for a moment in the signal's light.
The truce was signed, but the attack goes on.   15

We helped to choose these fields we crawl upon.
Sired in caskets, born to die at night,
We had the notion it was dawn.
The truce was signed, but the attack goes on.

Randall Jarrell   *(1914–1965)*

Jerome

Each day brings its toad, each night its dragon.
Der heilige Hieronymus—his lion is at the zoo—
Listens, listens. All the long, soft, summer day
Dreams affright his couch, the deep boils like a pot.
As the sun sets, the last patient rises,   5
Says to him, *Father;* trembles, turns away.

Often, to the lion, the saint said, *Son.*
To the man the saint says—but the man is gone.
Under a plaque of Gradiva, at gloaming,
The old man boils an egg. When he has eaten   10

JEROME   The poet superimposes on a modern psychiatrist the image of St. Jerome (340?–420), traditionally portrayed (notably by Albrecht Dürer) as a desert hermit or in his study translating the Bible into Latin. He is usually shown with a lion. On one occasion when a lion with a wounded paw interrupted his lecture and sent his disciples into flight, Jerome drew out a thorn and dressed the wound; and the lion remained faithfully with his benefactor. **9. plaque of Gradiva:** the frontispiece of Wilhelm Jensen's novel *Gradiva* shows a bas relief of a girl stepping along gracefully; Freud did a study of this novel that shows how repressed sexual desires reappear in neurotic patterns.

He listens a while. The patients have not stopped.
At midnight, he lies down where his patients lay.

All night the old man whispers to the night.
It listens evenly. The great armored paws
Of its forelegs put together in reflection,   15
It thinks: *Where Ego was, there Id shall be.*
The world wrestles with it and is changed into it
And after a long time changes it. The dragon

Listens as the old man says, at dawn: *I see*
—There is an old man, naked, in a desert, by a cliff.   20
He has set out his books, his hat, his ink, his shears
Among scorpions, toads, the wild beasts of the desert.
I lie beside him—I am a lion.
He kneels listening. He holds in his left hand

The stone with which he beats his breast, and holds   25
In his right hand, the pen with which he puts
Into his book, the words of the angel:
The angel up into whose face he looks.
But the angel does not speak. He looks into the face
Of the night, and the night says—but the night is gone.   30

He has slept. . . . At morning, when man's flesh is young
And man's soul thankful for it knows not what,
The air is washed, and smells of boiling coffee,
And the sun lights it. The old man walks placidly
To the grocer's; walks on, under leaves, in light,   35
To a lynx, a leopard—he has come:

The man holds out a lump of liver to the lion,
And the lion licks the man's hand with his tongue.

John Berryman   *(1914–1972)*

A Prayer for the Self

Who am I worthless that You spent such pains
and take may pains again?
I do not understand; but I believe
Jonquils respond with wit to the teasing breeze.

---

16. **Where Ego . . . be:** a reversal of Freud's famous remark, "Where Id was, there Ego shall be," at the close of *New Introductory Lectures*, ch. 21.
A PRAYER 1. **Who . . . pains:** Cf. "What is man, that thou are mindful of him?" (Psalms 8:4).

Induct me down my secrets. Stiffen this heart   5
to stand their horrifying cries, O cushion
the first the second shocks, will to a halt
in mid-air there demons who would be at me.

May fade before, sweet morning on sweet morning,
I wake my dreams, my fan-mail go astray,   10
and do me little goods I have not thought of,
ingenious & beneficial Father.

Ease in their passing my beloved friends,
all others too I have cared for in a traveling life,
anyone anywhere indeed. Lift up   15
sober toward truth a scared self-estimate.

Alun Lewis   (1915–1944)

The Peasants

The dwarf barefooted, chanting
Behind the oxen by the lake,
Stepping lightly and lazily among the thorntrees
Dusky and dazed with sunlight, half awake;

The women breaking stones upon the highway,   5
Walking erect with burdens on their heads,
One body growing in another body,
Creation touching verminous straw beds.

Across scorched hills and trampled crops
The soldiers straggle by.   10
History staggers in their wake.
The peasants watch them die.

Robert Lowell *(1917–)*

After the Surprising Conversions

September twenty-second, Sir: today
I answer. In the latter part of May,
Hard on our Lord's Ascension, it began
To be more sensible. A gentleman
Of more than common understanding, strict   5
In morals, pious in behavior, kicked
Against our goad. A man of some renown,
An useful, honored person in the town,
He came of melancholy parents; prone
To secret spells, for years they kept alone—   10
His uncle, I believe, was killed of it:
Good people, but of too much or little wit.
I preached one Sabbath on a text from Kings;
He showed concernment for his soul. Some things
In his experience were hopeful. He   15
Would sit and watch the wind knocking a tree
And praise this countryside our Lord has made.
Once when a poor man's heifer died, he laid
A shilling on the doorsill; though a thirst
For loving shook him like a snake, he durst   20
Not entertain much hope of his estate
In heaven. Once we saw him sitting late
Behind his attic window by a light
That guttered on his Bible; through that night
He meditated terror, and he seemed   25
Beyond advice or reason, for he dreamed
That he was called to trumpet Judgment Day
To Concord. In the latter part of May
He cut his throat. And though the coroner
Judged him delirious, soon a noisome stir   30
Palsied our village. At Jehovah's nod
Satan seemed more let loose amongst us: God
Abandoned us to Satan, and he pressed
Us hard, until we thought we could not rest

AFTER THE SURPRISING CONVERSIONS **2. I answer:** The speaker is Jonathan Edwards (1703–58), the Calvinist theologian and preacher, at the time (1735) minister at Northampton, Mass., which was undergoing an intense religious revival. The poem is based on an account (in the form of a letter) of the conversion and subsequent suicide of his uncle, Josiah Hawley, in Edwards' *A Faithful Narrative of the Surprising Work of God in the Conversion of Many Hundred Souls* (1736), better known as the *Narrative of Surprising Conversions.* **3. Lord's Ascension:** the Feast of the Ascension of Christ into Heaven, forty days after Easter. **4. sensible:** effectual.

Till we had done with life. Content was gone. 35
All the good work was quashed. We were undone.
The breath of God had carried out a planned
And sensible withdrawal from this land;
The multitude, once unconcerned with doubt,
Once neither callous, curious nor devout, 40
Jumped at broad noon, as though some peddler groaned
At it in its familiar twang: "My friend,
Cut your own throat. Cut your own throat. Now! Now!"
September twenty-second, Sir, the bough
Cracks with the unpicked apples, and at dawn 45
The small-mouth bass breaks water, gorged with spawn.

Mary Winslow

Her Irish maids could never spoon out mush
Or orange-juice enough; the body cools
And smiles as a sick child
Who adds up figures, and a hush
Grips at the poised relations sipping sherry 5
And tracking up the carpets of her four
Room kingdom. On the rigid Charles, in snow,
Charon, the Lubber, clambers from his wherry,
And stops her hideous baby-squawks and yells,
Wit's clownish afterthought. Nothing will go 10
Again. Even the gelded picador
Baiting the twinned runt bulls
With walrus horns before the Spanish Belles
Is veiled with all the childish bibelots.

Mary Winslow is dead. Out on the Charles 15
The shells hold water and their oarblades drag,
Littered with captivated ducks, and now
The bell-rope in King's Chapel Tower unsnarls
And bells the bestial cow
From Boston Common; she is dead. But stop, 20
Neighbor, these pillows prop
Her that her terrified and child's cold eyes
Glass what they're not: our Copley ancestress,
Grandiloquent, square-jowled and worldly-wise,
A Cleopatra in her housewife's dress; 25
Nothing will go again. The bells cry: "Come,

MARY WINSLOW   The poet's grandmother. **7. Charles:** the Charles River. **8. Charon, the Lubber:** the mythical ferryman of the dead across the Styx. "Lubber" means "clumsy." **19–20. cow . . . Common:** the Boston Common originally served as a pasture for cows. **23. our Copley ancestress:** one whose portrait was made by the celebrated American painter, John Singleton Copley (1738?–1815).

Come home," the babbling Chapel belfry cries:
"Come, Mary Winslow, come; I bell thee home."

Skunk Hour

(For Elizabeth Bishop)

Nautilus Island's hermit
heiress still lives through winter in her Spartan cottage;
her sheep still graze above the sea.
Her son's a bishop. Her farmer
is first selectman in our village;   5
she's in her dotage.

Thirsting for
the hierarchic privacy
of Queen Victoria's century,
she buys up all   10
the eyesores facing her shore,
and lets them fall.

The season's ill—
we've lost our summer millionaire,
who seemed to leap from an L. L. Bean   15
catalogue. His nine-knot yawl
was auctioned off to lobstermen.
A red fox stain covers Blue Hill.

And now our fairy
decorator brightens his shop for fall;   20
his fishnet's filled with orange cork,
orange, his cobbler's bench and awl;
there is no money in his work,
he'd rather marry.

One dark night,   25
my Tudor Ford climbed the hill's skull;

SKUNK HOUR   **5. first selectman:** senior town officer. **our village:** "a declining Maine
sea town" (Lowell). **9. Queen Victoria's century:** the nineteenth century; Victoria was
queen of England from 1837 to 1901. **15. L. L. Bean:** a Maine mail-order dealer in
sports equipment and clothing. **18. A red . . . Hill:** "The red fox stain was merely
meant to describe the rusty reddish color of autumn on Blue Hill, a Maine mountain
near where we were living. I had seen foxes playing on the road one night, and I think
the words have sinister and askew suggestions" (Lowell). **25. One . . . night:** "I hoped
my reader would remember John of the Cross's poem" (Lowell)—a poem about a girl
stealing forth one dark night for an ecstatic meeting with her divine lover. "My night is
not gracious, but secular, puritan, and agnostical. An Existentialist night. Somewhere in
my mind was a passage from Sartre or Camus about reaching some point of final darkness where the one free act is suicide. Out of this comes the march and affirmation, an
ambiguous one, of my skunks in the last two stanzas" (Lowell).

I watched for love-cars. Lights turned down,
they lay together, hull to hull,
where the graveyard shelves on the town. . . .
My mind's not right. 30

A car radio bleats,
"Love, O careless Love. . . ." I hear
my ill-spirit sob in each blood cell,
as if my hand were at its throat. . . .
I myself am hell; 35
nobody's here—

only skunks, that search
in the moonlight for a bite to eat.
They march on their soles up Main Street:
white stripes, moonstruck eyes' red fire 40
under the chalk-dry and spar spire
of the Trinitarian Church.

I stand on top
of our back steps and breathe the rich air—
a mother skunk with her column of kittens swills the garbage pail. 45
She jabs her wedge-head in a cup
of sour cream, drops her ostrich tail,
and will not scare.

Waking in the Blue

The night attendant, a B. U. sophomore,
rouses from the mare's-nest of his drowsy head
propped on *The Meaning of Meaning.*
He catwalks down our corridor.
Azure day 5
makes my agonized blue window bleaker.
Crows maunder on the petrified fairway.
Absence! My heart grows tense
as though a harpoon were sparring for the kill.
(This is the house for the "mentally ill.") 10

What use is my sense of humor?
I grin at Stanley, now sunk in his sixties,
once a Harvard all-American fullback,

35. I . . . hell: adapted from Satan's words in Milton's *Paradise Lost* (iv.75) as he
makes his way to Eden to spy on and tempt Adam and Eve: "Which way I fly is Hell;
my self am Hell."
WAKING 1. B. U.: Boston University. 3. The Meaning of Meaning: a book by C. K.
Ogden and I. A. Richards (1920). 10. house . . . ill: McLean's, a private mental
hospital near Boston (see 1. 25).

(if such were possible!)
still hoarding the build of a boy in his twenties,   15
as he soaks, a ramrod
with the muscle of a seal
in his long tub,
vaguely urinous from the Victorian plumbing.
A kingly granite profile in a crimson golf-cap,   20
worn all day, all night,
he thinks only of his figure,
of slimming on sherbet and ginger ale—
more cut off from words than a seal.

This is the way day breaks in Bowditch Hall at McLean's;   25
the hooded night lights bring out "Bobbie,"
Porcellian '29,
a replica of Louis XVI
without the wig—
redolent and roly-poly as a sperm whale,   30
as he swashbuckles about in his birthday suit
and horses at chairs.

These victorious figures of bravado ossified young.

In between the limits of day,
hours and hours go by under the crew haircuts   35
and slightly too little nonsensical bachelor twinkle
of the Roman Catholic attendants.
(There are no Mayflower
screwballs in the Catholic Church.)

After a hearty New England breakfast,   40
I weigh two hundred pounds
this morning. Cock of the walk,
I strut in my turtle necked French sailor's jersey
before the metal shaving mirrors,
and see the shaky future grow familiar   45
in the pinched, indigenous faces
of these thoroughbred mental cases,
twice my age and half my weight.
We are all old-timers,
each of us holds a locked razor.   50

---

27. **Porcellian**: an exclusive Harvard undergraduate club. 38. **Mayflower**: The poet is himself the member of a distinguished old American Protestant family (although a Roman Catholic convert for a time), which included a number of writers and statesmen; this theme is suggested in the "pinched, indigenous faces" of l. 46.

For the Union Dead

"Relinquunt Omnia Servare Rem Publicam."

The old South Boston Aquarium stands
in a Sahara of snow now. Its broken windows are boarded.
The bronze weathervane cod has lost half its scales.
The airy tanks are dry.

Once my nose crawled like a snail on the glass;   5
my hand tingled
to burst the bubbles
drifting from the noses of the cowed, compliant fish.

My hand draws back. I often sigh still
for the dark downward and vegetating kingdom   10
of the fish and reptile. One morning last March,
I pressed against the new barbed and galvanized

fence on the Boston Common. Behind their cage,
yellow dinosaur steamshovels were grunting
as they cropped up tons of mush and grass   15
to gouge their underworld garage.

Parking spaces luxuriate like civic
sandpiles in the heart of Boston.
A girdle of orange, Puritan-pumpkin colored girders
braces the tingling Statehouse,   20

shaking over the excavations, as it faces Colonel Shaw
and his bell-cheeked Negro infantry
on St. Gaudens' shaking Civil War relief,
propped by a plank splint against the garage's earthquake.

Two months after marching through Boston,   25
half the regiment was dead;
at the dedication,
William James could almost hear the bronze Negroes breathe.

Their monument sticks like a fishbone
in the city's throat.   30
Its Colonel is as lean
as a compass-needle.

FOR THE UNION DEAD **Epigraph:** "They gave up everything to save the Republic," a version of Charles W. Eliot's inscription on the statue on Boston Common dedicated to Col. Robert Gould Shaw, leader of the first Negro regiment from Boston in the Civil War. The statue, by Augustus Saint-Gaudens (1897), shows Shaw on horseback leading his troops.

He has an angry wrenlike vigilance,
a greyhound's gentle tautness;
he seems to wince at pleasure,   35
and suffocate for privacy.

He is out of bounds now. He rejoices in man's lovely,
peculiar power to choose life and die—
when he leads his black soldiers to death,
he cannot bend his back.   40

On a thousand small town New England greens,
the old white churches hold their air
of sparse, sincere rebellion; frayed flags
quilt the graveyards of the Grand Army of the Republic.

The stone statues of the abstract Union Soldier   45
grow slimmer and younger each year—
wasp-waisted, they doze over muskets
and muse through their sideburns . . .

Shaw's father wanted no monument
except the ditch,   50
where his son's body was thrown
and lost with his "niggers."

The ditch is nearer.
There are no statues for the last war here;
on Boylston Street, a commercial photograph   55
shows Hiroshima boiling

over a Mosler Safe, the "Rock of Ages"
that survived the blast. Space is nearer.
When I crouch to my television set,
the drained faces of Negro school-children rise like balloons,   60

Colonel Shaw
is riding on his bubble,
he waits
for the blessèd break.

The Aquarium is gone. Everywhere,   65
giant finned cars nose forward like fish;
a savage servility
slides by on grease.

---

44. Grand . . . Republic: the Northern (Union) forces in the Civil War. **60.
drained . . . school-children:** during the resistance to desegregation of Southern
schools.

Lawrence Ferlinghetti *(1919–)*

A Coney Island of the Mind: 17

This life is not a circus where
the shy performing dogs of love
     look on
as time flicks out
    its tricky whip   5
      to race us thru our paces
Yet gay parading floats drift by
    decorated with gorgeous gussies in silk tights
    and attended by moithering monkeys
       make-believe monks   10
      horny hiawathas
   and baboons astride tame tigers
    with ladies inside
   while googly horns make merrygoround music
and pantomimic pierrots castrate disaster   15
    with strange sad laughter
 and gory gorillas toss tender maidens heavenward
  while cakewalkers and carnie hustlers
   all gassed to the gills
    strike playbill poses   20
  and stagger after every
      wheeling thing
While still around the ring
    lope the misshapen camels of lust
   and all us Emmett Kelly clowns   25
     always making up imaginary scenes
with all our masks for faces
     even eat fake Last Suppers
      at collapsible tables
   and mocking cross ourselves   30
      in sawdust crosses

And yet gobble up at last
     to shrive our circus souls
   the also imaginary
      wafers of grace   35

A CONEY ISLAND **8. gorgeous gussies:** girls resembling "Gorgeous Gussie" Moran, an American tennis player, best known on the courts for her daring costumes. **9. moithering:** laboring; babbling. **15. pierrots:** sad-faced, ineffectual clowns. **18. cakewalkers:** strutting dancers. **carnie:** carnival, circus. **25. Emmett Kelly:** a famous clown. **35. wafers of grace:** communion wafers.

Robert Duncan *(1919–   )*

This Place Rumord to Have Been Sodom

might have been.
Certainly these ashes might have been pleasures.
Pilgrims on their way to the Holy Places remark
this place. Isn't it plain to all
that these mounds were palaces? This was once   5
a city among men, a gathering together of spirit.
It was measured by the Lord and found wanting.

It was measured by the Lord and found wanting,
destroyd by the angels that inhabit longing.
Surely this is Great Sodom where such cries   10
as if men were birds flying up from the swamp
ring in our ears, where such fears that were once
desires walk, almost spectacular,
stalking the desolate circles, red eyed.

This place rumord to have been a City surely was,   15
separated from us by the hand of the Lord.
The devout have laid out gardens in the desert,
drawn water from springs where the light was blighted.
How tenderly they must attend these friendships
or all is lost. All *is* lost.   20
Only the faithful hold this place green.

Only the faithful hold this place green
where the crown of fiery thorns descends.
Men that once lusted grow listless. A spirit
wrapped in a cloud, ashes more than ashes,   25
fire more than fire, ascends.
Only these new friends gather joyous here,
where the world like Great Sodom lies under fear.

The world like Great Sodom lies under Love
and knows not the hand of the Lord that moves.   30
This the friends teach where such cries
as if men were birds fly up from the crowds
gatherd and howling in the heat of the sun.

THIS PLACE   When Lot was visited in Sodom by two angels, the men of Sodom
wanted to assault the angels sexually, and God destroyed the city by raining down fire
and brimstone (Genesis 19:1–28). **3. Holy Places:** e.g., Bethlehem, Jerusalem.

In the Lord Whom the friends have named at last Love
the images and loves of the friends never die.   35

This place rumord to have been Sodom is blessd
in the Lord's eyes.

Richard Wilbur   (1921–   )

Love Calls Us to the Things of This World

The eyes open to a cry of pulleys,
And spirited from sleep, the astounded soul
Hangs for a moment bodiless and simple
As false dawn.
                 Outside the open window
The morning air is all awash with angels.   5

Some are in bed-sheets, some are in blouses,
Some are in smocks: but truly there they are.
Now they are rising together in calm swells
Of halcyon feeling, filling whatever they wear
With the deep joy of their impersonal breathing;   10

Now they are flying in place, conveying
The terrible speed of their omnipresence, moving
And staying like white water; and now of a sudden
They swoon down into so rapt a quiet
That nobody seems to be there.
                        The soul shrinks   15

From all that it is about to remember,
From the punctual rape of every blessèd day,
And cries,
          "Oh, let there be nothing on earth but laundry,
Nothing but rosy hands in the rising steam
And clear dances done in the sight of heaven."   20

Yet, as the sun acknowledges
With a warm look the world's hunks and colors,
The soul descends once more in bitter love
To accept the waking body, saying now
In a changed voice as the man yawns and rises,   25

LOVE CALLS   The title is from St. Augustine's commentary on the Psalms. **2. spirited:**
in one sense, stolen or kidnapped. **9. halcyon feeling:** warmth and buoyancy, evoking
the days when the halcyon (kingfisher) supposedly nests on the sea and calms it.

"Bring them down from their ruddy gallows;
Let there be clean linen for the backs of thieves;
Let lovers go fresh and sweet to be undone,
And the heaviest nuns walk in a pure floating
Of dark habits,
                keeping their difficult balance."   30

Beasts

Beasts in their major freedom
Slumber in peace tonight. The gull on his ledge
Dreams in the guts of himself the moon-plucked waves below,
And the sunfish leans on a stone, slept
By the lyric water,   5

In which the spotless feet
Of deer make dulcet splashes, and to which
The ripped mouse, safe in the owl's talon, cries
Concordance. Here there is no such harm
And no such darkness   10

As the selfsame moon observes
Where, warped in window-glass, it sponsors now
The werewolf's painful change. Turning his head away
On the sweaty bolster, he tries to remember
The mood of manhood,   15

But lies at last, as always,
Letting it happen, the fierce fur soft to his face,
Hearing with sharper ears the wind's exciting minors,
The leaves' panic, and the degradation
Of the heavy streams.   20

Meantime, at high windows
Far from thicket and pad-fall, suitors of excellence
Sigh and turn from their work to construe again the painful
Beauty of heaven, the lucid moon
And the risen hunter,   25

Making such dreams for men
As told will break their hearts as always, bringing
Monsters into the city, crows on the public statues,

---

26. gallows: in one sense, clotheslines.
BEASTS 13. werewolf's . . . change: the change of the resistant man into a devouring
wolf is triggered by the moonlight. 18. minors: sounds in a minor key. 19. degradation:
wearing away of earth. 25. risen hunter: the constellation Orion.

Navies fed to the fish in the dark
Unbridled waters.   30

Advice to a Prophet

When you come, as you soon must, to the streets of our city,
Mad-eyed from stating the obvious,
Not proclaiming our fall but begging us
In God's name to have self-pity,

Spare us all word of the weapons, their force and range,   5
The long numbers that rocket the mind;
Our slow, unreckoning hearts will be left behind,
Unable to fear what is too strange.

Nor shall you scare us with talk of the death of the race.
How should we dream of this place without us?—   10
The sun mere fire, the leaves untroubled about us,
A stone look on the stone's face?

Speak of the world's own change. Though we cannot conceive
Of an undreamt thing, we know to our cost
How the dreamt cloud crumbles, the vines are blackened by frost, 15
How the view alters. We could believe,

If you told us so, that the white-tailed deer will slip
Into perfect shade, grown perfectly shy,
The lark avoid the reaches of our eye,
The jack-pine lose its knuckled grip   20

On the cold ledge, and every torrent burn
As Xanthus once, its gliding trout
Stunned in a twinkling. What should we be without
The dolphin's arc, the dove's return,

These things in which we have seen ourselves and spoken?   25
Ask us, prophet, how we shall call
Our natures forth when that live tongue is all
Dispelled, that glass obscured or broken

In which we have said the rose of our love and the clean
Horse of our courage, in which beheld   30
The singing locust of the soul unshelled,
And all we mean or wish to mean.

ADVICE TO A PROPHET   **22. Xanthus:** "Hephaestus, invoked by Achilles, scalded the
river Xanthus (Scamander) in *Iliad* xxi" (Wilbur).

Ask us, ask us whether with the worldless rose
Our hearts shall fail us; come demanding
Whether there shall be lofty or long standing 35
When the bronze annals of the oak-tree close.

Anthony Hecht *(1922–   )*

The Dover Bitch

A Criticism of Life

for Andrews Wanning

So there stood Matthew Arnold and this girl
With the cliffs of England crumbling away behind them,
And he said to her, "Try to be true to me,
And I'll do the same for you, for things are bad
All over, etc., etc." 5
Well now, I knew this girl. It's true she had read
Sophocles in a fairly good translation
And caught that bitter allusion to the sea,
But all the time he was talking she had in mind
The notion of what his whiskers would feel like 10
On the back of her neck. She told me later on
That after a while she got to looking out
At the lights across the channel, and really felt sad,
Thinking of all the wine and enormous beds
And blandishments in French and the perfumes. 15
And then she got really angry. To have been brought
All the way down from London, and then be addressed
As sort of a mournful cosmic last resort
Is really tough on a girl, and she was pretty.
Anyway, she watched him pace the room 20
And finger his watch-chain and seem to sweat a bit,
And then she said one or two unprintable things.
But you mustn't judge her by that. What I mean to say is,
She's really all right. I still see her once in a while
And she always treats me right. We have a drink 25
And I give her a good time, and perhaps it's a year
Before I see her again, but there she is,
Running to fat, but dependable as they come,
And sometimes I bring her a bottle of *Nuit d'Amour*.

THE DOVER BITCH   See Matthew Arnold's "Dover Beach"; the dictum that poetry is
"a criticism of life" is also Arnold's. **29. Nuit d'Amour:** Night of Love (a perfume).

Third Avenue in Sunlight

Third Avenue in sunlight. Nature's error.
Already the bars are filled and John is there.
Beneath a plentiful lady over the mirror
He tilts his glass in the mild mahogany air.

I think of him when he first got out of college,   5
Serious, thin, unlikely to succeed;
For several months he hung around the Village,
Boldly T-shirted, unfettered but unfreed.

Now he confides to a stranger, "I was first scout,
And kept my glimmers peeled till after dark.   10
Our outfit had as its sign a bloody knout,
We met behind the museum in Central Park.

Of course, we were kids." But still those savages,
War-painted, a flap of leather at the loins,
File silently against him. Hostages   15
Are never taken. One summer, in Des Moines,

They entered his hotel room, tomahawks
Flashing like barracuda. He tried to pray.
Three years of treatment. Occasionally he talks
About how he almost didn't get away.   20

Daily the prowling sunlight whets its knife
Along the sidewalk. We almost never meet.
In the Rembrandt dark he lifts his amber life.
My bar is somewhat further down the street.

Birdwatchers of America

> *I suffer now continually from ver-
> tigo, and today, 23rd of January,
> 1862, I received a singular warning:
> I felt the wind of the wing of mad-
> ness pass over me.*
> BAUDELAIRE, *Journals*

It's all very well to dream of a dove that saves,
    Picasso's or the Pope's,

THIRD AVENUE   The poem is set in New York City. **7. Village:** Greenwich Village.
10. glimmers: old-fashioned slang for "eyes." **12. museum:** the Metropolitan Museum
of Art, located on the edge of Central Park. **23. Rembrandt:** the seventeenth-century
Dutch painter, noted for his treatment of light and shade.

The one that annually coos in Our Lady's ear
                    Half the world's hopes,
And the other one that shall cunningly engineer   5
The retirement of all businessmen to their graves,
                    And when this is brought about
Make us the loving brothers of every lout—

But in our part of the country a false dusk
                    Lingers for hours; it steams   10
From the soaked hay, wades in the cloudy woods,
                    Engendering other dreams.
Formless and soft beyond the fence it broods
Or rises as a faint and rotten musk
                    Out of a broken stalk.   15
There are some things of which we seldom talk;

For instance, the woman next door, whom we hear at night,
                    Claims that when she was small
She found a man stone dead near the cedar trees
                    After the first snowfall.   20
The air was clear. He seemed in ultimate peace
Except that he had no eyes. Rigid and bright
                    Upon the forehead, furred
With a light frost, crouched an outrageous bird.

Philip Larkin   (1922–   )

An Arundel Tomb

        Side by side, their faces blurred,
        The earl and countess lie in stone,
        Their proper habits vaguely shown
        As jointed armor, stiffened pleat,
        And that faint hint of the absurd—   5
        The little dogs under their feet.

        Such plainness of the pre-baroque

BIRDWATCHERS   2. **Picasso's . . . Pope's:** Pablo Picasso made several famous sketches of the dove of peace, some used as Communist Party propaganda; the Pope's is the dove as a symbol of the Holy Ghost.
AN ARUNDEL TOMB   A tomb belonging to an earl of that title (Arundel Castle in Sussex was built in the twelfth century); the details of the tomb effigies are typical of many medieval figures, later to be succeeded by more elaborate and ornate baroque tomb designs.

Hardly involves the eye, until
It meets his left-hand gauntlet, still
Clasped empty in the other; and
One sees, with a sharp tender shock,
His hand withdrawn, holding her hand.

They would not think to lie so long.
Such faithfulness in effigy
Was just a detail friends would see:
A sculptor's sweet commissioned grace
Thrown off in helping to prolong
The Latin names around the base.

They would not guess how early in
Their supine stationary voyage
The air would change to soundless damage,
Turn the old tenantry away;
How soon succeeding eyes begin
To look, not read. Rigidly they

Persisted, linked, through lengths and breadths
Of time. Snow fell, undated. Light
Each summer thronged the glass. A bright
Litter of birdcalls strewed the same
Bone-riddled ground. And up the paths
The endless altered people came,

Washing at their identity.
Now, helpless in the hollow of
An unarmorial age, a trough
Of smoke in slow suspended skeins
Above their scrap of history,
Only an attitude remains:

Time has transfigured them into
Untruth. The stone fidelity
They hardly meant has come to be
Their final blazon, and to prove
Our almost-instinct almost true:
What will survive of us is love.

Church Going

Once I am sure there's nothing going on
I step inside, letting the door thud shut.
Another church: matting, seats, and stone,

9. **gauntlet:** glove. 27. **glass:** the stained glass of the church which contains the tomb. 29. **ground:** the churchyard outside. 40. **blazon:** record of virtues or achievements; also, coat of arms.

And little books; sprawlings of flowers, cut
For Sunday, brownish now; some brass and stuff   5
Up at the holy end; the small neat organ;
And a tense, musty, unignorable silence,
Brewed God knows how long. Hatless, I take off
My cycle-clips in awkward reverence,

Move forward, run my hand around the font.   10
From where I stand, the roof looks almost new—
Cleaned, or restored? Someone would know: I don't.
Mounting the lectern, I peruse a few
Hectoring large-scale verses, and pronounce
"Here endeth" much more loudly than I'd meant.   15
The echoes snigger briefly. Back at the door
I sign the book, donate an Irish sixpence,
Reflect the place was not worth stopping for.

Yet stop I did: in fact I often do,
And always end much at a loss like this,   20
Wondering what to look for; wondering, too,
When churches fall completely out of use
What we shall turn them into, if we shall keep
A few cathedrals chronically on show,
Their parchment, plate and pyx in locked cases,   25
And let the rest rent-free to rain and sheep.
Shall we avoid them as unlucky places?

Or, after dark, will dubious women come
To make their children touch a particular stone;
Pick simples for a cancer; or on some   30
Advised night see walking a dead one?
Power of some sort or other will go on
In games, in riddles, seemingly at random;
But superstition, like belief, must die,
And what remains when disbelief has gone?   35
Grass, weedy pavement, brambles, buttress, sky,

A shape less recognizable each week,
A purpose more obscure. I wonder who
Will be the last, the very last, to seek
This place for what it was; one of the crew   40
That tap and jot and know what rood-lofts were?
Some ruin-bibber, randy for antique,
Or Christmas-addict, counting on a whiff
Of gown-and-bands and organ-pipes and myrrh?
Or will he be my representative,   45

CHURCH GOING   **25. pyx:** the container which holds the consecrated wafer of the Communion. **30. simples:** herbal cures. **41. rood-lofts:** a loft or gallery forming the top of a rood-screen, which bears a rood (crucifix) on it and separates the nave from the choir of the church. **44. gown-and-bands:** formal priestly dress.

Bored, uninformed, knowing the ghostly silt
Dispersed, yet tending to this cross of ground
Through suburb scrub because it held unspilt
So long and equably what since is found
Only in separation—marriage, and birth,   50
And death, and thoughts of these—for which was built
This special shell? For, though I've no idea
What this accoutred frowsty barn is worth,
It pleases me to stand in silence here;

A serious house on serious earth it is,   55
In whose blent air all our compulsions meet,
Are recognized, and robed as destinies.
And that much never can be obsolete,
Since someone will forever be surprising
A hunger in himself to be more serious,   60
And gravitating with it to this ground,
Which, he once heard, was proper to grow wise in,
If only that so many dead lie round.

Love Songs in Age

She kept her songs, they took so little space,
   The covers pleased her:
One bleached from lying in a sunny place,
One marked in circles by a vase of water,
One mended, when a tidy fit had seized her,   5
   And colored, by her daughter—
So they had waited, till in widowhood
She found them, looking for something else, and stood

Relearning how each frank submissive chord
   Had ushered in   10
Word after sprawling hyphenated word,
And the unfailing sense of being young
Spread out like a spring-woken tree, wherein
   That hidden freshness sung,
That certainty of time laid up in store   15
As when she played them first. But, even more,

The glare of that much-mentioned brilliance, love,
   Broke out, to show
Its bright incipience sailing above,
Still promising to solve, and satisfy,   20
And set unchangeably in order. So
   To pile them back, to cry,
Was hard, without lamely admitting how
It had not done so then, and could not now.

---

46. ghostly: in its older sense, sacred. 53. frowsty: stale, musty. 56. blent: blended, fused.

Louis Simpson (1923–   )

On the Lawn at the Villa

On the lawn at the villa—
That's the way to start, eh, reader?
We know where we stand—somewhere expensive—
You and I *imperturbes*, as Walt would say,
Before the diversions of wealth, you and I *engagés*.   5

On the lawn at the villa
Sat a manufacturer of explosives,
His wife from Paris,
And a young man named Bruno,

And myself, being American,   10
Willing to talk to these malefactors,
The manufacturer of explosives, and so on,
But somehow superior. By that I mean democratic.
It's complicated, being an American,
Having the money and the bad conscience, both at the same time.   15
Perhaps, after all, this is not the right subject for a poem.

We were all sitting there paralyzed
In the hot Tuscan afternoon,
And the bodies of the machine-gun crew were draped over the balcony.
So we sat there all afternoon.   20

Alan Dugan (1923–   )

Funeral Oration for a Mouse

This, Lord, was an anxious brother and
a living diagram of fear: full of health himself,
he brought diseases like a gift
to give his hosts. Masked in a cat's moustache
but sounding like a bird, he was a ghost   5

ON THE LAWN   **4. imperturbes . . . Walt:** a joke at Walt Whitman's use of French
phrases, as in the title of his poem, "Me Imperturbe" ("Untroubled Me"). **5. engagés:**
politically committed to liberal or leftist causes.

of lesser noises and a kitchen pest
for whom some ladies stand on chairs. So,
Lord, accept our felt though minor guilt
for an ignoble foe and ancient sin:
    the murder of a guest   10
who shared our board: just once he ate
    too slowly, dying in our trap
from necessary hunger and a broken back.

Humors of love aside, the mousetrap was our own
    opinion of the mouse, but for the mouse   15
    it was the tree of knowledge with
    its consequential fruit, the true cross
and the gate of hell. Even to approach
    it makes him like or better than
its maker: his courage as a spoiler never once   20
impressed us, but to go out cautiously at night,
    into the dining room—what bravery, what
    hunger! Younger by far, in dying he
was older than us all: his mobile tail and nose
spasmed in the pinch of our annoyance. Why,   25
then, at that snapping sound, did we, victorious,
    begin to laugh without delight?

Our stomachs, deep in an analysis
    of their own stolen baits
(and asking, "Lord, Host, to whom are we the pests?"),   30
    contracted and demanded a retreat
from our machine and its effect of death,
    as if the mouse's fingers, skinnier
than hairpins and as breakable as cheese,
    could grasp our grasping lives, and in   35
    their drowning movement pull us under too,
into the common death beyond the mousetrap.

Actual Vision of Morning's Extrusion

Gray smoke rose from the morning ground
and separated into spheres. The smoke
or fog of each sphere coiled upon itself
like snakes at love, and hardened into brains:
the corals in the ocean of first light.   5
These brains grew shells. Mother of pearl, out

FUNERAL ORATION   **17. consequential fruit:** momentous outcome, inevitable result (i.e., the Crucifixion and the possibility of damnation follow from the Fall, the eating of the fruit of the Tree of Knowledge).

MORNING'S EXTRUSION   **1–2 Gray . . . spheres:** suggesting the explosion of the atomic bomb in the coral atoll of Eniwetok, producing a brain-shaped cloud.

clattered the bones! Two ivies intertwined
ran down them searchingly, the red and white
of arteries and nerves, and found their ends.
Nerves hummed in the wind: the running blood,   10
in pulsing out a heart, induced a warm,
red haze of flesh around a hollow tube,
writhing with appetite, ejection, love,
and hardened in the temperature of dawn.
"Done!" said the clocks, and gave alarm.   15
Eyes popped into heads as tears amazed.
All hair stood out. All moved and rose
and took a breath: two gasping voids
turned blue with it around the heart.
Shocked into teeth and nails and wrapped   20
in winding sheets of skin, all souls walked
to test their creatures in their joints,
chinks, and armors as the walking dead,
curious as to what the water, partial sun-light,
ground and mobile air, combined   25
reactively, could have in mind.

On Alexander and Aristotle, on a Black-on-Red Greek Plate

The linear, encircled youth
acclaimed his limits running
in the bottom of a plate
with "he's a handsome lad"
scratched anyhow around   5
him as a joke or hint
of love. A northern prince,
finishing his cereal beneath
a Grecian tutor's smile,
would see the one clear line   10
appear, become a youth,
and run off on the way
from breakfast to the city
through an alphabet
circumferenced by art.   15
This is doubt's breakfast
in a school of Gordian knots:

21. **winding sheets:** the traditional burial garments of a corpse. 26. **reactively:** perhaps an allusion to nuclear reaction.

ON ALEXANDER AND ARISTOTLE   3, **plate:** an ancient Greek decorated terracotta plate, with black designs and inscriptions fired on the clay. 7. **northern prince:** Alexander, son of Philip of Macedon and the pupil of Aristotle (the "Grecian tutor" of l. 9, and "The Philosopher" of l. 25). 17. **Gordian knots:** Alexander was shown the knot tied by the peasant Gordius and told that whoever undid it would rule over the whole East. "It is thus I perform the task," Alexander exclaimed as he cut it with his sword.

in ending at the genitals,
where it began, the line
is doubled on itself and tied   20
unclearly in a bow knot
with dangles. The lewd
scratches mar design well.
Which way can princes turn
with The Philosopher behind   25
them and the Greeks in front?

If cooks can shatter art
then love is menial, and boys
can use it to be gods
in thirty-some-odd years.   30
That was doubt's breakfast
in the school of Gordian tricks:
"To have good government
thinkers should form the king,"
so when he took his way   35
he took Real armies with him:
Athens crumbled in the Seen
of Alexander's sober frown
and tricked his looking to go on
to Porus and the elephants   40
and drunkenness in Babylon.

James Dickey *(1923–   )*

The Fiend

He has only to pass by a tree   moodily walking   head down
A worried accountant   not with it   and he is swarming
He is gliding up the underside light of leaves   upfloating
In a seersucker suit   passing window after window of her building.
He finds her at last, chewing gum   talking on the telephone.   5
The wind sways him softly   comfortably sighing   she must bathe
Or sleep.   She gets up, and he follows her along the branch

---

30. thirty . . . years: Alexander died at the age of 33 (356–323 B.C.). **33–34. To have
. . . king:** paraphrasing Plato, *The Republic*, Book 5, 473 C: "until philosophers are
kings, or the kings and princes of this world have the spirit and power of philosophy
. . . cities will never have rest from their evils." **37. Athens crumbled:** It fell to Alexander in 335 B.C. **40. Porus:** the Indian king whose army, with two hundred elephants,
was overcome by Alexander in the battle of the Hydaspes (326 B.C.). When Porus
was captured, Alexander asked him how he expected to be treated. When he replied,
"Like a king," Alexander restored him to his throne. **41. Babylon:** where Alexander
died of a fever.

Into another room.   She stands there for a moment   and the teddy
      bear
On the bed feels its guts spin as she takes it by the leg and tosses
It off.   She touches one button at her throat, and rigor mortis   10
Slithers into his pockets, making everything there—keys, pen
and secret love—stand up.   He brings from those depths the knife
And flicks it open   it glints on the moon one time   carries
Through the dead walls   making a wormy static on the TV screen.
He parts the swarm of gnats that live excitedly at this perilous level   15
Parts the rarefied light high windows give out into inhabited trees
Opens his lower body to the moon.   This night the apartments are
      sinking

To ground level   burying their sleepers in the soil   burying all floors
But the one where a sullen shopgirl gets ready to take a shower,
Her hair in rigid curlers, and the rest.   When she gives up   20
Her aqua terry-cloth robe the wind quits in mid-tree   the birds
Freeze to their perches round his head   a purely human light
Comes out of a one-man oak   around her an energy field   she stands
Rooted   not turning to anything else   then begins to move like a
      saint
Her stressed nipples rising like things about to crawl off her   as he gets   25
A hold on himself.   With that clasp she changes   senses   some-
      thing

Some breath through the fragile walls   some all-seeing eye
Of God   some touch that enfolds her body   some hand come up
      out of roots
That carries her as she moves   swaying   at this rare height.
      She wraps
The curtain around her and streams.   The room fades.   Then coming   30
Forth magnificently   the window blurred from within   she moves in a
      cloud
Chamber   the tree in the oak currents sailing   in clear air keeping
      pace
With her white breathless closet—he sees her mistily part her lips
As if singing to him, come up from river-fog   almost hears her as if
She sang alone in a cloud   its warmed light streaming into his branches   35
Out through the gauze glass of the window.   She takes off her bathing
      cap
The tree with him ascending   himself and the birds all moving
In darkness together   crumbling the bark in their claws.
By this time he holds in his awkward, subtle limbs the limbs

Of a hundred understanding trees.   He has learned what a plant is like   40
When it moves near a human habitation   moving closer the later it is
Unfurling its leaves near bedrooms   still keeping its wilderness life
Twigs covering his body with only one way out   for his eyes into inner
      light
Of a chosen window   living with them night after night   watching

Watching with them at times their favorite TV shows   learning—   45
Though now and then he hears a faint sound: gunshot, bombing,
Building-fall—how to read lips: the lips of laconic cowboys
Bank robbers   old and young doctors tense-faced   gesturing savagely
In wards and corridors   like reading the lips of the dead

The lips of men interrupting the program at the wrong time   50
To sell you a good used car on the Night Owl Show   men silently re-
        porting
The news out the window.   But the living as well, three-dimensioned,
Silent as the small gray dead, must sleep at last   must save their lives
By taking off their clothes. It is his beholding that saves them:
God help the dweller in windowless basements   the one obsessed   55
With drawing curtains this night. At three o'clock in the morning
He descends   a medium-sized shadow   while that one sleeps and
        turns
In her high bed in loss   as he goes limb by limb   quietly down
The trunk with one lighted side. Ground upon which he could not explain
His presence he walks with toes uncurled from branches, his bird-move-
        ments   60
Dying hard. At the sidewalk he changes   gains weight   a solid citizen

Once more. At apartments there is less danger from dogs, but he has
For those a super-quiet hand   a hand to calm sparrows and rivers,
And watchdogs in half-tended bushes lie with him watching their women
Undress   the dog's honest eyes and the man's the same pure beast's   65
Comprehending the same essentials. Not one of these beheld would ever
        give
Him a second look   but he gives them all a first look that goes
On and on   conferring immortality while it lasts   while the suburb's
        leaves
Hold still enough   while whatever dog he has with him holds its breath
Yet seems to thick-pant   impatient as he with the indifferent men   70
Drifting in and out of the rooms   or staying on, too tired to move
Reading the sports page   dozing   plainly unworthy   for what
        women want
Dwells in bushes and trees: what they want is to look outward,

To look with the light streaming into the April limbs   to stand straighter
While their husbands' lips dry out   feeling that something is there   75
That could dwell in no earthly house: that in poplar trees or beneath
The warped roundabout of the clothesline   in the sordid disorder
Of communal backyards   some being is there in the shrubs
Sitting comfortably on a child's striped rubber ball filled with rainwater
Muffling his glasses with a small studious hand against a sudden   80
Flash of houselight from within   or flash from himself   a needle's
        eye
Uncontrollable   blaze of uncompromised being. Ah, the lingerie
Hung in the bathroom! The domestic motions of single girls living to-
        gether

A plump girl girding her loins against her moon-summoned blood:
In that moon he stands   the only male lit by it, covered with leaf-
    shapes.   85
He coughs, and the smallest root responds   and in his lust he is set
By the wind in motion. That movement can restore the green eyes
Of middle age   looking   renewed   through the qualified light
Not quite reaching him where he stands again on the usual branch
Of his oldest love   his tie not loosened   a plastic shield   90
In his breast pocket full of pencils and ballpoint pens given him by sales-
    men
His hat correctly placed to shade his eyes   a natural gambler's tilt
And in summer wears an eyeshade   a straw hat Caribbean style.
In some guise or other he is near them when they are weeping without
    sound
When the teen-age son has quit school   when the girl has broken up   95
With the basketball star   when the banker walks out on his wife.
He sees mothers counsel desperately with pulsing girls face down
On beds full of overstuffed beasts   sees men dress as women
In ante-bellum costumes with bonnets   see doctors come, looking oddly
Like himself   though inside the houses   worming a medical arm   100
Up under the cringing covers   sees children put angrily to bed
Sees one told an invisible fairy story   with lips moving silently as his
Are also moving   the book's few pages bright. It will take years
But at last he will shed his leaves   burn his roots   give up
Invisibility   will step out   will make himself known to the one   105
He cannot see loosen her blouse   take off luxuriously   with lips
Compressed against her mouth-stain   her dress   her stockings
Her magic underwear.   To that one he will come   up frustrated
    pines
Down alleys   through window blinds   blind windows   kitchen
    doors
On summer evenings. It will be something small that sets him off: 110
Perhaps a pair of lace pants on a clothesline   gradually losing
Water to the sun   filling out in the warm light with a well-rounded
Feminine wind as he watches   having spent so many sleepless nights
Because of her   because of her hand on a shade always coming down
In his face   not leaving even a shadow stripped naked upon the brown
    paper   115
Waiting for her now in a green outdated car with a final declaration
Of love   pretending to read   and when she comes and takes down
Her pants, he will casually follow her in   like a door-to-door salesman
The godlike movement of trees stiffening with him   the light
Of a hundred favored windows   gone wrong somewhere in his glasses   120
Where his knocked-off panama hat was   in his painfully vanishing hair.

Pursuit from Under

Often, in these blue meadows,
I hear what passes for the bark of seals

And on August week ends the cold of a personal ice age
Comes up through my bare feet
Which are trying to walk like a boy's again   5
So that nothing on earth can have changed
On the ground where I was raised.

The dark grass here is like
The pads of mukluks going on and on

Because I once burned kerosene to read   10
Myself near the North Pole
In the journal of Arctic explorers
Found, years after death, preserved
In a tent, part of whose canvas they had eaten

Before the last entry.   15
All over my father's land

The seal holes sigh like an organ,
And one entry carries more terror
Than the blank page that signified death
In 1912, on the icecap.   20
It says that, under the ice,

The killer whale darts and distorts,
Cut down by the flawing glass

To a weasel's shadow,
And when, through his ceiling, he sees   25
Anything darker than snow
He falls away
To gather more and more force

From the iron depths of cold water,
His shadow dwindling   30

Almost to nothing at all, then charges
Straight up, looms up at the ice and smashes
Into it with his forehead
To splinter the roof, to isolate seal or man
On a drifting piece of the floe   35

Which he can overturn.
If you run, he will follow you

PURSUIT FROM UNDER   **9. mukluks:** Eskimo boots made of sealskin or reindeer skin.
12. Arctic explorers: possibly a reference to Robert F. Scott and his companions who
reached the South Pole in 1912, but perished on the return journey. Scott's diaries,
kept up until his death, give a moving account of his experiences.

Under the frozen pane,
Turning as you do, zigzagging,
And at the most uncertain of your ground   40
Will shatter through, and lean,
And breathe frankly in your face

An enormous breath smelling of fish.
With the stale lungs staining your air

You know the unsaid recognition   45
Of which the explorers died:
They had been given an image
Of how the downed dead pursue us.
They knew, as they starved to death,

That not only in the snow   50
But in the family field

The small shadow moves,
And under bare feet in the summer:
That somewhere the turf will heave,
And the outraged breath of the dead,   55
So long held, will form

Unbreathably around the living.
The cows low oddly here

As I pass, a small bidden shape
Going with me, trembling like foxfire   60
Under my heels and their hooves.
I shall write this by keroscne,
Pitch a tent in the pasture, and starve.

Denise Levertov *(1923–   )*

The Rainwalkers

An old man whose black face
shines golden-brown as wet pebbles
under the streetlamp, is walking
two mongrel dogs of dis-
proportionate size, in the rain,   5
in the relaxed early-evening avenue.

63. **starve:** perhaps with some of its old meaning, "die."

The small sleek one wants to stop,
docile to the imploring soul of the trashbasket,
but the young tall curly one
wants to walk on; the glistening sidewalk   10
entices him to arcane happenings.

Increasing rain. The old bareheaded man
smiles and grumbles to himself.
The lights change: the avenue's
endless nave echoes notes of   15
liturgical red. He drifts

between his dogs' desires.
The three of them are enveloped—
turning now to go crosstown—in their
sense of each other, of pleasure,   20
of weather, of corners,
of leisurely tensions between them
and private silence.

The Jacob's Ladder

The stairway is not
a thing of gleaming strands
a radiant evanescence
for angels' feet that only glance in their tread, and need not
touch the stone.   5

It is of stone.
A rosy stone that takes
a glowing tone of softness
only because behind it the sky is a doubtful, a doubting
night gray.   10

A stairway of sharp
angles, solidly built.
One sees that the angels must spring
down from one step to the next, giving a little
lift of the wings: 15

and a man climbing
must scrape his knees, and bring
the grip of his hands into play. The cut stone
consoles his groping feet. Wings brush past him.
The poem ascends.   20

THE JACOB'S LADDER   The ladder seen by Jacob in his dream (Genesis 28:12): "and behold a ladder set up on the earth, and the top of it reached to heaven: and behold the angels of God ascending and descending on it."

". . . Else a Great Prince in Prison Lies"

All that blesses the step of the antelope
all the grace a giraffe lifts to the highest leaves
all steadfastness and pleasant gazing, alien to ennui,
dwell secretly behind man's misery.

Animal face, when the lines   5
of human fear, knots of a net, become transparent
and your brilliant eyes and velvet muzzle
are revealed, who shall say you are not the face of a man?

In the dense light of wakened flesh
animal man is a prince. As from alabaster   10
a lucency animates him from heel to forehead.
Then his shadows are deep and not gray.

Our Bodies

Our bodies, still young under
the engraved anxiety of our
faces, and innocently

more expressive than faces:
nipples, navel, and pubic hair   5
make anyway a

sort of face: or taking
the rounded shadows at
breast, buttock, balls,

the plump of my belly, the   10
hollow of your
groin, as a constellation,

how it leans from earth to
dawn in a gesture of
play and   15

wise compassion—
nothing like this
comes to pass

ELSE A GREAT PRINCE   See John Donne, "The Ecstasy": "So must pure lovers' souls
descend/T'affections and to faculties,/Which sense may reach and apprehend,/Else a
great prince in prison lies."

in eyes or wistful
mouths.
   I have   20

a line or groove I love
runs down
my body from breastbone
to waist. It speaks of
eagerness, of   25
distance.

   Your long back,
the sand color and
how the bones show, say
what sky after sunset
almost white   30
over a deep woods to which

rooks are homing, says.

Earth Psalm

I could replace
God for awhile, that old ring of candles,
that owl's wing brushing the dew
off my grass hair.
If bended knee calls up   5
a god, if the imagination of idol
calls up a god, if melting
of heart or what was written as
bowels but has to do
      not with shit but with salutation of   10
      somber beauty in what is mortal,
calls up a god by recognition and power of
longing, then in my forest
God is replaced awhile,
awhile I can turn from that slow embrace   15
to worship *mortal*, the summoned
god who has speech, who has wit
to wreathe all words, who laughs
wrapped in sad pelt and without hope of heaven,
who makes a music turns the heads   20
of all beasts
as mine turns, dream-hill grass
standing on end at echo even.

EARTH PSALM   **9. bowels:** in the old sense (because they were once regarded as the
center of tender and sympathetic emotions), pity, compassion.

O Taste and See

The world is
not with us enough.
O taste and see

` the subway Bible poster said,
meaning **The Lord,** meaning   5
if anything all that lives
to the imagination's tongue,

grief, mercy, language,
tangerine, weather, to
breathe them, bite,   10
savor, chew, swallow, transform

into our flesh our
deaths, crossing the street, plum, quince,
living in the orchard and being

hungry, and plucking   15
the fruit.

Gloria C. Oden (1923–   )

Review from Staten Island

The skyline of New York does not excite me
(ferrying towards it) as mountains do in snow-steeped
            hostility to sun.
There is something in the view—spewed up from water
            to pure abandonment in air—   5
            that snakes my spine with cold
and mouse-tracks over my heart.

Strewn across the meet of wave and wind, it seems
the incompleted play of some helter-skeltering child whose
            hegira (as all   10

O TASTE AND SEE   **1–2. world . . . enough:** Cf. Wordsworth's sonnet, "The world is
too much with us; late and soon,/Getting and spending, we lay waste our powers."
REVIEW FROM STATEN ISLAND   **10. hegira:** journey; originally the flight of Mohammed
from Mecca to Medina.

our circles go) has not yet led him back, but will, ripe
                    with that ferocious glee which
                    can boot these building-blocks
to earth, then heel under.

One gets used to dying living. Growth is an   15
end to many things—even the rose disposes of summer—
                    but still I
wince at being there when the relentless foot kicks down;
                    and the tides come roaring over
                    to pool within   20
the unlearned depths of me.

Donald Justice *(1925–   )*

Men at Forty

Men at forty
Learn to close softly
The doors to rooms they will not be
Coming back to.

At rest on a stair landing,   5
They feel it moving
Beneath them now like the deck of a ship,
Though the swell is gentle.

And deep in mirrors
They rediscover   10
The face of the boy as he practices tying
His father's tie there in secret

And the face of that father,
Still warm with the mystery of lather.
They are more fathers than sons themselves now.   15
Something is filling them, something

That is like the twilight sound
Of the crickets, immense,
Filling the woods at the foot of the slope
Behind their mortgaged houses.   20

Kenneth Koch *(1925–   )*

Permanently

One day the Nouns were clustered in the street.
An Adjective walked by, with her dark beauty.
The Nouns were struck, moved, changed.
The next day a Verb drove up, and created the Sentence.

Each Sentence says one thing—for example, "Although it was a dark rainy
    day when the Adjective walked by, I shall remember the pure and sweet
    expression on her face until the day I perish from the green, effective
    earth."   5
Or, "Will you please close the window, Andrew?"
Or, for example, "Thank you, the pink pot of flowers on the window sill
    has changed color recently to a light yellow, due to the heat from the
    boiler factory which exists nearby."

In the springtime the Sentences and the Nouns lay silently on the grass.
A lonely Conjunction here and there would call, "And! But!"
But the Adjective did not emerge.   10

As the adjective is lost in the sentence,
So I am lost in your eyes, ears, nose, and throat—
You have enchanted me with a single kiss
Which can never be undone
Until the destruction of language.   15

Robert Bly *(1926–   )*

Laziness and Silence

I

On a Saturday afternoon in the football season,
I lie in a bed near the lake,
And dream of moles with golden wings.

While the depth of the water trembles on the ceiling,
Like the tail of an enraged bird,
I watch the dust floating above the bed, content.   5

I think of ships leaving lonely harbors,
Dolphins playing far at sea,
Fish with the faces of old men come in from the blizzard.

II

A dream of moles with golden wings   10
Is not so bad; it is like imagining
Waterfalls of stone deep in mountains,
Or a wing flying alone beneath the earth.

I know that far out in the Minnesota lake
Fish are nosing the mouths of cold springs,   15
Whose water causes ripples in the sleeping sand,
Like a spirit moving in a body.

It is Saturday afternoon. Crowds are gathered,
Warmed by the sun, and the pure air.
I thought of this strange mole this morning,   20
After sleeping all night by the lake.

Robert Creeley *(1926–   )*

I Know a Man

As I sd to my
friend, because I am
always talking,—John, I

sd, which was not his
name, the darkness sur-   5
rounds us, what

can we do against
it, or else, Shall we &
why not, buy a goddamn big car,

drive he sd, for   10
christ's sake, look
out where yr going.

The Crisis

Let me say (in anger) that since the day we were married
we have never had a towel
where anyone could find it,
the fact.
                Notwithstanding that I am not
simple to live with, not   5
my own judgment, but no
matter.
                There are other things:

to kiss you is not
to love you.
                Or not so simply.

Laughter releases rancor, the quality of mercy is not   10
strained.

Wait for Me

                . . . give a man his
                I said to her,

                manliness: provide
                what you want I

                creature comfort   5
                want only

                for him and herself:
                ᴍᴏʀᴇ 30. You

                preserve essential
                think marriage is   10

                hypocrisies—
                everything?

                in short, make a
                Oh well,

                home for herself,   15
                I said.

THE CRISIS   **10–11. the quality . . . strained:** Portia's words in Shakespeare's *Merchant of Venice*, IV.i.184.

The Way

My love's manners in bed
are not to be discussed by me,
as mine by her
I would not credit comment upon gracefully.

Yet I ride by the margin of that lake in   5
the wood, the castle,
and the excitement of strongholds;
and have a small boy's notion of doing good.

Oh well, I will say here,
knowing each man,   10
let you find a good wife too,
and love her as hard as you can.

Heroes

In all those stories the hero
is beyond himself into the next
thing, be it those labors
of Hercules, or Aeneas going into death.

I thought the instant of the one humanness   5
in Virgil's plan of it
was that it was of course human enough to die,
yet to come back, as he said, *hoc opus, hic labor est.*

That was the Cumaean Sibyl speaking.
This is Robert Creeley, and Virgil   10
is dead now two thousand years, yet Hercules
and the *Aeneid*, yet all that industrious wis-

dom lives in the way the mountains
and the desert are waiting
for the heroes, and death also   15
can still propose the old labors.

HEROES   **4. Hercules:** in a fit of madness he slew his wife and children, and Apollo required him as penance to serve for twelve years the king Eurystheus, who imposed twelve great labors on him. **8. hic opus . . . est:** the Cumaean Sibyl's warning to Aeneas as he is about to go to the underworld to visit the dead: the descent is easy, but to return again, "This is the task, this the toil" (*Aeneid,* vi.126–29).

Allen Ginsberg (1926–   )

America

America I've given you all and now I'm nothing.
America two dollars and twentyseven cents January 17, 1956.
I can't stand my own mind.
America when will we end the human war?
Go fuck yourself with your atom bomb.   5
I don't feel good don't bother me.
I won't write my poem till I'm in my right mind.
America when will you be angelic?
When will you take off your clothes?
When will you look at yourself through the grave?   10
When will you be worthy of your million Trotskyites?
America why are your libraries full of tears?
America when will you send your eggs to India?
I'm sick of your insane demands.
When can I go into the supermarket and buy what I need with my good
    looks?   15
America after all it is you and I who are perfect not the next world.
Your machinery is too much for me.
You made me want to be a saint.
There must be some other way to settle this argument.
Burroughs is in Tangiers I don't think he'll come back it's sinister.   20
Are you being sinister or is this some form of practical joke?
I'm trying to come to the point.
I refuse to give up my obsession.
America stop pushing I know what I'm doing.
America the plum blossoms are falling.   25
I haven't read the newspapers for months, everyday somebody goes on trial
    for murder.
America I feel sentimental about the Wobblies.
America I used to be a communist when I was a kid I'm not sorry.
I smoke marijuana every chance I get.
I sit in my house for days on end and stare at the roses in the closet. 30
When I go to Chinatown I get drunk and never get laid.
My mind is made up there's going to be trouble.
You should have seen me reading Marx.
My psychoanalyst thinks I'm perfectly right.
I won't say the Lord's Prayer.   35

AMERICA **20. Burroughs:** William Burroughs, novelist, author of *Naked Lunch*. **27. Wobblies:** members of the revolutionary Industrial Workers of the World, organized in Chicago in 1905 and active in major strikes as late as 1928.

I have mystical visions and cosmic vibrations.
America I still haven't told you what you did to Uncle Max after he came
    over from Russia.

I'm addressing you.
Are you going to let your emotional life be run by Time Magazine?
I'm obsessed by Time Magazine.   40
I read it every week.
Its cover stares at me every time I slink past the corner candystore.
I read it in the basement of the Berkeley Public Library.
It's always telling me about responsibility. Businessmen are serious.
    Movie producers are serious. Everybody's serious but me.
It occurs to me that I am America.   45
I am talking to myself again.

Asia is rising against me.
I haven't got a chinaman's chance.
I'd better consider my national resources.
My national resources consist of two joints of marijuana millions of genitals
    an unpublishable private literature that goes 1400 miles an hour and
    twentyfive-thousand mental institutions.   50
I say nothing about my prisons nor the millions of underprivileged who
    live in my flowerpots under the light of five hundred suns.
I have abolished the whorehouses of France, Tangiers is the next to go.
My ambition is to be President despite the fact that I'm a Catholic.

America how can I write a holy litany in your silly mood?
I will continue like Henry Ford my strophes are as individual as his auto-
    mobiles more so they're all different sexes.   55
America I will sell you strophes $2500 apiece $500 down on your old
    strophe
America free Tom Mooney
America save the Spanish Loyalists
America Sacco & Vanzetti must not die
America I am the Scottsboro boys.   60

---

57. Tom Mooney: American labor leader (1883–1942) convicted of a part in the bomb killings at the San Francisco Preparedness Day parade in 1916; his death sentence was commuted to life imprisonment in 1918, and finally—after much popular protest in behalf of his innocence—he was pardoned in 1939. **58. Spanish Loyalists:** those loyal to the Spanish Republic, defeated in the civil war (1936–39) by the conservative forces of General Francisco Franco. **59. Sacco & Vanzetti:** Nicola Sacco and Bartolomeo Vanzetti, Italian-American anarchists, were charged with a robbery and murder that took place in Massachusetts in 1920. Much of the evidence against them was suspect, and their conviction was in part a result of anti-radical sentiment; but a new trial was denied both by the Massachusetts Supreme Court and by a special governor's committee, and they were executed in 1927. **60. Scottsboro boys:** nine blacks accused of rape of two white girls, all but one (who was 13 years old) sentenced to death in April 1931. The case went to the Supreme Court and was returned to the Alabama courts, where it dragged on for years, ending in dismissal of the charges against several of the defendants. The Scottsboro case became a propaganda cause of the Communists, but it was wider in its appeal and won national attention for several years.

America when I was seven momma took me to Communist Cell meetings
    they sold us garbanzos a handful per ticket a ticket costs a nickel and
    the speeches were free everybody was angelic and sentimental about the
    workers it was all so sincere you have no idea what a good thing the
    party was in 1935 Scott Nearing was a grand old man a real mensch
    Mother Bloor made me cry I once saw Israel Amter plain. Everybody
    must have been a spy.
America you don't really want to go to war.
America it's them bad Russians.
Them Russians them Russians and them Chinamen. And them Russians.
The Russia wants to eat us alive. The Russia's power mad. She wants to
    take our cars from out our garages.   65
Her wants to grab Chicago. Her needs a Red Readers' Digest. Her wants
    our auto plants in Siberia. Him big bureaucracy running our filling-
    stations.
That no good. Ugh. Him make Indians learn read. Him need big black
    niggers. Hah. Her makes us all work sixteen hours a day. Help.
America this is quite serious.
America this is the impression I get from looking in the television set.
America is this correct?   70
I'd better get right down to the job.
It's true I don't want to join the Army or turn lathes in precision parts
    factories, I'm nearsighted and psychopathic anyway.
America I'm putting my queer shoulder to the wheel.

James Merrill (1926–   )

The Broken Home

    Crossing the street,
    I saw the parents and the child
    At their window, gleaming like fruit
    With evening's mild gold leaf.

    In a room on the floor below,   5
    Sunless, cooler—a brimming
    Saucer of wax, marbly and dim—
    I have lit what's left of my life.

61. **garbanzos**: chickpea seeds. **Scott Nearing**: sociologist and political writer. **mensch**: manly man. **Mother Bloor**: Ella Reeve Bloor, member of the Communist national committee and a well-known speaker. **Israel Amter**: at the time Chairman in New York State of the Communist Party. **plain**: echoing Robert Browning's "Ah, did you once see Shelley plain,/And did he stop and speak to you?/And did you speak to him again?" ("Memorabilia," ll. 1–3).

I have thrown out yesterday's milk
And opened a book of maxims.   10
The flame quickens. The word stirs.

Tell me, tongue of fire,
That you and I are as real
At least as the people upstairs.

My father, who had flown in World War I,   15
Might have continued to invest his life
In cloud banks well above Wall Street and wife.
But the race was run below, and the point was to win.

Too late now, I make out in his blue gaze
(Through the smoked glass of being thirty-six)   20
The soul eclipsed by twin black pupils, sex
And business; time was money in those days.

Each thirteenth year he married. When he died
There were already several chilled wives
In sable orbit—rings, cars, permanent waves.   25
We'd felt him warming up for a green bride.

He could afford it. He was "in his prime"
At three score ten. But money was not time.

When my parents were younger this was a popular act:
A veiled woman would leap from an electric, wine-dark car   30
To the steps of no matter what—the Senate or the Ritz Bar—
And bodily, at newsreel speed, attack

No matter whom—Al Smith or José Maria Sert
Or Clemenceau—veins standing out on her throat
As she yelled *War mongerer! Pig! Give us the vote!*,   35
And would have to be hauled away in her hobble skirt.

What had the man done? Oh, made history.
Her business (he had implied) was giving birth,
Tending the house, mending the socks.

Always that same old story—   40
Father Time and Mother Earth,
A marriage on the rocks.

BROKEN HOME   **31. Ritz Bar:** a fashionable Paris bar. **33. Al Smith:** Governor of New York, and Democratic candidate for President in 1928. **José Maria Sert:** Spanish mural painter. **34. Clemenceau:** Georges Clemenceau, French statesman and premier (1906–09; 1917), known as "the Tiger of France." **36. hobble skirt:** long skirt that impeded walking, popular just before the First World War.

One afternoon, red, satyr-thighed
Michael, the Irish setter, head
Passionately lowered, led   45
The child I was to a shut door. Inside,

Blinds beat sun from the bed.
The green-gold room throbbed like a bruise.
Under a sheet, clad in taboos
Lay whom we sought, her hair undone, outspread,   50

And of a blackness found, if ever now, in old
Engravings where the acid bit.
I must have needed to touch it
Or the whiteness—was she dead?
Her eyes flew open, startled strange and cold.   55
The dog slumped to the floor. She reached for me. I fled.

Tonight they have stepped out onto the gravel.
The party is over. It's the fall
Of 1931. They love each other still.

She: Charlie, I can't stand the pace.   60
He: Come on, honey—why, you'll bury us all!

A lead soldier guards my windowsill:
Khaki rifle, uniform, and face.
Something in me grows heavy, silvery, pliable.

How intensely people used to feel!   65
Like metal poured at the close of a proletarian novel,
Refined and glowing from the crucible.
I see those two hearts, I'm afraid,
Still. Cool here in the graveyard of good and evil,
They are even so to be honored and obeyed.   70

. . . Obeyed, at least, inversely. Thus
I rarely buy a newspaper, or vote.
To do so, I have learned, is to invite
The tread of a stone guest within my house.

Shooting this rusted bolt, though, against him,   75
I trust I am no less time's child than some
Who on the heath impersonate Poor Tom
Or on the barricades risk life and limb.

---

66. **proletarian novel**: novel glorifying the working class, popular in the 1930s. 71. **stone guest**: In Mozart's *Don Giovanni*, Giovanni kills the Commander whose daughter he has seduced. Later the statue of the Commander stalks into Giovanni's house and Giovanni is consumed by the flames of Hell. 77 **Poor Tom**: the madman's disguise adopted by the persecuted Edgar in Shakespeare's *King Lear*.

Nor do I try to keep a garden, only
An avocado in a glass of water—   80
Roots pallid, gemmed with air. And later,

When the small gilt leaves have grown
Fleshy and green, I let them die, yes, yes,
And start another. I am earth's no less.

A child, a red dog roam the corridors,   85
Still, of the broken home. No sound. The brilliant
Rag runners halt before wide-open doors.
My old room! Its wallpaper—cream, medallioned
With pink and brown—brings back the first nightmares,
Long summer colds, and Emma, sepia-faced,   90
Perspiring over broth carried upstairs
Aswim with golden fats I could not taste.

The real house became a boarding-school.
Under the ballroom ceiling's allegory
Someone at last may actually be allowed   95
To learn something; or, from my window, cool
With the unstiflement of the entire story,
Watch a red setter stretch and sink in cloud.

Frank O'Hara *(1926–1966)*

Ode to Joy

We shall have everything we want and there'll be no more dying on the
    pretty plains or in the supper clubs
for our symbol we'll acknowledge vulgar materialistic laughter over an
    insatiable sexual appetite
and the streets will be filled with racing forms
and the photographs of murderers and narcissists and movie stars will
    swell from the walls and books alive in steaming rooms to press
    against our burning flesh not once but interminably
as water flows down hill into the full-lipped basin   5
and the adder dives for the ultimate ostrich egg
and the feather cushion preens beneath a reclining monolith that's
    sweating with post-exertion visibility and sweetness near the grave
    of love

                                                    No more dying

We shall see the grave of love as a lovely sight and temporary near the
    elm that spells the lovers' names in roots

and there'll be no more music but the ears in lips and no more wit but
    tongues in ears and no more drums but ears to thighs   10
as evening signals nudities unknown to ancestors' imaginations
and the imagination itself will stagger like a tired paramour of ivory
    under the sculptural necessities of lust that never falters like a
    six-mile runner from Sweden or Liberia covered with gold
as lava flows up and over the far-down somnolent city's abdication
and the hermit always wanting to be lone is lone at last
and the weight of external heat crushes the heat-hating Puritan whose
    self-defeating vice becomes a proper sepulcher at last that love may live   15

Buildings will go up into the dizzy air as love itself goes in and up the
    reeling life that it has chosen for once or all
while in the sky a feeling of intemperate fondness will excite the birds to
    swoop and veer like flies crawling across absorbèd limbs
that weep a pearly perspiration on the sheets of brief attention
and the hairs dry out that summon anxious declaration of the organs as
    they rise like buildings to the needs of temporary neighbors pouring
    hunger through the heart to feed desire in intravenous ways
like the ways of gods with humans in the innocent combination of light   20
and flesh or as the legends ride their heroes through the dark to found
great cities where all life is possible to maintain as long as time which
    wants us to remain for cocktails in a bar and after dinner lets us live
    with it
                                          No more dying

W. D. Snodgrass (1926–   )

These Trees Stand . . .

These trees stand very tall under the heavens.
While *they* stand, if I walk, all stars traverse
This steep celestial gulf their branches chart.
Though lovers stand at sixes and at sevens
While civilizations come down with the curse,   5
Snodgrass is walking through the universe.

I can't make any world go around *your* house.
But note this moon. Recall how the night nurse
Goes ward-rounds, by the mild, reflective art
Of focusing her flashlight on her blouse.   10
Your name's safe conduct into love or verse;
Snodgrass is walking through the universe.

Your name's absurd, miraculous as sperm
And as decisive. If you can't coerce

One thing outside yourself, why you're the poet!   15
What irrefrangible atoms whirl, affirm
Their destiny and form Lucinda's skirts!
She can't make up your mind. Soon as you know it,
Your firmament grows touchable and firm.
If all this world runs battlefield or worse,   20
Come, let us wipe our glasses on our shirts:
Snodgrass is walking through the universe.

"After Experience Taught Me . . ."

After experience taught me that all the ordinary
Surroundings of social life are futile and vain;

    I'm going to show you something very
    Ugly: someday, it might save your life.

Seeing that none of the things I feared contain   5
In themselves anything either good or bad

    What if you get caught without a knife;
    Nothing—even a loop of piano wire;

Excepting only in the effect they had
Upon my mind, I resolved to inquire   10

    Take the next two fingers of this hand;
    Fork them out—kind of a "V for Victory"—

Whether there might be something whose discovery
Would grant me supreme, unending happiness.

    And jam them into the eyes of your enemy.   15
    You have to do this hard. Very hard. Then press

No virtue can be thought to have priority
Over this endeavor to preserve one's being.

    Both fingers down around the cheekbone
    And setting your foot high into the chest   20

No man can desire to act rightly, to be blessed,
To live rightly, without simultaneously

    You must call up every strength you own
    And you can rip off the whole facial mask.

THESE TREES   16. irrefrangible: unbreakable, indivisible.

Wishing to be, to act, to live. He must ask   25
First, in other words, to actually exist.

    And you, whiner, who wastes your time
        Dawdling over the remorseless earth,
    What evil, what unspeakable crime
        Have you made your life worth?   30

Mementos, 1

Sorting out letters and piles of my old
    Canceled checks, old clippings, and yellow note cards
That meant something once, I happened to find
    Your picture. *That* picture. I stopped there cold,
Like a man raking piles of dead leaves in his yard   5
    Who has turned up a severed hand.

Still, that first second, I was glad: you stand
    Just as you stood—shy, delicate, slender,
In that long gown of green lace netting and daisies
    That you wore to our first dance. The sight of you stunned   10
Us all. Well, our needs were different, then,
    And our ideals came easy.

Then through the war and those two long years
    Overseas, the Japanese dead in their shacks
Among dishes, dolls, and lost shoes; I carried   15
    This glimpse of you, there, to choke down my fear,
Prove it had been, that it might come back.
    That was before we got married.

—Before we drained out one another's force
    With lies, self-denial, unspoken regret   20
And the sick eyes that blame; before the divorce
    And the treachery. Say it: before we met. Still,
I put back your picture. Someday, in due course,
    I will find that it's still there.

The Men's Room in the College Chapel

Here, in the most Unchristian basement
of this "fortress for the Christian mind,"
they close these four gray walls, shut out shame,
and scribble of sex and excrement,

draw bestial pictures and sign their name—   5
the old, lewd defiance of mankind.

The subversive human in his cell—
burn his vile books, stamp out his credo,
lock him away where no light falls,
and no live word can go back to tell   10
where he's entombed like Monte Cristo—
still, he'll carve his platform in the walls.

In need, men have painted the deep caves
to summon their animal, dark gods;
even the reviled, early Christians   15
prayed in catacombs to outlawed Good,
laid their honored dead and carved out graves
with pious mottos of resistance.

This is the last cave, where the soul
turns in its corner like a beast   20
nursing its wounds, where it contemplates
vengeance, how it shall gather to full
strength, what lost cause shall it vindicate,
returning, masterless and twisted.

A. R. Ammons (1926–   )

Runoff

By the highway the stream downslope
could hardly clear itself
through rubbish and slime but by

that resistance gained a cutting
depth equal to its breadth   5
and so had means to muscle into

ripples and spill over angled
shelves:
and so went on down in a long

THE MEN'S ROOM IN THE COLLEGE CHAPEL   **8. credo:** statement of belief. **11. Monte Cristo:** the hero of Alexandre Dumas' novel *The Count of Monte Cristo*, who is imprisoned in a dungeon for fourteen years.

curve, responsively slow to the   10
sizable ridge it
tended

and farther on down, quiet and clear,
never tipping enough to break sound,
slowed into marshy landrise and burst   15

into a bog of lupine and mirrored:
that was a place! what a place!
the soggy small marsh, nutgrass and swordweed!

Cut the Grass

The wonderful workings of the world: wonderful,
wonderful: I'm surprised half the time:
ground up fine, I puff if a pebble stirs:

I'm nervous: my morality's intricate: if
a squash blossom dies, I feel withered as a stained   5
zucchini and blame my nature: and

when grassblades flop to the little red-ant
queens burring around trying to get aloft, I blame
my not keeping the grass short, stubble

firm: well, I learn a lot of useless stuff, meant   10
to be ignored: like when the sun sinking in the
west glares a plane invisible, I think how much

revelation concealment necessitates: and then I
think of the ocean, multiple to a blinding
oneness, and realize that only total expression   15

expresses hiding: I'll have to say everything
to take on the roundness and withdrawal of the deep dark:
less than total is a bucketful of radiant toys.

Corsons Inlet

I went for a walk over the dunes again this morning
to the sea,
then turned right along
     the surf
               rounded a naked headland   5
               and returned
     along the inlet shore:

it was muggy sunny, the wind from the sea steady and high,
crisp in the running sand,
     some breakthroughs of sun   10
   but after a bit

continuous overcast:

the walk liberating, I was released from forms,
from the perpendiculars,
     straight lines, blocks, boxes, binds   15
of thought
into the hues, shadings, rises, flowing bends and blends
       of sight:

           I allow myself eddies of meaning:
yield to a direction of significance   20
running
like a stream through the geography of my work:
   you can find
in my sayings
          swerves of action   25
          like the inlet's cutting edge:
      there are dunes of motion,
organizations of grass, white sandy paths of remembrance
in the overall wandering of mirroring mind:

but Overall is beyond me: is the sum of these events   30
I cannot draw, the ledger I cannot keep, the accounting
beyond the account:

in nature there are few sharp lines: there are areas of
primrose
     more or less dispersed;
disorderly orders of bayberry; between the rows   35
of dunes,
irregular swamps of reeds,
though not reeds alone, but grass, bayberry, yarrow, all . . .
predominantly reeds: 40

I have reached no conclusions, have erected no boundaries,
shutting out and shutting in, separating inside
      from outside: I have
      drawn no lines:
      as   45

manifold events of sand
change the dune's shape that will not be the same shape
tomorrow,

so I am willing to go along, to accept
the becoming   50
thought, to stake off no beginnings or ends, establish
          no walls:

by transitions the land falls from grassy dunes to creek
to undercreek: but there are no lines, though
          change in that transition is clear   55
          as any sharpness: but "sharpness" spread out,
allowed to occur over a wider range
than mental lines can keep:

the moon was full last night: today, low tide was low:
black shoals of mussels exposed to the risk   60
of air
and, earlier, of sun,
waved in and out with the waterline, waterline inexact,
caught always in the event of change:
          a young mottled gull stood free on the shoals   65
          and ate
to vomiting: another gull, squawking possession, cracked a crab,
picked out the entrails, swallowed the soft-shelled legs, a ruddy
turnstone running in to snatch leftover bits:

risk is full: every living thing in   70
siege: the demand is life, to keep life: the small
white blacklegged egret, how beautiful, quietly stalks and spears
          the shallows, darts to shore
                              to stab—what? I couldn't
          see against the black mudflats—a frightened   75
          fiddler crab?

                    the news to my left over the dunes and
reeds and bayberry clumps was
                    tall: thousands of tree swallows
                    gathering for flight: 80
                    an order held
      ,   in constant change: a congregation
rich with entropy: nevertheless, separable, noticeable
                    as one event,
                              not chaos: preparations for   85
flight from winter,
cheet, cheet, cheet, cheet, wings rifling the green clumps,
beaks
at the bayberries:
          a perception full of wind, flight, curve,   90
          sound:

the possibility of rule as the sum of rulelessness:
the "field" of action
with moving, incalculable center:

in the smaller view, order tight with shape: 95
blue tiny flowers on a leafless weed: carapace of crab:
snail shell:
        pulsations of order
        in the bellies of minnows: orders swallowed,
broken down, transferred through membranes 100
to strengthen larger orders: but in the large view, no
lines or changeless shapes: the working in and out, together
      and against, of millions of events: this,
          so that I make
          no form of 105
          formlessness:

orders as summaries, as outcomes of actions override
or in some way result, not predictably (seeing me gain
the top of a dune,
the swallows 110
could take flight—some other fields of bayberry
      could enter fall
      berryless) and there is serenity:

      no arranged terror: no forcing of image, plan,
or thought: 115
no propaganda, no humbling of reality to precept:

terror pervades but is not arranged, all possibilities
of escape open: no route shut, except in
      the sudden loss of all routes:

      I see narrow orders, limited tightness, but will 120
not run to that easy victory:
      still around the looser, wider forces work:
      I will try
    to fasten into order enlarging grasps of disorder, widening
scope, but enjoying the freedom that 125
Scope eludes my grasp, that there is no finality of vision,
that I have perceived nothing completely,
      that tomorrow a new walk is a new walk.

James Wright *(1927–   )*

A Presentation of Two Birds to My Son

Chicken. How shall I tell you what it is,
And why it does not float with tanagers?
Its ecstasy is dead, it does not care.
Its children huddle underneath its wings,
And altogether lounge against the shack,   5
Warm in the slick tarpaulin, smug and soft.

You must not fumble in your mind
The genuine ecstasy of climbing birds
With that dull fowl.
When your grandfather held it by the feet   10
And laid the skinny neck across
The ragged chopping block,
The flop of wings, the jerk of the red comb
Were a dumb agony,
Stupid and meaningless. It was no joy   15
To leave the body beaten underfoot;
Life was a flick of corn, a steady roost.
Chicken. The sound is plain.

Look up and see the swift above the trees.
How shall I tell you why he always veers   20
And banks around the shaken sleeve of air,
Away from ground? He hardly flies on brains;
Pockets of air impale his hollow bones.
He leans against the rainfall or the sun.

You must not mix this pair of birds   25
Together in your mind before you know
That both are clods.
What makes the chimney swift approach the sky
Is ecstasy, a kind of fire
That beats the bones apart   30
And lets the fragile feathers close with air.
Flight too is agony,
Stupid and meaningless. Why should it be joy
To leave the body beaten underfoot,
To mold the limbs against the wind, and join   35
Those clean dark glides of Dionysian birds?
The flight is deeper than your father, boy.

A PRESENTATION **36. Dionysian:** ecstatic, like the worship of Dionysus, the god of
wine, often a frenzied and mindless ritual.

A Blessing

Just off the highway to Rochester, Minnesota,
Twilight bounds softly forth on the grass.
And the eyes of those two Indian ponies
Darken with kindness.
They have come gladly out of the willows   5
To welcome my friend and me.
We step over the barbed wire into the pasture
Where they have been grazing all day, alone.
They ripple tensely, they can hardly contain their happiness
That we have come.   10
They bow shyly as wet swans. They love each other.
There is no loneliness like theirs.
At home once more,
They begin munching the young tufts of spring in the darkness.
I would like to hold the slenderer one in my arms,   15
For she has walked over to me
And nuzzled my left hand.
She is black and white,
Her mane falls wild on her forehead,
And the light breeze moves me to caress her long ear   20
That is delicate as the skin over a girl's wrist.
Suddenly I realize
That if I stepped out of my body I would break
Into blossom.

W. S. Merwin   (1927–   )

The Owl

These woods are one of my great lies
I pretend
oh I have always pretended they
were mine
I stumble **among**   5
the smaller **lies**
as this night falls and
of my pretenses likewise
some
and your voice   10
begins

who need no hope to
hunt here who
love me
I retreat before   15
your question as before my own
through old branches who
am I hiding
what creature in the bowels quaking
that should not be raised   20
against the night
crying its truth at last

No I who
love you
find while I can some light to crawl into   25
maybe
I will never answer
though your dark lasts as·my own does
and your voice in it without hope
or need of it   30
calling what I call calling
me me *You*
who are never there

The Chaff

Those who cannot love the heavens or the earth
beaten from the heavens and the earth
eat each other
those who cannot love each other
beaten from each other   5
eat themselves
those who cannot love themselves
beaten from themselves
eat a terrible bread
kneaded in the morning shrouded all day   10
baked in the dark
whose sweet smell brings the chaff flying like empty hands
through the turning sky night after night
calling with voices of young birds
to its wheat   15

Charles Tomlinson *(1927–)*

The Picture of J. T. in a Prospect of Stone

What should one
wish a child
and that, one's own,
emerging
from between   5
the stone lips
of a sheep-stile that divides
village graves
and village green?
—wish her   10
the constancy of stone.
—But stone
is hard.
—Say, rather,
it resists   15
the slow corrosives
and the flight
of time
and yet it takes
the play, the fluency   20
from light.
—How would you know
the gift you'd give
was the gift
she'd wish to have?   25
—Gift is giving
gift is meaning:
first
I'd give
then let her   30
live with it
to prove
its quality the better and
thus learn
to love   35
what (to begin with)
she might spurn.
—You'd
moralize a gift?

THE PICTURE OF J.T.   Cf. Andrew Marvell, "The Picture of Little T. C.," and John
Ashbery, "The Picture of Little J. A."

—I'd have her   40
   understand
      the gift I gave her.
—And so she shall
   but let her play
      her innocence away   45
emerging
   (as she does)
      between
her doom (unknown),
   her unmown green.   50

John Ashbery *(1927–   )*

The Picture of Little J. A. in a Prospect of Flowers

> "He was spoilt from childhood by
> the future, which he mastered
> rather early and apparently without
> great difficulty."
>
> —BORIS PASTERNAK

I

Darkness falls like a wet sponge
And Dick gives Genevieve a swift punch
In the pyjamas. "Aroint thee, witch."
Her tongue from previous ecstasy
Releases thoughts like little hats.   5

"He clap'd me first during the eclipse.
Afterwards I noted his manner
Much altered. But he sending
At that time certain handsome jewels
I durst not seem to take offense."   10

In a far recess of summer
Monks are playing soccer.

II

So far is goodness a mere memory
Or naming of recent scenes of badness
That even these lives, children,   15

THE PICTURE OF LITTLE J. A. Cf. Andrew Marvell, "The Picture of Little T. C." and
Charles Tomlinson, "The Picture of J. T." 3. **Aroint thee, witch**: begone, witch
(Shakespeare, *Macbeth*, I.iii.6).

You may pass through to be blessed,
So fair does each invent his virtue.

And coming from a white world, music
Will sparkle at the lips of many who are
Beloved. Then these, as dirty handmaidens   20
To some transparent witch, will dream
Of a white hero's subtle wooing,
And time shall force a gift on each.

That beggar to whom you gave no cent
Striped the night with his strange descant.   25

III

Yet I cannot escape the picture
Of my small self in that bank of flowers:
My head among the blazing phlox
Seemed a pale and gigantic fungus.
I had a hard stare, accepting   30

Everything, taking nothing,
As though the rolled-up future might stink
As loud as stood the sick moment
The shutter clicked. Though I was wrong,
Still, as the loveliest feelings   35

Must soon find words, and these, yes,
Displace them, so I am not wrong
In calling this comic version of myself
The true one. For as change is horror,   40
Virtue is really stubbornness

And only in the light of lost words
Can we imagine our rewards.

Anne Sexton   (1928–   )

Her Kind

I have gone out, a possessed witch,
haunting the black air, braver at night;
dreaming evil, I have done my hitch
over the plain houses, light by light:
lonely thing, twelve-fingered, out of mind.   5

A woman like that is not a woman, quite.
I have been her kind.

I have found the warm caves in the woods,
filled them with skillets, carvings, shelves,
closets, silks, innumerable goods;   10
fixed the suppers for the worms and the elves:
whining, rearranging the disaligned.
A woman like that is misunderstood.
I have been her kind.

I have ridden in your cart, driver,   15
waved my nude arms at villages going by,
learning the last bright routes, survivor
where your flames still bite my thigh
and my ribs crack where your wheels wind.
A woman like that is not ashamed to die.   20
I have been her kind.

Moon Song, Woman Song

I am alive at night.
I am dead in the morning,
an old vessel who used up her oil,
bleak and pale boned.
No miracle. No dazzle.   5
I'm out of repair
but you are tall in your battle dress
and I must arrange for your journey.
I was always a virgin,
old and pitted.   10
Before the world was, I was.

I have been oranging and fat,
carrot colored, gaped at,
allowing my cracked o's to drop on the sea
near Venice and Mombasa.   15
Over Maine I have rested.
I have fallen like a jet into the Pacific.
I have committed perjury over Japan.
I have dangled my pendulum,
my fat bag, my gold, gold,   20
blinkedy light
over you all.

HER KIND   **19. my ribs . . . wind:** that is, her bones are broken on the wheel, a torture instrument.

So if you must inquire, do so.
After all I am not artificial.　　　　　25
I looked long upon you,
love-bellied and empty,
flipping my endless display
for you, you my cold, cold
coverall man.

You need only request　　　　　30
and I will grant it.
It is virtually guaranteed
that you will walk into me like a barracks.
So come cruising, come cruising,
you of the blast off,　　　　　35
you of the bastion,
you of the scheme.
I will shut my fat eye down,
headquarters of an area,
house of a dream.　　　　　40

In the Beach House

The doors open
and the heat undoes itself,
everyone undoes himself,
everyone walks naked.
Two of them walk on the table.　　　　　5
They are not afraid of God's displeasure.
They will have no truck with the angel
who hoots from the fog horn
and throws the ocean into the rocks outside.
One of them covers the bedstead.　　　　　10
One of them winds round the bedpost
and both of them beat on the floor.

My little cot listens in
all night long—
even with the ocean turned up high,　　　　　15
even with every door boarded up,
they are allowed the lifting of the object,
the placing themselves upon the swing.
Inside my prison of pine and bedspring,
over my window sill, under my knob,　　　　　20
it is plain that they are at
the royal strapping.

Have mercy, little pillow,
stay mute and uncaring,

hear not one word of disaster! 25
Stay close, little sour feather,
little fellow full of salt.
My loves are oiling their bones
and then delivering them with unspeakable sounds
that carry them this way and that 30
while summer is hurrying its way in and out,
over and over,
in their room.

X. J. Kennedy (1929–   )

First Confession

Blood thudded in my ears. I scuffed,
    Steps stubborn, to the telltale booth
Beyond whose curtained portal coughed
    The robed repositor of truth.

The slat shot back. The universe 5
    Bowed down his cratered dome to hear
Enumerated my each curse,
    The sip snitched from my old man's beer,

My sloth pride envy lechery,
    The dime held back from Peter's Pence 10
With which I'd bribed my girl to pee
    That I might spy her instruments.

Hovering scale-pans when I'd done
    Settled their balance slow as silt
While in the restless dark I burned 15
    Bright as a brimstone in my guilt

Until as one feeds birds he doled
    Seven Our Fathers and a Hail
Which I to double-scrub my soul
    Intoned twice at the altar rail 20

Where Sunday in seraphic light
    I knelt, as full of grace as most,

FIRST CONFESSION   10. Peter's Pence: specifically, Roman Catholic annual contribution to the expenses of the Vatican; generally, a contribution to any collection. 18. Seven . . . Hail: seven repetitions of the Lord's Prayer and a "Hail Mary," recited as penance.

And stuck my tongue out at the priest:
A fresh roost for the Holy Ghost.

In a Prominent Bar in Secaucus One Day

To the tune of "The Old Orange Flute"
or the tune of "Sweet Betsy from Pike"

In a prominent bar in Secaucus one day
Rose a lady in skunk with a topheavy sway,
Raised a knobby red finger—all turned from their beer—
While with eyes bright as snowcrust she sang high and clear:

"Now who of you'd think from an eyeload of me   5
That I once was a lady as proud as could be?
Oh I'd never sit down by a tumbledown drunk
If it wasn't, my dears, for the high cost of junk.

"All the gents used to swear that the white of my calf
Beat the down of the swan by a length and a half.   10
In the kerchief of linen I caught to my nose
Ah, there never fell snot, but a little gold rose.

"I had seven gold teeth and a toothpick of gold,
My Virginia cheroot was a leaf of it rolled
And I'd light it each time with a thousand in cash—   15
Why the bums used to fight if I flicked them an ash.

"Once the toast of the Biltmore, the belle of the Taft,
I would drink bottle beer at the Drake, never draft,
And dine at the Astor on Salisbury steak
With a clean tablecloth for each bite I did take.   20

"In a car like the Roxy I'd roll to the track,
A steel-guitar trio, a bar in the back,
And the wheels made no noise, they turned over so fast,
Still it took you ten minutes to see me go past.

"When the horses bowed down to me that I might choose,   25
I bet on them all, for I hated to lose.
Now I'm saddled each night for my butter and eggs
And the broken threads race down the backs of my legs.

"Let you hold in mind, girls, that your beauty must pass
Like a lovely white clover that rusts with its grass.   30

IN A PROMINENT BAR   1. **Secaucus:** an industrial town in northern New Jersey. 8. **junk:** narcotics. 14. **cheroot:** cigar. 17–19. **Biltmore . . . Astor:** various fine, or once-fine, hotels in New York City. 21. **Roxy:** a huge, ornate movie palace.

Keep your bottoms off barstools and marry you young
Or be left—an old barrel with many a bung.

"For when time takes you out for a spin in his car
You'll be hard-pressed to stop him from going too far
And be left by the roadside, for all your good deeds,   35
Two toadstools for tits and a face full of weeds."

All the house raised a cheer, but the man at the bar
Made a phonecall and up pulled a red patrol car
And she blew us a kiss as they copped her away
From that prominent bar in Secaucus, N.J.   40

Adrienne Rich *(1929–   )*

The Roofwalker

for Denise Levertov

Over the half-finished houses
night comes. The builders
stand on the roof. It is
quiet after the hammers,
the pulleys hang slack.   5
Giants, the roofwalkers,
on a listing deck, the wave
of darkness about to break
on their heads. The sky
is a torn sail where figures   10
pass magnified, shadows
on a burning deck.

I feel like them up there:
exposed, larger than life,
and due to break my neck.   15

Was it worth while to lay—
with infinite exertion—
a roof I can't live under?
—All those blueprints,
closings of gaps,   20
measurings, calculations?
A life I didn't choose
chose me: even
my tools are the wrong ones

for what I have to do. 25
I'm naked, ignorant,
a naked man fleeing
across the roofs
who could with a shade of difference
be sitting in the lamplight 30
against the cream wallpaper
reading—not with indifference—
about a naked man
fleeing across the roofs.

Novella

Two people in a room, speaking harshly.
One gets up, goes out to walk.
(That is the man.)
The other goes into the next room
and washes the dishes, cracking one. 5
(That is the woman.)
It gets dark outside.
The children quarrel in the attic.
She has no blood left in her heart.
The man comes back to a dark house. 10
The only light is in the attic.
He has forgotten his key.
He rings at his own door
and hears sobbing on the stairs.
The lights go on in the house. 15
The door closes behind him.
Outside, separate as minds,
the stars too come alight.

Thom Gunn (1929–)

Modes of Pleasure

I jump with terror seeing him,
Dredging the bar with that stiff glare
As fiercely as if each whim there
Were passion, whose passion is a whim:

The Fallen Rake, being fallen from 5
The heights of twenty to middle age,

And helpless to control his rage,
So mean, so few the chances come.

The very beauty of his prime
Was that the triumphs which recurred   10
In different rooms without a word
Would all be lost some time in time.

Thus he reduced the wild unknown.
And having used each hour of leisure
To learn by rote the modes of pleasure,   15
The sensual skills as skills alone,

He knows that nothing, not the most
Cunning or sweet, can hold him, still.
Living by habit of the will,
He cannot contemplate the past,   20

Cannot discriminate, condemned
To the sharpest passion of them all.
Rigid he sits: brave, terrible,
The will awaits its gradual end.

The Corridor

A separate place between the thought and felt
The empty hotel corridor was dark.
But here the keyhole shone, a meaning spark.
What fires were latent in it! So he knelt.

Now, at the corridor's much lighter end,   5
A pierglass hung upon the wall and showed,
As by an easily deciphered code,
Dark, door, and man, hooped by a single band.

He squinted through the keyhole, and within
Surveyed an act of love that frank as air   10
He was too ugly for, or could not dare,
Or at a crucial movement thought a sin.

Pleasure was simple thus: he mastered it.
If once he acted as participant
He would be mastered, the inhabitant   15
Of someone else's world, mere shred to fit.

He moved himself to get a better look
And then it was he noticed in the glass

Two strange eyes in a fascinated face
That watched him like a picture in a book. 20

The instant drove simplicity away—
The scene was altered, it depended on
His kneeling, when he rose they were clean gone
The couple in the keyhole; this would stay.

For if the watcher of the watcher shown 25
There in the distant glass, should be watched too,
Who can be master, free of others; who
Can look around and say he is alone?

Moreover, who can know that what he sees
Is not distorted, that he is not seen 30
Distorted by a pierglass, curved and lean?
Those curious eyes, through him, were linked to these—

These lovers altered in the cornea's bend.
What could he do but leave the keyhole, rise,
Holding those eyes as equal in his eyes, 35
And go, one hand held out, to meet a friend?

On the Move

'Man, you gotta Go.'

The blue jay scuffling in the bushes follows
Some hidden purpose, and the gust of birds
That spurts across the field, the wheeling swallows,
Have nested in the trees and undergrowth.
Seeking their instinct, or their poise, or both, 5
One moves with an uncertain violence
Under the dust thrown by a baffled sense
Or the dull thunder of approximate words.

On motorcycles, up the road, they come:
Small, black, as flies hanging in heat, the Boys, 10
Until the distance throws them forth, their hum
Bulges to thunder held by calf and thigh.
In goggles, donned impersonality,
In gleaming jackets trophied with the dust,
They strap in doubt—by hiding it, robust— 15
And almost hear a meaning in their noise.

Exact conclusion of their hardiness
Has no shape yet, but from known whereabouts

They ride, direction where the tires press.
They scare a flight of birds across the field:
Much that is natural, to the will must yield.
Men manufacture both machine and soul,
And use what they imperfectly control
To dare a future from the taken routes.

It is a part solution, after all.
One is not necessarily discord
On earth; or damned because, half animal,
One lacks direct instinct, because one wakes
Afloat on movement that divides and breaks.
One joins the movement in a valueless world,
Choosing it, till, both hurler and the hurled,
One moves as well, always toward, toward.

A minute holds them, who have come to go:
The self-defined, astride the created will
They burst away; the towns they travel through
Are home for neither bird nor holiness,
For birds and saints complete their purposes.
At worst, one is in motion; and at best,
Reaching no absolute, in which to rest,
One is always nearer by not keeping still.

20

25

30

35

40

John Hollander (1929–   )

Jefferson Valley

The tops of the spruces here have always done
Ragged things to the skies arranged behind them
Like slates at twilight; and the morning sun
Has marked out trees and hedgerows, and defined them
In various greens, until, toward night, they blur
Back into one rough palisade again,
Furred thick with dusk. No wind we know can stir
This olive blackness that surrounds us when
It becomes the boundary of what we know
By limiting the edge of what we see.
When sunlight shows several spruces in a row,
To know the green of a particular tree
    Means disbelief in darkness; and the lack
    Of a singular green is what we mean by black.

5

10

Movie-Going

Drive-ins are out, to start with. One must always be
Able to see the over-painted Moorish ceiling
Whose pinchbeck jazz gleams even in the darkness, calling
The straying eye to feast on it, and glut, then fall
Back to the sterling screen again. One needs to feel   5
That the two empty, huddled, dark stage-boxes keep
Empty for kings. And having frequently to cope
With the abominable goodies, overflow
Bulk and (finally) exploring hands of flushed
Close neighbors gazing beadily out across glum   10
Distances is, after all, to keep the gleam
Alive of something rather serious, to keep
Faith, perhaps, with the City. When as children our cup
Of joys ran over the special section, and we clutched
Our ticket stubs and followed the bouncing ball, no clash   15
Of cymbals at the start of the stage-show could abash
Our third untiring time around. When we came back,
Older, to cop an endless series of feels, we sat
Unashamed beneath the bare art-nouveau bodies, set
High on the golden, after-glowing proscenium when   20
The break had come. And still, now as always, once
The show is over and we creep into the dull
Blaze of mid-afternoon sunshine, the hollow dole
Of the real descends on everything and we can know
That we have been in some place wholly elsewhere, a night   25
At noonday, not without dreams, whose portals shine
(Not ivory, not horn in ever-changing shapes)
But made of some weird, clear substance not often used for gates.
Stay for the second feature on a double bill
Always: it will teach you how to love, how not to live,   30
And how to leave the theater for that unlit, aloof
And empty world again. "B"-pictures showed us: shooting
More real than singing or making love; the shifting
Ashtray upon the mantel, moved by some idiot
Between takes, helping us learn beyond a trace of doubt   35
How fragile are imagined scenes; the dimming-out

MOVIE-GOING **3. pinchbeck:** sham, spurious. **5. sterling:** alluding to "silver screen," the old cliché for movies. **6. stage-boxes:** unused because of sight-angles in a theater converted to films. **13–14. our cup . . . over:** Cf. "my cup runneth over," Psalms 23:5. **14. special section:** reserved for unaccompanied children. **19. art-nouveau:** in the curving shallow forms of early twentieth-century design. **20. after-glowing:** when the house lights are on, with the suggestion of sexual "afterglow." **23. dole:** portion; but also anciently, pain, grief, lamentation. **25. wholly elsewhere:** alluding to the theological conception of the divine as "wholly other," transcending human experience and comprehension. **27. ivory . . . horn:** referring to the gates through which, in Greek myth, false and true dreams passed as they sped up to earth. **32. "B"-pictures:** cheaply made movies used as second features to fill a "double bill."

Of all the brightness of the clear and highly lit
Interior of the hero's cockpit, when the stock shot
Of ancient dive-bombers peeling off cuts in, reshapes
Our sense of what is, finally, plausible; the grays   40
Of living rooms, the blacks of cars whose window glass
At night allows the strips of fake Times Square to pass
Jerkily by on the last ride; even the patch
Of sudden white, and inverted letters dashing
Up during the projectionist's daydream, dying   45
Quickly—these are the colors of our inner life.

Never ignore the stars, of course. But above all,
Follow the asteroids as well: though dark, they're more
Intense for never glittering; anyone can admire
Sparklings against a night sky, but against a bright   50
Background of prominence, to feel the Presences burnt
Into no fiery fame should be a more common virtue.
For, just as Vesta has no atmosphere, no verdure
Burgeons on barren Ceres, bit-players never surge
Into the rhythms of expansion and collapse, such   55
As all the flaming bodies live and move among.
But there, more steadfast than stars are, loved for their being,
Not for their burning, move the great Characters: see
Thin Donald Meek, that shuffling essence ever so
Affronting to Eros and to Pride; the pair of bloated   60
Capitalists, Walter Connolly and Eugene Pallette, seated
High in their offices above New York; the evil,
Blackening eyes of Sheldon Leonard, and the awful
Stare of Eduardo Cianelli. Remember those who have gone—
(Where's bat-squeaking Butterfly McQueen? Will we see again   65
That ever-anonymous drunk, waxed-moustached, rubber-legged
Caught in revolving doors?) and think of the light-years logged
Up in those humbly noble orbits, where no hot
Spotlight of solar grace consumes some blazing hearts,
Bestowing the flimsy immortality of stars   70
For some great distant instant. Out of the darkness stares
Venus, who seems to be what once we were, the fair
Form of emerging love, her nitrous atmosphere
Hiding her prizes. Into the black expanse peers
Mars, whom we in time will come to resemble: parched,   75
Xanthine desolations, dead Cimmerian seas, the far
Distant past preserved in the blood-colored crusts; fire

---

48. asteroids: here the supporting players. 53–54. Vesta . . . Ceres: asteroids revolving around the sun between the orbits of Mars and Jupiter. 58. Characters: here character actors, constantly reenacting the same distinctive types. 65. bat-squeaking: a
reference to her remarkably high-pitched voice. 73. nitrous atmosphere: the enshroud-
ing atmosphere of the planet Venus. 76. Xanthine: yellow; but see also Richard Wilbur's "Advice to a Prophet," ll. 21–22 and note (p. 415). Cimmerian: in a region of
perpetual darkness, fabled in antiquity; cf. the "Cimmerian desert" of Milton's
"L'Allegro" 1. 10 (p. 128).

And water both remembered only. Having shined
Means having died. But having been real only, and shunned
Stardom, the planetoids are what we now are, humming   80
With us, above us, ever into the future, seeming
Ever to take the shapes of the world we wake to from dreams.

Always go in the morning if you can; it will
Be something more than habit if you do. Keep well
Away from most French farces. Try to see a set   85
Of old blue movies every so often, that the sight
Of animal doings out of the clothes of 'thirty-five
May remind you that even the natural act is phrased
In the terms and shapes of particular times and places.
Finally, remember always to honor the martyred dead.   90
The forces of darkness spread everywhere now, and the best
And brightest screens fade out, while many-antennaed beasts
Perch on the housetops, and along the grandest streets
Palaces crumble, one by one. The dimming starts
Slowly at first; the signs are few, as "Movies are   95
Better than Ever," "Get More out of Life. See a Movie" Or
Else there's no warning at all and, Whoosh! the theater falls,
Alas, transmogrified: no double-feature fills
A gleaming marquee with promises, now only lit
With "Pike and Whitefish Fresh Today" "Drano" and "Light   100
Or Dark Brown Sugar, Special." Try never to patronize
Such places (or pass them by one day a year). The noise
Of movie mansions changing form, caught in the toils
Of our lives' withering, rumbles, resounds and tolls
The knell of neighborhoods. Do not forget the old   105
Places, for everyone's home has been a battlefield.

I remember: the RKO COLONIAL; the cheap
ARDEN and ALDEN both; LOEW'S LINCOLN SQUARE's bright shape;
The NEWSREEL; the mandarin BEACON, resplendently arrayed;
The tiny SEVENTY-SEVENTH STREET, whose demise I rued   110
So long ago; the eighty-first street, sunrise-hued,
RKO; and then LOEW's at eighty-third, which had
The colder pinks of sunset on it; and then, back
Across Broadway again, and up, you disembarked
At the YORKTOWN and then the STODDARD, with their dark   115
Marquees; the SYMPHONY had a decorative disk
With elongated 'twenties nudes whirling in it;
(Around the corner the THALIA, daughter of memory! owed
Her life to Foreign Hits, in days when you piled your coat
High on your lap and sat, sweating and cramped, to catch   120
"La Kermesse Heroique" every third week, and watched

---

118. Thalia: a theater named for the Muse of comedy, one of the daughters of Memory. 121. "La Kermesse Heroique": a French film, also known as *Carnival in Flanders*, directed by Jacques Feyder (1935).

Fritz Lang from among an audience of refugees, bewitched
By the sense of Crisis on and off that tiny bit
Of screen) Then north again: the RIVERSIDE, the bright
RIVIERA rubbing elbows with it; and right   125
Smack on a hundredth street, the MIDTOWN; and the rest
Of them: the CARLTON, EDISON, LOEW'S OLYMPIA, and best
Because, of course, the last of all, its final burst
Anonymous, the NEMO! These were once the pearls
Of two-and-a-half miles of Broadway! How many have paled   130
Into a supermarket's failure of the imagination?

Honor them all. Remember how once their splendor blazed
In sparkling necklaces across America's blasted
Distances and deserts: think how, at night, the fastest
Train might stop for water somewhere, waiting, faced   135
Westward, in deepening dusk, till ruby illuminations
Of something different from Everything Here, Now, shine
Out from the local Bijou, truest gem, the most bright
Because the most believed in, staving off the night
Perhaps, for a while longer with its flickering light.   140

These fade. All fade. Let us honor them with our own fading sight.

Adam's Task

> *"And Adam gave names to all cat-*
> *tle, and to the fowl of the air, and*
> *to every beast of the field . . ."—*
> Gen. 2:20

Thou, paw-paw-paw; thou, glurd; thou, spotted
   Glurd; thou, whitestap, lurching through
The high-grown brush; thou, phant-footed,
   Implex; thou, awagabu.

Every burrower, each flier   5
   Came for the name he had to give:
Gay, first work, ever to be prior,
   Not yet sunk to primitive.

Thou, verdle; thou, McFleery's pomma;
   Thou; thou; thou—three types of grawl;   10
Thou, flisket; thou, kabasch; thou, comma-
   Eared mashawk; thou, all; thou, all.

---

122. Fritz Lang: (b. 1890), distinguished German director who escaped from Germany and began to work in the United States in 1936. **129. Nemo:** Latin for "no one" (hence "anonymous").

Were, in a fire of becoming,
    Laboring to be burned away,
Then work, half-measuring, half-humming,   15
    Would be as serious as play.

Thou, pambler; thou, rivarn; thou, greater
    Wherret, and thou, lesser one;
Thou, sproal; thou, zant; thou, lily-eater.
    Naming's over. Day is done.   20

The Bird

from the Yiddish of Moishe Leib Halpern

Well, this bird comes, and under his wing is a crutch,
And he asks why I keep my door on the latch;
So I tell him that right outside the gate
Many robbers watch and wait
To get at the hidden bit of cheese,   5
Under my ass, behind my knees.

Then through the keyhole and the crack in the jamb
The bird bawls out he's my brother Sam,
And tells me I'll never begin to believe
How sorely he was made to grieve   10
On shipboard, where he had to ride
Out on deck, he says, from the other side.

So I get a whiff of what's in the air,
And leave the bird just standing there.
Meanwhile—because one never knows,   15
I mean—I'm keeping on my toes,
Further pushing my bit of cheese
Under my ass and toward my knees.

The bird bends his wing to shade his eyes
—Just like my brother Sam—and cries,   20
Through the keyhole, that *his* luck should shine
Maybe so blindingly as mine,
Because, he says, he's seen my bit
Of cheese, and he'll crack my skull for it.

It's not so nice here anymore.   25
So I wiggle slowly towards the door,
Holding my chair and that bit of cheese
Under my ass, behind my knees,
Quietly. But then as if I care,
I ask him whether it's cold out there.   30

They are frozen totally,
Both his poor ears, he answers me,
Declaring with a frightful moan
That, while he lay asleep alone
He ate up his leg—the one he's lost.   35
If I let him in, I can hear the rest.

When I hear the words "ate up," you can bet
That I'm terrified; I almost forget
To guard my bit of hidden cheese
Under my ass there, behind my knees.   40
But I reach below and, yes, it's still here,
So I haven't the slightest thing to fear.

Then I move that we should try a bout
Of waiting, to see which first gives out,
His patience, there, behind the door,   45
Or mine, in my own house. And more
And more I feel it's funny, what
A lot of patience I have got.

And that's the way it's stayed, although
That was some seven years ago.   50
I still call out "Hi, there!" through the door.
He screams back " 'Lo, there" as before.
"Let me out" I plead, "don't be a louse"
And he answers, "Let me in the house."

But I know what he wants. So I bide   55
My time and let him wait outside.
He enquires about the bit of cheese
Under my ass, behind my knees;
Scared, I reach down, but, yes, it's still here.
I haven't the slightest thing to fear.   60

Robert Pack *(1929–   )*

Everything Is Possible

I am becoming a god!
At last!
I knew I could make it.
You always told me so.
I knew I could never rest   5
Until I did it.

Now in my left hand, see
My first made meadow.
Let there be a fox
With a magnificent, wandering, rufous tail   10
Echoing windward behind it.
Does that please you?
And behind that stone
I have shaped
Like a head emerging   15
From the bristle of cut sheaves
Is the vixen's den lit
With the polished eyes of her cubs.
Do you like that?
And there in repose in my right hand   20
Pulses a lake,
You can hear the roots
Of the willow trees sucking
Toward the source of its flow.
What color fish   25
Shall I put in it?
Shall I make them symmetrical?
Shall I fleck them
With random dots
And inscrutable blotches?   30
Everything is possible!
You always told me so.
Let there be a child!
May I plant him inside you
And let him grow   35
To tend the fox and tend the fish,
Humming the meadow,
Whistling the shape of the lake?
Could we rest then?
Would you like that?   40
Would that then make us free?

The Pack Rat

Collector of lost beads, buttons, bird bones,
Catalogue-maker with an eye for glitter,
Litter lover, entrepreneur of waste—
Bits of snail-shell, chips of jugs, red thread,
Blue thread, tinfoil, teeth; fair-minded thief   5
(Leaving in my pocket when I slept,
A pine cone and two nuts for the dime you stole);
Reasonable romancer, journeying more
Than half a mile to meet a mate, split-eared
Lover with a bitten tail (your mate mates rough),   10

You last all courtship long, you stick around
When the brood comes, unlike most other rats;
Payer of prices, busy with no dreams,
But brain enough to get along; moderate
Music maker with moderate powers, thumping   15
The drum of frightened ground with both hind feet
Or scraping dry leaves till the still woods chirp;
Simple screamer seized by the owl's descent,
One scream and one regret, just one; fellow,
Forebear, survivor, have I lost my way?   20

Gregory Corso (1930–   )

Marriage

Should I get married? Should I be good?
Astound the girl next door with my velvet suit and faustus hood?
Don't take her to movies but to cemeteries
tell all about werewolf bathtubs and forked clarinets
then desire her and kiss her and all the preliminaries   5
and she going just so far and I understanding why
not getting angry saying You must feel! It's beautiful to feel!
Instead take her in my arms lean against an old crooked tombstone
and woo her the entire night the constellations in the sky—

When she introduces me to her parents   10
back straightened, hair finally combed, strangled by a tie,
should I sit knees together on their 3rd degree sofa
and not ask Where's the bathroom?
How else to feel other than I am,
often thinking Flash Gordon soap—   15
O how terrible it must be for a young man
seated before a family and the family thinking
We never saw him before! He wants our Mary Lou!
After tea and homemade cookies they ask What do you do for a living?
Should I tell them? Would they like me then?   20
Say All right get married, we're losing a daughter
but we're gaining a son—
And should I then ask Where's the bathroom?

O God, and the wedding! All her family and her friends
and only a handful of mine all scroungy and bearded   25
just wait to get at the drinks and food—

MARRIAGE **2. faustus hood:** like that of the scholar-magician hero of Christopher
Marlowe's play *Dr. Faustus.*

And the priest! he looking at me as if I masturbated
asking me Do you take this woman for your lawful wedded wife?
And I trembling what to say say Pie Glue!
I kiss the bride all those corny men slapping me on the back   30
She's all yours, boy! Ha-ha-ha!
And in their eyes you could see some obscene honeymoon going on—
Then all that absurd rice and clanky cans and shoes
Niagara Falls! Hordes of us! Husbands! Wives! Flowers! Chocolates!
All streaming into cozy hotels   35
All going to do the same thing tonight
The indifferent clerk he knowing what was going to happen
The lobby zombies they knowing what
The whistling elevator man he knowing
The winking bellboy knowing   40
Everybody knowing! I'd be almost inclined not to do anything!
Stay up all night! Stare that hotel clerk in the eye!
Screaming: I deny honeymoon! I deny honeymoon!
running rampant into those almost climactic suites
yelling Radio belly! Cat shovel!   45
O I'd live in Niagara forever! in a dark cave beneath the Falls
I'd sit there the Mad Honeymooner
devising ways to break marriages, a scourge of bigamy
a saint of divorce—

But I should get married I should be good   50
How nice it'd be to come home to her
and sit by the fireplace and she in the kitchen
aproned young and lovely wanting my baby
and so happy about me she burns the roast beef
and comes crying to me and I get up from my big papa chair   55
saying Christmas teeth! Radiant brains! Apple deaf!
God what a husband I'd make! Yes, I should get married!
So much to do! like sneaking into Mr Jones' house late at night
and cover his golf clubs with 1920 Norwegian books
Like hanging a picture of Rimbaud on the lawnmower   60
like pasting Tannu Tuva postage stamps all over the picket fence
like when Mrs Kindhead comes to collect for the Community Chest
grab her and tell her There are unfavorable omens in the sky!
And when the mayor comes to get my vote tell him
When are you going to stop people killing whales!   65
And when the milkman comes leave him a note in the bottle
Penguin dust, bring me penguin dust, I want penguin dust—

Yet if I should get married and it's Connecticut and snow
and she gives birth to a child and I am sleepless, worn,
up for nights, head bowed against a quiet window, the past behind me,   70

---

60. **Rimbaud**: Arthur Rimbaud (1854–91), French symbolist poet. 61. **Tannu Tuva**: area of southern Siberia, an independent people's republic 1921–44, now part of the USSR.

finding myself in the most common of situations a trembling man
knowledged with responsibility not twig-smear nor Roman coin soup—
O what would that be like!
Surely I'd give it for a nipple a rubber Tacitus
For a rattle a bag of broken Bach records	75
Tack Della Francesca all over its crib
Sew the Greek alphabet on its bib
And build for its playpen a roofless Parthenon

No, I doubt I'd be that kind of father
not rural not snow no quiet window	80
but hot smelly tight New York City
seven flights up, roaches and rats in the walls
a fat Reichian wife screeching over potatoes Get a job!
And five nose running brats in love with Batman
And the neighbors all toothless and dry haired	85
like those hag masses of the 18th century
all wanting to come in and watch TV
The landlord wants his rent
Grocery store Blue Cross Gas & Electric Knights of Columbus
Impossible to lie back and dream Telephone snow, ghost parking—	90
No! I should not get married I should never get married!

But—imagine If I were married to a beautiful sophisticated woman
tall and pale wearing an elegant black dress and long black gloves
holding a cigarette holder in one hand and a highball in the other
and we lived high up in a penthouse with a huge window	95
from which we could see all of New York and even farther on clearer days
No, can't imagine myself married to that pleasant prison dream—

O but what about love! I forget love
not that I am incapable of love
it's just that I see love as odd as wearing shoes—	100
I never wanted to marry a girl who was like my mother
And Ingrid Bergman was always impossible
And there's maybe a girl now but she's already married
And I don't like men and—
but there's got to be somebody!	105
Because what if I'm 60 years old and not married,
all alone in a furnished room with pee stains on my underwear
and everybody else is married! All the universe married but me!

Ah, yet well I know that were a woman possible as I am possible
then marriage would be possible—	110

---

74. **Tacitus:** Roman historian (A.D. 55–117). 76. **Della Francesca:** Piero della Francesca (1420–92), Italian Renaissance painter. 83. **Reichian:** follower of Wilhelm
Reich, a psychoanalyst who placed special value on the achievement of full orgasm. 86.
hag masses: black masses celebrated by witches (?).

Like SHE in her lovely alien gaud waiting her Egyptian lover
so I wait—bereft of 2,000 years and the bath of life.

Ted Hughes *(1930–   )*

Hawk Roosting

I sit in the top of the wood, my eyes closed.
Inaction, no falsifying dream
Between my hooked head and hooked feet:
Or in sleep rehearse perfect kills and eat.

The convenience of the high trees!   5
The air's buoyancy and the sun's ray
Are of advantage to me;
And the earth's face upward for my inspection.

My feet are locked upon the rough bark.
It took the whole of Creation   10
To produce my foot, my each feather:
Now I hold Creation in my foot

Or fly up, and revolve it all slowly—
I kill where I please because it is all mine.
There is no sophistry in my body: 15
My manners are tearing off heads—

The allotment of death.
For the one path of my flight is direct
Through the bones of the living.
No arguments assert my right: 20

The sun is behind me.
Nothing has changed since I began.
My eye has permitted no change.
I am going to keep things like this.

Pennines in April

If this country were a sea (that is solid rock
Deeper than any sea) these hills heaving

111. **SHE:** the age-old but unfadingly beautiful heroine of Rider Haggard's novel, *She*
(1887). **gaud:** elaborate finery or ceremony.
PENNINES IN APRIL   The Pennines are a range of hills in northern England.

Out of the east, mass behind mass, at this height
Hoisting heather and stones to the sky
Must burst upwards and topple into Lancashire.   5

Perhaps, as the earth turns, such ground-stresses
Do come rolling westward through the locked land.
Now, measuring the miles of silence
Your eye takes the strain: through

Landscapes gliding blue as water   10
Those barrelings of strength are heaving slowly and heave
To your feet and surf upwards
In a still, fiery air, hauling the imagination,
Carrying the larks upward.

Reveille

No, the serpent was not
One of God's ordinary creatures.
Where did he creep from,
This legless land-swimmer with a purpose?

Adam and lovely Eve   5
Deep in the first dream
Each the everlasting
Holy One of the other

Woke with cries of pain.
Each clutched a throbbing wound—   10
A sudden, cruel bite.
The serpent's head, small and still,

Smiled under the lilies.
Behind him, his coils
Had crushed all Eden's orchards.   15
And out beyond Eden

The black, thickening river of his body
Glittered in giant loops
Around desert mountains and away
Over the ashes of the future.   20

Gary Snyder (1930–   )

Milton by Firelight

Piute Creek, August 1955

"O hell, what do mine eyes
        with grief behold?"
Working with an old
Singlejack miner, who can sense
The vein and cleavage   5
In the very guts of rock, can
Blast granite, build
Switchbacks that last for years
Under the beat of snow, thaw, mule-hooves.
What use, Milton, a silly story   10
Of our lost general parents,
        eaters of fruit?

The Indian, the chainsaw boy,
And a string of six mules
Came riding down to camp   15
Hungry for tomatoes and green apples.
Sleeping in saddle-blankets
Under a bright night-sky
Han River slantwise by morning.
Jays squall   20
Coffee boils

In ten thousand years the Sierras
Will be dry and dead, home of the scorpion.
Ice-scratched slabs and bent trees.
No paradise, no fall,   25
Only the weathering land
The wheeling sky,
Man, with his Satan
Scouring the chaos of the mind.
Oh Hell!   30

Fire down
Too dark to read, miles from a road
The bell-mare clangs in the meadow

MILTON BY FIRELIGHT   1–2. "O hell . . . behold": Satan's outcry on first seeing Adam and Eve (*Paradise Lost,* iv.358).

That packed dirt for a fill-in
Scrambling through loose rocks   35
On an old trail
All of a summer's day.

Kyoto: March

A few light flakes of snow
Fall in the feeble sun;
Birds sing in the cold,
A warbler by the wall. The plum
Buds tight and chill soon bloom.   5
The moon begins first
Fourth, a faint slice west
At nightfall. Jupiter half-way
High at the end of night-
Meditation. The dove cry   10
Twangs like a bow.
At dawn Mt. Hiei dusted white
On top; in the clear air
Folds of all the gullied green
Hills around the town are sharp,   15
Breath stings. Beneath the roofs
Of frosty houses
Lovers part, from tangle warm
Of gentle bodies under quilt
And crack the icy water to the face   20
And wake and feed the children
And grandchildren that they love.

Sylvia Plath   (1932–1963)

Suicide Off Egg Rock

Behind him the hotdogs split and drizzled
On the public grills, and the ochreous salt flats,
Gas tanks, factory stacks—that landscape
Of imperfections his bowels were part of—
Rippled and pulsed in the glassy updraft.   5

---

37. **All . . . day**: Cf. Milton's description of how Mulciber, thrown by Jove, fell from heaven: "from morn/To noon he fell, from noon to dewy eve,/A summer's day" (*Paradise Lost*, i.742–44).

SUICIDE   **2. ochreous**: light brownish yellow. **5. glassy updraft**: the heat waves that produce the wavering images of distorting glass panes.

Sun struck the water like a damnation.
No pit of shadow to crawl into,
And his blood beating the old tattoo
I am, I am, I am. Children
Were squealing where combers broke and the spindrift   10
Raveled wind-ripped from the crest of the wave.
A mongrel working his legs to a gallop
Hustled a gull flock to flap off the sandspit.

He smoldered, as if stone-deaf, blindfold,
His body beached with the sea's garbage,   15
A machine to breathe and beat forever.
Flies filing in through a dead skate's eyehole
Buzzed and assailed the vaulted brainchamber.
The words in his book wormed off the pages.
Everything glittered like blank paper.

Everything shrank in the sun's corrosive   20
Ray but Egg Rock on the blue wastage.
He heard when he walked into the water

The forgetful surf creaming on those ledges.

The Bee Meeting

Who are these people at the bridge to meet me? They are the villagers—
The rector, the midwife, the sexton, the agent for bees.
In my sleeveless summery dress I have no protection,
And they are all gloved and covered, why did nobody tell me?
They are smiling and taking out veils tacked to ancient hats.   5

I am nude as a chicken neck, does nobody love me?
Yes, here is the secretary of bees with her white shop smock,
Buttoning the cuffs at my wrists and the slit from my neck to my knees.
Now I am milkweed silk, the bees will not notice.
They will not smell my fear, my fear, my fear.   10

Which is the rector now, is it that man in black?
Which is the midwife, is that her blue coat?
Everybody is nodding a square black head, they are knights in visors,
Breastplates of cheesecloth knotted under the armpits.
Their smiles and their voices are changing. I am led through a beanfield.   15

Strips of tinfoil winking like people,
Feather dusters fanning their hands in a sea of bean flowers,
Creamy bean flowers with black eyes and leaves like bored hearts.
Is it blood clots the tendrils are dragging up that string?
No, no, it is scarlet flowers that will one day be edible.   20

Now they are giving me a fashionable white straw Italian hat
And a black veil that molds to my face, they are making me one of them.
They are leading me to the shorn grove, the circle of hives.
Is it the hawthorn that smells so sick?
The barren body of hawthorn, etherizing its children.   25

Is it some operation that is taking place?
It is the surgeon my neighbors are waiting for,
This apparition in a green helmet,
Shining gloves and white suit.
Is it the butcher, the grocer, the postman, someone I know?   30

I cannot run, I am rooted, and the gorse hurts me
With its yellow purses, its spiky armory.
I could not run without having to run forever.
The white hive is snug as a virgin,
Sealing off her brood cells, her honey, and quietly humming.   35

Smoke rolls and scarves in the grove.
The mind of the hive thinks this is the end of everything.
Here they come, the outriders, on their hysterical elastics.
If I stand very still, they will think I am cow parsley,
A gullible head untouched by their animosity,   40

Not even nodding, a personage in a hedgerow.
The villagers open the chambers, they are hunting the queen.
Is she hiding, is she eating honey? She is very clever.
She is old, old, old, she must live another year, and she knows it.
While in their fingerjoint cells the new virgins   45

Dream of a duel they will win inevitably,
A curtain of wax dividing them from the bride flight,
The upflight of the murderess into a heaven that loves her.
The villagers are moving the virgins, there will be no killing.
The old queen does not show herself, is she so ungrateful?   50

I am exhausted, I am exhausted—
Pillar of white in a blackout of knives.
I am the magician's girl who does not flinch.
The villagers are untying their disguises, they are shaking hands.
Whose is that long white box in the grove, what have they accomplished,
    why am I cold?   55

The Moon and the Yew Tree

This is the light of the mind, cold and planetary.
The trees of the mind are black. The light is blue.
The grasses unload their griefs on my feet as if I were God,
Prickling my ankles and murmuring of their humility.

Fumy, spiritous mists inhabit this place   5
Separated from my house by a row of headstones.
I simply cannot see where there is to get to.

The moon is no door. It is a face in its own right,
White as a knuckle and terribly upset.
It drags the sea after it like a dark crime; it is quiet   10
With the O-gape of complete despair. I live here.
Twice on Sunday, the bells startle the sky—
Eight great tongues affirming the Resurrection.
At the end, they soberly bong out their names.

The yew tree points up. It has a Gothic shape.   15
The eyes lift after it and find the moon.
The moon is my mother. She is not sweet like Mary.
Her blue garments unloose small bats and owls.
How I would like to believe in tenderness—
The face of the effigy, gentled by candles,   20
Bending, on me in particular, its mild eyes.

I have fallen a long way. Clouds are flowering
Blue and mystical over the face of the stars.
Inside the church, the saints will be all blue,
Floating on their delicate feet over the cold pews,   25
Their hands and faces stiff with holiness.
The moon sees nothing of this. She is bald and wild.
And the message of the yew tree is blackness—blackness and silence.

Tulips

The tulips are too excitable, it is winter here.
Look how white everything is, how quiet, how snowed-in.
I am learning peacefulness, lying by myself quietly
As the light lies on these white walls, this bed, these hands.
I am nobody; I have nothing to do with explosions.   5
I have given my name and my day-clothes up to the nurses
And my history to the anesthetist and my body to surgeons.

They have propped my head between the pillow and the sheet-cuff
Like an eye between two white lids that will not shut.
Stupid pupil, it has to take everything in.   10
The nurses pass and pass, they are no trouble,
They pass the way gulls pass inland in their white caps,
Doing things with their hands, one just the same as another,
So it is impossible to tell how many there are.

THE MOON   15. yew tree: commonly planted in church graveyards. 17. Mary: the
Virgin Mary.

My body is a pebble to them, they tend it as water   15
Tends to the pebbles it must run over, smoothing them gently.
They bring me numbness in their bright needles, they bring me sleep.
Now I have lost myself I am sick of baggage—
My patent leather overnight case like a black pillbox,
My husband and child smiling out of the family photo;   20
Their smiles catch onto my skin, little smiling hooks.

I have let things slip, a thirty-year-old cargo boat
Stubbornly hanging on to my name and address.
They have swabbed me clear of my loving associations.
Scared and bare on the green plastic-pillowed trolley   25
I watched my tea-set, my bureaus of linen, my books
Sink out of sight, and the water went over my head.
I am a nun now, I have never been so pure.

I didn't want any flowers, I only wanted
To lie with my hands turned up and be utterly empty.   30
How free it is, you have no idea how free—
The peacefulness is so big it dazes you,
And it asks nothing, a name tag, a few trinkets.
It is what the dead close on, finally; I imagine them
Shutting their mouths on it, like a Communion tablet.   35

The tulips are too red in the first place, they hurt me.
Even through the gift paper I could hear them breathe
Lightly, through their white swaddlings, like an awful baby.
Their redness talks to my wound, it corresponds.
They are subtle: they seem to float, though they weigh me down,   40
Upsetting me with their sudden tongues and their color,
A dozen red lead sinkers round my neck.

Nobody watched me before, now I am watched.
The tulips turn to me, and the window behind me
Where once a day the light slowly widens and slowly thins,   45
And I see myself, flat, ridiculous, a cut-paper shadow
Between the eye of the sun and the eyes of the tulips,
And I have no face, I have wanted to efface myself.
The vivid tulips eat my oxygen.

Before they came the air was calm enough,   50
Coming and going, breath by breath, without any fuss.
Then the tulips filled it up like a loud noise.
Now the air snags and eddies round them the way a river
Snags and eddies round a sunken rust-red engine.
They concentrate my attention, that was happy   55
Playing and resting without committing itself.

The walls, also, seem to be warming themselves.
The tulips should be behind bars like dangerous animals;

They are opening like the mouth of some great African cat,
And I am aware of my heart: it opens and closes   60
Its bowl of red blooms out of sheer love of me.
The water I taste is warm and salt, like the sea,
And comes from a country far away as health.

Mark Strand *(1934–   )*

Keeping Things Whole

In a field
I am the absence
of field.
This is
always the case.   5
Wherever I am
I am what is missing.

When I walk
I part the air
and always   10
the air moves in
to fill the spaces
where my body's been.

We all have reasons
for moving.   15
I move
to keep things whole.

Eating Poetry

Ink runs from the corners of my mouth.
There is no happiness like mine.
I have been eating poetry.

The librarian does not believe what she sees.
Her eyes are sad   5
and she walks with her hands in her dress.

The poems are gone.
The light is dim.
The dogs are on the basement stairs and coming up.

Their eyeballs roll,   10
their blond legs burn like brush.
The poor librarian begins to stamp her feet and weep.

She does not understand.
When I get on my knees and lick her hand,
she screams.   15

I am a new man.
I snarl at her and bark.
I romp with joy in the bookish dark.

The Remains

for Bill and Sandy Bailey

I empty myself of the names of others. I empty my pockets.
I empty my shoes and leave them beside the road.
At night I turn back the clocks;
I open the family album and look at myself as a boy.

What good does it do? The hours have done their job.   5
I say my own name. I say goodbye.
The words follow each other downwind.
I love my wife but send her away.

My parents rise out of their thrones
into the milky rooms of clouds. How can I sing?   10
Time tells me what I am. I change and I am the same.
I empty myself of my life and my life remains.

From a Litany

Let the shark keep to the shelves and closets of coral.
Let cats throw over their wisdom.
Let the noble horse who rocks under the outlaw's ass eat plastic turf.
For no creature is safe.
Let the great sow of state grow strong.   5
Let those in office search under their clothes for the private life.
They will find nothing.
Let them gather together and hold hands.
They shall have nothing to hold.
Let the flag flutter in the glass moon of each eye.   10
Let the black-suited priests stand for the good life.

FROM A LITANY   Suggested by Christopher Smart's *Jubilate Agno* (see pp. 198–201).

Let them tell us to be more like them.
For that is the nature of the sickness.
Let the bodies of debutantes gleam like frigidaires.
For they shall have sex with food.   15
Let flies sink into their mothers' thighs and go blind in the trenches of
    meat.
Let the patient unmask the doctor and swim in the gray milk of his mind.
For nothing will keep.
Let the bleak faces of the police swell like yeast.
Let breezes run like sauce over their skins.   20
For this kingdom is theirs.
Let a violet cloak fall on the bleached hair of the poetess.
Let twilight cover the lost bone of her passion.
For her moon is ambition.
Let the dusty air release its sugars.   25
Let candy the color of marlin flesh build up on the tables.
For everyone's mouth is open.
Let the wind devise secrets and leave them in trees.
Let the earth suck at roots and discover the emblems of weather.

LeRoi Jones / Imamu Amiri Baraka   *(1934–   )*

Preface to a Twenty Volume Suicide Note

(for Kellie Jones, born 16 May 1959)

Lately, I've become accustomed to the way
The ground opens up and envelops me
Each time I go out to walk the dog.
Or the broad edged silly music the wind
Makes when I run for a bus—   5

Things have come to that.

And now, each night I count the stars,
And each night I get the same number.
And when they will not come to be counted
I count the holes they leave.   10

Nobody sings anymore.

And then last night, I tiptoed up
To my daughter's room and heard her
Talking to someone, and when I opened

The door, there was no one there . . .   15
Only she on her knees, peeking into

Her own clasped hands.

An Agony. As Now.

I am inside someone
who hates me. I look
out from his eyes. Smell
what fouled tunes come in
to his breath. Love his   5
wretched women.

Slits in the metal, for sun. Where
my eyes sit turning, at the cool air
the glance of light, or hard flesh
rubbed against me, a woman, a man,   10
without shadow, or voice, or meaning.

This is the enclosure (flesh,
where innocence is a weapon. An
abstraction. Touch. (Not mine.
Or yours, if you are the soul I had   15
and abandoned when I was blind and had
my enemies carry me as a dead man
(if he is beautiful, or pitied.

It can be pain. (As now, as all his
flesh hurts me.) It can be that. Or   20
pain. As when she ran from me into
that forest.
        Or pain, the mind
silver spiraled whirled again the
sun, higher than even old men thought
God would be. Or pain. And the other. The   25
yes. (Inside his books, his fingers. They
are withered yellow flowers and were never
beautiful.) The yes. You will, lost soul, say
'beauty.' Beauty, practiced, as the tree. The
slow river. A white sun in its wet sentences.   30

Or, the cold men in their gale. Ecstasy. Flesh
or soul. The yes. (Their robes blown. Their bowls
empty. They chant at my heels, not at yours.) Flesh
or soul, as corrupt. Where the answer moves too quickly.
Where the God is a self, after all.)   35

Cold air blown through narrow blind eyes. Flesh,
white hot metal. Glows as the day with its sun.
It is a human love, I live inside. A bony skeleton
you recognize as words or simple feeling.

But it has no feeling. As the metal, is hot, it is not,   40
given to love.

It burns the thing
inside it. And that thing
screams.

Audubon, Drafted

For Linda

It does not happen. That love, removes
itself. (I am leaving, Goodbye!
                          Removes
itself, as rain, hard iron rain
comes down, then stops. All those   5
eyes opened for morning, close with
what few hours given them. With tears,
or at a stone wall, shadows drag down.

I am what I think I am. You are what
I think you are. The world is the   10
one thing, that will not move. It is
made of stone, round, and very ugly.

THEMATIC AND GENERIC
TABLE OF CONTENTS

493

GLOSSARY

abstract: a word that is so general that it does not suggest any specific attributes; "love," "happiness," "beauty" are abstract. See *diction.*

alexandrine: a six-foot line in iambic meter (iambic hexameter), named for the conventional French line of twelve syllables; in English it is sometimes used in the triplets of Augustan verse, where the standard couplet is extended to a third rhyming line of greater length; also used as the last line of the Spenserian stanza.

allegory: a dramatic or narrative structure in which the main actors embody general principles such as moral qualities (Lucifera, or Pride, and the other Seven Deadly Sins in *The Faerie Queene*, Book I, Canto iv) or historical forces (as in W. B. Yeats's "Leda and the Swan"). For a discussion of the problems connected with allegory, see Introduction.

alliteration: the repetition of initial consonants, sometimes reinforced by similar sound patterns within words as well: "When to the sessions of sweet silent thought/I summon up remembrance of things past, . . ." (Shakespeare, Sonnet 30).

allusion: a brief reference to a person, event, or earlier work of literature that the reader is expected to recognize: "No! I am not Prince Hamlet, nor was meant to be . . ." (T. S. Eliot, "The Love Song of J. Alfred Prufrock").

ambiguity: two or more meanings (sometimes contradictory, sometimes complementary) in a single word or phrase, as in the use of "straits" as both literal sea passages and as tribulations of spirit in John Donne's "Hymn to God, My God, in My Sickness": "That this is my southwest discovery,/*Per fretum febris,* by these straits to die."

anapest, anapestic: see *meter.*

antithesis: see *couplet.*

archaism: a word whose form or sense is obsolete, for example, Spenser's deliberate usage in *The Faerie Queene*, Book I, Canto iv, stanza 28: "His life was nigh unto deaths doore yplast,/And thred-bare cote, and cobled shoes he ware,/Ne scarse good morsell all his life did tast,/But both from backe and belly still did spare."

archetype: an image, character, or event that recurs in literature and suggests primitive myth or evokes other patterns of deep and scarcely conscious feeling (such as the death-rebirth archetype discussed in the Introduction).

assonance: a repetition of the same or similar vowel sounds, as the *a, e,* and *i* sounds in Hart Crane's "Voyages II": "—And yet this great wink of eternity,

/Of rimless floods, unfettered leewardings,/Samite sheeted and processional where/Her undinal vast belly moonward bends,/Laughing the wrapt inflections of our love. . . ."

ballad: a narrative poem, usually in quatrains (typically with alternating four- and three-foot lines that rhyme *abab*), sometimes with a refrain; usually abrupt and condensed in narrative, stressing the surprise of the reversal or final revelation (see "Sir Patrick Spence" and "The Twa Corbies"). The *literary ballad* imitates the form and often adapts it to more complex purposes, as in Coleridge's "The Rime of the Ancient Mariner" or W. H. Auden's "As I Walked Out One Evening." A more straightforward use of traditional ballad form in a modern poem is X. J. Kennedy's "In a Prominent Bar in Secaucus One Day."

bathos: literally, sinking; a sudden drop from the exalted to the ridiculous, whether unconscious or deliberate.

blank verse: unrhymed iambic pentameter, common in Elizabethan drama, later used as the English heroic or epic meter by Milton (*Paradise Lost*) and Wordsworth (*The Prelude*), among others. Increasingly, after James Thomson's *The Seasons* (written in the mid-eighteenth century in imitation of Milton), it became a typical meter for reflective and descriptive poetry as well as narrative.

bucolic: see *pastoral.*

burlesque: the imitation of other literary works which renders them ludicrous by using incongruous idiom, characters, or events. Among the specific forms one can distinguish *parody*, which applies specific mannerisms or conventions of a style to incongruous materials (see Anthony Hecht, "The Dover Bitch"); *travesty*, which re-creates the original character or incidents of a work such as Virgil's *Aeneid* in low and scurrilous language or incidents; the *mock-heroic*, which applies an exalted style to seemingly trivial characters and events. See *mock-heroic.*

caesura: see *couplet* and *meter.*

carpe diem: Latin for "seize the day," a conventional motif in love poetry in which the lover urges his mistress to live and love in the present while she is young instead of deferring pleasure to the future, as in Marvell's "To His Coy Mistress."

chiasmus: see *couplet.*

closed couplet: see *couplet.*

conceit: an extended comparison of unlike things, as in the *Petrarchan conceit* that compares at length a mistress to a cruel divinity or the lover's grief to natural disaster, as in Sir Thomas Wyatt's "My Galley Chargèd with Forgetfulness." The Metaphysical poets, and particularly John Donne, overturned the conventionality of the Petrarchan conceit by finding obscure and unexpected comparisons. As Dr. Samuel Johnson wrote of the Metaphysicals' conceits: "The most heterogeneous ideas are yoked by violence together; nature and art are ransacked for illustrations, comparisons, and allusions. . . ." Donne's image of the lovers as compasses in "A Valediction: Forbidding Mourning" is often cited, and all of his poems, like many of Marvell's, supply instances. One can find a modern example in W. H. Auden's "In Memory of W. B. Yeats": "The provinces of his body revolted,/The squares of his mind were empty,/Silence invaded the suburbs,/The current of his feeling failed: he became his admirers."

concrete: a word or phrase that evokes a number of specific attributes, such as "rusty, garden spade," which suggests size, color, texture, shape, and so on. See *diction*.

condensation: see *wit*.

connotation and denotation: strictly speaking, the connotation would be the attributes conveyed by a word, as opposed to the objects to which these apply; thus the qualities implied by "hardness" would be the connotation of the word and their instances the denotation. But connotation is usually applied to the suggested meanings or implications a word carries in addition to its precise and explicit meaning (which is often called its denotation). A poet like Dylan Thomas sometimes exploits this second sense of connotation more than denotation: "All the sun long it was running, it was lovely, the hay/Fields high as the house, the tunes from the chimneys, it was air/And playing, lovely and watery/And fire green as grass" ("Fern Hill"). See *diction*.

convention: any poetic feature or form that is generally understood or accepted and is recognized as part of a system or code. Poetic conventions include the use of rhyme, of stanza form, and of traditional genres (ballad, pastoral, epic) whose forms are often signaled by more specific and limited conventions, such as (in the case of epic) the invocation to the muse.

couplet: a pair of rhymed lines; most often iambic tetrameter, as in Andrew Marvell's "To His Coy Mistress," or iambic pentameter, as in most of Dryden's and Pope's poetry. The iambic tetrameter coupled with elaborate and humorous rhymes (often forced) was used for burlesque by Samuel Butler in *Hudibras* (1662) and later by Matthew Prior and Jonathan Swift. An example can be taken from Swift's "Baucis and Philemon": "Found his head filled with many a system,/But classic authors—he ne'er missed 'em." The *heroic couplet*, named for its use as an English epic meter, is iambic pentameter; and it may be open or closed. In the *open couplet*, the syntactic sense carries on beyond the couplet, and the closure achieved by the rhyme is given less emphasis. The *closed couplet* tends to complete its sense within the two lines, and it develops—in Dryden and Pope—an elaborate internal structure. There is usually a pause at the end of the first line and another, lesser one (called a *caesura*, literally, a cutting) somewhere near the middle of each line, but varying in position with the sense of the words. These units, the halves and quarters of the closed couplet, may be used for *antithesis*, a contrast between units, or even for *chiasmus*, where a crisscrossing of units is achieved, as in Pope's line, "A fop her passion, and her prize, a sot," or in a more complicated structure: "The thriving plants//ignoble broomsticks made,/Now sweep those alleys//they were born to shade" (*To Burlington*, 97–98). Here we can see chiasmus in the parallelism of the first and fourth quarters (flourishing shade trees) as well as the second and third (broomsticks sweeping).

dactyl, dactylic: see *meter*.

decorum: see *style*.

denotation: see *connotation*.

diction: the choice of words, as when the poet may choose a dignified or low word, an abstract or concrete, or a general or particular one to refer to the same object. The poet may or may not wish to make use of all these attributes in his poem; a poem like Gerard Manley Hopkins' "Pied Beauty" finds significance in "dappling" (or the coupling of attributes), and this requires vivid instances of high concreteness. Emily Dickinson may move between abstract and concrete diction, as in "Crumbling Is Not an Instant's Act." In eighteenth-century poetry we often find a general noun rendered more specific and concrete by an adjective: both "finny tribe" and "scaly breed" (examples of *periphrasis,* a roundabout or indirect way of naming) refer to fish as one of the kinds of creatures in a society, while evoking some distinctive attribute that recalls their concrete look and form. Each choice of diction is a way of bringing a certain kind of meaning to bear on the object that is named. See the Introduction and *connotation and denotation.*

dramatic irony: see *irony.*

dramatic monologue: a poem spoken by one character to another who is present but silent (opposed to a soliloquy, where the speaker is alone), as in Robert Browning's "My Last Duchess." In contrast to a meditation, which may be addressed to another person, the dramatic monologue attempts to reveal (often through unconscious self-exposure) a distinctive personality in the speaker.

eclogue: see *pastoral.*

elegy: a formal lament for the death of a personal friend or public figure, as in Milton's "Lycidas" or W. H. Auden's "In Memory of W. B. Yeats." The lament may take a pastoral form derived from Greek and Roman traditions (Bion, Moschus, and Virgil are among the most celebrated models), in which the myth of the poet as shepherd is created and conventions are employed that may, as in Milton's poem, be turned to new uses. The elegy usually seeks to expand the immediate sense of loss to a more impersonal consideration of such themes as the status of poetry, the significance of death, and the possibilities of metaphorical if not literal rebirth.

elision: the partial or complete suppression of one vowel before another ("th' intending lines") or the suppression of a weak syllable within a word ("pow'r," "heav'n") for the sake of metrical regularity.

enjambment: the use of run-on lines where the sense does not require or permit a full pause between lines, as opposed to end-stopped lines.

epic: a heroic poem, usually in high or elevated style, on a great action performed by a hero, usually of almost superhuman warlike powers. Homer's *Iliad* and *Odyssey* and Virgil's *Aeneid* provide the great classical examples, and Milton's *Paradise Lost* the greatest English instance. In Milton's poem, because of its peculiar subject and content, one cannot easily identify a single hero, and in fact Milton disdains the outward trappings of martial heroism (although he represents them in the war in heaven of Book VI) in order to celebrate the heroism of Christian humility. While the strict form of heroic action may be absent, one can see something like epic dimensions in Wordsworth's *The Prelude* and at least an evocation of epic themes in Tennyson's *Idylls of the King.* Among the conventions of epic are the invocation of the muse, the epic question (as in *Paradise Lost*, Book I, ll. 27–33), and the extended, seemingly irrelevant epic simile (that draws into the poem realms not directly presented or visions of a life far removed from the scene of battle and conflict). See *mock-heroic.*

epigram: usually a very short poem, concise, witty, and sharply pointed, as in Alexander Pope's "Epigram. Engraved on the Collar of a Dog which I Gave to his Royal Highness": "I am his Highness' dog at Kew;/Pray, tell me Sir, whose dog are you?"

false wit: see *wit.*

fancy: see *wit.*

feminine rhyme: see *rhyme.*

figures of speech: departures from literal or conventional use of language, most notably in metaphor, where the qualities or action of one kind of thing are assigned, without explanation, to another: "A rosy sanctuary will I dress/ With the wreathed trellis of a working brain" (John Keats, "Ode to Psyche"). See *metaphor* for further discussion. Other figures that are commonly identified are these:
simile: an explicit comparison, using "like" or "as," between different kinds of things: "The tangled bine-stems scored the sky/Like strings of broken lyres" (Thomas Hardy, "The Darkling Thrush").
synecdoche: a part of something used for the whole, as in Milton's reference to the corrupt clergy in "Lycidas" as "blind mouths."
metonymy: the name of an object used for something else closely associated with it, as the crown for the king, or: "In every voice, in every ban,/The mind-forged manacles I hear" (William Blake, "London").
zeugma: literally, a yoking; the use of one word in two parallel grammatical constructions with a telling difference of meaning: "Here thou, Great Anna! whom three realms obey,/Dost sometimes counsel take—and sometimes tea" (Pope, *The Rape of the Lock,* Canto III, ll. 7–8).

foot: a unit of measure in verse consisting of stressed and unstressed syllables. For a more complete discussion, see Introduction and *meter.*

free verse (or **vers libre**): rhythmic but not regularly metrical verse of varying line lengths that follows the cadences of spoken language, as in the poetry of Walt Whitman or William Carlos Williams.

genre: a traditional literary form or "kind," such as epic, satire, romance, tragedy; each perhaps constituting a distinctive "vision" of experience. See Introduction.

georgic: a poem about rural or agricultural life, recounting and celebrating daily labors rather than evoking idyllic simplicity or ease. In Jonathan Swift's "Description of a City Shower" we find an instance of a mock-georgic, the ironic application of the convention to the life of the city.

heroic couplet: see Introduction and *couplet.*

iamb, iambic: see *meter.*

idyll: see *pastoral.*

image: a concrete, pictorial, sensuously apprehended detail, which may acquire metaphorical or symbolic meaning; in fact, the term is often applied to those concrete terms that lend themselves to metaphorical use. Certain images may, under repeated use, grow into symbolic patterns in a poem. See Introduction.

imitation: see *satire.*

irony: a way of speaking or writing that implies a meaning different from or additional to the one explicitly stated. It is sometimes confused with *sarcasm,* which is a special case of irony, usually obvious because it implies a meaning flatly contradictory to the one expressed and a meaning, moreover, that is highly critical if not actually hostile. In *Socratic irony* the speaker professes innocence or ignorance while in fact revealing real insight and leading others to question their own overconfident beliefs. In *dramatic irony* a character speaks in ignorance of events or of a future fate known to the audience or to other characters, like Oedipus seeking the cause of the plague in Thebes without knowing that he is the man he seeks. In *romantic irony* a poet like Byron may create an illusion which he himself punctures by a sudden drop in tone (see *bathos*) or by calling attention to his own manipulation of language or characters. The most general sense of irony, as it is used in modern criticism, is the simultaneous adoption of somewhat conflicting attitudes and a consequent awareness of all that may be opposed to any single view that is expressed; it may be contrasted with naive or simple-minded awareness, and it is sometimes equated with "maturity," or an awareness of the full complexity of experience. See Introduction.

levels of style: see *style.*

literary ballad: see *ballad.*

lyric: a short poem, which, while it may be dramatic or narrative, finds its most distinctive form in a direct expression of strong feeling (e.g., John Keats's "Ode on Melancholy" or Henry Vaughan's "The Retreat"); originally, a poem sung to the accompaniment of a lyre, the term is now used of any poem whose structure is meditative or deliberative: sonnets, odes, elegies, hymns, love songs, and so on.

masculine rhyme: see *rhyme.*

metaphor: a term for a specific figure of speech, it has also been used more generally for the entire process of oblique or nonliteral statement. Particular words are metaphorical in that they bring together two diverse objects through a common term ("The winds come to me from the fields of sleep" in Wordsworth's "Intimations of Immortality" or "Out of the whinnying green stable/On to the fields of praise" in Dylan Thomas's "Fern Hill"). But we may also speak of the larger metaphors of the "Ancient Mariner" or regard W. B. Yeats's system of cycles in "The Second Coming" as a great metaphor that brings together historical change and varieties of human temperament. The term has been used to cover all forms of analogy and analogical thinking, including those unconscious "pictures" of reality we may live by without full awareness of what we are taking for granted. I. A. Richards contributed the terms "tenor" and "vehicle" to the discussion of metaphor. The *tenor* of a metaphor is the implicit relationship it presents (e.g., the brave man in contrast to most men), the *vehicle* the verbal form or image in which the "tenor" is carried or suggested ("He is a lion among jackals"). See Introduction.

Metaphysical poetry: a term applied to the "school" of seventeenth-century poets who use learned and often violently incongruous conceits: John Donne, George Herbert, Andrew Marvell, Richard Crashaw, Henry Vaughan, Thomas Traherne, Abraham Cowley. With the revival and frequent imitation of these poets in the early twentieth century, the term was often applied to poetry that shows their influence, notably that of T. S. Eliot. Other modern poets who show great awareness of the earlier Metaphysical poets are W. B. Yeats, Hart Crane, and, in his early work, Robert Lowell; but in their poetry the influence of English poets is often fused with that of nineteenth-century French Symbolist poets. See *symbol*.

meter: the stress patterns of formal verse, which serve as poetic norms with which the poet plays, often as a kind of counterpoint to ordinary speech rhythms. Only a feeble poetry or doggerel matches meter and speech rhythms very closely, and yet the pressure of meter as a controlling norm is felt in the loosest of metrical verse. (For the complete abandonment of meter, see *free verse*.) The names of the standard meters are based on the feet (units of syllables) that tend to dominate in a line or a poem:

> iambic ("indeed")
> trochaic ("glory")
> anapestic ("at a loss")
> dactylic ("mournfully")
> spondaic ("shipwreck")

Only the first two feet have been extensively used in a sustained fashion for serious poems, with certain exceptions, such as Longfellow's dactylic *Evangeline* ("This is the forest primeval, the murmuring pines and the hemlocks . . ."). Most lines will contain different degrees of stress, which may vary as there is conflict or convergence of metrical accents with that of normal speech rhythms and the stress may be emphasized by pitch or other sound patterns.

The lines or verses of English poetry take their names from the number of feet they contain:

1 monometer	5 pentameter
2 dimeter	6 hexameter (when iambic, *alexandrine*)
3 trimeter	7 heptameter
4 tetrameter	

A pause created by speech rhythm usually falls at one or two notable points in the line and is called a *caesura*. It may fall within a foot or between feet, and its variation contributes to the reduction of metrical monotony. The following two excerpts indicate the use of the caesura:

> They heard and were abashed //, and up they sprung
> Upon the wing, // as when men wont to watch
> On duty, sleeping // found by whom they dread,
> Rouse and bestir themselves // ere well awake.
>> (Milton, *Paradise Lost*, Book I, ll. 331–4)

> And now, with gleams // of half-extinguished thought,
> With many recognitions // dim and faint,
> And somewhat // of a sad perplexity,
> The picture of the mind // revives again . . . .
>> (Wordsworth, *Tintern Abbey*, ll. 58–61)

For a further discussion of meter, see the Introduction.

metonymy: see *figures of speech*.

mock-heroic: the most important form of burlesque. We can see it used by poets of different periods: Spenser, Pope, Byron, T. S. Eliot. In its strictest form, the mock-heroic follows the conventions of classical epic, particularly in the use of elevated diction, but instead of treating heroic themes it treats commonplace or familiar experience. The mock-heroic may move toward satiric exposure of the lack of heroism, or toward some questioning of the heroic vision (see *irony*), or toward a sense of satiric incongruity.

motif: a recurring image, character, series of events, or the like, in poetry or prose. See *theme*.

myth: a story or group of stories, perhaps once taken literally, that accounts for the origin of things, for man's moral condition, for particular rituals or names that survive. The term has been extended in recent years to mean any narrative or dramatic pattern that commands wide belief (the myth of success, usually combining both hard work and unexpected reward, with the suggestion that failure is a moral or social stigma). In its literary sense, it usually signifies a pattern that has some kind of traditional, even primitive, claim on feeling and imagination (such as the quest motif, the testing of the hero by riddles, the descent into darkness and rebirth into life). Such patterns are uncovered beneath the surface of contemporary experience as a way of relating it to the past and of giving it the resonance of universal experience. See Introduction for further discussion of *myth and archetype*.

neoclassical: a term applied, sometimes misleadingly, to poetry that shows conscious imitation of classical models and may aspire to attitudes regarded as typical of Greek or Roman antiquity; in fact, the term has led to an exaggerated view of the imitativeness of eighteenth-century poetry, which often departs tellingly from its classical models, when it uses them at all.

New Criticism: a critical movement deriving from different sources (I. A. Richards, Ezra Pound, T. S. Eliot) that emphasized the need for close scrutiny of individual poems, with full attention to the subtle working of their language and the complex or ironic attitudes this might convey. In order to achieve this close and subtle scrutiny, these critics refused to be restricted by historical generalizations, by biographical surmises, or by social explanations. They insisted on studying poetry, in T. S. Eliot's words, "primarily as poetry and not another thing." They sought freedom to explore the poem as far as possible in its own terms, and to do this they needed to suppress efforts to derive the poem from something simpler or better known, like biography or history. Among the chief figures in the movement are John Crowe Ransom, Cleanth Brooks, Robert Penn Warren, R. P. Blackmur, and Allen Tate; the most philosophical and refined theorist allied with this group is W. K. Wimsatt.

occasional poetry: poems written to celebrate or commemorate specific events or anniversaries, such as W. B. Yeats's "Easter, 1916" or the birthday odes written for the king by the poet laureate, on more trivial occasions, it may become *vers de société*, at its best in Pope's "Epistle to Miss Blount, on Her Leaving the Town, after the Coronation" but also to be found in the same poet's "On a Lady who P—st at the Tragedy of *Cato*."

octave: see *sonnet*.

ode: usually a solemn lyric poem, often a long one, in an elevated style; its ultimate model is the long celebratory poems written by the classical Greek poet Pindar on public occasions. The range of the English ode is great: it may celebrate the power of music (Dryden), the drowning of a favorite cat (Gray), intimations of immortality (Wordsworth), a Grecian urn (Keats), or the Confederate dead (Allen Tate). The true Pindaric ode was based on choral action and fell into three major divisions (strophe, antistrophe, and epode) and was regular in form, if rhapsodic in language. While the Pindaric odes in English sometimes follow this form (as in Thomas Gray's "The Bard"), the more influential odes of Abraham Cowley turned the Pindaric into a freely varied long form, falling into stanzas of varying length and pattern. The Horatian ode is simpler, using one stanzaic form throughout, as in Andrew Marvell's Horatian ode on Cromwell or in Keats's odes.

onomatopoeia: the imitation in words of the sounds they describe, as "buzz," "hiss," "screech," etc. See, for example, "the weak-eyed bat,/With short shrill shriek, flits by on leathern wing" (William Collins, "Ode to Evening").

open couplet: see *couplet.*

ottava rima: see *stanza.*

oxymoron: see *paradox.*

paradox: contradictory words or phrases that may be reconciled when one explores their metaphoric nature, as in "The bird would cease and be as other birds/But that he knows in singing not to sing" (Robert Frost, "The Oven Bird"). A special case is *oxymoron*, where two terms seem to cancel each other out, as in "very tragical mirth," such Petrarchan love-terms as "freezing flames," or Milton's "darkness visible." Paradox has sometimes been extended to cover the implicit conflicts to be seen in *irony*, that is, the inconsistency of alternative views that might simultaneously be taken of the same object or situation.

parallelism: similarity or repetition of phrasing, idea, or grammatical construction, as in

> Not youthful kings in battle seized alive,
> Not scornful virgins who their charm survive,
> Not ardent lovers robbed of all their bliss,
> Not ancient ladies when refused a kiss . . .
> E'er felt such rage, resentment, and despair,
> As thou, sad virgin, for thy ravished hair.
> (Pope, *Rape of the Lock*, Canto IV, ll. 3–6, 9–10)

paraphrase: the technique of restating in other words the meaning of a text; most poetic texts are sufficiently complex so that only by an overlapping series of paraphrases can one begin to render their full implications.

parody: see *burlesque.*

pastoral: strictly, a poem about the life of the shepherd (Latin, "pastor"), as written by Theocritus in Greek and Virgil in Latin. The strict pastoral has a set of conventions that often recur (the debate about rival mistresses, the wager, the lament for unrequited love, the mourning of the death of a fellow shepherd). In Spenser's *Shepherd's Calendar* there are twelve poems, one for each month of the year; in Pope's *Pastorals* four, one for each season. John Gay in *The Shepherd's Week* wrote mock-pastorals, burlesquing the celebration of rural life by stressing its coarse rusticity; he wrote six poems for the days of the week, allowing the shepherds a silent sabbath. The term has been extended to cover works of various kinds that explore the superiority of a simple life to that of city or court; Shakespeare's treatment of the Forest of Arden in *As You Like It* is an example. One can speak accordingly of a "pastoral" treatment of working-class life, of imaginary utopias placed in benign climates, of heroes who lack the worldliness of more corrupt or simply more reality-bound men. Related terms are *eclogue* (literally, a selection), derived from the title of Virgil's pastoral poems; *bucolic* (from the Greek for herdsman); *idyll*, from the term applied to Theocritus' poems; *georgic*, from the Greek for ploughman. See also *georgic, elegy.*

pastoral romance: see *romance.*

pathetic fallacy: a term invented by John Ruskin to name the investing of inanimate objects with human feelings, as in "The moon doth with delight /Look round her when the heavens are bare" or "Land and sea/Give themselves up to jollity" (both from Wordsworth's ode, "Intimations of Immortality"). The term, once applied adversely, is now used as a neutral description of a common device.

periphrasis: see *diction.*

persona: the fictitious or semifictitious character assumed by the poet as the speaker of his poem, as the lover in Marvell's "To His Coy Mistress," the narrator in Byron's *Don Juan*, or the dramatic voice of Pope in his satiric dialogues. The persona has a consistency that is usually simpler than the full character of the actual poet; it is created in order to produce a dramatic or rhetorical situation of special clarity or to account (as in Shelley's "An Indian Serenade") for an intense and extravagant idiom, and the limitations of the persona may be used for ironic effect, as with the unreliable narrator in fiction or the speaker in the dramatic monologue. An example of the latter is the self-satisfied Duke who speaks in Browning's "My Last Duchess," unconscious of the way in which he exposes his own cruelty.

personification: the process of attributing human presence to abstract forces or inanimate objects (for the latter, see *pathetic fallacy*): "Can Honor's voice provoke the silent dust,/Or Flattery soothe the dull cold ear of Death?" (Thomas Gray, "Elegy Written in a Country Churchyard"). See also *allegory* and Introduction.

Petrarchan conceit: see *conceit.*

quatrain: see *stanza.*

rhetorical figures: see *figures of speech.*

rhyme: the matching of final sounds of lines; sometimes an approximate matching, as in imperfect "slant" or "near" rhymes. *Masculine rhymes* end with a stressed syllable, *feminine* with an unstressed. By elaborate rhymes (called "double" or "triple" if they involve two or three syllables), comic effects can be achieved, as in Byron's "What men call gallantry, and gods adultery,/ Is much more common where the climate's sultry" (*Don Juan* I, stanza 63). But the full effect of rhyme depends not merely on the number of syllables but on the surprise or aptness of the meanings it conveys. As W. K. Wimsatt has shown, there is in the strongest rhymes a telling congruity or incongruity of sense that the sound seems to confirm. Many poets use rhyme, however, as a pattern of regularity like meter, imposing its order in counterpoint to speech rhythms, but not necessarily calling attention to itself.

rime royal: see *stanza.*

romance: a long narrative, in verse or prose, in which events are surprising, magical, or miraculous. In this genre, characters tend to be simple and plots complex. Classical romances, such as Apuleius' *Golden Ass*, provide a prototype, but the most familiar instances are medieval and courtly in setting, and the Arthurian legends are the most famous in English. Later adaptations are to be found in Keats's "The Eve of St. Agnes" and Tennyson's *Idylls of the King*, and many romance elements survive, in altered and ironic form, in T. S. Eliot's *The Waste Land*. The *pastoral romance* is a common species, as in Sidney's *Arcadia* or in portions of Shakespeare's comedies, for example in *As You Like It* and *The Winter's Tale.*

romantic irony: see *irony.*

sarcasm: see *irony.*

satire: a mode of presenting experience as ridiculous or comtemptible; it excludes sympathy through deliberately maintaining detachment or a sense of distance and usually implies a standard on which its mockery or scorn is based. Satire can range from gentle irony to savage invective; Horace tends to provide a model for the former, Juvenal for the latter. Both wrote formal verse satires, customarily short poems voicing the sentiments of a persona, and the form was imitated by such poets as Donne, Dryden, Pope, and Johnson. The last two wrote so-called *imitations*, which were free adaptations of a recognizable original, applied to their own contemporary scene and meant to be read beside the original text. There are satiric elements in many works that are not pure satires, and the works may range from Shakespeare's *Troilus and Cressida* to Byron's *Don Juan*. Later instances occur in such poems as Ezra Pound's "Portrait d'une Femme," A. D. Hope's "Coup de Grâce," "and Gregory Corso's "Marriage."

sentimentality: a term applied to works or attitudes which exhibit or demand a degree of emotion they do not earn by what they say or present; in general, an excessive or self-indulgent cultivation of feelings, usually tender and pathetic ones, although the term has been applied as well to some versions of would-be sardonic understatement. The estimation of what is excessive varies from reader to reader, as it does from age to age.

sestet: see *sonnet.*

simile: see *figures of speech.*

Socratic irony: see *irony.*

sonnet: a rhyming lyric poem of fourteen lines, usually reflective but sometimes dramatic, especially in sonnet sequences, where shifting attitudes are revealed in the speaker. The Petrarchan or Miltonic sonnet consists of an eight-line *octave* and a six-line *sestet*; the Shakespearian sonnet of three *quatrains* and a final *couplet*. Rhyme schemes vary, but the most common in the Miltonic sonnet is *abbaabba cdecde*, in the Shakespearian *abab cdcd efef gg.*

Spenserian stanza: see *stanza*.

spondee, spondaic: see *meter*.

sprung rhythm: a term devised by Gerard Manley Hopkins for a free meter derived in part from Old and Middle English verse; the stressed syllables alone are counted, and they may stand alone or be accompanied by a varying number of unstressed syllables. Hopkins's verse compensated for this rhythmic freedom with elaborate effects of assonance and alliteration, as in "Fall, gall themselves, and gash gold-vermilion" ("The Windhover").

stanza: a division of a poem, usually repeated throughout in the same form, that is, with the same kind of lines and rhyme schemes. The *couplet* consists of two rhyming lines; the *quatrain* of four lines which may rhyme, if at all, in various patterns (*abab, aabb, axby*, etc.). We can see *tercets* (three rhyming lines) in Robert Herrick's "Upon Julia's Clothes," and an adaptation of Dante's *terza rima* (where interlocking tercets rhyme *aba bcb cdc*, etc.) in Shelley's "Ode to the West Wind." Longer stanzas are *ottava rima* (eight lines in iambic pentameter, rhymed *abababcc*), used notably in Byron's *Don Juan*; the *Spenserian stanza* (*ababbcbcc*), where the iambic pentameter is varied with a final alexandrine, or hexameter; and *rime royal*, seven lines of iambic pentameter rhymed *ababbcc*.

stock responses: preconceived ideas, such as the familiar notions of robbers as swaggering, freedom-loving adventurers, of mothers as lovable old ladies in rocking chairs, of childhood as a period of prolonged rapture and security, that I. A. Richards calls "acquired, stereotyped, habitual responses" to experience that block our awareness of novel or complex views.

style: the manner of expressing ideas or emotions characteristic, to a degree, of an age or, more distinctively, of a particular writer. Traditional rhetoric recognized *levels of style*, notably high (epic, tragedy), middle (satire, meditation), and low (burlesque, pastoral). Occasionally critics have found a correlation between levels of style and the kind of audience or subject (high, court; middle, city; low, country). Levels of style represent a choice for the poet, who may achieve his subtlest effects by sudden shifts of level. The full impact of these variations of style depends on the reader's recognizing the claims of *decorum*, that is, of the appropriateness of a given style to a given subject or of a particular word to a level of style. Although these claims are not met consistently—in variations they are deliberately defied—they provide a grammar of style from which departures gain their significance. See Introduction.

sublime: extreme elevation or rapture, cultivated through images of infinite space or unimaginable spans of time, through the dramatization of virtually superhuman intensity of heroism or evil, or through an idiom that collapses under the strain of emotion or vision and awakens a sense of the ineffable. The Greek critic Longinus is its earliest theorist, and Edmund Burke and Immanuel Kant its late eighteenth-century theorists.

symbol: in general, that which refers to something beyond itself, as in mathematical or map-reading symbols, or such traditional religious and political symbols as the cross and the scepter. The term is extended to cover those repeated images that acquire some consistency of suggested meaning within a poem, such as greenness in Andrew Marvell's "The Garden" or the various marks of social organization in William Blake's "London." The symbol is often regarded as open-ended, suggestive, and inexhaustible in contrast with the more limited and definable meanings of allegory; such a contrast is useful as long as it does not degenerate into a simple pairing of praise and blame and does not neglect the overlap between such terms. Symbolism as a literary movement, notably in later nineteenth-century France and twentieth-century England, is marked by a rejection of explicit statement or narrative and a cultivation of obliquity and density of meaning, often achieved by allusion to earlier literature (as in T. S. Eliot) or to traditional but newly interpreted myth (as in W. B. Yeats, as well as Eliot). See Introduction.

synecdoche: see *figures of speech*.

synesthesia: an attempt to fuse different kinds of sensation by describing one in terms of another, as in Keats's account of wine, "Tasting of Flora and the country green,/Dance, and Provençal song, and sunburnt mirth!" ("Ode to a Nightingale").

tenor: see *metaphor*.

tercet: see *stanza*.

terza rima: see *stanza*.

theme: the central idea or thesis of a work, that is, the governing view taken of its subject; sometimes used loosely for the subject itself (old age, love, martial heroism) and more narrowly for particular *motifs* such as the earthly paradise, the star-crossed lovers, the deification of the hero. The term is useful as a way of stating briefly the governing structural principle or standard of relevance in a poem; the theme in itself may be familiar and common, but it may also serve to order a new range of experience. See Introduction.

tone: the attitude adopted by the poet toward his material: reverential, mocking, quizzical, patronizing, and so on. The tone of a poem may be the expression of a persona adopted as the speaker; it may be directly conveyed through the choice of a level of style; and it may be a source of irony.

tradition: a body of conventions shared by a group of writers, usually from one age to another, such as the classical tradition or the tradition of formal verse satire. Within a given tradition the poet will achieve his own variations, which gain import from the system of expectations built up in the past and now significantly altered.

travesty: see *burlesque*.

trochee, trochaic: see *meter*.

trope: a "turn" from literal to figurative use of language. See *metaphor* and *figures of speech*.

true wit: see *wit*.

vehicle: see *metaphor*.

vers libre: see *free verse*.

wit: in its original sense intelligence and skill, and used from the Renaissance to the eighteenth century to designate the creative or inventive faculties of poets. During the seventeenth century and increasingly in the eighteenth century the term was also used in the more restricted sense of a clever and surprising juxtaposition of disparate things or ideas, usually in one ambiguous term (later called "condensation" in Sigmund Freud's analysis of wit and of dream processes). The eighteenth century distinguished between *false wit*, which found trivial likenesses or devised pointless puns, and *true wit*, which found significant likenesses and thus achieved imaginative discovery. The term *fancy* was often used for the power of relating disparate ideas; only if confirmed by judgment did it reveal genuine truths and deserve the name of *true wit*. In the nineteenth century, Coleridge distinguished between imagination (the true creative power) and fancy (the reshuffling of familiar ideas and phrases). See Introduction.

zeugma: see *figures of speech*.

INDEX OF AUTHORS, TITLES, AND FIRST LINES

When the first line of a poem supplies the title, only a first-line entry is given.

B 5
C 6
D 7
E 8
F 9
G 0
H 1
I 2
J 3
4